JEWISH VIEWS OF THE AFTERLIFE

Simcha Paull Raphael

JASON ARONSON, INC.
Northvale, New Jersey
London

First Jason Aronson Inc. softcover edition—1996

This book was set in 11pt. Goudy Oldstyle.

For credits, see page 457.

Library of Congress Cataloging-in-Publication Data

Raphael, Simcha Paull.
    Jewish views of the afterlife / Simcha Paull Raphael.
        p. cm.
    Includes bibliographical references and index.
    ISBN 0-87668-583-1 (hardcover)
    ISBN 1-56821-938-5 (softcover)
    1. Future life—Judaism—History of doctrines. 2. Eschatology,
Jewish—History of doctrines. 3. Immortality—Judaism—History of
doctrines. 4. Resurrection (Jewish theology)—History of doctrines.
    I. Title.
    BM635.R37 1994
    296.3'3—dc20   94-10597

Manufactured in the United States of America. Jason Aronson Inc. offers books and cassettes. For information and catalog write to Jason Aronson Inc., 230 Livingston Street, Northvale, New Jersey 07647.

Dedicated to

Leslie Tibor Erdos, ע'ה
1951–1973

David Nathanson, ע'ה
1950–1971

Todd Martin Geiger, ע'ה
1956–1976

Contents

Foreword

A PERSONAL MEMORY

The topic of this book, the fate of the soul after death, as seen in the source texts of Jewish tradition, has deeply concerned me ever since I awakened to my own thinking.

In 1939 I was fourteen and a half and we were refugees in Belgium. Hitler had just taken over Austria, where I grew up. I felt as if all of my roots were cut from under me. The specter of not being left to live out all my allotted years because of Hitler was in the foreground of my mind. I was angry with God. I wanted to have some people in God's place so I could vent my frustration and anger on them. One Shabbat afternoon I decided to visit an Orthodox youth fellowship, Pirchei Agudat Yisrael, where I could count on them to study a text of the Mishnah, *Pirkei Avot*, the Ethics of the Fathers.

The lesson always begins with "All of Israel has a share in the World-to-Come." I think to myself: "Oy, will I give it to them!" I go there prepared with all of my ammunition and sure enough, sitting opposite me at the head of the table is a young man, with a Talmud folio before him; he begins to read this Mishnah. Before long, after he translates the first part, I jump into the conversation and I put out all of my denial: "The World-to-Come! Pie in the sky! Nobody has ever come back from there! Baloney! Opiate of the masses! This is only to enslave and deceive people! You rob them in this world but promise that they'll get something in the next world." And as I start to pour my pent-up anger, the people around the table are getting furious, ready to tear me apart. But the signal from their leader at the head of the table is to stay calm and let me finish.

When I finish, he says to me, "Would you like to hear from someone who agrees with you?" I say, "Sure enough!" At this point, I can't back out of it. He begins to read for me Maimonides' Mishnah commentary on the section he has just read, which deals with the issue of the afterlife. Maimonides debunks the popular gross ideas of the folktales arising from a naive understanding of Torah and Talmud, and then proceeds to refine them to a most sophisticated subtlety.

Hearing this reading touched me in a deep way, and at that moment I began to make my deep commitment to Judaism. I now had a sense that there exists this spirituality beyond what I saw as the fairy-tale language used in the Talmud. And with the debunking there came the affirmation that there really was something there. But this something that was there was much more subtle and much more spiritual than what I had heard up to that time. With this affirmation, the issues about God and soul took on greater clarity for me.

THE AUTHOR

I am delighted that this work, *Jewish Views of the Afterlife*, is now being published. On the very first day I met Simcha Raphael, in 1976, we had a conversation about life after death in Jewish tradition. As I see it, the unfolding of his own life destiny is expressed in the writing of this book. His life pursuits and studies have equipped him with the critical capacity of academic scholarship, with the vision of a mystic and the insight of a transpersonal psychologist. All of this he has used in his pastoral counseling with the dying and bereaved, and the wisdom of his experience in doing this holy work suffuses the spirit of this work.

Jewish Views of the Afterlife is reflective of the new genre of Jewish-renewal literature. It is an amalgam of the emerging cosmology with the metaphysics of Jewish mysticism. Simcha Raphael, who has participated in the evolution of Jewish renewal, brings forward valuable ancient traditions and makes them available and accessible in content and in spirit to the concerned citizens of the next millennium.

THIS IS AN IMPORTANT BOOK

There are those who have written about these "last" and ultimate things as if they did not apply to them. Books like these can be written "objectively," academically, by doing conceptual thinking. However, it makes a great deal of difference if one approaches a subject in what Professor Abraham Joshua Heschel used to call the method of situational thinking. This is a book that, with all of the conceptual material it contains, it is nonetheless anchored in an awareness of our existential situation.

We are dealing here with material that seems to scandalize the rational, everyday mind. If it were not described by those seers endowed with a "fantastic" vision, we would not be able to approach this issue at all. We cannot and must not approach this subject with the attitude of nineteenth-century scientism, asking, "Who has ever come back from there?" This is not material that has hard, laboratory-repeatable, empirical data behind it. But given that one looks at the prima facie anecdotal reports on our own and other traditions, one meets countless reports that rivet one's attention and demand that one look into them for the paramount patterns they share.

There are people who have been researching in what we may call borderline sciences, studying psychic phenomena, parapsychology and the near-death and out-of-body experiences. Often, in their studies, they quote Hindu and Tibetan Buddhist texts and compare them with the reported phenomena. Whenever I as a Jew read that material, I felt that tradition, and the teachings I received about the afterlife were confirmed by these outside sources. And yet I also experienced a very deep frustration and regret that our Jewish sources were not part and parcel of their conversations.

In the 1950s, when I was searching for this type of information for myself, I began by looking in the library's subject catalog. I got to know names of authors who had written about postmortem survival. One day, I ventured into the stacks and discovered an entire section in the Dewey Decimal system filed under number 133. I still remember it well! There facing me on the library shelves—far beyond anything I ever imagined— were all kinds of studies of what the philosophers and the religious writers had to say about the world beyond death.

To my delight, one day I discovered thirty volumes of Arcana Celestia, written by the Swedish mystic Emanuel Swedenborg, and I opened one to see what was inside. How surprised I was to see an amazing Midrash on the Torah interspersed with observations that Sweden-borg, trained as a scientist, made when in one of his altered states. He was able to visit realms that compare with our *m'tivta d'r'qia'*, the Acad-emy on High. Swedenborg knew these worlds as the realms of good and of truth. In the Jewish mystical tradition of Kabbalah, one would speak of similar worlds described by Swedenborg—the worlds of Yetzirah, and of Briyah, and the Gan Eden below and the Gan Eden above. Here I had found Jewish Kabbalah, in a different cultural garb.

To my surprise, another author I found was Sir Arthur Conan Doyle. He had been for me just the creator of the Sherlock Holmes mysteries until I discovered, also in those 133 stacks, how he and Sir Oliver Crookes had worked together in the British Societies for Psychical Research, applying their intellectual acumen to the question "What happens to us after we die?" The Societies for Psychical Research, in this country and in England, produced many works concerning communing with the departed, mediumship and other psychic phenomena, and studies of the near-death experience and life after death. It became very clear to me that the literature on this subject was enormous.

About the time I was reading about the afterlife, I also started to pay attention to spiritualism. I visited people working as mediums and settings in which spirits of the dead purportedly came through. I discov-ered that these kinds of encounters brought about a deeply surprising experience of authentic and truthful material being communicated. This also gave me an understanding of what I read in the writings of the psy-chic Edgar Cayce, and in the kabbalistic text *Shaar Ha-Gilgulim*, a medi-eval text on the reincarnation of souls.

And yet, as I read through all these kinds of studies, I realized that what we Jews had to say about such topics never entered into the dis-course. It was no wonder! The first translations of Jewish classics from the Hebrew were done by rationalists. They were ashamed to make avail-able texts that would expose the kinds of mystical writings that the Jew-ish historian Heinrich Graetz rejected as irrational superstition. They did not translate works dealing with otherworldly matters such as soul and afterlife, so these sources did not get to be known in German or English translations. Sure enough, the Yiddish author Y. L. Peretz could tell sto-ries about *Yenne Velt*—"the other world"—but that was safe enough for translation since it was seen as folklore. As long as it did not philosophi-cally contradict the *Religion der Vernunft*—"Religion of Reason"—as Ju-daism was understood to be, the rationalists felt safe. In this way, our teachings on the afterlife remained unknown to the world at large. For many Jews, the thirst for knowing something about our teachings regarding the mystical journey of the soul was not quenched.

For me personally, the matter became crucial about 1950 when the late Lubavitcher Rebbe, Rabbi Yossef Yitzchak Schneersohn, passed on. Suddenly, without access to the master's guidance, we were bereft. I often pondered, how can I contact the Rebbe? At one point, I even offered his son-in-law and successor to train as a medium so that the *hasidim* would be able to consult the late Rebbe and continue to receive his guidance. In the first year after his father-in-law's demise, Rabbi Menachem Mendel Schneersohn, *z'l*, insisted that he was not the Rebbe but that he was merely the chief of operations for the late Rebbe. "The Rebbe, Rabbi Yossef Yitzchak, is the leader of the generation. What difference does it make if he is in this world or the other world?" was how he put it. "Medium?" he said. "If the Rebbe wants to come through, he'll find his ways to come through. We don't have to provide jumping tables. Let him go direct to each individual *hasid* in visions, apparitions, or dreams. The Rebbe knows how to move around the narrow limits." And, in truth, for a while, I received his guidance in dreams. In this way, my concerns about and interests in the issue of the afterlife were sharpened by the loss of my master's physical guidance and reinforced by the dream apparitions. As a result of these experiences, I began to look at the classical doctrines on postmortem survival with a fresh eye.

DOCTRINE AND EXPERIENCE

Classical Jewish belief is very clear: there is this world, *Olam Ha-Zeh*, and there is the World to Come, *Olam Ha-Ba*. At birth the soul enters the body and at death leaves it and continues to survive. This belief is referred to in Jewish sources as *hash'arat ha-nefesh*—literally "the survival of the soul." There is judgment and reward and punishment in the afterlife. According to the *Ethics of the Fathers*, we are to give our report or reckoning, our *din va-heshbon*, before God for a lifetime lived, and expect that we would be judged by God after death. Additionally, there is Gan Eden—paradise, and Gehinnom—purgatory. All of these beliefs are articles of faith in the Orthodox world, where they are read about in traditional sources and taken seriously. However, for most people these worlds beyond death are seen as some supernal reality that is not directly accessible to human experience within this world. There is an unbridge-able reality gap between what is believed, because one has to believe it, and what one actually experiences.

Even among those who, as a matter of doctrine, affirm a belief in divine postmortem reward and retribution, there is very little awareness of the specific teachings found in the tradition. If you were to say, "Do I have to believe that?" people would say, "Yes, that's what you have to believe." If I were to retort, "Can you show me where in Jewish litera-ture such teachings can be found?" only a few could cite chapter and verse. They will affirm existence of a life after death as a part of their creedal commitments, their *ani ma'amin*, but believe that it is a reality of another kind, not accessible to us here.

It is this type of thinking that divides the *mitnagged* from the *hasid*, the rationalist from the mystic. For the mystically inclined, the underly-ing question is always, when I perform a commandment, does it have a certain psychospiritual effect on my connection with God? How does the fulfillment of a commandment impact upon my being, my soul, my con-sciousness? For the rationally thinking *mitnagged*, on the other hand, there is an unbridgeable chasm between the transcendent reality and personal human experience. In other words, it doesn't matter if one has a direct experience of some deeper level of consciousness. What is im-portant to the rationalist is that God's will is fulfilled on this plane. There is no notion about what a *mitzvah*, or commandment, is beyond that. Clearly, this dividing line between two types of mind, rationalist and mystic, affects the way people think about the questions explored in this book.

As you read, you will discover just how much mystical literature is available and how, over the course of millennia, Judaism has tradition-ally accepted the existence of an ontological or ultimate reality in the life after death. Only in the last one hundred years has the rationalist mind-set hidden this mystical point of view in the closet.

As human beings, we have deep hunches about the afterlife. But there has been much denial about death in general and about one's own mortality. The reason this conversation does not come out of the closet is that although we have deep hunches about it, we do not have socially acceptable means to talk about it. A tradition provides a person with a socially acceptable means to enter the conversation. By hearkening back to the tradition, I can go back to these intuitive feelings, the hunch that there exists an afterlife. To find this conversation written about, and taken seriously, is of great support to people who have had their insights and intuitions confirmed in a social way. This book thus becomes an invitation to this conversation, and its publication at this point is timely and much needed.

A MEDITATION ON THE EVOLUTION OF IDEAS AND SOULS

What I have learned in my encounter with the question about life after death leads me to the following meditation. The early parts of the Bible know not of an afterlife above or in heaven. There is a region known as Sheol, the netherworld—Hades. In that region all souls, righteous and wicked, abide (including the patriarch Jacob, who says that he shall surely "go down to Sheol" and Samuel, the prophet, who is raised from Sheol by the Medium of Ein Dor). Scripturally, the dead sleep in the dust and await the time they will be raised from their graves.

Apparently, at that time there had not yet taken hold a belief in a heavenly afterlife in which the blessed and vindicated souls abide. We find in the "intertestamental period" the extracanonical texts of the Apocrypha, and in them there are already other beliefs about the afterlife that in the talmudic period become distinct visions of heavens and hells. In the Middle Ages and the Renaissance, especially after the publication of the Zohar, there are complete geographies of the seven levels of Gehinnom and the many mansions of the heavens. Around this time, teachings on reincarnation make their appearance after having been denied in earlier times. What is one to believe today, in the welter of seemingly conflicting notions of afterlife found throughout history? Are these beliefs really in conflict, each one contradicting the other? Or perhaps they are philosophical ideas that reflect various stages in the evolution of both the ideas of soul and the soul matter of the world?

As I started looking through history I saw a growth in the history of ideas. In my meditations I often contemplate the cycles, the patterns, as they unfold. Patterns, rather than specific details, give us the deeper insights. For me, the deepest midrashic process is to discover patterns that are embedded in the ancient texts. As we wrestle with the meaning of these texts, they begin to issue forth new insights and patterns that we then apply to our readings of other texts.

When I bring together what I have learned from the study of psychology, and from my own introspection, I discover the existence of similar developmental patterns. I frequently ask myself if the development of the stages of the afterlife only deals with ideas or if there is a deeper pattern that reflects the evolution of the soul itself. I see in the variety of teachings on the afterlife a parallel to the long evolutionary process in which consciousness arises from single cells, to sexual reproduction in animals, and at last reaches that of human beings. After many millennia of evolution, human souls emerge out of, and at death return to, a primordial pool. Thus, for instance, in Judges 2:10 we find the statement that "an entire generation was gathered into its ancestors." As a soul discarnate, one returns to the "ancestors" after a lifetime. This is to be taken as an ontological reality and not as a mere figure of speech.

Through the process of evolution, more and more consciousness emerges with each life cycle. The experience of each lifetime creates a deeper and stronger imprint of specific personality molded on the spiritual substance of the individual soul. Through her evolving biology, the earth has produced the now-enhanced matrix of the human soul. That soul matrix proceeded so far that it now reached that level where it could even think about the process of thought, thus reaching the sophistication in which it would turn its thought to the meaning of life and to what happens after death.

With the close of the biblical period, we are talking about judgment before God, purgatory, and a heavenly life after death. But at that time and at that level of evolution, we see only one individual life cycle. Then centuries later there is the introduction of the possibility of multiple lifetimes, many cycles. Notions of reincarnation appear in religious texts all over the world. So too people report "déjà vu" phenomena and relate their experiences of recalling past lives. These testimonies enter the stream of popular culture, again suggesting that the ontological reality of people's lives, as well as the inner consciousness, reflects what is found in the text, and vice versa.

As you read this book you will do well to remember that the various statements about the fate of the soul after death not only represent ideas found in texts but also describe phases in the long journey of the soul's evolution.

AFTER-DEATH CARE

Another important consideration this book raises is, How are we to help those who die and those who have died? I think often about those dying now who are making their way through to the other side and the problems they are likely to encounter. I pray that they are getting help from those who come to meet them on the other side.

From Jewish texts, we know of states of the after-death experience in which the soul is disoriented and confused. Our sources speak of *Hibbut Ha-Kever*, the pangs of the grave, and *Olam Ha-Tohu*, the world of confusion. How do we understand the reality of these states for people who are now dying or who are recently deceased? Are there any traditional models of care for the souls of the dead? From the legacy of Hasidism, we know that the Baal Shem Tov used to talk about *Tikkun Ha-Neshamot*, "the fixing or mending of souls." Before Shabbat he would help all of those souls that had passed during the week to make their reconciled entry into the world beyond. It was known that on Friday afternoons, he would say a long *Minhah Amidah*, afternoon silent prayer, and using deeply concentrated prayer, would act as a guide on behalf of the souls of the dead. Similarly, in the premodern Jewish world there were lay societies—the *Hevrah Tehillim* and *Hevrah Mishnayot*—who took upon themselves to provide after-death care by reciting Psalms, the *Kaddish* prayer, and selected texts of the Mishnah.

Even now in this age of the epidemics of cancer, AIDS, and other ravaging diseases, we need adepts to do this type of sacred rescue work. Members of the Jewish burial society, the *Hevrah Kaddisha*, could learn to offer such help to those who have died; ideally, each *Hevrah Kaddisha* group could have its own set of hospice workers to help people make the transition from life to what lies beyond. These and other possibilities are a natural outgrowth of the research on Jewish ideas of the hereafter gathered together in this book. With a deeper knowledge of Judaism's afterlife traditions, individuals and communities can be more adequately equipped and motivated to create cooperative institutions dedicated to postmortem care of the soul.

THE RESURRECTION

Finally, in reflecting on ideas about the afterlife, I turn to the question of the meaning of *Tehiyyat Ha-Metim*, resurrection of the dead. Each day

I recite several times the traditional Jewish formula "Blessed are You who revives the dead." In what way can one affirm this ancient principle of the faith the Sages and Maimonides teach as an essential component to being a believing Jew?

I do not believe that the crypts will open up in cemeteries and corpses will crawl out of them. Do I believe that at some time at the end of days the individual cells of my remains will be reconstituted? How many bodies have I worn out in only one lifetime already? We keep on changing. I cannot claim that this body will rise at the time of the resurrection. Which one of my various bodies, from which incarnation, which time in history? So I ask myself, how can I say I believe in the resurrection of the dead and mean it?

I believe that the resurrection occurs when dead matter proceeds to become a conscious, living being. This resurrection seems to be happening to the totality of this planet right now, at this very moment. On the cusp of the twenty-first century, this planet is waking up, being raised from being merely dead matter to becoming aware, conscious, alive. In paying attention to the emerging conscious ecology, we are part of this miraculous process of the rising from the dead. As human beings, we are becoming part of the planet's consciousness. In the language of the Lovelock-Margolis "Gaia hypothesis," we serve as the cells of the global brain. We are hearing the message of the planet earth, saying to us: "You can no longer do what you are doing to me. You have to change your ways. You have to collaborate with me." As we begin to awaken and hear this message, we begin to collaborate with earth's awakening and healing!

I believe *Tehiyyat Ha-Metim* is the resurrection of matter. In the past we used to think of matter dead and unconscious. Today, in this age of nuclear technology, genetic engineering, and supercomputers, matter is becoming alive to us! We speak of atoms, molecules, and cells as strings of information. Biologists have discovered genetic consciousness as encoded in DNA and RNA. With the advent of the computer, we now think of the memory as resident in silicon, a stone chip. Our thinking about matter and the physical world has undergone a shift from death to life.

Tehiyyat Ha-Metim, the resurrection of the dead, can then mean the coming to total awareness of the planet as a living organism with which we are connected. As beings in connection with the holographic planet mind, we will be augmented in consciousness and enriched by all other conscious beings!

This meditation on the evolution of the soul follows the way of the evolution. In this flow of thought, the disparate statements regarding the fate of the soul become of one piece. We meet the treasured pearls not separately but as part of a whole string, one in succeeding connection with the other. The teachings of Jewish tradition on the soul and its afterlife destiny can in this way be seen in a unified field theory, as a part of the greater whole.

Mazel Tov to us that this book is being made available as an aid in this process.

Zalman M. Schachter-Shalomi

Preface

In 1978, as a graduate student at the California Institute of Integral Studies, I first began systematic research on the topic of life after death in Judaism. If I knew then what I know now, I probably would have never attempted to write this book. Because of both the breadth and depth of the material, the task was more than I ever imagined it to be. At every juncture of the way, I was continually amazed—even more so, overwhelmed—at the magnitude of Jewish teachings on the afterlife. It has been one of the most challenging tasks of my life to immerse myself in this material, to endeavor to make sense of what Jewish sages wrote about the life after death, and to come away with a deeper appreciation of the ultimately unknown mysteries of life and death.

As I demonstrate throughout this book, teachings on life after death have always been part and parcel of the Jewish spiritual legacy. Although I have gathered together the most extensive compilation of Jewish afterlife sources available in one place, and have attempted to produce a resource book that has scholarly integrity, in no way is this book exhaustive. After more than fifteen years, *Jewish Views of the Afterlife* still feels to me like a work-in-progress. I have no doubt that each chapter—on the afterlife in biblical, apocryphal, rabbinic, medieval, kabbalistic, and hasidic Judaism—could be developed into a complete book in and of itself. It is my intention to inform both Jews and non-Jews about the afterlife in Judaism, and to inspire Jewish scholars to further investigate the uncharted maps and untranslated texts of Jewish teachings on the afterlife journey of the soul.

Like many a scholar, I have often worked in isolation on this book. Yet along the way, there were a number of people whose support must be acknowledged. First and foremost of all, my parents, Harold and Rose Paull, have been behind me all along. They gave me a deep appreciation of Jewish life and the opportunities for education that prepared me for this project. Each in their own way helped me to see this book through to completion.

Reb Zalman Schachter-Shalomi encouraged me to take on the task of researching and writing this book. Reb Zalman is a Jewish visionary and one of the great teachers of our age. For me, it was truly an honor that he was willing to be an adviser to this project and was available throughout the writing of this book to lend his wisdom and understanding. I hope I have done my teacher proud in bringing out the hidden legacy of Jewish afterlife teachings, and any shortcomings of this book are my own.

I am especially grateful to Michael Benjamin of Benjamin's Park Memorial Chapel. Colleague, friend, a mensch among men, Michael is an individual who deeply understands Jewish sacred traditions of death and dying. I learned a great deal from Michael during the years I worked with him in establishing the Benjamin Institute, a death-awareness education-and-bereavement support program, run in conjunction with a Jewish funeral home in Toronto, Ontario. As a result of Michael's progressive visionary work as a Jewish funeral director, I had the opportunity for practical experience working with the bereaved and learned how to bridge theory and practice, discovering the applicability of Jewish afterlife teachings in helping people to cope with the reality of grief and loss.

My wife, Geela Rayzel Robinson Raphael, accompanied me on the roller-coaster ride of this project. She shared my excitement when I discovered whole new pieces of the Jewish afterlife tradition and helped me wade through the times when writing this book felt more like death than afterlife. Throughout she has been both wife and friend, and as a rabbi herself, has continually offered invaluable scholarly input.

A number of friends, colleagues, and teachers read selections of the manuscript or offered me advice in pursuing research. With genuine appreciation, I acknowledge the support and scholarly input received from Robert Goldenberg and Herbert Levine. Above and beyond the call of duty, they helped me fine-tune the scholarship within this book. In addition, I offer my thanks to Art Green, Elliott Isenberg, Aryeh Streikowsky, Kalman Neumann, Marian Meyers, and Myriam Klotz, all of whom lent advice or editorial support. Finally, special thanks to Janet Warner of Jason Aronson Inc., who supported me through the editing process to final publication.

In addition, a number of individuals and foundations offered financial assistance for this project, and I want to express my due thanks. While completing my doctoral dissertation, an early version of this book, I received funding from the Samuel and Saidye Bronfman Foundation, Montreal, Quebec; Micha Taubman, of the Emet Foundation, formerly of San Rafael, California; the Kern Foundation, of Wheaton, Illinois, which offered me a fellowship to study at the Krotona Institute of Theosophy, in Ojai, California; Rabbi Yossi Wosk, of Vancouver, British Columbia; and James Raymond, of the Gamma Rho Foundation, Montreal, Quebec. In recent years, Mitchell and Natalie Robinson have provided support toward the completion of this book, along with a deep personal belief in my professional potential. Their generous assistance has made life much easier for me and my family over the past seven years. To all of these people, I thank you for making this work possible. As this book is birthed into the world, know that the fruit of your philanthropic caring will be shared widely with others.

As a death-awareness educator, throughout the past decade I have taught courses and offered workshops and lectures on the theme of life after death in Judaism, sharing various facets of this book with literally thousands of people in Canada, the United States, and Israel. So often I was deeply touched with how valuable, even precious, this material seemed to the men and women I met. "Judaism does uphold a belief in life after death!" many would exclaim, often with tears in their eyes. On many occasions, I have seen a bereaved individual move toward resolution with a dead parent or spouse, just by becoming aware of Judaism's wisdom about survival of the soul after death. Throughout the years, the thirsty and deeply appreciative response of my students continually served to motivate and inspire me to see this project through to completion. As rabbinic tradition asserts, מתלמידי יותר מכולם—"From my students I have learned most of all." I am forever grateful for the opportunity to be a teacher and owe a deep sense of gratitude to the many people with whom I had wonderful conversations about the personal and spiritual relevance of Jewish views of the afterlife.

Finally, in a prayerful spirit, I offer my thanks to the Holy Blessed One who has sustained me, nurtured me, and brought me to this moment.

Simcha Paull Raphael, Ph.D.
Philadelphia

Chapter 1

A Personal Journey

At the age of four, I encountered death for the first time when my maternal grandmother suddenly disappeared from my life. Faced with the absence of a person who had been a deep source of love and nurturance, I probingly questioned all the adults around me as to her whereabouts. In response to my innocent, yet persistent inquiries, I was told that Bubby had died and gone to Heaven. However, no one ever explained to me exactly why she died, or why she left without even a good-bye.

As a result of that early experience, the remaining years of my childhood were spent looking toward the heavens. Night after night I prayed to God for Bubby Mina's peace, and found myself communicating with the spirit of a dead grandmother who perpetually radiated love and protection. Although I did not know it then, at a very early age seeds were planted that would inspire and motivate the writing of this book on Jewish views of the afterlife.

Throughout the years of late adolescence and early adulthood, death was a frequent visitor in my world. Growing up in the 1960s, when my contemporaries were attracted to drugs and fast cars, I lived through the deaths of all too many young people. The highway or the hospital intensive care unit claimed the lives of several friends and family members I loved deeply.

In my early twenties death impacted upon my life in an irreversible

1

way, when two very close friends died suddenly—one in a car accident, the other from a massive brain hemorrhage. I discovered the stark reality that someone I loved could be alive one day and dead the next. One cold winter's day in 1973, my life was changed forever as I stood witness while the body of a beloved friend, a young man of twenty-two, was lowered into the frozen earth. With an aching, numb heart, I found myself wondering, as people often do: what happened to the life force once animating this body? Was this the end? Was there a soul that somehow lived on? Was there any ultimate meaning to life and death? This ordeal catalyzed a profound and ongoing process of wrestling with questions about death, immortality, and postmortem survival, a process that has continued to this day.

Encounters with death have led me into the depths of spiritual despair and personal disintegration. And yet, out of the alienation, suffering, and grief, I have discovered an invisible thread of spiritual purpose and destiny pervading human life itself. From the meaninglessness of death, I learned to find meaning, purpose, and faith in my own life. Seeing the obvious temporality of the human condition, and yet feeling the infinite, transcendent nature of love between people, I have come to see death as but an expression of the unfolding of the divine on the plane of human existence. Death can be cruel and painful; for many it is. Yet, in my own life, death has been a spiritual teacher, a source of much inspiration, and a catalyst for genuine spiritual growth.

In dealing with the intensity of my grief reaction, I found myself continually drawn to the study of death and the afterlife in modern psychology and in the great religions of the world. Teachings on life after death in Eastern religions were often easy to track down. Since the 1960s there have been innumerable gurus, swamis, and lamas popularizing Hindu and Buddhist spirituality in the West. For a time, in the 1970s, teachings on reincarnation, yoga philosophy, and meditation were almost normative—after all, the Beatles had meditated with the Maharishi Mahesh Yogi, who was a frequent guest on late-night television. Nonetheless, my thirsting Jewish soul ached to find Judaism's wisdom on life after death. But, as many have discovered, it was not easy to find Jewish writings on the afterlife. Most modern studies describe Jewish rituals of dying and mourning, but only in perfunctory ways make reference to a postmortem existence.

However, with the encouragement of Rabbi Zalman Schachter-Shalomi, I was appropriately led to begin a systematic exploration of little-known Jewish traditions on the hereafter. And once my pursuit had begun, I continually unearthed more and more treasures of Jewish wisdom on the afterlife journey of the soul. Almost fifteen years in the making, this book, which in an earlier form was submitted as a doctoral dissertation at the California Institute of Integral Studies, is a product of a lifelong personal quest to understand the mysteries of life, death, and beyond.

A CATALOG OF IMAGES AND THEMES ON THE AFTERLIFE

Jewish Views of the Afterlife is a survey of ideas of life after death throughout the history of Judaism. The task of this book is to explore the emergence of Jewish teachings on individual survival after death, and document how various afterlife conceptions were formed and transformed as Judaism evolved.

Essentially a study of Jewish texts, *Jewish Views of the Afterlife* is designed as a tour through history—imagine this book as a "Traveler's Guide to the Afterlife." In the pages that follow we will time travel through four thousand years of Jewish cultural development. Each chapter depicts the understanding of the afterlife and the nature of the postmortem journey developed in a particular period of Jewish history. We will investigate the sacred texts produced in each era and ask: how did Judaism conceive of the fate of the individual after death? And further, what are the teachings, tales, and traditions found in these texts that reveal to us Jewish ideas of the hereafter?

The overall intention of this Jewish guide to the afterlife is to provide a phenomenological description of the ever-changing notions of life after death uncovered in each historical period, in each set of sacred texts. What ultimately emerges from our historical excursion is a multidimensional catalog, rich in imagistic diversity, broad in philosophical scope, portraying the myriad conceptions of life after death in Judaism.

As we will discover, at no point is it really appropriate to speak simply of *the* Jewish view of the afterlife. Just as Judaism and Jewish culture developed and changed repeatedly through contact with other world civilizations, so Jewish afterlife teachings evolved rapidly during the course of four millennia. In almost every era of history we uncover many parallel and sometimes even conflicting ideas on life after death existing side by side. Four thousand years of Jewish thought about postmortem survival can be confusing. For this reason, in exploring the voluminous legacy of Jewish writings, we endeavor to demonstrate how new ideas evolved, merged with earlier conceptions of the afterlife, and ultimately led to entirely new formulations about the mysterious fate of the individual after physical death. We also portray the unique style of afterlife texts in each era, as well as the common elements that characterize Jewish conceptions of the hereafter throughout history.

CONTENT OF THE BOOK

In Chapter 2, "Is There Afterlife after Auschwitz?," we set the foundation for this study, discussing, in broad strokes, the whole issue of the afterlife in modern Judaism. This chapter elucidates the various forces that have made the topic of life after death problematic in the Judaism of the twentieth century.

Chapter 3, "Biblical Roots of Jewish Views of the Afterlife," inaugurates the historical journey. Here, we explore the emergence of biblical notions of individual postmortem survival. Although an important and necessary starting point, the Hebrew Bible is certainly not a definitive source for understanding Jewish ideas of life after death. However, certain Jewish notions of life after death are seeded in biblical times. For this reason, the exploration of biblical writings sets the stage for understanding further Jewish philosophical thinking about the hereafter.

Chapter 4, "Tours of Heaven and Hell in Apocryphal Literature," investigates the literary creations of Hellenistic Judaism. In the Apocrypha and Pseudepigrapha we discover apocalyptic and visionary depictions of the afterlife and uncover an important stream of Jewish tradition, one that has been obscured and is not widely known in modern Judaism.

In Chapter 5, "The World to Come in Rabbinic Judaism," we cull through over five centuries of diverse, and often incongruous, rabbinic texts. What emerges from a study of Mishnah, Talmud, and Midrash is a fascinating collage of teachings on the life after death. At no point does rabbinic literature convey a monolithic conception of the hereafter. Rather, what we find is an exceptionally broad spectrum of images and themes elucidating the fate of the dead in various realms of the afterlife.

Chapter 6, "Visionary Tours of the Afterlife in Medieval Midrash," takes us into the little-known world of medieval legendary Midrash. Here we encounter exotic visionary depictions of the afterlife, unparalleled in

Jewish tradition. In order to make this unique material more widely available, in this chapter we present English translations of fourteen primary source texts on the afterlife.

In Chapter 7, "Immortality of the Soul in Medieval Philosophy," we investigate the writings of the medieval Jewish philosophers, surveying the afterlife teachings of Saadia Gaon, Moses Maimonides, Gersonides, and Nahmanides. In medieval Jewish philosophy we find an attempt to harmonize rationalistic philosophy and traditional Jewish notions of survival of the soul after death.

Within Kabbalah, a Jewish mystical tradition that developed especially during the twelfth to sixteenth centuries, can be found an exceptionally well developed notion of the soul and its fate after death. In Chapter 8, "The Afterlife Journey of the Soul in Kabbalah," we examine the *Zohar* and other kabbalistic writings and present an outline of the most extensive philosophy of life after death found in Judaism. In so doing, we also document the emergence of new Jewish ideas on the afterlife, including *gilgul*, transmigration of souls, or reincarnation—a little-known Jewish concept.

In Chapter 9, "Death and the Afterlife in Hasidic Tales," we enter into the world of hasidic literature. Here we find a series of stories and legends about various hasidic masters, depicting the awe-inspiring ways in which they died, and reports of how, after death, they allegedly maintained communication with the living. These stories, which reflect more of a folk than a philosophical tradition, demonstrate yet another aspect of the diverse Jewish legacy on the afterlife.

Chapter 10 brings the historical survey to its natural junction, presenting "A Contemporary Psychological Model of the Afterlife." This is an original model of the afterlife journey, based on a synthesis of modern consciousness research, transpersonal psychology, studies of near-death experiences, and traditional Jewish sources. This model outlines the various stages of the soul's journey after death, and as a summary to the book, presents my own quintessential view of the afterlife in Judaism.

A WORD ON THE SOURCES

In writing this book I have endeavored to be as expansive as I could be in presenting Jewish material on the afterlife. A glance at the bibliography reveals the wide-ranging Jewish, psychological, philosophical, comparative religion, and death and dying resources brought together in this study. Hopefully, the breadth and eclecticism of my training in Jewish studies, comparative religion, and psychology have not been at the cost of depth in any one area. But I recognize that as a Jewish scholar, I am a generalist. I believe my own unique contribution to this topic lies in the contemporary psychological and spiritual view of the afterlife that I map out in the final chapter. I have done all I can to bring scholarly integrity and depth to the exploration of Jewish sources in this book. Nonetheless, I know there are still unmined resources on life after death in Judaism.

In the area of Kabbalah and Hasidism, I worked with somewhat defined sources. Chapter 8 on "The Afterlife Journey of the Soul in Kabbalah" draws largely from Zohar, which is only one layer of kabbalistic tradition, albeit an important one. I know that there are other very rich and extensive kabbalistic writings on the afterlife and reincarnation; for now, such writings still await further scholarly investigation. Similarly, in Chapter 9 on "Death and the Afterlife in Hasidic Tales" I focus predominantly on hasidic stories, and little on other genres of hasidic literature. The truth is, there is still a lot more scholarly work to be done to fully bring to light the richness of afterlife traditions in Hasidism and in Kabbalah. Nonetheless, I believe this book does justice in portraying teachings on life after death in the Jewish mystical tradition.

Finally, the scholar of modern Judaism may be disappointed to discover that I do not do an extensive survey of what early modern Jewish theologians had to say about the afterlife. Part of the problem is that they did not have much to say. As I point out in the next chapter, "Is There Afterlife after Auschwitz?," in the modern era Judaism does not have an extensive tradition on the afterlife. Ideas about life after death take a back seat to rationalism and scientific materialism. I use Chapter 2 to set the groundwork for the rest of the book. Though I mention the ideas of people like Hermann Cohen and Leo Baeck, I present more of a synopsis than a survey of modern Judaism's view of the life after death. And even though as early as 1767 Moses Mendelssohn authored a treatise on immortality of the soul entitled *Phaedon*, this book has no Jewish content. It is designed as an explication of Plato's philosophy of the soul in light of modern psychology but does not refer at all to traditional Jewish ideas of the afterlife. For this reason, I do not include Mendelssohn's *Phaedon* in this book.[1]

With most of the primary source material I used—specifically, Hebrew Bible, Talmud, rabbinic Midrash, medieval Midrash, *Zohar*, and

Hasidism—I worked predominantly with original Hebrew or Aramaic sources that are also available in English translation. As much as possible I went back and forth between English translations and the original Hebrew and Aramaic sources. When quoting directly from the ancient texts, at times I modified previously translated sources to create translations that reflect a contemporary and, where possible, nonsexist God language.

In introducing each chapter, I give an overview of the sources on the afterlife in each era. The specialist and the scholar will discover that the bibliography and footnotes provide detailed documentation of the primary and secondary sources available for studying afterlife teachings within each period of Jewish history. However, where possible I have included textual references to primary sources within the body of the book. Therefore, the general reader will still be able to appreciate the breadth of Jewish afterlife teachings, with or without any footnotes.

HOW TO READ THIS BOOK

There are three different ways that I read books. Some books I read with a pencil: those are usually scholarly writings, works of philosophy, treatises that require uninterrupted intellectual concentration, books written to educate the mind and intellect.

There are other books I read straight through from start to finish, stopping neither for notes nor for footnotes. These books tend to be authored in a somewhat more popular style. Even if nonfiction, they are frequently written as first-person narrative; these are not books about how to think, but more about how to live, books written for the heart and soul.

Then there are those books that I can randomly open up at any page and read for a while, stopping to savor each word image, maybe spending half an hour on two or three pages. These are books of wisdom rather than knowledge; they are filled with images and with poetry, designed to illuminate and awaken the soul.

Personally, I think *Jewish Views of the Afterlife* is one of those books that can be read with a pencil. Designed to be a resource book of teachings on life after death, it is filled with complex concepts and intricate texts covering almost forty centuries of Jewish life. As a scholarly book, it can be read straight through, but it can also be used as a reference work

for people investigating Jewish thought and experience in different periods of history.

But this book is more than just an academic text. I believe it can
also be read randomly, associatively, allowing the imagistic material to
act upon the higher mind, the intuition, the soul. My experience as a
bereavement psychologist tells me that people buy and read books on
death, dying, and the afterlife, not only to educate the mind, but also to
heal the heart and to quench the thirsting of the soul. For some readers,
the academic content of this book is going to be satisfying in and of itself. But for others, it may not be. If this is the case for you, I suggest you
read the next chapter, which sets the context of the book as a whole.
But then, feel free to wander through history—read individual chapters,
or bits and pieces of the different chapters. Reflect on the themes of the
afterlife encoded in different texts; savor the intensity of the images about
the soul and its wandering through the postmortem realms; turn to the
summary at the end of each chapter for a cognitive overview of the central themes that develop in a particular period. If you choose to read this
book in a nonlinear, intuitive fashion, be sure to spend a good deal of
time reading through the collection of primary source texts in Chapter 6
on "Visionary Tours of the Afterlife in Medieval Midrash." This is very
fascinating material and will transform your ideas about what Jews believe about life after death. Also, Chapter 9, "Death and the Afterlife in
Hasidic Tales," is more of a collection of stories and gives a very different portrayal of ideas about life after death. Finally, however you use this
book, be sure to read Chapter 10, "A Contemporary Psychological Model
of the Afterlife." I think this chapter, more than any other, has the ability to speak to people who are investigating the topic of death and the
afterlife with some personal thought about the eventual fate of mortal
human beings.

Above all, when reading this book, remember that Jews have written and thought about life after death for millennia, and there is no right
or wrong answer to the questions we human beings have about dying and
death. In each era Jewish sages have contributed their own new perspectives to understanding the nature of the hereafter, and the final word
has not been said about what happens to human beings after death.

This book has been written as one individual's attempt to make some
sense of the enigma of human mortality. Writing it has been my own way
of wrestling with the uncertainty of what lies beyond the transition between life and death. As a scholar of religion, I have brought together a

vast collection of Jewish texts and traditions on death and the afterlife. As a psychologist, I have presented in contemporary psychological terms how I understand the essence of Jewish teachings on the postmortem journey of the soul. And, finally, as a mortal human being, I humbly recognize that, ultimately, there are no final answers to the mystery of life and death.

Chapter 2

Is There Afterlife after Auschwitz?[1]

DO JEWS BELIEVE IN THE AFTERLIFE?

There is a story told about an eighty-five-year-old Jewish woman who was in a convalescent hospital dying. Her concerned daughter wanted to do all she could to help the elderly woman in her final days and weeks. She made plans to visit the hospital to read her mother selections from the *Tibetan Book of the Dead*, a religious text with elaborate descriptions of what one encounters subsequent to physical death.

Just stop for a moment and contemplate that scene. An elderly Jewish woman, likely raised on gefilte fish and chicken soup, is close to the end of her life. Her baby-boomer daughter, a product of Dr. Spock and the Beatles, is willingly ready to read her mother contents of a sixteenth-century Buddhist deathbed manual. That scene is suggestive of a cultural mix possible only in the age of the global village.

A psychologist working with dying patients cautioned the young woman against reading her mother the contents of this death manual created by Tibetan Buddhist monks. He explained that the arcane symbolism and deathbed meditations of the *Tibetan Book of the Dead* would frighten and confuse the elderly woman, rather than help her understand the process and experience of dying. Instead, the daughter was advised to go and read her dying mother old Yiddish love songs.[2]

Given the circumstances, it appears that Yiddish love songs were the appropriate substitute. The scene of an elderly, dying Jewish woman being read Yiddish love poetry suggests a much greater quality of cultural harmony than the intrusion of Tibetan Buddhist deathbed meditations. Yet an important question emerges from this anecdote: Why are Yiddish love songs the recommended resource for assisting a Jewish person at the time of death?

Throughout the world, there are religious texts on dying and death specifically designed to provide assistance at the time of passage from this world. The Buddhists have the *Tibetan Book of the Dead*; there is an *Egyptian Book of the Dead*; Hindus, Moslems, and most Native American cultures have traditions about survival in the afterlife. Even medieval Christianity produced a genre of literature entitled *Ars Moriendi*, or "The Art of Dying," which discusses the postmortem fate of the soul. Is there a Jewish tradition on the afterlife journey of the soul or specific Jewish texts that can be of help to people at the time of death? What exactly are the Jewish resources for guiding a person through the transition from life to death?

When dealing with dying, grief, loss, and the inevitability of human mortality, people frequently ask the question "Is there life after death?" As to be expected, Jews more specifically inquire: "Does Judaism believe in an afterlife?" This question frequently creates a quandary for Jews and non-Jews alike. The reality is that the whole topic of life after death in Judaism is perplexing and problematic.

When asked "What do Jews believe about life after death?," individuals respond with a variety of answers that invariably demonstrate both confusion and a paucity of information available on the hereafter in Jewish tradition. "Jews believe in life after death, but there are no details to speak of" is a common answer. Or "Jews believe that the soul is eternal, and after death one lives on as a soul." Another recurring theme frequently expressed is "Jews believe that there is a resurrection of the dead that will take place after the Messiah comes." "My grandmother told me to burn my fingernails so I won't have to go looking for them at the time of the resurrection," said one individual. With some variation many often claim that "Jews believe in a World to Come, *Olam Ha-Ba*, and eventually one enters this world." In a similar vein, others say: "When I was young and my father died, I was told he was with God in heaven. We believe in heaven." It is clear that Jews believe many different things about life after death. However, when pressed for additional details or an enhanced philosophical exploration of this topic, even among those who are well versed in Jewish thought, there is not a great deal more information forthcoming. Simply put, most modern Jews are vastly unaware of Jewish teachings on the afterlife. Why?

Well, there is one additional answer that always emerges when asking people about Jewish beliefs in the afterlife. And this answer, expressed in the following anecdote, is really central to this whole problem about the afterlife in Judaism.

Recently, a rabbi was lecturing a group of nurses on "Bio-Medical Ethics: The Jewish Approach." When asked by a member of the audience, "Does Judaism believe in an afterlife?" forthrightly the rabbi replied: "Judaism celebrates life and the living. It dwells on life here rather than on the hereafter as other religious faiths do. Life is precious, the here and the now."[3]

This response, which is absolutely characteristic of modern Judaism's attitude toward the afterlife, is the singularly most problematic Jewish belief about life after death today. Why? Because it is simply not true!

Yes, Judaism does value life, here and now, over and above a future death and eternal life.[4] As Abraham Joshua Heschel so eloquently expressed: "The cry for a life beyond the grave is presumptuous if it is not accompanied by a cry for eternal life prior to death."[5] Yes, it is accurate to maintain that Judaism has a life-affirming, this-worldly orientation that proclaims the sanctity and significance of physical plane life. This world, divinely given for humanity to enjoy, appreciate, and sanctify, has always been very important for Judaism, because within the context of physical, embodied life one can fulfill the divine commandments, or mitzvot. There is no doubt that Judaism is committed to tikkun olam—the "mending of the world"—the total transformation of the sociopolitical realm of human existence. But this does not imply there is no Jewish belief in an afterlife. To deny or politely bypass Jewish notions of life after death is a pedagogical error promulgated by all too many instructors of Judaism.

Somehow, in the twentieth century, Judaism has been proclaimed as a "here and now" religion. As an inadvertent result, both Jews and non-Jews have come to believe that Judaism does not have any conception of a life after death. It is therefore not surprising that when seeking accessible resources for responding to the crisis of death, many turn to other traditions such as the *Tibetan Book of the Dead* or read Yiddish love poetry for spiritual solace. It is the intention of this book to demonstrate that Judaism does have a belief in life after death. More to the point, there exists a profound and extensive legacy of Jewish teachings on the afterlife. Over the course of four millennia, Judaism evolved and promulgated a multifaceted philosophy of postmortem survival, with doctrines comparable to those found in the great religions of the world. In short, Jews have always believed in life after death.

THE PREMODERN JEWISH LEGACY ON THE AFTERLIFE

To illustrate how pervasive afterlife teachings have been in premodern Judaism, and as a foretaste of the content of this book, consider the following vignettes of Jewish literary history.

In 1626, in Mantua, Italy, Rabbi Aaron Berachia ben Moses of Modena authored a text entitled *Maavor Yabok*, literally "Crossing the River Yabok." (In Genesis 32 Jacob crossed the River Yabok, the metaphor used in the title of this text.) *Maavor Yabok* is a compilation of writings on death, dying, and the philosophy of the afterlife. Based on the kabbalistic philosophy of the soul expounded by Isaac Luria, this text is replete with descriptions of the soul's experiences at the time of death, and beyond.[6] More than any other Hebrew book, *Maavor Yabok* may be considered the "Jewish Book of the Dead."

Produced specifically for the *Hevrah Kaddisha*, or Burial Society, of Mantua, this text was rapidly accepted in both Ashkenazic and Sephardic Jewish communities of the time. Over the course of two centuries, *Maavor Yabok* was printed in more than twenty editions and became the standard *Hevra Kaddisha* manual for Jews in Southern, Central, and Eastern Europe.[7] Although untranslated, this text is still in print today.

Another text worthy of note is *Nishmat Hayyim*, "The Soul of Life," by Rabbi Menasseh ben Israel,[8] a scholar, commercial entrepreneur, and political statesman who negotiated with Oliver Cromwell for permission for Jews to reenter England. Originally a Marrano who reembraced Judaism when he migrated from Spain to Amsterdam in the early 1600s, Menasseh ben Israel was the first rabbi and spiritual leader of the Amsterdam Jewish community.[9]

In the author's introduction to *Nishmat Hayyim*, he relates how he was lying awake one night, when a *Malakh*, an angel or spirit guide, appeared to him at his bedside. The visionary being then dictated, or channeled, to Menasseh ben Israel a treatise on *din gilgul neshamot*, literally "the law of the revolution of souls"—reincarnation. *Nishmat Hayyim* is an eclectic text that presents a survey of Jewish beliefs on such topics as immortality of the soul, the nature of the astral body, the death-moment itself, postmortem judgment, the afterlife wanderings of the soul, and other conceptions of the hereafter found in rabbinic and kabbalistic sources.

Additionally, while most people have heard of *The Divine Comedy*, Dante's epic poem on heaven, hell, and purgatory,[10] almost completely unknown is the poetic chronicle of life in the afterlife written by Immanuel Ha-Romi, a thirteenth-century Italian Jew. A contemporary of Dante, Ha-Romi authored an elaborate text that portrays his visionary journeying through the postmortem worlds.[11] Based on ancient rabbinic traditions of the afterlife, this text is one of many legendary creations of the medieval period that describe with ornate detail the divine judgment experienced at the time of death and the Jewish afterlife realms of heaven and hell—known as Gan Eden, the Garden of Eden, and Gehenna, or purgatory. As visionary and imagistic as anything produced by Dante, such texts are not isolated literary products, outside the canon of Jewish tradition. Philosophically based in Torah and Talmud, they are part of an extensive and popularized Jewish afterlife tradition and as Jewish as Moses and Manishewitz wine!

Thus, as these examples suggest, it is not that Judaism lacks a belief in the afterlife. Rather, the contents of many of these earlier teachings have been lost due, in part, to the changing nature of modern Jewish society. Over the course of the past century, as Jews left behind the traditional ghetto lifestyle of premodern Europe, there has been increasing assimilation and a rapid diminuation of commitment to the study and practice of Judaism. And in the twentieth century, as the center of Jewish life shifted from Europe to North America, and from a Hebrew and Yiddish linguistic environment to an English-speaking one, knowledge of and interest in premodern Jewish teachings on the afterlife have been lost.

Assuming the young woman mentioned above had been aware of Jewish afterlife teachings, because they were written in a language and cultural metaphor alien to her, she might not have found them very helpful as she attempted to deal with the immediacy of her dying mother's needs.[12] The simple truth of the matter is that modern Jewish life is desperately lacking and passionately seeking adequate spiritual resources for dealing with death and dying.

Standing on the cusp of the twenty-first century, we are living through an era of changing perspectives on dying and death. The time is ripe for a reclaiming of ancient Jewish afterlife traditions and the creation of a contemporary model of the afterlife that makes Jewish postmortem teachings accessible to individuals dealing with death, dying, and bereavement today. Such is the goal of this book.

WHAT HAPPENED TO THE AFTERLIFE?

The chapters that follow explore the theme of life after death in the Bible, Apocrypha, Mishnah, Talmud, rabbinic and medieval Midrash, medieval philosophy, Kabbalah, and hasidic tales. In depicting the evolution of afterlife teachings, we will encounter a plethora of premodern teachings on the immortality of the soul, the fate of wandering deceased spirits, postmortem judgment, individual reward and punishment, mythical visions of hell and heaven, reincarnation, resurrection, as well as innumerable rabbinic and hasidic folktales that express a belief in the soul's continued survival after death.

The sheer volume of the material covered in this book reflects just how extensive is the premodern Jewish afterlife tradition. And yet, from this stage in history we are forced to ask: What happened to the afterlife in Judaism? If there is in fact such a legacy of traditional Jewish beliefs in the hereafter, then where has it gone? Why has modern Judaism lost touch with the whole notion of life after death?

The answer to this series of questions is not simple. Both historical and contemporary factors, from within Judaism itself and as a result of cultural transformation in the Western world, have led to the deemphasis of teachings about the fate of the individual after death. Presently, we will examine some of these factors.

Biblical Judaism's Inherent Ambivalence toward the Afterlife

First of all, in the early biblical period, there is a conscious attempt made to keep a distance from the realm of the deceased. The result is a biblical text frequently asserting that any interaction between the living and the dead is in violation of God's law.

For example, in 1 Samuel 28, King Saul travels to the Witch of En-Dor and requests of her to evoke the spirit of the deceased Prophet Samuel. After some preliminary conversation, she summons from the netherworld an aged, godlike figure—the prophet Samuel himself—who delivers a somewhat disheartening message to the king. While this tale points to the existence of a postmortem realm of the dead, there is something else quite strange going on. In embarking upon his nocturnal visit to the medium from En-Dor, Saul had disguised himself in clothing other than his royal, military garb to avoid being recognized. Why the disguise? Because he himself had "expelled all the mediums and wizards from the land" (1 Samuel 28:3). Thus, there are two contradictory attitudes co-existing simultaneously: on the one hand, it is clear that there were those engaged in oracular communication with the dead—even King Saul himself elected to do so. On the other hand, there had been an official condemnation of necromancy and spiritualistic practices.

Evidence suggests that, at least in the early biblical period, there was an association between communion with the dead and paganistic, idolatrous practices condemned by the monotheistic biblical writers. Thus, in Deuteronomy, condemnation of both mediumship and child sacrifice appear side by side:

> Let no one be found among you who sacrifices his son or daughter in the fire, who practices divination or sorcery, interprets omens, engages in witchcraft, or casts spells, or who is a medium or spiritist or who consults the dead. (Deuteronomy 18:10–11)

Similarly, in Leviticus, there is further evidence establishing a clear distance from the realm of the ancestral dead. Whenever an Israelite high priest came into contact with a dead body, he was automatically regarded as contaminated and, consequently, seen as unfit for divine service in the tabernacle (Leviticus 21:11–12). And why is the priest to avoid contact with dead bodies? The likelihood is that various forms of necromancy were indigenous to religious practice of the ancient Near East; there were undoubtedly pagan priests in ancient Mesopotamia who practiced various forms of communing with the dead.[13] But the monotheistic Hebrews were commanded to distinguish themselves from such idolatrous practices, and the biblical writers harshly condemned both physical and spiritistic forms of contact with the world of the dead. In the biblical worldview, to commune with the dead—even more, to assume that the dead actually survive after death—was at times regarded as a form of idolatry itself.

Because of this view, we find in biblical Judaism a deep reticence about the dead and an obvious reluctance to elucidate any overt notion or belief in an afterlife. Even to this day an individual who is a *kohen* or descendant of priestly lineage, whether a rabbi or a layperson, is prohibited from coming into contact with a dead body. Based on a ritual taboo instituted almost four thousand years ago, in response to ancient Near Eastern idolatry, today there are many Jews who are completely unable to deal with any physical aspect of death, prohibited to do so by religious law. And even more, this ancient taboo has insidiously affected four thousand years of Jewish thought and leaves modern Judaism with a somewhat tainted, negative attitude toward life after death.

Eschatology: Individual and Collective

To further understand why modern Judaism is often confused about the afterlife, we need to know the difference between individual and collective eschatology. Eschatology is a theological and philosophical term derived from the Greek *eschatos*, meaning "last" or "farthest." It is the study of religious and philosophical teachings concerned with that which occurs at "the end of days," that is, at the time "farthest" from the present. An exceptionally broad subject, eschatology includes topics such as life after death; reincarnation and postmortem survival of the soul, as well as teachings about the end of time and history; theories of resurrection of body and/or soul; last judgment; messianic redemption of the world; and the ultimate destiny of the entire universe.

Scholars make a distinction between individual and collective eschatology. Whereas collective eschatology is concerned with the collective future of humanity and the cosmic order at the end of time and history, individual eschatology focuses specifically on the destiny of each unique human being after death. While the two often overlap, when thinking about Jewish afterlife teachings it is useful to understand the difference between these two facets of eschatology: individual, the unique person; collective, the whole nation, the world.

Within Judaism the focus has often been on collective rather than individual eschatology—on the fate of God's chosen nation at the end of time, rather than on the afterlife experiences of the individual. In light of the covenant at Sinai, the Israelite people collectively stood in a direct relationship with God. God's actions impacted upon the nation as a whole, and vice versa, the behavior of the nation Israel determined God's response. Given this relationship, redemption, according to the biblical worldview, implies redemption of the entire Israelite nation, not the individual Israelite. The question is not what happens after death, but rather what will happen to the nation at a future time when God will save and transform the world. The very idea of an individual relationship with God, distinct from the collective Israelite nation, does not emerge prior to the sixth century B.C.E. Even then, collective teachings about ultimate redemption at the end-of-days, messianic renewal, establishment of a divine kingdom on earth, last judgment, and, eventually, resurrection of the dead, all take precedence over beliefs in an individual hereafter.[14] Thus, collective eschatology, at least in the biblical period, always supersedes individual afterlife eschatology.

When we investigate rabbinic Judaism, we find a somewhat confused view of the afterlife. In rabbinic tradition the term *Olam Ha-Ba*, or the "World to Come," is frequently used in reference to a future postmortem life. But it is often unclear whether this World to Come is inaugurated immediately after an individual's death or in the distant future, at the end of time and history when the world will be redeemed.

For example, in one rabbinic text we find this statement: "My law will guide you in your path in this world; it will watch over you in your sleep, at the hour of death; and when you wake, it will converse with you in the *Olam Ha-Ba*" (*Sifre* on Leviticus 18:4).

This passage suggests that *Olam Ha-Ba* is a postmortem world one enters immediately after death. However, elsewhere the Talmud expresses a different point of view:

> Not like this world will be the World to Come. In this world one has the trouble to harvest grapes and press them; but in the World to Come a person will bring a single grape in a wagon or a ship, store it in the corner of his house, and draw from it enough wine to fill it a large flagon. . . . There will not be a grape which will not yield thirty measures of wine (*Ketubbot* 111b).

Here the World to Come is not a postmortem world but rather an era that begins at the end of time and history with the onset of the messianic kingdom. The World to Come seems more like a time of global supertechnology than anything having to do with death and life after death.

Thus, in rabbinic literature, collective and individual eschatological teachings are frequently fused and confused. No clear distinction is made between philosophical teachings on the ultimate fate of the nation at the end of time and teachings on the destiny of the individual in the hereafter.

However, just because collective eschatology is often the dominant stream in early Judaism does not mean that there was never any belief in an individual afterlife. This is a misreading of history, and contemporary interpreters of Jewish thought, like Herschel Matt, who claim "the main line of rabbinic Judaism does not teach the survival of the soul,"[15] choose to see only the collective eschatological strands within Judaism. This totally ignores the fact that after the Babylonian exile, in the sixth century B.C.E., the conception of an individual postmortem survival begins to slowly emerge and that in early and later rabbinic literature there are teachings on the immortality of the soul. Even more, from the twelfth century C.E. onward, an increasingly sophisticated series of teachings on the afterlife journey of the soul are produced in the mystical and mythical literature of medieval Judaism.

The Influence of Moses Maimonides

Another explanation for the modern confusion about life after death can be found in the approach to the afterlife of Moses Maimonides, the most famous Jewish scholar of the medieval period. A committed traditional Jew, Maimonides was a rationalistic philosopher who endeavored to reconcile Jewish tradition with the emerging philosophical worldview of medieval times.

Although he affirms the existence of an immortal soul, when speaking of Olam Ha-Ba, the World to Come, Maimonides describes it as an otherworldly realm, totally beyond human comprehension. "As to the blissful state of the soul in the World to Come, there is no way on earth in which we can comprehend or know it," declares Maimonides quite explicitly.[16] With this statement, Maimonides, like other rationalistic Aristotelians of the medieval age, created an unbridgeable chasm between matter and spirit, between human and divine realms. Matter is matter, spirit is spirit, and ne'er the twain shall meet is the dictum of the

Maimonidean view. This point of view has successfully wedged a gap between the spiritual and human realms, thereby convincing many people that contemplating the question of life after death is a task beyond human ability.

Today, Maimonides' belief that the spiritual life of the World to Come is beyond human comprehension persists within Judaism. In spite of the demise of the rationalistic, Aristotelian worldview, we find these philosophical conceptions echoed in *The Jewish Way in Death and Mourning*, one of the most widely read modern books on death and Judaism. In discussing the afterlife, Maurice Lamm reiterates Maimonides' point of view, saying that, in spite of the Jewish belief in immortality, there are no details available on the afterlife. Why? Because "flesh-and-blood man cannot have any precise conception of the pure, spiritual bliss of the world beyond."[17] This is an uncritical acceptance of Maimonides' philosophical rationalism that ignores the mystical and mythic streams of Judaism wherein are found magnificent textual depictions of the afterlife realms.

And similarly, one generation earlier, the modern German-Jewish theologian Leo Baeck, in his classic of modern Jewish thought, *The Essence of Judaism*, likewise echoed Maimonides' views of the afterlife, stating quite explicitly:

> We need but recall the pitying derision with which Maimonides dismissed as antiquated child's play all these fantasies and sensuous conceptions of the world beyond. Basic to Judaism, was the imageless spiritual conception of immortality, which permits not representation, hardly even a verbal one.[18]

As I see it, Maimonides' philosophical dualism actually makes it problematic to understand the nature of Jewish teachings on the afterlife. The Maimonidean point of view has caused modern Judaism to price the afterlife out of the market, so to speak. If the spiritual life of the World to Come is so lofty, according to Maimonides, human beings cannot even come close to understanding it; at least this is the logic that emanates from a reading of Maimonides. Thus, with the Maimonidean influence as a background, it is no wonder that modern Jews have trouble reflecting on the whole question of a life after death.

In contemporary culture, Maimonides' Aristotelian dualism, like Newtonian physics, is no longer adequate. To effectively wrestle with many of the philosophical and spiritual questions of our age, we will have to develop a Jewish model that reflects the emerging consciousness of the late twentieth century. Certainly, with regard to the topic of immortality and life after death, there is no doubt that we have to go beyond Maimonides and beyond the rationalistic stream of Judaism, to discover a way of seeing the afterlife journey of the soul in terms that speak to our contemporary point of view.

The historical evidence examined thus far has delineated factors within Jewish tradition that have made teachings on the afterlife seem vague and obscure to modern Jews. There are, however, others factors at play that have made it difficult for twentieth-century Judaism to rightfully and proudly claim the legacy of Jewish afterlife teachings.

Rationalism, Psychoanalysis, and Death of the Afterlife

Belief in a life after death can be found in cultures across the globe and throughout the history of civilization. According to Sir James George Frazer, one of the early anthropologists, preliterate societies always upheld some form of belief in individual postmortem survival.[19] Archaeological discoveries dating as far back as 50,000 B.C.E. indicate that in the early Stone Age people were buried with food, tools, and other implements, "sent on their journey to the eternal hunting ground, into a realm where a divinity perhaps had its residence."[20] Other archaeological finds from Mesopotamia and Africa reveal a widespread practice of supplying foodstuffs and other provisions to the dead, indicating that ancient humanity believed in ongoing communication between the realm of the dead and the world of human mortals. It was a mutual relationship in which the living provided physical nourishment for the deceased, who, in turn, would bestow blessings and offer assistance with the ongoing demands of physical life.[21] In addition to the archaeological evidence, textual studies reveal widespread beliefs in an eternal realm of the dead in both the ancient and historical religions of the world.[22]

Whereas in the past, belief in a supreme being and a life after death were almost universal, in the modern era, these once traditional creeds have eroded. Influenced by the philosophical dictates of René Descartes, the scientific worldview emphasized the value of objective, observable dimensions of human experience, rejecting the relevance of nonobservable, internal, subjective, or spiritual phenomena. As a consequence of the Enlightenment, Western culture has given increasingly less credence to any and all human experiences that have "nonrational" aspects associated with them. In the opening decades of the twentieth century, with the growth of scientific rationalism, logical positivism, and psychoanalysis, god, angels, souls, mystical visions, and the idea of individual survival after death were progressively eliminated from the agenda of intellectual inquiry, replaced by an unwavering commitment to rationalism.

In a scientific, rationalistic universe death is seen as the final cessation of life. Since consciousness is regarded as an epiphenomenon of the brain, there can be no awareness separate from the body. When the body dies, a person dies and that is the end. As the philosopher Bertrand Russell wrote, in 1903: "All the evidence goes to show that what we regard as our mental life is bound up with brain structure and organized bodily energy. Therefore it is rational to suppose that mental life ceases when the body ceases."[23] According to the modern scientific worldview, the notion of survival of the soul after death is a nonoption. Once the brain waves cease functioning, life is over. No soul. No afterlife. No heaven. Dead is dead. It is this view of life and death that has become the predominant intellectual point of view in the twentieth century.

The materialistic point of view regarding life after death finds expression, in almost a comical way, in the following passage by Nikita Khrushchev, written soon after the Soviet Union began exploratory space travel:

> As to paradise in heaven, we heard about it from the priests. But we wanted to see for ourselves what it was like, so we sent our scout there, Yuri Gagarin. He circled the globe and found nothing in outer space—just complete darkness, he said, and no garden at all, nothing that looked like paradise. We thought the matter over and decided to send another scout. We sent Herman Titov and told him to fly around a bit longer this time and take a good look—Gagarin was only up there for an hour and a half, and he might have missed it. He took off, came back and confirmed Gagarin's conclusion. There's nothing up there, he reported.[24]

One individual who had a monumental impact in promulgating the materialistic, rationalistic attitude toward the afterlife was Sigmund Freud. As a scholar intrigued with the inherent nature of culture, Freud wrote extensively on human beliefs in god, religion, death, and immortality.

In his early writings, Freud paid little attention to the theme of death. However, in his forties, Freud recovered from a serious illness, and was also deeply affected by his father's impending death. As the biographies of his life reveal, as Freud became increasingly preoccupied with fears of dying, he continually wrestled the meaning of death and with questions about postmortem survival in a world beyond.[25] These personal concerns were reflected in a number of important writings from the latter half of his life—*Totem and Taboo, Civilization and Its Discontents, The Future of an Illusion,* and *Moses and Monotheism,* among others—in which he investigated human religiosity and the origins of beliefs in immortality and divine retribution.

Yet as a product of nineteenth-century European thought, Freud's own philosophical worldview precluded any belief in God, a soul, or an afterlife. Freud was an atheistic Jew who regarded religion as a "universal obsessional neurosis" that reflected a regression to infantile forms of behavior. To relate to a God, according to Freud, was but a childish yearning for a relationship with one's father. Just as a young child yearns for the protection of a father, similarly, in times of vulnerability and helplessness adults respond by yearning for a suprahuman figure, a God who can guarantee security and protection against the hostile forces of life. For Freud, the very idea of God is a human creation, a distorted expression of humanity's wish for security. As civilization matures, that is, becomes increasingly rational, human beings will recognize the fallacy of all religious beliefs. Ultimately, suggests Freud, religion will be rightfully superseded by rationalism, empirical science, and psychoanalysis itself.[26]

In *Totem and Taboo* Freud examines early humanity's response to death and offers his reflections on the evolution of ideas of the hereafter. The so-called primitive, he explains, could neither understand nor conceive of the idea of physical death. In response to human mortality, the primitive invented the idea of spirits and postmortem survival:

> Man could no longer keep death at a distance, for he had tasted it in his pain about the dead; but he was nevertheless unwilling to acknowledge it, for he could not conceive of himself as dead. So he devised a compromise; he conceded the fact of his own death as well, but denied it the significance of annihilation. . . . It was beside the dead body of someone he loved that he invented spirits. . . . His persisting memory of the dead became the basis for assuming other forms of existence and gave him the conception of a life continuing after apparent death.[27]

In "Thoughts for the Times on War and Death" Freud further develops his thinking on postmortem conceptions. Here, too, he declares that early humanity created the idea of a hereafter in response to the stark reality of death. "What came into existence beside the dead body of a loved one," he writes, "was . . . the doctrine of the soul and the belief in immortality." He goes on to explain:

> It was only later that religions succeeded in representing this afterlife as the more desirable, the truly valid one, and in reducing the life which is ended by death to a mere preparation. After this, it was no more than consistent to extend life backwards into the past, to form the notion of earlier existences, of the transmigration of souls and of reincarnation, all with the purpose of depriving death of its meaning as the termination of life.[28]

These two passages are characteristic of Freudian thought and reflect the attitude toward life after death that has persisted throughout the twentieth century. Essentially, for Freud the very notion of life after death is a psychological creation of the human mind. To believe in an afterlife, or even to show any concern with ideas about heaven and the survival of the soul, is a denial of the reality of death, a defense against the inherent fear of annihilation and extinction.

Freud's ideas on the afterlife influenced an entire generation of psychoanalysts, psychiatrists, and other helping professionals, as well as philosophers and social scientists. As a result, until very recently, the whole topic of postmortem survival has been ignored or regarded with great suspicion, or as an embarrassment, in psychology, philosophy, and even theology.

There is no doubt the rationalistic, secularizing forces of the modern era have left their impact within the Jewish world. Even well before Freud, the materialistic, rationalistic view of the afterlife influenced the intellectual development of the German-Jewish philosopher Hermann Cohen (1842–1918). As a leader of an entire generation of neo-Kantian Jewish thinkers, Cohen was embarrassed by the Jewish doctrine of life after death.[29] In his classical study *Religion of Reason out of the Sources of Judaism*, Cohen reinterpreted traditional Jewish conceptions of immortality. The individual alone does not survive after death, he maintained, although a person's legacy does, as part of the evolving history of humanity: "only in the infinite development of the human race toward the ideal spirit of holiness can the individual soul actualize its immortality."[30] Furthermore, biblical metaphors for death, such as "And thou shalt go to thy fathers" and "He is gathered to his people," Cohen regarded as symbolic of "the historical living on of the individual in the historical continuity of the people."[31]

This belief, often referred to as "social immortality," has persisted for over a century and has become an increasingly widespread modern Jewish response. However, many people do not realize that this adaptation to the rationalist worldview completely ignores the traditional Jewish perspective that there is an immortal soul that survives bodily death. Even so-called experts within the Jewish world mistakenly promulgate the materialistic, rationalistic point of view in the public arena. As recently as 1989, when asked by a Newsweek journalist about Jewish views of afterlife, Rabbi Terry Bard, the director of Pastoral Services at Boston's Beth Israel Hospital, explained that after the individual dies, dead is dead—"what lives on are the children and a legacy of good works."[32]

It is no wonder that the issue of life after death is problematic for modern Jews. But this is part of a larger spiritual alienation in which questions of faith, God, religious experience, and the inner life are perplexing to an entire generation of Jews influenced by the intellectual climate of the past century. Generally speaking, social issues, politics, education, and fund-raising are given due consideration in Jewish communities and congregations. But spirituality, the experience of a personal, intimate relationship with God and the mystical exploration of the soul and its nature in life and death, has not been high on the agenda of the North American Jewish community. However, this is beginning to shift. As we explore below, evidence suggests that an increasing interest in spirituality and spiritual renewal has taken root, at least within specific segments of the North American Jewish community.[33]

The Influence of Christianity

Let us explore another factor affecting modern Jewish perspectives on life after death, by reflecting, somewhat speculatively, on the interaction between Judaism and ideas about life after death within Christianity.

For over a decade, I have worked as a Jewish death awareness educator, assisting people in wrestling with psychological and spiritual questions about death, dying, and life after death. Whenever I ask individuals to explore the images they hold about the hereafter, what emerges are not Jewish ideas of the afterlife, but Christian ones. Invariably people imagine a radiant heaven with pearly gates populated by cherubic angels and a subterranean hell with a burning inferno, more often than not attended by an evil-looking taskmaster who punishes the sinful. Even people who do not believe in an afterlife find that automatically such visual pictures emerge in their imagination. Why? Because such images are so deeply embedded in the consciousness of Western culture.

Reflect on this for a moment. Before reading on, conjure in your mind a picture of the realms of heaven and hell. Notice what images come to mind. Do not read on yet, but take a moment and do this brief exercise now.

Do you see Adam? Abraham? Moses? The radiant presence of the *Shekhinah*, the divine feminine aspect of God? Seven regions of heaven? Seven realms of hell, presided over by the angel of death? These are the images found in Jewish sources. Yet the likelihood is that the afterlife images that come to mind—for both Jews and non-Jews—are closer to medieval Christian art than to the motifs represented in Jewish mysticism or legend. This exercise reveals the extent to which Christian notions of life after death have permeated Jewish awareness, at a very deep, unconscious level.

For almost two thousand years eternal life, heaven, and hell have been the predominant themes of Christian doctrine. From the very beginning, Christianity promised eternal life and paradise to anyone who repented in the name of Jesus Christ. During the second to fifth centuries, Christianity evolved from a marginal Jewish sect to the dominant religious authority in the Roman world. During this time, the Church fathers, notably Irenaeus and St. Augustine, further expounded Christian creeds about an otherworldly paradise and the torments of hell.[34] In the thirteenth century, Dante's *Divine Comedy* mapped out very exceptionally picturesque and graphic images of heaven and hell, which became canonical Christian dogma, promulgated throughout the Byzantine world and Europe. Eventually, Christianity's teachings on heaven and hell were depicted artistically in the creations of European painters such as Michelangelo, Hieronymus Bosch, Jan van Eyck, and William Blake.[35] Because of the strong biblical prohibition against graven images, Jews did not take to art in the same way as Christians did. Therefore, what was infused into the visual awareness of Western society were Christian afterlife beliefs, not those of the Jews. To this day, Christian images of life after death, and the philosophical ideas behind them, remain pervasive in the minds of both non-Jews and Jews.

When examining the history of Jewish-Christian relations, there is no doubt that Christianity's belief in eternal life impacted upon the Jews, but in a very negative sense. As a rule, when Jews refused to accept the promise of heavenly paradise and eternal life, in the name of the Messiah Jesus, they were ostracized, persecuted, tortured, or put to death. And it was very common for Christian notions of heaven and hell to be employed in ways quite abusive to the Jews. The prevalent teaching for centuries was that if an individual Jew did not embrace Christianity, he or she was destined, not to the pearly gates of heaven, but to the damnation of hell. For example, in 1442 the Council of Florence proclaimed that "none of those outside the Catholic Church, not Jews, nor heretics, nor schismatics, can participate in eternal life, but will go into the eternal fire prepared for the devil and his angels, unless they are brought into it [the Catholic Church] before the end of life."[36] That was five hundred years ago. Yet, to this day, this teaching remains infused in the minds of many Christians, in spite of the Second Vatican Council and the ongoing contemporary efforts to eliminate anti-Semitism and other forms of racism.

Centuries of anti-Jewish persecution left its toll on the modern Jewish psyche. In reaction to the omnipresence of Christian teachings on heaven and hell, it seems as if, collectively, many Jews have rejected, in totality, the whole idea of a postmortem life. If the operating cultural assumption was that non-Christians could not enter heaven, then many Jews decided to completely opt out of the whole system, abandoning belief in both heaven and hell and a life after death.

We see this very overtly in the anecdote mentioned above about the nurse who asked the rabbi if Judaism had a belief in the afterlife. The rabbi, you will recall, maintained that Judaism "dwells on life here rather than on the hereafter *as other religious faiths do.*" What are the "other religious faiths" to which the rabbi is referring? Likely not Buddhism and Hinduism, but Christianity. In other words, it is almost as if the underlying assumption expressed here is that "Christians believe in all that stuff about heaven, hell, and eternal life. But we Jews don't!"

This is a totally absurd assumption, one that ignores the legacy of almost three millennia of Jewish writings on life after death. Given the historical factors operating, however—the prevalence of Christian iconography of the afterlife in Western consciousness, the use of heaven and hell teachings as part of the systematic oppression of the Jews, and the increasing inaccessibility of traditional Jewish teachings in modern times—it is little wonder this belief has been promulgated.

Not surprisingly, this view that Christians believe in the afterlife and Jews do not is substantiated by modern social science surveys. A Gallup poll in 1952 asked the question "Do you think that your soul will live on after death?" While 85 percent of Catholics and 80 percent of Protestants answered yes, by contrast only 35 percent of Jews responded affirmatively. In 1965 the numbers were even lower: 83 percent of Catholics and 75 percent of Protestants answered yes, whereas only 17 percent of Jewish respondents believed their souls would live on after death. The remaining 83 percent of the Jews polled said either "no" or "don't know." The results of these two studies can be found in Table 2–1.[37]

These comparative statistics are not insignificant. They suggest that Jews, dramatically more than Catholics and Protestants, have been affected by the secularizing tendencies of the modern period. But perhaps this can be explained even more clearly by looking at another unique Jewish experience of the twentieth century—the Holocaust—which might further explain why modern Jews have quite ostensibly rejected the belief in the soul's survival after death.

Is There Afterlife after Auschwitz?

One other factor unconsciously influencing modern Judaism's perspective on life after death is the experience and impact of the Holocaust. Undeniably, the Holocaust has been a powerful force operating upon the psyche of twentieth-century Jews. The overwhelming nature of the murder perpetuated against Jews by the Nazis has made it difficult for modern Jews to really reflect on the whole issue of life after death.

TABLE 2-1   AFTERLIFE BELIEFS AMONG CATHOLICS, PROTESTANTS, AND JEWS

Religion (%)	1952			1965		
	Yes	No	Don't Know	Yes	No	Don't Know
Catholics	85	4	11	83	3	14
Protestants	80	5	15	78	7	15
Jews	35	24	41	17	46	37

To understand this more fully, ask yourself the following: Is there afterlife after Auschwitz? No doubt you have not heard that question asked before. Auschwitz evokes images of suffering and death. But after Auschwitz, the Jewish response has been to focus energy on life and re-birth, not on the hereafter.

In the era immediate following the Holocaust, the mandate of the Jewish people was a very functional and practical one: to resettle refu-gees, to build a Jewish homeland, and to guarantee the ongoing survival of Jewish life around the world. Imagine, or remember, what it was like in 1945, as the discovery and the liberation of concentration camps began. Could the task at hand have been accomplished if Judaism emphasized a philosophical preoccupation with the state of the souls of six million dead? What would have taken place in the years after World War II if Judaism had a proclivity to contemplate the transcendental wanderings of the souls of six million dead Jews? Even now this is an awesome thought, one that evokes a jarring sense of discomfort.

In the aftermath of the Holocaust, the memory of the six million was best honored by affirming the continuity of Jewish existence, not by focusing on the postmortem fate of the dead. Such a mission was too monumental and too overwhelmingly painful to even contemplate. After Auschwitz it was difficult, if not impossible, for Judaism, collectively, to relate to the idea of an afterlife. Modern Judaism, at least in the forty years after the liberation of the concentration camps, simply could not integrate the Jewish philosophy of the immortal soul with the reality of the Holocaust. So it was best ignored, left to the private sphere but not the public arena of religious life, except for Yizkor services, when the six million martyrs were remembered.

Looking retrospectively on the decades after World War II, it was quite utilitarian and adaptive for modern Judaism to lose touch with the legacy of Jewish teachings on the afterlife. The spirit of the times of the fifties, sixties, and seventies necessitated building a socially responsive and intellectually viable Judaism. Within the context of a post–World War II North American Judaism, there has not been any room for a con-cern with spirituality and disembodied souls in the hereafter. It may well be that for many Jews, raised in the shadow of the Holocaust, there was simply no need for a philosophy of the afterlife.

In recent times, however, there has been a progressive yearning for spirituality and spiritual renewal. Standing on the threshold of the twenty-first century, we find ourselves in a critical time of societal transformation and a revolution in human consciousness. Perhaps now, some fifty years after the Holocaust, it is time to rediscover the Jewish spiritual legacy that was buried in the ashes of Auschwitz. In this era, as a more evolved and accepting approach to death, dying, and bereavement is being developed in Western culture, the time is ripe for bringing to light the full legacy of Jewish teachings on death and the afterlife.

CULTURAL CONTEXT

In defining the parameters of this book, we need to explore two important contemporary cultural trends that form the background to our investigation of life after death in Judaism: (1) the Jewish renewal movement and (2) thanatology, the interdisciplinary study of death and dying.

The first trend, the Jewish renewal movement, is best described as a contemporary concern with the renaissance of spirituality in the Jewish community. The second trend, thanatology, is a discipline of study in and of itself, and as a social movement can be regarded as the growing societal interest in all dimensions of death, dying, and bereavement. Written at the crossroads of these two trailblazing movements, *Jewish Views of the Afterlife* is both a contribution to and a product of Jewish renewal and contemporary thanatology.

The Jewish Renewal Movement

Behind the writing of this book is the overt influence of a new spirit emerging within contemporary Judaism known as the Jewish renewal movement, a diverse movement of individuals and communities dedicated to the creative revitalization of all facets of Jewish spiritual life.

The Jewish renewal movement is both a social and a religious force. As a social force, this movement is creating new participatory forms of worship and celebration and evolving an egalitarian, feminist Judaism in which women are participating in and contributing to Jewish life as never before. As a religious force, this renewal movement is creating a new theological understanding of the meaning and role of religion in a person's life. The dualistic, human-divine understanding is being replaced by an imminent theology, which recognizes the inherent unity of the individual, the divine, and the environment.

Earlier antecedents of this movement appeared in the 1960s, during the era of antiwar protest, psychedelic drugs, and hippies. As a response to religious alienation within the synagogues and the bureaucratic, hierarchical organization of Jewish community life, a Jewish counterculture coalesced. In places like New York and Boston young people who had rejected the structures of the community began evolving radical new forms of Jewish expression. In study, prayer, and ritual celebration, the writings of individuals like Henry David Thoreau, Martin Luther King, Jr., and Abby Hoffman were fused with ancient teachings from the Hebrew prophets and the Psalms. Reflecting the radical social consciousness of the times, this countercultural movement planted the seeds of a unique American contribution to Jewish culture. Most noteworthy, during this era an important publication was conceived—*The Jewish Catalog*, a do-it-yourself manual for Jewish practice, which has been a continuing source of inspiration to people searching for practical guidelines to the renewal of Judaism.[38]

During the 1970s this revitalizing force in the Jewish world became known as "New Age Judaism." At this time, Eastern religions and the human potential movement had become very popular, attracting many Jewish adherents. Influenced largely by Rabbi Zalman Schachter-Shalomi and the communities he founded, such as the Aquarian Minyan of Berkeley, and the B'nai Or Religious Fellowship, an innovative form of Judaism emerged, blending mystical Jewish traditions with Yoga, Tibetan Buddhism, Zen, Sufism, and other esoteric philosophies, along with the consciousness practices of humanistic and transpersonal psychology. Many who had studied with Eastern gurus and lamas returned to the Jewish fold, practicing a renewed style of Judaism that emphasized meditation, spirituality, and the pursuit of expanded consciousness over and above rationality and rote ritual.

Although certainly not a mainstream movement, New Age Judaism became a strong force for the rediscovery and resurrection of the mystical, spiritual side of Judaism. Inspired by the new forms of spirituality pioneered in this period, many were challenged to learn more about the Jewish past and to bring to light treasured ancient resources of Jewish mysticism and spirituality. This process of reclaiming the spiritual legacy of the past has continued through the years, affecting Jewish learning, liturgy, and practice.

Also during the late 1960s an entirely new phenomenon in American Jewish life appeared on the scene, the *Havurah*. Derived from the Hebrew *haver*, or "friend," *Havurah* literally means "fellowship" or "friendship circle." *Havurot* are small communities of men and women who gather on a regular basis for prayer, Torah study, and the celebration of Shabbat, holy days, and life-cycle rituals. In contrast to the styles of mainstream congregations, *Havurot* tend to be empowering rather than alienating. They are usually peer led and emphasize creative experimentation in liturgy and a "do-it-yourself," participatory form of Jewish practice.

Although originally an outgrowth of the early countercultural movement, today there are both independent *Havurot* and those operating in conjunction with existing synagogues. There are also a number of different national organizations that serve to network *Havurot* communities in the United States and Canada, as well as in Israel, Europe, and South America. The *Havurah* movement, as a whole, may be regarded as an early forerunner of the Jewish renewal movement. It was only in the early 1980s that the term "Jewish renewal" was first coined to describe the process of individual empowerment and collective spiritual rebirth that had been in place for over fifteen years.

Today the Jewish renewal movement synthesizes the various innovative trends that have emerged over the decades and is articulating a vision of where Judaism is evolving in the twenty-first century. In a sense, Jewish renewal is a process of reframing Jewish practice in light of the ancient wisdom of the past and the emerging paradigm of the postmodern age. Jewish renewal also expresses the contemporary search for spiritual meaning characteristic of this time in history.

The post–World War II promise that science would fulfill all human needs has not materialized. Even with all kinds of profound technological innovations—satellites, computers, fax machines, and fiber optics, to name a few—the quality of human life in the Western world continues to decline. Drugs have taken their toll on countless lives; families seem to be in jeopardy; fatal diseases like AIDS are spreading, not disappearing; the toxicity of the earth and its atmosphere is only now being understood. With all this going on, more and more people find themselves deeply questing for personal meaning. What's it really all about? The question is no longer "Is God dead?" but rather "How can I, as an individual, personally access God in my own life and enhance the quality of life for myself and the people around me?" We are living in an age of transition characterized by spiritual hunger. People are longing for functional resources that offer meaning, a connection with the transcendent, and an ability to experience the deep layers of the human psyche wherein genuine healing can be found.

In such a time of spiritual questioning, many alienated Jews are turning back to their roots. Even previously commited Jewish men and women are looking beyond the legalistic, rational dimensions of Judaism for an internal experience of transformation. Many people, young and old alike, are searching to unearth the ancient wisdom of the Jewish past and make it viable for daily life in this age.

As a result, there is a burgeoning interest in the mystical, mythical, and apocalyptic traditions of Judaism. As it turns out, there is so much more to Judaism than meets the eye, so much that has been covered over by rationalism, secularization, and cultural assimilation. Through the process of Jewish renewal, scholars and practitioners alike are being motivated to unearth the sacred past. Over the past decade, more and more traditional Jewish texts have been translated into English, and this process is continuing. In addition, a number of leading Jewish teachers are creating a new genre of American Jewish spiritual writings. Topics such as mysticism, meditation, magic, folk religion, healing, altered states of consciousness, as well as reincarnation and life after death, are emerging on the agenda of study, not only in small study circles, but also in well-respected academies of Jewish learning. Greater and greater numbers of Jews and non-Jews are becoming passionately interested in the long-lost legacy of Jewish spirituality and mysticism.

Against this background, this book is being written. The spiritual search inherent to Jewish renewal has provided the impetus to ask the following questions: What is the ancient legacy of Jewish teachings on the afterlife? And, how can this heritage be made accessible and relevant to the contemporary world?

This book contributes to the work of Jewish renewal in three distinct ways. First, as a survey of Jewish teachings on life after death through the ages, *Jewish Views of the Afterlife* makes a substantial addition to the growing body of knowledge of Jewish spirituality and mysticism. In particular, little-known kabbalistic and Midrashic teachings on the soul and its postmortem destiny are mapped out here, designed to be accessible to all.

Second, this book presents a contemporary contribution to current Jewish thought. In the spirit of Jewish renewal, a contemporary model of the afterlife is developed, based on the recent developments in transpersonal psychology and consciousness research. This model synthesizes the ancient past with the most innovative cultural trends and in so doing attempts to facilitate the process of bringing Judaism and Jewish thought into the future.

Finally, Jewish renewal is interested in renewing traditional rituals to give them a sense of meaning and in evolving new forms of practice that honor the individual need for spiritual fulfillment and understanding. The spiritually oriented view of the afterlife presented in the final chapter recognizes that consciousness survives bodily death. This point of view has implications in how we understand and practice the rituals associated with dying and grieving. Awareness that a spiritual connection between the living and the deceased persists, even after death of the body, can totally transform the ways in which we look at every facet of the human encounter with death. The spiritual view of the afterlife developed in this book has the potential to reinvigorate and bring new meaning to all the traditional Jewish ritual practices of death and mourning, from dying and the deathbed, to burial, funeral, and the various bereavement rituals of *shivah, Kaddish, Yahrzeit,* and *Yizkor.* In the long run, reclaiming the ancient Jewish tradition of the afterlife and making it relevant to our times will totally revolutionize the way Jewish communities care for the elderly, sick, dying, and bereaved.

Thanatology: The Interdisciplinary Study of Death and Dying

In the society at large, something of great significance is happening: slowly but surely death has come out of the closet. When the history of the twentieth century is written, the years after 1960 will be regarded as an extraordinary era in which the collective understanding of death was profoundly altered.

Behind this changing perspective on death is an interdisciplinary field of inquiry known as thanatology, the study of death and dying. Its name is derived from Thanatos, the mythological Greek god of death, who was a twin of Hypnus, the god of sleep. A relatively recent creation, thanatology is an amalgam of research on the various aspects of death, dying, and bereavement. History, philosophy, religion, anthropology, sociology, parapsychology, and consciousness research, as well the helping professions of psychology, social work, psychiatry, nursing, and medicine, intermingle in the quest to understand the multidimensional experience of death.

As a result of developments in thanatology over the past three decades, death has become a topic of significant social concern and an area for study and professional training. For example, today there are probably over 200,000 courses on death and dying taught annually in the

United States alone, many more worldwide.[39] Each year, hundreds of
articles and scores of books on death, dying, and related topics are published.[40] The professional field of thanatology is continually diversifying
and permeating various humanistic and scientific disciplines.

Elisabeth Kübler-Ross, a Swiss psychiatrist known to many as the
"death and dying lady," has contributed much to the area of thanatology.
Working against the medical establishment, she inaugurated the transformation of attitudes toward death in modern society. Whereas sex was
the cultural taboo in Victorian times, it was replaced in the twentieth
century by the topic of death. As individuals like Geoffrey Gorer have
noted, by the mid-twentieth century death had become the pornogra-
phy of society, a subject about which people were profoundly uncom-
fortable to speak.[41]

But Kübler-Ross is the "Sigmund Freud of death and dying." Just as
Freud's theories on sexuality revolutionized cultural values and attitudes
toward sex in the early part of this century, so Kübler-Ross's pioneering
work with the dying has served to open discussions on death. Already
her lifework has transformed Western views of death as profoundly as
Freud's catalyzed a revolution in sexuality and sexual mores. In the aftermath of Kübler-Ross, the taboo on death has been broken.

The story of Kübler-Ross's early work with dying patients is almost
legendary in thanatological literature.[42] As a psychiatrist at the University of Chicago in the mid-1960s, Kübler-Ross went to hospital wards in
search of dying patients to interview. She was repeatedly told: "We have
no dying patients here." With both fear and denial pervasive in the medical profession, it was completely unheard of for a doctor to relate to patients in terms of their personal experience of dying.

Kübler-Ross persisted. She began to receive an increasing number
of referrals and was soon dedicating her time to interviewing terminally
ill patients to understand what it was like for those approaching death.
From a simple willingness to listen to dying people, Kübler-Ross inaugurated a growing cultural movement concerned with improving the quality of life for the dying and bereaved and their families.

Kübler-Ross's work with terminally ill patients, dying children, and,
more recently, persons with AIDS has continually challenged the cultural fear and denial of death. Undoubtedly, the seed planted by Kübler-
Ross in the 1960s took root in the seventies, and multiplied and prolifer-
ated in the eighties and beyond. Over the years, as a result of this
pioneering work, there has been an exponential increase in human knowl-

edge about death and mourning, coupled with significant developments in the area of care for the dying and bereaved. Today there is a much greater honesty and openness in the face of death. Dying individuals are given more opportunity to speak about their feelings with family members and attending medical staff. More and more frequently, conscious effort is made to meet the social, emotional, and spiritual needs of the dying, along with the medical and physical ones. Generally, there is a marked concern for enhancing the quality of life for dying individuals, whether they are in hospital settings or in the home.

Kübler-Ross also had an important impact on attitudes toward bereavement. There was a time when people tiptoed around those in mourning, speaking in hushed tones, not wanting to upset them by bringing up the subject of death or grief. Today we understand more clearly how important it is for bereaved individuals to tell their grief story, over and over again if necessary. Increasingly, there is a growing number of resources available to meet the needs of the bereaved, as well as a growing cadre of helping professionals who are able to diagnose and treat the many different aspects of bereavement. The standard psychiatric manual, *DSM-III*, lists "Normal Bereavement Reaction" as a classification of mental health, giving due understanding to the serious and transitional nature of the bereavement experience.[43]

On the whole, medical and mental health professionals, as well as clergy, are now being taught how to relate more effectively to the dying and bereaved, learning to enter into their world and understand the emotional and psychological experiences associated with death and grief. There are also greater numbers of professional education conferences dealing specifically with the whole area of death care. And finally, numerous innovative community programs have been created to deal with the needs of dying and bereaved individuals and their families. Residential and home hospice centers, bereavement support groups, grief-counseling clinics, and death-awareness education programs run by hospitals, social work agencies, even funeral directors have become increasingly common. Clearly, Kübler-Ross has had her impact.

Even more than all of this, there are a variety of new developments forcing people to rethink questions about the meaning of life and death itself. Biotechnological advances such as heart transplants, frozen embryos, and suicide machines make it clear that science is not value neutral, and as a culture we need to evolve bioethics and spiritual principles corresponding with the evolution of technology. In addition, near-death experiences, the visionary reports of people who have been declared clinically dead and then brought back to life, have forced medical doctors and scientists to reopen the whole question about life after death and rethink the materialistic definition of death. We are seeing an increasing integration of ancient wisdom with modern science; as a consequence, radical new perspectives are being developed not only on the dying process, but on that which occurs after death.

It is obvious that there has been a significant shift away from the fear and denial of death toward a more accepting, compassionate view of human mortality. The reality of AIDS has forced people to talk and think about death and mortality. Prime-time television characters now openly struggle with grief and loss. Bereaved and terminally ill people appear on talk shows for nationally broadcast rap sessions on parental grief, suicide, SIDS ("sudden infant death syndrome"), and a variety of other types of bereavement. And in recent years, several movies have attempted to depict visions of the survival of the soul after death.

We are in the midst of a total cultural transformation that is bringing about the emergence of a revised understanding of death and dying. In place of the materialistic view that biological death is the final end of life, a spiritual view of death and life is emerging. Increasingly, a new paradigm is being articulated in the mental health professions and the biological sciences, one that gives due recognition to the perennial wisdom of the ages, encoded in the esoteric traditions of the world, and understands that death is not the end of life but merely a transition to a different state of consciousness.

Against this background, there is little doubt that Judaism, in the fullness of its ancient wisdom, has a contribution to make to the new ways of understanding the experiences of dying and death.

Kübler-Ross, the Holocaust, and a New Jewish Vision of the Afterlife

One other anecdote about Elisabeth Kübler-Ross suggests that the rebirth of the Jewish approach to the afterlife may have emerged from the Holocaust itself.

It was at the Maidanek concentration camp in 1945 that Kübler-Ross, a relief worker, became fascinated with the mystery of the human encounter with death. Surveying the vacant concentration camp, she was overwhelmed by the presence of death—the stench in the air, the chimney of the crematorium, the barbed wire, the boxes of baby shoes, jewelry, and women's hair, and above all, the scribbling found on the walls of the empty barracks. There, amid the graffiti and hundreds of initials carved into the five-tiered wooden bunks, she noticed countless drawings of butterflies. Perhaps days or only hours before dying in the gas chambers, adults and children left behind their final message—butterflies—the symbol of hope and rebirth, the symbol of the eternal human soul. This curious juxtaposition of images of life and death left a profound impression on the young Kübler-Ross, and ultimately motivated her to study death and dying.[44]

The Holocaust obliterated the traditional Jewish life of Eastern Europe, wiping out so many of the spiritual leaders who had direct access to Judaism's sacred legacy of mystical teachings about the soul and its afterlife pilgrimage. In a strange way, it is almost as if the Jewish afterlife, and the spiritual worldview behind those holy teachings, died in Nazi death camps. Yet the tragedy of the Holocaust inspired Elisabeth Kübler-Ross to investigate the mysteries of dying and death. Perhaps like the phoenix rising from the ashes, Kübler-Ross's work in contemporary thanatology now gives us the motivation and inspiration to reclaim, to resurrect Judaism's spiritual approach to death and the afterlife.

And yet, even though in the aftermath of the Kübler-Ross death-and-dying revolution there have been thousands of contributions documenting medical, psychological, sociological, anthropological, and spiritual perspectives on death and dying, within the Jewish community relatively little new material has been written in the past three decades.[45] Kübler-Ross herself noted this paradox:

> I have always wondered why the Jews as a people have not written more on death and dying. Who, better than they, could contribute to understanding of the need to face the reality of our own finiteness?[46]

Even with Kübler-Ross's cultural influences, the psychic grip of the Holocaust has pervaded and Jews have avoided writing on death, dying, and the afterlife. But this dearth of Jewish writings on death—like the view that Jews do not believe in an afterlife—is a modern phenomenon. Throughout the history of Judaism, Jewish sages have authored all types of resources not only on the afterlife, but on all aspects of the encounter with death. Perhaps now, as a new millennium dawns, it is time to unbind the psychic shackles of the Holocaust and begin a process of integrating traditional Jewish wisdom on death, dying, mourning, and the spiritual journey of the soul in the afterlife with new emerging perspectives on the psychology of death and dying.

Circumstances of the times necessitate reclaiming the wisdom of Jewish death traditions. We are living in an era in which people live longer; as a result, there is an increased concern with both the quality of life and the quality of death. Within the Jewish community there are increasing numbers of elderly Jews, and this will be the trend of the coming decades, as the baby-boom generation deals with parents who are aging and dying. In our communities, the debilitating illnesses of Alzheimer's, cancer, and AIDS continue to directly affect the lives of countless families. As a society, we desperately need all the information and resources available to enable us to deal more effectively with death.

There is a great need today for a spiritually oriented, community-based approach to death and dying. The spirit of the times requires a conscious method for empowering individuals and families to deal effectively with terminal illness, dying, funerals, mourning, and bereavement. I believe that one of the best ways to meet this need is to tap into the rich, unmined legacy of Jewish afterlife teachings. These are found not only in the Bible, rabbinic literature, and in Maimonides, but also in ancient Jewish apocalyptic writings, in medieval Midrash, in the Zohar and other texts of Jewish mysticism, and in the teachings of the hasidic masters.

Fifty years after Auschwitz it is time to resurrect the ancient Jewish tradition on the afterlife journey of the soul and to make those teachings available in a language and style appropriate for contemporary Jewish life, in the metaphor of the psychology of consciousness. The Tibetan Book of the Dead may well be sufficient for Tibetan monks. But now there is a need to develop a Jewish Book of the Dead, or more appropriately a Jewish Book of Life, that will be a manual for dying Bubbys and Zaidyes and their children and grandchildren. Now we need to bring to life Jewish wisdom on the mysteries of death and the immortal soul, so that the next generation of Jewish life will be lived with greater fullness and with a profound sense of the spiritual significance of life and death. This book is one man's humble attempt in that direction.

Chapter 3

Biblical Roots of Jewish Views of the Afterlife

THE HISTORICAL CONTEXT

Our journey through Jewish history begins in the biblical period, an era of almost two thousand years during which time Judaism emerged as a religious force in the ancient Near Eastern world. For the sake of chronological understanding, the biblical period can be divided into three distinct eras, reflecting the changing historical circumstances of the Israelite people: (1) *early biblical period*—from Abraham to the Exodus from Egypt, c. 1800–1250 B.C.E.; (2) *preexilic biblical period*—from the conquest of Canaan at the time of Joshua to the Babylonian exile, c. 1250–586 B.C.E.; and (3) *postexilic biblical period*—from the Babylonian exile to the Hellenistic era, c. 586–200 B.C.E.[1] During each of these eras, a plethora of biblical traditions developed and were encoded in written form; it is generally assumed that biblical texts were written from the tenth to the fifth century B.C.E.[2]

The task of understanding the earliest layers of Jewish afterlife teachings is not a simple one. Throughout the biblical era, ideas about survival beyond the grave were in a process of constant flux. From the time of Abraham, there were various traditions about contact with the dead in a hereafter, often paralleling similar beliefs and practices among other ancient Near Eastern cultures. However, with the development and strengthening of monotheism, after the year 1000 B.C.E., new beliefs about the afterlife emerged. In some instances, early ideas about the fate of the dead continued to persist for centuries, lingering reminders of the antiquated past. In other instances, ancient and newly fashioned perspectives blended and formed radically innovative conceptions of the afterlife. Absolutely nowhere in the Bible do we find a unified view about life after death that reflects postmortem beliefs of the entire biblical era, or even of any one period.

The biblical text is a historical amalgam, a melange of centuries of experience, and it is very common to encounter early and later conceptions of the afterlife subtly interwoven within the various strata of sacred writings. Because of this, it is not possible to present a strictly chronological delineation of biblical teachings on the afterlife. Instead, we will look thematically at the origin and evolution of various confusing and contradictory notions of survival after death during successive periods of biblical history.

In textual writings describing life in the early biblical period, we find no specific philosophical teachings about the afterlife. In exploring this period, the best way to understand beliefs about life after death is through an examination of burial and funerary practices, and an examination of attitudes toward death and dying reflected in biblical narratives. By looking at various ritual practices associated with death and burial, almost in an anthropological sense, we will be able to deduce attitudes toward immortality and life after death in the centuries prior to and soon after conquest of the land of Canaan.

In the later biblical periods, with the more philosophically oriented writings of the prophets and the Psalmist, we begin to see the emergence of notions of individual immortality and postmortem survival. Through an analysis of biblical writings, we can discover the earliest philosophical development of Jewish afterlife beliefs and chronicle the progressive transformation of these beliefs over a period of almost a thousand years.

This book has as its predominant focus the postmortem destiny of the individual. In this chapter, we will explore what the Hebrew Bible teaches about the afterlife fate of each unique human being. However, it is essential to understand that within the biblical worldview the ultimate fate of the individual cannot be understood apart from that of the entire nation. Simply put, within the biblical context, it is impossible to study Jewish views of the individual afterlife experience without reference to Judaism's prophetic teachings on the eventual destiny of all the people of Israel at the end-of-days. As we noted earlier, throughout the Bible individual and collective eschatology, or teachings on the fate of individual Israelites and on the national collectivity of Israel, are intimately intertwined.

From its inception, biblical Judaism, or Israelite religion, divinely inspired by the monotheistic God YHVH,[3] was concerned exclusively with the collective destiny of the nation and not at all with the postmortem fate of the individual Israelite per se. In patriarchal and Mosaic times, even in the days of the Israelite tribal confederacy, the Bible has nothing to say about the fate of the individual after death, and there is certainly no notion of an individual afterlife experience for the soul. There is not even a clear conception of an individual apart from the collective, nor any idea of a soul separate from the body.[4] These are notions that emerge later in the biblical era.

In exploring the terrain of biblical texts, we will see that only after the sixth century B.C.E. do any conceptions of an afterlife fate for the individual begin to appear within Judaism. Even then, concern with the collective destiny of the Israelite nation—eschatological teachings on messianic redemption and resurrection of the dead—remains the central foundation of Judaism's worldview.[5]

In this chapter we will demonstrate early Israelite concerns about the fate of the dead and document specific stages in the development of Jewish conceptions of the postmortem destiny of the individual person. In doing so, we will map out the biblical foundation for all later Jewish teachings on the afterlife journey of the soul.

THE EARLY BIBLICAL PERIOD

The Family Tomb

The patriarchs—Abraham, Isaac, and Jacob—are the founders of biblical Judaism. For almost three thousand years people have been reading, rereading, and remembering the tales of their lives, chronicled in Genesis. By closely examining how our biblical ancestors lived, and even more, how they died, we can sense how they related to the inevitability of human mortality and the ways in which they conceived of life after death.

An excellent place to start our exploration of biblical Judaism is in the seventeenth or sixteenth century B.C.E., around the time when Jacob supposedly lived. Imagine this scene: Jacob, father of thirteen children and leader of the Israelite tribes, is on his deathbed. Knowing the end of his life is at hand, he calls together his sons to bestow his parting blessings. Then, in a noble and dignified fashion, Jacob gives final instructions:

> "I am about to be gathered to my kin. Bury me with my fathers in the cave which is in the field of Ephron the Hittite, the cave which is in the field of Makhpelah, facing Mamre, in the land of Canaan, the field that Abraham bought from Ephron the Hittite for a burial site—there Abraham and his wife Sarah were buried; there Isaac and his wife Rebekah were buried; and there I buried Leah—the field and the cave in it, bought from the Hittites." When Jacob finished his instructions to his sons, he drew his feet into the bed, and, breathing his last, he was gathered to his people. (Genesis 49:29–31, 33)

With an acute clarity, this passage portrays—at least symbolically—the biblical notion of death. Like Abraham (Genesis 25:8) and Isaac (Genesis 35:29) before him, Jacob was "gathered to his people." To die, in the language of the Bible, is to return to the company of one's ancestral family.

This conception of death is evident for most of the biblical era. After granting Moses a glimpse of the Land of Canaan, God tells him: "You too will be gathered to your kin, just as your brother Aaron was" (Numbers 27:13). And it is said of King Solomon, that at the time of his physical demise, he "slept with his ancestors" (1 Kings 11:43).

As an ancient Near Eastern civilization, biblical Judaism was tribal in nature. The central social organism was the family clan. Like the Bedouins of today, the early Hebrews traversed the deserts in large extended families, living, working, and worshiping together. The individual clans or tribes were led by a patriarch who had experienced a divine revelation and established a family-based cult of worship.[6] And as they lived, so they died—in the company of all family members—and were buried in family tombs.

Upon his deathbed, Jacob is surrounded by members of the family clan. We can imagine that not only his children but his grandchildren, great-grandchildren, and other extended family were present to hear the final words of this great patriarchal leader. In his final exhortations, Jacob unequivocally emphasizes the importance of being buried in the family sepulcher, the Cave of Makhpelah. With a deliberate precision, he repeats the specific details regarding the purchase and location of Makhpelah and names those family members already buried there. What we see is that here Jacob is saying more than "Listen, children, this is where I own a burial plot!" Through his parting words, Jacob communicates to his sons what is essentially a spiritual request: "Just as I lived my life as part of an ancestral clan, make sure I am buried with my ancestors at Makhpelah." For Jacob, and for the early biblical Hebrews, death meant entering the ancestral realm of the family tomb so that upon departing from this world he would be "gathered to his people."[7]

All the patriarchs and matriarchs, with the exception of Rachel (see Genesis 35:19–20), were buried in the family grave, the Cave of Makhpelah. This phenomenon of a family tomb recurs for centuries in biblical times. King David was laid to rest in the Citadel of David, another family tomb (1 Kings 2:10), where later kings of Judah, including Rehoboam (1 Kings 14:31), Asa (1 Kings 15:24), Jehoshaphat (1 Kings 22:51), Uzziah (2 Kings 15:7), Jotham (2 Kings 15:38), and Ahaz (2 Kings 16:20) were also buried. And the first king of Israel, Saul, and his son Jonathan were buried in the tomb of Saul's father, Kish. In this case, heroic effort is made by Saul's concubine, Ritzpah, to protect the bodies of those desecrated by the Gibeonites, until they are recaptured and given proper burial with their ancestors, in the family tomb (2 Samuel 21:1–14).

The family tomb is the central symbol for understanding early biblical notions of the hereafter. Over and over, in the Torah and in later biblical writings, great importance is placed on being buried beside one's family members. As Herbert Brichto suggests, it is "not mere sentimental respect for the physical remains [that is] . . . the motivation for the practice, but rather an assumed connection between proper sepulture and the condition of happiness of the deceased in the afterlife."[8]

Burial in the family grave served to reconnect the departed one with a society of previously dead ancestors. This society was believed to exist in the tomb itself or perhaps in the surrounding locality.[9] Death itself was not seen as a cessation of existence. On the contrary, to be gathered to one's ancestors implied but a passage to another realm where departed family spirits cohabited and the activities of kith and kin continued within the sacred ancestral society of the family tomb.

Through the image of the family tomb, traces of a belief in a continued postmortem experience can be found in the early biblical period. However, as in life, so in death; as yet, there is no individual self-consciousness apart from the group, tribe, or family clan. The individual is conceived of as property of the family, with no sense of separate, individualized existence. Even though there are individual leaders—Abraham, Isaac, Jacob, Moses, David, Solomon—their individuality is important only insofar as they represent the nation as a whole. At this stage in biblical history, the notion of a personal immortality does not yet exist.

Feeding the Dead

The Hebrews, or as they were later called, the Israelites, shared common patterns of religious expression with other peoples of the ancient Near East. Therefore, by looking at funerary practices described in the Bible as well as in extrabiblical sources, we can discover additional information on postmortem beliefs in the early biblical period.

One rather curious phenomenon that appears throughout the ancient Near East is the ritual act of feeding the dead. Family clan members sensed a continued contact with the deceased, who were believed to be residing in the locale of the family tomb. Since the dead were removed from the earthly domain, the living felt it necessary to provide for their ongoing well-being, and they would do so by bringing food and drink to the burial ground. For us today that may seem quite strange, but within the ancient world, it was a mutually beneficial arrangement between the living and the ancestral dead. The living would provide physical sustenance to the dead; in turn, the deceased ancestors would be expected to provide guidance and protection to the living.[10]

There is abundant evidence attesting to various forms of this practice of feeding the dead. Egyptian funerary art frequently depicts the image of a deceased person seated at a lavish banquet table, surrounded by food presented to him by family members. Farther to the north, excavations at Gezer, dating from c. 4000 to 2000 B.C.E., demonstrate that the Canaanites similarly evolved a custom of serving food and drink to the deceased. Graves have been unearthed, with hollow tubes at the headstone that allowed for depositing foodstuff in the tomb. This practice seems to have been normative in the ancient Near East for centuries; and as late as the seventh century B.C.E., we find an inscription in the name of the Assyrian king Ashurbanipal proclaiming: "The rules for making offerings to the dead and libations to the ghosts of the kings my ancestors . . . I reintroduced. I did well unto god and man, to dead and living."[11]

Further archaeological finds reveal that the custom of feeding the dead was also practiced by the biblical Israelites. For example, a sepulchral chamber unearthed at Megiddo contained a cone-shaped trough, undoubtedly designed for transporting some form of liquid food substance to the subterranean antechamber below. Similar archaeological evidence has been found elsewhere, suggesting this may have been a common practice.[12] Certainly the textual material of the Hebrew Bible substantiates this view.

Thus, for example, Deuteronomy 26:14 describes a ritual confession recited when presenting agricultural tithes to the Temple priesthood. As part of the prescribed confession, the person bringing the tithe would publicly disclaim having given any food to the dead:

> I have not eaten of it [the consecrated food] while in mourning; I have not cleared out [consumed] any of it while I was unclean, and I have not deposited any of it with the dead. I have obeyed the voice of YHVH, my God; I have done just as You commanded me.[13]

Two other texts refer to special foods that were offered to the dead. Hosea 9:4 reads: "It will be for them like the food of mourners; all who partake of which are defiled." Jeremiah 16:6–7 clearly states: "Great and small alike will die in this land. . . . They will not break bread for a mourner, to comfort him for bereavement, nor offer one a cup of consolation for the loss of his father or mother." Much later, the Apocryphal author Ben Sirach ridicules the custom of feeding the dead: "Good things spread out before a mouth that is closed are like piles of food spread on a grave" (Ecclesiasticus 30:18).

The condemnatory attitude toward feeding the dead reflected in the Bible indicates that this particular type of mourning ritual was in all likelihood carried out in the early biblical period. Why would the act need to be condemned so strongly if it hadn't been practiced by the people of Israel? It may be that this ritual took the form of a sacrifice presented as an offering when consulting the dead.[14] However, with the passing of time, as prophetic monotheism became the dominant religious force, this practice was subsequently condemned as idolatrous.

Nonetheless, the combination of archaeological information and textual material indicates that throughout the early centuries of the biblical period there was a sense of ongoing interaction between the living and the dead. Although one cannot speak of a philosophical conception of the afterlife, there is nonetheless a simple, unsophisticated perception that existence continues after the physical body has been laid to rest in the family tomb.

Funerary Practices: *Bamot*

Another element from the early biblical period that sheds light on beliefs in a postmortem realm are the *bamot*, or "high places." The *bamot* were sanctuaries of cultic worship, both Canaanite and Israelite, at times dedicated to deities other than YHVH. Although monotheistic in its founding revelation at Sinai, Israelite religion retained elements of Canaanite worship for centuries. Kings of Israel and Judah—Solomon, Rehoboam, Jehoshapat, and Jehoash, to name a few—built and offered sacrifices and incense on the *bamot*.[15] Condemned repeatedly by later biblical writers, the *bamot* nonetheless were important centers of Israelite religious worship.

Structurally, the *bamot* were large elevated platforms, ranging from six to twenty-five yards in diameter. They were built of stone, approximately six feet above the surrounding ground, with a flight of stairs leading up to the platform.[16] The *bamot* were altars used for cultic worship, often adorned with an *asherah*, or sacred pole associated with the goddess Asherah or Anath, and a *massebah*, an upright stone that symbolized the male deity.[17] 1 Kings 14:23, for example, lists all these elements of religious worship together: "For they also built high places [*bamot*] for themselves and pillars [*massebot*, plural of *massebah*] and Asherim, on every high hill, under every leafy tree."

Archaeological research demonstrates the structural similarity between the *bamot* and funeral mounds in the ancient Near East, and a number of biblical scholars have suggested that the *bamot* may have also functioned as burial sites where specific funerary practices were carried out.[18] Certain textual passages support this point of view. For example, the way in which Ezekiel 43:7 refers to both *bamot* and burial suggests the use of *bamot* as a place for burial: "The House of Israel and their kings must not again defile My holy name by their apostasy and by the corpses of their kings in their high places [*bamot*]." Furthermore, the *massebah*, or stele, associated with the *bamot* was often utilized to mark a grave. For example, Jacob erected a *massebah* on Rachel's burial site (Genesis 35:20). The Canaanite sanctuary excavated at Hazor revealed the existence of numerous *massebot*, which were likely used to mark a burial ground.[19]

Although speculative, it may well be that certain cultic acts associated with the *bamot* were utilized to commune with the realm of the deceased ancestral family. Perhaps sacrifices and the dispensing of food and drink to the dead were carried out upon the *bamot*. Certainly the evidence suggests that there was a concern with the realm of the dead during early biblical times, and it is clear that some form of ritualized interaction between the living and the dead was inherent to the earliest historical layers of Judaism.

Funerary Practices: *Teraphim*

Another phenomenon that may be associated with biblical funerary practices were the *teraphim*, translated as "household gods," or "images." In a somewhat cryptic story in Genesis 31, Rachel steals the *teraphim* of Laban, her father; she hides them in a camel saddle and sits upon them. When Laban comes searching for them she innocently responds: "Let not my lord take it amiss that I cannot rise before you; for the way of women [the period of women] is upon me" (Genesis 31:35).

What exactly were the *teraphim*? From the Genesis story of Rachel, they appear to be small and portable carved images, with an apparent religious significance. However, in 1 Samuel 19, they appear as life-size, perhaps even having a human form. When David is being pursued by King Saul's men, his wife Michal helps him escape through a window. Then "she took the *teraphim* [household idols] and laid it on the bed, and covered it with a cloth; and at its head she put a net of goats' hair" (1 Samuel 19:13) to deceive Saul's messengers into believing it was David's figure. When they arrive looking for David, she tells them: "He is sick," and quickly sends them away.

It may be that the *teraphim* were associated with death and the postmortem ancestral realm. Etymologically, the Hebrew word *teraphim* can be related to the word *rephaim*, meaning "ghosts" or "shades."[20] R. H. Charles has suggested that the *teraphim* were actual images of dead ancestors utilized as oracular devices when consulting the deceased.[21] There is certainly indication that the *teraphim* were used for some sort of divinatory purposes. According to the medieval biblical commentator Nahmanides, the *teraphim* were used to gain knowledge of future events.[22] This is inferred in both Judges 17:5 and Hosea 3:4, which mention the *teraphim* along with the *ephod*, a known ancient divinatory device. In Zechariah 10:2 divination is even more clearly implied: "The *teraphim* speak deceit, diviners see visions that lie; they tell dreams that are false, they give comfort in vain."[23] These passages do not specifically intimate any connection to the postmortem realm of the dead; however, 2 Kings 23:24 lists necromancers, wizards, *teraphim*, and idols as abominations to God, and thus links the *teraphim* with the condemned practice of necromancy, consulting the dead.[24] While these activities and ritual objects were not sanctioned by the prophets, they persisted as cultic remnants of early Israelite religion.

Both the *teraphim* and the *bamot*, as well as the existence of family tombs and the practice of feeding the dead, all point to an early biblical belief in the postmortem survival of an ancestral family clan. But there is no detailed information offered on just what occurs after death, nor is there any description of the nature of the postmortem realm. What we can say, however, is that in the early centuries of the biblical era there existed at least a primitive conception of a relationship between the living and the dead. There is additional textual evidence to suggest this was the case.

Necromancy, *Ob*, and Familiar Spirits

The story of Saul and the witch of En-Dor is a classic example of biblical evidence alluding to an ancient practice of communing with the dead. In the face of a military crisis, King Saul sought out a woman who could contact the spirit of the deceased prophet Samuel on his behalf. Of significance in this narrative is the term used in the Hebrew text. In 1 Samuel 28:7, Saul gives explicit instruction to his courtiers to find for him a *baalat eishet ob*, literally "a woman who has mastery over *ob*." The term *ob* can be translated as "familiar spirit" or "ghost." What is implied by *baalat eishet ob* is an individual who has the ability to contact and communicate with ghosts, or spirits of the deceased. It is very clear here that Saul solicited the services of a medium.

Although *ob* occurs repeatedly in the Hebrew Bible, there is some variation in its use. In a number of places, *ob* is specifically a spirit or ghost of the dead; elsewhere, it is understood as the individual who engages in contact with these spirits, that is, a medium or necromancer.

Thus, for example, in the following passages *ob* is used to indicate a spirit of the dead. Deuteronomy 18:11 condemns the individual who casts spells or consults ghosts (Hebrew: *shoel ob*) or familiar spirits (*yidd'oni*, from the verb *yada*, "to know"), or who inquires of the dead (*doresh el ha-metim*). Similarly, we find in Leviticus 20:27 this injunction: "A man or woman who has a ghost (*ob*) or a familiar spirit (*yidd'oni*) shall be put to death. They will be pelted with stones—their bloodguilt will be upon them."

On the other hand, in the following passages *ob* is used in a different sense, as one who communicates with the dead. Thus, in 2 Kings 23:24 Josiah also did away with the necromancers (*ha-ovot*, plural of *ob*) and the mediums (*ha-yidd'onim*), the household gods (*teraphim*), and the fetishes—"all the detestable things that were to be seen in the land of Judah and Jerusalem." And Isaiah 8:19 states: "And when they will say to you consult the mediums (*ha-ovot*) and the wizards, who whisper and mutter, should not a people inquire of their God? Why consult the dead on behalf of the living?"

W. O. E. Oesterley attempts to clarify various uses of the term *ob* by suggesting that "first it was believed that a ghost, or *Ob*, actually appeared to the diviner; [later] the diviner believed himself or herself to be 'possessed' by the ghost, and thus came to be called by the same name."[25] These seem to be types of spiritualistic communication, and when the term *ob* appears, what is implicit is a process of interaction between the living and the dead. The repeated biblical indictment of this otherworldly communication suggests that necromancy was likely a time-honored tradition, one with a widespread folk-level interest.[26] Even more, there was probably a thriving guild of En-Dor-type practitioners of the condemned art of spiritualistic mediumship. Thus, there is little doubt that we have here yet another ancient phenomenon indicative of a belief in life after death. Put together, all the evidence—on ancestral family tombs, feeding the dead, the cultic use of *teraphim* and *bamot*, and the practice of necromancy—undoubtedly suggests that our biblical ancestors were not only cognizant of a hereafter realm, but found various means to engage in an ongoing interactive process of communication with the dead.

SHEOL—THE AFTERLIFE PHILOSOPHY
OF ISRAELITE RELIGION

Origins

From the twelfth century B.C.E. onward, new conceptions of life after death began to emerge among the Israelites. Developing slowly and in successive stages, these new conceptions formed the historical basis for later Jewish teachings on the afterlife.

With the traditions of the Mosaic revelation at Sinai, a nation was born. Referred to as B'nai Yisrael—the Children of Israel—this new nation was characterized by a monotheistic theology and a national-political consciousness: belief in one God who had taken upon Himself to redeem and sustain His elected people. Progressively, the nomadic family clan and the tribe were superseded by the notion of the unified Israelite nation as the primary social unit. This shift in the political-social consciousness of the nation had a direct bearing on conceptions of death and the postmortem realm.

As the idea of collective Israel evolved, it was believed that all the graves of family, tribe, or nation united into one. This was a logical extension of existing beliefs: multiple tribes and family clans; many family graves and different ancestral realms for the dead; one tribe, or rather, one nation; hence, one postmortem ancestral realm. Just as the living tribes unified, so the realms of the ancestral dead merged; this unified collectivity of the dead became known as Sheol,[27] a conception that became increasingly important in the Israelite worldview.

Sheol was a subterranean realm in which the relations and customs of earthly life were reproduced. Upon death, one descended deep beneath the earth and entered the depths of Sheol. In an early biblical text, Jacob says to Reuben: "If any harm came to him [Benjamin] on the journey you are to undertake, you would send me down to Sheol with my white head bowed in grief" (Genesis 42:38).[28] Later, by the time of Isaiah, the subterranean imagery associated with Sheol becomes even more descriptive: "Your magnificence has been flung down to Sheol . . . underneath a bed of maggots and over you a blanket of worms" (Isaiah 14:11). Even more, Sheol is envisioned as an all-consuming, cavernous beast, whose "bones are strewn at the mouth of Sheol" (Psalm 141:7); Sheol "has enlarged herself, and opened her mouth without measure" (Isaiah 5:14).

The etymological origins of the word *Sheol* are not very clear. One possible derivation is from the Hebrew root *shaal*, "to ask." Hence, Sheol is a place of inquiry where one inquires of the dead, an obvious reference to the condemned practice of necromancy. A second possible derivation is from the Hebrew word *sho'al*, "a hollow hand"; thus, Sheol is a hollow place (beneath the ground). However, neither of these etymological conjectures are considered definitive.[29]

Mythologically, the notion of Sheol has parallels in other religious traditions. The biblical Israelites and the ancient Babylonians shared common beliefs in a postmortem underworld: both Sheol and the Babylonian Aralu are conceived of as being located beneath the earth.[30] Similarly, S. G. F. Brandon suggests that the description of Sheol, particularly in Job 10:21–22, is a Hebrew equivalent of the Mesopotamian *kur-nu-gi-a*, the "land of no return."[31] And finally, the Israelite notion of Sheol has a resemblance to the Greek Hades, the underworld domain depicted in the *Iliad* and the *Odyssey*.[32]

Characteristics of Sheol

One of the main attributes of Sheol, at least in the early stages of development as a postmortem concept, was its amoral character. Existence in Sheol was neither good nor bad; it was an underground domain of the dead, completely beyond the care and control of God. YHVH was a national God, dedicated primarily to His people, the Israelites, and to the land He had promised for generations. According to the three-tiered ancient biblical worldview, YHVH dwelt in the heavenly sphere, human beings inhabited the earthly realm, and the ancestral dead resided deep within the depths of Sheol.[33] After death, the individual was completely removed from the human realm in which God's moral jurisdiction was operant.[34] Thus, Samuel is found in Sheol after his death (1 Samuel 28:3ff.), but it is not a realm of torment or punishment; it is simply the domain of the dead. The negative, punitive aspects that later characterized Sheol were almost completely lacking in its original conception. Therefore, rich and poor, kings and sinners (Job 3:11ff.), all went to Sheol upon their death.[35]

Some additional images depicting the character of Sheol in both the pre- and postexilic biblical periods include the following: It was considered a land of dust (Daniel 12:2) and disorder (Job 10:22). Sheol had different divisions or chambers (Proverbs 7:27), was provided with gates (Psalm 9:14, 108:18), and was secured with bars (Job 17:16). And, finally, Sheol was below the sea (Job 26:5) and without light (Job 10:21). Put together, these images paint a picture of Sheol as a bleak and forlorn subterranean realm.[36]

Abbadon, Bor, and Shakhat

While *Sheol* is the term most frequently used to describe the underground domain of the dead, on occasion in later biblical texts three other synonymous terms are used: *Abbadon*, meaning "ruin" or "destruction"; *Bor*, meaning "the pit"; and *Shakhat*, meaning "corruption."

Abbadon, from the root word meaning "to perish," appears four times in the Hebrew Bible, in juxtaposition with either Sheol or death. The congruence between Abbadon and a postmortem underworld is apparent: "Is your love declared in the grave, your faithfulness in Abbadon [Destruction]"? (Psalm 88:11). "Abbadon and Death say, 'Only a rumor of it has reached our ears'" (Job 28:22). "Sheol is naked before him and Abbadon has no covering" (Job 26:6). Finally, in Proverbs 15:11, there is a very clear correlation between the two terms: "Sheol and Abbadon lie open before YHVH—how much more the minds of men!"

In Isaiah 14:15, Sheol and Bor appear in parallel juxtaposition, again suggesting a similarity of usage: "You will be brought down to Sheol; to the depth of the Pit [Bor] (Isaiah 14:15). Elsewhere in Isaiah we find: "And they will be gathered together as prisoners are gathered in the Pit" (Isaiah 24:22). In Ezekiel Bor is clearly a reprehensible underground realm:

> I will bring you down, with those who go down to the Pit [Bor], to the people of old. I shall set you in the lowest parts of the earth, like places desolate of old, with those who go down to the Pit, and you shall not be inhabited and shall not radiate splendor in the land of the living. (Ezekiel 26:20)

The term *Shakhat* appears in Isaiah 38:17: "You saved my life from the Pit of Destruction [Shakhat]." Most English translations of the biblical text do not make a clear distinction between *Shakhat* and *Bor*, suggesting the similarity of meaning in the two terms; nonetheless, a netherworld of torment is implied. Shakhat, like Sheol, is beneath the earth: "They will bring you down to the Pit [Shakhat], in the heart of the sea you will die a violent death" (Ezekiel 28:8). "I sank to the base of the mountains; the bars of the earth closed on me forever; Yet you brought my life up from the Pit [Shakhat]" (Jon. 2:6). Finally: "For you, O God, will bring them down to the nethermost Pit [*Be'er Shakhat*], those murderous treacherous men" (Psalm 55:24).

Abbadon, Bor, and Shakhat all connote the negative, abysmal aspects of the after-death realm of Sheol. From their occurrence in the biblical text, it is clear that ideas of an underworld abode of the dead were inherent to the ancient Israelite worldview.

The Inhabitants of Sheol: The *Rephaim*

Those beings in Sheol were given a specific name, at least in later biblical texts, where they are called *rephaim*—ghosts, shades, or literally, weak ones, powerless ones. In eight different passages, the term *rephaim* refers quite specifically to the ghostlike inhabitants of Sheol. Thus, for example, Psalm 88:10 states: "Do You work wonders for the dead? Do the *rephaim* rise up to praise You?" In Isaiah and Job we find the statements "They are dead, they can never live. *Rephaim*, they can never rise" (Isaiah 26:14) and "The *rephaim* tremble beneath the waters and their denizens. Sheol is naked before Him . . ." (Job 26:5–6). Proverbs, also a late text, uses the same term in speaking of the dead in Sheol: "He does not know that the *rephaim* are there, that her guests are in the depths of Sheol" (Proverbs 9:18); "A man who strays from the path of prudence, Will rest in the company of *rephaim*" (Proverbs 21:16).

There is also another context for the term *rephaim*. According to ancient biblical myth, the *rephaim* were originally a people of great physical stature—giants—dwelling in the Land of Canaan prior to the Conquest. They are mentioned in Genesis 14:5 and 15:20. It has even been suggested that the *rephaim* may be equated with the antediluvian race, the *nephilim*, referred to in Genesis 6:4.[37] A juxtaposition of Deuteronomy 2:10–11 and Numbers 13:33 bears this out. Deuteronomy 2:10–11 states: "It [the wilderness of Moab] was formerly inhabited by the Emim, a people great and numerous, and as tall as the Anakim. Like the Anakim, they are counted as *rephaim*; but the Moabites called them Emim." In the words of Numbers 13:33: "We saw *nephilim* there—the Anakites are part of the *nephilim*—and we looked like grasshoppers to ourselves, so we must have looked to them." Thus, as later rabbinic Midrash claims, the equation is *nephilim* equals Anakim equals Emim equals *rephaim*.[38] All well and good, but what does this have to do with the abode of the dead?

Ancient Hebrew myth propounds that the original antediluvian race of giants, called at different times *nephilim* or *rephaim*, was destroyed by God and banished to the underworld.[39] According to the conjecture of Oesterley, "In the course of time, when this ancient myth had been gradually toned down, the name of *rephaim* was used as a general designation of all the departed in the underworld."[40] Thus, the *rephaim*, at a certain point in history, came to be known as the dead, the shades in the underworld of Sheol. But most references to *rephaim* as the ghostly dead come from the postexilic period, so what we have here is really a later notion, dating from after the sixth century B.C.E.

Before we can travel the next step of the journey historically, we need to understand one other important aspect of the ancient biblical view of Sheol.

Sheol, *Nefesh Met*, and the Biblical Conception of Death

Associated with the biblical conception of Sheol was a very specific understanding of death. Death was not conceived of as a complete annihilation, the termination of existence, but rather as a diminution of energy. Life and death were seen as poles of a continuum of vital energy. In life, the energy, or *nefesh*, was dynamically present; in sickness, it was weakened; and in death, there was a maximum loss of vitality. As Johs. Pederson puts it:

> Life and death are not sharply distinguished spheres, because they do not mean existence or nonexistence. Life is something which one possesses in a higher or lower degree. If afflicted by misfortune, illness or something else . . . then one has only little life, but all the more death. He who is ill or otherwise in distress may say that he is dead, and when he recovers, he is pulled out of death.[41]

Within the biblical context, death was perceived as the progressive depletion of the *nefesh*—breath, vital energy, life force, or spirit. But the Hebrew word *nefesh* does not imply a soul, or spirit, in contradistinction to a body. The differentiation between body and soul, with the accompanying notion of a soul exiting the body upon death, was totally foreign in early biblical times and did not emerge in the Jewish consciousness until many centuries later. *Nefesh* was understood in a unitive way as the totality of being—"man does not have *nefesh*, he is *nefesh*, he lives as *nefesh*."[42] While alive, a human being is considered a *nefesh hayyah* (Genesis 2:7), a living *nefesh*, a vital psychophysical entity. Once dead, the individual becomes a *nefesh met* (Leviticus 21:11; Numbers 6:6), a dead *nefesh*, a depotentiated psychophysical entity.

The *nefesh hayyah*, the living person, dwelt with family clan, tribe, or nation in the terrestrial realm. Upon death, the individual descended into the subterranean realm and as a *nefesh met* dwelt in the grave, in the family tomb, and eventually in Sheol, the abode of the ancestral dead.

Thus, for our biblical ancestors, the termination of earthly life was not in any way a complete or final cessation of being. After the energy required to sustain life dissipated to an extreme, the individual claimed a place in Sheol where existence undeniably continued, but in a weakened, faded condition.[43]

In ancient Israel at this time—between the tenth and eighth centuries B.C.E.—there is still no conception of a postmortem judgment associated with Sheol, nor any philosophy of an individual soul. Death is regarded as a depotentiated state of being—*nefesh met*—and Sheol, an afterlife realm of devitalized existence removed from God's control. This conception of death and the afterlife reflects the fusion of early ideas about the postmortem survival of the ancestral family clan with the newer concept of Sheol. However, this particular understanding of Sheol is only one stage in the evolution of a concept of life after death. Biblical teachings on Sheol did not remain static but began undergoing numerous changes concurrent with changing theology. As the God of Israel eventually became the God of the entire world, the power of YHVH extended throughout the created universe, including Sheol. This theological shift paved the way for the development of an individual postmortem eschatology and a notion of personal immortality.

THE TRANSITION TO YHVH'S MONOTHEISM

Monotheism and Changing Conceptions of Sheol

The monotheistic ideal heralded in the Sinai traditions was not instantly and unequivocally accepted by the Israelite people. For centuries following the settlement of Canaan, Baal, Asherah, and other deities were worshiped along with YHVH. As late as the seventh century B.C.E., nonmonotheistic elements of religious practice continued to exist, although they were repeatedly condemned by the spiritual leaders of Israel and Judah.

The religious history of the biblical period prior to the Babylonian exile is a chronicling of the progressive evolution of monotheism. It is a history of over six centuries during which time the monotheism of YHVH became the predominant religious force. Throughout this period, Jewish conceptions of the postmortem realm likewise evolved and were directly affected by the successful emergence of monotheism.

As indicated above, originally Sheol was the netherworld where the deceased ancestors dwelt, a realm often associated with nonmonotheistic aspects of worship such as the *bamot* and *teraphim* and related cultic practices. However, as YHVH's monotheism came to predominate in the religious life of the Israelite people, idolatrous practices and the accompanying beliefs were purged. Consequently, the understanding of Sheol underwent a radical shift.

First of all, it was necessary to eliminate the earlier notions of Sheol as a nonmoral realm beyond God's dominion, in which the dead possessed superhuman knowledge of earthly events and communicated with the living. Subsequently, Sheol came under YHVH's control and became moral and retributive; that is to say, Sheol became a place of punishment for the wicked. And finally a new development in the evolution of Jewish afterlife philosophy emerged: incorporated into the conception of Sheol was the notion of a spiritualized, individual postmortem future, attainable through direct communion with YHVH. Over the course of centuries, the conception of a personal life after death eventually made its appearance within Jewish tradition.

We will now travel a journey of approximately three to four hundred years documenting the specific stages involved in the emergence of biblical Judaism's conception of an individual immortality.

YHVH's Power Extends to Sheol

The first important shift in the Israelite conception of Sheol came about with the increase and strengthening of YHVH's power. Once YHVH came to be regarded as the one and only God of the universe, God's power widened and could now save human beings from the clutches of Sheol. Thus, Psalm 49:15 states: "But God will redeem my soul from the power of Sheol, and will receive me." And a similar point of view appears in Psalm 116:2: "The cords of death surrounded me and the pains of Sheol seized me. And I called upon the name of YHVH . . . and He saved me."

In the Book of Kings, YHVH's power over Sheol and death is expressed through His prophets Elijah (1 Kings 17:22) and Elisha (2 Kings 4:35), both of whom are able to bring the dead back to life.

Of Elisha, the story is told that

> Elisha came into the house, and there was the boy, laid out dead on his couch. He went in, shut the door behind the two of them, and

prayed to YHVH. Then he mounted [the bed] and placed himself over the child. He put his mouth on its mouth, his eyes on its eyes, and his hands on its hands: as he bent over it. And the body of the child became warm. He stepped down, walked once up and down the room, then mounted and bent over him. Thereupon the boy sneezed seven times, and the boy opened his eyes. (2 Kings 4:32–35)

In a similar vein, the story of Elijah reviving a dead child expresses with certainty how it is YHVH's power, more than Elijah's, that is at the core of this supernatural feat:

After a while, the son of the mistress of the house fell sick, and his illness grew worse until he had no breath left in him. She said to Elijah, "What harm have I done to you, O man of God, that you should come here to recall my sin and cause the death of my son?" "Give me the boy," he said to her; and taking him from her arms, he carried him to the upper chamber where he was staying, and laid him down on his own bed. He cried out to YHVH, and said: "O YHVH, my God, will you bring calamity upon this widow whose guest I am, and let her son die?" Then he stretched out over the child three times, and cried out to YHVH, saying: "O YHVH, my God, let this child's life [nefesh] return to his body!" YHVH heard Elijah's plea; the child's life [nefesh] returned to his body, and he revived. (1 Kings 17:17–22)

Sheol: A Land of Forgetfulness and a Realm of Silence

In consequence of the establishment of God's authority over the domain of Sheol, there was a radical alteration in the power attributed to the inhabitants of the underworld. In its earliest conception, Sheol was a world unto itself paralleling the human realm; those in Sheol were not inert but rather possessed life, knowledge, and the power to interact with and even counsel the living.[44] Thus, faced with military adversity, King Saul summoned the prophet Samuel from Sheol, soliciting guidance (1 Samuel 28:12–20); and Rachel, long after her death, is said to weep for her children, the exiled Israelite nation, refusing to be comforted (Jeremiah 31:15).

However, according to a later view, the dead in Sheol have absolutely no knowledge of what transpires in the earthly realm. Job 14:21 speaks of how a dead man's "sons come to honor [him], and he knows it not. . . . Only when his flesh is on him does he feel pain, and while his soul is within him does he mourn." Or, in the words of the Psalmist: "I am set apart with the dead, like the slain who lie in the grave, whom you remember no more, who are cut off from your care" (Psalm 88:5). In this new conception of Sheol, the dead "shall not awake nor be raised out of sleep" (Job 14:12). Ecclesiastes, dating from the late biblical period, also echoes this conception of Sheol: "The living know they will die: but the dead know nothing, nor do they have any more a reward; for the memory of them is forgotten" (Ecclesiastes 9:5). Thus, Sheol is completely and totally depotentiated. In the words of the Psalmist, "the dead cannot praise YHVH" (Psalm 116:17), for Sheol is a "land of forgetfulness" (Psalm 88:12) and a realm of silence (Psalm 94:17).

Sheol Becomes a Realm of Postmortem Retribution

At this point, a number of important conceptual changes take place in the biblical understanding of Sheol. YHVH has gained control over the subterranean realm of the dead, and the occupants of Sheol no longer have personal power. Next, Sheol begins to take on a retributive quality—it becomes a realm in which the adversaries of Israel receive due punishment.

Recall that originally, Sheol was simply a habitation of the ancestral dead with no special moral, retributive function; there were no distinct realms for the wicked and the righteous, and no reward or punishment. The ideas we often take for granted today when thinking about life after death were not even in the consciousness of the Israelite people at this point in history. However, by the end of the sixth century B.C.E. Israel had encountered a series of formidable foes. Assyria had vanquished the northern kingdom of Israel in the eighth century B.C.E., and less than two hundred years later, Babylonia conquered and exiled the southern kingdom of Judah. These sociopolitical circumstances were reflected in a radically transformed conception of the postmortem underworld. What surfaced at this time was a philosophical notion envisioning eventual chastisement, even decimation, of Israel's enemies in Sheol. In response to the reality of military defeat and exile, by the sixth century B.C.E. Sheol came to be seen as a place of punishment for the enemies of YHVH and of Israel.

At first, this retributive conception of Sheol was seen only within the context of the collective historical-political destiny of Israel. For example, Isaiah 14 speaks of how the king of Babylon and "all the kings of the nations" (Isaiah 14:9) who have risen up against Israel will "be brought down to Sheol, to the depths of the pit" (Isaiah 14:15). Similarly, Ezekiel 32 condemns Israel's enemies Egypt, Assyria, and "the daughters of mighty nations" (Ezekiel 32:18)—they will all be destroyed, cast down to Sheol.

What we encounter here is the very first layer of afterlife teachings in which there is an association of Sheol, death, and retribution. What later becomes central to Jewish conceptions of life after death arises for the first time only in the sixth century B.C.E. But even here, this notion of retributive punishment in the hereafter is bound up exclusively with collective eschatological thinking. At this point, the rebuke of the afterlife is not for the individual, but for the wicked nations. Those punished in Sheol are enemies of the Israelite community, punished for a national iniquity against God's chosen people, and not at all because of any personal sin.[45]

Retribution and Individual Responsibility

In the next stage, an evolutionary breakthrough occurs in Jewish teachings of the afterlife; it is a slight, yet profound shift representing a distinct turning point in the creation of a philosophical conception of individual immortality.

At the time of Jeremiah—who was a likely witness to the Babylonian conquest[46]—the concept of individual retribution, and hence individual responsibility, finally enters Jewish thought. In the Book of Jeremiah, every person is to be held responsible for his or her own sin. It is a theme first glimpsed in prophetic literature and echoed repeatedly throughout the later history of Judaism.

Jeremiah, heralding the words of God, proclaims: "In those days they will say no longer, 'Parents have eaten sour grapes, and the children's teeth are set on edge.' But every one shall die for his own sins: whosoever eats sour grapes, his teeth will be set on edge" (Jeremiah 31:29–30).

With this declaration by Jeremiah there emanates a new notion of the individual in relation to God. For the first time, we glimpse the possibility of an individual destiny set apart from the collective fate of the entire nation. John Hick explains this shift in terms of the unfolding history of Judaism in the sixth century B.C.E.:

So long as the stream of national life continued in full spate the individual was carried along in it, and the immortality of the nation
did not require an individual immortality for its separate members.
But with the crushing Babylonian conquest of Judah in the sixth
century and the exile of so many of Jerusalem's leading citizens, faith
in continuing national existence was shaken and the individual became more conscious of his own personal status and destiny.[47]

In place of the collective Israelite nation, with the Babylonian exile
the individual person becomes the primary religious unit. A similar shift
is evidenced elsewhere during this period—for example, in the Greek
world, with the creation of the individual citizenship within the Greek
polis, or city-state, and in India, with the appearance of Buddhism. At
this point in history the uniqueness of the individual is recognized over
and above that of the collective.[48] As a result of this shift, for the first
time in biblical history each individual is given a degree of moral freedom and hence, the ability to shape his or her ultimate fate.

In Ezekiel, this notion of individualism is carried even further. As a
prophet whose writings also date from the time of the Babylonian exile,
Ezekiel teaches that every soul is the property of God, not merely that of
the family and nation. "Consider," says YHVH, "all lives are Mine; the
life of the parent and the life of the child are both Mine. The person who
sins, only he will die" (Ezekiel 18:4).

Now, instead of one's destiny being mediated through the destiny
of the nation, every unique individual stands in a direct and immediate
relationship to God. Thus, if each individual stands apart from the collectivity, a new question emerges: who will be punished and who will be
saved by YHVH from Sheol? According to Ezekiel, it depends entirely
on the quality of the individual life lived:

> The person who sins, he alone shall die. A child shall not share the
> burden of a parent's guilt, nor shall a parent share the burden of a
> child's guilt; the righteousness of the righteous shall be accounted
> to him alone, and the wickedness of the wicked shall be accounted
> to him alone. (Ezekiel 18:20)

Here, the doctrine of an individual moral retribution is articulated
very explicitly. From this time onward, each individual is to be punished
or rewarded in direct proportion to their sin or righteousness during their
lifetime.[49] Proverbs teaches that "for an intelligent [righteous] man, the

path of life leads upward, In order to avoid Sheol below" (Proverbs 15:24); but those who are wicked are condemned by YHVH to the reprisals of the subterranean refuge. Elsewhere it is taught that the one who seeks a path of righteousness achieves life, "but to pursue evil, leads to death" (Proverbs 11:19). The concept of individual responsibility is a necessary transitional step in the creation of a Jewish notion of a personal afterlife. However, at this point, Sheol is not yet that postmortem spiritual immortality for the righteous. Reward for the God-abiding person, although it is a "delivery from death" (Proverbs 10:2), is experienced through divine reward in earthly life, not in the hereafter. The righteous individual is given due reward within the earthly sphere (Proverbs 11:31), not through an immortal existence in the afterlife. Thus, at this stage the polarity of divine retribution is as follows: the good live, the wicked die and are condemned to Sheol. In neither Jeremiah nor Ezekiel is there any direct reference to the notion of a divine life beyond the grave for the righteous. That is glimpsed for the first time only in the Book of Job, a text dating from the late biblical period.

The Dawning of an Individual Immortality

Jewish philosophical thinking, in the period surrounding the Babylonian exile, contained within it one essential problem: how could one account for the suffering of the righteous? The doctrine of divine retribution, which taught that there was a direct correspondence between one's actions and one's life situation, guaranteed Sheol for the wicked and a blessed earthly existence for those who faithfully abided by the ways of YHVH. As long as the righteous experienced good fortune and divine benevolence, this doctrine presented no problems. However, when the upright and faithful were plagued by suffering and anguish, the doctrine began to break down. How could the suffering of the righteous be explained if YHVH was truly a god of justice? This is the problem addressed in the Book of Job.

Job was a "blameless and upright [man] who feared God and shunned evil" (Job 1:1). Yet a series of calamities befell Job, killing his family, destroying his property, and leaving him physically pain-stricken. All along, in spite of his suffering and grief, he was convinced of his innocence. Believing his life was one of exemplary piety, Job could find no justice in the circumstances of his fate. Bitterly tormented, he struggled to understand the ways of divine retribution and to maintain faith in the face of a perceived desertion by God.

The Book of Job is a classical allegorical text focusing on the themes of faith and divine justice in Judaism. One passage in this text seems to some, especially R. H. Charles, to point toward the possibility of an immortal spiritual existence subsequent to death. From the depths of his anguish, Job exclaims:

> For I know that that my Redeemer lives,
> And at last he will stand upon the earth;
> and after my skin has been thus destroyed,
> Then from my flesh shall I see God. (Job 19:25–26)[50]

For the first time in biblical literature, the possibility of an immortal, spiritual existence subsequent to physical death may here be glimpsed. Job, if Charles is right, envisions a postmortem life wherein the soul, after death, continues to exist in a spiritual relationship with God—"after my skin will have been peeled off, I would behold God."

This is a seed for later developments in the evolution of Jewish afterlife teachings. However, at this point the notion of a transcendental, spiritual afterlife for the righteous is still not given full expression, nor is it central to Job's worldview. The possibility of an individual postmortem immortality is at most glimpsed for a fleeting moment by Job.[51] But this seed idea later flowers and becomes central in Jewish afterlife philosophy.

Although the value of the individual had been proclaimed by Jeremiah, Ezekiel, and Job, this dawning notion of a personal postmortem immortality did not become the predominant Jewish view of the afterlife in biblical times. Even while the incipient notion of a personal spiritual hereafter was infusing itself into the consciousness of Judaism, it never replaced or eliminated the pervasive concern with the postmortem fate of YHVH's Israelite nation.

COLLECTIVE ESCHATOLOGY AND THE END-OF-DAYS

Background

Thus far we have traced the early development of a biblical philosophy of personal immortality. As we noted above, teachings on the collective destiny of Israel influenced all later beliefs about the afterlife in Judaism. Therefore, to complete our historical trek through the biblical period, we have to backtrack in time and examine the broader collective eschatology found within the Hebrew Bible—in particular, conceptions about divine judgment and the end-of-days. Although the textual depictions of these collective notions do not impart information on the individual postmortem experience, they are important philosophical and eschatological dimensions of the biblical world. As such, they are central in the evolution of all subsequent Jewish teachings on life after death.

Historically, the idea of a national collectivity was central to the biblical worldview. According to the Book of Genesis, Abraham was promised that his descendants would become as numerous as the heavenly stars and would inherit the land of Canaan (Genesis 17:8). The covenant between Abraham and God was symbolically engraved in the flesh by circumcision and reaffirmed for Isaac (Genesis 26:24), Jacob/Israel (Genesis 28:13ff.), and Moses (Exodus 3:13ff.). In the mythic understanding of ancient Israel, the covenantal relationship between YHVH and the Israelite nation was reasserted at Sinai. Through the giving of the Ten Commandments, a group consciousness was formed: one nation, one Torah, one God who had promised the people they would inherit the Land of Canaan. This notion of a collective destiny for the entire nation underlies all eschatological thinking throughout the biblical period.

Prophetic Visions of the Future: Nationalistic and Universal

After the conquest of Canaan, a nationalistic theology developed in which YHVH's connection with the land and the people remained central. With the creation of the political entity of the Israelite monarchy, eschatological visions of the future took on a nationalistic-political character. The prophets envisioned a future time of blessedness for the Israelite nation. Through divine intervention, the awaited "day of YHVH" would come about, and Israel's foes would be conquered and defeated (Isaiah 13:9). In turn, a new era would be inaugurated in which the nation would enjoy ongoing material prosperity:

> A time is coming—declares YHVH—when the ploughman shall meet the reaper, and the treader of grapes him who holds [the bag] of seed; when the mountains shall drip sweet wine, and all the hills

shall wave [with grain]. . . . and they shall plant vineyards and drink
their wine; they shall till gardens and eat their fruit. (Amos 9:13–14)

During the eighth century B.C.E. the doctrine of the coming kingdom of YHVH entered prophetic literature. It was envisioned that the
future would bring about God's dominion upon earth and a time of peaceful social and political existence for the entire nation of Israel (Hosea
14:6–8). Originally, no mention was made of a Messiah in connection
with the coming kingdom. In later times, however, it was believed that a
descendant of the Davidic lineage would herald the coming of a messianic period (Jeremiah 23:5) and preside over a kingdom in which the
former glory of ancient Israel would be restored.[52]

In the preexilic biblical period, conceptions of the end-of-days were
exclusively nationalistic. Since YHVH was a national God, concerned
only with the fate of the nation, it was Israel alone that would be redeemed. Alongside this nationalistic conception of the end-of-days, there
gradually developed a conception that YHVH's power had extended to
include the whole world. Thus, certain prophetic writings reflect a more
universal image of the end-of-days. In Isaiah, for example, it is envisioned
that YHVH would eventually become the God of all the nations, with
Jerusalem becoming the spiritual center of the entire world:

> In the days to come,
> The Mountain of YHVH's house
> Shall stand form above the mountains
> And tower above the hills;
> And all the nations
> Shall gaze on it with joy,
> And the many peoples shall go and say:
> "Come, Let us go up to the Mountain of YHVH
> To the House of the God of Jacob;
> That he may instruct us in His ways,
> And that may walk in His paths."
> For Torah [the instruction] shall come forth from Zion,
> The word of YHVH from Jerusalem. (Isaiah 2:2–3)

Conceptions of Divine Judgment

The notion of a divine postmortem judgment, which is central in
rabbinic Judaism's teachings on life after death, has its roots in the collective eschatology of the biblical period. What later becomes a complex

and elaborate afterlife conception was originally understood exclusively in terms of the national destiny of the Israelite people.[53]

In early prophetic literature, divine judgment is spoken of in national-political terms. YHVH judges the nations: Israel; Israel and Judah; and the "other nations," *goyim*, gentiles. There is no sense of individual judgment; all the people of the nation merit the punishment or reward collectively.

In Amos and Hosea, judgment is directed against Israel: "You alone have I singled out, of all the families of the earth—that is why I will call you to account for all your iniquities" (Amos 3:2). In Isaiah and Micah, judgment for iniquities is levied against the southern kingdom of Judah (Isaiah 1:1–20; Micah 3:12). Isaiah prophesies the coming of a divine kingdom (Isaiah 1:26); but first, there will be a divine judgment and a purging of evil before the nation can be restored (Isaiah 2:12–22).

An important development in the notion of divine judgment takes place in the Book of Zephaniah. Here, YHVH's judgment is universal, directed against all the inhabitants of the earth: "I will sweep everything away from the face of the earth" (Zephaniah 1:2); "I will also punish on that day everyone who steps over the threshold" (Zephaniah 1:9).

In Ezekiel, judgment is conceived of in a dual sense. YHVH's judgment will be directed against both Israel and the other nations. For the nations, judgment will be collective; all will be punished and/or destroyed (Ezekiel 25:8ff.). For Israel, however, judgment will be based on the merit of each individual. The sinful wicked will be annihilated by God's wrathful vengeance. The righteous Israelite will be saved, and thereby selected to participate in the coming kingdom of YHVH (Ezekiel 11:17–21; 36:25–32).

With Ezekiel, an important and subtle philosophical transformation takes place: individual and collective conceptions of divine judgment merge for the first time. God's judgment and retribution, according to Ezekiel, will take into account the accrued merit of each individual Israelite. Participation in the future redemption of the nation will depend upon the merit of each individual person's life. The righteous individual Israelite will be awarded a share in YHVH's messianic collective. This is a significant development in the evolution of an individual philosophy of the afterlife.

Thus far, there is no sense that God's collective judgment will occur in a postmortem realm. Judgment takes place in the human realm and through the unfolding of history, not in an afterworld. There is, however, the beginning of a sense of divine judgment for the individual, corresponding with the rise of the doctrine of individualism and individual retribution in the sixth century B.C.E.

The Final Transition

After Jeremiah, Ezekiel, and Job, individual and collective conceptions of divine judgment begin to blend and mutually influence each other. On the one hand, the individual finally emerges out of the nation and can now stand before God in individual judgment. On the other hand, through Zoroastrian influence, a cosmic, dualistic, transcendental, and universalistic eschatology enters Judaism.[54] As a result of the meeting of these two philosophical trends, Jewish postmortem teachings in the late biblical period become incredibly complex, permeated with conceptions of the Last Judgment, the mythic-historical end-of-days, and the doctrine of resurrection. It was believed that the individual, the nation, the world, and ultimately the entire cosmic order would be subjected to divine judgment. After centuries of concurrent but separate development, collective and individual eschatology—notions about the nation and the individual—finally merged into one elaborate system.

What evolved was a new philosophical synthesis that totally transformed Judaism's understanding of the postmortem world of Sheol. In the final centuries of the biblical era, Sheol came to be seen as a temporary abode of rest for the righteous, where they awaited the eventual coming kingdom of YHVH.

The key in this new transition was the emergence in the late biblical era of the doctrine of resurrection. The righteous who merited redemption waited for an indefinite time in Sheol; then they were resurrected from the dead to participate in the flowering messianic kingdom. This new conception was an evolutionary leap in Jewish postmortem eschatology and radically affected all subsequent Jewish teachings on life after death.

RESURRECTION—THE SYNTHESIS OF INDIVIDUAL AND COLLECTIVE ESCHATOLOGY

Introduction

The doctrine of resurrection is a belief that the dead will live again at some future time, be united with their physical bodies, and participate in the triumph of a divine messianic kingdom on earth. This conception—which in rabbinic terms is called *tehiyyat ha-metim*[55]—originated in the late biblical period and to this day remains central to traditional Jewish teachings on the afterlife.[56]

Resurrection was an organic and necessary next step in the development of biblical conceptions of the afterlife. We have seen the broader background of a belief in the collective redemption for the entire nation; we have also noted the slow evolution of a conception of individual immortality after the sixth century B.C.E. Resurrection was a philosophical integration of all that had come before. First of all, it synthesized two prevailing beliefs of the postexilic biblical period: (1) the belief in the future redemption of the Israelite nation and the establishment of a divinely inspired social order and (2) the notion of divine retribution for the righteous.[57] Second, it was based on the ancient Hebrew belief in the organic unity of the human person: although there was a temporary separation from the body at the time of death, according to the doctrine of resurrection, body and spirit, or consciousness, would eventually be reunited.

The doctrine of resurrection provided a satisfactory philosophical answer to prevalent questions about divine justice and vindication for the righteous individual: If there would eventually be a redemption for the righteous, what would happen to the God-abiding person prior to the inauguration of YHVH's kingdom? Would he or she be condemned to suffer in Sheol? According to the doctrine of resurrection, the righteous were guaranteed God's justice and a place in the coming messianic kingdom. However—and here again there is a new development in the Jewish afterlife philosophy—first there would be a period of waiting in Sheol. Then, at the end-of-days the dead would be revived and return to full physical vitality as participants in the divine kingdom of YHVH. At this point, even though there is a sense of postmortem existence, recompense for the righteous is not with an individual, solitary immortality, but with a blessed resurrected life together with the entire nation.[58]

National Resurrection in Ezekiel

The image of the resurrection of the dead appears for the first time in the Book of Ezekiel, which dates from the early sixth century B.C.E. In a well-known passage, Ezekiel envisions a valley of dry, dismembered bones being transformed into animated, life-filled human bodies:

The hand of YHVH came upon me. He took me out by the spirit of YHVH, and set me down in the valley. It was full of bones. He led me all around them; there were very many of them spread over the valley, and they were very dry. He said to me, "O mortal [son of man], can these bones live again?" I replied, "O Lord YHVH, only you know." And He said to me, "Prophesy over these bones, and say to them, O dry bones, hear the word of YHVH. Thus says the Lord YHVH to these bones: I will cause breath to enter into you, and you shall live again. I will lay sinews upon you, and cover you with flesh, and form with skin over you. And I will put breath into you, and you shall live again. And you will know that I am YHVH." I prophesied as I had been commanded. And while I was prophesying, suddenly there was a sound of rattling, and the bones came together, bone to matching bone. . . . I prophesied as He commanded me. The breath entered them, and they came to life and stood up on their feet, a vast multitude. (Ezekiel 37:1–8, 10)

Here, Ezekiel's vision of a resurrection is a national/collective one.[59] Written subsequent to the Babylonian exile, what is envisioned is the total revivification of the fallen Israelite nation. No doubt, this image of the redemption of the fallen dead provided a sense of hope and vision to the dispirited exiles.

Interestingly, the scene of the dead bones in this vision is reminiscent of a Zoroastrian funeral ground. Zoroastrian religious practitioners did not bury their dead, but rather allowed bodies to lie exposed to the elements and to birds of prey, believing that after the Judgment Day, Ahura Mazda would gather together all the scattered bones.[60] This is certainly the motif in the above-quoted passage, and it is likely that during his sojourn of exile in Babylonia, Ezekiel himself was influenced by these Zoroastrian ideas.[61]

The text continues and describes a return to the soil of Israel:

And he said to me, "O mortal, these bones are the whole House of Israel. They say, 'Our bones are dried up, our hope is gone; we are doomed.' Prophesy therefore and say to them: 'Thus said the Lord YHVH: I am going to open your graves, and lift you out of your graves, O My people, and bring you to the land of Israel. And you shall know that I am YHVH, when I have opened your graves, and lifted you out of your graves.'" (Ezekiel 37:11–13)

In symbolic form, the message here is that although it appears impractical for dismembered bodies and piles of dead bones to be brought to life, and similarly, it may seem doubtful that the exiled nation of Judah can ever be returned to the land, in both cases the impossible is made possible through the miracle of divine intervention.[62] The nation will be brought to life; the people will be returned to the land.

Although this prophecy is a new departure in the eschatological beliefs of the postexilic period, it is nonetheless consistent with earlier notions of collective redemption. According to prophetic teachings, the people have been promised redemption at the end-of-days. But if the bodies are dead and the bones remained scattered, how can people participate in God's promised kingdom? In Ezekiel's teachings, to revive the dead is simply the means by which to guarantee Israel's national redemption and the coming messianic kingdom.

In this passage from Ezekiel we encounter another notable development in the evolution of biblical conceptions of the afterlife. Here, Ezekiel envisions that God's redemptive powers will operate within a postmortem realm. From this point on, God's judgment and its results are no longer limited to the earthly domain. Even after death, the entire national collectivity can be rewarded by YHVH, with an eventual complete and total physical resurrection from the realm of the dead.[63]

The doctrine of the resurrection of the dead first appeared in the early postexilic period and gained increasing popularity and acceptance.[64] But it took at least three full centuries until this notion became widely recognized as a normative doctrine in the Jewish world.[65]

Resurrection in Isaiah

The conception of resurrection appears again in Isaiah, in a passage that can be dated as late as 334 B.C.E.:[66]

Oh, let your dead revive! Let corpses arise! Awake and shout for joy, You who dwell in the dust!—For your dew is like the dew on fresh growth; You make the land of the shades come to life. (Isaiah 26:19)

Here, associated with resurrection, we find the image of dew as a life-giving force—a motif familiar to Canaanite mythology.[67] This passage contains the first biblical reference to the notion of resurrection for the individual person, apart from the national collectivity. It is the righteous Israelite who, at the end-of-days, will be redeemed through physical resurrection. But together, both the nation and the righteous individual will receive the blessedness of YHVH. Thus, we see that here Isaiah successfully blends individual and collective postmortem conceptions into a coherent unity. Through physical resurrection the individual, as part of the redeemed Israel nation, is guaranteed a divine postmortem existence.

At this point, the righteous dead must remain in Sheol, awaiting the advent of the coming kingdom. In Isaiah, Sheol is conceived of as a godless, unspiritual realm where the dead are cut off from communion with God and, at least for a limited time, exist in an interim realm awaiting the time of resurrection. Once again Jewish afterlife philosophy goes through an evolutionary shift. With Isaiah, the beginnings of the final transformation of the postmortem realm of Sheol are evidenced: Sheol now becomes a resting, intermediate abode for the righteous of Israel.[68] This conception was developed more fully in the subsequent two to three centuries.

Resurrection in Daniel

The Book of Daniel, dating from the second century B.C.E., is one of the latest additions to the Hebrew Bible. It is an apocalyptic text with elaborate mystical speculation on the end of time and history.[69] The historical context for this book is the era of the Syrian king Antiochus IV, who had conquered Jerusalem, desecrated the Temple, and prohibited Jewish worship. In this book, Daniel envisions a mythical end-of-days, a major battle against the forces of destruction, which will culminate in deliverance and include a postmortem resurrection:

> There will be a time of trouble, the like of which has never been since the nation came into being. At that time, your people will be rescued, all who are found inscribed in the book. Many of those that sleep in the dust of the earth will awake, some to eternal life, others to reproaches, to everlasting abhorrence. (Daniel 12:1–2)

By the time of Daniel, the doctrine of resurrection was familiar to the Judean people living under Hellenistic rule. But here, an important new dimension is added. For the first time, not only the righteous, but likewise the wicked will be resurrected from the depths of Sheol. While the righteous Israelites will be included in the coming messianic kingdom—"your people will be rescued" (Daniel 12:1)—the wicked will be punished and condemned "to reproaches, to everlasting abhorrence" (Daniel 12:2).

Thus, with the Book of Daniel, Jewish postmortem teachings become apocalyptic and dualistic in nature. The ultimate fate of each individual person will be determined by a final judgment that will take place after death—at the end-of-days. Then, reward or punishment will be dispensed as merited. At this stage there emerges a clear dualistic conception of judgment—the possibility of reward or punishment—applied for the first time specifically to the postmortem world.

Daniel's vision of resurrection for both the righteous and the wicked is a seed idea for the notion of heaven and hell that characterizes later Jewish and Christian afterlife teachings. Thus, at the very end of the biblical period, that which was to be of central importance in apocryphal and rabbinic literature—a clear dualistic sense of postmortem punishment and reward—was first conceived.

The Importance of Resurrection in Jewish Eschatology

Soon after its inception, the doctrine of resurrection assumed a position of primary importance in Judaism. Although originally a product of Zoroastrian influence, resurrection was rapidly integrated into the mainstream of Jewish postmortem philosophy.

With the evolution of the philosophy of resurrection, three important developments took place in Jewish afterlife eschatology over a period of three centuries. First, resurrection transformed the understanding of Sheol into an intermediate realm where the righteous await divine redemption at the end-of-days. Second, the doctrine of resurrection envisioned that the result of God's divine judgment would occur within a postmortem realm. And finally, with the Book of Daniel, divine retribution developed a dualistic aspect to it, teaching that eventually there would be a postmortem judgment for both the righteous and the wicked.

Even with these innovative aspects, the doctrine of resurrection assumed a position of primary importance in Judaism soon after its inception. Over the course of two to three centuries resurrection was rapidly integrated into the mainstream of Jewish postmortem philosophy. The reason for this successful inclusion within Jewish thought is that the philosophy of resurrection provided a bridge between the past and the future, between collective and individual eschatology. By linking the basic Israelite notion of a collective, national redemption with the newly evolving doctrine of individual retribution and personal immortality, the new doctrine of resurrection encompassed all existing eschatological conceptions.

Resurrection was an evolutionary development totally consistent with Judaism's past, yet, at the same time, it provided an impetus toward the future. With Daniel's teachings on the resurrection came an entirely new view of a final postmortem judgment. This was a notion that acknowledged the importance of the individual's relationship to God, without sacrificing the long-standing sense of collective identity that had always been fundamental to Judaism. It is precisely because it synthesized individual and collective eschatology that the doctrine of resurrection came to hold such an important place in the subsequent course of Jewish conceptions of the afterlife. As we continue our journey through Jewish history, we will see that the biblical doctrine of resurrection continues to play a significant role in subsequent Jewish teachings on life after death.

SUMMARY

In this chapter we have traced the evolutionary development of the postmortem philosophy of the biblical period. Before we travel the next stage on our historical journey, let us summarize what we have discovered until now about the nature of Judaism's conceptions of life after death in biblical times.

1. In the early biblical period, there is no written philosophical speculation on the postmortem experience. However, there were a number of ancient traditions—burial in ancestral family tombs, feeding the dead, use of *teraphim*, cultic worship on the *bamot*, and forms of necromancy—all of which suggest that there was an ongoing concern with the existence of the dead in a subterranean netherworld.

2. Throughout the biblical period, the notion of Sheol, as a realm of the dead, underwent a series of successive transformations. Originally, it was conceived of as a godless, amoral eternal abode

for all who had died. In the second stage, it became an eternal abode for the wicked. And finally, in the third stage, Sheol was seen as an intermediate resting abode for the righteous Israelites, and a permanent abode for the wicked. The transformations of Sheol corresponded to the changes in the theology of Judaism.

3. There are only scant traces of the notion of individual immortality throughout the Bible. Because of the collective vision upon which Judaism was founded, the collective redemption of the nation always remained as the primary concern for the Israelite people.

4. In the postexilic biblical period, the incipient idea of individualism brought forth at least a preliminary conception of individual immortality. But this never emerged as a dominant theme in biblical times, and textual references to an individual postmortem world are rarely found in the Hebrew Bible. Throughout the biblical period, individual and collective eschatological notions coexisted and were eventually blended together.

5. With the doctrine of resurrection of the dead, individual and collective eschatology became synthesized. The result was a new conception of a postmortem judgment for both the wicked and the righteous. This was an evolutionary step paving the way for the idea of heaven and hell in later Judaism.

6. Notions of the hereafter developed in biblical times remained as the foundation for all future Jewish conceptions of the afterlife experience.

Chapter 4

Tours of Heaven and Hell in Apocryphal Literature

THE HISTORICAL CONTEXT

As we continue our journey through Jewish history, we now enter the apocryphal period, the postbiblical era that bridges biblical and rabbinic Judaism. The apocryphal period spans four centuries, from 200 B.C.E. to 200 C.E., during which time Jewish writers in and outside of Palestine produced a unique collection of literature known as the Apocrypha and the Pseudepigrapha.

The texts of the Apocrypha and the Pseudepigrapha are valuable resources for understanding the development of Jewish ideas on immortality and life after death. Before investigating specific apocryphal texts, we will examine the literary and historical background of these sacred writings from late antiquity.

In the closing years of the biblical period, Jews were living under the benevolent rule of the Persian Empire. After the return from exile in Babylonia, Ezra and Nehemiah successfully resettled the land of Judah (renamed Judea), reconstructed the Jerusalem Temple, and instituted religious reforms that led to a renaissance of Jewish life.

The year 334 B.C.E. heralded an entirely new period of history as Alexander the Great conquered the Persian Empire and immediately began establishing Greek colonies throughout the Mediterranean region. Within little more than a decade, Alexander brought about a widespread political and cultural penetration of Hellenism into the ancient world and established the cultural tenor of the subsequent three to four centuries.[1]

When Alexander died in 323 B.C.E. at the age of thirty-three, he left no biological heirs to his newly acquired empire. As a result, a period of civil war ensued. Eventually his empire was divided among his generals— Ptolemy, who seized rule in Egypt, and Seleucus, who ruled over Syria. Palestine, where the Jews were living, was under Ptolemaic domination until 200 B.C.E., when it was conquered by Antiochus III, the Seleucid ruler.

But regardless of whether the Ptolemaic or Seleucid dynasty ruled, the cultural predominance of Hellenism left an indelible imprint on all peoples that it touched. Judaism could not and certainly did not remain isolated from the surrounding Hellenistic environment. That environment was replete with religious sects and sages, philosophers seeking wisdom, ecstatic visionaries, and sectarian mystics, all of whom were responding to the ever-changing political circumstances of the times. There was also an apocalyptic spirit prevalent in those centuries, a collective yearning for salvation that would completely transform the nature of the sociopolitical world. Not unlike our own times, the ancient Greco-Roman world stood on the verge of a "new age," and every conceivable brand of religiosity existed within the pluralistic Mediterranean basin. Imagine the cultural ambiance and the cross-fertilization of ideas that existed in such an environment where there was a confluence of Persian, Greek, Gnostic, Jewish, and eventually Christian philosophies! It was a time of spiritual ferment and profound religious creativity, a period about which scholars continue to discover more and more archaeological and textual information.[2]

It was within such a socioreligious environment that the Jews of Palestine and Alexandria[3] created a collection of sacred writings that have come to be known as the Apocrypha (a Greek word meaning "hidden away") and Pseudepigrapha (also Greek—"false or spurious writings"). Together the Apocrypha and Pseudepigrapha form a very rich and diverse body of literature that has been classified into various categories of apocalyptic, historical, legendary, prophetic, and didactic, or moralistic, writings.[4] What is common to all of these writings is that they have not been formally included within the Hebrew Bible.

Strictly speaking, the Apocrypha refers to those texts excluded from the Hebrew canon but included in the Septuagint, the Greek translation of the Bible, known in Hebrew as *Targum Ha-Shivim*. In the fourth century C.E. St. Jerome incorporated these texts in the Vulgate, or Latin, translation of the Bible, and in 1546 the Council of Trent recognized these sacred texts as canonical.[5] To this day there are approximately fifteen individual apocryphal texts included in the Catholic Bible.[6]

The Pseudepigrapha, on the other hand, refers to those texts that never received official canonical status within either Judaism or Christianity. Like the Apocrypha, many texts of the Pseudepigrapha are legendary and apocalyptic in character. They are replete with visionary revelations; are usually ascribed to ancient biblical figures such as Enoch, Abraham, Elijah, and Moses; build upon themes expressed in the Hebrew Bible; and purport to contain divine instruction about the impending fate of humanity at the end-of-days.[7]

The Fourth Book of Ezra, a pseudepigraphic text dating from the late first century C.E., presents a legendary chronicling of the divine origins of the noncanonical literature of the Apocrypha and Pseudepigrapha. The text describes Ezra's vision instructing him to prepare for the writing of the sacred scriptures, assisted by five scribes specifically trained for this purpose:

> And the Most High gave understanding to the five men, and by turns they wrote what was dictated. . . . They sat forty days, and wrote during the daytime, and ate their bread at night. . . . And when the forty days were ended, the Most High spoke to me saying, "Make public the twenty-four books that you wrote first and let the worthy and the unworthy read them; but keep the seventy that were written last, in order to give them to the wise among your people." (4 Ezra 14:42–47)

Here, "the twenty-four books that you wrote first"[8] refer to the texts of Hebrew Bible, and "the seventy that were written last" speak of those noncanonical writings now known as Apocrypha and Pseudepigrapha. What we see at play in this passage is a process of using these texts themselves to attribute divine origins to the very writings that were never given canonical status by the Rabbis. It may work well as a literary form but politically, so to speak, it obviously did not succeed. Divine origin or not, the Rabbis did not accept the canonicity of the Apocrypha and Pseudepigrapha.

In the closing decades of the first century C.E. the issue of the authenticity and canonicity of sacred writings was of primary importance for the Rabbis of Yavneh. With the destruction of the Jerusalem Temple and the increasing spread of Christianity, it was necessary to provide clear boundaries as to what "officially" constituted Judaism. Although the evidence suggests that there were discrepant opinions regarding the status of even such texts as Esther, Ecclesiastes, and Song of Songs,[9] it appears that the process of canonization of the Hebrew Bible was more or less complete by around 90 C.E.[10]

At this time, most of the apocryphal and pseudepigraphic texts had already been written, some in Greek, others in either Hebrew or Aramaic, the vernacular of the Jewish world. The scholarly Rabbis, however, rejected these writings as being inauthentic, lacking in divine status, or else simply heretical. As a result, apocryphal and pseudepigraphic texts were designated as *sefarim hitzonim*, or "extraneous books," and excluded from the Hebrew canon. The Mishnah documents the rabbinic attitude toward these noncanonical writings with a rather serious statement to the effect that one who reads the extraneous books (*sefarim hitzonim*) will have no share in the world to come (M. *Sanhedrin* 10:1). The term *hitzonim* clearly has the connotation of heresy, and in another mishnaic passage (M. *Megillah* 8:8) we find a reference to *hitzoniut*—understood here as heresy or sectarianism—that is, "those who follow their own way and not the ways of the Rabbis."[11]

What took place after the first century C.E. was an obvious spurning of a body of literature that had been produced within a Jewish milieu. Authored at a time when there was not a normative orthodoxy operating within the Jewish world, the Apocrypha and Pseudepigrapha reflect significant elements of the spectrum of Jewish beliefs existing prior to and immediately following the destruction of the Jerusalem Temple. There is increasing evidence that these texts, even though they convey the apocalyptic and syncretistic temperament of the Greco-Roman era, were nonetheless widely read and accepted within the Jewish world. For example, at the synagogue of Dura-Europas, dating from c. 245 C.E., artistic representations are found not only of Moses and Joshua, but of Ezra, and especially Enoch, who represents the apocryphal and apocalyptic traditions of Judaism.[12] Furthermore, the discovery of fragments of the

Book of Enoch at Qumran suggest that this and other noncanonical texts captivated the Jewish spirit throughout this period of history.[13] Yet, with the emerging hegemony of the Rabbis after the year 70 C.E., apocryphal and pseudepigraphic texts, the *sefarim hitzonim*, were progressively eliminated from the Jewish tradition of transmission and over time were vanquished from the mainstream of Jewish life. Today apocryphal and pseudepigraphic texts have no place within traditional Jewish study.[14] However, a number of these texts were translated from Hebrew and Aramaic into Greek, and into such languages as Latin, Syriac, Arabic, Armenian, Ethiopic, Coptic, Slavonic, and Georgian, languages of both the Roman and Eastern Orthodox churches. These texts did gain popularity in Christian circles, and it was through transmission within the Church that the texts survived into the modern period.

Because the Pseudepigrapha never received any canonical status whatsoever, there was never any strictly defined list of pseudepigraphic texts. The classic English-language source on the Pseudepigrapha, R. H. Charles's *Apocrypha and Pseudepigrapha of the Old Testament in English*,[15] was published in 1913 and contains approximately thirty-two different texts. A critical Hebrew edition of the Apocrypha and Pseudepigrapha, based on and translated from Greek manuscripts, was edited by Abraham Kahana, in 1936, and published under the title *Ha-Sefarim Ha-Hitzonim*.[16]

In recent years a two-volume collection of texts, *The Old Testament Pseudepigrapha*,[17] edited by James H. Charlesworth, has become the main English source on the Pseudepigrapha and includes far more material than that contained in the Charles edition. With the discovery of the Dead Sea Scrolls, and the Nag Hammadi Library—a series of Gnostic texts from a somewhat later era—the boundaries of definition of the Pseudepigrapha have become far more fluid than envisioned even fifty years ago, and it is clear that the period of 200 B.C.E. to 200 C.E. represents a most fruitful and creative time in Jewish literary activity.

In this chapter we will use the designation "apocryphal period" to describe the 400-year span during which the Apocrypha and Pseudepigrapha were produced; we will use the term "apocryphal literature" to cover both the Apocrypha and the Pseudepigrapha.

Our goal in this phase of the journey through Jewish history is to trace the evolution of images and themes of the afterlife in the apocryphal period. First, we will look at the relationship between views of the hereafter in apocryphal literature and in earlier biblical texts, then document the continued emergence of new apocryphal postmortem conceptions. We will also look briefly at apocryphal teachings on divine judgment and resurrection.

RELATIONSHIP TO BIBLICAL
CONCEPTIONS OF AFTERLIFE

As in the biblical period, in apocryphal times we find that various conceptions of the afterlife coexist. Sometimes mutually incompatible beliefs appear in two different texts, or even occasionally within the same text, many of which are collated collections of writings. It is usually impossible to find any clear historical demarcation indicating when one particular set of postmortem teachings fall into disuse and when newer ones become predominant in the popular mind or in the philosophical schools of the time. There are varying strata of afterlife conceptions coexisting in apocryphal literature. Some date back close to the time of the Babylonian exile; others are replicated and come to predominate in rabbinic tradition; yet other images of the postmortem journey of the soul appear briefly in this era but do not reemerge in Jewish thought until after the year 1000 C.E., when they become increasingly common in medieval legendary Midrash and in the early kabbalistic writings.

The preexilic biblical conception defining Sheol as a lifeless realm of the dead continued to hold sway among the Jews of late antiquity as late as the second century C.E. However, at this stage in Jewish history this view is a lingering remnant of an older philosophical outlook, often identified with the Sadducees, who rejected the notion of the resurrection of the dead, and not a predominant belief. Nonetheless, we find a number of texts that depict Sheol as a world void of life, vitality, consciousness, or awareness.[18]

The Second Book of Baruch, a text attributed to a Sadducean author,[19] describes how "the righteous sleep at rest in the earth" (2 Baruch 11:5) in an unfeeling, silent realm of the dead and hear neither the anguish nor the cries of the living. In the oblivion of Sheol, the dead are better off than the living, who continue to experience suffering of the human realm (2 Baruch 11:4–7). Here, in a metaphor similar to the "land of forgetfulness" described in the Psalms (Psalm 88:12), the window between the living and the dead is closed. As in many biblical texts dating from the time of the early monarchy to the Babylonian exile— c. 1000–600 B.C.E.—Sheol is a realm of silence.

Ecclesiasticus, also known as the Wisdom of Ben Sirach, is one of the earlier apocryphal texts. It was originally written in Hebrew c. 180 B.C.E. and translated into Greek by the author's grandson approximately 132 B.C.E.[20] This text, which was well known to the talmudic Rabbis,[21] portrays an accepting attitude toward death and a philosophical conception of Sheol not unlike that of the classical biblical view.

Fear not death, says Ben Sirach, for it is the nature of all human beings to die, "the Lord's decree for all living creatures, so why try to argue with the will of the Most High?" (Ecclesiasticus 41:4). Death is an inevitability of human life: "Like foliage growing on a bushy tree, some leaves falling, others growing, so are the generations of flesh and blood; one dies, another is born" (Ecclesiasticus 14:19). Whether one has lived ten, a hundred, or even a thousand years, in the final analysis, after death the duration and even the quality of one's life won't really matter—"its length will not be held against you in Sheol" (Ecclesiasticus 41:4). Sheol, in this context, is an amoral realm of the dead where one can take no pleasure (Ecclesiasticus 14:17), where there is no light (Ecclesiasticus 22:11), and where one cannot praise the Lord (Ecclesiasticus 7:28).

Jubilees, written in the late second century B.C.E.,[22] echoes earlier biblical conceptions of the afterlife in using the phrase "slept with his fathers" or "was gathered to his fathers" to describe the deaths of Abraham (Jubilees 23:1), Isaac (Jubilees 36:1), and Jacob (Jubilees 45:15). But in this text, the conception of Sheol is blended with newer elements of Jewish postmortem beliefs. In the Book of Jubilees we see the emergence of a dualistic aspect to the afterlife realm. For the wicked sinner, Sheol is a place of judgment (Jubilees 7:29, 22:22, 24:31). Evildoers "will go down into Sheol . . . into the place of judgment they will descend. And into the darkness of the depths they will all be removed with a cruel death" (Jubilees 7:29). But of the righteous it is written: "[T]heir bones will rest in the earth and their spirits will increase in joy" (Jubilees 23:31).

This last passage demonstrates an important shift in philosophical orientation, characteristic of apocryphal literature. Sheol is not simply a neutral amoral hereafter, as it is seen in the preexilic biblical era. Now, there are separate postmortem fates for the wicked, who are condemned to darkness in Sheol, and for the righteous, who merit an immortalized eternal life. In addition to this dualistic notion of separate postmortem destinies for the righteous and for the wicked, we see in the apocryphal period the development of a dualism of body and soul—a radically new idea that did not exist in biblical times.

As we have already discovered, in the Hebrew Bible body and *nefesh* are closely aligned. The living are referred to as *nefesh hayyah*, living *nefesh*, or spirit; the dead are understood to be *nefesh met*, the dead *nefesh*—shades, ghosts, or *rephaim*—that cohabit the subterranean realm of Sheol. In the apocryphal Jewish writings, however, there is a new notion of spirit, or soul, totally distinct from the physical body—while bones lie in the earth, the surviving spirit experiences an increase in joy. This is a new departure in the development of Judaism's postmortem philosophy. As D. S. Russell notes, in the texts of the Apocrypha and Pseudepigrapha

> the departed are actually described as "souls" or "spirits" in a manner quite unlike anything that has gone on before. Sometimes in this connection the word "soul" alone is used; sometimes the word "spirit" is used; at other times both "soul" and "spirit" are found side by side. Thus, even in some of the earliest apocalyptic writings, "soul" and "spirit" are used as synonymous terms to describe the form of a man's survival immediately after death.[23]

As an example of this dualistic separation of body and spirit, we find in the Apocalypse of Moses[24] the statement that "Adam . . . has gone out of this body" (Apocalypse of Moses 32:4). Adam's physical death is described as the departure of his soul (Apocalypse of Moses 13:6) or the giving up of his spirit (Apocalypse of Moses 31:4). There is a sense of a discarnate spirit or a soul, a postmortem entity that exists distinct from the physical body. What is implied by the separation of body and spirit is the notion of an individualized, personal postmortem survival. Upon death, body and spirit separate; the human personality survives as a distinct disembodied entity, then receives due reward or punishment based on individual merit.

This understanding of the postmortem destiny of the individual is a new development in the evolution of Jewish afterlife teachings and, as we will see, leads to increasingly elaborate depictions of the reward and punishment in the postmortem realms of paradise and hell.

THE BOOK OF ENOCH (1 ENOCH)

The Enochic Traditions within Judaism

Enoch, according to the Book of Genesis, is the seventh descendant of Adam and Eve. From the sparse four-sentence biography found in the first book of the Torah, we know little about Enoch's life. What we do know, however, is that "Enoch walked with God; then he was no more; for God took him" (Genesis 5:24). Enoch is a biblical character who never died; according to tradition, he was transported from the earth to the heavenly realms. These rather brief and cryptic details about Enoch left plenty of room for speculation about Enoch's cosmic wanderings. Around the third century B.C.E., perhaps even earlier, there developed a literary tradition chronicling the visionary journeys throughout the heavenly and underworld realms taken by Enoch and other biblical ancestors.

There are three pseudepigraphic books of Enoch, and each of them is a composite literary creation that delineates Enoch's assorted mystical journeys. The Enoch texts were produced by various writers spanning a period of over five hundred years, beginning in the third century B.C.E.[25]

The full manuscript of 1 Enoch has been preserved in Ethiopic and is usually referred to as the Ethiopic Book of Enoch, in contradistinction to 2 Enoch, known as the Slavonic Book of Enoch, or 3 Enoch, the Hebrew Book of Enoch. When R. H. Charles did his pioneering work translating apocryphal texts, he dated the earliest sections of 1 Enoch in the second century C.E. However, with the discovery of Aramaic fragments of 1 Enoch at Qumran, scholarly consensus now dates sections of the Book of Enoch even earlier. J. T. Milik has demonstrated that "The Book of Watchers," chapters 1 through 36 of 1 Enoch, can be dated as early as the third century B.C.E., while chapters 72 to 82, a unit that has been entitled "The Book of the Heavenly Luminaries," may be even older.[26] This material, regarded as "the oldest surviving Jewish documents of religious character outside the Bible,"[27] was composed prior to the Maccabean revolt and antedates sections of Daniel by close to a half century.

It is difficult to know the impact of the books of Enoch in their time. However, the fact that this text survived, and that many different recensions were produced over the course of centuries, attests to the popularity of the Enoch tradition. The visionary journeys of 1 Enoch, which link back thematically to the divine visions in Ezekiel, had an inspirational impact on later Jewish writers, eventually becoming a central motif in a unique genre of visionary literature—the Merkavah mysticism of the second to fourth centuries C.E.[28]

We will now explore images of the postmortem worlds found in 1 Enoch and, in so doing, delineate the new conceptions of the afterlife that emerge out of the terrain of Enoch's visionary tours of heaven and hell.

Sheol as a Punitive Realm for the Wicked

The word *Sheol* appears repeatedly in 1 Enoch. It is understood very clearly as being a realm of retribution for the wicked: "Woe to you who spread evil to your neighbors!" declares Enoch, "for you will be slain in Sheol" (1 Enoch 99:11). Sinners who deny the name of the Lord of the Spirits and who are morally corrupt "are cast into the oppressive Sheol" (1 Enoch 63:10).

Underlying this conception of Sheol is the notion of individual retribution that had developed in the postexilic biblical period. Each individual is responsible for the consequences of his or her actions and is rewarded or punished according to merit. Although in 1 Enoch Sheol is seen as a realm of punishment, it is clear from the text that we are not actually talking about an individual retribution immediately after death. Instead, here the notion of Sheol appears within a sweeping mythic vision of the end-of-time, when there will be a collective judgment, with subsequent reward or punishment. "In those days," says Enoch—this phrase signifying an eschatological future—"Sheol will open her mouth, and [the sinners] will be swallowed up into it and perish" (1 Enoch 56:7–8). So at least based on this passage, we cannot conclude that there is in 1 Enoch a concept of individual punishment after death, only the idea of retributive chastisement at a future time of judgment.

Enoch's Tour of Sheol

Chapter 17 of 1 Enoch begins the first of a series of journeys through the unseen worlds. Enoch is lifted up into what is described as "the place of the ones appearing like the flaming fire." He is guided through the whirlwind in the mountain, into chambers of light and thunder, through the waters of life, then shown the storerooms of the wind and the foundations of the earth, the firmament of the heaven—the very pillars of heaven, as well as the sun and stars and beyond (1 Enoch 17–18).

Enoch's next tour takes him even further, as the third century B.C.E. text describes, and he eventually finds himself in the place where "the spirits of the souls of the dead assemble" (1 Enoch 22:3). From the literary record of Enoch's journey, we see a multileveled and complex understanding of Sheol emerge in the Jewish mind-set of the late Second Temple period.

A very important passage in chapter 22 describes Enoch's entry into Sheol:

> And then I went to another place and Uriel showed me on the west side a great and high mountain of hard rock and inside it four beautiful corners, deep and very smooth, and the place was deep and dark to look at. At that moment Raphael, one of the holy angels who was with me, responded to me; and he said: "These beautiful corners are here in order that the spirits of the souls of the dead should assemble into them—they are created so that the souls of the children of the people should gather here. They prepared these places in order to put the souls of the people there until their day of their judgment and the appointed time of great judgment is upon them." (1 Enoch 22:1–4)

Here, Sheol is a gathering place for the dead, who are assembled together waiting until the time of great judgment. Notice that at this point, Sheol has a rather interesting geography to it: it is comprised of four different corners, or compartments—R. H. Charles's translation speaks of "four hollow places." There are specific divisions for the "spirits of the children of the people who were dead" (1 Enoch 22:5) who assemble in this specially designated area.

Enoch continues speaking with the angel Raphael and asks questions regarding the divisions within Sheol:

> At that moment I raised a question regarding the judgment of all. "For what reason is one separated from the other?" And he answered me saying: "These three (sic!) were made to separate the spirits of the dead. This division has been made for the spirits of the righteous, where there is a bright fountain of water. And this has been created for sinners, when they die and are buried in the earth and judgment has not been executed upon them in their lifetime. Here their great spirits are separated for this great torment of the accursed forever, in order that [there may be] recompense for their spirits. There he will bind them forever. And this division has been made for the spirits of those who bring suit, who make disclosure concerning [their] destruction, when they were murdered in the days of the sinners. And this division has been created for the spirits of men who are not pious, but sinners. . . . Their spirits will not be punished on the day of judgment, nor will they be raised from there." (1 Enoch 22:8–13)[29]

This passage and the textual material surrounding it are somewhat cryptic, and the exact divisions of Sheol are not very clear. There has been scholarly discussion as to whether three or four categories of the dead are described here.[30] Either way, there is now a stratification in Sheol—there is a separation of the righteous and the wicked, with sinners assigned to specific localities in this netherworld region of divine castigation.

This depiction of Sheol is yet another revolutionary breakthrough in the evolution of Judaism's philosophy of the afterlife destiny of the soul. Now Sheol has become diversified, serving a dual function. On the one hand, it is conceived of as an intermediate abode for the righteous who still will receive divine recompense at a later time; on the other hand, it is a final eternal abode for the wicked who have already been punished.

Gehenna

With the First Book of Enoch another new conception enters Jewish postmortem philosophy—the notion of Gehenna as a place of eternal damnation. On his cosmic voyage, Enoch is shown "the accursed valley" and told that it is for those who are "accursed forever." Those sinners who have not been judged in their lifetime will first experience the suffering and "great pain" of Sheol (1 Enoch 22:11). Then, at the time of a future judgment, they will be removed from Sheol and transferred to "the accursed valley," which, in Jewish tradition, was known as Gei Hinnom, the "Valley of Hinnom," later simply called Gehinnom, or Gehenna.

To backtrack briefly, the roots of this notion of Gehenna go back to the biblical age. *Gehenna* is an Aramaic word based on the Hebrew expression *Gei Hinnom*—the "Valley of Hinnom"—referred to in Joshua (Joshua 15:8) and Jeremiah (Jeremiah 7:30–34). This Valley of Hinnom was a location south of Jerusalem where, in the period of the Israelite monarchy, idolatrous child sacrifices to Moloch were offered. This practice was condemned by the prophets and many Judean kings as a total abomination to the loyalty-demanding YHVH. Although the ritual sacrifices were finally wiped out in the seventh century B.C.E., *Gei Hinnom* came to be associated with depravity and evil. The term *Gei Hinnom* continued to maintain its original geographical connotations, referring to the condemned site of child sacrifices.[31]

However, sometime between the third and second centuries B.C.E. the word *Gehinnom* came to be associated with the realm of punishment for the dead. Although not used explicitly in the Book of Daniel, it is implied in the phrase "some to shame and everlasting abhorrence" (Daniel 21:2). With Enoch, the idea of Gehenna emerges into the foreground, entering the ever-diversifying repertoire of postmortem conceptions. What we notice at this point, however, is that Gehenna and Sheol are considered to be synonymous, and, in 1 Enoch, these terms are used interchangeably.

Here is a clear example of how these two terms are juxtaposed, used within the context of a passage that is referring to the resurrection of the dead:

> In those days, Sheol will return all the deposits which she had received and hell [Gehenna] will give back all that which it owes. And he shall choose the righteous and the holy ones from among the risen dead, for the day when they shall be selected and saved has arrived. (1 Enoch 51:1–3)

Within the same passage there is reference to two different realms of the dead, but the differentiation is ambiguous. We really cannot glean any substantial information suggesting a real difference between these two realms. Generally, as the term Gehenna came into use in this era, it was no different than Sheol. In 1 Enoch, and in other apocryphal texts, these two postmortem conceptions are identical, at least for a short period of time.

Sheol as a Realm of Torturous Punishment

Associated with Sheol in this period of Jewish history are very strong, harsh images of punishment, affliction, and torment. Sheol never appears as a desirable place to be; it is usually rather dreadful. In the texts of the Apocrypha, we find a proliferation of depictions of torture, punishment, darkness, fire, burning, and so on. The Book of Enoch, interestingly enough, is a precursor to an entire genre of literature—referred to as "Tours of Hell"[32]—that describes with vivid detail the torments and punishments of the underworlds. In the "tour of hell" given to our antediluvian hero of 1 Enoch, Sheol is unequivocally a realm of postmortem punishment, and it is described with far more imaginative detail than anything we have observed thus far in Jewish afterlife literature.

First Enoch 54, for example, describes how on "the great day of judgment" even lofty rulers will be subjected to burning fire, imprisonment chains, and iron fetters of immense weight before finally being cast into the abyss of complete condemnation (1 Enoch 54:1–6).

Elsewhere we encounter a similar negative fate ascribed to those souls condemned to Sheol: "Woe unto you sinners who are dead! . . . You yourselves know that they will bring your souls down to Sheol; and they shall experience evil and great tribulation—in darkness, nets and burning flame" (1 Enoch 103:7).

Other Images of Gehenna/Sheol

While there is a diverse collection of horrific images associated with Sheol at this point, we do not yet see any comprehensive structural pattern in place. The well-developed "Tour of Hell" motif, which comes into place somewhat later, is in a nascent state at this time. However, to understand the historical evolution of afterlife teachings, it is useful to observe and to catalog recurring motifs and themes of postmortem torment in this period which bridges biblical and rabbinic Judaism. Thus, the following passages from 1 Enoch illustrate the landscape of the underworld in the apocryphal era.

Fire and Burning

In numerous places Gehenna is described as an "abyss . . . full of fire (1 Enoch 90:26ff.) or a place where there is "a burning worse than fire" (1 Enoch 100:9).

We find more of these images of fire and burning in a section of 1 Enoch (chapters 91–104) dating from the early first century C.E.,[33] which speaks of Sheol/Gehenna as follows:

> Therefore they shall be wanting in doctrine and wisdom, And they shall perish thereby together with their possessions. And with all their glory and their splendour, and in shame and in slaughter and in great destitution, their spirits shall be cast into the furnace of fire. (1 Enoch 98:3)

In a similar vein, 1 Enoch 90 describes how the fallen angels and shepherds are subjected to judgment and condemnation to burning by fire:

And behold, they were all bound, I saw, and they all stood before Him. And the judgment was held . . . and they were judged and found guilty, and went to the place of condemnation, and they were cast into an abyss, full of fire and flaming, full of pillars of fire. And those seventy shepherds were judged and found guilty, and they were cast into that fiery abyss. And I saw at that time how a like fire of abyss was opened in the midst of the earth, full of fire, and they were judged and found guilty and cast into this fiery abyss, and they burned. . . . (1 Enoch 90:23–26)

Total Destruction

In those days Sheol shall open its jaws, And they will be swallowed up therein, and their destruction will be at an end; Sheol will devour the sinners in the presence of the elect. (1 Enoch 56:8)

Woe to you who spread evil to your neighbors; for you shall be slain in Sheol. Woe to you who make deceitful and false measures. And to them who cause bitterness on the earth. For they shall be utterly condemned. (1 Enoch 99:11–12)

The Wicked in Sheol as a Spectacle for the Righteous

And He will deliver them to the angels for punishment. . . . And they shall be a spectacle for the righteous and for His elect. . . . (1 Enoch 62:11–12)

Eternal Punishment

Know that their soul will be made to descend into Sheol, and they shall be wretched in their great tribulation. And into darkness and chains and a burning flame where there is grievous judgment shall your spirits enter; and the great judgment shall be for all the generations of the world. Woe to you, for you shall have no peace. (1 Enoch 63:10)

Paradise/Heaven

Along with a dualistic conception of Sheol as a realm for both the wicked and the righteous, there emerged in apocryphal literature yet another entirely new conception of Jewish afterlife philosophy—the notion of Paradise, or Heaven, as the abode for the righteous following the last judgment. While the wicked are repeatedly warned of future punishment, the righteous are told:

> Be hopeful, because formerly you have pined away through evil and toil. But now you will shine like the lights of heaven, and you shall be seen; and the windows of heaven will be opened for you . . . you are about to be making a great rejoicing like the angels of heaven. (1 Enoch 104:2, 4)

Prior to the first century B.C.E. Heaven, or Paradise (the Hebrew term is *Pardes*, meaning "orchard"), had been the abode of only two individuals: Enoch and Elijah, both of whom had never died, but ascended to the heavenly realms. However, in the apocryphal era, Heaven becomes somewhat democratized and is conceived of as the final resting place of the righteous and the elect. Thus, in 1 Enoch, we find this philosophical view fully stated: "All the holy ones who are in heaven will bless Him, and all the elect who dwell in the garden of life" (1 Enoch 61:12). Elsewhere Paradise is conceived of as a "garden of righteousness" (1 Enoch 77:3) and the "garden of the righteous" (1 Enoch 90:23).

Thus, we find an increasing diversification within apocryphal literature, leading to the emergence of a conception of Heaven/Paradise as a realm distinct and separate from Sheol/Gehenna. This dualism becomes even more pronounced in the rabbinic period, as well as in all later Jewish afterlife teachings.

The World That Is to Become

Finally, there is one last image we uncover in 1 Enoch. Planted as a seed in the apocryphal period, it is a motif that takes root and emerges only in rabbinic eschatology, where it becomes a major philosophical theme. 1 Enoch 71 speaks of a mythic being known as "the Antecedent of Time" who, along with the angels, "proclaims peace in the name of the world that is to become" (1 Enoch 71:15). This phrase is an echoing of the rabbinic notion of *Olam Ha-Ba*—the World to Come—around which all rabbinic motifs of collective and individual immortality are built. At this point, however, only this and no more is said regarding this "world that is to become."

Significance of 1 Enoch in the Evolution
of Jewish Afterlife Beliefs

In and of itself, 1 Enoch is not predominantly concerned with life after death. Enoch's entry into the hereafter is not as a dead being; remember, he is a cosmic traveler, guided through the postmortem spheres on his far-reaching and mysterious tour of the universe. Nonetheless, as we have seen, 1 Enoch is filled with an innovative collection of postmortem motifs, and as such, bequeaths to the Jewish afterlife tradition a rich, philosophical legacy. In this frequently ignored apocalyptic text, we find three important themes that emerge for the first time in late antiquity and subsequently have a considerable effect on the development of Jewish teachings on life after death.

First of all, in 1 Enoch we encounter a clear dualism of body and soul. At the end of the second century B.C.E., the notion of a dualistic separation between eternal spirit and mortal body emerges as a fully integrated philosophical concept, at least within the Hellenistic Jewish world. As a result, sacred writings of the apocryphal period speak about a postmortem soul, or spirit, existing totally independent of the physical body. Long after mortal destruction of the body, this spirit persists, experiencing due compensation in the postmortem realm.

Second, we find in 1 Enoch the beginnings of a dualism of heaven and hell, Paradise and Gehenna, or Sheol. The domain of disembodied spirits described in 1 Enoch as Paradise, Heaven, is a region of the universe allocated specifically for the enjoyment of the righteous. Paradise exists in opposition to Gehenna, or Sheol, a negative purgational world of torments and punishments. In Enochic literature we see the beginnings of the Jewish tradition of the visionary tours of heaven and hell.

Finally, 1 Enoch reflects an emerging multidimensionality of the postmortem realms. At the dawn of the millennium, born out of the Greco-Roman, Judeo-Egyptian, Gnostic environment, there arises a vast macrocosmic picture of the universe—apocalyptic tradition is born, and within that tradition more and more secrets and mysteries of the afterlife realms are revealed. The postmortem realm seen by Enoch is multitiered. At this point, it is only four-leveled, but later we will find increasingly complex depictions of the afterlife, leading eventually to a seven-leveled heaven and hell. From this point on, the postmortem realms become multidimensional and increasingly complex, with more information provided on the afterlife experiences of the soul.

As we journey through Jewish history, we find that 1 Enoch is a pivotal text in the development of Jewish tenets of the afterlife. Images and motifs of life after death found in 1 Enoch represent a philosophical evolutionary leap. With 1 Enoch, Jewish sages begin defining more elaborately the nature of the mysterious realm of the dead; even more, they begin placing the realm of the dead within a greater schema of the universe.

2 ENOCH—THE BOOK OF THE SECRETS OF ENOCH

The Book of the Secrets of Enoch, or 2 Enoch, is an enigmatic apocalyptic text, authored anonymously in a Judeo-Hellenistic environment during the first century C.E. Like its predecessor, this text describes Enoch's ascent into the higher worlds where the mysteries of creation are revealed to him. There are parallels to Egyptian mythology found in 2 Enoch, and we may assume that it was written in Egypt and edited into its present form by a Hellenistic Jew.[34] With its focus on angelology, astronomy, astrology, and calendrical systems, 2 Enoch is a cryptic text and, as George W. E. Nickelsburg notes, "a testimony to the religious thought of some presently unknown sector of ancient Diasporan Judaism."[35] For over twelve hundred years, knowledge that such a text ever existed was lost to both Judaism and Christianity. However, in 1892 manuscripts of Enochic literature were found in Russia and Serbia, and have since been translated into English.[36]

We find the afterlife themes of Heaven/Paradise and Sheol/Gehenna occurring in 2 Enoch. The incipient conception of Heaven, or Paradise, is developed further as Enoch's visionary journey takes him through a total of seven heavens. He is told at the very beginning that "you will ascend with us to heaven today" (2 Enoch 1:8), and this ascent takes him through seven different heavens.

Enoch is shown the third heaven where the postmortem realms are to be found. From the third heaven he looks downward and glimpses a locale referred to as Paradise, an inconceivably pleasant place "where rest is prepared for the righteous" (2 Enoch 42:3). This realm of Paradise is described in a unique and elaborate way, as follows:

And that place is inconceivably pleasant. And I saw all the trees in full flower. And their fruits were ripe and pleasant-smelling, with every food in yield and giving off profusely a pleasant fragrance. And in the midst of them was the tree of life, at that place where the Lord takes a rest, when he goes up into paradise. And that tree is of indescribable pleasantness and fine fragrance, and more beautiful than any other created thing that exists. And from every direction it has an appearance which is gold-looking and crimson and with the form of fire. And it covers the whole of Paradise. And it has something of every orchard tree and of every fruit. . . . And two springs come forth, one a source of milk and honey, and a source which produces oil and wine. And they come out into the paradise of Eden. . . . And there is no unfruitful tree there, and every place is blessed. And there are three hundred angels very bright, who look after Paradise; and with never-ceasing voice and pleasant singing they worship the Lord every day and hour. (2 Enoch 8:1–8)

The lush and elaborate depiction of Paradise here represents a new development in Jewish afterlife thought—it is clearly the first time this kind of ornate imagery is applied to Paradise. Although today these types of images are taken for granted when thinking about the notion of heaven, it is important to recognize that this kind of imaginative reflection does not appear within Judaism until this time, approximately the first century C.E., contemporaneous with the emergence of both Christianity and rabbinic Judaism.

Elsewhere in the text, Enoch experiences another heavenly ascent "into the Paradise of Eden" (notice the juxtaposition of these two terms in one place), which is understood here as a realm of eternal life. Enoch describes seeing

angels of flame, singing victory songs, never silent . . . rejoicing at the arrival of the righteous . . . waiting with joyful anticipation to have dinner with delightful enjoyments and riches that cannot be measured, and joy and happiness in eternal light and life. (2 Enoch 42:3–6)

Following his vision of the realm of the righteous, Enoch is transported to "the place of terrible and various tortures"—in other words, Gehenna. Interestingly, this realm is also found within the third heaven. In the cosmic schema of 2 Enoch, the realms of the dead, Gehenna and

Paradise, coexist in distinct regions of the third heavenly sphere. Thus, we now have a much more complex pattern of the universe than that of biblical times. And, as 2 Enoch depicts this realm of torment, we see once again a new development—the blossoming of a rich, imagistic language of trial, tribulation, and woe:

> And those two men led me up on to the Northern side, and showed me there a very terrible place, and there were all manner of tortures in that place: Cruel darkness and unillumined gloom, and there is no light there, but murky fire constantly flames aloft, and there is a fiery river coming forth, and that whole place is everywhere fire, and everywhere there is frost and ice, thirst and shivering, while the bonds are very cruel, and the angels fearful and merciless, bearing angry weapons, merciless torture, and I said, "Woe, woe, how very terrible is this place," and those men said to me: This place, O Enoch, is prepared for those who dishonour God, who on earth practice sin against nature, which is child-corruption after the sodomistic fashion, magic-making, enchantments and devilish witchcrafts, and who boast of their wicked deeds, stealing, lies, calumnies, envy, rancour, fornication, murder, and who, accursed, steal the souls of men, who seeing the poor take away their goods and themselves wax rich, injuring them for other men's goods; who being able to satisfy the empty, made the hungering to die; being able to clothe, stripped the naked; and who knew not their creator, and bowed down to lifeless Gods, who cannot see or hear, vain gods, who also built hewn images and bow down to unclean handiwork, for all these is prepared this place amongst these, for eternal inheritance. (2 Enoch 10:1–6)

The imagery continues further, as Enoch describes "the key-holders and the guards of the gates of hell standing, as large as serpents, with their faces like lamps that have been extinguished, and their eyes aflame, and their teeth naked down to their breasts" (2 Enoch 42:1).

All of the above selections from 2 Enoch are characteristic of the new forms of eschatological teachings surfacing in the first century C.E. Increasingly, there is a multileveled complexity ascribed to the postmortem worlds, as well as intricate detailed descriptions of both netherworld punishment and heavenly delight. The depictions of the realms of the dead first developed in the Enoch texts are similar to the afterlife visions found in later Midrash and kabbalistic literature. From the apocryphal era onward, we can speak not only of philosophical conceptions of the afterlife, but also of mythical descriptions of Paradise and Hell.

3 ENOCH, OR THE HEBREW BOOK OF ENOCH

The Third Book of Enoch is a pseudepigraphic writing, attributed to the Palestinian rabbi Ishmael who lived in the early second century C.E. There has been much controversy as to the dating of this text, with scholars suggesting a point of origination anywhere from the first to the twelfth century C.E.[37] Gershom Scholem dates 3 Enoch close to the year 500 C.E. and has shown the connection of this text to the *hekhalot* literature, a genre of Jewish writings, replete with descriptions of mystical palaces one encounters on the sacred journey of the chariot.[38] In fact, this Enochic book begins with Rabbi Ishmael describing his ascent "to the height to behold the vision of the chariot," where he enters a series of seven palaces, "one inside the other" (3 Enoch 1:1–2).

Originally written in Hebrew, this text has been termed "The Hebrew Book of Enoch," although for centuries it circulated within Jewish mystical circles as *Sefer Ha-Hekhalot*—"The Book of the Heavenly Palaces."[39] Manuscripts of this text were popular among Hasidei Ashkenaz and the Spanish kabbalists beginning in the tenth century. Based on certain rabbinic traditions, 3 Enoch reflects the esoteric doctrines of talmudic Judaism.

With regard to the evolution of Jewish views of the afterlife, we find in 3 Enoch a number of pertinent motifs. In this unique text there are numerous images of the postmortem worlds identical to those found in other apocryphal writings. However, given the late dating of this text, in many instances these afterlife concepts are blended philosophically with newer ideas of the afterlife that emerged only in the rabbinic period.

We find in 3 Enoch the association of Heaven, or *Pardes*, with Gan Eden, the Garden of Eden, the term used in rabbinic literature to refer to the heavenly abode of the righteous. Chapter 5 of 3 Enoch speaks of the Divine Presence—the *Shekhinah*—at the gates of the Garden of Eden:

> [A]nyone who gazed at the brightness of the *Shekhinah* [the feminine aspect of God] was not troubled by flies or gnats, by sickness or pain; malicious demons were not able to harm him, and even angels had no power over him. When the Holy One, blessed be he, went out from the garden to Eden, and from Eden to the garden, from the garden to heaven, and from heaven to the garden of Eden, all gazed at the bright image of his Shechina and were unharmed. (3 Enoch 5:5–6)

Notice the use of the terms—garden, Eden, heaven, and Garden of Eden—although here they are not used in any postmortem sense. However, the process of differentiating the heavens continued in the pseudepigraphic writings, as well as in early and later rabbinic texts. By the time of 3 Enoch, in the fifth century C.E., it was taken as a given that the structure of the universe included seven realms of heaven.

Chapters 41 through 48 of 3 Enoch form a unit entitled "The Sights of Heaven," and within this material are conceptions of the afterlife we have not seen thus far. On his journeying through the cosmos, Rabbi Ishmael is shown "the souls of the righteous who have already been created and have returned and the souls of the righteous who have not yet been created" (3 Enoch 43:1). A conception exists here of a storehouse of souls—in Hebrew, *guf ha-briyot*—a notion that had already been developed at this point in rabbinic literature.[40]

Continuing the journey, Rabbi Ishmael is shown "the place where the wicked stand, and where the souls of the intermediate stand" (3 Enoch 44:1). Here we see the creation of a third category of human souls: besides the righteous, who are in a realm unto themselves, there are also souls of an intermediate category who experience a fate somewhat different from the wicked. The passage below elaborates on this threefold designation and demonstrates the integration of afterlife philosophy and Jewish angelology that had developed over the course of centuries:

> The souls of the wicked are brought down to Sheol by two angels of destruction, Zaapiel and Samkiel. Samkiel is in charge of the souls of the intermediate, to support them and purify them from sin, through the abundant mercies of the Omnipresent One. Zaapiel is appointed to bring down the souls of the wicked from the presence of the Holy One, blessed be he, from the judgment of the Shechina to Sheol to punish them with fire in Gehinnom with rods of burning coal.

> [Rabbi Ishmael was further shown that] the faces [of the wicked] looked like human faces, but their bodies were like eagles. Moreover, the faces of the intermediate were a greenish color, on account of their deeds, for they are tainted until purified of their iniquity by fire. And the faces of the wicked souls were as black as the bottom of a pot, because of the multitude of their wicked deeds. (3 Enoch 44:1–6)

At this stage in the evolution of Jewish afterlife teachings, we again see a entirely new concept coming to birth. Here the emergence of an intermediate category of sinners includes with it the possibility of post-mortem purification. Life after death is not simply Heaven/Paradise for the righteous or Hell/Gehenna for the wicked. The realms of the here-after expand once again; now there is a specifically designated locale for souls of the intermediate type who, after being purified from defilement, seem to be able to merit the same rewards as the righteous.[41] In the next phase of Jewish life, in the rabbinic period, we will see how this notion of purification and purgation became central to Judaism's diverse philoso-phy of the afterlife journey of the soul.

Finally, we find within 3 Enoch important teachings on the theme of postmortem judgment. Below, we will explore the theme of divine judgment within the broader scope of other apocryphal and pseudepi-graphic literature. We will also investigate the unique contribution of 3 Enoch with regard to judgment after death.

THE FOURTH BOOK OF EZRA

The Fourth Book of Ezra is an apocalyptic writing that dates from the late first century C.E.[42] Originally written in Hebrew, an expanded form of this text appears in the Apocrypha, entitled 2 Esdras. Through the years only Latin manuscripts, with later Christian emendations and ad-ditions, have survived. There is no evidence indicating the influence of either Egyptian Judaism or the Dead Sea community at Qumran, and modern scholarship points to Jewish Palestine, some thirty years after the Roman destruction of Jerusalem, as the point of origin of this text.[43]

Throughout the text, Salathiel, who is identified with Ezra the Scribe, experiences a series of seven visions, all the while engaged in a dialogue with an accompanying angel. In chapter 7 of 4 Ezra we encoun-ter a lengthy eschatological vision, the most complete description of the postmortem experience in all apocryphal literature.

First, Salathiel is told of a coming messianic kingdom, a time of fu-ture judgment when "the pit of torment will appear [and] the furnace of Hell will be disclosed," and opposite these will be "the Paradise of de-light [and] the place of rest" (4 Ezra 7:36). Here we see the juxtaposi-tion of Paradise and Hell, or Gehenna, in the same text—a sign that there is an increasing clarification of the overall Jewish afterlife schema.

Salathiel continues his conversation with the angel accompanying him and asks a question that was obviously at the base of philosophical inquiry in this era:

> I answered and said: "If I have found favor in your sight, my lord, show this also to your servant: whether after death, as soon as everyone one of us yields up his soul, we shall be kept in rest until those times come when you will renew the creation, or whether we shall be tormented at once?" (4 Ezra 7:75)

This is an important question, one that remained central to Jewish postmortem philosophy for close to a thousand years. Postulated on a belief in the resurrection of the dead, the question is essentially this: given that there will be a resurrection at the end-of-days, is there a process of judgment that takes place more immediately after death? Phrased another way the question is not unlike those of our day: what happens to the soul immediately after death of the physical body?

The remainder of chapter 7 is an answer to this question, and in a lengthy passage that has been titled "The Salathiel Apocalypse" we find a discussion on the "intermediate state" of the soul between death and judgment:

> Now, concerning death, the teaching is: When the decisive decree has gone forth from the Most High that a man will die, as the spirit leaves the body to return again to him who gave it, first of all it adores the glory of the Most High. And if it is one of those who have shown scorn and not kept the way of the Most High, and who have despised his Law, and who have hated those who fear God—such spirits shall not enter into habitations but shall immediately wander about in torments, ever grieving and sad in seven ways. . . .

> [The text then goes on to describe each of the seven ways, ending with the last:] The seventh way, which is worse than all the ways that have been mentioned, because they will utterly waste away in confusion and be consumed with shame, and will wither with fear at seeing the glory of the Most High before whom they have sinned while they were alive, before whom they are to be judged in the last times. (4 Ezra 7:78–81, 87)

Now this is the order of those who have kept the ways of the Most High, when they will be separated from their mortal body.

During the time that they lived in it, they laboriously served the Most High, and withstood danger every that they might keep the Law of the Lawgiver perfectly. Therefore this is the teaching concerning them: First of all, they shall see with great joy the glory of him who receives them, for they shall have rest in seven orders.

[The text goes on to describe each of the seven orders, ending with the last:] The seventh order, which is greater than all that have been mentioned, because they shall rejoice with boldness, and shall be confident without confusion, and shall be glad without fear, for they hasten to behold the face of him whom they served in life and from whom they are to receive their reward when glorified. This is the order of the souls of the righteous. . . . (4 Ezra 7:88–92, 98–99)

This lengthy passage documents what might be considered an emerging prototype of the first century C.E. belief in the afterlife. At the end-of-days there will be a divine judgment, followed by the resurrection of the dead—that is the classical collective eschatology of the biblical period. The new apocryphal teaching, building on the teachings evidenced in 1 Enoch, maintains that at the time of death the righteous and the wicked enter an intermediate state and according to merit are assigned to one of seven heavens, or one of seven realms of torment. This intermediate state is one in which there are preliminary awards and punishments, and wherein one experiences a foretaste of the judgment that awaits at the end-of-days.[44]

As Salathiel continues his discussion with the angel, he once again asks an important question about the fate of the soul immediately after death:

I answered and said: "Will time therefore be given to the souls after they have been separated from the bodies, to see what you have described to me?" He said to me: "They shall have freedom for seven days, so that during these seven days they may see the things of which you have been told [the seven realms for the wicked and for the righteous], and afterward they shall be gathered into their habitations. (4 Ezra 7:100–101).

What is observed here is the mapping out of yet another stage of the afterlife journey. Salathiel is told of the existence of a special seven-day period immediately following the soul's separation from the body, even prior to the time that righteous and wicked souls are assigned to their intermediate abodes.

So 4 Ezra envisions a philosophy of life after death that has a number of phases to it. First, immediately following physical death, there is a seven-day period when the soul peruses the variety of possible postmortem options. Subsequent to this is a time wherein souls, by virtue of individual merit, are assigned to abodes designated for either the wicked or the righteous. And finally, at the end of days there is a divine judgment and, in turn, the penultimate resurrection of the dead.

This afterlife text found in 4 Ezra, chapter 7, represents the integration of individual and collective eschatology. Beliefs about the entire nation at the end of time and history and about the fate of the individual subsequent to death are successfully blended together. However, as we will see in the remainder of this chapter and the next, as in biblical times, there continued to be an ongoing tension between the concept of an afterlife for the individual, and notions of the collective destiny of the entire Israelite nation. In fact, the integration of individual and collective postmortem eschatological teachings evidenced in 4 Ezra is not at all indicative or characteristic of later talmudic views of the afterlife.

INDIVIDUAL IMMORTALITY
IN APOCRYPHAL LITERATURE

In most apocryphal and pseudepigraphic texts, the doctrine of resurrection remains the central belief underlying all conceptions of life after death. Even though teachings on Gehenna/Sheol and Paradise/Heaven emerged during this era, nonetheless belief in a collective future-time resurrection persisted as the essential background for all Jewish speculation on the afterlife.

However, alongside teachings on the resurrection, the idea of an individual afterlife immortality surfaced during the apocryphal period, and this is an interesting and curious phenomenon to note. In various ways, Greek philosophy and its idea of the immortal soul infused itself into Judaism, especially within the Alexandrian Jewish community. As a result, a philosophical worldview that precludes the notion of last judgment and resurrection, coupled with speculation on the soul's immortal existence immediately after death, can be found in a number of apocryphal texts written in the Egyptian Jewish community.[45]

The Wisdom of Solomon affords the best evidence of the fusion of Greek and Jewish ideas. Written by a well-educated, Hellenized Jew in the first century C.E. and attributed to King Solomon, this text found its way into the Catholic Bible. Such Hellenistic texts are of a totally different genre than the Enochic, or other apocalyptic, writings. There are no cosmic visions here, no lush imagistic depictions of a macrocosmic journey through realms of heaven or hell. Instead we read the pearls of wisdom left behind by the author of a wisdom text.

Wisdom of Solomon is concerned with the whole question of death and human immortality. "Better to have no children yet to have virtue," says the Book of Wisdom, "since immortality perpetuates its memory" (Wisdom of Solomon 4:1). What we encounter here, plain and simple, are philosophical intimations of an immortalized afterlife existence.

The Wisdom text continues:

> But the souls of the virtuous are in the hands of God,
> no torment shall ever touch them
> In the eyes of the unwise, they did appear to die,
> their going looked like a disaster,
> their leaving us, like annihilation;
> but they are in peace.
> If they experienced punishment as men see it,
> their hope was rich with immortality;
> slight was their affliction, great will their blessings be.
> (Wisdom of Solomon 3:1–4)

We see a very different kind of focus in these writings. There is no backdrop of final judgment or resurrection, nor any concern with Sheol or Paradise. In this text, the righteous enter into God's presence immediately after death and experience immortality—it is a far more simple eschatology based on the Greek view of the eternal soul. Albeit a minority view, this belief in an eternal spiritualized immortality is certainly a legitimate Jewish belief during the apocryphal period, part of the pluralistic plethora of first-century Judaism.

In a similar vein, a number of other apocryphal and pseudepigraphic texts reflect this Greek philosophical strain in Judaism. The Book of

Jubilees, which dates from the late second century B.C.E., offers a promise of blessed immortality for the righteous. The eternal spirit will survive, but after death absolutely no physical resurrection will take place:

> And their bones will rest in the earth
> and their spirits will increase joy,
> and they will know that the Lord is an executor of judgment
> and shows mercy to hundreds and thousands and to all that love
> Him. (Jubilees 23:31)

In the Psalms of Solomon, dating from the first century B.C.E., there
is once again an acclamation of an immortal afterlife. We find the statement that "those who fear the Lord shall rise up to eternal life, and their
life shall be in the Lord's light, and it shall never end" (Psalms of Solomon
3:16). Similarly, according to the Testament of Asher, "if anyone is peaceful with joy he comes to know the angel of peace and enters eternal life"
(Testament of Asher 6:6), or elsewhere, "those who die for the sake of
God live unto God" (4 Maccabees 16:25). Implied in all these passages
is the view that there will be no resurrection of the dead, but rather a
divine spiritual existence right after death.

Finally, even in 1 Enoch there are references to a belief in immortality. Given that 1 Enoch is such an eclectic text, it is not surprising that
teachings on eternal life coexist with beliefs about resurrection. In a
number of places throughout 1 Enoch we find an affirmation of eternal
life for the righteous, over and above the conception of ultimate resurrection: "The spirits of those who died in righteousness shall live and
rejoice, their spirits shall not perish (1 Enoch 103:4). Elsewhere, we find
clear indications of a belief in immortality, as Enoch is told that "the righteous ones shall be in the light of the sun and the elect ones in the light
of eternal life which has no end" (1 Enoch 58:3).[46]

This idea of individual immortality is not found in the apocryphal
and pseudepigraphic writings of Palestinian Judaism. It never replaced
the doctrine of the resurrection of the dead for the Palestinian authors,
as it did for those from Alexandria. Nonetheless, it was a very important
development in the evolution of Jewish ideas on the afterlife. It represents an explicit conception of an individual, eternal existence after death.
This is but one stream of Jewish afterlife teachings in the apocryphal era,
however, and even in the subsequent period of rabbinic Judaism individual immortality never became the predominant belief regarding life
after death.

DIVINE JUDGMENT

Divine Last Judgment of the Nations

The motif of divine judgment is basic to apocryphal literature. Although the texts of the Apocrypha and Pseudepigrapha demonstrate a wide spectrum of teachings regarding God's judgment, the central conception is that at the end-of-days there will occur a last judgment, "the great event toward which the whole universe is moving and which will vindicate once and for all God's righteous purpose for men and all creation."[47]

Judgment, according to the philosophical assumptions in apocryphal texts, is inherently part of the cosmic order. Thus, according to 4 Ezra: "When the Most High made the world . . . he prepared the judgment and the things that pertain to the judgment" (4 Ezra 7:70).

The background to all teachings on divine judgment, as to be expected, is the biblical conception of a universal, cosmic judgment at the end-of-days. For example, the Testament of Moses, (10:4–7) speaks of a time when "the earth will tremble, even to its ends shall it be shaken. . . . The sun will not give light. . . . God the Most High will . . . come to work vengeance on the nations. . . ."

Similarly, the last judgment envisioned in 1 Enoch echoes the prophetic vision of divine judgment:

> The God of the Universe, the Holy Great One, will come forth from his dwelling. . . . And great fear and trembling shall seize them unto the ends of the earth. Mountains and high places will fall down and be frightened. And high hills shall be made low; and they shall melt like a honeycomb before the flame. And earth shall be rent asunder and all that is upon the earth shall perish. (1 Enoch 1:3ff)

Divine Last Judgment of the Righteous and the Wicked

However, apocryphal literature goes far beyond biblical tradition, and throughout we find the notion of separate judgments for the wicked and for the righteous. As 1 Enoch propounds:

> There shall be a judgment upon all including the righteous. And to all the righteous he will grant peace. He will preserve the elect. . . .

They will belong to God and they will prosper and the light of God
will shine unto them. . . . He will destroy the wicked ones and cen-
sure all flesh on account of everything that they have done, that
which the sinners and the wicked ones committed against him.
(1 Enoch 1:8–9)

This notion of qualitatively different judgments for the wicked and
for the righteous is a baseline assumption in apocryphal literature. It is
an eschatological belief that entered the mainstream of Jewish thought
by the end of the Second Temple period and was integrated with prevailing notions of the resurrection of the dead. We see this in the Book
of Jubilees, dating from the second century B.C.E.:

And then the Lord will heal his servants, and they will rise up and
see great peace. And they will drive out their enemies and the righteous ones will see and give praise, and rejoice forever and ever with
joy; and they will see all of their judgments and all of their curses
among their enemies . . . they will know that the Lord is an execu-
tor of judgment; and he will show mercy to hundreds and thousands,
to all who love him. (Jubilees 23:30–31)

Judgment of the Individual and the Recording of Human Deeds

Generally, in earlier apocryphal texts, the idea of last judgment is
bound up with the salvation of the entire nation. The righteous person
is redeemed along with the collective. However, in later writings there is
more and more emphasis on the individual person.[48] Building on the conceptions of individualism put forth in Ezekiel and Jeremiah, we find the
proliferation of the belief that judgment will take into account accrued
individual merit: "And when the whole of creation, visible and invisible,
which the Lord has created, shall come to an end, then each person will
go to the Lord's great judgment" (2 Enoch 65:6).

As the notion of individual judgment evolved, it led to the development of an entirely new eschatological motif. In apocryphal writings
we find the idea that each individual's actions are recorded—"all your
sins are being written down every day" (1 Enoch 104:7)—and at the time
of judgment the record of one's deeds are evaluated, and reward or punishment is apportioned accordingly. This idea is articulated in 1 Enoch
as follows: "He shall judge all the works of the holy ones in heaven above,
weighing in the balance their deeds" (1 Enoch 61:8).

Elsewhere in 1 Enoch a similar view is expressed:

I swear to you sinners by the Holy Great One that all your evil deeds
are revealed in the heavens. None of your deeds of injustice are covered and hidden . . . [they are] written down every day in the presence of the Most High . . . until the day of your judgment. (1 Enoch
98:6–7)

Similarly, in the Testament of Abraham we find a description of a
judgment scene in which angelic beings evaluate a person's deeds:

The two angels, the one on the right and the one on the left, these
are those who record sins and righteous deeds. The one on the right
records righteous deeds, while the one on the left records sins. And
the sunlike angel, who holds the balance in his hand . . . weighs
the righteous deeds and the sins. . . . (Testament of Abraham
13:9–10)

At the time of judgment each person's deeds will be evaluated and
judgment meted out accordingly. This recording of deeds leads to the
beginnings of a motif in Jewish afterlife teachings—what may be appropriately called a "life review"[49]—the idea that after death, a person witnesses the contents of his or her own life and a higher divine force evalu-
ates the ethical and moral basis of a person's life. This motif, which recurs
in subsequent periods of Jewish thought, is evidenced quite clearly in
2 Enoch:

[O]n the day of the great judgment every measure and every weight
and every scale will be exposed as in the market; and each one will
recognize his measure, and according to measure, each shall receive
his reward. (2 Enoch 44:5)

In 3 Enoch the theme of the recording of one's deeds is developed
even further. We find numerous references to a book, or specific books—
some form of divine repository—in which all human actions are recorded.
Also in 3 Enoch we find a description of how God judges the world, and
in so doing consults "the books of the living and the books of the dead"
(3 Enoch 28:7). This motif of a divine data bank of human actions recurs frequently; a number of other metaphors are used throughout the
text. Elsewhere, the text of 3 Enoch describes how an angel "takes out

the scroll box in which the book of records is kept, and brings into the presence of the Holy One, blessed be he" (3 Enoch 27:2). The text also speaks of "records concerning the inhabitants of the earth"(3 Enoch 18:19), a book in which all the doings of the world are recorded (3 Enoch 30:2), a book of fire and flame (3 Enoch 32:1); and books in which are recorded all wicked deeds (3 Enoch 44:9).

Divine Judgment before a Heavenly Court of Law

In developing the notion of individual judgment, 3 Enoch envisions that the postmortem divine judgment occurs within the context of a heavenly court of law. Thus, it is stated that "the Holy One, blessed be he, . . . sits upon the throne of judgment and judges the whole world in truth" (3 Enoch 26:12).

There are a number of judgment scenes depicted in 3 Enoch, and these form one of the main motifs of the entire text. Thus, we find the following description of divine judgment:

> When the Holy One, blessed be he, sits on the throne of judgment, Justice stands on his right hand, Mercy, on his left, and Truth stands directly facing him. When a man enters his presence for judgment, a staff as it were, extends toward him from the splendor of Mercy and takes a position in front of him. At once the man falls prostrate, and all the angels of destruction fear and shrink from him. . . . (3 Enoch 31:2)

Elsewhere, there is an even more elaborate depiction of the judgment:

> Every day when the Holy One, blessed be he, sits on the throne of judgment and judges the world, with the books of the living and the books of the dead open before him, all the celestials stand before him in fear, dread and trembling. When the Holy One, blessed be he, sits in judgment on the throne of judgment, his garment is white like snow, the hair of his head is as pure wool, and he is covered all over with righteousness. . . . The Watchers and the holy ones stand before him like court officers before the judge; they take up and debate every single matter and they close each case that comes for judgment before the Holy One, blessed be he. . . . (3 Enoch 28:7–8)

It is interesting to note that in the above passages judgment takes place "every day." Scholarly textual study indicates that the judgment described in 3 Enoch is not a final last judgment but, in fact, one that takes place immediately after death. The emphasis in this text, which probably dates from the fifth century C.E., is on an individual postmortem judgment and not on a divine judgment subsequent to the resurrection of the dead.[50]

Individual and Collective Judgment Synthesized

An additional unique eschatological motif associated with the theme of divine judgment appears in the Testament of Abraham. This second-century C.E. text speaks of three separate judgments. First, a person will be judged by another human being—Abel, the son of Adam. Second, at the end-of-days there will be a judgment by the tribes of Israel. And finally, everyone will undergo a divine judgment—"they shall be judged by the Master God of all; and thereafter the fulfillment of that judgment will be near" (Testament of Abraham 13:6–8).

What we see in this rather unique conception of judgment is the essential tension characterizing Jewish afterlife teachings—the intertwining of notions of individual postmortem judgment and the collective judgment of all people at the end-of-days.[51] The author of the Testament of Abraham has endeavored to harmonize these two, sometimes conflicting, sometimes compatible notions. The integration that exists here is perhaps somewhat artificial, a later Christian editing that introduces a notion of judgment by the twelve tribes that has little precedent or antecedent in Jewish thought.[52] By way of conclusion, the tension between individual and collective notions of judgment and postmortem survival is never fully resolved in apocryphal literature.

RESURRECTION

Background

Teachings about the resurrection of the dead became increasingly important during the apocryphal period. Within four centuries after first appearing in Ezekiel and Isaiah, and later in Daniel, the notion of a physical postmortem resurrection emerged as a normative religious belief for

Jews of late antiquity. Simply put, the resurrection of the dead at the end-of-time is a theme underlying most, although not all, eschatological teachings of apocryphal literature.

In spite of the influence of Greek teachings on the immortal soul, the Jewish view of unity of body and soul persisted through the course of centuries. This ancient biblical belief found expression in apocryphal and pseudepigraphic writings about the resurrection, which envisioned the ultimate unity—or rather, reunification—of body and soul.

We will now look briefly at a number of apocryphal teachings on resurrection. As to be expected, there is certainly no monolithic Jewish view of resurrection, but many different ideas coexisting with other, often contradictory, afterlife beliefs.

2 Maccabees: Resurrection of Fallen Israelites

Second Maccabees, chapters 6–7, an early text dating from c. 100 to 40 B.C.E., speaks of resurrection. The emphasis here is clearly on resurrection only for the Israelite. The text affirms that God does "not see fit to deal with us [i.e., the Israelites, the Jews] as He does with the other nations" (2 Maccabees 6:15). The narrative of the text describes the story of the murder of a woman and her seven sons by King Antiochus, and contains dialogue between one of the sons and the king. As he is being tortured, the son says to the king: "Better to be killed by men and cherish God's promise to raise us again. There will be no resurrection to life for you!" (2 Maccabees 7:14). In other words, "Kill me if you will, but I am going to be resurrected."

Interestingly enough, it is likely that the Maccabean revolt of 167 B.C.E. was the historical context that led to the rapid emergence of the concept of resurrection.[53] In the religious war against Syrian-Greek domination, many Jewish warriors were wiped out in battle. Since they were fighting for God's justice, it strengthened belief that they would eventually be vindicated for their life sacrifice, and would be delivered up from the realm of the dead.

The text of 2 Maccabees relates how certain slain Jewish warriors were found to have in their possession "amulets sacred to the idols of Jamnia" (2 Maccabees 12:40), which were clearly prohibited by Jewish law. Upon discovering the idols, Judah Maccabee offered penance on behalf of the fallen men and arranged to send a sin offering to Jerusalem. The text describes what he did as "a fit and proper act in which he took due account of the resurrection" (2 Maccabees 12:43).

The text goes on to say:

> For if he had not been expecting the fallen to rise again it would have
> been foolish and superfluous to pray for the dead. But since he had
> in view the wonderful reward for those who die a godly death, his
> purpose was a holy and pious one. And this was why he offered an
> atoning sacrifice to free the dead from their sin. (2 Maccabees
> 12:44–45)

What is implied in this story is that the expiation and prayers of the
living have the power to affect the fate of the dead at the time of the
resurrection. This development in Jewish postmortem thought is based
on the notion of an intermediate realm in which the righteous dead await
their fate until the time of the resurrection.

Resurrection of All Humanity/Resurrection of the Righteous

Throughout apocryphal literature the question is often raised regarding who will be resurrected at the end-of-days.

In a number of texts the view is very clear that all humanity will be
resurrected. Four Ezra speaks of "the nations that have been raised from
the dead" (4 Ezra 7:37), thus implying resurrection, not only for Israelites, but all humanity. In another text the implication is likewise that all
humanity are resurrected: "The earth will surely give back the dead at
that time . . . as it has received them so it will give them back" (2 Baruch
50:2).

The Testament of Benjamin speaks of how "Enoch, Seth, Abraham,
Isaac, and Jacob shall be raised up" and at the same time "also all men shall
rise, some unto glory and some unto shame" (Testament of Benjamin
10:6–8). Likewise, the Testament of Judah echoes this view in stating
that "Abraham, Isaac, and Jacob will be resurrected to life. . . . And those
who die in sorrow shall be raised in joy" (Testament of Judah 25:1, 4).

Sibylline Oracles 4:181–183 echoes this idea of resurrection for all
and states that "God himself will again fashion the bones and ashes of
men and shall raise up mortals once more as they were before" (Sibylline
Oracles 4:181–183). However, here the notion of resurrection for all,
occurs alongside references to resurrection only for the righteous. Thus,
while the wicked will be condemned to "the repulsive recesses of
Gehenna," they "that are pious shall live on earth again" (Sibylline
Oracles 4:181–183).

1 Enoch: Resurrection of the Righteous

As one of the earliest apocryphal texts, 1 Enoch contains teachings on the resurrection. But remember, this text is an edited compilation, and because of this, there is no unitary view about resurrection found within 1 Enoch. Earlier and later historical strands of teachings about the fate of the dead appear side by side, and the text is full of often conflicting, interwoven teachings about resurrection and the postmortem destiny of human beings.

Underlying 1 Enoch is an inherent dualism: sin and righteousness yield very distinct results; as a consequence, after death the wicked and the righteous are subjected to very different types of experiences. This conception is reflected quite clearly in teachings about resurrection.

1 Enoch envisions a divine postmortem resurrection for the righteous:

In those days, Sheol will return all the deposits which she had received and hell will give back all that which it owes. And he shall choose the righteous and the holy ones from among the risen dead, for the day when they shall be selected and saved has arrived. (1 Enoch 51:1–3)

Similarly:

Then they shall be glad and rejoice in gladness and they shall enter into the holy place; its fragrance shall penetrate their bones, long life will they live on earth such as your fathers lived in their days. (1 Enoch 25:6)

While resurrection is for the righteous, sinners can expect a different fate. As we discussed earlier, 1 Enoch envisions a postmortem realm for sinners, a place "created for the spirits of men who are not pious, but sinners. . . . Their spirits will not be punished on the day of judgment, nor will they be raised from there" (1 Enoch 22:12–13). For the wicked, there is no resurrection.

Similarly, 1 Enoch 48:9–10 speaks of no resurrection, but what is implied is a denial of resurrection for the wicked sinner:

I shall deliver them into the hands of my elect ones like grass in fire and like lead in the water, so they shall burn before the face of the holy ones and sink before their sight, and no place will be found for them . . . they shall fall on their faces, they shall not rise up again. . . . (1 Enoch 48:9–10)

The teaching underlying this passage does not deny the doctrine of resurrection, but rather, maintains that only the righteous will merit the reward of physical resurrection.

Elsewhere in 1 Enoch, however, there are very different views about resurrection, reflecting the assortment of Jewish eschatological beliefs of the late Second Temple period. In contrast to other passages on resurrection, 1 Enoch 104:2, 4, 6 asserts a belief in heavenly immortality—"You will shine as the lights of heaven . . . as the angels in heaven. . . . You will become companions of the host of heaven"—and is thus a philosophical denial of the doctrine of resurrection. This denial of resurrection is based on an affirmation of the Greek view of the immortal soul. There is no resurrection—the righteous enter an immortal heavenly afterworld. The text is based on a philosophical worldview that precludes belief in the postmortem resurrection of the body.

In other places within 1 Enoch there is also a denial of resurrection but in a very different philosophical context than the above passage. In the complex pool of apocalyptic eschatology of late antiquity can be found remnants of the ancient biblical notion of Sheol, a view that was asserted by the Sadducees. Here there is no resurrection, because the dead remain in a lifeless state in a subterranean realm of darkness:

> As we die, so do the righteous die. What then have they gained by their deeds? Behold, like us they have died in grief and in darkness, and what have they more than we? From now on we have become equal. What will they receive or what will they receive forever? Behold they have surely died; and from now on they shall never see light forever. (1 Enoch 102:6–8)

More clearly, the text goes on:

> Have you seen the righteous? . . . they perished and became like those who were not and descended into Sheol—and their spirits too—with anguish. (1 Enoch 102:11)

We see here in 1 Enoch the existence of a much earlier biblical notion of Sheol, coexisting with newer teachings about resurrection and the postmortem fate of the individual.

In some sense this examination of Jewish sources on afterlife has come full circle. The First Book of Enoch demonstrates the complex multidimensional Jewish view of the afterlife in the apocryphal era. While new conceptions of the immortality, resurrection, separate realms for the wicked and the righteous, and heavenly record books emerge in the Enoch texts, there are also to be found teachings about Sheol and the afterworld that predate the close of the biblical period.

Resurrection within the Postmortem Scheme of Jewish Life in the Apocryphal Era

One last text that needs to be noted in looking at resurrection in the Apocrypha is 4 Ezra (2 Esdras). As part of the postmortem depictions presented in chapter 7, "The Salathiel Apocalypse," the text speaks of a time when the Most High will be in communication with the "nations that have raised from the dead" (4 Ezra 7:37). There is a clear assumption of a belief in resurrection, and it is resurrection for the righteous ones of all humanity.

But this belief in resurrection is part of the entire schema of postmortem beliefs depicted so elaborately in 4 Ezra. Resurrection occurs at the end of time; this belief always remains the end point of Jewish eschatology. Prior to that metahistorical event, there is a judgment based on individual merit, and righteous and wicked souls are assigned to specific intermediate realms of reward and punishment, where they await the resurrection. This is the structural schema that remains as the foundation for all further Jewish afterlife teachings.

Even with the influence of the Greek doctrine of the soul, Jewish teachings on postmortem immortality never supplanted the primacy of belief in physical resurrection. Throughout subsequent eras of Jewish life, the notion of the physical resurrection of the body persists as the background to any and all developments in Judaism's teachings on life after death.

SUMMARY

The apocryphal period is pivotal in the development of Jewish afterlife teachings. Within the plethora of apocryphal and pseudepigraphic texts are to be found a complex series of ideas about the afterlife survival of the human soul. Based on the material discussed in this chapter, the following observations can be made about the evolutionary development of Judaism's conceptions of life after death in the apocryphal period:

1. There is a growing diversification of the postmortem worlds evidenced in apocryphal literature. Sheol comes to be seen as a stratified realm in which there are separate and distinct regions for the righteous and the wicked.

2. During the apocryphal period a dualistic conception of the hereafter emerges. Sheol, or Gehenna, comes to be seen as the abode of the wicked; Paradise, or Heaven—an entirely new postmortem concept—becomes the abode of the righteous.

3. Elaborate depictions of Gehenna and Paradise are presented, for the first time, in apocryphal literature. Within certain texts, afterlife teachings take on a mythic, imagistic form and are the precursors to the creation of a tradition of visionary tours of heaven and hell.

4. In Alexandrian Judaism the doctrine of an eternal, individual immortality becomes increasingly popular, replacing the notion of the physical resurrection of the dead.

5. In spite of beliefs about the individual immortal soul, collective eschatological doctrines of divine judgment and resurrection still remain as the baseline foundation of afterlife beliefs in the apocryphal period. The popularization of the doctrine of the resurrection of the dead during this era was accompanied by a new understanding of Sheol as an intermediate realm where the dead lay in waiting until the time of resurrection.

6. Given that apocryphal and pseudepigraphic texts never received canonical status in rabbinic Judaism, the impact of these texts within the Jewish world dissipated over time. However, the imagistic visionary stream of apocryphal afterlife teachings, while not predominant in rabbinic Judaism, reappears almost a thousand years later in medieval Midrash and in Kabbalah.

7. Within the writings of the Apocrypha and Pseudepigrapha are to be found important conceptions linking the afterlife teachings of the biblical period with those developed in the subsequent era of rabbinic Judaism.

Chapter 5

The World to Come in Rabbinic Judaism

THE HISTORICAL CONTEXT

In our continuing investigation of Jewish teachings on life after death, we enter the world of rabbinic Judaism. In this chapter, we will examine a profoundly extensive data bank of Jewish law and lore produced over a period of close to a thousand years—Mishnah, Talmud, and Midrash—and discover what the Rabbis had to say about immortality and the afterlife. But first, some relevant background, to set the stage for our entry into the world of rabbinic Judaism.

Rabbinic Judaism was born out of crisis and destruction. In the year 70 C.E. the Jerusalem Temple was decimated by the Romans, the city of Jerusalem ransacked and laid to waste. Up until that time, Jewish religious practice had been centered on sacrificial worship and a Temple priesthood. Every aspect of the religious life—daily rituals, the annual pilgrimage festivals, and the entire agricultural system of priestly tithing—could no longer be continued without the Temple, which had been the central Jewish institution for over a thousand years. As a result, after the year 70 C.E. it became essential for the Jewish people to discover entirely new forms for serving the divine and for maintaining the continuity of Jewish life.

The spiritual leaders of this crucial era were the Rabbis, the teachers and interpreters of Torah. In recognizing the need to adapt Judaism to the changed circumstance precipitated by the loss of the Temple, the Rabbis were able to successfully spearhead a far-reaching religious transformation in Jewish life. Since they had the Torah, the only surviving spiritual possession of the Jews after 70 C.E., the Rabbis searched within this sacred text for functional guidelines and spiritual direction for continuing to live a spiritual life in the absence of Temple and priesthood. In the subsequent centuries rabbinic Judaism emerged and created a radically transformed Jewish religion centered on individual and group prayer and the study of Torah and other sacred texts.[1]

There is a famous legend about Rabbi Yohanan ben Zakkai that tells the tale of the shift Judaism experienced with the destruction of the Temple. It is said that during the siege of Jerusalem, ben Zakkai was placed in a coffin by his students, who were then able to carry him past the Roman sentry on the pretext that they were going to bury their teacher outside the city walls. Once outside the besieged city, ben Zakkai made his way to Rome, where he requested of Vespasian, the Roman general and emperor-to-be, permission to set up an academy of learning at Yavneh, a town to the northwest of Jerusalem (*Avot de Rabbi Natan* 4). With Vespasian's approval, ben Zakkai established a center of learning at Yavneh that was to have a profound impact on the next era of Judaism. In the final years of the first century, Yavneh became the most important academy of learning in the Jewish world. The religious creativity that emerged from Yavneh spawned a spiritual renewal that enabled Judaism to survive the catastrophe of the year 70 C.E. Within one generation after the destruction of the Temple, the era of priestly worship had become history and the Rabbis of Yavneh had successfully created the theological, liturgical, and legalistic foundation for the subsequent development of rabbinic Judaism.[2]

Originally, the spiritual discourses of the Rabbis were passed down through a process of oral transmission from student to disciple. But by the second century C.E., it became necessary to record the discussions, conclusions, and new legislation emerging from various rabbinic schools. What developed over the course of five hundred to a thousand years was a vast body of literature that reflected the ongoing creative ferment of rabbinic Judaism.

The earliest rabbinic teachings were recorded in a document called the Mishnah (from the verb *shanah*, meaning "to repeat"), which was compiled in the late second century C.E. by the Palestinian rabbi Yehudah Ha-Nasi. Between the third and fifth centuries, an extensive commentary on the Mishnah, known as the Gemara (from the Aramaic root, *gmr*, like the Hebrew root, *lmd*, meaning "to study"), was written. Gemara and Mishnah together are referred to as the Talmud. Since there were centers of learning in Babylonia and Palestine, two separate Talmuds were compiled: the Babylonian Talmud and the Jerusalem, or Palestinian, Talmud. The former is more extensive, edited with greater precision and often regarded as the more authoritative of the two. Within the Talmud can be found a diverse assortment of legalistic and allegorical literature—stories, ethical parables, biblical exegeses, aphorisms, transcripts of legal debates, and so on—addressing all facets of Jewish life. For over fifteen centuries the Talmud has been a traditional pillar of the religious life in Judaism.[3]

In addition to the legalistic discourse in the Talmud, the Rabbis also developed a new form of interpreting Torah known as Midrash, from the Hebrew word *darash*, "to expound or investigate." Midrash is an extensive body of literature, predominantly legendary, but at times legalistic in nature, that provides homiletical interpretation and explanations of contradictory or confusing passages in the Torah. Whereas the editing and compilation of the Talmud was complete by the end of the fifth century C.E., subsequent generations of rabbinic leaders continued to compose Midrash for centuries.[4] The earlier *midrashim* (plural of Midrash), which date from the second and third centuries C.E., are known as Midrash *Halakhah*, "legalistic Midrash," and are often used to justify particular religious laws. These contain a minimal amount of material on life after death and rabbinic eschatology. The later *midrashim*, referred to as Midrash *Aggadah*, "legendary Midrash," tend to be more mythic in style and, in presenting homiletical interpretation of Torah, often discourse on the fate of the individual after death. By the medieval period, Midrash *Aggadah* developed into quite an elaborate form replete with mythic and legendary depictions of the supernal realms.

Within both Talmud and Midrash are found vast collections of teachings on immortality and the afterlife journey of the soul. These teachings are based on the conceptions of the afterlife found in the Hebrew Bible and apocryphal literature. But rabbinic postmortem teachings frequently move in new directions and have a character of their own, building upon the past, but reflecting the unique spiritual word view of the Rabbis.

As in biblical and apocryphal writings, nowhere in rabbinic litera-ture do we find a single, systematized statement on the Jewish under-standing of life after death. There is certainly no such thing as a talmudic tractate on the hereafter, and given the eclectic and broad-ranging na-ture of rabbinic literature itself, it is unrealistic to even speak of *the* rab-binic view of the afterlife. What we find instead are thousands of indi-vidual rabbinic teachings on various facets of death and the hereafter, randomly interspersed throughout talmudic and midrashic literature. And, just as in the biblical and apocryphal period, many distinct and disparate notions of the afterlife coexist, some related to collective res-urrection of the dead, others to individual immortality. Over the course of centuries the Rabbis formulated and elucidated a wide variety of di-verse and often contradictory ideas on life after death, and the legacy they left behind is in no way systematic or monolithic.

For the Rabbis, the Torah itself was an integrated system that re-quired further study and investigation. Codifying and systematizing ex-isting teachings was not their primary form of literary activity. Instead, the Rabbis were more interested in interpreting and understanding the sacred legacy of the past, encoded in Torah and Mishnah. The goal of their investigation of Torah was to establish guidelines for religious prac-tice, rather than to explicate a particular metaphysical doctrine.[5] When-ever the Rabbis did venture into any discussion on life after death, they did so by literary interpretation of biblical texts and not by philosophical speculation. Unlike the sages of ancient Greece, the Rabbis did not spend much time contemplating and writing about the origins, nature, and func-tions of the soul; and, unlike the apocryphal authors, rarely did they describe mystical voyages into the realms of the dead. The doctrine of divine retribution and postmortem reward and punishment interested the Rabbis far more than the esoteric mysteries of the soul (which did emerge as a predominant focus in the medieval kabbalistic period).[6] Above all else, the Rabbis were concerned with ethical action within the context of embodied, daily life. At the root of rabbinic teachings on the afterlife is always the question of the relationship between moral action in life and divine recompense after death. Ultimately, for the Rabbis of the Talmud and Midrash, what mattered was the way in which a human being served God and fulfilled the commandments while alive, for it was such action that inevitably determined one's fate in the hereafter.

Our goal at this stage of the journey through Jewish history is to show the diversity of afterlife teachings found in the texts of rabbinic Judaism.[7] As appropriate, we will discuss how rabbinic ideas built upon afterlife conceptions of the Bible and apocryphal literature and note particular evolutionary developments in the afterlife teaching found in different talmudic and midrashic sources. Above all, what emerges in this chapter is a fascinating collage of various recurring images and themes of life after death produced by the Rabbis over the course of over a thousand years of Jewish life.

OLAM HA-BA/THE WORLD TO COME— VARYING CONCEPTIONS

This World/The World to Come

Throughout rabbinic literature, a number of philosophical ideas and conceptual terms appear for the first time in Jewish thought and usually are accepted as a given by the Rabbis with little introduction or prefatory comment.[8] One such term, commonly used in the Talmud and Midrash in reference to the future life after death, is *Olam Ha-Ba*—"the World to Come." The notion of *Olam Ha-Ba* frequently appears juxtaposed with the term *Olam Ha-Zeh*—"this world" of physical plane life. *Olam Ha-Ba* is a spiritual world of a completely different order than *Olam Ha-Zeh*. In the words of the talmudic tractate *Berakhot*: "*Olam Ha-Zeh* is not at all like *Olam Ha-Ba*" (*Berakhot* 17a).

According to Mishnah *Avot*, "Better is one hour of bliss in the World to Come [*Olam Ha-Ba*] than the whole of life in this world [*Olam Ha-Zeh*]" (M. *Avot* 4:17). Such a statement would seem to suggest that rabbinic Judaism placed a priority on the spiritual world, above and beyond the ongoing life of day-to-day existence. Oddly enough, however, the very same Rabbi who made the above statement also said: "Better is one hour of repentance and good works in this world [*Olam Ha-Zeh*] than the whole life of the World to Come [*Olam Ha-Ba*]" (M. *Avot* 4:17).

There is a kind of paradoxical dualism in these two statements. On first glance, it is not clear which is more important—this world or the World to Come. The way in which these two apparently conflicting ideas are juxtaposed in the same text suggests that there was never primacy of importance given to this world over *Olam Ha-Ba*, or vice versa. The two—ongoing daily life and the transcendental spiritual realm—stood in an organic relationship with each other, both having importance in their own right.

The Rabbis, unlike the early Christians, never emphasized a postmortem spiritual existence over and above life in the world.[9] Nowhere do we find a craving or yearning for death and never a denial of the importance of this earthly plane. In fact, the second-century sage Shimon bar Yohai and his son were purportedly punished by a divine messenger because they judgmentally sneered at a man plowing a field and exclaimed: "They forsake life eternal and engage in life temporal." For this, he and his son had to spend a full year doing penance in an isolated cave (*Shabbat* 33b). Another story, which reflects a similar point of view, is told about King Solomon and the death of his father, King David:

> When King David died, Solomon, his son sent this inquiry to the *Bet Ha-Midrash*: "My father is dead and lying in the sun; and the dogs of my father's house are hungry, what shall I do?" They sent back this answer: "Feed the dogs first and then attend to your dead father. . . . living dogs take precedence over a dead king." (*Shabbat* 30b)

This is a rather strange anecdote, especially given the sanctity Judaism has always given to the handling of the dead. However, what we have here is a rabbinic way of emphasizing the importance of earthly existence, over and above any postmortem reality.[10] In the rabbinic view, earthly life is to be lived fully and appreciated because it is in this plane of existence that one can serve God directly through fulfillment of the divine commandments, or *mitzvot*. It is within this world that the individual carries out a relationship with the divine, and not only in a transcendent realm.

For the Rabbis, the ongoing tension between *Olam Ha-Zeh* and *Olam Ha-Ba* served to motivate and inspire a person to ethical and moral actions. Rabbinic leaders encouraged their followers to concentrate on study, prayer, and compassionate deeds (M. *Avot* 1:2) in order to merit the rewards of the World to Come.

In the tractate *Berakhot*, a story is told about the second-century rabbi Eliezer. Once when Rabbi Eliezer was ill, his students came to visit, and they requested of him: "Master, teach us the ways of life whereby we may be worthy of the life of the World to Come." He responded by setting out guidelines for living an ethical life:

Be careful of the honor of your colleagues; restrain your children from [meaningless] recitation; and seat them between the knees of the disciples of the Sages; and when you pray, know before whom you stand; and on that account you will be worthy of the life of the World to Come. (*Berakhot* 28b).

For Rabbi Eliezer, as for the Rabbis that followed him, one lived daily life with an awareness that one would eventually stand accountable before God in the World to Come. The world beyond awaits each individual, and the god-fearing person is repeatedly reminded that: "This world [*Olam Ha-Zeh*] is like a vestibule to the World to Come [*Olam Ha-Ba*]; prepare yourself in the vestibule that you may enter the hall" (M. *Avot* 4:16). In the same vein, with regard to that vital spiritual relationship between this life and the higher life in *Olam Ha-Ba*, Rabbi Joshua ben Levi is reported to have said: "Whoever utters songs of praise to God in this world [*Olam Ha-Zeh*] shall be privileged to do so in *Olam Ha-Ba*" (*Sanhedrin* 91b).

What Is *Olam Ha-Ba*?

The conception of *Olam Ha-Ba* in rabbinic tradition is not always precise. The Rabbis often did not define particular concepts with an unbending, explicit clarity. As a result, it is very common to find contradictory points of view within rabbinic literature. On the positive side, because of this tendency, later generations of Rabbis were not limited by dogmatic formulations, and therefore had great freedom to expand and interpret existing concepts.[11] This is certainly the case with regard to rabbinic afterlife teachings, which reflect a number of clearly discrepant points of view.

Thus, for example, in an early Midrash found in *Sifre Deuteronomy*, *Olam Ha-Ba* is not described with any well-defined visual picture. According to the legend, the people of Israel are gathered in the presence of Moses, and he is asked: "Tell us what goodness the Holy Blessed One will give us in the World to Come?" In a style that hardly demonstrates the vast wisdom ascribed to the man, Moses responds: "I do not know what I can tell you. Happy are you for what is prepared for you" (*Sifre Deuteronomy* 356). This is a somewhat cryptic passage. Is Moses suggesting that he knows something that the people are not to be told of? Or is he, too, in the dark about the what *Olam Ha-Ba* is really like? Either way, we get little information from Moses about the shape and texture of *Olam Ha-Ba*.

On the other hand, another tradition offers a more vivid impression:

> In the World to Come there is no eating, or drinking nor procreation or commerce, nor jealousy, or enmity or rivalry—but the righteous sit with crowns on their head and enjoy the radiance of the *Shekhinah* [Divine Presence]. (*Berakhot* 17a)

The main problem we encounter in exploring the notion of *Olam Ha-Ba* is that rabbinic literature is often ambiguous, reflecting the dichotomy we saw in the biblical period between individual and collective conceptions of the afterlife. Exactly how is *Olam Ha-Ba* seen in the teachings of the Rabbis? Is the World to Come a postmortem realm that the individual enters immediately after death? Is it a messianic age at the end of time and history? Or is *Olam Ha-Ba* the period that is inaugurated by the resurrection of the dead? The truth is that, as we noted earlier, collective and individual eschatological themes are fused and often confused in rabbinic literature. In certain sources, *Olam Ha-Ba* is uniquely associated with teachings about collective redemption and resurrection, but in other places *Olam Ha-Ba* is conceived of as an afterlife realm for the individual.

One late rabbinic text, a devotional poem from the Sabbath liturgy, presents a systematic differentiation between the various possible conceptions of *Olam Ha-Ba*:

> There is none to be compared beside You, O Lord our God, in this world, neither is there any beside You, O Lord our King, for the life of the world to come [*Ha-Olam Ha-Ba*]; there is none but You, O our Redeemer, for the days of the Messiah; neither is there any like unto You, O our Savior, for the resurrection of the dead.[12]

Within this passage we see a four-stage continuum from this life, to the postmortem world (here understood as *Olam Ha-Ba*), to the messianic era, to the time of resurrection. However, this schematic breakdown from a much later period of time is not characteristic of all rabbinic writings.[13] Midrash *Tanhuma*, for example, states quite the opposite: "After the Days of the Messiah come the *Olam Ha-Ba* and the Holy One, Blessed Be He appears in His glory and shows His mighty arm" (*Tanhuma*, *Ekev*, 7). Throughout Talmud and Midrash there are varied and divergent teachings on *Olam Ha-Ba*, and there is no simple or ordered schema of eschatological concepts. If we are to understand rabbinic conceptions of immortality and life after death, we have to look closely at individual descriptions of *Olam Ha-Ba* and clarify if a text is referring to a postmortem realm or a messianic era.

Olam Ha-Ba and the End-of-Days

In an early rabbinic text, a mishnaic source dating from the second century, we find that *Olam Ha-Ba* is not understood as a postmortem realm. Chapter 10 of Mishnah *Sanhedrin* addresses the question of who will have a share in the World to Come. Within the Mishnah we find the following statement: "The generation of the Flood have no share in the World to Come" (M. *Sanhedrin* 10:3). Others who will be denied the World to Come include three specific kings of Israel—Jeroboam, Ahab, and Manasseh; the men of Sodom; the spies who entered Israel and reported back to the wandering Israelites in the desert; the generation of the wilderness; and even those who deny that the resurrection of the dead is prescribed by the Torah (M. *Sanhedrin* 10:2–3).[14]

From the context of this mishnaic text, it is clear that the Rabbis are speaking about a resurrection of the dead at the end of time, not an immortal life subsequent to physical death. The text refers to various generations of Israelites that have already died. The concern is focused on whether or not they will be resurrected, or at least whether they will make an appearance and be judged by God. The overall content of the chapter indicates that here the Rabbis see *Olam Ha-Ba* as an era at the end-of-days, a future time when divine judgment will be meted out and many will be brought back to physical life. The Rabbis of the Mishnah do not usually talk about what the afterlife region itself will look like; rather, they are concerned with the more ethically centered question of who will merit *Olam Ha-Ba* at the end-of-time. In Mishnah *Sanhedrin*, as in many places within early rabbinic literature, there is no demonstrated interest in the experiences of the soul immediately after death.

Throughout both early and later rabbinic literature, passages abound depicting *Olam Ha-Ba* as a utopian, messianic era that will manifest within

a sociopolitical context. This *Olam Ha-Ba*, similar to the divine kingdom envisioned by the prophets, will be characterized by righteousness,
social justice for all, and material prosperity.[15]

According to a passage in tractate *Ketubbot*, which was previously
quoted in Chapter 2:

> Not like this world will be the World to Come. In this world one has
> the trouble to harvest grapes and press them; but in the World to
> Come a person will bring a single grape in a wagon or a ship, store it
> in the corner of his house, and draw from it enough wine to fill it a
> large flagon. . . . There will not be a grape which will not yield thirty
> measures of wine. (*Ketubbot* 111b)

Such a description gives absolutely no indication of a heavenly afterlife; rather, what we encounter here is a futuristic vision of an earthly
utopia—*Olam Ha-Zeh*, this world, transformed. This eschatological
theme is echoed in numerous other places. For example, the Talmud
states that in the World to Come "grain will be produced after fifteen
days and trees will grow fruit after one month" (P. *Taanit* 64a); "the land
of Israel will grow loaves of the finest flour and garments of the finest
wool" (*Ketubbot* 111b); and "women will bear children daily and the trees
will produce fruit daily" (*Shabbat* 30b).

Elsewhere in rabbinic literature *Olam Ha-Ba* is likewise portrayed
as a posthistorical period in which the nation of Israel shall be redeemed.
Pirke de Rabbi Eliezer, for example, in an exegetical discussion of
Deuteronomy 32:39 states:

> The Holy Blessed One said: "I am" in this world, and "I am" in the
> World to Come; I am the one who redeemed Israel from Egypt; and
> I am the one who, in the future, will redeem them at the end of the
> fourth kingdom. . . . (*Pirke de Rabbi Eliezer*, chapter 24)

Again, here there is not even a hint of any postmortem belief in an
immortal afterlife. *Olam Ha-Ba* is envisioned as a time of collective redemption guided by divine intervention. After millennia of humiliation
and unjust oppression, having been made to "appear lowly in this world,"
in *Olam Ha-Ba* Israel will finally be vindicated by God's justice and will
"inherit the world from end to end" (*Leviticus Rabbah* 36:2).[16]

In a similar vein, the Midrash *Tanhuma* describes the redemption
of Israel in the World to Come:

The Holy Blessed One said to Israel, In this world, I will set you blessings and curses, good fortune and disasters, but in *Olam Ha-Ba* I will remove you from the curses and disasters and bless you, so that all who behold you will declare you to be a people of the blessed. (*Tanhuma, Reeh,* 4)

What is noteworthy about the above examples is that they span close to five centuries of rabbinic literary activity—*Leviticus Rabbah* being dated around 450 C.E. and *Tanhuma* and *Pirke de Rabbi Eliezer* as late as the ninth century.[17] In both early and later rabbinic texts, *Olam Ha-Ba* is still conceived of in terms of the collective eschatology that was basic in the biblical era. The notion that at the end-of-days God would redeem all the nation maintained its philosophical importance for Jews down through history. However, on a parallel track a series of rabbinic teachings were developed about individual survival in an immortal life after death.

Olam Ha-Ba as a Postmortem Realm

One question that repeatedly concerned the Rabbis was: exactly when would *Olam Ha-Ba* transpire? As early as the second century there were certain sages who taught that *Olam Ha-Ba* would commence immediately following physical death. This notion, which assumes a philosophy of individual immortality, did find popular expression throughout the rabbinic period, but it never became a predominant view and was always philosophically overshadowed by the ancient biblical belief in the unity of body and soul and their eventual reunification through the resurrection of the dead.[18] Nonetheless, there is explicit textual evidence depicting the idea of *Olam Ha-Ba* as a postmortem afterlife realm.

Thus, for example, in one anecdote told about Rabbi Abahu, it was said that at the moment when he "was about to depart from this life, he beheld all the good things that were stored up for him in *Olam Ha-Ba,* and he rejoiced" (*Exodus Rabbah* 52:3). Similarly, another Midrash cites an individual on the verge of being martyred, who cries out: "Tomorrow, my portion will be with them in the *Olam Ha-Ba*" (*Sifre Deuteronomy* 307). No doubt we are speaking here of a postmortem *Olam Ha-Ba* in these cases. In another midrashic text, this conception is given prominent expression in the following statement:

My law will guide you in your path in this world; it will watch over
you in your sleep, at the hour of death; and when you awake, it will
converse with you in the Olam Ha-Ba. (Sifre Leviticus 18:4; see also
M. Avot 6:9)

Elsewhere, we find Rabbi Yohanan teaching that Olam Ha-Ba is a
postmortem realm, entirely different from the time of future redemption,
designated as Yemot Ha-Mashiah, the "Days of the Messiah":

All our prophets foretell only what will happen in the Yemot Ha-
Mashiah. But as for Olam Ha-Ba [understood as the world beyond
the grave] "no eye has seen, and no ear has heard, O God, beside
You" [Is. 650:3], but God alone knows what He prepared for him
that waits for them. (Berakhot 34b)

Another passage, dating from the ninth century C.E., indicates quite
clearly once again that Olam Ha-Ba, at least sometimes, was conceived
of as a postmortem realm for the dead:

The sages have taught us that we human beings cannot appreciate
the joys of the future age. Therefore, they called it "the coming world"
[Olam Ha-Ba], not because it does not yet exist, but because it is
still in the future. "The World to Come" is the one waiting for man
after this world. But there is no basis for the assumption that the
world to come will only begin after the destruction of this world.
What it does imply is that when the righteous leave this world, they
ascend on high, as it is said: "How great is the goodness, O Lord,
which you have in store for those who fear you, and which, toward
those who take refuge in you, you show in the sight of men. [Psalms
31:20]. (Tanhuma, Vayikra 8)

In all of these rabbinic texts, the World to Come is an individual
afterlife realm. However, within the vast canon of talmudic and midrashic
literature, there is no doubt that this philosophical notion was never a
central or exclusive rabbinic dogma. The postmortem conception of Olam
Ha-Ba always remained secondary to the view that Olam Ha-Ba was a
collective time of redemption at the end-of-days. Even a thousand years
after the notion of individual postmortem deliverance first appeared in
Judaism, at the time of the Babylonian exile, the prophetic vision of a
future collective redemption still predominated Jewish eschatological
thinking.

Divine Judgment and *Olam Ha-Ba*

Fundamental to all teachings about *Olam Ha-Ba* is the rabbinic doctrine of divine judgment—the idea that with the onset of the World to Come, human beings are subjected to God's reckoning. We find both individual and collective notions of divine judgment coexisting in rabbinic literature. Echoing prophetic eschatology, the Rabbis speak of the judgment of the entire nation at the end-of-time, with the onset of *Olam Ha-Ba*. At the same time, there is an increasingly well-articulated belief that after death each individual person stands in judgment before God.

According to some sources, collective judgment in the World to Come is not only for the people of Israel, but for all nations. Midrash *Tanhuma* teaches that "in *Olam Ha-Ba* the Holy Blessed One will sit with the Elders of Israel like a President of a *Beth Din* and judge gentile nations" (*Tanhuma, Kedoshim* 1).

Another source details the process of judging the gentile nations:

> In *Olam Haba*, the Holy Blessed One will take a scroll of the Torah, set it upon his lap, and say, "Let him who occupied himself therewith come and receive his reward." Immediately the nations of the world gather together and come in disorder. The Holy Blessed One says to them, "Do not enter before Me in disorder, but let each nation present itself together with its teachers." (*Avodah Zarah* 2a)

The text continues and describes how first Rome, then Persia appear before God lauding their many accomplishments in the world. Rome describes the many marketplaces and bathhouses built. Persia claims that many wars have been won and many bridges built. But in the end, both are condemned because they have not accepted the Torah and its principles. Israel, who has accepted the Torah is praised and glorified (*Avodah Zarah* 2a, b). This talmudic text passage reaffirms the fundamental rabbinic belief that learning Torah and serving God through *mitzvot* is the best insurance policy to guarantee benevolent judgment in *Olam Ha-Ba*.

We also find in rabbinic texts the conception of an individual judgment in *Olam Ha-Ba*. According to an early rabbinic source: "You will in *Olam Ha-Ba* have to give account and reckoning before the supreme King of Kings, the Holy Blessed One" (M. *Avot* 4:29). During this experience of postmortem judgment, the individual is shown a review of all the deeds of his or her life (*Taanit* 11a). Based on the merit of his or her actions, the person is duly rewarded or punished: the righteous merit Gan Eden, the Garden of Eden, and the wicked are punished in Gehenna, the realm of punitive retribution (*Midrash Psalms* 31, 120a; *Hagigah* 15a).

The Rabbis also question if it is the body, the soul, or both that will be judged following death. According to one source, it was only the soul:

> In *Olam Ha-Ba* the soul and body will stand in judgment. What will the Holy Blessed One do? He will overlook the body and censure the soul, and when it pleads, "Master of the Universe! The two of us sinned alike, so why do You overlook the body and censure me?" He answers, "The body comes from below where people sin; but you come from above where sin is not committed. Therefore I overlook the body and censure you." (*Leviticus Rabbah* 4:5)

But elsewhere, in an earlier text, the idea is expressed that both body and soul stand before God in judgment:

> The Holy Blessed One puts the soul back into the body and judges them both as a single being. He calls on the heavens to bring forth the soul and he calls on the earth below so that he can judge the body along with it. (*Sanhedrin* 91a)

There are many more texts illuminating the motif of divine judgment. As we explore other rabbinic afterlife conceptions, we will see how this notion of divine judgment is a philosophical underpinning characteristic of the rabbinic worldview as a whole. Even more, the notion of divine judgment, both individual and collective, remained central to Jewish ideas about life after death throughout all subsequent eras of Jewish history.

PHENOMENA OF THE AFTER-DEATH JOURNEY

The Moment of Death, and Beyond

In addition to philosophical speculation on *Olam Ha-Ba*, the Rabbis discussed the death experience and offered a cornucopia of teachings on how they envisioned that sacred event.[19] The legacy they leave to us is neither monolithic nor even normative. Instead, we find a diverse collage of ideas about the death moment and beyond that we will now explore.

First of all, they taught that 903 different kinds of death were created in the world.[20] While the most difficult and painful death is due to the croup, a form of choking, the easiest is a "death by the kiss," a painless departure of the soul, likened to the experience of "drawing a hair out of milk" (*Berakhot* 8a; see also *Mo'ed Katan* 28a). Such is the way of death for the truly righteous person. According to tradition, Abraham, Isaac, Jacob, Aaron, Moses, and Miriam died in this effortless way (*Baba Batra* 17a). But such a gentle death was in no way universally guaranteed. For a wicked person, death could be like "pulling tangled rope through a narrow opening . . . [or] working a nail out of the gullet . . . [or] pulling wool shearings out of thorns" (*Midrash on Psalms* 11:6). Other metaphors describing the death moment suggest that it was believed to be an experience of agitation and travail:

> How does the soul depart? R. Yohanan said: Like rushing waters from a channel (when the sluice bars are raised); R. Hanina said: Like swirling waters from a channel; R. Samuel said: Like a moist and inverted thorn tearing its way out of the throat. (*Ecclesiastes Rabbah* 6: 6, 1)

Repeatedly, the Rabbis leave little doubt that a righteous life is clearly a ticket to a less painful, more blissful type of death. It is said that the righteous are made aware of their day of death, so that "they shall bequeath their crowns to their children" (*Numbers Rabbah* 19:17). In addition, as they are about to depart from this world, God shows the righteous the reward due to them, and they rejoice in such sublime vision (*Exodus Rabbah* 52:3; see also *Genesis Rabbah* 62:2).

A number of other phenomena are reported to occur with the onset of death. At the very moment of death, as the soul leaves the body, there is a reverberating noise made, resounding throughout the world. According to Midrash *Exodus Rabbah*: "There are three sounds which go from one end of the world to the other, yet the creatures therein hear nothing. These are: the day, rain, and the soul when it departs the body" (*Exodus Rabbah* 5:9; see also *Genesis Rabbah* 6:7, *Yoma* 20b). A later midrashic tradition claims there are five instances when this indistinct sound is heard:

The voices of five objects of creation go from one end of the world to the other, and their voices are inaudible. When people cut down the wood of the tree which yields its fruit; when the serpent sloughs off its skin; when a woman is divorced from her husband; when the infant comes forth from its mother's womb; [and] when the soul departs from the body, [in each of these cases] the cry goes forth from one end of the world to another, and the voice is not heard. (*Pirke de Rabbi Eliezer*, chapter 34)

Recognizing the active relationship between the living and the souls of the dead, the Rabbis assert that the roaring sound emitted at the moment of death can be quelled by words of prayer of the sages (*Yoma* 21a).

Exactly where the Rabbis got their information about what happens at the time of death is never discussed. And in no way do they attempt to present a systematic, organized depiction of the dying process itself. What we do find in the Talmud and Midrash are statements revealing quite clearly that existence beyond the limits of mortal life was of vital concern to the Rabbis. Once we begin investigating rabbinic reflections on death and beyond, it becomes instantly obvious that the Rabbis operated from the assumption that there continued to be conscious awareness long after the demise of the body.

The Postmortem Life Review

Another phenomenon of the death moment, according to the Rabbis, is the postmortem life review. At the time of death, an individual is shown a panoramic vision of the deeds of his or her life: "When a man departs to his eternal home all his deeds are enumerated before him and he is told: Such and such a thing have you done, in such and such a place on that day" (*Taanit* 11a). The deceased acknowledges the review of life events, and even signs the record shown to him. Admitting to the justice of the verdict, the individual then says: "Rightly have You judged me" (*Taanit* 11a). In the course of the life review, all the details of a person's life experience are completely revealed. According to the Talmud: "Even superfluous remarks that pass between husband and wife are recorded against him in the hour of death" (*Hagigah* 5b).

How is it that such a vision of life activities is apparent at the time of one's physical demise? According to Midrash *Pesikta Rabbati*, while alive, each individual has angels specifically assigned to keep records of all his or her deeds, both righteous and wicked. Because of this, upon death the inherent truth of one's life is unequivocally apparent and transparent:

> Angels are assigned to every human being. And every day they record his deeds, so that everything he does is known to the Holy Blessed One, and everything is put down on his record and marked with a seal. When a man is righteous, his righteousness is recorded; when a man does wrong, his wrongdoing is recorded. Accordingly, when a righteous man arrives at the end of his days, his recording angels precede him into heaven singing his praise. . . . But when a wicked man dies, a man who did not bring himself to turn in repentance to God, the Holy Blessed One, says to him: "Let your soul be blasted in despair! How many times did I call upon you to repent, and you did not." (*Pesikta Rabbati* 44:8)

What we see here is a clearly articulated rabbinic notion that after death, each person must account directly for his or her actions. This notion of an individual postmortem life review, common in rabbinic literature and also in later kabbalistic texts, has numerous parallels in other religious traditions around the world.[21]

The Angel of Death

Throughout rabbinic literature there are repeated references to an Angel of Death who makes his presence known at the time of one's departure from the world.[22] Although the Hebrew term *malakh ha-mavet* eventually becomes normative in Jewish tradition and the subject of much Jewish folklore,[23] it is clearly a rabbinic creation and does not appear in the Hebrew Bible. There are, however, a few possible biblical antecedents of this motif, embodying the idea that death manifests as a destroying angel, wrenching human beings from the world of the living.

Thus, Proverbs 17:11 uses the term *malakh akhzari*, meaning "a stern messenger," and it is understood in this context as a personification of death. In 2 Kings 19:35, Isaiah 37:36, and 1 Chronicles 21:12, 30, the angel who wreaks mortal devastation upon humanity is given the appellation "Angel of YHVH," suggesting that God actively appoints a celestial messenger to bring the destruction of death to human beings. Elsewhere, in 2 Samuel 24:16 and 1 Chronicles 21:15 another phrase appears, *malakh ha-mashkhit*, "the destroying angel," which seems to most clearly represent a forerunner to the rabbinic conception of the Angel of Death.[24]

In later rabbinic literature (*Targum Jonathan*, Genesis 3:6; *Deuteronomy Rabbah* 11:10) the Angel of Death is given the name Samael, derived from a combination of the words *sam*, meaning "poison," and *el*, meaning "God"; hence, the angel of god who brings about the poison of death. This idea developed out of a belief that Samael, the Angel of Death, terminates the life of a person by the use of drops of gall or wormwood poison, often inflicted with a sword.[25] This motif, expressed quite clearly in the following talmudic passage, is developed even further in the ornate mythological afterlife texts of the medieval period:

> It is said of the Angel of Death that he is full of eyes. When a sick person is about to depart, he stands above his head-pillow with his sword drawn out of his hand, and a drop of gall hanging on it. As the sick person beholds it, he trembles and opens his mouth [in fright]; he then drops it into his mouth. It is from this that he dies, from this that [the corpse] deteriorates, from this that his face becomes greenish. (*Avodah Zarah* 20b)

Obviously an ominous creature whose impending presence was often announced by the howling of dogs (*Baba Kamma* 60b), the Angel of Death was equated with the primary human enemies—Satan and the evil inclination *yetzer hara* (*Baba Batra* 16a). In fact, in many cases the terms Satan, *malakh ha-mavet*, Samael, and *yetzer hara* are utilized interchangeably.[26]

Notwithstanding the viciousness of this messenger of doom, there were methods for keeping the Angel of Death at bay, the two principal ones being giving charity and learning Torah. According to one source: "When anyone dispenses righteous charity in secret, God diverts the Angel of Death from him and the members of his household" (*Midrash Proverbs* 21:14; see also *Baba Batra* 11a, *Shabbat* 156b). Additionally, it was taught that at the time of the giving of the Torah at Sinai, the Angel of Death held no power over the Israelites (*Pirke de Rabbi Eliezer*, 47; see also *Avodah Zarah* 5a). As a consequence, engaging in the study of Torah was almost always a potent and efficacious technique for warding off the malevolent executing angel. Legend has it that King David was able to elude the Angel of Death through unrelenting immersion in the

Torah. As the end of King David's life approached, "every Sabbath day he would sit and study all day. On the day that his soul was to be at rest, the Angel of Death stood before him but could not prevail against him because learning did not cease from his mouth" (*Shabbat* 30b). Only by deceptively distracting him from his studies was the infamous *malakh ha-mavet* finally able to claim the soul of Israel's second king.

Other Angels Encountered at the Time of Death

Besides *malakh ha-mavet*, other angelic beings are involved in the process of death. One cohort of the Angel of Death is Dumah, caretaker of the souls of the departed. The two collaborate, and Dumah's responsibilities begin when the Angel of Death completes his work:

> [After the Angel of Death removes the soul from a person's body] the man dies right away, but his spirit comes out and sits on the tip of the nose until the body begins to decay. As decay sets in, the spirit, weeping, cries out to the Holy Blessed One, saying: "Master of the universe, where am I to be taken?" Immediately Dumah takes the spirit and carries it to the courtyard of the dead, to join the other spirits. (*Midrash on Psalms* 11:6; see also *Hagigah* 5a, *Berakhot* 18b, *Shabbat* 152b)

Also involved in the postmortem process of the soul are the recording angels, mentioned earlier, who chronicle the life history of each person. At the time of death, these angels present to God the cumulative record of a person's life; based on that tally sheet, each individual is given due reward or punishment.

In addition, the Talmud maintains that after death, two other angels stand at either end of the world and toss the souls of the wicked back and forth, traversing the entire distance from one end of the earth to the other (*Shabbat* 152b). Elsewhere, it is taught that at the moment of death, a trio of angelic beings accompany the soul of the deceased individual. According to Midrash *Pesikta Rabbati*:

> The elder R. Hiyya said: "When a holy man leaves this world, three companies of angels attend him, one saying: "Let him come in peace" (Isaiah 57:2); another saying: "Let him rest in his bed" (Isaiah 57:2); and another walking before him in silence, as the verse concludes

"walking before him" (Ibid.). (*Pesikta Rabbati* 2:3; see also *Ketubbot* 104a)

As is typical of rabbinic literature, we never see any formally standardized teachings about the events occurring after death, nor any about the various angels said to be part of the postmortem experience. But what we do find in this legendary material are mythological images of the afterlife that are frequently expounded upon in later medieval Midrash, as well as in kabbalistic literature.

FATE OF THE DEAD IN THE GRAVE

Do the Dead Feel Pain?

Another topic broached in rabbinic discourse was whether the dead have any conscious awareness, more specifically, whether the body actually experienced physical pain after being laid to rest in the grave. Although there were divergent opinions on this issue, the prevailing belief among the Rabbis was that the body of the deceased maintained sensitivity for some time after death.[27] This point of view is attributed to a saying in the name of Rabbi Isaac, who asserted that "worms are as painful to the dead as a needle in the flesh of the living" (*Berakhot* 18b; *Shabbat* 13b). According to the Rabbis, the process of experiencing pain in the grave had the function of enabling atonement for sins committed while alive.[28] Thus, tractate *Sanhedrin* teaches: "The atonement of man for his sins starts from the moment the body begins to feel the pains [of the pressure] of the grave" (*Sanhedrin* 47b). The term here for "pains of the grave" in Aramaic is *tzarah de-kavra*. While this notion is not developed any further during the talmudic era, as we will see in subsequent chapters, the belief that a physical, body-centered purification process occurs soon after death was developed quite significantly in later Jewish tradition.

Are the Dead Aware of the Living?

Also of concern to the Rabbis was the extent to which spirits of the dead were cognizant of the living. A variety of talmudic anecdotes suggest that, in point of fact, this was the case.[29] For example, it is said that the Babylonian sage Rav told his colleague Rabbi Samuel ben Shilath: "Be fervent in my funeral eulogy, for I will be standing there" (*Shabbat* 152b). In addition, the Talmud maintains that when a deceased sage is acknowledged for his teaching, or when a *halakhah*, a Jewish legal ordinance, is uttered in his name, then the lips of that person move gently while in the grave (*Sanhedrin* 90b; *Yebamot* 97a).

Rabbi Abahu was of the belief that the deceased could hear all that was said in their presence until the lid of the grave was sealed. Other Rabbis disagreed, asserting that the dead continued to hear the living until the process of physical decomposition had taken place (*Shabbat* 152b). These two differing points of view were based on different proof texts:

> He who says, until the flesh rots away—because it is written, "But his flesh upon him has pain, and his soul within him mourns" [Job 14:22]. He who says, until the top-stone [i.e. coffin lid][30] closes [the grave], because it is written, "and the dust returns to the earth as it was [and the spirit returns unto God]" [Ecclesiastes 12:7]. (*Shabbat* 152b)

Elsewhere, it is apparent that the operating rabbinic belief is that the dead communicate with both the human realm (*Baba Batra* 58a) and the heavenly realms (*Baba Metzia* 85b), wherein they petition for mercy on behalf of the living (*Taanit* 16a). Thus, in one instance, it was reported that after his death, Rabbi Yossi appeared to Rabbi Ze'iri in a dream and informed him about the various Rabbis with whom he kept company in the Heavenly Academy (*Baba Metzia* 85b).

The following lengthy anecdote communicates a clear belief in the ongoing interaction between the living and the dead and affirms the rabbinic view that spirits of the deceased continue to have awareness long after burial in the grave:

> It is related that a certain pious man gave a *denar* to a poor man on the eve of New Year in a year of drought, and his wife scolded him, and he went and passed the night in the cemetery, and he heard two spirits conversing with one another. Said one to her companion: My dear, come and let us wander about the world and let us hear from behind the curtain [screening the Divine Presence] what suffering is coming on in the world [in the aftermath of the divine judgment at the time of the New Year]. Said her companion to her: I am not

able, because I am buried in a matting of reeds. But do you go, and whatever you hear tell me. So the other went and wandered about and returned.

Said her companion to her: My dear, what have you heard from behind the curtain? She replied: I heard that whoever sows after the first rainfall will have his crop smitten by hail. So the man went and did not sow until after the second rainfall, with the result that everyone else's crop was smitten and his was not smitten. The next year he again went and passed the night in the cemetery, and heard the two spirits conversing with one another. Said one to her companion: Come and let us wander about the world and hear from behind the curtain what punishment is coming upon the world. Said the other to her: My dear, did I not tell you that I am not able because I am buried in a matting of reeds? But do you go, and whatever you hear, come and tell me. So the other went and wandered about and returned.

She said to her: My dear, what have you heard from behind the curtain? She replied: I heard that whoever sows after the later rains will have his crop smitten with blight. So the man went and sowed after the first rain with the result that everyone else's crop was blighted and his was not blighted. Said his wife to him: How is it that last year everyone else's crop was smitten and yours was not smitten, and this year everyone else's crop is blighted and yours is not blighted? So he related to her all his experiences.

The story goes that shortly afterward a quarrel broke out between the wife of that pious man and the mother of the child [whose spirit the man had heard conversing in the cemetery], and the former said to the latter, Come and I will show you your daughter buried in a matting of reeds. The next year the man again went and spent the night in the cemetery and heard those conversing together. One said: My dear, come and let us wander about the world and hear from behind the curtain what suffering is coming upon the world. Said the other: My dear, leave me alone; our conversation has already been heard among the living. . . . This would prove that they know? Perhaps some other man after his decease went and told them. (*Berakhot* 18b; see also *Avot de Rabbi Natan* 3)

In the same vein is the following story:

Ze'iri deposited some money with his landlady, and while he was away visiting Rab she died. So he went after her to the cemetery and said to her, Where is my money? She replied to him: Go and take it from under the ground, in the hole of the doorpost in such and such a place, and tell my mother to send me my comb and my tube of eye-paint by the hand of So-and-so who is coming here today. (*Berakhot* 18b)

Necromancy

Even with the folk-level belief in spirits of the dead, the Rabbis still had to wrestle with the issue of necromancy and the practice of formal spiritistic communion. Although the kinds of stories we have just read were plentiful among the Jews of Babylonia and Palestine, at the same time, the Rabbis were the beneficiaries of the ancient biblical injunction against communication with the dead, as expressed in both Leviticus and Deuteronomy. This prohibition was forcefully rearticulated in the Mishnah:

> A *baal ob* [he that has a familiar spirit] is the pithom [ventriloquist, necromancer] who speaks from his armpit. The *yidd'oni* [wizard] is one who speaks from his mouth. These two are stoned; while he who inquires of them transgresses a formal prohibition. (M. *Sanhedrin* 7:7)

Within the Talmud we see that the practice of necromancy was discussed quite openly, as the Rabbis attempted to develop their own understanding of the ancient biblical terms *baal ob* and *yidd'oni*—necromancers and wizards (*Sanhedrin* 65a–65b). While Rabbi Katrina called necromancers liars and blatantly denied any truth in necromancy (*Berakhot* 59a), this was in no way a widespread view. On the whole, we do not find a denial of the practice of calling up spirits from the dead, and one individual—a proselyte named Onkelos ben Kalonymous—raised up from the dead the soul of Emperor Titus (*Gittin* 56b). The likelihood is that the Rabbis maintained a middle-of-the-road position with regard to necromancy: not officially accepting it as a formal practice within the canon of Jewish law, but at the same time not overtly discrediting the practice of necromantic incantation, which probably did have folk-level support.[31]

Experiences of the Soul in the Days Following Death

Another concern addressed by the Rabbis is the fate of the soul of the deceased in the subsequent days after death. On this theme, we find a number of sources indicating that initially—during the first three days—

the soul remains in close proximity to the body, trying to reenter it. However, with the onset of physical decomposition, the soul departs and continues its postmortem wanderings.[32] We find two statements in the Midrash specifically asserting this point of view:

> Bar Kappara taught: Until three days [after death] the soul keeps on returning to the grave, think that it will go back [into the body]; but when it sees that the facial features have become disfigured, it departs and abandons it [the body]. (*Genesis Rabbah* 100:7)

> R. Abba ben R. Pappai and R. Joshua of Siknin said in the name of R. Levi: For three days after death the soul hovers over the body, intending to reenter it, but as soon as it sees its appearance change, it departs. (*Leviticus Rabbah* 18:1)

Another midrashic text speaks of a seven-day period in which the soul sojourns back and forth from the gravesite where the body is interred to its former home base:

> All the seven days of mourning the soul goes forth and returns from its former home to its sepulchral abode, and from its sepulchral abode to its former home. After the seven days of mourning, the body begins to breed worms and it decays and returns to dust as it originally was . . . and returns to the place whence it was given, from heaven, as it is said, "And the soul returns unto God who gave it" [Ecclesiastes 12:7]. (*Pirke de Rabbi Eliezer*, chapter 34)

What we see going on here is the early development of rabbinic traditions about the postmortem wanderings of the soul. Eventually, in the kabbalistic period, these ideas are developed even further.

However, for now, as we continue to map out the motifs of the afterlife in rabbinic Judaism, we will explore teachings about the postmortem realms of Gehenna and Gan Eden.

GEHENNA—THE REALM
OF POSTMORTEM PUNISHMENT

Names of Gehenna

Central to the afterlife teachings of the Rabbis is the notion of Gehenna, or Gehinnom,[33] the biblically derived appellation for the realm of postmortem punishment. Whereas in apocryphal literature both Sheol and Gehenna appear interchangeably, in the rabbinic era Gehenna is the term used most frequently to describe the afterlife realm of punitive retribution. Given a great deal of attention in rabbinic literature, the concept of Gehenna rapidly emerged as a central pillar of Jewish afterlife belief.

In the tractate *Erubin*, Rabbi Joshua ben Levi lists seven of the original names for Gehenna, basing each on a specific biblical passage: Sheol (Jonah 2:2); *Abbadon*, or Destruction (Psalm 88:12); *Be'er Shakhat*, or Corruption (Psalm 16:10); *Bor Sha'on*, or Horrible Pit and *Tit Ha-Yaven*, or Miry Clay (Psalm 40:3); *Tzalmavet*, or Shadow of Death (Psalm 107:10); and *Eretz Ha-Takhtit*, the Netherworld, which is a tradition[34] (*Erubin* 19a). These seven names are not fixed and others are used elsewhere. According to *Midrash on Psalms*, the seven names of Gehenna are Sheol, Abbadon (Destruction), *Tzalmavet* (Shadow of Death), *Eretz Takhtit* (Netherworld), *Eretz Neshiyah* (Realm of Forgetfulness), Gehinnom, and *Dumah* (Silence) (*Midrash on Psalms* 11:6).[35]

As traditions about Gehenna evolved, the seven different names came to represent seven different regions or stories within Gehenna, to which the wicked dead are judiciously dispatched. Thus, according to one source: "Behold! There are seven habitations for the wicked . . . according to their works . . ." (*Midrash on Psalms* 11:6). While we do not find any earlier apocryphal tradition about seven levels of Sheol, it may well be that 4 Ezra 7:80–81, the Salathiel Apocalypse, is a precursor to this idea that there are seven realms in which the wicked are punished. There we find mention of seven different ways the wicked grieve for their sins:

> And if it is one of those who have shown scorn and not kept the way of the Most High, and who have despised his Law, and who have hated those who fear God—such spirits shall not enter into habitations but shall immediately wander about in torments, ever grieving and sad in seven ways. (4 Ezra 7:80–81)

Origins of Gehenna

The Rabbis had a sense of time that was more often mythical than historical. Even though, as a philosophical concept, the notion of Gehenna did not appear before the sixth century B.C.E. and there is absolutely no mention of this postmortem realm in the creation narratives of Genesis, it was no problem for the Rabbis to assert that Gehenna was fashioned on the second day of creation, along with the firmament, angels, and fire (*Genesis Rabbah* 4:6, 11:9).

Other teachings within rabbinic literature went even further, asserting that Gehenna was included in the original design of the universe and is among the seven things created before the world (*Pesahim* 54a; *Midrash on Proverbs* 8:22; *Sifre Deuteronomy* 37).[36] According to one tradition, the creation of Gehenna actually predates creation by two thousand years (*Midrash on Psalms* 90:12). These kinds of conflicting traditions were neither uncommon nor problematic for the Rabbis, and certainly not of ultimate importance to their understanding of Gehenna.

Gehenna and the Ethical Worldview of Rabbinic Judaism

When the Rabbis discuss Gehenna, characteristically, they are concerned with the ethical and moral implications of this afterlife realm. The idea of a world of postmortem punishment was very real to the Rabbis and their disciples. They saw Gehenna as an abode of punishment for the person who did not live a righteous life in accordance with the ways of God and Torah (*Exodus Rabbah* 2:2). That belief was central to their daily lives. Although the Rabbis did define the nature of Gehenna itself, and with increasingly precise detail, the plethora of rabbinic teachings on Gehenna were meant to inspire an individual to lead an ethical life and to practice the fulfillment of *mitzvot*, or commandments. At every point, the intention behind the doctrine of Gehenna was not to infuse life with fear, but to encourage godliness and holy acts. Ultimately, threat of punishment in Gehenna was used by the rabbinic leaders to motivate the ordinary, average Jew to engage wholeheartedly in a life of Torah and *mitzvot*.

Throughout rabbinic literature, the Rabbis dealt with questions about who would and who would not be condemned to the punishment and retribution of Gehenna. Not surprisingly, the scholarly Rabbis claimed that a person who makes scoffing, "derogatory remarks about a scholar after [his] death is cast into Gehenna" (*Berakhot* 19a). Other people, who were obviously part of their daily milieu, such as the rich men of Babylon (*Betzah* 32b), a teacher who "causes a community to sin" (*Yoma* 89a), one who practices idolatrous worship (*Taanit* 5a), and a person who speaks lewdly (*Shabbat* 33a), were all believed to be condemned to Gehenna.

In the day-to-day dealings of the world, even one learned in Torah had to avoid specific activities or behaviors that might cause one to merit Gehenna. Thus, we find the following talmudic teaching, which gives a glimpse of the values and ethics of the Rabbis:

> If a man counts money from his hand into the hand of a woman so as to have the opportunity of gazing at her, even if he can vie in Torah and good deeds with Moses our teacher, he shall not escape the punishment of Gehenna. (*Berakhot* 61a)

Other sins that, according to the Rabbis, brought upon oneself the postmortem punishments of Gehenna were incest (*Erubin* 19a), idolatry (*Taanit* 5a; *Midrash on Proverbs* 6:1), adultery (*Sotah* 4b), pride (*Avodah Zarah* 18b), haughtiness (*Baba Batra* 10b), anger and losing one's temper (*Nedarim* 22a), teaching a pupil who was not worthy (*Hullin* 133a), and following the advice of one's wife (*Baba Metzia* 59a).[37]

Even though they articulated high standards of morality, the Rabbis were practical-minded people and often proposed specific actions and spiritual practices that individuals could make use of in their daily lives in order to avoid Gehenna. This is spelled out in general terms in the *Midrash on Proverbs* where Rabbi Eliezer asks Rabbi Joshua: "What should a man do to escape the judgment of Gehenna?" The reply, quite simply, was: "Let him occupy himself with good deeds" (*Midrash on Proverbs* 17:1). In a similar vein, another text suggests that "he who has Torah, good deeds, humility and fear of heaven will be saved from punishment [in Gehenna]" (*Pesikta Rabbati* 50:1). While the study of Torah is undeniably an important method for avoiding Gehenna—"people who study Torah will be released from torments of Gehenna" (*Midrash on Proverbs* 1:5, 2:21)—in some cases, Torah alone is not sufficient:

> If the person who comes before God has [knowledge of] Torah in hand, but none of Mishnah, God turns his face away from him, whereupon the wardens of Gehenna overpower him like wolves of the steppe, fall upon him, and fling him into its midsts. (*Midrash on Proverbs* 10:17)

The Rabbis enumerate a variety of other specific activities that can help a person avoid the punishments of Gehenna: giving charity, sharing one's bread with the poor, tithing money to teachers and their pupils, and developing an attitude of humility (*Pesikta Rabbati* 50:1).[38] In addition, the Talmud teaches that visiting the sick (*Nedarim* 40a), teaching Torah to the son of an ignoramus (*Baba Metzia* 85a),[39] and observing the commandments of eating three meals on the Sabbath (*Shabbat* 118a), all work to save a person from the retribution of Gehenna. Even more, tractate *Berakhot* describes a simple practice that anyone can follow, that is, saying the Shema not only daily (*Berakhot* 15b), but with clarity: "If in reciting the Shema, one pronounces the letters distinctly, Gehenna is cooled for him" (*Berakhot* 15a). Finally, even to the very last, there remains the rabbinic belief in the possibility of personal redemption by turning back to God through *teshuvah*, or repentance. The Talmud teaches that even at the very gates of Gehenna, it is still possible to repent before God, receive divine mercy, and be granted exemption from the realm of postmortem punishment (*Erubin* 19a).

The theology behind the Rabbis' view of Gehenna seems quite simple: a person who sins merits the punishment of Gehenna; but Gehenna can be avoided by practicing a whole system of good deeds, or ethical actions, that is, the *mitzvot*.

Within the rabbinic worldview, Gehenna was neither a fixed nor a guaranteed experience after death. In addition to the benevolent actions in one's life, in certain cases, there were other ways of being exempted from the torments of Gehenna. For example, if a person's life was filled with suffering—such as the case of a poor person, one afflicted with bowel diseases, or one held in captivity by an oppressive government—then such an individual would be exempt from "seeing the face of Gehenna" (*Erubin* 41b). At the root of the rabbinic notion of Gehenna was an idea of an equitable sense of divine justice in operation, which, although not always obvious in life, would be made apparent to everyone upon death.

Duration of Punishment in Gehenna

The Rabbis often discuss the duration of punishment in Gehenna. The generally accepted belief was that the punitive tortures of Gehenna are time-limited, not eternal. Eternal punishment was never accepted as a doctrinal belief in rabbinic Judaism. Gehenna was conceived of as a temporary abode widely believed to last a maximum of twelve months. This idea is reflected in both early and later texts.

The tractate *Shabbat* stipulates that "the punishment of the wicked in Gehenna is twelve months" (*Shabbat* 33b). Similarly, we find elsewhere in the Talmud the view that both Jewish and gentile sinners are sent to Gehenna and punished there for a period of twelve months (*Rosh Ha-*

Shanah 17a). Even the generation of the Flood, among the more notorious evildoers in biblical history, were believed to have spent only a maximum of twelve months in the Gehenna (M. *Eduyyot* 2:10; *Genesis Rabbah* 28:8).

However, rabbinic literature does assert that certain classes of sinners are eternally condemned to Gehenna. In particular, heretics, informers, and scoffers (Hebrew: *epikorsim*), as well as people who have rejected the words of Torah and denied the belief in the resurrection, are sentenced to Gehenna "for all generations" (*Rosh Ha-Shanah* 17a). Another tradition maintains that only "one who commits adultery with a married woman, publicly shames his neighbor, or fastens an evil epithet upon his neighbor" descends to Gehenna and never reascends (*Baba Metzia* 58b).

Even though there is evidence of a belief in the enduring punishment of Gehenna, it is accurate to say that the notion of eternal damnation never became predominant within the rabbinic worldview. The Rabbis always maintained that in addition to its punitive aspects, Gehenna served as a realm of purgation and purification. During the twelve-month period in Gehenna, the soul goes through a process of purification and atonement, and, as described in Midrash *Pesikta Rabbati*, "after going down to Gehenna and receiving the punishment due him, the sinner is forgiven from all his iniquities, and like an arrow from the bow he is flung forth from Gehenna" (*Pesikta Rabbati* 53:2). After this experience, the soul is sufficiently purified and able to enter the supernal postmortem realm of Gan Eden, the Garden of Eden (*Exodus Rabbah* 7:4).

This belief stands in sharp contrast to the Christian notion of hell and damnation reflected in St. Augustine's *City of God*, an eschatological text from this same time period, c. fourth century.[40] Whereas St. Augustine's teachings have influenced Christian (and hence, Western) society by emphasizing the notion that sin leads to eternal suffering in hell, rabbinic sources, on the other hand, definitely did not exclusively focus on punishment and damnation but rather always taught that Gehenna was a transitional purificatory experience for the soul. As we will see in subsequent chapters, this idea is developed even further in the medieval period.

Diverse Characteristics of Gehenna

In addition to the ethical aspects of the concept of Gehenna, rabbinic writings portray a variety of imagistic impressions of this postmortem domain of retribution and torment. Talmudic and midrashic texts provide descriptive detail on the characteristics, qualities, and dimensions of Gehenna and the types of punishments received in that realm. Of course, there is never one consistent picture or image presented. Instead, rabbinic tradition builds on earlier textual material, continually changing and diversifying the descriptions of Gehenna.

The best way to capture the rabbinic style is through the following collage of texts portraying various mythic images of Gehenna.[41]

The Dimensions of Gehenna

While certain rabbinic teachers claim that Gehenna "had no limit in size" (*Taanit* 10a), others attempt to portray the dimensions of this realm, at least in relative terms. Thus, the Talmud also teaches that

> the world is a sixtieth a part of Gan Eden and Gan Eden is a sixtieth a part of Gehenna; consequently the whole world is in comparison to like the lid of a pot. Some declare that Gan Eden is limitless in extent and others say the same of Gehenna. (*Taanit* 10a)

But generally, the dimensions of Gehenna cannot be fixed with great precision. In fact, another tradition has it that Gehenna itself can expand in proportion to the number of wicked sinners:

> The wicked say tauntingly, "How many myriads can Gehenna hold? Two hundred myriads? Three hundred myriads? How can it ever hold the many myriads more of the wicked who appear in every generation?" To them the Holy Blessed One replies: By your downfall! As you increase in the world, Gehenna, too, increases, growing wider and deeper and broader every day. (*Pesikta Rabbati* 41:3)

Location of Gehenna

Generally, the Rabbis assumed that Gehenna was to be found beneath the earth. A number of early rabbinic texts speak of how sinners "go down to Gehenna" (*Rosh Ha-Shanah* 16b; M. *Avot* 5:22). This idea that Gehenna is found in a subterranean region is, in all probability, a vestige of the biblical notion that Sheol is beneath the earth, in the ground where the dead reside.[42]

The Rabbis were not content simply to accept that Gehenna was beneath the earth; they also reflected upon where it might be found. Some suggested it existed in the East, others that it was in the West (*Baba Batra* 84b). One tradition locates Gehenna "above the firmament" (*Tamid* 32b); another suggests it was found "at the left hand of God" (*Pesikta de-Rav Kahana* 191a).

Entrances to Gehenna

According to one tradition there are seven doors of entry into Gehenna (*Pirkei de Rabbi Eliezer*, chapter 53). But in no way is this a fixed number, and according to another source, there are three entrances to Gehenna:

> Gehenna has three [entrances]: One in the wilderness, a second in the sea, and a third in Jerusalem. Another tradition tells, there are two date-palms in the valley of Ben-Hinnom from between which smoke ascends and that is the entrance of Gehenna. (*Erubin* 19a)

Another midrashic text claims there are two gates of entry into the postmortem realm of retribution:

> R. Abba bar Kahana taught: Sheol [i.e., Gehenna] has two gates, an inner and an outer. Whenever a man's life is taken without God's permission [as by suicide or murder], his soul must finish out in the outer regions of Sheol [i.e., Gehenna] the remainder of the years he was to live. That Sheol [i.e., Gehenna] has more than one gate [i.e., several regions] is intimated in the verse: "I said: In the noontide of my days I shall go, even to the gates of Sheol" (Isaiah 38:10). (*Pesikta Rabbati* 24:1)

Elements of Gehenna—Fire, Snow, Hail

Of the various elements of Gehenna, the principal one is a fire of abnormal intensity: "[Ordinary] fire is a sixtieth of [the fire of] Gehenna" (*Berakhot* 57b). And:

> "A fiery stream issued forth and came before Him" [Daniel 7:10]. Whence does it originate? From the sweat of the holy *Hayyot*. And whence does it empty itself? Upon the heads of the wicked in Gehenna; as it is said, "It shall burst upon the head of the wicked" [Jeremiah 23:19]. (*Hagigah* 13a)

In another instance it is stated that "Gehenna is half fire and half hail" (*Exodus Rabbah* 51:7). And elsewhere, another opinion includes the element of snow:

> The Holy Blessed One judges the wicked in Gehenna for twelve months. At first he afflicts them with itching; after that with fire, at which they cry out "O! O!" and then with snow, at which they cry out "Woe! Woe!" (P. *Sanhedrin* 29b)

Elements of Gehenna—Brimstone and Smoke

Another element of Gehenna is brimstone: "Why does a man's soul shrink from the odor of brimstone? Because it knows that it will be judged therein in the World to Come" (*Genesis Rabbah* 51:3).

In addition, there is the element of smoke: "Gehenna is narrow on the top and wide below" (*Sifre Deuteronomy* 35:7, 149b); the reason for this is "its mouth is narrow so that its smoke may be retained therein" (*Menahot* 99b).

Darkness of Gehenna

Finally, there are numerous textual references to Gehenna as a place of darkness:

> The wicked are darkness, Gehenna is darkness, the depths are darkness. I lead the wicked to Gehenna and cover them with the depths. (*Genesis Rabbah* 33:1)

> They who descend to Gehenna will be judged by nothing else than darkness; as it is said, "A land of darkness, as darkness itself" [Job 10:22]. (*Tanhuma, Noah* 1)

> And Moses stretched forth his hand toward heaven, and there was thick darkness [Exodus 10:22]. Where did the darkness originate? From the darkness of Gehenna. (*Tanhuma, Bo* 2)

> With what are the wicked covered in Gehenna? With darkness . . . "And darkness was upon the face of the deep" [Genesis 1:2]. This refers to Gehenna—a proof that the darkness which came upon the Egyptians was from Gehenna. (*Exodus Rabbah* 14:3)

What we have delineated here is only a cross section of the imagery associated with Gehenna. Teachings about Gehenna were integral to rabbinic ideas about life after death, and the Rabbis took a great deal of "theological license" in painting a wretched and forlorn picture of life in Gehenna. From what we have seen here, the Rabbis certainly had a far more elaborate notion of Gehenna than is found in either biblical or apocryphal tradition. But rabbinic Judaism was only a stopping point along the way in developing Jewish conceptions of a realm of postmortem torment. Later generations—both the medieval midrashists and the kabbalists—delineated the topography of Gehenna, and its multifaceted types of suffering, anguish, and torture with even more loathsome and lurid detail.

GAN EDEN AND BEYOND

The Location and Creation of Gan Eden

Yet another term used in rabbinic literature to refer to the afterlife is *Gan Eden*, the Garden of Eden. This term first appears in the Hebrew Bible, although there it is never used as a postmortem concept.[43] Apocryphal literature, as we have seen, does make use of the term to describe a mythical afterlife realm. By the time of the Talmud and Midrash, we find within Judaism a proliferation of teachings describing the qualities and characteristics of Gan Eden.

Rabbinic teachings speak of two different Gardens of Eden: one, the celestial Garden of Eden, is where the souls of the righteous dwell; the other, located in the terrestrial spheres, is a garden of lush vegetation and abundant fertility. The boundaries between these two realms are not always clearly discernible.[44] Is paradise to be found in the celestial realms? Or upon the earth?

There are talmudic teachings that are based on the geographical parameters delineated in Genesis 2:10–14, which specifically locate Gan Eden on earth. Thus, we find in tractate *Erubin*: "If Gan Eden is located in the Land of Israel its entrance is Beth-Shean; if in Arabia its entrance is Beth-Gerem" (*Erubin* 19a). Another tradition teaches that Gan Eden is found in Africa (*Tamid* 32b). However, through the course of history, Gan Eden has come to be understood primarily as a heavenly realm where the souls of the righteous reside.

Typical of rabbinic literature, there are often opposing and contradictory traditions regarding Gan Eden. For example, one generally accepted
belief was that Gan Eden had existed prior to creation. Teachings delineated in both Talmud and Midrash claim that "seven things were created
before the world was created: Torah, repentance, the Garden of Eden,
Gehenna, the Throne of Glory, the Temple and the name of the Messiah"
(*Pesahim* 54a; see also *Midrash on Proverbs* 8:22, *Sifre Deuteronomy* 37,
Nedarim 39b, and *Pirke de Rabbi Eliezer*, chapter 3). Another tradition,
however, places the creation of Gan Eden on the third day:

> The Holy Blessed One created three objects on each day: on the first,
> heaven and earth and light; on the second, the firmament, Gehenna
> and the angels; on the third, trees, herbs and the Garden of Eden.
> (*Genesis Rabbah* 11:9)

Within the ethical-retributive schema of rabbinic Judaism, Gan
Eden and Gehenna are intrinsically related to each other. "Why has God
created Gan Eden and Gehenna?" asks a sixth-century Midrash. "That
one might deliver from the other" (*Pesikta de-Rav Kahana* 30, 191b) is
the answer. Another Midrash suggests that the link between them is not
only spiritual but also geographic. According to *Pesikta Rabbati*,

> Why did the Holy Blessed One create Gehenna and Gan Eden? So
> that one can behold the other. How much space is between them?
> R. Yohanan said: The breadth of a wall. R. Hanina said: The breadth
> of a hand. But the Rabbis said: The two are right up against each
> other. (*Pesikta Rabbati* 52:3)

With regard to the relationship between these two realms, a Midrash
states quite simply: for the person "who treasures up religious acts and
good deeds, behold there is Gan Eden; while for him who does not lay
up religious acts and good deeds, behold there is Gehenna" (*Genesis
Rabbah* 11:9). Similarly, in a passage from *Exodus Rabbah* it is taught that
"he who keeps the Torah has entry to Gan Eden, but he who does not
keep it is faced with Gehenna" (*Exodus Rabbah* 2:2).

Before the righteous enter Gan Eden, God shows them the place
they might have merited in Gehenna; similarly, the wicked sentenced to
Gehenna are first shown the place they might have been accorded in Gan
Eden (*Midrash on Psalms* 6:6, 31:6). Thus, according to rabbinic thought,
just as Gehenna serves as a reminder and a warning for the righteous of

the dangers of straying from God's ways, Gan Eden exists to provide inspiration for sinners to lead a holy, God-fearing life. It is this ethical theme that underlies the rabbinic doctrine of Gan Eden.

Gan Eden: Messianic or Postmortem?

As we found with the notion of *Olam Ha-Ba*, it is not always clear whether the Rabbis conceived of Gan Eden as a postmortem or a posthistorical realm, as an afterlife domain, or as a utopian paradise inaugurated through divine redemption of the human plane. In numerous rabbinic sources, it is obvious that the righteous enter Gan Eden, not after death, but at the time of *Olam Ha-Ba*—at the end-of-days. This is very clear in the statement found in *Exodus Rabbah*: "[I]n the Messianic Age God will establish peace for [the nations] and they will sit at ease and eat in Gan Eden" (*Exodus Rabbah* 15:7). Other sources speak of how, in the *Olam Ha-Ba* of the future, the righteous in Gan Eden will experience great delight and joy in being in the presence of God:

> In *Olam Ha-Ba* the Holy Blessed One will arrange a dance for the righteous in Gan Eden, He sitting in their midst; and each one will point to Him with his fingers, exclaiming, "Lo, this is our God, and we have waited for Him and He will save us; this is the Lord, we have waited for Him, we will be glad and rejoice in His salvation" [Isaiah 25:9]. (*Taanit* 31a)
>
> In *Olam Ha-Ba*, the Holy Blessed One will prepare a banquet for the righteous in Gan Eden, and there will be no need to provide balsam or perfumes, because a north wind and a south wind will sweep through and sprinkle all the romantic plants of Gan Eden so that they will yield their fragrance. (*Numbers Rabbah* 13:2)

Because the above two passages do not make reference to the dead in any way, it is not clear whether the Gan Eden referred to is seen as a final resting place for the dead; there is also the possibility that it is an intermediate abode where the righteous wait until the time of resurrection. This kind of obscurity highlights the ongoing dilemma we continue to find when studying Jewish afterlife teachings, a problem that is inherent in the nature of Jewish eschatology. Given the strength of the belief in the resurrection of the dead, which is central to rabbinic thought, we can assume, however, that these passages refer to a Gan Eden at the end-of-days, and not to an individual, immortal afterlife realm.

However, under the influence of the Greek doctrine of the preexistence of the soul, the conception that souls enter an immortal afterlife
continued to infuse itself into rabbinic tradition.[45] As a result, we find
other strands of rabbinic teachings that indicate that the soul of the departed person enters Gan Eden immediately after death.[46] For example,
Pesikta Rabbati speaks of the righteous people who study Torah, and

> everyday of their lives, with all parts of their bodies, bless, hallow,
> and proclaim My [God's] oneness—these, when they die, I lay down
> with great honor under the tree of life in Gan Eden; and I give them
> rest in their graves. (*Pesikta Rabbati* 50:1)

Undoubtedly, the Gan Eden here is an afterlife realm.

Similarly, there is a famous talmudic legend about the death of Rabbi
Yohanan ben Zakkai. Just prior to passing from this world, ben Zakkai
questions whether he will enter Gehenna, or Gan Eden, and it is clear
he is talking about a postmortem Gan Eden. The legend is as follows:

> When R. Yohanan ben Zakkai fell ill, his disciples went into to visit
> him. When he saw them he began to weep. His disciples said to him:
> "Lamp of Israel, pillar of the right hand, mighty hammer! Why are
> you weeping?" He replied: "If I were being taken today before a king
> of flesh and blood who is here today and tomorrow in the grave,
> whose anger, if he should be angry with me, does not last forever,
> who if he imprisons me, does not imprison me forever and who, if he
> puts me to death does not put me to everlasting death, and whom I
> can persuade with words and bribe with money, even so I would
> weep. Now that I am being taken before the supreme King of Kings,
> the Holy Blessed One, who lives and endures for ever and ever,
> whose anger, if He is angry with me, is an everlasting anger, who if
> He imprisons me, imprisons me forever, who if He puts me to death
> puts me to death forever, and whom I cannot persuade with words
> or bribe with money! Moreover, there are two roads before me, one
> leading to Gan Eden and the other to Gehenna, and I do know by
> which I shall be taken. Shall I not weep?" (*Berakhot* 28b; see also
> *Avot de Rabbi Natan* 25)

These passages demonstrate that speculation about Gan Eden as
an immortal realm of the righteous dead was part of rabbinic Judaism.
However, this was never a predominant point of view, and certainly never
surpassed or replaced beliefs about Gan Eden as a collective transcen-

dent messianic world. Obviously, two different conceptions of Gan Eden—as an immortal afterlife realm and as a final resting place at the end-of-time—coexisted. However, the biblically based notion that soul and body remain united in the grave until the resurrection did continue to dominate rabbinic afterlife teachings for centuries.[47]

Mythic Descriptions of Gan Eden

Generally speaking, in the Talmud we do not find very elaborate depictions of Gan Eden and the conditions of life therein. However, within Midrash, and particularly in later *midrashim*, we see the development of increasingly extensive descriptions of the geography of Gan Eden. *Sifre Deuteronomy*, echoing the Book of Enoch, envisions that "there are seven groups of the righteous in Gan Eden, one higher than the other" who dwell within seven different divisions or stories of Gan Eden, which are called Presence, Courts, House, Tabernacle, Holy Hill, Hill of the Lord, and Holy Place (*Sifre Deuteronomy* 10:67a).

In a parallel teaching, found in *Midrash on Psalms*, we find the following:

> Seven classes will stand before the Holy Blessed One in the World to Come. . . .[48] The first class sits in the company of the King and beholds His presence. . . . The second dwells in the house of the King. . . . The third ascends to the *hill* to meet the King. . . . The fourth is in the court of the King. . . . The fifth is in the Tabernacle of the King. . . . The sixth is in the holy hill of the King. . . . The seventh is in the palace of the King. . . . (*Midrash on Psalms* 11:7, 51a)

In a much later rabbinic text, a vivid portrayal of life in Gan Eden is presented. Although this text, *Yalkut Shimoni*, is ascribed to Rabbi Joshua ben Levi, a third-century mystically inclined Rabbi, it appears in a collection of rabbinic *midrashim* from the thirteenth century and likely dates from that time.[49] This text is exceptionally visual and demonstrates the way in which mythic portrayals of Gan Eden, and also Gehenna, began to emerge out of the rabbinic imagination:

> Gan Eden has two gates of ruby, by which stand sixty myriads of ministering angels. The luster of the face of each of them glistens like the splendor of the firmament. When a righteous person arrives,

they divest him in white robes of the clouds of glory, set two crowns upon his head, one made of gems and pearls and the other of gold . . . place eight myrtles in his hand and praise him saying: "Go eat your food in joy." They take him into a place where are brooks of water, surrounded by eight hundred varieties of roses and myrtles. Each person has a chamber allotted to him according to the honor due him. From it issues four streams, one of milk, one of wine, one of balsam, and one of honey; and above every chamber there is a golden vine studded with thirty pearls, each one of them glistening like the brilliance of the planet Venus. . . .

In every corner of Gan Eden there are eighty myriad species of trees, the most inferior of them being finer than all the aromatic plants [of this world]; and in each corner are sixty myriads of ministering angels singing in pleasant tones. In the center is the Tree of Life, its branches covering the whole of Gan Eden, containing five hundred thousand varieties of fruit all differing in appearance and taste. Above it are the clouds of glory, and it is smitten by four winds so that its odor is wafted from one end of the world to the other. Beneath it are the disciples of the sages who expounded the Torah, each of them possessing two chambers, one of the stars and the other of the sun and moon. Between every chamber hangs a curtain of glory, behind which lies Eden. (*Yalkut Shimoni, Bereshit* 20)[50]

What we find in this text is a specific concern with the content of the supernal worlds, and less of an emphasis on the ethics of reward and punishment. In a sense, this text is a bridge between the Midrash of the early Rabbis and the ornate visionary writings on the afterlife that characterize medieval Midrash. For those who claim that Judaism does not have a concern with the details of the afterlife, this particular text, and the tradition that it spawns, is a direct contradiction. In Chapter 6 we will more fully explore these types of visionary texts on the afterlife.

Beyond Gan Eden: The Divine Treasury of Souls

There is one additional rabbinic afterlife concept that, although not extensively developed in talmudic and midrashic writings, is important nonetheless in the overall Jewish schema of the hereafter. In a number of places the Rabbis speak of something called *otzar*, or "divine treasury." It is a realm, seemingly beyond, or in the highest region of Gan Eden, where the souls of the righteous gather. According to one Midrash: "Both the souls of the righteous and those of the wicked alike ascend above, but those of the righteous are placed in the divine treasury [*otzar*], while those of the wicked are cast about on earth" (*Ecclesiastes Rabbah* 3:18).

This divine treasury, or *otzar*, is often equated with *tzror ha-hayyim*— translated as "bond of life," "bundle of life," or "treasury of life"—a term that appears but once in the Bible, in the First Book of Samuel. There, Abigail, who was to become King David's wife, says: "If any man sets out to pursue you, and take your life, your life shall be bound up in the bond of life [*tzror ha-hayyim*] with the Lord your God; but he will fling away the lives of your enemies as from the hollow of a sling [*kaf ha-kela*]" (1 Samuel 25:29). Through homiletical interpretation, the Rabbis (but even more, the kabbalists) came to understand the term *tzror ha-hayyim* as referring to a transcendent realm of souls. Thus, we find in *Avot de Rabbi Natan* the statement "the souls of all the righteous are in safekeeping under the Throne of Glory, as it is said: 'Your life shall be bound up in the bond of life [*tzror ha-hayyim*] with the Lord your God'" (1 Samuel 25:29) (*Avot de Rabbi Natan* 12).

The philosophical context behind this notion of *otzar*, or *tzror ha-hayyim*, is the idea that there exists a divine holding tank of a sort, a gathering place for souls in the highest spheres. This comes out of the ancient Greek idea of the preexistence of the soul. According to this doctrine, which made its way into Judaism during the first centuries after the destruction of the Temple, before souls are born, they are gathered together in a transcendent domain awaiting birth; then, after death, there is a supernal sphere to which such souls return.

Parallel with the notion of *otzar* are rabbinic teachings about a storehouse where souls abide prior to physical embodiment, often referred to as *guf*, meaning "body."[51] We find reference to this idea of preexistence of souls in a teaching ascribed to the Tanna Rabbi Yossi: "The Messiah will not come before the souls which are in the *guf* have entered physical life" (*Avodah Zarah* 5a; see also *Nidarim* 13b, *Yeb.* 62a–63b,[52] *Genesis Rabbah* 24:4, *Leviticus* 15:1). Rabbi Meir also teaches that the souls of the righteous, and the souls (*ruhot*) and spirits (*neshamot*) not yet born, who reside in the *guf*, are found in the seventh heaven, Arabot, one of the traditional names for Gan Eden (*Hagigah* 12b).[53]

So it came to be believed that all preexistent souls descended into incarnation from this *guf*; and after death righteous souls returned to the *otzar*, or divine treasury hidden under the Throne of Glory (*Shabbat* 152b; see also *Pesikta Rabbati* 2:3). At this stage in the evolution of Jewish afterlife thought, the Rabbis do not spell out any clear relationship between *otzar* and Gan Eden. They are simply two coexisting notions, with Gan Eden clearly being the realm given most importance when speaking of the fate of the righteous dead. But as we will see later, the kabbalists developed this idea of a divine treasury of souls even further.

RESURRECTION OF THE DEAD

Resurrection—A Fundamental Rabbinic Doctrine

Our exploration of rabbinic views of the afterlife is incomplete without at least some discussion of the doctrine of resurrection, which by the first century C.E. had become a prevalent belief in Judaism. If there was any one canonized dogma of rabbinic Judaism, it was the belief that there would be a collective resurrection at the end-of-days.[54] Differing views about this eschatological doctrine was at the root of the polarization between the Sadducees and the Pharisees. The former completely rejected the notion of postmortem reward and punishment, and along with it, the belief in bodily resurrection. In place, they taught that the soul totally ceased its existence at the time of death.

According to the historian Josephus, who records Sadducean views:

> The Sadducees . . . take away fate entirely, and suppose that God is not concerned in our doing or not doing what is evil; and they say, that to act what is good, or what is evil, is at men's own choice, and that the one or the other belongs so to every one, that they may act as they please. They also take away the belief of the immortal duration of the soul, and the punishments and rewards in Sheol.[55]

On the other hand, the Pharisees, in the words of Josephus, "believe that souls have an immortal vigor in them . . . [and the] power to revive and live again."[56] Precursors of the rabbinic era, the Pharisees assiduously upheld a belief in reward and punishment, which, as a corollary, assumed a physical resurrection for the righteous dead. It was this notion that eventually prevailed, as the pharisaic/rabbinic worldview emerged as the predominant tradition in the first century C.E. Even in the Gospels we see how Jesus, obviously a product of early-first-century Judaism, tacitly accepted the pharisaic belief in a resurrection of the dead for all humanity.[57]

In very little time, rabbinic Judaism, heir to the pharisaic legacy, purged any and all opposition to belief in physical resurrection. According to the Jewish historian Salo Baron:

> Talmudic Judaism . . . eliminated all "heresies" from the life of the people for centuries to come. As early as the second century, Celsus, an informed writer, knew nothing about the Sadducean denial of resurrection and simply stated that the Jews shared with the Christians the belief in the ultimate resurrection of the dead.[58]

Through the process of homiletical textual exegesis, the Rabbis continually validated and reasserted the primacy of their belief in resurrection. There is frequent discussion among the Rabbis as to where in the Torah belief in resurrection can be found. Responses like the ones below are characteristic of talmudic discourse on the subject:

> Sectarians [minim[59]] asked Rabban Gamliel: "Whence do you know that the Holy Blessed One will resurrect the dead to life?" He answered them citing the Torah, Prophets and Writings. From the Torah: for it is written: "And the Lord said to Moses, Behold you shall sleep with your fathers; and this people will rise up" [Deuteronomy 31:16]. From the Prophets: as it is written: "Your dead men shall live, together with my dead bodies shall they arise. Awake and sing, you that dwell in the dust; for your dew is as the dew of herbs, and the earth shall cast out its dead." [Isaiah 26:19]; from the Writings: as it is written, "And the roof of your mouth, like the best wine of my beloved, like the best wine, that goes down sweetly, causing the lips of those who are asleep to speak" [Song of Songs 7:9]. (Sanhedrin 90b)
>
> R. Meir asked, Whence is the resurrection derived from the Torah? As it is said, "Then will Moses and the children of Israel sing this song unto the Lord" [Exodus 15:1]. It is not said "sang" but "will sing"; hence the Resurrection is deducible from the Torah. R. Joshua ben Levi asked, Whence is the resurrection derived from the Torah? As it is said, "Blessed are they that dwell in Your house, they will still be praising You" [Psalm 84:4]. It is not stated, "They have praised You" but "will still be praising You" [in Olam Ha-Ba]; hence the resurrection is deducible from the Torah. (Sanhedrin 91b)

Rapidly, the doctrine of resurrection became a central dogma of rabbinic teachings, as important as belief in the divine origin of the

Torah.[60] Thus, in the second-century Midrash, *Sifre Deuteronomy*, we find the unequivocal, perhaps somewhat revisionist statement that "there is no section of the Torah which does not imply the doctrine of Resurrection, but we have not the capacity to expound it in this sense" (*Sifre Deuteronomy* 306). Further, linking belief and practice through the development of liturgy, the Rabbis incorporated the theme of resurrection into daily prayer, making it a pivotal component of the *Tefillah*, or "Eighteen Benedictions" prayer:

> You are mighty forever, my Lord; You resurrect the dead; You are powerful to save. He sustains the living with loving kindness, resurrects the dead with great mercy, supports the falling, heals the sick, releases the bound, fulfills His trust to those who sleep in the dust. Who is like You, mighty One! And who can be compared to You, King, who brings death and restores life, and causes deliverance to spring forth. Blessed are You, who revives the dead.[61]

Including this prayer in liturgical worship established resurrection doctrine as a central pillar in the theological worldview of the Rabbis and effectively excluded from communal worship those who did not accept the primacy of belief in resurrection.[62] The prayer on resurrection, called in Hebrew *tehiyyat ha-metim*, is still recited daily in traditional Jewish liturgy. For over two thousand years the doctrine of the resurrection of the dead has been a fundamental tenet of Judaism.

Who Will Be Resurrected?

The Rabbis frequently addressed the question of who will be resurrected at the end-of-days. There was no uniformly accepted belief. Rather, rabbinic literature displays a wide diversity of opinions on this question.

In some instances, a universal belief is put forth that everyone—Jew and gentile, righteous and wicked—will be resurrected: "They that are born are destined to die and the dead be brought to life again" (M. *Avot* 4:29). Other passages, however, claim that "the resurrection is reserved for Israel" (*Genesis Rabbah* 8:6).

Other Rabbis, however, believed that only the righteous would be resurrected:

> More important is a day of rain than the resurrection of the dead, since the Resurrection is for the righteous and not the wicked, whereas rain is for both the righteous and the wicked. (*Taanit* 7a)

In a similar vein, it was believed that "those who are ignorant of Torah will not live again; as it is said, 'They are dead, they shall not rise'" [Isaiah 26:4] (*Ketubbot* 111b). And of those who denied a belief in resurrection, it was claimed: "Since a person repudiated belief in the resurrection of the dead, he will have no share in the resurrection" (*Sanhedrin* 90a).[63]

There was also a great deal of speculation on where the resurrection would take place. Frequently, the idea was put forth that it would occur in the Holy Land; only those who died in Israel would be resurrected:

> Those who die outside the land of Israel will not live again . . . and those who die in the land of My delight will live again, but those who do not die there will not. . . . Even a Canaanite maidservant in the land of Israel is assured of inheriting the World to Come. (*Ketubbot* 111b)

Given the large number of Jews living—and dying—outside the Land of Israel, this belief presented certain problems. Did it mean that all those pious talmudic sages living in the Babylonian community were to be denied resurrection? To solve this problem, two different types of solutions were evolved. First, there was a concrete attempt to resolve the problem by arranging for burial in Palestine. It became common practice for Jews of the Diaspora—predominantly in Babylonia—to be buried in the country where they died; then, after physical decomposition, the bones were gathered in ossuaries and transported to Israel for secondary burial in places such as Sanhedria and Beit Shearim, well-known burial sites in talmudic times.[64]

A second solution was more metaphoric, or perhaps metaphysical. While agreeing that the Holy Land would be the site of the resurrection, certain Rabbis claimed that the bodies of those buried elsewhere would be spontaneously transported to Israel in order that they may be brought back to life.[65] According to one Midrash, at the time of the resurrection

> God will make underground passages for the righteous who, rolling through them like skin bottles will get to the Land of Israel, and when they get to the Land of Israel, God will restore their breath [soul] to them. (*Pesikta Rabbati* 1:6; see also P. *Ketubbot* 35b)

Interestingly enough, even to this day, it is a custom in the Diaspora to bury a person with a small stick, or dowel, placed in the casket. Since the operating belief is that the resurrection will begin in the Holy Land, at the designated time of redemption, the person will be able to burrow through the earth to the Land of Israel and participate fully in the miracle of resurrection. In addition, a small satchel of earth from the Mount of Olives in Jerusalem is sprinkled in the casket, once again a symbolic act connecting the deceased to the Land of Israel where the resurrection is to begin. While many people are often unaware of these customs[66]—and they are customs, not legal, halakhic dictates—they do reflect how belief in resurrection has pervaded Jewish practice and persisted over the course of almost two millennia.

Resurrection and the Immortality of the Soul

As rabbinic conceptions of life after death evolved and changed over the centuries, there was eventually a successful integration of the notions of individual immortality and resurrection of the dead. The prevalent belief came to be that upon death the individual soul first entered the purgative realm of Gehenna; after twelve months it entered the paradisical abode of Gan Eden, where it remained until the time of the collective resurrection of the dead at the end-of-days. But this clearly integrated synthesis of individual and collective postmortem teachings was not always apparent throughout much of the rabbinic period. As in biblical times, individual and collective conceptions of the afterlife are confused in rabbinic literature. The differentiated stages of the afterlife experience are only the culmination of over a thousand years of postmortem reflection and writing on the part of the Rabbis. This multistage understanding of the hereafter is expanded and built on in the medieval and kabbalistic periods of Judaism.

SUMMARY

In this chapter we have explored the central themes and conceptions of the afterlife experience in rabbinic literature. From the material presented, the following observations can be made about the nature of Jewish postmortem teachings in the rabbinic period:

1. Rabbinic afterlife teachings were never organized and systematized into a consistent whole. As a result, there are many di-

vergent, contradictory, and often ambiguous notions of the afterlife. Both individual and collective postmortem conceptions are
often intertwined and coexist in rabbinic literature.

2. *Olam Ha-Ba*—the "World to Come"—is the most frequently
used term in rabbinic writings on the afterlife. However, it is often
unclear whether this refers to a postmortem realm or to a messianic era at the end-of-days. In the early and late rabbinic period,
there are traditions in which *Olam Ha-Ba* is seen as a postmortem realm, but this was never a predominant point of view in
rabbinic literature.

3. Rabbinic literature contains ample material on the fate of the
individual after death, including discussions about various phenomena of the death experience, encounters with the Angel of
Death and other postmortem angelic beings, and tales of ongoing contact between the dead and the living. From both philosophical teachings and folk-level anecdotes, it is clear that the
Rabbis believed that after bodily death there continued to be
conscious awareness for the individual soul.

4. In rabbinic literature, Gehenna is the realm of postmortem punishment. Both the Talmud and Midrash describe with increasingly lurid detail the nature and topography of this realm. Although there are strands of teachings about eternal punishment,
Gehenna is generally understood to be a temporary purgative
abode where the soul abides for only twelve months. Inherent
in the rabbinic conception of Gehenna is the notion of an individual soul that undergoes a process of postmortem purgation
and purification.

5. Rabbinic texts present numerous descriptions of Gan Eden, the
postmortem realm of paradise for the righteous. In later *midrashim*,
descriptions of Gan Eden become increasingly elaborate and
mythic in nature.

6. Beyond Gan Eden is the realm called *tzror ha-hayyim or otzar*, a
divine storehouse for all souls.

7. Resurrection of the dead was a fundamental eschatological belief in rabbinic Judaism, taking a central place in rabbinic theology.

8. During the rabbinic period, a multistage conception of the afterlife emerges that combines individual and collective postmortem teachings. Gradually, it came to be believed that the indi-

vidual would first experience the purgations of Gehenna for twelve months, followed by a time of divine bliss in Gan Eden. Then, at the end-of-days there would be a collective resurrection of both body and soul of the dead.

9. Rabbinic conceptions of the afterlife became the foundation on which all later Jewish postmortem beliefs were based.

Chapter 6

Visionary Tours
of the Afterlife
in Medieval Midrash

THE HISTORICAL CONTEXT

As we continue our journey tracing the evolution of Jewish teachings on life after death, we now enter the medieval era where we will discover a little-known and rather exciting treasury of Jewish writings on the afterlife.

By the end of the ninth century, most classical rabbinic texts had been completed; the Talmud was a finished product, and many of the homiletical *midrashim* on the books of the Bible were in the final stages of compilation.[1] From the end of the Geonic period onward, especially during the tenth to fourteenth centuries, a more elaborate form of legendary Midrash began to appear in the medieval Jewish world. In Babylonia and later in Europe, there was a proliferation of legendary narratives—best referred to as medieval visionary Midrash—that explore various historical, ethical, apocalyptic, and eschatological themes.[2] Among this unique genre of Jewish literature appear a good number of texts that chronicle the experiences of the individual soul after death and mythically depict the torments of Gehenna and the supernal realms of Gan Eden.

As it turns out, medieval visionary Midrash is a great source for Jewish teachings on the afterlife. With depictions of the postmortem worlds that range from the macabre to the sublime, these texts are full of graphic details of life after death, no less fantastic than Dante's *Divine Comedy*. For this reason, this chapter will present a series of primary source medieval midrashic texts on the afterlife. Rather than offer a secondary source thematic analysis of texts, as done with the biblical, apocryphal, and rabbinic material, here we will allow the texts to speak for themselves and demonstrate the extent of medieval Judaism's teachings on the hereafter. Largely unknown to the modern world, these midrashic writings are a gold mine for understanding how Jews envisioned the postmortem torments of the grave, the punishments of Gehenna, and the celestial rewards of Gan Eden.

THE SOURCES

Medieval visionary Midrash is a strange breed of Jewish writings, and not much is known about the origins and the authors of many of these afterlife texts. While some are clearly based on legendary teachings found in rabbinic writings, others display similarities to motifs found in *Zohar* and other kabbalistic writings. In many of the texts from this period, there are clearly thematic textual links to the ancient apocryphal writings, specifically those that detail Enoch's sojourns in hell and paradise. Similarly, there are parallels between some of the texts and the mystical *hekhalot* literature, which describe sojourning through the heavenly realms. Although these visionary midrashic writings never received the same kind of rabbinical support that other legalistic and ethical writings did, there is no doubt that they were very popular in their time, and as literary fantasy, managed to capture the imagination of the masses.[3]

Some medieval midrashic texts were lost for centuries, rediscovered only with the publication of documents from the Cairo Geniza;[4] others found their way into medieval anthologies such as *Sefer Zikhronot*,[5] or kabbalistic texts like *Reishit Hokhmah*.[6] However, to date, there has been a dearth of scholarly work on this genre of Jewish afterlife teachings; due to the rationalistic bias underlying nineteenth and early-twentieth-century Jewish scholarship, fantasy visions of heaven and hell have not been given much attention by most researchers. With the exception of the early translation work of Moses Gaster,[7] selections included in Louis Ginzberg's *Legends of the Jews*,[8] a brief essay on "Sins and Their Punishments" by Saul Lieberman,[9] the recent study of Martha Himmelfarb investigating the *Tours of Hell*,[10] and material found in the collection of translations by David Stern and Mark Jay Mirsky entitled *Rabbinic Fantasies*,[11] most material on medieval midrashic teachings on the afterlife are found exclusively in Hebrew texts and manuscripts.

The texts presented below appear in a number of different Hebrew sources. *Beit Ha-Midrash* is a six-volume anthology of little-known *midrashim* and apocryphal writings edited in the mid-nineteenth century by Adolph Jellinek, a German-Jewish scholar.[12] This is the best anthology to consult to get a flavor of medieval visionary Midrash, and most of the texts in this chapter are found there.

Another excellent anthology that contains medieval midrashic texts is *Otzar Midrashim*, edited by J. D. Eisenstein.[13] This is an alphabetical anthology of texts, and under the headings of "Gan Eden" and "Gehenna" are approximately ten individual texts on the afterlife.

Batei Midrashot is a two-volume anthology of texts from the Cairo Geniza, edited by Abraham Wertheimer.[14] The text entitled *Gedulat Moshe*—"The Revelation of Moses"—is found there.

Reishit Hokhmah, by Elijah de Vidas, is a sixteenth-century kabbalistic ethical treatise.[15] In chapters 12 and 13 appear medieval midrashic writings on life after death.

Finally, although technically not medieval Midrash, the last text included in this chapter is by Immanuel Ha-Romi, an Italian Jew who composed an elaborate poetic description of hell and heaven entitled *Ha-Tophet V'Ha-Eden*, which appears in a collection of his writings entitled *Mahbarot Immanuel*.[16]

With one exception, all the texts that appear here have been translated into English by Moses Gaster. Most are taken from an anthology by Gaster entitled *Chronicles of Jerahmeel*, which is a partial translation of a larger anthology of medieval *midrashim* entitled *Sefer Zikhronot*. Completed in 1325, *Sefer Zikhronot* was compiled by Eleazar ben Asher Ha-Levi, a copyist and anthologist who lived in the Rhine provinces of Germany. Eleazar ben Asher Ha-Levi gathered together extant material from a variety of different sources—"records of all events and incidents which have happened from the creation of the world until the present day"[17]—creating an epic of the Jewish people that blends both history and legend.[18]

In Gaster's translation, *Chronicles of Jerahmeel*, there are approximately twelve texts specifically related to the journeying of the soul in the afterlife.[19] Another text, *Gedulat Moshe*, is translated by Gaster in *Studies and Texts in Folklore, Magic, Medieval Romance, Hebrew Apocrypha and Samaritan Archaeology*.[20] The material from Immanuel Ha-Romi's *Ha-Tophet V'Ha-Eden* appears in English in a translation by Hermann Gollancz.[21]

Using Gaster as a basis, I have culled through his translations, eliminating his use of King James English in order to make the material more readable. I have also compared his versions with material found in Jellinek, Eisenstein, Wertheimer, and de Vidas, amending Gaster's translation in a number of instances. Although there will be some introduction and analysis of the texts to make it easier to enter this medieval world for the first time, I do believe the texts speak for themselves. My intention in this chapter is to make available these unique texts that document the Jewish concern—and a somewhat passionate one at that—for the details of the soul's journeying after death. No doubt, after reading this chapter, it will be quite difficult for anyone to continue to affirm the erroneous belief that Jews have few details about the afterlife.

What follows is a compendium of translations of medieval legendary texts on the afterlife. I have endeavored to collate families of texts that describe the soul's fate after death: in *Hibbut Ha-Kever* ("The Pangs of the Grave"), Gehenna, and Gan Eden. The last two texts—*Gedulat Moshe* and selections from *Ha-Tophet V'Ha-Eden*—combine Gehenna and Gan Eden themes together.

HIBBUT HA-KEVER TEXTS

In this section, there are three related texts forming *Masekhet Hibbut Ha-Kever*—"Tractate of the Pangs of the Grave." These texts are built on the rabbinic belief that immediately after death both the body and soul of the deceased go through a process of physical torment. By the medieval period, the idea of *din ha-kever*, or "judgment of the grave," had become normative within Judaism. The texts that follow describe with lurid details the nature of this judgment process directly after death. We find in this series of texts a more detailed phenomenology of the afterlife than anything we have seen until now.

What I have titled "Philosophical Introduction" to the *Hibbut Ha-*

Kever is a late rabbinic Midrash, in the names of Rabbi Abahu and Rabbi Jose. In the Hebrew editions of *Masekhet Hibbut Ha-Kever* this text is appended as a fourth chapter. The content of the text certainly sets the tone for a consideration of the topic of *Hibbut Ha-Kever* and goes well as an introductory selection. While there is some description of an individual's after-death visions, above all the text emphasizes the rabbinic ethical worldview—that the study of Torah and the fulfilling of the *mitzvot* are the best way to live one's life, and hence the most efficacious antidote for avoiding postmortem punishment. This continues to be the foundational belief underlying the postmortem philosophy of medieval Midrash.

The text entitled *Rabbi Isaac ben Parnach from Gehinnom* often appears as chapter 1 of *Masekhet Hibbut Ha-Kever*, minus the opening two verses. This text builds on earlier rabbinic Midrash and describes the Angel of Death and the companies of three ministering angels that escort the righteous; the text goes even further and speaks about five angels of destruction that approach the wicked at the hour of death.

The third text, usually appearing as chapter 2 of *Masekhet Hibbut Ha-Kever*, speaks of three days of judgment in the grave. After giving a detailed account and reckoning, the individual is judged measure for measure. Punishment is meted out in accordance with the nature of the sin. Verbal transgressions merit a torturing of the lips, hearing sinful words earns punishment of the ears, gazing at sinful acts results in torture of the eyes, and so on. This theme of the punishment fitting the crime is developed more extensively in the Gehenna texts and characterizes this genre of visionary postmortem literature.

Also found in the text is the notion of three kinds of judgment: in the grave, that is, *Hibbut Ha-Kever*; in Gehenna, and interestingly enough, in heaven (the Hebrew word in the text is *Din Shamayim*).

Besides the English translations presented here, which are found in Gaster's *Chronicles of Jerahmeel*, there are other Hebrew fragments of *Hibbut Ha-Kever* midrashic material.

"Philosophical Introduction" to *Hibbut Ha-Kever*[22]

1. Rabbi Abahu told the parable of three different men. One tills the ground, another works in silver and gold, and the third studies Torah. When the time approaches for him who tills the ground to die, he says to his household, "Give me some of my

work, so that I do not go to the next world empty-handed." To which they reply, "You are foolish. Have you not worked the field? and Torah has already said, 'The earth and its fulness belong to God,' therefore you have nothing of your own to bring."

2. When the end of him who works in silver and gold arrives, he says to his household, "Give me some of my labor, that I may not go to the next world empty-handed." But they reply, "You are foolish. You have worked in this world in silver and gold. Torah has already said, 'Mine is the silver, and Mine is the gold, says the Lord'; therefore you have nothing of your own to bring."

3. When the time arrives for him who studies Torah to quit this world, he says to his household, "Give me of my labor, that I may not go to the next world empty-handed." To him they say, "O you pious and righteous person, how can we give you [the fruits] of your labor? Have you not constantly occupied yourself with the Torah? But the Holy Blessed One will grant you the reward of your work, and shall receive you with good grace. The ministering angels shall go forth to meet you and exclaim, 'Come in peace'; and concerning you Scripture says, 'Then shall your light break forth as the morning.'"

4. Rabbi Jose says, "If you desire to know the reward of the righteous in the world to come, come here and learn it from what has befallen Adam. He was commanded to perform an easy precept, and because he transgressed it, the Holy Blessed One punished him and all subsequent generations with many kinds of death. Therefore the sages have said that, on the contrary, whoever studies and observes the Torah and performs good deeds shall be delivered from the punishment of Gehinnom and the sorrows of the grave [Hibbut Ha-Kever]." Rabbi Abahu mentions one of the proverbial sayings of Rabbi Isaac that the end of a man is death, the end of animals is slaughter, and all are destined to die.

5. Rabbi Jose says, "Come here and see the difference existing between man and animals; the latter are slain and flayed, and are not subjected to any judgment: while with reference to man, how many chastisements and troubles does he bear in this world; and after his death, if he is a righteous man, his judgment is delayed; but if he is wicked, he is brought before the tribunal every year between Passover and Pentecost, as it is said, 'And they shall go forth and look upon the carcasses of the men, and it shall be at every new moon.'"

6. After man's death he is seen by all the other dead, and he appears to each just as they last saw him alive: some see him as a youth, others as an old man, just as each saw him before his own death, so that they should not think that any man lives forever, and say when we were among the living we saw this or that man, and now how many hundreds of years have passed since we have seen them alive?

7. Therefore, when one dies the angel who guards the dead makes his soul assume various forms, so that all shall recognize him by seeing him just as they saw him in life. Then, in the event of one being condemned afterward to Gehinnom, he is enveloped with smoke and brimstone, so that one should not see the punishment of the other; and none should be put to shame before the other, except those who have publicly put others to shame.

8. Every man after death is brought to judgment, even if he should belong to the section of the righteous, still, after a time his sins are visited. Thus Samuel said to Saul, "Tomorrow you shall be in my division." Was not Samuel in Ramah and Saul in another place? The explanation is that he [Samuel] referred to the soul when he said, "You will be with me in my division." And we see that after a long lapse of time the house of Saul was judged on account of Saul and on account of the house of blood. Thus, the house of Saul was visited. Although he was called "the chosen of the Lord," yet His seed was judged.

Rabbi Isaac ben Parnach mi Gehinnom
(Preamble to Masekhet Hibbut Ha-Kever)[23]

1. Rabbi Isaac ben Parnach has said that all man's iniquities are engraved upon his bones, as it is said, "Their iniquities shall be upon their bones," and all his merits shall be engraved upon his right hand, as it is said, "The Lord is your guard and your protection on your right hand."

2. Rabbi Joshua ben Levi says that man's merits and sins are not testified to until the day of his death. Even frivolous conversation, which is not accounted as a sin, is mentioned only at the time of his death, as it is said, "For behold He who has formed the mountains and created the wind will tell man what his conversation has been."

Chapter 1 of *Masekhet Hibbut Ha-Kever* begins here:

3. Thus at his death three ministering angels come to him, one the Angel of Death, one a scribe, and a third who is appointed to accompany them. They say to him, "Arise, for your end has come." To which he replies, "I shall not rise, for my end has not yet arrived."

4. Then the scribe proceeds to number his days and years. At that moment the man opens his eyes and sees the Angel of Death, whose length extends from one end of the world to the other; he quakes exceedingly and falls upon his face.

5. From the sole of his [the angel's] foot to the crown of his head he is full of eyes, his clothing is of fire, his covering of fire, he is surrounded by fire, he is all fire. In his hand he carries a fiery blade, from which hangs a bitter drop. This drop causes first death, then decomposition and the lividness of appearance, but man does not die until he has seen the Holy Blessed One, as it is said, "For no man shall see Me and live; but when he dies he shall see Him, as it is said, 'Before Him there shall bend all those who go down to the dust when he ceases to live.'"

6. Then the man confesses everything he has done in the world. His mouth bears witness, and the Lord writes it down. "By Myself have I sworn, says the Lord, that from My mouth shall go forth righteousness."

7. If he is a man of perfect righteousness, his soul is handed over to its owner. But if a man of consummate wickedness, he stiffens the neck and allows his evil inclination to prevail over him; hence, the sages have said that a wicked man's evil inclination prevails over him even at his death.

8. Rabbi Eliezer has said that just as he is stiff-necked in this world, so is he at the Day of Judgment, as it is said, "The wicked shall see and be angry."

9. At the death of the righteous man, three companies of ministering angels come to him. The first company says, "A righteous man has perished from the earth." The second company says, "Let him in peace come and rest upon the couches." The third company says, "He goes the straight path."

10. But at the death of the wicked, five angels of destruction come to him and say, "The wicked shall return to Sheol."

Masekhet Hibbut Ha-Kever—
"Tractate of the Pangs of the Grave"[24]

1. Rabbi Eliezer's pupils asked him, "What judgment is there in the grave?" He replied, "When a man quits this world, the Angel of Death comes to him and sits by his grave, and beating it with his hands, says, 'Tell me your name.' 'Flesh and blood is my name. It is revealed and known to Him who said, and the world was. But I do not know what my name is.' Then immediately the soul reenters his body. He stands up and is brought to judgment."

2. Rabbi Joshua ben Levi says, "They bring a chain of iron, half of it burning like fire, half as cold as ice, and they beat him with it. At the first stroke his limbs get separated; at the second, his bones are scattered. Then the ministering angels gather them together, and restoring him, beat him a third time, and demand of him an account and reckoning, and judge him measure for measure.

3. "On the second day they judge him in the same manner.

4. "On the third day they judge him further, and they punish his two eyes, his two hands, his two feet and his two ears, his mouth and his tongue. Why are his eyes punished? Because he looked with them upon transgression. Why his ears? Because he heard sinful utterances with them. Why his lips? Because he uttered with them words of foolishness. And why his tongue? Because he has testified falsely with it. Why his two hands? He committed violence and robbery with them. Why his two legs? Because he hastened with them to transgression." Rabbi Yehudah says, "Whoever has gone to a married woman shall hang ignominiously in Gehinnom; and whoever slanders his neighbor shall be suspended by his tongue."

5. Rabbi Meir, in the name of Rabbi Joshua, says, "The judgment in the grave is more severe than that in Gehinnom, for in Gehinnom only they are judged who are thirteen years old and upwards; but in the grave, stillborn children and perfectly righteous men, and even sucklings, are brought to judgment." Hence the sages have said, "He who dwells in the Land of Israel and dies on Sabbath eve at the time of the blowing of the *shofar*, as long as the sun shines he shall not see the judgment in the grave; while he who loves righteousness and chastisement, charitable deeds and hospitality to strangers, although not living in the Land

of Israel, shall see neither the judgment of the grave nor that in Gehinnom, as it is said, 'From the midst of trouble' refers to the beating in the grave. 'From the depth of Sheol I cried.' This refers to the punishment in Gehinnom."

6. Ben Azay says, "There are three kinds of judgments, one more severe than the other; moreover, they are all inflicted in the presence of the Holy Blessed One." "But," asks Rabbi Akiva, "are they all in the Holy Blessed One's presence?" "Clearly the angels inflict the judgment in the grave [Din Hibbut Ha-Kever] and also that in Gehinnom, but only the judgment of heaven [Din Shamayim] alone is inflicted in the presence of the Holy Blessed One!" Three days are given over to the judgment in the grave, three days to that in Gehinnom, and three days to the judgment in heaven.[25] If there is no charge against a man, he is not brought up for judgment; but if there are charges against him, the judgment may last long.

7. The punishment of transgressing Israelites is twelve months in Gehinnom, as it is said, "And it shall come to pass at the renewal of the new moon and at the renewal of the Sabbath." Just as the weeks form a cycle, so the months form an annual cycle, and then shall all flesh prostrate themselves before the Holy Blessed One. Rabbi Yohanan ben Nuri says, "The time extends from Passover until Pentecost, as it is said, 'And from one festival to the other,' during which the sabbaths are counted." Some sinners are judged in Gehinnom from Passover until Pentecost, after which time they are acquitted; others, again, such as the consummately wicked of Israel, obtain no rest for the whole twelve months.

8. "While others who have violated the whole of the Torah and the precepts and have sinned against the Torah of God, going the idolatrous way of the nations, shall have their bodies and souls burnt. Gehinnom vomits them out, and the north wind scatters them, so that they become ashes under the soles of the feet of the righteous, as it is said, 'And on account of the doings of the wicked, behold they shall become ashes beneath your feet on the day when I execute judgment.'

9. "Further, those who leave the community, the apostates, traitors, renegades, scoffers, those who despise the holy days, deny the resurrection of the dead and the divinity of Torah are swallowed up by Gehinnom; the doors are locked upon them, and

there they are left a prey to eternal punishment, as it is said, 'And they go forth and look upon the carcasses of those that have transgressed against Me, for their worm shall not die, neither shall their fire be quenched.'"

GEHENNA TEXTS

Next, we will look at a series of five texts that elaborate on the theme of punishment in Gehenna. The texts presented, all of which appear in English translation in Chronicles of Jerahmeel, form the corpus of Masekhet Gehinnom.

Like Masekhet Hibbut Ha-Kever, Masekhet Gehinnom, or "Tractate of Gehinnom," is a compendium of various texts that exists in a number of different recensions. In a broad sense, Masekhet Gehinnom can be best seen as a family of texts that build on the theme of sins and their punishments.

These texts are in the tradition of visionary "Tours of Hell" that grow out of the Book of Enoch and relate historically, at least in a general sense, to Jewish Merkavah literature. There are comparable visionary tours of the punishments of hell in both Christian and Muslim traditions.[26]

In the "Tours of Hell" texts, characteristically, one individual is guided through the hell realms, often accompanied by an angel.[27] Here, as in many Gan Eden texts, it is Rabbi Joshua ben Levi who is given guided tour of the habitations of the dead. According to Jewish legend, Joshua ben Levi was able to outsmart the Angel of Death and entered the realms of Gan Eden alive.[28] Like Enoch, Joshua ben Levi became the subject of Jewish visionary writings. He is often depicted as the one who meets Elijah, the Messiah, and other notables as he travels through the arcane multidimensional realms of the universe where the righteous dead and the tortured wicked are to be found.

The first chapter of Masekhet Gehinnom speaks of two bands of angels at the entrance to Gehinnom, three gates through which one enters, and five different kinds of fire. These are images that bear resemblance to the portrayal of Gehenna in rabbinic writings. What is evidenced here is the unfolding of the midrashic process. Old motifs and themes are elaborated upon, and, in contrast with earlier talmudic and midrashic texts, there is an increasing complexification of images in the medieval writings.

A major theme in the *Masekhet Gehinnom* texts is that of sins and their punishments. In some of the texts that follow, we find a recurrence of the motif of specific postmortem punishment meted out based on the nature of one's sins. Individual senses and body parts are tortured in retribution for behavioral transgressions involving such senses, limbs, genitals, breasts, hair, and so on.

Essentially, the operating principle working here is the biblical notion of "an eye for an eye, a tooth for a tooth" (Exodus 21:24; Leviticus 24:20), which is an underpinning in legal codes throughout the ancient Near East. Even in the rabbinic period, this principle operates, evidenced, for example, in Mishnah *Sotah* 1:8–9.[29]

On the value of these Gehenna texts, Saul Lieberman writes:

> The investigation of the visions of Gehenna is not only of interest to lovers of mysticism and folklore, but has a much broader scope. At times, there is reflected in these visions men's views on judicial justice, on sin and its punishment. Moreover, some of the cruel punishments used by the Roman authorities were inserted into Gehenna from real practice, and the authors were only speaking of the ordinary custom.[30]

The tortures detailed in the Gehenna texts do appear as macabre to our modern sentimentalities, but they are really no more so than *Twin Peaks*, *Robo-Cop*, and other media epics of violence and torture. These *midrashim* have a moralizing quality to them, and undoubtedly this was one of the goals of the original authors. "Don't sin with your mouth, or your mouth will be tortured!" "Don't sin with your hand, or your hand will be tortured!" This is the message that the *Masekhet Gehinnom* texts endeavor to communicate to the Jewish masses of the medieval world.

The text entitled *Compartments of Gehenna* is built on the rabbinic teachings on the seven names of Gehenna. The compartments here are named Sheol, Beer Shakhat, Tit Ha-Yaven, Shaarei Mavet, Abbadon, Shaarei Tzalmavet, and Gehinnom.

In *Rabbi Joshua ben Levi and the Seven Compartments of Gehinnom* the names of the compartments are not mentioned, but in each compartment is to be found an accompanying angel that is named in this text.

The Hebrew word for "compartment" is *madorei*, which is a play on the word *madura*, or "fireplace." Hence, we might say that there are seven fiery realms of Gehenna in these texts, with accompanying angels of destruction.[31]

Table 6-1 outlines the contents of the realms of Gehenna evidenced in the final two texts of this section.

Masekhet Gehinnom—"Tractate of Gehinnom"[32]

1. It is said: "Who can stand before its might, who can withstand the fury of its wrath?" (Nahum 1:6). Rabbi Abahu opened his homily with the verse: "*Aluka* has two daughters called *Hab Hab*" (Proverbs 30:15).[33] Rabbi Eliezer says that these are the two bands of angels that stand at the Gates of Gehinnom and say, "Come! come!" Why is it named Gehinnom (Valley of Wailing)? Because the voice of its wailing traverses the world from one end to the other. And why is it called *Tofteh* ("enticer")? Because all enter there enticed by their evil inclination.

Chapter 1 begins here:

2. Rabbi Yohanan began his homily with the verse "Passing through the valley of weeping, they make it a valley of springs" (Psalm 84:7). This means to say that the sinner confesses, just as the leper confesses; and he says: "I have committed such and such a transgression in that place, on that day in the presence of So-and-so, in that society."

TABLE 6-1 COMPARTMENTS OF GEHENNA

Name	Angel	Inhabitants	Leader
1. Sheol		open pits and fiery lions	
2. Beer Shakhat	Kushiel	ten nations of world	Absalom
3. Tit Ha-Yaven	Shabtil	seven nations of world	Korah and company
4. Shaarei Mavet	Maktiel	four nations of the world	Jeroboam
5. Abbadon	Hushiel	seven nations	Ahab
6. Shaarei Tzalmavet	Parhiel		Micah
7. Gehinnom		six nations of the world	Elisha b. Abuya

3. Gehinnom has three gates: one at the sea, the other in the wilderness, and the third in the inhabited part of the world. That at the sea is alluded to in Jonah: "Out of the belly of Sheol cried I, and you heard my voice" (Jonah 2:3). That in the wilderness, of which it is said: "So they and all that appertained to them went down alive into Sheol" (Numbers 16:30). And that in the inhabited portion of the world in Isaiah: "Says the Lord, whose fire is in Zion and His furnace in Jerusalem" (Isaiah 31:9).

4. Five different kinds of fires are in Gehinnom: one devours and absorbs; another absorbs and does not devour; another devours but does not absorb; while another, again, neither devours nor absorbs. There is further the fire that devours fire.

5. There are coals big as mountains, and coals big as hills, and coals huge like the Dead Sea, and coals like huge stones. There are rivers of pitch and sulfur flowing and fuming and seething.

6. The punishment of the sinner is thus: the Angels of Destruction throw him to the flame of Gehinnom; this opens its mouth wide and swallows him, as it is said, "Therefore Sheol has enlarged herself and opened her mouth without measure, and their glory and their multitude and their pomp, and he that is joyful, shall do down in it" (Isaiah 5:14). This all happens to him who has not done one single pious act that would incline the balance toward mercy.

7. While that man who possesses many virtues and good actions and learning, and who has suffered much, he is saved from Gehinnom, as it is written, "Yea, though I walk through the valley of the shadow of death, I will fear no evil, for You are with me; Your rod and Your staff shall comfort me" (Psalm 23:4). "Your rod" means the suffering, and "Your staff" signifies the law.

Chapter 2 begins here:

8. Rabbi Yohanan began: "The eyes of the wicked shall fail, and refuge is perished from them, and their hope shall be the giving up of the ghost" (Job 11:20). That means, a body that is never destroyed, and whose soul enters a fire that is never extinguished; of these speaks also the verse, "For their worm shall not die, neither shall their fire be quenched" (Isaiah 66:20).

Masekhet Gehinnom—"Tractate of Gehinnom" (continued)[34]

1. Rabbi Joshua ben Levi said, "Once upon a time I was walking on my way, when I met the Prophet Elijah. He said to me, 'Would you like to be brought to the Gate of Gehinnom?' I answered, 'Yes!' So he showed me men hanging by their hair, and he said to me, 'These were the men that let their hair grow to adorn themselves for sin.' Others were hanging by their eyes; these were they that followed their eyes to sin, and did not set the Holy Blessed One before them. Others were hanging by their noses; these were they that perfumed themselves to sin. Others were hanging by their tongues; these were they that had slandered. Others were hanging by their hands, these were they that had stolen and robbed. Others were hanging ignominiously; these were they that had committed adultery. Others were hanging by their feet; these were they that had run to sin. He showed me women hanging by their breasts; these were they that uncovered their breasts before men, to make them sin.

2. "He showed me further men that were fed on fiery coals; these were they who had blasphemed. Others were forced to eat bitter gall; these were they that ate on fast days.

3. "He showed me further men eating fine sand; they are forced to eat it, and their teeth are broken; and the Holy Blessed One says to them, 'O you sinners! when you used to eat that which you stole and robbed it was sweet in your mouth; now you are not able to eat even this,' as it is said, 'You have broken the teeth of the wicked' (Psalm 3:8).

4. "He showed me further men who are thrown from fire to snow, and from snow to fire; these were they that abused the poor who came to them for assistance; therefore are they thus punished, as it is said, 'You have caused men to ride over our heads; we went through fire and through water.' He showed me others who were driven from mountain to mountain, as a shepherd leads the flock from one mountain to another. Of these speaks the verse: 'Like sheep they are appointed to Sheol; death shall be their shepherd; and the upright shall have the dominion over them in the morning; and their form shall waste away in Sheol, leaving behind their dwelling'" (Psalm 49:15).

5. Rabbi Yohanan said, "For every sin there is an angel appointed
to obtain the expiation thereof; one comes first and obtains his
expiation, then follows another and so on until all the sins are
expiated. As with a debtor who has many creditors, and who
come before the king to claim their debts, and the king delivers
him to them, and says, 'Take him and divide him between yourselves,' so also is the soul delivered in Gehinnom to cruel angels, and they divide it among themselves."

Chapter 3 begins here:

6. Three descend to Gehinnom forever, and do not ascend anymore—the man who commits adultery, who blames his neighbor in public, and who is guilty of perjury. Others say those who
seek honor for themselves by slandering their neighbors, and
those who make intrigues between man and wife in order to create strife among them.

7. On the eve of the Sabbath the sinners are led to two mountains
of snow; there they are left until the end of the Sabbath, when
they are taken back from there and brought again to their former
places. An angel comes and thrusts them back to their former
place in Gehinnom. Some of them take, however, snow and hide
it in their armpits to cool them during the six days of the week,
but the Holy Blessed One says to them: "Woe to you who steal
even in Gehinnom," as it is said, "Drought and heat consume
the snow waters, so does Sheol those who have sinned" (Job
24:19). That means to say, "They sin even in Sheol."

Chapter 4 begins here:

8. Every twelve months the sinners are burned to ashes, and the
wind disperses them and carries those ashes under the feet of
the righteous, as it is said, "And you shall tread down the wicked,
for they shall be ashes under the sole of your feet" (Malachi 3:21).
Afterward, their soul is returned to them, they are released from
Gehinnom, and they come out black as the blackness of a pot,
and they acknowledge the justice of their punishment and say,
"You have rightly sentenced us and rightly judged us. With You
is righteousness and with us shame, as it is with us today."

Punishments of Gehenna[35]

1. There are five kinds of punishments in Gehinnom, and Isaiah saw them all. He entered the first compartment and saw there two men carrying pails full of water on their shoulders, and they pour that water into a pit, which, however, never fills. Isaiah said to the Holy Blessed One, "O You who unveils all that is hidden, unveil to me the secret of this." And the Spirit of the Lord answered, "These are the men who coveted the property of their neighbors, and this is their punishment."

2. He entered the second compartment, and he saw two men hanging by their tongues; and he said, "O You who unveils the hidden, reveal to me the secret of this." He answered, "These are the men who slandered, therefore they are thus punished."

3. He entered the third compartment, and he saw there men hanging by their organs. He said, "O You who unveils the hidden, reveal to me the secret of this." And He answered, "These are the men who neglected their own wives, and committed adultery with the daughters of Israel."

4. He entered the fourth compartment and saw there women hanging by their breasts, and he said, "O You who unveils the hidden, reveal to me the secret of this." And he answered, "These are the women who uncovered their hair and rent their veil, and stay in the open marketplace to suckle their children, in order to attract the gaze of men and to make them sin; therefore they are punished thus."

5. He entered the fifth compartment and found it full of smoke. There were all the princes, chiefs, and great men, and Pharaoh, the wicked, presides over them and watches at the gate of Gehinnom, and he says unto them, "Why did you not learn from me when I was in Egypt?" Thus he sits there and watches at the gates of Gehinnom.

6. There are seven compartments in Gehinnom, and in each of them are 7,000 rooms, in each room 7,000 windows, in each window [recess] there are 7,000 vessels filled with venom, all destined for slanderous writers and iniquitous judges. It is to that that Solomon alludes when he says, "And you mourn at your latter end when your flesh and your body are consumed."

7. The other nations, however, and the idolators are punished in the seven compartments of Gehinnom, in each compartment for twelve months. And the River of Light [*Nehar Dinur*] flows from beneath the Throne of Glory and falls over the heads of the sinners, and the sound travels from one end of the world to the other.

8. All these punishments are prepared for the apostates, for those who deny the resurrection of the dead, for the renegades, slanderers, and traitors. Of these King Solomon said, "Their evil shall be as bitter as wormwood." None of these are saved unless they repent, acquire learning, and perform pious deeds. But at the end the Holy Blessed One will have pity on all His creatures, as it is said, "For I will not always chide, nor keep anger forever, for the spirit shall pass before Me and the souls which I have made" (Psalm 103:9).

Compartments of Gehenna[36]

1. There are besides in every compartment 7,000 holes [crevices], and in every hole there are 7,000 scorpions. Every scorpion has 300 slits [cavities]: in every slit are 7,000 pouches of venom, and from each of these flow six rivers of deadly poison. When a man touches it, he immediately bursts, every limb is torn from him, his body is cleft asunder, and he falls dead upon his face. The Angels of Destruction collect his limbs, set them aright, and revive the man and place him upon his feet, and take their revenge upon him anew. This takes place in the uppermost compartment, which is called Sheol. The height thereof is 300 years' journey, the width 300 years' journey, and its length the same.

2. The second compartment is Beer Shakhat, of the same height, width, and length. The third is Tit-Hayaven, of equal size. The fourth is Shaarei Mavet, of the same size. The fifth, Abbadon, of the same size. The sixth, Shaarei Tzalmavet, of the same size. The seventh, Gehinnom, of the same size. Thus the length of hell is altogether 6,300 years' journey. [We read further that the fire of Gehinnom is one-sixtieth of the fire of Shaarei Tzalmavet, and so of every consecutive compartment until the fire of Sheol.] Sheol consists half of fire and half of hail [ice], and when the sinners contained therein emerge from the fire they are tortured

by the hail [ice], and when they emerge from the hail [ice] the fire burns them, and the angels who preside over them keep their souls within their bodies. As it is said, "For their worm shall not die, neither shall their fire be quenched."

3. Every day the Angel of Death comes and drives them on like cattle from mountain to valley and from valley to mountain, as it is said, "They are sent down to Sheol like sheep; death acts like a shepherd unto them." The Angels of Destruction punish the sinners for twelve months in Gehinnom. After twelve months they revive their bodies and lower them to Shaarei Mavet, where they are again punished for twelve months. Then they are lowered into Shaarei Tzalmavet, and after twelve months' punishment they are lowered into Tit-Hayaven, and again after twelve months' punishment they are lowered into Beer Shakhat. Thence, after the same lapse of time, to Abbadon, and finally, after twelve months' punishment, they are lowered then into Sheol, where they are seen by the righteous, who say, "O Lord, who are merciful to all Your creatures, let it be enough for them!" But the Holy Blessed One answers, "It is not yet enough, for they have destroyed My temple, and have sold My children as slaves among the nations." Then they are lowered to Arqa, and placed beneath the river of fire that flows from beneath the Throne of Glory, and he who is lowered into Arqa ascends no more.

4. Above Arqa is Tehom, and above Tehom is Tohu. Above this is Bohu, and above Bohu is the sea [Yam], and above the bottom of the sea are the waters. Above the waters is the inhabited world, on the surface of which rise the mountains and dales. This earth is inhabited by man and beasts, by the birds of the air and the fish of the sea. Therein is Torah, charity, and piety, and the fear of the Lord.

5. At the time of judgment 6,000 angels of trembling surround man and lead him to the place of judgment, where they weigh his merit and his guilt in the balance. Then if his guilt turns the scale they lead him to Gehinnom and hand him over to the angels of terror, and these again to the angels of anguish, and these to the angels of trembling; the angels of trembling then to the Angels of Destruction, who hand him over to the Angel of Death. He throws him into the depth of Gehinnom, as it is said, "And the angel of the Lord punishes him."

6. If, however, his merits turn the scale, they lead him to the gates
   of Gan Eden and hand him over to the ministering angels, who
   hand him over to the Angels of Peace, and these to the Angels
   of Mercy, who bestow great honor upon him in Gan Eden.

Rabbi Joshua ben Levi and the Seven Compartments of Gehinnom[37]

1. After this I implored [the Messiah] and said, "Show me
   Gehinnom, which I desire to behold." But he would not allow
   me. And I said to him, "Why will you not let me see it?" To
   which the Messiah answered and said, "It is not meant for the
   righteous to see it, for there are no righteous people in
   Gehinnom."

2. I then sent to the angel Kushiel[38] that he might measure
   Gehinnom from beginning to end; but he was not able to do
   so, because at that time Rabbi Ishmael, Rabbi Shimon, son of
   Gamliel, and ten other righteous men were put to death. I tried,
   but could not succeed.

3. After this, I went to the angel Kushiel, who went with me until
   I came before the fire at the Gates of Gehinnom. The Messiah
   [also] went with me, and when the wicked in Gehinnom saw
   the light of the Messiah, they rejoiced and said, "This one will
   bring us forth from this fire." They showed me then a compartment in Gehinnom, which I entered, and, going round it, I
   measured it.

4. Rabbi Joshua said, "When I measured the first compartment of
   Gehinnom, I found it to be one mile in length and breadth, and
   behold, there were many open pits in which were lions, and the
   lions were of fire. There were also two brooks, and when the
   wicked people fall therein, they are swallowed up, and lions of
   fire standing above cast them into the fire.

5. When I measured the second compartment, I found it as the
   first, and I asked the same questions as I asked about the first,
   and they made the same reply. There were in it some of the
   nations of the world, presided over by Absalom, and one nation says to the other, "If we have sinned, it is because we did
   not wish to accept the law; but you, what sin have you committed?" And they reply, "We have committed the same sin as

you." And they say to Absalom, "If you have not listened, your ancestors have done so. And why have you then been punished in such a manner?" "Because," he replied, "I did not listen to the exhortations of my father."

6. An angel stands with a rod of fire, and this angel that smites them is named Lahatiel. He orders the other angels to throw them down and to burn them, and one by one they are brought in, and after smiting them, they are cast upon the fire and burned until all the people have been consumed. After this, Absalom is brought in to be smitten, when a voice is heard to say, "Do not smite him nor burn him because he is one of the sons of those whom I love, who said on Mount Sinai, 'We shall do, and we shall hear.'" After they have finished smiting and burning the wicked these emerge from the fire just as if they had not been burnt; they are then smitten again, and again thrust into the fire, and this is repeated seven times every day and three times every night. But Absalom is saved from all this because he is one of the sons of David.

7. The third compartment contains seven nations of the world, who are judged in the same manner, and Korah and his company are with them. The name of him who smites them is Shaftiel. But Korah and his company are saved from all this, because they exclaimed on Mount Sinai, "We shall do, and we shall hearken."

8. The fourth compartment contains four nations of the world, with Jeroboam to preside over them, and the one who smites them is named Machtiel. But Jeroboam is delivered from all these punishments, because he descended from those who exclaimed, "We shall do, and we shall hearken."

9. In the fifth compartment they are judged likewise. It contains seven nations, with Ahab among them, and he who smites them is named Khutriel. But Ahab is delivered from all this, because his ancestors said on Mount Sinai, "We shall do, and we shall hearken."

10. The sixth compartment, containing ten nations of the world, is judged likewise, and Micah is among them, and the angel who smites them is named Pusiel. But Micah is rescued from all this, because his ancestors also exclaimed on Mount Sinai, "We shall do, and we shall hearken."

11. The seventh compartment contains six nations of the world, which are judged in the same manner, and among them is Elisha ben Abuya; and the angel who smites them is named Dalkiel. But one cannot see the other [compartments] on account of the darkness, for the darkness that existed before the creation of the world is now there.

GAN EDEN TEXTS

This section consists of four texts in which different facets of Gan Eden are described. The first text, *Masekhet Gan Eden*, or "Tractate of Gan Eden," is the earliest of the collection here. This text first appears in the thirteenth-century midrashic anthology *Yalkut Shimoni* and is a link back to the previous chapter on rabbinic views of the afterlife. The translation presented here is a more elaborate version of the mythic Gan Eden text presented in Chapter 5. In *Beit Ha-Midrash* Jellinek incorrectly titled this text *Seder Gan Eden*.[39] However, the text often appears as the first chapter of *Masekhet Gan Eden*. With elaborate, ornate imagery the text describes the gates of Gan Eden and the fate awaiting the righteous dead when they enter the heavenly realm.

The next text, *Rabbi Joshua ben Levi and the Seven Compartments of Gan Eden*, is connected with the Gehenna text we looked at earlier that describes Rabbi Joshua ben Levi's tour of the seven realms of punishment. In some editions, the two texts appear together; in other cases, separately. Here the seven compartments of Gan Eden are not named. What is described are the inhabitants of each of the seven realms which include proselytes; penitents; the patriarchs and those Israelites who departed Egypt, and those who lived in the desert; the perfect, the faithful, and the righteous; the Messiah, the son of David; those who died while performing a pious act; and those who died from illnesses caused through the sins of Israel.

Life in Gan Eden on the Sabbath, or *Seder Gan Eden*, is a small text that describes the activities of the dead on Sabbath. Here, we learn that all the dead of Israel rest on the Sabbath. Along with this emerges the view that when the Sabbath arrives, all souls are released from Gehenna and permitted to enter and taste of the bliss of Gan Eden.

Gan Eden and the World to Come, which goes by the Hebrew title *Seder Gan Eden*, is by far the most elaborate and complete text describing the realms of Gan Eden. Originally, this text was incorporated within the body of a book entitled *Orhot Hayyim*, or *The Ways of Life*, also known as *Tzavaat Rabbi Eliezer*, or *The Ethical Will of Rabbi Eliezer*. This is a moralistic and ethical treatise, written in the Middle Ages, which consists of two parts: an ethical will from Rabbi Eliezer the Great to his son[40] and the text *Seder Gan Eden*, which appears below. In early manuscripts of *Orhot Hayyim*, these two sections appeared together, although later they are separated.[41]

According to Gershom Scholem, *Seder Gan Eden* was most likely produced in the kabbalistic circles of the thirteenth century; there is even speculation that Moses de Leon himself may have been the author of this visionary depiction of Gan Eden.[42] Thus, while *Seder Gan Eden* technically belongs to the literature of the *Zohar*, it is characteristically a form of medieval legendary Midrash and for that reason is included in this chapter. We see in this text the full-grown development of the tradition of visionary depictions of the afterlife.

The landscape of Gan Eden, according to this text, contains the following phenomena: First of all, there are three outer walls surrounding Gan Eden, with gates and accompanying angels. At each wall are to be found specific categories of righteous. Furthermore, the outer wall seems to be a transit station for those being sent to Gehinnom to receive punishment, and for those who are returning from there having already suffered due affliction.

Within Gan Eden itself, there are seven realms of the righteous, wherein are to be found accompanying angels and deceased biblical ancestors who are given the task of leadership of a specific realm. In the first realm are those who are called Righteous, and angels named Aralim. It is Joseph the righteous, son of Jacob, who is head of this realm. In the second realm are those who are called Upright, and angels named Hashmalim. Phineas, the son of Eleazar, is head of this realm. In the third realm are those who are called Perfect, and angels named Tarshishim.[43] Eleazar, son of Aaron the priest, is head of this realm. In the fourth realm are those who are called Holy. Aaron the priest is head of this realm. In the fifth realm are those who are penitents. Angelic beings named Ophanim and the angel Barkiel are found in this realm. Manasseh, king of Judah, is appointed as head of this realm. In the sixth realm are found unsinning schoolchildren, Metatron, the Angel of the Countenance, as well as the Cherubim. Joshua, the attendant of Moses, is head of this realm. In the seventh realm are those who are called Perfect and angelic beings called "holy Hayyot." Abraham, Isaac, and Jacob are appointed over this realm.

Interestingly, what appears in *Seder Gan Eden* is a delineation of the dwelling places of the righteous women in Gan Eden.[44] In the first dwelling is Batyah, the daughter of Pharaoh. In the second dwelling is Yokheved, the wife of Amram. In the third dwelling is Miriam the prophetess. In the fourth dwelling is Hulda the prophetess. In the fifth dwelling is Abigail. Beyond this point, one find the matriarchs: Sarah, Rebecca, Rachel, and Leah.

As Chava Weissler has shown,[45] this motif of women in Gan Eden is amplified in later Jewish literature, particularly in Yiddish devotional writings of the sixteenth to nineteenth centuries. What is found here in *Seder Gan Eden* is likely the earliest text that elucidates the nature of the heavenly realms where women can occupy themselves with study of Torah.

Also mentioned in *Seder Gan Eden* are a number of additional heavenly palaces—the Palace of Splendor (*Hekhal Nogah*), the Palace of the Messiah (elsewhere called "the bird's nest," or *kan ha-tzippor*),[46] the Palace of the Heads of the Academies, and the Palace of the Nut (*Hekhal Ha-Egoz*). These are found deep within the interior regions of Gan Eden.

At the very end, the text describes the existence of three walls surrounding the heavenly Gan Eden [*Gan Eden shel Malah*]. The first is called "The Whisper of the Secret Staircase"; the second, "The Movement of the Lord's Laborer"; the third, "The Garden of the Royal Cloak."

The power of the text lies in its imagery and is most certainly among the most descriptive of all Jewish writings on Gan Eden.

Masekhet Gan Eden—"Tractate of Gan Eden" ("The Gates of Gan Eden")[47]

1. Thus says Rabbi Joshua ben Levi: Gan Eden has two gates of carbuncle, and sixty myriads of ministering angels keep watch over them. Each of these angels shine like the radiance of the heavens. When the righteous person approaches them, the angels remove from him the clothes in which he had been buried, and clothe him with eight robes of the clouds of glory, and place upon his head two crowns, one of precious stones and pearls, and the other of gold, and they place eight myrtles in his hand and praise him, and say to him, "Go and eat your bread with joy." And they

lead him to a place full of waters surrounded by 800 species of roses and myrtles. Each one has a canopy according to his merits, as it is said, "For over all the glory shall be spread a canopy."

2. Through Gan Eden flow four rivers, one of oil, the other of balsam, the third of wine, and the fourth of honey. Every canopy is overgrown by a vine of gold, and thirty pearls hang down from it, each of them shining like [the planet] Venus, the morning star.

3. In every canopy there is a table of precious stones and pearls, and sixty angels stand at the head of every righteous person, saying to him, "Go and eat with joy of the honey for you have truly wrestled with the Torah," of which it is said, "And it is sweeter than honey," and drink of the wine preserved from the six days of Creation, for you have truly wrestled with the Torah, and she is compared to wine, as it is said, "I would cause you to drink of spiced wine." The least fair of the [angels of the righteous] is as beautiful as Joseph and Rabbi Yohanan [ben Zakkai], and as the grains of the pomegranate lit up by the rays of the sun. And there is no night, as it is said, "And the light of the righteous is as the shining light."

4. And everyday the Holy Blessed One creates for the righteous in Gan Eden four unique transformations in accordance with the phases of the day: In the first phase, the individual is changed into a child. He enters the realm for children, and tastes the joys of childhood. In the second phase, the individual is changed into a youth. He enters the realm of youth, and enjoys the delights of youth. In the third phase, the individual is changed into a middle-aged person. He enters the realm of the middle-aged, and enjoys the delights of middle-age. In the fourth phase, the individual is changed into an elder. He enters the realm of elders, and enjoys the pleasures of elders.

5. And in every corner of Gan Eden there are eighty myriads of trees, and the least among them is even more glorified than all the sweet-smelling spice trees. In every corner there are sixty myriads of ministering angels singing with sweet voices, and the tree of life and its flowering branches stands in the middle and overshadow all of Gan Eden; and it has fifteen thousand tastes,[48] and each one unique. No taste, smell, or image of one is at all like the other.

6. And the tree of life has forty-eight branches, each one as the fullness of the entire world. And from each one come an additional seven branches, reaching upward, as it is written in Torah: "She is a tree of life to those who cleave unto her."

7. Hanging over this tree of life are seven clouds of glory, and the winds blow upon it from all four directions, and its fragrance travels from one end of the world to the other. Underneath it sit the scholars who explain the Torah. Over each of them are spread two canopies, one of stars and the other of sun and moon, and each canopy has seventy divine curtains made of the clouds of glory. And deep within Gan Eden are found 310 worlds, [derived by numerical computation, or *gematria*, from the passage] as it is written: "That I may cause those that love Me to inherit Substance (Proverbs 7:21) [the numerical value of the Hebrew word for "substance"—שׁי—is equivalent to 310].

8. Here are [found] the seven compartments of the righteous. In the first are the martyrs, as, for instance, Rabbi Akiva and his companions. In the second, those who were drowned. In the third, Rabbi Yohanan ben Zakkai and his disciples. The fourth group consists of those who were covered by the cloud of glory. The fifth group is that of the penitents, for the place occupied by a penitent not even a perfectly just man can occupy. The sixth group is that of children who have not yet tasted sin in their lives. The seventh group is that of the poor, who, notwithstanding their poverty, studied the Torah and the Talmud and had followed a moral life. Of these speaks the verse, "For all that put their trust in You rejoice, and they shout for ever for joy" (Psalm 5:11).

9. And the Holy Blessed One sits in their midst, and expounds to them the Torah, as it is said, "My eyes shall be upon the faithful of the land, that they that dwell with Me" (Psalm 101:6). And God has not yet fully unveiled the glory that awaits the pious in the world to come, as it is said, "The eye has not seen, O God, beside You, that which You do for him that waits for Him" (Isaiah 64:4).

Rabbi Joshua ben Levi and the Seven Compartments of Gan Eden (*Maaseh de R. Joshua ben Levi*)[49]

1. Rabbi Joshua ben Levi was a pious man. When the time approached that he should leave this world, the Holy Blessed One

said to the Angel of Death, "Go and fulfill whatever his wish may be." He went to him and said to him: "The time has come for you to leave this world, but now tell me what you wish, that I may fulfill it."

2. As soon as Rabbi Joshua heard this, he said: "I pray, show me my place in Gan Eden." He answered and said: "Come and I will show it to you." Rabbi Joshua answered and said, "Give me your sword, so that you should not frighten me." And he gave him his sword.[50] So they went together until they reached the wall of Gan Eden. There being outside the wall, the Angel of Death lifted Rabbi Joshua from the ground and placed him upon the crest of the wall, and said to him: "Behold your place in Gan Eden."

3. At that moment Rabbi Joshua jumped down from the wall and fell into Gan Eden. The Angel of Death caught him by his mantle and said to him, "Get out of there!" But Rabbi Joshua swore by the name of God that he would not do so. The Angel of Death had no power to enter therein. The ministering angels seeing this said to the Holy Blessed One: "Master of the Universe, behold what Rabbi Joshua has done! By force has he taken possession of his portion in Gan Eden." The Holy Blessed One answered: "Go and see if he has ever broken his oath, then shall this oath of his be likewise void and null." They searched and could not find any such case. So they came and said: "He has never broken his oaths in his lifetime." And the Holy Blessed One answered: "If it be so, let him remain there."

4. When the Angel of Death saw this, he said to Rabbi Joshua: "Give me now my sword back." But Rabbi Joshua did not fulfill his request until a Heavenly Voice [Bat-Kol] came forth and said: "Give him the knife, for it is of necessity for His creatures."

5. Rabbi Joshua then said to him: "Swear to me that you will not show it anymore to the creatures at the moment when you take their souls." [For up to that time the Angel of Death used to kill men openly, as one slaughters animals, and he showed it even to the suckling in the bosom of their mother.] At that hour he swore to him, and Rabbi Joshua returned the knife to him.

6. After that began the Prophet Elijah to proclaim and to cry out aloud to the righteous: "Clear the way for the son of Levi."

7. He went and saw Rabbi Joshua sitting in the compartment of the righteous, and he asked him: "Are you the son of Levi?"

And he answered: "Yes." He asked again: "Have you seen a rainbow in your lifetime?" Again Rabbi Joshua answered: "Yes." And he replied: "Then if this is so, you are not the son of Levi."—In fact it had not been the case. Now Rabbi Joshua had not seen a rainbow, but he did not wish to boast of it and to ascribe it to his own merits. He had asked him about the rainbow, for it is the sign of the covenant between the Holy Blessed One and the world; and when the rainbow appears then the Holy Blessed One [remembers] and pities His creatures; but when there lives a righteous person, there is no longer any necessity for a rainbow, as through his merits the world is saved. As it is said: "And the righteous is the foundation of the world" (Proverbs 10:25). Therefore did he ask him about the rainbow.

8. The Angel of Death went to Rabbi Gamaliel and told him: "So and so has Rabbi Joshua done to me." Rabbi Gamaliel answered and said: "He served you right. But now please go and tell him I request him to search through Gan Eden and Gehinnom and their mysteries and write them down and send it to me, if there are gentiles in Gan Eden, and Israelites in Gehinnom."

9. The Angel of Death went, and Rabbi Joshua answered: "I will do so."

10. Thereupon Rabbi Joshua went and searched throughout Gan Eden and he found therein seven compartments, each of twelve myriads of miles in width, and twelve myriads of miles in length; the measure of their width being the same as that of their length.

11. The first compartment corresponds to the first gate of Gan Eden. Here dwell the proselytes who had embraced Judaism of their own free will, not from compulsion. The walls are of glass and the paneling of cedar. As I tried to measure it the inhabitants rose to prevent me from doing it. Obadiah the righteous, who presides over them, rebuked them and said: "What are your merits that this man should dwell here with you?" (for they wished to retain him there). Thereupon they allowed him to measure it.

12. The second compartment corresponds to the second gate of Gan Eden. It is built of silver and the paneling of cedar. Here dwell those who repent, and Manasseh, son of Ezekiah, presides over them.

13. The third compartment, facing the third gate, is built of silver and gold. Here dwell Abraham, Isaac, and Jacob, and all the

Israelites who came out of Egypt, and the whole generation who had lived in the desert, and all the kings [princes], with the exception of Absalom. There is also David, and Solomon, and Kilab, son of David, still alive, and all the kings of the house of Judah, with the exception of Manasseh, who presides over those who repent. Over these here preside Moses and Aaron. Here are the precious vessels of silver and gold, and jewels, and canopies, and beds, and thrones, and lamps of gold, and precious stones and pearls. And I asked: "For whom are all these prepared?" And David answered and said: "They are for those who still dwell in the world from where you have come." And I asked: "Is here perhaps one also from the gentiles, at least from my brother Esau?" And he answered and said: "No; because the Holy Blessed One gives the reward of every good deed they do in their lifetime in that world, but after death they go down to Gehinnom; while the sinners in Israel get their punishment in their lifetime in the world, but after death they obtain the merit of their good deed here." As it is said: "And he pays."

14. The fourth compartment, facing the fourth gate of Gan Eden, is beautifully built, like to the first compartment, but its paneling is of olive wood. Here dwell the perfect, the faithful, and the righteous. Why is the paneling of olive wood? Because their life has been bitter to them as olive wood.

15. The fifth compartment is built of onyx stones and of precious stones, crystal, and bdellium; and through its midst flows the River Gihon, which illumines the upper world. The walls are of silver and gold, and a perfume breathes through it more exquisite than the perfume of Lebanon. And beds of silver and gold are there prepared, covered with violet and purple covers, woven by Eve, and mixed with scarlet and made of goat's hair, a palanquin of the wood of Lebanon; the pillars are of silver, the bottom of gold, the seat of it of purple. Herein lies the Messiah, the son of David, who is the love of the daughters of Jerusalem, the midst thereof is love. The Prophet Elijah takes the head of the Messiah and places it in his bosom and says to him: "Be quiet and wait, for the end draws near." On every Monday and Thursday and Sabbath and Holy Day, the Patriarchs, and all the tribes, and Moses and Aaron and David and Solomon and every king of Israel and of the House of David, comfort him, and say to him: "Be quiet and wait and rely upon

your Creator, for the end draws near." Also Korah and his company and Dathan and Abiram and Absalom come to him on
every Wednesday, and ask him: "When will the end of our mis-
ery come? When will you reveal yourself?"

16. He answers them and says: "Go to your Patriarchal ancestors
and ask them." And when they hear of their Patriarchal ancestors they feel ashamed [shy] and do not ask any further.

17. When I came to the Messiah he asked me: "What is Israel doing
in the world from which you come?" And I answered and said:
"Every day they await you in their captivity among the nations
of the world, which oppresses them." He immediately raised His
voice and wept.

18. In the sixth compartment dwell those who died through performing a pious act.

19. In the seventh compartment dwell those who died from illnesses
caused through the sins of Israel.[51]

20. Said Rabbi Joshua ben Levi: "After having seen this I wrote to
Rabbi Gamaliel and the elders of Israel, and I told them all what
I had seen in Gan Eden. . . . May the Compassionate Almighty
save us from the judgment of Gehinnom and give us a share in
the World to Come, along with the righteous and the just."

Life in Gan Eden on the Sabbath (*Seder Gan Eden*)[52]

1. The sages tell that the dead have a large habitation, in front of
which there flows a brook from Gan Eden, and by the side of this
brook is a field. On every Sabbath eve between the afternoon
and evening services the souls of the dead go forth from their
secret abode and eat on this field and drink from this brook.

2. And every Israelite who drinks water between the afternoon and
evening services of the Sabbath robs the dead. When the con-
gregation on Sabbath eve exclaim, "Bless the Lord, who is
blessed," they return to their graves, and the Holy Blessed One
revives them and causes them to stand upon their feet alive.

3. And all the dead of Israel rest on the Sabbath, and all stand up
alive from their graves, and great multitudes come before the
Holy Blessed One and sing praises unto Him upon their graves,
and going to the synagogues, prostrate themselves before Him,
as it is said, "The pious exult in honor, and they sing upon their
resting places."

4. Every Sabbath and every new moon they rise from their graves, and coming before the Divine Presence, prostrate themselves before Him, as it is said, "And the people of the earth shall worship Me, on Sabbaths and on the new moons" (Ezekiel 46:3). What is meant by the people of the earth? Those who are hidden in the earth, as it is written, "And it shall come to pass that on each new moon and upon each Sabbath all flesh shall come to worship Me" (Isaiah 66:23).

Gan Eden and the World to Come (*Seder Gan Eden*)[53]

The Outer Wall

There are three walls around Gan Eden, and all are of fire. The outer wall is of black fire, which is both visible and invisible. The flaming sword around the outer wall turns itself around it (Genesis 3:24). There are four gates in the outer wall with a distance of 120 cubits from one gate to the other. The flaming sword revolves all day and night, is never still, and consumes all green grass and everything within a mile's distance from the garden. There is a distance of 600 mile's distance from the garden. There is a distance of 600 cubits between that outer wall and the second wall. There are the pious of the gentiles, their kings who have rescued the Israelites, and those proselytes who do not fittingly implement the fear of the Lord in all its implications. From the time of the afternoon sacrifice onward, the angels of destruction are gathered together to take them away from there and lead them to Gehinnom. All will be crying aloud when the angel appointed over them, whose name is Azriel, will come and seize them and deliver them from their hands. They will return from the afternoon sacrifice and before the evening prayer three times they will cry to Abraham in a loud voice. That angel will then return and seize them as in the beginning. All this is so as to afflict them. There in that outer wall will also be those who do righteousness in public, but not in the name of Heaven. These will be sorry for themselves three times a day, and two angels will seize them and rescue them from the hands of the destroying angel. All those who have received their punishment in Gehinnom and are coming out from there will be accompanied by three ministering angels, who will bring them to the place of the revolving, flaming sword. There they will receive their purification and enter into this outer wall, and there they will stand and enjoy a trifle of the luster of the countenance of the righteous who are within, but they will not cause them distress. All those wicked ones who were contemplating to do repentance before they left the world and after they had received their punishment will enter this wall and wait there until the sanctifying of the day on the eve of the Sabbath. The breezes inside Gan Eden will go up from the angel Hariel, who brings all these in and shows them their designated places of pleasure. When the winds go up toward the crevice of the rock, he [the angel] gives them a place which they enter at the termination of the Sabbath. At the time when the Israelites are saying the prescribed holy prayer, all the winds descend to their dwelling places, each one knowing his appointed place and his exact location.

The Second Wall

The second wall is of green and red fire, and the angel Peniel is appointed over them. There, within that wall, are those who enabled their sons to learn Torah. Although they [the children] did not succeed, yet they [the parents] tried [to impart learning] to them. There are those who were men of action, who were immediately ready to listen to the words of the Torah and moral teachings. There the light from the pleasantness of the righteous remains with them only for an instant and immediately vanishes. All those who expect the Messiah and all those who see the Messiah from there once every day [are there]. On the sixth day, at the time when the Israelites try to rest, all the palaces in the Garden tremble. The inner palace where the Messiah is called "the bird's nest." The Messiah goes out from there with all the righteous ones accompanying him. He wears garments of vengeance that are destined for the salvation of Israel. All enter with him and the fathers when he goes out from there and stands in the midst of the Garden, in the place of the pillar, which is in the center. He will take hold of the four signet rings that are in the four corners of the Garden and will shout so loudly as to cause the firmament above the Garden to tremble.

Gan Eden and all its effects were created before the world was created—all its plants, the firmament that is over them, and the ground under it. After 1,361 years, 3 hours, and 2 minutes, heaven and earth were created. The ground of the Garden [came into existence thus]: When the Holy Blessed One created Gan Eden, he took snow from under the Throne of Glory from which he called into being the ground of the Garden. This ground of the Garden both touches and does not touch the land that is above all the countries. The firmament that is over the Garden reflects all the colors of a paved work of a sapphire stone (Exodus 24:10). The name of the Holy Blessed One is engraved in the middle of the firmament. There are four signet rings at the four corners of the firmament and four Ophanim in every signet. In the midst of the firmament is a pillar, and this pillar is projected from the ground of the Garden until it is seized before the Throne of Glory and is covered by the cloud of glory. The angel Gabriel, dressed in linen, stands over it. Once a day he seizes the signet rings of the firmament, and the pillar that revolves, and the firmament surrounding [it on which are engraved] the letters of the Ineffable Name protruding, glittering, ascending, and descending. A voice proclaims, "Prepare yourselves, O righteous saints. Blessed are you that you have merited this. Who has heard or seen [things] like these?" When the music sounded, the firmament was moved by the man dressed in linen. It removes itself, stands still, and the pillar sounds its note, going up and down while the light continues shining, a pleasant light from above that pillar. The righteous will stand before that light and enjoy it until midnight. At midnight, when the Holy Blessed One comes to enter with the righteous, they will hear a voice encircling the firmament. Then the pillar will sound its note, the ground of the Garden will be raised, and the righteous will arise from their canopies to meet their Maker. The whole Garden will be filled with his glory. At that hour the male and female spirits will be mated as when they were created. From that pleasant desire of theirs to see the pleasant one of the Lord, all bearing fruit, and their fruit will produce spirits for proselytes just as Abraham and Sarah produced spirits for proselytes. Blessed is the one who merits in this age to be found in that hour with the joy of the Torah!

The light of the brilliance of the Holy Blessed One will remain in Gan Eden, but it will ascend and all the righteous ones will go out and be nourished from it, just as are the heavenly, ministering angels. At that time when the Messiah goes out and seizes the four signet rings and shouts loudly, shaking all the firmament that is over the Garden, the seven angels attending him will say, "Keep still, O chosen one of the Lord, for the time has already arrived when the wicked kingdom will be uprooted from its place." The voice will be heard from the synagogues and houses of study, where [the worshipers] will say with all their might, "Amen! May his great Name be blessed forever, and unto eternity!" Then the Holy Blessed One will shake the firmament and two tears will fall to the Great Sea. The righteous will enter together with the Messiah into that palace called "the bird's nest."

The Third Wall

The third wall is composed of light mixed with darkness, and it is before Gan Eden. From there on the interest of the Garden is in its ascents, pleasures, and buildings. It is like the paved work of sapphire stone whose plant ascends for the benefit of the spirits of the four winds that blow upon it from the four corners. These spirits are from the subject of the [living] beast that is under the God of Israel. This is the beast that the waters breed from the Upper Eden [Eden Ha-Elyon], which "eye has not seen, O God, except you, who works for those who wait for him" (Isaiah 64:3). Inside this wall is the brightness that has appeared like the glory of the Lord. From there on the righteous, who are the spirits, dwell. When they enter there they are immediately embodied by the upper air that blows in the Garden, and they are dressed in it like a pure and holy garment. That garment is of the same pattern that was in this world. With this garment, they walk and recognize each other, each as it befits him.

The Seven Realms of the Righteous in Gan Eden[54]

First Realm

There are seven realms of the righteous in Gan Eden, with seven canopies separated from each other according to their realms. The first realm of those who are called righteous, and they are all those who keep the holy covenant in this world and who controlled their evil impulses and faithfully observed the commands of the Torah. Opposite them from above were those angels named Aralim. The chief of this realm is Joseph the righteous, son of Jacob. He ministers in the first canopy, which is the first palace in Gan Eden.

Second Realm

The second realm is of those who are called the upright. They are just in their ways and all the things they do in this world [they do] with an upright heart. They have no thoughts of evil things, for all their deeds are upright before their Creator. Facing them above are those angels who are called Hashmalim. These are in front of the realm of the righteous. Concerning these two groups, it is said, "The righteous will praise your name; the just will dwell before you" (Psalm 140:14). The chief of this realm is Phineas, the son of Elazar who ministers in this canopy, which is the second palace in Gan Eden.

Third Realm

The third realm consists of those who are called perfect and who pace this world with a perfect heart and do not entertain impure thoughts of the ways of the Holy Blessed One. They have tried to attain the realms of the first ones in righteousness and equity within their hearts, and they have kept the words of the Torah and the commandments. Facing them above are those angels, the ministers of the Most High who are called Tarshishim. The head of this realm is Elazar, son of Aaron the priest, who ministers in this canopy, which is the third palace in Gan Eden.

Fourth Realm

The fourth realm is of those who are called holy. They are the ones of whom it is written, "They are for the holy ones who are in the land, my noble ones. All my desire is in them" (Psalm 16:3). These possess all the keys of the gates of Gan Eden. When the pillar that is in the center of the Garden moves and plays of its own accord, then the firmament that is over Gan Eden returns. Those who went out first to meet their Creator draw near to the pillar. The man dressed in linen seizes the four signet rings that are in the firmament, and the pillar of the firmament strikes the signet ring that is in the heart of the firmament. Then all the trees in the Garden sing for joy and burst forth in paeans of praise, and the glory of the God of Israel comes, concerning whom it is said, "Behold the glory of the Lord God of Israel comes from the holy way, and the land will reflect his glory" (Ezekiel 43:1). This is Gan Eden. The realm of these holy ones began first by saying, "Holy, holy, holy is the Lord of hosts" (Isaiah 6:3; Psalm 72:19). Over the realm of these holy ones is Aaron, the priest of his holy God.

Fifth Realm

The fifth realm is of the repentant who broke the brass doors and returned to their Creator in a fitting manner. Facing them above is the realm of the attendants of the Holy One on high. The place of their realm is called Ophanim, and there is none who can reach their realm, because it is very high. The pleasant one of the Name reaches them because of the brilliance of the repentance from on high which "eye has not seen" (Isa. 64:3). All the righteous ones are scorched by the canopy of these. Even the wicked ones in Gehinnom see the brilliance of their realm and cry out, "Master of the Universe, there is favoritism in this, for both we and these in this great canopy have all sinned together and have transgressed the Torah. Why do they enjoy this great realm while we live in the thick darkness of the pit of Gehinnom?" At once the angel Barkiel appears for them and says, "Fools that you are! When you were in the world, you were content to go out [of the world]. These of your fellows who sinned like you finally meditated glory." Manasseh, king of Judah, is appointed over them.

Sixth Realm

The sixth realm is that of the schoolchildren who have not sinned. This is a more intimate realm than the others, and every day Metatron, the Angel of the Countenance [Hebrew: *Sar Ha-Panin*], descends by way of the pillar and teaches them the Torah. Their compartment is greater than all the others. At midnight, they go up to the academy above, and the Holy Blessed One teaches them Torah in which they take delight. Facing them above are those called Cherubim, of whom it is said, "Who teaches knowledge and who understands the report? Those who are weaned from milk, taken from the breast" (Isaiah 28:9). The chief of this division below is Joshua, the young man who was the attendant of Moses.

Seventh Realm

The seventh realm is one whose members are called *Hasidim* and which is the most inward of all. Facing [the members] from above is the realm of the *Hayyot* that are called the "holy *Hayyot*." Over it [the realm] are appointed Abraham, Isaac, and Jacob. The name, Adam, has been placed over the door of this palace. There are seven gates in this seventh wall, corresponding to the seven realms. Each of these realms enters into a gate above that realm, and guards stand over every gate. The group of the righteous enter through theirs; and thus [it is with] every single realm of these seven realms.

Contents of the Garden

In Gan Eden, from the wall inward, there is a thick cloud, but its surroundings are brilliant. On the north side, there is a curtain that is separated from the brilliance and a greenish fire divide them from the rest of the spirits of the Garden. There the palaces are hidden because of the righteous and pure women that were in Israel. On the side of the east wind there is a palace that is hidden and closed. It is called the Palace of Splendor [Hebrew: *Hekhal Nogah*]. This palace is built like heaven itself for purity, and surrounding all its walls are signs projecting and dazzling, some ascending and some descending. These wind their way from here and descend there on the other side. Whereas those letters that are on the other side fly from there and rest there, changing with each other, and never becoming confused.[55] No one can stop them, because they do not cease even for an instant. Flowers [in the form of] lattice work display four colors of dazzling brilliance there. On the Sabbath day, the Messiah with the patriarchs enters there, and the letters chip themselves off. Those who read them are very glad, and no one knows how this happens.

In that palace, and before that open gate, and there inside that curtain are statues of those killed at Lydda and the ten martyred by the Romans. It is from there that the Messiah rises and enters. When he sees those statues he will raise his voice and roar like a lion. All the Garden and all the righteous will tremble. The pillar in the center of the Garden will tremble and ascend and descend. The four Ophanim will be summoned there, and they will seize the four signet rings. The firmament will revolve, and the voice will be heard on high. The Holy Blessed One will shed two tears on the pillar below. The Ophanim will enter [the Palace of] the Messiah, and all the patriarchs will enter the door of the front gate which is in that palace. There they will see all the realms of the righteous ones of Lydda and the ten martyred by the Romans [at the time of the Bar Kokhba revolt, i.e., Rabbi Akiba and his colleagues]. They will all, including the Messiah, be standing, and the Ophanim will ascend to the King of kings, the Holy Blessed One. He will swear to them that he will wear garments of vengeance and wreak their vengeance on the gentiles, as it is said, "He will judge those nations, filling them with corpses" (Psalm 110:6). They will return to the Messiah. They and the patriarchs will approach [the Palace of] the Heads of the Academies who are there and will rejoice at the new interpretations of the Torah that rejuvenate every individual in this world. From there all the deans of all the academies will go to the academy of our teacher Moses (peace be upon him). Moses and all the righteous ones who belonged to the generation of the wilderness will sit before him and learn the Torah. He will interpret for them the reception of the Torah according to that which he received from on high.[56]

The Seven Realms of the Women in Gan Eden

First Realm

In Gan Eden, on the north side, are seven prepared realms and palaces for the righteous women in Israel who performed meritorious deeds for the Holy Blessed One by giving charity and from the merits of the Torah for their children. In the first realm will be found Batyah, the daughter of Pharaoh. How many will be righteous women that are there? All those who reared orphans, showed kindness to scholars, showing the hospitality of their husbands, and giving charity secretly. Every day they are crowned with a shining crown of the splendor of the *Shekhinah*, and they proclaim over it [the house], "Blessed are you who fortify and continue the growth of the branch of splendor in the world."

Second Realm

In the second realm there are many righteous women of Israel. There is Yokheved, the wife of Amram, who is chief over them. Three times a day they proclaim with respect to her: "Blessed are you that you have merited bearing a son whose head and feet stood among the thick cloud."

Third Realm

In the third realm there is Miriam the prophetess, with whom the righteous women stand. All those who encourage their husbands [to walk in] the good way and in the service of their Creator. In every realm, there are canopies of tranquility, and well-known angels have been appointed over every realm.

Fourth Realm

In the fourth realm is Hulda the prophetess and many pious women who reside in that division.

Fifth Realm

In the fifth realm there is Abigail, and with her are many righteous women, dwelling in confidence, each in her own canopy.

From there on are those of the matriarchs: Sarah, Rebecca, Rachel, and Leah. At midnight when the Holy Blessed One enters with the righteous, a voice calls in the Garden: "You are righteous, prepare yourselves to meet your Maker! Blessed are you who have merited all this glory." At that time, the souls will blossom forth and each of them will be paired together suitably and according to the realm of their works. They will see and attain their realm of their works. They will see and attain their realm with joy, "Eye has not seen, O God, except you [who works for those who wait for him" (Isaiah 64:3).

Scholars

In Gan Eden there is a dean of the academy in the Palace of the Nut [Hekhal Ha-Egoz]. That is the Palace of Splendor, which is closed up and hidden. Near it is the Palace of "the bird's nest"[57] and is called "[The academy of] Rav Gadeil, the youth." He reveals all the deep and secret things of the Torah that are made crystal clear by him. All the righteous desire to be near him. He was born in the days of the religious persecution [of Hadrian] and was studying the Torah in a cave when he was only seven years old. The enemies came and found him and cut him up into pieces. His soul ascended to Gan Eden. It is said that like the appearance of a rainbow that is in a cloud on a rainy day, so is the radiance that surrounds this place. It is like the appearance of the glory of the Lord. The Holy Blessed One raised him [Gadiel] before him and swore to him that he would cause him to inherit the Palace of Splendor and that he would reveal in Gan Eden the secret and deep things that are in the Torah and that had not been disclosed previously. All the righteous ones who are in Gan Eden long eagerly to see him and to hear from him the deep things in the Torah and its secrets.

When he goes out, the letters of the Ineffable Name protrude and dazzle over his head, and all the righteous ones are happy. He entered, fell on his face, and wept bitterly because he did not merit having a son in this world. Then Joshua ben Yehozedek, the high priest, stood over him and seized him and made him stand on his feet. Then he said to him, "Arise! My associates are yours. My associates are your sons!" Rabbi Yohanan ben Zakkai fasted seven fasts so that he might see him. They showed him the hidden things of seven firmaments in a dream. Finally, all of them had seen him like the brightness of the firmament; seventy angels surrounded him; and there were fifty keys in his hand. There were many groups of righteous ones before him and the letters of the Ineffable Name hovered over his head. They were soon hidden, and no one could any longer see him. They used to ask him, "How long will you permit us to see this version of the bow that is in the cloud?" The sages returned to his father and found that he had never looked at the physical form of a man or at the rainbow of his covenant, that his hand never reached [the area] from his navel downwards, and that he did not arise from the study of the Torah in order to pursue the ways of the world. There was no other righteous man in the world who suffered such hardship and yet did not say a word outside of the Torah or the ways of the Torah. He fathered this son, and he died. When his mother gave him birth, she died and he was left an orphan. He grew up amidst hardship; yet he studied much Torah, and because they killed him, he merited all this [splendor].

The Righteous

All the righteous will see each other, and they will know and recognize with a mature knowledge that lacks nothing. When the souls ascend on the evening of the Sabbath to Upper Gan Eden [*Gan Eden Ha-Elyon*], they proclaim many announcements above and below. They all strip themselves of that garment and go up to Gan Eden. There in the firmament of the heavens stands Michael the great prince. There is an altar before him, and all the souls of the righteous will sacrifice on that altar. Then will come a spirit of fragrance because they performed [good] deeds in this world. The Holy Blessed One will restore to [each man] his spirit, for with the spirit with which they depart will they come into this world. That spirit returns and is restored to him. For this reason human beings return to their first cause. At that time, when Michael offers the sacrifice of the souls, he restores [each man's] spirit to him, and they bring him inside. There is a time when the Holy Blessed One restores [a man's] spirit to him, but he does not bring him inside. In the latter case, the spirit returns here and there and roams to and fro to Gehinnom. When he brings him inside, to his bosom, he enters the earthly Gan Eden [*Gan Eden shel Ha-Aretz*] Once inside there, they [then] bring him into the heavenly Gan Eden [*Gan Eden shel Malah*].[58] If you are surprised that a man's soul goes out of his mouth, it is written, "He breathed into his mouth the soul of life" (Genesis 2:7). He raises [the soul] from the altar with the love of the fragrance and brings it forth from its midst to the heavenly Gan Eden.

The Heavenly Garden

The heavenly Gan Eden is that which the Lord God planted, a place of Upper Eden, as it is written, "The Lord planted a Garden in the east of Eden" (Genesis 2:8). That Garden is to the north side of heaven as is earthly Jerusalem, as it is said, "Mount Zion, in the far north, [the city of the great king]" (Psalm 48:3). The heavenly Gan Eden is beneath a screen under the God of Israel. It is square at the four corners of the firmament, which is like the terrible frost. Six mirrors brightly shine around it, and the sixth planet [Venus] resembles a river that flows into the midst of the Garden. It goes out from the Upper Eden and enters the midst of the Garden. From there it divides and becomes four heads. One head is [that of] Michael the great prince, and faces Pishon, the first [river] that is beneath the earthly Gan Eden [*Gan Eden shel Matah*].[59] The second head is [that of] the man Gabriel, dressed in linen. He faces the second river that is in the earthly Gan Eden, named Gihon. The third head is [that of] Nuriel, which faces the river Euphrates. In the earthly Gan Eden, a river goes out from Eden and waters all those plants. From there, that river divides and becomes four, just as it is in heaven. In the earthly Gan Eden, there is a tree of life in the midst of the Garden, and close to it is the tree of the knowledge of good and evil. In the tree of life, there are things that are closed off and hidden. When the Holy Blessed One enters the Garden with the righteous, the tree of life gives forth a fragrance that permeates the whole Garden. That fragrance [means] life for all the righteous who are there. It all spreads out, and the leaves shout for joy. The righteous dwell in its shade. Every New Moon and festival they sit down [to eat] of delicacies. Its fruit is life and rest. "Its leaf does not wither. In all that it does, it prospers" (Psalm 1:3). How is it said, "His leaf does not wither, and all that he does prospers"? What does the Holy Blessed One do, entering the Nut Garden that is before the Garden, and his beloved ones who are in the ten realms and the righteous sit in the shade of the tree? A fountain of blessing cascades and falls upon the head of every righteous person. When the dew falls upon him, he goes and stands in the eastern gate before the nut Garden and there he prostrates himself before the cloud of his glory. The Holy Blessed One asks and he answers, learns whatever he learns, and departs. Thus every righteous person does. The Holy Blessed One rejoices very much with them. He comes and stands near that tree of life. The cloud turns away, and the righteous come and prostrate themselves before that shining light of his glory above.

Three Walls around Heavenly Gan Eden

While on this subject, there are three walls [around] the heavenly Gan Eden. One is called the "Secret Whisper"; the second is called "The Movement of the Lord's Laborer"; the third is called "The Garden of the Royal Cloak." The names of the Holy Blessed One are on every wall.

The first wall is called "The Whisper of the Secret Staircase." It is that of which Solomon said by way of parable, "My dove is in the cleft of the rock, in the covert of the cliff" (Song of Songs 2:14). No soul enters the heavenly Gan Eden except on Sabbaths and festivals, which are called "the Sabbath of the Lord," because in them souls take delight, as it is written, "You shall call the Sabbath a delight" (Isaiah 58:13). This wall is of fire that consumes fire, and there are angels that were created on the second day. When they draw near to this wall they sing a song. They draw near to enter, and they are scorched by the licking of that fire. They return at the New Moons as at the beginning. Concerning them, it is said, "They are new every morning. Great is your faithfulness" (Lamentations 3:23). The secret of the flaming sword revolves around this wall, and two Cherubim guard the Garden. Between all the walls, there stand Seraphim, according to their kind, guarding and holding vigil. There the River of Light [Nehar Dinur] surrounds, winds around, leading and going forth with thousands of thousands and myriads of myriads using it. All the angels who are appointed over the nations [stay] around that river until the river [reaches] a high place and the ladder that Jacob saw in a dream is seen in it (Genesis 28:12). That ladder is the one used by the young man Metatron, who is placed higher than his colleagues, a distance of five hundred years. All the princes appointed over the nations approach the ladder: some ascend while others descend. All who go up have a kingdom; all who go down enter into the River of Light, and are licked up there, and the kingdom departs from them.

The second wall is called "The Lord's Laborer." It is a light shining for the righteous, and the Holy Blessed One labors continually in this light that "eye has not seen, O God, except you, laboring for those who wait for him" (Isaiah 64:3). This Gan Eden is above 390 firmaments. The first veil and firmament [contain] clouds and a dwelling in which are Jerusalem, the house of the sanctuary, the altar, the dwelling, the abode, and the heaven. In the heavens are the seven hidden things of life, as well as mysteries of peace and blessing. The souls of the righteous are higher than all those firmaments.

The Firmaments

Come and see how many numerous firmaments the Holy Blessed One created. There is neither number nor place for the heavens of the Most High. They are the place of all worlds and all firmaments, "Eye has not seen, O God, except you" (Isaiah 64:3). Every single world is a world by itself, and every world is divided into a thousand worlds except for the veil where there is time that exceeds a thousand [worlds] and also that does not exceed a thousand. The remaining six are 6,000 worlds and are held to each other three times; they are 18,000 worlds. No one enters them except the Holy Blessed One, as it is said, "The chariots of God, twice ten thousand thousands doubled" (Psalm 68:18), which are nonexistent, because no one knows them except the one who ascends. This Gan Eden is directed toward the clouds, where they grind manna for the righteous, and their mills are placed in the clouds, where they grind the manna. The clouds enter the Garden and above toward the tree, which is the secret of the central pillar in Gan Eden below [*Gan Eden shel Matah*]. This pillar is in the midst of the Garden above and leads downward. From it are drawn all the good things of the Garden and all its delicacies. This pillar is bounded by twelve diagonal borders, and that tree is the place from which souls come forth. All twelve of its boundaries and this tree have their roots in Lebanon where is the Throne of Glory above. Lebanon faces the Lebanon above and it has seventy-two trees planted in the house of the Lord. There are forty-two branches, and all the princes of the world are suspended from it. There are thirty-six diagonal lines altogether, and it [the tree] is bounded by the corners of the world. The wind has nine in the East, nine in the North, nine breezes in the South, and nine in the West. In the middle of the Garden where the trunk of the tree is, the holy people are held, and they took their lot. On this tree there are fifty gates, and each of them is a gate for those who are righteous in their faith to enter. From the trunk of the tree that is in the midst of the Garden the souls blossom forth. There are no winds, because the winds are on the other tree below, and the souls from the upper tree are hidden, as we have said.

OTHER VISIONARY TEXTS

The text that follows, *Gedulat Moshe*—"The Revelation of Moses"—also goes by the name *Ke-Tapuah B-Atzei Ha-Yaar*—"Like an Apple Tree among the Trees of the Forest." Translations by Moses Gaster and Louis Ginzberg, and the Hebrew version by Abraham Wertheimer, are all based on slightly different versions of the manuscript. We can assume that *Gedulat Moshe* was in circulation for some time, and went through a number of different recensions. Saul Lieberman notes an Islamic influence within the text, suggesting that it originated in Arabic-speaking countries.[60] Indeed, an Arabic translation of the text does exist.[61] The edition that appears in *Batei Midrashot* is based on a Yemenite manuscript found among the Cairo *Genizah* fragments.[62]

According to Wertheimer, the text is quite late and may date from the fifteenth, or even sixteenth, century.[63] However, there is no doubt that the text reflects much older traditions[64] and is, in a sense, the completion of centuries of developing medieval Judaism's tradition of the tours of heaven and hell. What we have here is the most elaborate medieval text on the afterlife, which brings together images of Gehenna and Gan Eden parallel with the texts we have seen thus far.

In this text, Moses goes on a sojourn through the postmortem realms. First, he travels in the company of the angel Metatron and is shown each of the seven heavens, where he meets specific angels, or groups of angelic beings. He then meets up with the angel Nasargiel, the Guardian of Gehinnom, who escorts him through the realms of torture in Gehinnom. The descriptions of the punishments of Gehenna are similar to those appearing earlier. Here, however, the punishments are elaborated even more, and we can see how a tradition is developed and amplified over centuries.

This long text ends with Moses being told by the Heavenly Voice [*Bat-Kol*]:

> Moses . . . even as you have seen the reward which is preserved for the righteous in the future world, so also shall you be worthy and shall you and all the righteous ones be worthy to see the days of the

World to Come [*Olam Ha-Ba*], and the rebuilding of the Temple
and the advent of the Messiah, and behold the beauty of the Lord,
and meditate in His Temple.

In the final analysis, even with this lengthly description of the postmortem realms, the ancient Jewish belief in the end-of-days, the notion
of *Olam Ha-Ba* as a time of collective redemption, remains as essential
to Jewish beliefs in the afterlife.

Gedulat Moshe—"The Revelation of Moses"[65]

1. As the apple tree among the forest, so is my beloved among
   the sons (Song of Songs 2:3). This applies to Moses, peace be
   upon him.
2. In that hour when the Holy Blessed One appeared to him at
   Mount Horeb, He said: "Go and bring out the children of
   Israel from Egypt, for I have heard their groaning, and I remembered the covenant, and the oath I swore to Abraham my servant."
3. Moses said: "O Master of the Universe, who am I that I should
   go to Pharaoh, and that I should bring forth the children of Israel
   out of Egypt?" (Exodus 3:11). God said: "You have humbled
   Yourself in saying, 'Who am I that I should go to Pharaoh?' but
   I will honor you [as it is said]: 'He that is of lowly spirit shall
   obtain honor' [Proverbs 19:23], and I will give the whole of
   Egypt into Your hands, and I will bring you up even near to my
   Throne of Glory; and I will show you the angels of the heaven."[66]
4. Thereupon the Holy Blessed One commanded Metatron, the
   Angel of the Countenance and said to him: "Go and bring
   Moses to the celestial regions with harps, and pipes, and drums,
   and dances, with joy, and songs, and praises." And Metatron
   answered and said: "O Master of the Universe, Moses is not able
   to ascend and see the angels, for there are angels who are of
   fire and he is only of flesh and blood."
5. Then the Holy Blessed One commanded Metatron: "Go and
   change his flesh into torches of fire, and his strength into the
   strength of Gabriel."[67] And Metatron went to Moses. When
   Moses beheld Metatron he trembled with fear, and said to him:
   "Who are you?"

6. And he answered: "I am Enoch, the son of Jared, your father's father. The Holy Blessed One has sent me to bring you up to His Throne of Glory."

7. Moses said: "I am only flesh and blood, and cannot look upon the angels." And Metatron changed Moses' tongue into a tongue of fire, and his eyes he made like the wheels of the heavenly chariot [*Merkavah*], and his power like that of the angels, and his tongue like a flame, and brought him up to heaven. Fifteen thousand angels were on the right hand, and 15,000 on the left, Metatron and Moses in the middle. In this way was Moses carried up to heaven.

8. Moses went up to the first heaven, which corresponds to the first day of the week; there he saw streams upon streams of water. And he observed that this heaven was full of windows, and at each window stood an angel. And Moses asked Metatron: "What are these windows?" And Metatron answered: "These windows are—the window of prayer, the window of request, the window of supplication, the window of crying [tears], the window of joy, the window of satiation, the window of famine, the window of poverty, the window of riches, the window of war, the window of peace, the window of pregnancy, the window of birth, the window of the treasures of rain, the window of dew, the window of smallness, the window of greatness, the window of death, the window of life, the window of disease among men, the window of disease among animals, the window of healing, the window of sickness, the window of health." And Moses saw great things past finding out, "yea marvelous things without number" (Job 9:10).

9. Moses went up to the second heaven, which corresponds to the second day of the week. There he saw an angel whose name is Nuriel.[68] His length is 300 parasangs high and he has a retinue of fifty myriads of angels; they are fashioned of fire and water, and their faces are turned toward the *Shekhinah* above; and all sing hymns, saying: "Great is the Lord and highly to be praised" (Psalm 145:3).

10. And Moses asked Metatron and said: "Who are those?" He answered: "These are the angels who are set over the clouds, the wind, and the rain; they go and fulfill the will of their Creator and return to their places and praise the Holy Blessed One."

And Moses asked: "Why have they their faces turned toward the *Shekhinah?*" And Metatron answered: "From that day when God created them until today they have not been moved from their position."

11. Moses went up to the third heaven, which corresponds to the third day of the week. There he saw an angel whose name is Sandalphon.[69] His length is a journey of 500 years. He has 70,000 heads, in each head 70,000 mouths, in each mouth 70,000 tongues, and in each tongue 70,000 sayings; before him stand 70,000 myriads of angels, all of white fire; they all praise and sing to God [and say: "Yours, O Lord, is the greatness and the power" (1 Chronicles 29:11)].

12. Moses asked Metatron: "Who are these? And what is their name?" And he answered: "Their name is Erelim; they are placed over the grass [herbs], and over the trees, and over the fruits, and over the corn; and they all go and fulfill the will of their Creator and return to their places."

13. Moses went up to the fourth heaven, which corresponds to the fourth day of the week. There he saw the Temple built; the columns of red fire; the sides of green fire; the thresholds of white fire; the hooks and the planks of blazing fire; the portals of carbuncle and the halls of sparkling gems. And he saw angels going in and praising the Holy Blessed One, and saying, as did King David, peace be upon him: "Bless the Lord, you angels of His, you mighty in strength, that fulfill his word" (Psalm 103:20).

14. Moses asked Metatron and said: "Who are these angels?" And Metatron answered: "These are the angels, who are placed over the earth, and over the sun, and over the moon, and over the stars, and over the planets, and over the constellations, and over the twenty-six [planetary] spheres, and ever sing they hymns to Him." And he saw two big stars, each of them as big as the whole earth; the name of one was Nogah [Venus] and the name of the other Maadim [Mars], one standing above the sun, and the other above the moon. Moses asked Metatron: "Why do these stand above those others?" And he said: "Nogah [Venus] lies upon the sun in summer in order to cool the world from the heat of the sun; while Maadim [Mars] lies upon the moon in order to warm the world from the cold of the moon."

15. Moses went up to the fifth heaven, which corresponds to the fifth day of the week, and he saw there troops of angels half of fire and half of snow, and the snow did not melt, nor was the fire extinguished, for God had established perfect harmony between the two elements, as it is said: "He makes peace in his high places" (Job 25:2) and all praise the Holy Blessed One.

16. And Moses asked Metatron: "What are these doing?" He said: "Since the day when God created them are they so." Moses asked: "What is their name?" and he answered: "These are the Erelim who are called Ishim [as it is said: 'Unto you, O *Ishim* [men], I call'" [(Proverbs 8:4), i.e., "I call you *Ishim*"].

17. Moses went up to the sixth heaven, which corresponds to the sixth day of the week. There he saw an angel whose length was 500 years' journey; his name was Uriel and he was wholly of hail, and by him stood thousands and myriads of angels, without number, and all sung praises to the One who said and the world was created[70] [as it is said: the heaven proclaims the glory of God (Psalm 19:2)].

18. Moses asked Metatron: "Who are these?" and he answered: "These are the *Irin U-Kadishin* ["the holy watchers"]" (Daniel 4:10–14).

19. Moses went up to the seventh heaven, which is like the Sabbath, and he saw an angel wholly of fire; and two angels who were fastened with chains of black and red fire; and each of them had the length of 500 parasangs.

20. Moses asked Metatron: "Who are these?" And he answered: "These are the angels *Af*, "Wrath," and *Hemah*, "Anger," and God created them during the six days of creation, that they should fulfill his will."

21. Moses replied: "I am afraid of these angels, and I cannot look on them." Thereupon Metatron embraced Moses, placed him in his bosom and said: "O Moses, beloved of God, servant of God, be not frightened." And Moses was immediately calmed.

22. After this Moses saw another angel, whose countenance was totally different from those of the other angels, for he was ugly and his height of 500 years' journey, and he was girded forty times around his waist. From the sole of the foot to the head he was full of fiery eyes, and whosoever looked at him, fell down in dread.

23. And Moses asked Metatron: "Who is this?" He answered: "This is Samael, the Angel of Death, who takes the souls of men." And he asked him: "Where is he now going?" And Metatron answered: "He goes to take the soul of Job the pious."

24. And Moses said before Holy Blessed One: "May it be Your will, O Lord, my God and God of my fathers, that You should not deliver me into the hands of this angel!"

25. Then he saw angels standing before Holy Blessed One, each of them having six wings. With two wings they covered their faces, so that they might not look upon the Shekhinah. With the other two wings they cover their feet, for they have the feet of a calf, and with the other two wings they fly and praise God. And they say "Holy, Holy, Holy the Lord of Hosts, the entire world is filled with Your Glory" (Isaiah 6:3). The length of each wing is 500 years' journey, and the width from one end of the world to the other. And Moses asked: "Who are these?" and Metatron answered: "These are the Holy Creatures [Hayyot Ha-Kodesh]."

26. And after that Moses saw an angel in the heaven called Arabot, that is, the seventh heaven, and this angel, whose name was Zagzagiel, who was teaching souls which were created by God at the time of the Creation and have been placed in paradise.[71] He teaches them in seventy languages in the college on high, and they answer: "Thus is the law of Moses given by tradition from Mount Sinai [as it is said: "The books were opened; they sat in judgment [dina] (Daniel 7:10). And there is no judge [dayan] other than Zagzagiel, who is the guardian of Torah and Wisdom." And he has the "horns of glory" [Hebrew: karnei ha-kavod]. He has also another name, they call him Jefefiyah, for the name of the guardian angel of the Torah is Iofiel]."

27. And Moses stood before the angel Zagzagiel and learned the ten mysteries, and afterward he said before the Holy Blessed One: "I will not depart from here unless You will give me good gifts, as it is written: 'For I gave you a good gift' (Proverbs 4:2). Therein are also the commandments, positive and negative, and not only this (I grant you) but also that the Torah shall be recorded in Your name, as it is written: 'Remember the Law of Moses, my servant' (Malachi 3:22)."

28. From whence do we know that Moses did actually ascend seven heavens? We learn it from the verse "And Moses ascended to

God." It is further written, "Elohim went up amidst the sounds of a shout [teruah], the sound of a shofar" (Psalm 47:6). Moses is therefore called Elohim like his Master, for it is said: "See I have made you as Elohim unto Pharaoh," therefore it is written: "Like an apple tree in the wood is my beloved among the sons" (Song of Songs 2:3). This is Moses, master of the prophets and servant of God; he is like an apple in odor and taste.

29. At that time a Heavenly Voice (Bat-Kol) came forth and said: "Moses, my servant! You have ascended the seven heavens, and I have shown you my treasures and I have given you my Torah. You have come and you have seen the Throne of Glory. Thus, you shall be worthy and you shall see two realms [Hebrew: pardesim, literally "orchards"], one of Gan Eden and one of Gehinnom."

30. Afterward the Holy Blessed One sent Gabriel and said to him: "Go with my beloved servant Moses and open Gehinnom!" Moses came and Gabriel opened Gehinnom for him, and Moses saw a burning fire.

31. And Moses said to Gabriel: "I cannot enter Gehinnom, that blazing fire." He said to him: "Moses, there is a fire that burns more than all the seven realms of Gehinnom, and yet when you tread it with your feet, it shall not burn you."

32. When Moses entered Gehinnom, the fire of Gehinnom withdrew 500 parasangs. And Nasargiel, the Guardian of Gehinnom, said to him: "Who are you?" He answered: "I am the son of Amram." The Guardian of Gehinnom answered: "This is not your place. Your place is in Gan Eden."

33. And Moses said: "I came to see the powerful works of the Holy Blessed One." Said the Holy Blessed One to Nasargiel, the Guardian of Gehinnom: "Go and show him Gehinnom, and the state of the wicked ones there."

34. Immediately Moses followed Nasargiel to the entrance to Gehinnom, like a pupil before his master, and entered Gehinnom together with him.

35. There he saw men tortured by the Angels of Destruction. Some of the sinners were hanged by their eyelids, some by their ears, some by their hands, and others by their tongues, and they cried bitterly. And he saw women hanging by their hair, by their breasts, and by their feet, hanging by chains of fire.

36. And Moses asked Nasargiel: "Why are these hanged by their eyes?" And he said: "Because they looked with an evil eye at fair women, and at married women, and at the money of their friends and neighbors, and gave false witness against their neighbors; and these that are hanged by their ears, are because they hear vain words and slander; and turn their ears away from hearing the words Torah.[72]

37. "And these that are hanging by their tongues? Because they speak negatively of others, and talk habitually of idle matters; and these that are hanging by their feet, because they walk in the slanderous ways of their friends, and do not go [walk] in the ways of fulfillling a commandment, nor walk to synagogue to pray to the Creator. And these that are hanged by their hands? Because they stole money from their friends, with their own hands; and murdered their comrades.

38. "And the men that are hanged by their sexual organs? Because they committed adultery. And the women hanging by their breasts? Because they used to uncover their breasts to nurse their children, and the young men would see this, desire them, and thus come to sin."[73]

39. And then Gehinnom cried with a bitter and loud voice, and said to Nesargiel: "Give me something to ease my hunger!" [Nesargiel] said to [Gehinnom]: "What should I give you?" "Give me the souls of the righteous." He said: "The Holy Blessed One will not give you the souls of the righteous."[74]

40. Moses descended to another location and saw two sinners hanged by their feet with their heads downward, and they cried by reason of the torture of Gehinnom, and from the soles of their feet to the crown of their head their bodies were covered with black worms, each worm 500 parasangs long. And these cry and lament, saying: "Woe unto us, for the terrible punishment of Gehinnom; would we could die." But they cannot die [as it is said: "You long for death but it comes not" (Job 3:21)].

41. Moses asked Nesargiel: "What acts have these committed?" And he answered: "These are those who swore falsely, and profaned the Sabbath and Holy Days; despised the learned and persecuted the orphans; and gave bad names to their neighbors, and bore false witness. Therefore has the Holy Blessed One delivered them to these worms to take vengeance on these."

And Moses asked: "What is the name of this place?" And he answered: "Aluka [as it is said]: Aluka ["leech"] has two daughters" (Proverbs 30:15).

42. Moses went then to another place. There were two sinners prostrated while two thousand scorpions were lashing, stinging, and tormenting them, and the tortured victims cried bitterly. Each scorpion has 70,000 heads, and each head has 70,000 mouths, and each mouth has 70,000 stings, and each sting has 70,000 vesicles filled with poison and venom, which these sinners are forced to drink down; and their eyes melt in their sockets from fear of the scorpions.

43. And Moses asked Nesargiel: "What have these committed?" And he answered: "These have squandered collective funds; they have taken bribery and elevated themselves above others; they have put their neighbors publicly to shame; they have delivered up their brother Israelite to the gentile; they denied the Torah of Moses our teacher, peace be upon him, and maintained that the Holy Blessed One did not create the world. Therefore the Holy Blessed One has handed them over to the scorpions to be avenged on them." And Moses said to Nesargiel, "What is the name of this place?" And he answered him: "*Tit Ha-Yaven* ["miry clay"]" (Psalm 40:3).

44. And Moses looked and he saw sinners standing in mud up to their navels [in this place called] Tit. And Angels of Destruction tie them up with chains of iron and lash them with fiery whips, and they take fiery stones and break with them their teeth, from morning until evening, and during the night they lengthen their teeth and break them anew next morning; [as it is said: "You have broken the teeth of the wicked" (Psalm 3:8)]. And they cry: "Woe unto us, woe unto us!" but nobody takes pity on them.[75]

45. Moses asked Nesargiel: "What have these committed?" He answered: "They ate foods that were ritually forbidden and foods cooked by gentiles; they were apostates and usurers; they wrote the ineffable name of God on amulets for gentiles; they used false weights; they stole money, and ate on the fast day of Kippur [for whosoever eats blood, or reptiles, or worms, and does not keep away from them is punished by being cut off], these are forever punished in Gehinnom, and therefore the Holy Blessed One has delivered them to the Angels of Destruction."

46. He saw there other wicked ones punished half in fire and half in snow; snow above and fire below. At night fire comes instead of snow; and during the day the snow comes instead of fire. Moses asked Nesargiel, saying: "Why are these punished half in fire, half in snow?" And he answered: "Because they are placed on the path of goodness and they walk the path of wickedness."

47. Then Nesargiel said to Moses: "Come and see how the wicked are punished in Gehinnom with fire." Moses answered: "I dread to go." But [Nesargiel, the Guardian of Gehinnom] answered: "Let the light of the *Shekhinah* go before you and fear not. The fire of Gehinnom shall not overpower you" [as it is said: "Yea, though I walk through the valley of the shadow of death I will fear no evil" (Psalm 23:4)].

48. Moses went and saw how the wicked were punished by fire, being half in fire and half in snow, with worms crawling up and down their bodies and a fiery collar round their necks, and the Angels of Destruction were beating them, and not allowing them to rest, except on Sabbath and Holy Days. Of these speaks the verse: "And they shall go forth and look upon the carcasses of the men that have transgressed against me, for their worm shall not die, neither shall their fire be quenched" (Isaiah 76:24).

49. And Moses asked Nesargiel: "What acts have these committed?" And he said: "This is the punishment for those who have committed adultery, incest, sodomy; and had intercourse with a menstruant; and committed idolatry, and murder, and who have cursed their parents or teacher. Therefore has God delivered them to the Angels of Destruction to be avenged on them." And Moses asked: "What is the name of this place?" And he answered: "The name of it is Abbadon."[76]

50. Thereupon Moses ascended from Gehinnom and said: "May it be Your will, O Lord, my God, and God of my fathers, that You may save me and Your people Israel from those places that I have seen in Gehinnom."

51. The Holy Blessed One said to Moses: "Moses, my servant, I have created two realms [Hebrew: *pardesim*]: Gan Eden and Gehinnom. Whosoever does good deeds enters into Gan Eden, and whosoever commits evil deeds goes down to Gehinnom" [as it is said: "I the Lord search the heart, I try the reins, even to give every man according to his ways, according to the fruit of his doings" (Jeremiah 17:10)].

52. Then Moses lifted up his eyes and beheld the angel Gabriel; and he fell down and bowed himself before him. And Holy Blessed One said to the angel Gabriel: "Go with Moses and show him Gan Eden."

53. And so Moses went with him, and entered into Gan Eden, and two angels appeared before him and said: "Has your time [to leave the world] arrived that you have come here?" Moses answered: "My time has not yet come; however, I have come to see the reward of the righteous in Gan Eden."

54. The angels began then to praise Moses and they said: "Praise be Moses! You have been found worthy to ascend seven heavens! Praise be the nation to whom such belongs."[77]

55. When Moses went into Gan Eden he saw an angel, whose name was Samsiel, the Guardian of Gan Eden, sitting under the tree of life.

56. And the angel approached him and asked: "Who are you?" He answered: "I am the son of Amram." He said to him: "Why did you come here?" And Moses answered: "In order to see the reward of the righteous in Gan Eden."

57. The Holy Blessed One said to Samsiel: "Go with Moses and show him Gan Eden." Then [the angel] took Moses by the hand, and they went both together. Moses looked up and saw seventy thrones fixed, one next to another; all made of precious stones, of emerald, sapphire, and diamond and precious pearls, and the foot of each was of gold and fine gold. And each throne was served by sixty ministering angels; and among the thrones was one greater than the others, and [this throne] was served by 120 ministering angels.

58. Moses inquired of [the angel] Samsiel and said: "Whose is that throne?" He answered: "It is the throne of your ancestral father Abraham."

59. Moses went immediately and approached Abraham. And Abraham asked: "Has your time come to leave the world, that you have come here?" Moses answered: "My time is not yet come, but I came to see the reward of the righteous in Gan Eden." Abraham then said: "Praise the Lord, for He is good; for His mercy endures forever" (Psalm 106:1).

60. Moses then went to Isaac and spoke with him in a similar manner. Moses then went to Jacob and spoke with him in a similar manner.

61. Then Moses asked Samsiel: "What is the length and width of Gan Eden?" The angel answered: "There is none who could measure the length and width of Gan Eden, for it is unlimited and boundless and immeasurable. And each and every throne, which is served by sixty ministering angels, is unlike one to another, for some of them are of silver, others of gold, others of copper, others of bdellium, others of ruby, topaz, and carbuncle, others of emerald, sapphire, and diamond, others of precious stones and pearls."

62. Moses asked [the angel Samsiel]: "For whom is this throne of pearls?" He answered: "It is for the scholars who study Torah day and night for the sake of heaven." "And for whom is this throne of precious stones?" "For the totally righteous." "And for whom is this throne of gold?" "For those who repent and return to their faith."[78] "And for whom is this throne of silver?" "For the righteous converts."

63. "And for whom is that throne of copper?" He answered: "For the wicked person, whose father is righteous; or for the righteous child whose father is wicked; because through the merits of the child the Holy Blessed One gives one a portion in Gan Eden; as you see in the case of Terah, who had worshiped all the idols in the world, but whom the Holy Blessed One gave a share in Gan Eden, as it is said: 'You shall go to your fathers in peace' (Genesis 15:15), thus announcing to him [Abraham] that God would give [his father also] a place in Gan Eden."

64. Afterward Moses looked and beheld a spring of living water welling up from underneath the tree of life and dividing into four streams that pass under the Throne of Glory, and they encompass Gan Eden from one end to the other. And under each throne there flow four rivers, one of honey, the second of milk, the third of wine, and the fourth of pure balsam. These all pass beneath the feet of the righteous, who are seated upon thrones.

65. When Moses saw all these godly and pleasant things he felt great joy, and exclaimed: "Oh! how great is Your goodness reserved for those that fear, bestowed on those who take shelter in you, for all humanity to see" (Psalm 31:19).

66. And Moses retired from there and went away. At that same moment a Heavenly Voice [Bat-Kol] manifested and said to Moses, our teacher, peace be upon him: "Moses, servant of God,

faithful in His house; even as you have seen the reward that is
preserved for the righteous in the future world, so also shall you
be worthy and shall you and all the righteous ones be worthy to
see the days of the World to Come, and the rebuilding of the
Temple and the advent of the Messiah, and behold the beauty
of the Lord, and meditate in His Temple."

Immanuel ben Solomon of Rome—*Ha-Tophet V'Ha-Eden*[79]

The final text of this chapter consists of selections from *Ha-Tophet
V'Ha-Eden*—"Hell and Heaven"—by Immanuel Ha-Romi, a thirteenth-
century Italian Jew. Unlike any of the previous texts, the selection that
follows is Hebrew Renaissance poetry, not medieval Midrash. Modeled
after, and in many respects comparable to, Dante's *Divine Comedy*, *Ha-
Tophet V'Ha-Eden* is a poetic rendition of Immanuel Ha-Romi's afterlife
visions. *Ha-Tophet V'Ha-Eden* is certainly one of the most unique pieces
of Jewish literature; there is really nothing quite like this poem among
all of Judaism's writings about death, immortality, and the afterlife. This
text is included here because it is visionary in nature and demonstrates
one more literary style utilized by Jews to express a deep concern with
the nature of the disembodied life after death.

The background to *Ha-Tophet V'Ha-Eden* is as follows. In Italy the
walls of the Jewish ghetto were more permeable than in other European
countries, and by the middle of the thirteenth century Jewish life had
been influenced by the creative spirit of the Renaissance. Immanuel ben
Solomon of Rome, who lived c. 1265 to 1330,[80] was from one of the leading Jewish Italian families. Himself a man of letters, Immanuel received
a diverse religious and secular education. He authored commentaries on
the Bible and a study of Hebrew grammar, as well as both religious and
secular Hebrew poetry.[81] Of his occupation, Cecil Roth notes:

> He seems to have been a rolling stone, wandering from place to place
> to earn his living, presumably as a house-tutor for the children of the
> wealthy loan-bankers who were establishing themselves throughout
> central Italy at this time. . . . He dabbled in medicine, perhaps not
> seriously. He had some reputation as a Hebrew stylist, and was used
> from time to time by Jewish communities . . . to write official cor-
> respondence for them. It is probable that he acted from time to time
> as cantor in the synagogue. But generally speaking one receives the
> impression of the familiar type of seedy, down-at-the-heels "literary

genius," drifting aimlessly from town to town and from protector to protector, trying his hand at all things in turn, and never quite fulfilling his early promise.[82]

Today, Immanuel is remembered for his poetry, much of which is found in a compilation entitled *Mahbarot Immanuel*, "The Compositions of Immanuel." Consisting of twenty-eight individual compositions, *Mahbarot Immanuel* is a large anthology of Ha-Romi's poetry that brings together epigrams, puns, satires, lampoons, elegies, epitaphs, religious poetry, narrative verses, and various other hymns, including what is thought to be an early version of the famous liturgical poem *Yigdal*.[83]

Within the *Mahbarot* are found love poems, quite passionate and erotic in nature. While *Mahbarot Immanuel* was one of the earliest Jewish books of poetry, printed in Brescia in 1491, the secular, sensualistic nature of his poetry offended the sensitivity of the pious Jewish world. As a result, the renowned sixteenth-century Jewish legalist Joseph Karo, author of the *Shulhan Arukh*, issued a ban prohibiting the reading of the poetry of Immanuel ben Solomon Ha-Romi.[84] After an edition of *Mahbarot Immanuel* was published in Constantinople in 1535, the book was not published again until the late eighteenth century in Berlin, influenced by the *Haskalah* movement's renewed interest in Renaissance poetry.[85]

Ha-Tophet V'Ha-Eden is the twenty-eighth and final composition of *Mahbarot Immanuel* and details the author's vision of paradise and hell (which he calls Tophet, a biblical site associated with the Valley of Hinnom, mentioned in Jeremiah 7:31, 19:6). In Immanuel's sixtieth year of life, one of his close friends and literary patrons, a wealthy loan-banker named Daniel, had died. Touched deeply by this loss, Immanuel composed *Ha-Tophet V'Ha-Eden* sometime between 1320 and 1330.[86] In this lengthy poem, written in sonnet form, he envisions his friend Daniel escorting him through the realms of Tophet and Eden.

Although not exclusively a religious or midrashic text, *Ha-Tophet V'Ha-Eden* nonetheless has qualities characteristic of Jewish apocalyptic literature. Just as in many of the other texts in this chapter, once again we see an individual being shown the netherworlds in the company of a deceased disembodied being. We also see in this text images parallel to texts like *Masekhet Gehinnom* and *Masekhet Gan Eden*. Immanuel describes specific punishments of the sinners in Tophet, and encounters the patriarchs and other biblical and rabbinic personages in Eden.

Most likely Immanuel Ha-Romi was acquainted with Jewish medieval afterlife texts. While Gollancz has shown literary parallels between the works of Dante and Immanuel,[87] in the critical edition of *Mahbarot Immanuel* by Dov Yardin there are elaborate footnotes demonstrating Ha-Romi's command of biblical, talmudic, and midrashic literature.[88] References to traditional Jewish images of the afterlife are elegantly interwoven in his visionary poetry.

The text below consists of assorted selections from the rather lengthy poem, which is too long to include in complete form here. The main problem with the translation is that Gollancz's language is quite dense. Published in England in 1921, Gollancz wrote in terse King James English. He also endeavored to keep the poetic style of Ha-Romi. While he succeeds at poetry, what is lost in translation is the exquisite use of biblical phraseology by Ha-Romi.

No doubt there is need for a more contemporary translation of *Ha-Tophet V'Ha-Eden*. However, to make this afterlife material accessible, I have excerpted large sections of Ha-Romi's text, maintaining Gollancz's English language translation. Even with the arcane English, what comes through is yet another dimension of the Jewish legacy on the afterlife.

Immanuel Laments His Friend's Death and Questions His Fate

Sixty years of my life had now passed,
and the pains of mortal had come on me fast,
when of a sudden a man full of life and deeds,
of piety too he had sown the seeds,
bade adieu to the worlds and its ways,
he was junior to me in years and days,
and as I dwelt on the sorrowful sight,
I was seized with pain, horror, and fright.

Then said I, woe to me, benighted fool!
Be ashamed and confounded, thou wretched tool
of transgression and sin, error and crime,
sunk in the depths of the mire of time.
Have not God and man by me been cursed,
more than my forbears in iniquity nursed?
Were I of a sudden to be called on high,
borne on the shoulders to the grave near by,
and my comrades would seek me in vain with a sigh,

what provision have I made on the journey to start,
when the desolate soul from the body shall part?
How shall I then speak and with judgment cope,
if for the mercy of Him who forgiveth I cannot hope?
While with musing such as these I the world forgot,
my heart with me was hot;[89]
with tears did the window of my frame unfold,
and as water poured out they rushed forth and rolled.
Grievous and mournful did I feel at my state,
thinking of my soul lost and my pitiful fate,
since, in tribute to Desire, I killed myself in hate.[90]
Then spake I, where is Daniel, the man of delight,[91] and so wise?
Would that I knew where to find thee, before thy seat I would rise!
I would ask, and thou wouldst tell me, and sate me from the stream
    of thy measure
and make known to me my end, and of my days the measure,[92]
aye, indeed, the place where I may rest, and find repose and leisure.

Daniel Appears to Immanuel in a Vision

Now, whilst I was deep in the slough of despond,
my tears flowing full as the pond,
while trying to gain the mastery sorrow and sighing
over my heart were trying,
there followed great darkness and fear,
the sense of the wierd,
and unto me a vision appeared . . .

Then came the fire, and the voice soft and slight,
and as the brightness of the sun, the sevenfold light,
when lo, and anon, an aged man man before me passed in a mantle
    clad,
methought the countenance of an angel of the Lord, he had . . .

As he spake to me, I grew more bold,
and of the hem of his garment I took hold.
I hugged and kissed the dust of his feet straightway,
and said unto him, O Lord to thee I do pray,
if I and my people can thy favour claim,
tell me, I beseech thee, what is thy name?
He answered and said, Daniel am I, by thee "man of delight" yclept,
when but of late thy eyes streams of water wept. . . .[93]

Open thine eyes, and around thee gaze;
understand the thing and the vision's ways!
I have thee been sent,
and I am come to do thee good,
so that wisdom of thee shall be understood . . .

Immanuel and Daniel Travel through the Netherworlds of Tophet

Then spake the man: Take firm hold of my skirt, as thou hast begun,
so that 'twixt thee and me, of space there be none;
for the place wither we turn parched hath been made by heat,
'tis orderless and nought but shade [Tzalmavet][94]—
called the Valley of Corpses, dead and decayed.
As I seized the hem of his cloak, fear with my feelings blended;
and as soon as we departed to go, we gradually felt we had descended;
the way was certainly not of an upward flight,
but one veiled in darkness and gloom bewildering fright.
The paths were all crooked, ever turning and winding;
we perceived the thunder's roar and the lightening's flash blinding.
Nought was heard but the sound of the tempest wild
and shrieks, as one giving birth to her firstborn child,
so that that day by me, "the Day of Wrath" was styled.
Lastly a shattered bridge we reached, 'neath which a gushing stream
    did flow
that seemed to snatch and sweep all things below—
I then began to feel my pulse grow slow.
At the head of the bridge a gate, where the flame of the Sword that
    turned[95] kept guard,
and the man to me did say, This the gate Shallecheth[96] is called, ill-
    starred,
to which they who from the world depart,
who in Tophet find their places,
direct their step, hitherward do turn their faces.
We move not hence one hour or two; we watch the throng
of those who pass from the earth in fullest measure, a myriad strong.
By the Angel of Death we see them brought
to the land of shade and darkness and drought;
we watch their corruption
and their further destruction;
we marvel not at their pain,
at their great sorrow's train,

for a froward generation were they, children from faith ready to part,
therefore the sword which they plied upon them has turned, and
    entered their heart. . . .[97]

Having crossed the bridge, to the nethermost parts of the earth we
    did reach,
and all who saw me exclaimed, "Why didst thou commit a breach?"
There did we see a land of gloom, a great funeral-pyre its claim;
its sparks of fire, burning with a mighty flame.
The stake was of fire and wood without end,
nor day nor night its force did it spend.
Then said the man: This is the pile that gleams,
burning as of brimstone the streams,
reserved for souls full of rebellion's dreams.
Wouldst thou know why the wicked are here, and what is their name?
Study closely the name on their forehead inscribed with shame. . . .[98]

The Punishments of Sinners in Tophet

And as we journeyed thence, we saw a man with his right hand and
    tongue and slit;
they had made of him a target, against which with darts from brazen
    bow they hit
so that thereby to the earth his very gall, pouring forth did flit.
Now, placed upon an iron grid, he would of roasting endure the pang;
again in bitter waters they would immerse him with a clang;
then again, him upon a wooden gallows would they hang;
at another time, with stones at him they would bang.
Then I asked the man who spake to me, why this situation,
what the cause and reason for his tribulation.
And he replied and said: His was a tongue that did speak vauntingly,
and in his heart iniquity did jamble jauntingly.
In his father's face he would spit and utter vile curse;
he would run and catch by the neck those who this rebel once did
    nurse.
He laboured his sire with blows which, time after time, had been
    given,
till at length the cries of the father reached the throne of Heaven:
it is on this account that he now in fire and water is riven.
The Lord thus unto him hath done, as he had once designed,
so that he and his associates shall no longer be held in mind;
the Lord our God has silenced them, they have ceased to grind. . . .[99]

Now, as we journeyed thence, men once in violent fleet,
dismembered to their thumbs and the toes of their feet,
hanging on gallows of trees, we did meet.
Their flesh was being eaten by some wild fowl and fierce,
and their eyes the young eagle and raven of the valley did pierce.
Hail and fire did upon them continuously rain;
their fruit from above, their root below, were caught in destruction's
    train.
As I looked on, like wax it melted my heart,
and I asked the man who spake to me if he would to me the cause
    impart.

He answered: The smoke of folly thro' their nostrils found its way;
hardened in spirit, they stiffened their necks for the fray;
roaring like whelps, they would pounce upon their prey;
therefore their stars are darkened, they have no day.
They were once in the Lord's band,
but they have departed from His land;
"going forth to gather and finding no store,"
they did covet houses and fields and rob them, thus breaking God's
    law;
"his yoke from off them they did shake"
and "with their wiles they themselves tyrants did make";
they stole and lied, and put into their vessels what they could take;
not content to gather of that which Thou to them didst give,
they changed the paths, and by stripping the garment of its orna-
    ment they would live.
For this they are now smitten, madness and blindness to them are
    doled;
and while e'en the fragments of the "Tables" were placed in the Ark
    of old,
these shall have no portion, nor will their memory in God's Temple
    have a hold.
Their lot is to drink the cup of reeling, and on to destruction be
    rolled. . . .[100]
We journeyed thence, and the sight our eyes did meet
of fifty men trampled on by flaming horses' feet,
whereas toils, "as water covering the sea," about them did beat.
Then said I, who are these upon whom the curse doth press,
and Judgment done its worst, of destruction and distress.
And he answered saying,

These be the men whose wickedness did the world oppress,
who the doors of the bath and washhouses did caress,
to glance at the women going and returning,
who by their ablutions their purification from uncleanness were
     earning,
They went after vanity, and became fools at the end,
a man neighing lustful for the wife of his friend;
they inquire, "Why all this?" the cause not knowing they pretend;
hence they are hurled to desolation where torments do rend,
where misfortune will upon them be bestowed,
for the boast of their lust upon their necks they did load. . . .[101]

We journeyed thence, and lo, there were pits full of serpents, poi-
     sonous and flying,
hundreds and thousands of lions and leopards tearing the dying,
and round about angels of death with their swords were plying,
and torrents of mighty waters in floods were lying,
making the hearts of onlookers gasp with sighing.
Then said I, Who are these that for destruction are eagerly trying?
He replied, These be they caught in witchcraft and divining,
necromancers, and magicians, conjuring with *teraphim*[102] and the
     false assigning,
with mumming and whispering their craft designing.
These are now by the angel of the Lord expelled repining,
and by the King's Word, the Lord of Hosts, despatched at full speed
     declining.
And it is because the earth has been entirely defiled by their corruption,
that the Lord's anger has been kindled against them to their destruc-
     tion. . . .[103]

Immanuel Learns the Reason for the Punishments of Tophet

Then I spake to the conversing angel:
O Lord, I am overwhelmed with pain at the sight,
my heart can no longer strength retain to look upon each single soul
and the fare which is each one's dole.
Yet having now seen in part what these individuals of agonies for
     themselves did win,
I would desire that thou make known to me the rule in general
     wherein
these sinners against themselves did sin,

so that they and what to them befel
may unto succeeding generations the moral tell.

And the man replied, Thy demand is just;
therefore what thou askest, fulfill I must.
Attend, then to all the things unto which I shall speak,
so that thereby they who are turned by my parable instruction may
    seek.

Know, my son, that these men who thou seest steeped in such
    sorrow,
some from the laws of science strange doctrines did borrow;
thereby their fellow to deceive they dared,
and these, being cast into the fowler's net, became ensnared.
Such teachings and scientific laws
are nought but traps, instruments of deception and its cause;
'tis on this account these men have to grapple with confusion's wars.

As for the others, their ear was deaf to sense,
and they concealed within their offence;
in secret they were wicked and sinful in feeling,
whilst they showed forth integrity, justice and meekness in outward
    dealing
so that men might put them in their trust,
and their goods and chattels unto their hands entrust;
these latter would find themselves betrayed at last,
caught in the net of destruction which these men had cast. . . .[104]
Some would utter Heaven's Name in vain,
making mention of it for the purpose of everything profane,
in regard to matters having no lofty and holy strain;
and therefore the ban upon them is lain. . . .[105]
Some again in the concerns of humanity took no share,
nor in act nor word did they show any care, saying,
"What business is this of ours? God cast them down, let Him them
    raise,"
but they did not divine what would befall them in after days;
this is why, by visitation and extermination, He drags them along in
    Death's own ways,
"whilst enlargement and deliverance would in the end rise for their
    fellow Jews from some other place,"
and as for these wicked ones, brimstone will be showered on their
    dwellings, and they will lose all grace.[106]

Immanuel Leaves Tophet and Enters Eden

Now as we went forth from Tophet and our thoughts were lost in dread,
whilst our faces were turned and our wings were spread
in the direction which the way to Eden doth tread,
soon as we from Tophet had journeyed forth travelwise,
we came to the top of a ladder placed on earth, the end of which to
  heaven did rise.[107]
And as on the higher steps we did alight,
the God of the World came into sight,
and there the heavens new and a new earth we saw;
therein was nothing foul, no loathsome flaw,
only a purified earth, where holiness is in store, and steps are
  prepared for the holy-souled
that lower, second and third degrees enfold.
There is the perfect light of which the wise have told,
that is a sevenfold light as that of the seven days of old.[108]
For what beauty and excellence therein is found!
No weariness is there, none who fall to the ground;
in those souls purity is rife,
"bound up as they are in the bundle of life"[109]
they shine forth as the brilliance of the sky,
and they become as bright luminaries in the world on high.

There are the souls of the innocent poor;
there the life which doth to eternity endure;
there is continuous joy and gladness, of interruptions no trace;
there is Sarah holding Isaac, her son, in a mother's embrace;
there is Rebecca impressing her kiss upon her son Jacob's face;
and there toward Joseph doth Rachel leap at skipping pace,
while Leah is lovingly at the doors of the children of her race.
There is Abraham, our father, in excellence hoary,
our chiefest of joys and the crown of our glory.
There are Moses and Aaron, of brothers the pair;
there are the Levites who the Ark did bear.
There is David rehearsing his psalmody's air,
and there are Judah's kings, passing before him as the host reviewed
  from the Temple stair.[110]
[The text goes on to list hundreds of other biblical and rabbinical
personages in Gan Eden.]

These appeared, and crowns upon their heads they had,
while in the garb of salvation and the mantle of righteousness they
  were clad;

partaking of one round of joy and gladness, exulting in song,
and feasting on the radiance of the *Shekhinah*[111] all day long.[112]

Now while we about the streets of Eden were turning,
and seeing what grade the men of Wisdom were earning,
I observed men filled with honor and majesty's spark,
compared with whose beauty sun and moon were dark.
A passage unto them was given in the region of the angels of heaven.
I recognized of these neither that on nor this,
and asked the man who spake to me the cause of their bliss.
"These are the pious among the gentile state,[113]
who by their intellect and wisdom have become great.
They rose on the steps of Learning's ladder in capacity to their rate,
and they did not with their forefathers mate,
who to a generation belonged that acted as a rebellious and
     stubborn violator,
whilst they with their intelligence searched out who formed them,
and who was Creator,
thro' whose goodness they into being came,
and who brought them forth from nothingness to something with a name,
and set them in this World's frame,
and what was the purpose of their creation, what was its aim.
And as of their fathers they enquired,
and reflected on the answer required,
they felt how these were bare and not what they desired,
and so they came to condemn their fathers' belief,
and determined to search the faiths of others for relief.
And as they passed the Faiths of all others under examination,
and found they were built upon a strong foundation,
whilst their own Faith for its folly deserved condemnation,
they did not say, by our Faith we shall stand,
for from our fathers as a tradition it has come into our hand;
but they choose of all the beliefs views such as seemed to them right,
upon which men versed in science had no cause to fight;
of these they took hold, to these they adhered with their might,
whereas those matters which all peoples would slight,
on these they turn their backs and banish them from their sight. . . .[114]

Ascending the Realms of Eden

And as we ascended Eden's heights,
we were destined to see tremendous sights,

for there were placed thrones exalted and high,
the marvel of miracles it seemed to my eye,
to feast upon which the mind could not itself satisfy.
Among these there was a shining throne, and the earth filled with
    its brightness;
it was "like the work of bright sapphire, and as the very heaven for
    clearness."[115]
And as for the footstool under its feet, its entire length was made up
    of electron
and it was my desire to sit thereon.
Whereupon I spake,
O my lord, for whom is this glorious throne of delight?
and for whom is the footstool, work of the sculptor's might?
And he replied: By thy life, the throne is reserved for the noblest of
    the pastors' scion,
for Judah spoken of as "the whelp of the lion"[116]
he who above his brethren did tower;
whilst the splendor which its ornamental blossoms doth shower
is "for the lawgiver that from between his feet shall not lose power"[117]
to be seated on this seat shall be thy dower,
and thou shalt be near him from that hour. . . .[118]

Now while we were in that honored station, ten canopies we saw,
that trappings of purple and scarlet coverings bore,
o'erlaid from within with gold, and set with every precious stone,
whilst the frame itself was a sapphire alone.
In them were placed thrones of weight and height,
worked in gold and filled with chrystolite,
with costly crowns of majesty and splendour,
compared with which the light of sun would darkness render.
Then said I, For whom are these canopies so rare,
these thrones and crowns of beauteous glare?

Then Daniel, man of delight, replied,
As thou livest, they are Ten royal Martyrs meed;
and I asked, Where are they in very deed?
We have been seeking them as the day, this has been our very need.
And Daniel answered,
They have journeyed hence with the Prince Michael,
and with them have gone *Rabbenu Ha-Kodesh*[119] and Samuel,
and these are bending low and worshiping before the Lord, the God
    of Israel,

praying on behalf of the existing remnant that a redeemer for it forth
    may spring,
for they have seen Israel's suffering,
and in great terror they their petition ply,
not giving Him rest until He pour forth Spirit from on high,
and hasten the final redemption's days,
when Jerusalem shall be established, and be made the world's
    object of praise. . . .[120]

Five Canopies in Gan Eden

Then he said unto me: Lift thine eyes and see;
understand the matter, comprehend the mystery.
And I raised my eyes, and saw five canopies each report,
beautiful in appearance and import,
with choice crowns of fairest gold, and he said unto me:
These are the canopies which honors unfold as the inheritance of
the Lord's servants who their pious acts are revealed,
such as upon the tablet of the heart of Time are sealed.

The first canopy of joy and gladness is for a certain perfect soul. . . .

Now the second canopy is for an honored one, captain of the
    host . . . ;

As for the third canopy, it is for a noble one. . . .

As for the fourth occupant, to the likeness of the son of God he might
    agree,
for he could easily ascend to the highest degree. . . .

The fifth canopy is for [a certain] scholarly Master. . . .[121]

And it came to pass, while we were in that honored station,
that Daniel, the man of delight, said unto me:
As thou livest, God hath presented thee with a goodly ration,
in having suffered thee to see of the past and the future things of
    wondrous worth,
and hast thee seen the guard of the holy ones and the prophets that
    do serve in Eden, God's garden from the world's birth,
the place of the wicked ones too, who have been brought down
    wonderfully from their mirth,
their souls grievously amid lions bemoaning joys of dearth.

Immanuel Encouraged to Record His Vision

Heaven hath shown thee this all,
that the world's children may know the fate which upon them shall fall.
Observe thou, therefore, all the things which thou seest, and write
    them for a memorial in a book,
placing them in the ark in some nook,
that the last generation for their guidance may look.
And as for thee, whilst thou art still in the life,
proclaim aloud (the voyage you took),
and make known to the men of thy generation
what sights thine eyes have stirred,
and what thine ears have heard.
And as for me, Daniel, who came forth to instruct thee with
    wisdom,
when first thou supplicatingly before me stand,
I will entrust thy spirit into thy Creator's hand,
who for His mercy's sake will into oblivion thy sins command.
Thou, now, turn thee to the left or to the right on thy ways,
and approach the goal, tranquilly awaiting thy lot at the end of
    days.[122]
And it came to pass when he had finished speaking these words,
that he was hid from my sight, and him I could no longer see.
I sought him eagerly indeed, but he was not to be found by me.
And as I was in the thick of the storm, roaming after him,
thinking peradventure I might find him,
I was aroused from my sleep,
and as I called to mind the things which I had seen in a vision,
I muttered aught, and then my terror was deep;
I feared for my life, and from my phantasy's dream I awoke,
and I roused my hand to write down that which my hearing and sight
    bespoke;
all my strength I employed, I omitted nought;
and may God, my highest joy, the rock of my strength, my refuge,
whose trust I sought,
who inspired me with confidence on my mother's breast from the
    hour when out of her womb I was brought,
deign to accept my speech:
and may my teaching, dropping upon the hearts of the noble among
    His people, with the blessing of rain be fraught,
my words impressing themselves upon the tablet of their heart,
so that I become not as those singing unto the dead,
or crying unto idols to take their part!

And now, as for me, my hands are unto heaven spread,
that whilst His breath is yet within me, I may merit to learn and teach,
    to observe, and in His precepts tread;
and that at the latter end, God's mercy may grant me support,
taking hold of my right
and give me my rest in honor in that place where it shall be my
    delight
to meet those who have brought righteousness unto the many, as
    the stars for ever and ever shining bright.[123]

SUMMARY

In this chapter we have entered into the mythic world of medieval Midrash. From the material presented the following observations can be made:

1. In the medieval period an extensive mythical tradition was developed that yielded a series of elaborate visionary texts delineating the fate of the soul in the afterlife. These texts reflect a continuation of apocryphal traditions and a blending of these earlier visionary traditions with the genre and motifs of narrative rabbinic Midrash.

2. There are three clusters of themes explored in medieval Midrash: (a) the fate of the soul immediately after death, as it experiences *Hibbut Ha-Kever*, the pangs of the grave; (b) the fate of the soul and the nature of its experiences in Gehenna, the postmortem realm of punishment; and (c) the fate of the soul and the nature of its experiences in the heavenly realm of Gan Eden, the Garden of Eden. There are at least a dozen texts that describe these various phases of the afterlife journey with profoundly lurid and painstaking detail.

3. Medieval afterlife teachings also found expression in another entirely different form, through the Renaissance poetry of Immanuel ben Solomon, Ha-Romi. Though not strictly a religious or sacred text, Ha-Romi's *Tophet V'Ha-Eden* demonstrate the concern Jews of the medieval period had with the experiences of the soul in the afterlife.

4. There has been little formal scholarship on medieval midrashic writings, and few of these afterlife texts have been made widely

accessible to English-speaking, modern Jews. However, medieval Midrash reveals both the breadth and depth of Jewish fascination with the afterlife, and this genre of literature is a gold mine for further study of the evolution of Jewish motifs of life after death.

Chapter 7

Immortality of the Soul in Medieval Philosophy

THE HISTORICAL CONTEXT

In this chapter we will investigate a genre of literature entirely different from all that we have seen until now. Contemporaneous with the creation of medieval visionary Midrash, there appeared within the Jewish world a significant stream of medieval philosophical writings. During a period of close to six centuries, renowned Jewish scholars produced a vast body of philosophical writings, hundreds of texts and treatises that blended rabbinic Judaism with the substance and character of Greek, Arabic, and Christian philosophy. Individuals such as Saadia Gaon, Solomon ibn Gabirol, Yehuda Ha Levi, Abraham ibn Ezra, Abraham ibn Daud, Maimonides, and Gersonides wrote extensively on a wide spectrum of topics including mathematics, astronomy, medicine, natural science, philosophy, and metaphysics.[1] Among the corpus of medieval philosophical writings are found a diverse assortment of teachings on the immortal soul and its postmortem destiny.

On our historical journey we are in the heart of the medieval period, c. 850 to 1450 C.E., a period of creative cultural interaction between Judaism, Christianity, and Islam. During this era there was a progressive movement of the intellectual centers of Jewry from Babylonia, first to Egypt, North Africa, and Spain, then to Italy and Provence, in the south of France. While the quality of Jewish life differed under Muslim or Christian domination, overall this period was characterized by the ascendance of philosophical speculation and rich cultural developments in science, language, and literature.[2]

Medieval philosophy certainly did not emerge in a vacuum. In the Jewish writings of this period, rabbinic thought is blended with the obvious influence of Neoplatonism, Aristotelianism, Christian scholasticism, and Arabic Kalam philosophy. Like their Muslim and Christian contemporaries, Jewish writers focused on the philosophical issues of medieval times. Those issues had to with proving the existence of God; with questions about the nature, unity, and attributes of the divine; and with the mysteries of creation, providence, and human freedom. Common to both Greek and Judeo-Christian-Muslim tradition was a belief in human immortality. This belief was popular in medieval philosophy, and as a result, over the course of centuries scores of texts on the immortality of the soul were written.[3]

CHARACTER OF MEDIEVAL WRITINGS ON THE AFTERLIFE

Although radically different from talmudic and midrashic literature, medieval philosophical teachings on immortality and the afterlife, nonetheless, presuppose a commitment to rabbinic tradition. Medieval Jewish philosophy reflects the attempted synthesis of rabbinic Judaism and Greek philosophical thought. Whereas Torah and Talmud were regarded as documents of divine revelation, the writings of Aristotle and other philosophers were but the outgrowth of human rationalism. However, in the spirit of the intellectual tenor of the times, the medievalists endeavored to demonstrate that there was no contradiction or conflict between the dictates of rationalism and the dogmas of rabbinic Judaism.[4] In those areas where Torah and philosophy seemed to conflict, the medieval Jewish philosophers venture to demonstrate "that either the conflict was apparent, or that a particular understanding of Torah should be followed."[5]

In our exploration of afterlife teachings in this era, we will see how the medieval philosophers repeatedly investigate traditional Jewish concepts of *Olam Ha-Ba*, Gehenna, Gan Eden, divine judgment, and resurrection in some very unique ways. Undoubtedly, the essential questions of the philosophers are not those of the early Rabbis, the midrashists, the apocalyptic writers, and certainly not those of the biblical ancestors and the prophets. We do not find in these writings visionary, mythic depictions of the soul's journeying in Gan Eden and Gehenna. Rather, medieval philosophy is of a much more abstract quality, filled with speculative inquiry regarding the immortal soul, its essential nature, and postmortem destiny. Within this genre of Jewish literature, the understanding of the hereafter is essentially philosophical in tone. The medieval philosophers were absorbed with questions about the essence, substantiality, and immortality of the soul. As Harry Blumberg notes:

> The discussion of the problem of immortality in medieval philosophy usually revolved about a number of pivotal questions regarding the soul, the body and the hereafter. What is the nature of the soul? Is it part of the body or has it separate existence? If it is part of the body, will the soul perish with the destruction of the body or is there some part of the soul which will survive? Can immortal souls acquire new knowledge after death? Are the rewards and punishments in the hereafter purely spiritual or are they material? To what degree do the intellectual and moral attainments of the individual during his lifetime after the immortality of the person?[6]

It is this kind of inquiry that characterizes medieval philosophical writings on the afterlife.

By blending talmudic and midrashic teachings with classical philosophy, medieval Jewish scholars forged new pathways in the intellectual history of Judaism. What emerged was a unique and hitherto unseen Jewish philosophy of immortality, yet another important genre among the diverse legacy of Jewish teachings on the afterlife.

MEDIEVAL TREATISES ON IMMORTALITY

Although there are characteristics common to all medieval Jewish philosophers, there is at the same time a great deal of variance among different authors. In presenting a representative sampling of medieval afterlife teachings, we will examine the following writings on immortality and life after death:

1. *Sefer Ha-Emunot Ve-Ha-Daot*, "The Book of Beliefs and Opinions," authored by Saadia Gaon.
2. Three specific writings by Maimonides: *Perek Helek* in the *Commentary on the Mishnah*, *Hilkhot Teshuvah* in *Mishneh Torah*, and *Maamar Tehiyyat Ha-Metim*, "Treatise on Resurrection."
3. *Milhamot Ha-Shem*, "The Wars of the Lord," by Gersonides, in particular, Book 1, "The Immortality of the Soul."
4. *Shaar Ha-Gemul*, "The Gate of Reward," by Nahmanides, an individual treatise found in his major work *Torat Ha-Adam*.

It is important to note that Nahmanides is not usually considered among the medieval philosophers. The style and content of his writing generally tends less toward the rationalistic-philosophical school of Judaism and more toward the mystical-kabbalistic tone. However, Nahmanides is a later contemporary of Maimonides, and in the text we will consider here, he responds directly to Maimonides' views of the afterlife. The writings of Nahmanides will help us bridge medieval philosophy and kabbalistic Judaism.

THE AFTERLIFE PHILOSOPHY OF SAADIA GAON

Introduction—The Life and Work of Saadia Gaon

Saadia Gaon (882–942), also known as Saadia ben Joseph Al Fayyumi, was the first eminent philosopher of medieval Judaism. Often considered to be "the father of medieval Jewish philosophy of religion,"[7] he was the first to systematically integrate classical Jewish doctrine with the philosophical traditions of his age. Born in Upper Egypt, Saadia received an excellent education in Jewish, Muslim, and secular literature. At a relatively young age, he had gained prominence as an erudite scholar. By the time of his departure from Egypt, at the age of twenty-three, Saadia had already compiled a Hebrew dictionary and lexicon, single-handedly generating interest in Hebrew philology and linguistics,[8] and had authored important polemical texts against the sectarian Karaite movement.

Saadia Gaon traveled a great deal during his lifetime, residing at different times in Palestine, Syria, and Babylonia. Not one to avoid conflict, he found himself embroiled in a number of religiopolitical disputations in the Jewish world. Very early in his career, he spearheaded the campaign against the heretical Karaite sect, authoring important philosophical polemics aimed at the founder of Karaism. Later, Saadia was at the center of a major controversy between Babylonian and Palestinian Jewry with regard to the affixing of the Jewish calendar. In 928 C.E. Saadia was invited to serve as spiritual leader, or Gaon, of the rabbinical academy at Sura, in Babylonia. The first foreigner to fill this post, he was soon replaced after becoming enmeshed in a legal disputation with the exilarch, or *Rosh Galuta*, the leader of the Jewish Babylonian community who was the political representative to the sultan.[9]

Saadia Gaon was deeply steeped in traditional Jewish learning, and wherever he lived was recognized as the intellectual giant of the Judaism of his day. At the same time, he was also a product of the confluence of intellectual forces in his time. Standing on the threshold of medieval philosophical developments, Saadia was personally influenced by the writings of Aristotle, which he read in Arabic, and by the Mu'tazilites, the philosophical rationalists of the Islamic world.[10]

During Saadia's lifetime, Islam was involved in the process of codifying the teachings of Mohammed. During the Middle Ages, nascent Islam crystallized a series of six dogmas, which included belief in God, His angels, His books, His messenger, the hereafter, and predestination.[11] Similarly, Saadia himself articulated a credo, affirming the following specific beliefs:

1. The existence of a Creator
2. Creation out of nothing
3. The Creator had no associates
4. The authority of revealed laws
5. Belief in miracles
6. Belief in reckoning and retribution
7. Belief in resurrection
8. Belief in redemption[12]

In Saadia's credo, the influences of Islam were integrated with an unflinching commitment to rabbinic Judaism. This eightfold credo—a precursor to the Maimonidean articles of faith—assumed as a baseline Jewish eschatological beliefs in divine judgment, resurrection, and collective redemption. Even though Saadia conceived of immortality and the soul in philosophical terms, he nonetheless maintained and reaffirmed rabbinic conceptions of the hereafter.[13]

Saadia wrote extensively on practically every subject explored by Jewish scholars of his era, authoring books on philology, theology, philosophy, cosmology, biblical exegesis, and Jewish law. Among his literary accomplishments are *The Book of Seasons*, a legalistic response to the fixing of the calendrical cycle; his commentary on *Sefer Yetzirah*; and his magnum opus, *Sefer Ha-Emunot Ve-Ha-Daot*, "The Book of Beliefs and Opinions,"[14] which contains his central ideas on afterlife and immortality.

Originally written in Arabic, *The Book of Beliefs and Opinions* (most often referred to simply as *Emunot Ve-Daot*) was the first systematic study of Jewish religious philosophy.[15] It comprises a series of ten treatises, originally written separately and then later, c. 933 C.E., compiled into a single text. As a whole, *Emunot Ve-Daot* follows the literary pattern of the Islamic Mu'tazilites focusing on two broad areas of philosophical inquiry: (1) the unity of God and (2) divine justice and human morality.[16]

In the first part of this text are found some of Saadia's finest writings on the creation of the world, God's unity, God's commandments, and divine revelation. The larger second half of the text contains Saadia's most important writings on the afterlife. Although elsewhere he does discuss the topic of immortality, the core of his ideas regarding life after death appear in four separate treatises of *Emunot Ve-Daot*, titled as follows: "Merits and Demerits," "The Essence of the Soul and Death and What Comes after Death," "The Resurrection of the Dead in this World," and "Reward and Punishment in the World to Come."[17] We will now examine the specific content of these philosophical treatises.

Saadia's Philosophy of the Soul

In order to understand Saadia's views of the afterlife, we need to investigate the essential assumptions inherent in his philosophy of the soul. For Saadia, there is absolutely no question as to whether or not the soul exists. The soul is a creation of God and the effects of its operation in the world are directly visible.[18] What is important to Saadia is how the soul came into being and, as a parallel concern, exactly what the essence of the soul is.

In answer to the question of origins, Saadia's basic assumption is that the soul is not preexistent, but rather, is created in the womb. As he writes in *The Book of Beliefs and Opinions*: "[M]an's soul has its origins in his heart simultaneously with the completion of the formation of his body . . . [as it is written in Scripture, the Lord] 'laid the foundation of the earth and formed the spirit of man within him' (Zachariah 12:1)."[19]

This belief in the creation of the soul in the embryo is essentially Aristotelian and, interestingly enough, conflicts with talmudic teachings about a preexistent "storehouse of souls"—or *guf*—in heaven (*Yebamot* 62a). However, for Saadia, at the moment when the embryo receives its soul, God's presence is manifest; because it is created by God, the soul has the power to attain immortality.[20] This is an important philosophical assumption that establishes an a priori belief in the soul's postmortem immortality.

In reflecting on the question of the soul's essence, Saadia affirms belief in the substantiality of the soul. Unlike Plato, Saadia Gaon rejects the idea of nonmateriality of the soul. For Saadia, the soul is comprised of a substance the quality of which

> is comparable in purity to that of the heavenly spheres. Like the latter it attains luminosity as a result of the light which it receives from God, [and as a result, its substance] becomes even finer than that of the [heavenly] spheres.[21]

For Saadia, the soul has substance, but it is a spiritual substance: a subtle, luminescent light that is fine, pure, and transparent like the heavenly spheres. Further illuminating the point, Saadia explains that

> [i]f someone were to remark, "But we never see the soul depart from the body," our reply would be, "That is due to its transparency and to its resemblance to the air in its fineness, just as we are unable to see the heavenly spheres on account of the purity of their substances and their transparency."[22]

Yet another basic assumption made by Saadia is that the soul is an indivisible unity. He rejects the idea that the soul is twofold—one part infinite and the other finite; one part rational and another perceptive. While there are specific faculties or powers of the soul—the threefold division of *nefesh* (appetitive awareness), *ruah* (the soul's ability to experience such powerful emotions as anger or courage), and *neshamah* (the power of reasoning and cognition)[23]—nonetheless, in the final analysis, Saadia maintains that "soul and body constitute one agent."[24] These separate faculties of the soul are made manifest through the soul's union with the physical body; however, at the time of death, when the soul exits from the body there is absolutely no division of these individual aspects.[25]

Reward and Punishment in *Emunot Ve-Daot*

Discussion of the concept of reward and punishment in Saadia Gaon's philosophy demonstrates an innovative synthesis of rabbinic tradition and medieval thought. For the Rabbis, as we have seen, an individual's postmortem reward or punishment is always a result of their ethical action in the world. Those who act honorably, and with divine intent, are rewarded appropriately; those who act sinfully, are punished. In some ways, it is quite a simple system of retributive cause and effect.

In medieval philosophy, however, the name of the game, so to speak, changes. The goal is not simply to serve God by doing good deeds. Rather, for the philosopher, the goal of human existence is to achieve a connection with the active intellect—what we might call the soul, or the higher mind. This is accomplished through the study of philosophy, which, according to the philosophers, in and of itself serves to purify the mind.

According to Saadia, all human conduct affects the very nature of the soul. Ethical, moral actions, in consonance with the dictates of Torah, polish the soul, making it bright and luminous. On the other hand, wicked actions soil, stain, and darken the soul. Pure souls that have been refined are exalted and ennobled, whereas soiled souls are degraded and based.[26] In *Emunot Ve-Daot* this is asserted by Saadia as follows:

> [W]hen the merits predominate in the soul, the latter is thereby purified and rendered luminous. . . . [On] the other hand, when the demerits are in the majority in it, the soul becomes turbid and darkened, as Scripture does indeed say of those who are in such a state: "They shall never see the light." (Psalm 49:20)[27]

As long as a person is alive, he or she is capable of *teshuvah*, or repentance; hence, a tarnished soul can be purified and cleansed through rightful action. However, once a human being is deceased, the possibility for purification of the soul is eliminated.[28]

According to Saadia, there exists a divine scorecard of every person's deeds: God "keeps a record of these merits and demerits for all His servants"[29] in "books and archives in which are recorded the deeds of the righteous as well as of the wicked"[30] (a motif evidenced earlier apocryphal and rabbinic writings). After death, a person is judged according to his or her deeds, hence according to the nature of the luminosity found in his or her soul. An individual's afterlife recompense is thus based on whether it is light or darkness that predominates in the soul. This postmortem conception, totally unique to medieval philosophy, is a radical reframing of the traditional rabbinic ethics of divine judgment.

With regard to the timing of postmortem retribution, Saadia remains consistent with biblical tradition, and contends that divine retribution will be apportioned with the onset of the World to Come, at the end-of-days.[31] However, in discussing the specific nature of reward and punishment in the hereafter, Saadia's philosophical bent is exhibited. He reconceptualizes rabbinic theology in terms unique to medieval philosophy, and declares

> that this reward and punishment will take the form of two very fine substances that our Master, exalted and magnified be He, will create at the time of the retribution, applying them to each of His servants in accordance with his desert. They will both consist of the same essence, an essence resembling the property of burning, luminous fire, that will shine for the righteous but not for the sinful, whilst it will burn the sinful but not the righteous.[32]

Simply stated, Saadia maintains that the reward of the righteous is luminescent light and the punishment of the wicked is a burning fire.[33] In the World to Come, each individual will experience these distinct powers of light and fire, based on his or her acquired merit. The righteous will have the inherent capacity to absorb light, whereas the wicked will be susceptible only to penetrating fire.[34]

In an interesting transposition of rabbinic theology, Saadia goes one step further and asserts that the light of the righteous is Gan Eden, the fire of the wicked, Gehenna.[35] Good and bad have been transformed into light and darkness, and Gan Eden and Gehenna are seen as reflections of the substantive light and darkness of the individual soul. Thus, by using the building blocks of rabbinic tradition, Saadia Gaon is able to transform the ethically based postmortem teachings of the Rabbis into an afterlife conception that reflects the substantive philosophy of the medieval age.

Resurrection and Reincarnation in *Emunot Ve-Daot*

On the topic of resurrection, Saadia Gaon reiterates classical rab-binic views of the resurrection of the dead. He uses a series of biblical passages to demonstrate the rationality of physical resurrection, and maintains that there will be a messianic redemption followed by resur-rection of the dead and the reuniting of body and soul.

In *Emunot Ve-Daot* Saadia asserts that there will actually be two distinct periods of resurrection. It is not that the individual will return to bodily life twice, but rather that there will be two separate and dis-tinct periods of resurrection—one in the messianic era, a second in the World to Come.[36] As Israel Efros notes: "[First] the righteous of Israel will arise in the messianic era and will no more die, but will be transferred to the world to come . . . [then] the others, Jews and non-Jews, will arise only in the hereafter."[37]

With regard to reincarnation, Saadia stands vehemently opposed to any such belief. As we will see in our study of Kabbalah, around this time the doctrine of reincarnation of souls began slowly gaining popu-larity among mystically oriented schools of Judaism. Such a view main-tained that the infinite soul would reenter another body in a future life-time. However, Saadia was philosophically at odds with any such belief because he maintained there was an essential unity of body and soul. The resurrection required a full and total reunion of body and soul; hence, the idea of reincarnation in another physical form, at least according to his view, was an utter impossibility.[38]

The main eschatological belief underlying Saadia's philosophy was the essential rabbinic view that the soul, after death, would separate from the body and remain in an intermediate state until the time of resurrec-tion, when it would be reunited with the physical body. It was this collec-tive eschatological view, over and above any other belief in either indi-vidual immortality of the soul or reincarnation, that was basic for Saadia Gaon.[39]

THE AFTERLIFE PHILOSOPHY OF MOSES MAIMONIDES

Introduction—The Life and Work of Maimonides

Moses ben Maimon (1135–1204), known as Maimonides or Rambam (acronym for Rabbi Moses ben Maimon), was the greatest philosophical mind of medieval Judaism. A rabbi, scholar, philosopher, jurist, and physician, he was widely recognized in his lifetime throughout the Jewish world, extending from France to Yemen.

Born in Cordova, Spain, Maimonides descended from a long line of Jewish jurists and legalists. Although the eleventh century had witnessed a creative flowering of Jewish culture in Spain, by the early years of the twelfth century, even prior to Maimonides' birth, Jewish life had been threatened by increasing religious persecution. In 1148, the year of his *bar mitzvah*, Maimonides and his family fled the threat of forced apostasy in Cordova. After almost a decade of wandering throughout southern Spain and northern Africa, the family settled in Fez, Morocco; then, after 1165, they moved for a short time to Acre, Palestine, ultimately, settling in Fostat, Egypt, near Cairo.

No doubt this period of exile and uprootedness affected the young Moses Maimonides, yet all the while his unbridled passion for Jewish learning continued unabated. During the years of his wanderings he began work on his *Commentary on the Mishnah* and also authored other minor treatises on Jewish thought.[40]

In Egypt Maimonides became head of the Jewish community of Old Cairo, and eventually also a physician in the royal court. Seeing patients by day, Maimonides would then spend the remainder of his time engaged in scholarly study. This was a fruitful and creative period, during which time Maimonides completed and published the two celebrated works that have guaranteed his legacy in Jewish history—*Mishneh Torah* (compiled in 1180) and *Guide to the Perplexed* (1190)—as well as other minor writings.

Maimonides died in 1204 and, as he had requested, was buried in Tiberias, where his grave remains a pilgrimage site. One of the all-time great minds of Judaism, posterity has likened Maimonides to the first Moses, leader of the biblical Israelites: "From Moses to Moses, there arose none like Moses"—so Jews have acclaimed of him for centuries.[41]

Maimonides' voluminous collection of writings on philosophy, Jewish law, and medicine were unrivaled in his time, although certainly not without controversy.[42] As a philosopher, he endeavored to systematically delineate principles of Judaism in light of the wisdom of Greek philosophy. As a legalist, he codified the entire corpus of biblical and rabbinic teachings into a vast legalistic text that has remained an authoritative guidebook for Jewish religious practice.

Even while alive, Maimonides had a compelling influence on Jewish life. But even more so, after his death the spiritual legacy he left behind has had an enduring impact on the subsequent course of all Jewish thought.[43] After Maimonides, practically all philosophical thinking, whether so intended or not, is some form of a response to or commentary on Maimonides. Even to this day, almost 800 years after his death, various writings of Maimonides are widely read and serve as the mainstream diet of traditional Jewish learning.

With regard to teachings on immortality and the afterlife, it is safe to say that eschatology is not the most widely discussed topic in Maimonidean writings. He hardly gives much consideration to the subject in the *Guide to the Perplexed*, although some of his views on immortality can be inferred from his writing on the nature of the soul therein, and in other texts.

There are three specific texts, however, where Maimonides discusses postmortem life: a section in his *Commentary on the Mishnah* entitled *Perek Helek*; a chapter entitled *Hilkhot Teshuvah* ("Laws of Repentance") in his famous *Mishneh Torah*; and finally, a lengthy treatment of the subject, "The Treatise on Resurrection," known in Hebrew as *Maamar Tehiyyat Ha-Metim*.

In these eschatological writings, Maimonides deals with two essential philosophical concerns. First, he takes it on himself to integrate philosophical notions of the immortal soul with the more imagistic afterlife teachings of the Talmud and Midrash.[44] Second, given the importance of the doctrine of divine retribution in Jewish life, Maimonides attempts to explain biblical and rabbinic conceptions of reward and punishment in philosophical terms. Thus, although based on traditional rabbinic conceptions of *Olam Ha-Ba*, Maimonides' writings reflect the philosophical style of medieval Judaism. The texts we will now explore focus on philosophical conceptions of immortality rather than on descriptive information regarding the postmortem wanderings of the soul.

Perek Helek: Eschatological Views at the Time of Maimonides

Maimonides began writing his *Commentary on the Mishnah* at the age of twenty-three, completing it approximately ten years later, in 1165. This text laid the foundation for Maimonides' recognition as a pioneering trendsetter in Jewish law. Within the *Commentary on the Mishnah* is a small, but well-known selection that discusses Jewish eschatology. Referred to as *Perek Helek*,[45] this selection is a commentary on Mishnah

Sanhedrin 10:1, which begins: "All Israelites have a share in the World to Come"—*Kol Yisrael yesh la-hem helek La-Olam Ha-Ba.*

In *Perek Helek* Maimonides assumes the role of the wise spiritual leader who endeavors to clarify for the Jewish populace misconceptions regarding the wide variety of rabbinic afterlife teachings. Given the unsystematized nature of rabbinic afterlife teachings, the lack of an authoritative view regarding the individual's postmortem fate, and the populist tendency to take legendary depictions of Gan Eden and Gehenna quite literally, Maimonides felt the need to articulate his own philosophical understanding of immortality and the afterlife.

To begin with, Maimonides surveys the variety of eschatological beliefs prevalent in the medieval Jewish world. He delineates five views regarding the ultimate good and evil the individual merits as a result of his or her actions in life.

One group, notes Maimonides, believes that the ultimate good is Gan Eden, "a place in which one eats and drinks without physical effort and without toil" and where there are houses of precious stones, luxurious silk beds, and rivers flowing with oil and wine.[46] Further, this group presumes that the ultimate evil is Gehenna, "a place of burning fire where bodies are burned and where human beings suffer various types of agonies."[47] Elaborate descriptions of the agonies and suffering in Gehenna are elucidated by this group, who use scriptural passages from Torah and teachings of the Rabbis to establish their point of view. Notice here that Maimonides refers to the same motifs evidenced in such texts as *Masekhet Gan Eden* and *Masekhet Gehenna*. No doubt he is referring to the medieval midrashists and the legendary aggadic traditions of the afterlife that were popular among the masses during this period.

A second group believes that the anticipated ultimate good is the Days of the Messiah. This will be an epoch of human history in which all people will be kings, the Messiah will live eternally, and "the earth will bring forth ready-woven garments and ready-baked bread and many similar impossible things."[48] Conversely, ultimate evil will be the failure of an individual to exist and take part in the manifestation of this messianic age.

The third group maintains that the ultimate good one can hope for is the resurrection of the dead, when the dead will be restored to life, returning to family and kindred, and participating in ongoing life activities forevermore. Evil, in this case, is the failure to be resurrected.[49]

A fourth group, contends Maimonides, believes that the ultimate

good one merits is the experiencing of physical pleasure and the realization of worldly ambitions, "such as fertility of the land, and abundant possessions, and many children, and long life, and bodily health, and peace
and security, and the presence of a Jewish king and dominion over our
enemies."[50] The evil one experiences for not following Torah's commandments is the absence of the above material comforts.

Finally, a fifth group of Jewish pundits—the majority, according to
Maimonides—maintains that the expected supreme reward is an inte-
gration of all of the above beliefs. First there will be the arrival of the
Messiah, who will subsequently resurrect the dead and "lead them to the
Garden of Eden, [where] they will eat and drink . . . and live in good
health, so long as heaven and earth endure."[51]

This brief survey indicates clearly that even in the time of
Maimonides, there was no singular, accepted eschatological belief among
the Jews. Notions of Gan Eden, Gehenna, the messianic era, and the resurrection of the dead were intermingled or confused.

Next, Maimonides prepares to offer his personal philosophical understanding of immortality and the afterlife by first asking: Do people
really think seriously about this ultimate goal of the World to Come? Does
anyone even think about the distinction between this ultimate goal of
the World to Come and the means of achieving this goal? Most people
do not sufficiently understand the full import of the doctrines of immortality, Olam Ha-Ba, and the resurrection, says Maimonides:

> Rarely does anyone ask whether the World to Come is the ultimate
> good. . . . Nor does one often find persons who distinguish between
> the ultimate good itself and the means which lead to the ultimate
> good. What people ask about—both among the masses and the
> learned—is how the dead will arise. They want to know whether they
> will be naked or clothed, whether they will arise in the same shrouds
> in which they were buried, with the same embroidery, style and
> beauty of sewing, or in a plain garment which merely covers their
> bodies. Or they ask whether, when the Messiah comes, there will
> still be rich men and poor men, weak men and strong men, and other
> similar questions.[52]

Here, Maimonides is suggesting that all too many Jews think about
immortality and life after death in fundamentalist or materialistic ways.
Notice that what we have here is a veiled condemnation of the medieval
Midrash, which as a mythic and populist tradition was an affront to

Maimonides' philosophical rationalism. But, according to Maimonides, those who understand Torah metaphorically, not simply in a fundamentalist or materialistic sense, can intuitively perceive Torah's profound spiritual teachings. To those individuals, Maimonides addresses himself with regard to the doctrine of *Olam Ha-Ba*. Then, shifting focus, he writes: "Now I can begin to discuss the matter with which I am really concerned."[53]

Perek Helek: The Immortal Spiritual World of *Olam Ha-Ba*

In many ways, Maimonides can be seen as a Jewish Aristotelian. This is very apparent in *Perek Helek*, where his notion of *Olam Ha-Ba* is dualistic in contrast to the worldview of biblical Judaism. Whereas in biblical thought, there is no inherent dualism of body and soul, for Maimonides, body is body, spirit is spirit; the two are of separate and distinct realms. Thus, in *Perek Helek* we find the view that

> Just as a blind man cannot perceive colors, nor a deaf man hear sounds, nor a eunuch feel sexual desire, so bodies [of human beings] cannot attain spiritual delights. And just as fish do not know the element of fire because they live in its opposite, so are the pleasures of the spiritual world unknown to this world of flesh.[54]

Although physical beings experience the delights of the body, according to Maimonides, the pleasures of the spiritual world are far beyond any possibility of human comprehension. The spiritual world, like the angels, stars, and planets, is eternal, existing outside the limited and bounded dimensions of physical existence. However, Maimonides envisioned the possibility that human beings could know the delights of the spiritual world after death through the process of the intellectual contemplation of God and the infinite mysteries of creation.[55]

As Julius Guttmann notes:

> [For Maimonides] knowledge is a preliminary condition for the immortality of the soul. [He] accepts the doctrine of acquired immortality, according to which only the actualization through knowledge of man's intellectual power leads to immortality. The immortality of the soul thus becomes the immortality of the knowing spirit. But this metaphysical idea also has a religious meaning; it is the communion with God, gained through knowledge which endows man with eternal life.[56]

According to Maimonides, through philosophical inquiry—understood as a process of intellectual self-advancement—one can come to know the spiritual world and, ultimately, attain immortality of the soul. This is an essential underpinning of Maimonides' view of the World to Come. For Maimonides, the rabbinic conception of *Olam Ha-Ba*, the World to Come, is regarded as being a disembodied state of existence wherein an immortal soul has acquired knowledge of the divine.

To further explicate this philosophical premise, the Rambam draws on a well-known talmudic text from tractate *Berakhot*: "In *Olam Ha-Ba* [the World to Come] there is no eating, nor drinking, nor washing, nor anointing, nor sexual intercourse; but the righteous sit with their crowns on their heads enjoying the radiance of the Divine Presence [*Shekhinah*]" (*Berakhot* 17a).

Using rabbinic hermeneutics, Maimonides elucidates this passage as follows: "With their crowns on their heads," he explains, "is the immortality of the soul in the intellectual sphere";[57] "and they delight in the radiance of the Divine Presence" means that "those souls derive bliss from what they understand of the Creator, just like the holy spirits and the other ranks of angels."[58] For Maimonides, the ultimate objective of life is to achieve this lofty sphere of existence and to become exalted like this group of sages.

In this interpretation, Maimonides alludes to his concept of the soul. As documented in other writings,[59] he presupposes a threefold Aristotelian division of the soul: (1) a vegetative aspect, which controls physical nourishment and procreation; (2) a sensory aspect, which governs movement, sense perception, and imagination; and (3) a rational aspect, which possesses the power of reasoning.[60] The first two aspects of the soul, according to Maimonides, disintegrate with the death of the physical body. The third aspect, however, the rational or intellectual faculty—"the form of the soul which has succeeded in comprehending concepts and universal truths"[61]—is bestowed by God and therefore does not perish at the time of death.[62] This latter aspect of the soul, being immortal, is the faculty that experiences *Olam Ha-Ba*.

Notice what has taken place: Maimonides has transformed traditional rabbinic notions of the afterlife into abstract medieval philosophy. Out of the legacy of the past an entirely new postmortem conceptualization has come into being. For Maimonides, the World to Come is a transcendent realm characterized by a blissful, harmonious mystical rapport between soul and divine creator. By wedding rationalistic philosophy and rabbinic eschatology, as he does in *Perek Helek*, Maimonides conceives of *Olam Ha-Ba* as a spiritual abode of the immortal soul that the righteous enter immediately after death.[63]

Perek Helek: Olam Ha-Ba and Divine Retribution

In the latter part of *Perek Helek* Maimonides presents the ethical basis of his philosophy of *Olam Ha-Ba*. Given that the World to Come is the ultimate good, what is the ultimate evil? For Maimonides, it is "the cutting off of the soul and its perishing so that it does not become perpetual [i.e., live eternally]."[64] This ultimate punishment is what is meant by the biblical concept of *karet*—or cutting off—as in the verse "That soul shall be utterly cut off" (Numbers 15:31). For those who do not live righteously, their soul shall be cut off both in this world and in the World to Come:

> It follows that if a person has deliberately and regularly chosen physical delights, has despised the truth and loved falsehood, he will be cut off [excluded] from that high level of being and remain isolated [cut off, unconnected] matter [*homer nihrat*].[65]

The way to perfection is through performance of the commandments, or *mitzvot*. For those who embark on this path, God will remove obstacles to their fulfillment "so that persons who strive to do the commandments will be healthy and secure until they have attained that degree of excellence through which they will merit the life of the World to Come."[66] The reward for following God's commandments is not simply physical life comfort, but rather the increased ability to fulfill additional commandments, as the Rabbis have taught: "The reward of a *mitzvah* is a *mitzvah* and the reward of a sin is a sin" (M. *Avot* 4:2). Through the fulfillment of divine commandments, one will ultimately achieve perfection and merit existence in the World to Come.[67]

In wrapping up his eschatological discussions in *Perek Helek*, Maimonides briefly mentions other rabbinic notions. Gan Eden is described as a physical locale of luxuriant abundance that God will reveal to humanity sometime in the future.[68] Gehenna is "a term denoting the suffering that will come upon the wicked."[69] And the Days of the Messiah is described as a time of political sovereignty for Israel, world peace, and material prosperity.[70] These concepts are all enunciated in posthistorical terms, referring not to a realm immediately after death, but to a future time when all humanity will be redeemed and judged by God.

With regard to the resurrection of the dead, Maimonides articulates this as an assumed doctrinal premise requiring no extensive elaboration:

> The resurrection of the dead is one of the cardinal principles established by Moses our teacher, peace be on him. A person who does not believe in this principle has no real religion. He certainly does not cleave to the Jewish religion. However, resurrection is only for the righteous.[71]

In the delineation of these notions, Maimonides' essential aim is to communicate an ethical retributive point of view. He is less interested in specific descriptions of the postmortem fate of the soul than in righteous behavior and the fulfillment of *mitzvot*. One should serve the Creator out of the spirit of love, not for the expressed goal of attaining *Olam Ha-Ba*. By practicing the *mitzvot* and avoiding sin, one can thereby cultivate virtue and attain perfection:

> When one attains complete humanity [becomes a perfect human being] he acquires what is of the nature of the perfect [fulfilled] human being, namely that there is no eternal force which can deny his soul eternal life. His soul is thus confirmed in that eternal existence which it has come to know—and this is the World to Come as we have explained.[72]

What we see in *Perek Helek* is the blending of both individual postmortem notions of the afterlife and collective, posthistorical eschatological teachings on the end-of-days. On the one hand, Maimonides envisions an immortal soul after death that communes directly with God. On the other hand, he views Gan Eden, Gehenna, the resurrection of the dead, and the Days of the Messiah in the collective eschatological terms characteristic of rabbinic thought. In *Perek Helek* Maimonides reframes rabbinic afterlife teachings in terms of medieval philosophy, all the while maintaining as an underpinning the traditional rabbinic doctrine of divine retribution.

Mishneh Torah: Hilkhot Teshuvah ("Laws of Repentance")

Mishneh Torah (literally, "repetition of the teaching of Torah") is a fourteen-volume compendium of Jewish law. Written in mishnaic Hebrew, it is a codification of the entire Torah, Prophets, Writings, Talmud, Midrash, and Geonic literature, presented in topical order. This gigantic task, a labor of more than a decade, had never been attempted prior to Maimonides' time. Initially, Maimonides was criticized by his contemporaries for straying too far from the original talmudic approach and taking the liberty of providing his own interpretation of numerous matters. However, the *Mishneh Torah* was rapidly recognized for its profound depth and breadth and widely distributed throughout the Jewish world. Completed in 1190, by the thirteenth century the *Mishneh Torah* had been translated into Latin and other languages. It has been described as "the epitome of Judaism in all its varied aspects" and "one of the most readily understood books in all Jewish literature."[73]

Within the *Mishneh Torah*, writings on eschatology and the afterlife are minimal. However, in the first volume of the *Mishneh Torah*, in a section entitled *Hilkhot Teshuvah* ("Laws of Repentance") are two brief chapters that specifically address the topic of *Olam Ha-Ba*. In terms of content, most of what appears here is essentially a reiteration of what was explicated in *Perek Helek*.

The following passages best convey the essence of Maimonides' teachings.

Olam Ha-Ba *Is an Immortal, Spiritual Realm*

> The ultimate and perfect reward, the final bliss which will suffer neither interruption not diminution is the life in the World to Come.[74]

> The good reserved for the righteous is life in the World to Come—a life which is immortal, a good without evil.[75]

Olam Ha-Ba *Is the Realm of the Disembodied Soul*

> In the World to Come, there is nothing corporeal, and no material substance; there are only souls of the righteous without bodies.[76]

Olam Ha-Ba *Is Reserved for the Righteous, not the Wicked*

> The reward of the righteous is that they will attain bliss and abide in
> this state of happiness [of *Olam Ha-Ba*]; the punishment of the wicked
> is that they will not attain this life but will be cut off and die [*karet*].[77]

> The severest retribution beyond which punishment can no fur-
> ther go, is that the soul shall be cut off and not attain the life here-
> after.[78]

Merit of Olam Ha-Ba *Is Based on One's Deeds and Knowledge*

> The Holy One, blessed is He, gave us this Law—a tree of life. Who-
> ever fulfills what is written therein and knows it with a complete and
> correct knowledge will attain thereby life in the World to Come. Ac-
> cording to the greatness of his deeds and abundance of his knowl-
> edge will be the measure in which he will attain that life.[79]

> If you have served God with joy, and observed His way, He will
> bestow upon you blessings and . . . [you will] thus attain life hereafter,
> and then it will be well with you in the world which is entirely blissful
> and you will enjoy length of days in an existence which is everlasting.[80]

Olam Ha-Ba *Is Beyond Human Comprehension*

> As to the blissful state of the soul in the World to Come, there is no
> way on earth in which we can comprehend or know it. For in this
> earthly existence we only have knowledge of physical pleasure. . . .
> But the bliss of the life hereafter is exceedingly great, and can only
> metaphorically be compared with earthly enjoyments. In reality, how-
> ever, there is no comparison between the bliss of the soul in the life
> hereafter and the gratification afforded to the body on earth by food
> and drink. That spiritual bliss is unsearchable and beyond compare.[81]

As we see in the above passages, Maimonides' understanding of
Olam Ha-Ba is expressed in philosophical and ethical terms. For
Maimonides, *Olam Ha-Ba* is a realm of the disembodied immortal soul,
beyond ordinary human comprehension. Only the righteous, by virtue
of the acquisition of knowledge, merit the bliss of *Olam Ha-Ba*. Overall,
Maimonides language is abstract, concerned more with the experience
of philosophical contemplation than with mythic details of the afterlife
journey of the soul.

Maimonides' "Treatise on Resurrection"

An interesting and heated controversy in the Judeo-Arabic world motivated Maimonides to write the "Treatise on Resurrection" in 1191. Two years earlier, he had received a letter from Yemen indicating that many of his coreligionists were denying belief in physical resurrection, claiming that biblical and rabbinic statements on the resurrection were intended as allegorical. In support of their heretical view, they had cited specific passages from Maimonides' writings. Maimonides' claim that *Olam Ha-Ba* was a disembodied spiritual world—evidenced in both the *Commentary on the Mishnah* and *Mishneh Torah*—left open the possibility of interpreting that he did not believe in the physical resurrection of the dead. The author of the letter requested clarification from Maimonides.

Maimonides responded with a brief statement reiterating the centrality of belief in the physical resurrection of the dead. He had hoped that this reply would suffice, but such was not the case. Two years later, Samuel ben Ali, head of the Baghdad Academy, authored an essay condemning Maimonides' eschatological views.[82] Rapidly, a wide-reaching controversy on the resurrection emerged within various Judeo-Arabic communities. The main point of contention centered on Maimonides' view that in the World to Come there would be no physical bodies. Thus, some asked, how would it be possible for reward and punishment to take place without physical bodies?[83]

Maimonides felt it necessary to respond to the challenges against his earlier writings on *Olam Ha-Ba*. Although he had previously affirmed a belief in the resurrection, he had not elaborated his views on the subject. Thus, in the "Treatise on Resurrection" he addressed the question at length, providing a more detailed explanation of this central rabbinic doctrine.

The entire "Treatise on Resurrection" is presented as a polemical response to Maimonides' critics—"to those ignorant people [who] understand exactly the opposite of the words which the writer sought to explain."[84]

Recapitulating the content of *Perek Helek* and *Hilkhot Teshuvah*, he reminds his readers that he had previously asserted that "the resurrection of the dead is a cornerstone of the Torah and that there is no portion [in the World to Come] for him that denies that it is part of the Torah of Moses, our Teacher."[85] To accuse him of denying that the soul will eventually return to the body, as Rabbi Samuel ben Ali had done, is both erroneous and false. Maimonides shows the fallacies in the argument of his most vocal critic, then goes on to categorically stipulate:

> And I say that the resurrection of the dead which is widely known and accepted among our people . . . and which is often cited in prayers and in legends and in supplications composed by the prophets and the greatest of our sages, and which are found throughout the Talmud and homiletical commentaries on Scripture, means that the soul will return to its body after separation. This is a premise about which there is no disagreement among the nation and this [matter] requires no interpretation. It is not permissible for any religious Jew to support a man who believes the opposite.[86]

Maimonides also offers his reasons for not having provided a more explicit discussion of resurrection in earlier writings. Since immortality of the soul is a natural phenomenon, he explains, it can be understood by intellectual or philosophical deduction.[87] But resurrection, on the other hand, is a miracle of divine intervention: "It is a matter outside the laws of nature and one cannot prove it in a speculative manner. . . . What, therefore, could we say further about it and why [should we discuss it] at length?"[88] Resurrection does not require an established proof; like belief in miracles, it must be accepted as a doctrine of faith.

Thus, Maimonides asserts:

> Verily, we vehemently deny and we cleanse ourselves before Almighty God of the [accusation attributed to us that we espouse the] treatise that the soul will never return to the body and that it is impossible for that to occur. For such a denial [in the resurrection of the dead] leads to the denial of all miracles [chronicled in the Bible] and the denial of miracles is equivalent to denying the existence of God and abandonment of our faith. For we do consider the resurrection of the dead to be a cardinal principle of the Torah.[89]

In writing "Treatise on Resurrection," Maimonides took the opportunity to clarify another central question in Jewish eschatology, that is, the relationship between the resurrection, the Days of the Messiah, and the World to Come. On this issue he diverged from the prevailing view, "which held that the resurrection of the dead and the world to come are a single continuum of spiritual existence."[90]

According to Maimonides, first there will be a physical resurrection. Souls will reenter their former bodies and individuals will function normally in the physical world and live a long life, "like the long life which will exist during the days of the Messiah."[91] However, this would still be a temporary existence. Eventually, the resurrected dead will once again return to the dust. Then, only the immortal soul will continue to exist. This will be the *Olam Ha-Ba*—a spiritualized state of existence in which "souls without bodies will exist like angels."[92]

With this attempted clarification from Maimonides, we begin to see contradictions inherent in his own philosophy. The way he speaks of *Olam Ha-Ba* here, it does not appear to be a realm of existence following physical death. Rather, in "Treatise on Resurrection" *Olam Ha-Ba* seems to be a state of spiritual immortality that transpires only at the end-of-days, after the time of physical resurrection. Thus, there appears to be a discrepancy between Maimonides' conception of *Olam Ha-Ba* as a spiritualized, postmortem realm and his doctrinal affirmation of belief in the resurrection of the dead.[93]

What we encounter here, once again, is the repeated confusion between collective and individual notions of eschatology characteristic of rabbinic thought. As we have seen, this confusion is inherent in rabbinic tradition, and as a result, it seems Maimonides did not perceive the need to elucidate any distinction between teachings on the postmortem fate of the individual and teachings on collective redemption. That wasn't his problem; in writing "Treatise on Resurrection" Maimonides' sole purpose was to defend himself against accusations that he did not affirm the rabbinic belief in physical resurrection. With that task accomplished, Maimonides had achieved his goal.

Maimonides—Individual or Collective Eschatology?

As a philosopher, Maimonides successfully bridged the scholastic philosophy of his era with traditional Jewish eschatology. In utilizing the conceptual framework of medieval philosophy, Maimonides does not attempt to provide any clear description of what occurs to the individual immediately after death. A close reading of the three Maimonidean texts reveals the perennial confusion of rabbinic Judaism between the notions of the World to Come at the end-of-days and that which transpires following the demise of the physical body. From the first two texts surveyed here, it appears that the spiritual immortality of the World to Come may be interpreted as being that of a postmortem realm; but according to the "Treatise on Resurrection," it becomes clear that Maimonides is referring to the World to Come subsequent to the resurrection. Thus, while Maimonides affirms the existence of an immortal soul, he says little about its fate from the time of bodily death until the resurrection.

It is also clear from Maimonides' writings that he does not postulate the existence of a postmortem intermediate realm in which the soul goes through various stages of purification.[94] As a dualist, he presents only two options: the cutting off of the soul for the wicked and a divine immortal World to Come for the righteous.

In elevating Jewish afterlife teachings to philosophical abstraction, the Rambam has not made it any easier to comprehend the specifics of the individual's postmortem fate. As noted earlier in Chapter 2, if anything, Maimonides' philosophy has made Jewish afterlife teachings too lofty to be understood by those unschooled in philosophical thought. Maimonides' belief that the spiritual life of the World to Come is beyond human comprehension has persisted within Judaism to this day. It may well be because of Maimonides' rationalistic philosophy that modern Judaism has found it difficult to understand the phenomenological content of the life-after-death experience.

THE AFTERLIFE PHILOSOPHY OF GERSONIDES

Introduction—The Life and Work of Gersonides

Levi ben Gershom (1288–1344), known as Gersonides among the Christians and Ralbag (acronym for Rabbi Levi ben Gershom) among the Jews, was another important and prolific medieval Jewish philosopher.

Born in Bagnols-sur-Cèze, in Provence, an autonomous country in what is now southern France, Gersonides was a versatile medieval scholar who made significant contributions to almost every branch of medieval knowledge. A master of both secular and Jewish learning, Levi ben Gershom authored treatises on mathematics, medicine, astronomy, philosophy, and metaphysics, as well as on biblical exegesis, liturgy, and Jewish law.[95]

Although there is a dearth of biographical information about Gersonides' life, intellectually, he certainly left his mark. In the centuries subsequent to his death, there is not a Jewish philosopher or theologian who does not make reference to Gersonides, whether directly or indirectly, whether agreeing or disagreeing with him.[96] Even to this day, the Ralbag's biblical commentaries are included in published editions of the Hebrew Bible, and his major philosophical treatise, which addresses the question of immortality of the soul, *Milhamot Ha-Shem*, or "The Wars of the Lord," is studied as part of the corpus of medieval Jewish philosophy.

Gersonides' fame, however, extended beyond the Jewish world. His philosophical and scientific writings, known to popes and other leading Christian clerics, were translated into Latin, and he was renowned as an astronomer and an inventor of an instrument used to measure the movement of heavenly bodies.[97] As a tribute to his contribution to astronomy, the "Rabbi Levi" crater on the moon was posthumously named in his honor.[98]

Gersonides spent his entire life in Provence and unlike Saadia Gaon, Maimonides, and ibn Ezra, did not travel to other regions of the Jewish world. With regard to his occupation, there has been conjecture that he was a physician. However, while he did have a theoretical understanding of medical issues and wrote on the topic, it is not certain that he actually worked as a physician. More likely, Gersonides' main source of financial support was money-lending, an activity that had become quite widespread among Jews in the medieval world. The likelihood is that Gersonides was independently wealthy, and as such was able to finance his lifelong involvement in scholarship.[99]

During the Middle Ages, with the demise of Babylonian Jewry and the progressive decline of Spanish Jewish culture, Provence became an increasingly important center of Jewish life. From the middle of the twelfth century many well-educated Spanish Jews resettled in Provence, bringing with them the intellectual currents of the Spanish Judeo-Arabic cultural synthesis. Spawned even further by a favorable relationship between the papacy and the Jews of Provence, Hebrew literacy and Jewish philosophy flourished there. By the fourteenth century, Provence had become one of the most intellectually vibrant and culturally creative centers of Western Europe, and Provencal Jewry emerged as the most philosophically sophisticated community in the Jewish world.[100]

Thus, the Provence of Levi ben Gershom was a worldly cultural environment, in which Jewish scholars were well versed in biblical and talmudic traditions and steeped in the emerging medieval studies of philosophy, mathematics, and astronomy. All this had a profound effect upon Gersonides and guided the direction of his philosophical scholarship.

The dominant philosophical influences on Gersonides were Moses Maimonides; the Arabic philosopher, Averroes, whose philosophical writings had been translated into Hebrew; and Aristotle, whose ideas Gersonides encountered indirectly through his study of Maimonides. Like other medieval philosophers, Gersonides dedicated himself to explaining Torah in light of rationalistic philosophy. Convinced of the paramount superiority of rationalism, Gersonides believed that reason was not in any way incompatible with a true understanding of Torah.[101] In instances when reason and rationalism seemed to conflict with the dictates of Torah and Jewish dogma, it was necessary to recognize that logical inference and deduction were limited and could not grasp the nature of direct revelation.[102] Although essentially a philosophical Aristotelian, Gersonides always maintained the primacy of Torah and revelation, and as he contends in his introduction to *The Wars of the Lord*:

> since there are here many profound problems [of philosophical inquiry], whose solutions are extremely difficult to achieve, it is fitting that the Torah guide us in the attainment of their true solutions.[103]

Immortality of the Soul in *Milhamot Ha-Shem*

Gersonides' central teachings on the afterlife are found in his major philosophical work, *The Wars of the Lord*, or *Milhamot Ha-Shem*, written over the course of two decades and completed in 1329. In this treatise Gersonides discusses theological and philosophical issues in a scholastic style, presenting extensive documentation on all previous views of a particular topic and finally delineating his own.[104] Described as "the most precise, thorough and consistent of all pro-Aristotelian works in rabbinic philosophical theology,"[105] this treatise is divided into six separate books that address the following topics: immortality of the soul; dreams, divination, and prophecy; divine knowledge; Divine Providence; cosmology; and the creation of the universe.[106]

In examining the issue of the immortality of the soul, the first question Gersonides asks is whether the soul is immortal, whether it has been created or if any aspect of it is preexistent.[107] This is the central question of the philosophers, and in *Wars* Gersonides spells out his answer.

Gersonides presupposes that the human being is comprised of both a material, or human, intellect and an acquired, or agent, intellect. The material intellect comes into existence with each unique individual person. It has a capacity for learning and acquiring knowledge, which it does during the course of a lifetime, gradually and cumulatively. The human intellect is a biopsychological predisposition within the human being "to receive sensory information and to transform them with the aid of the Agent Intellect into logical concepts."[108]

While the human intellect dies with the demise of the physical body, the agent intellect is immortal. The knowledge acquired through the vehicle of the human intellect survives as part of the agent intellect and is immortal. The Agent Intellect contains the knowledge accrued during one's life time, and after death, survives. Thus, for Gersonides, "human immortality consists of intellectual attainment."[109] As Feldman writes:

> Man is immortal in so far as he attains the intellectual perfection that is open to him. This means that man becomes immortal only if and to the extent that he acquires knowledge of what he can in principle know, e.g., mathematics and the natural sciences. This knowledge survives his bodily death and constitutes his immortality.[110]

After bodily death, all the knowledge one has accumulated during life is apprehended simultaneously and perpetually. Just as during life a person experiences pleasure from the act of intellectual contemplation, even more so, after death one is able to fully experience this intellectual enjoyment, without any interfering emotional or sensory distractions. This, according to Gersonides, is what is meant by the pleasure of the World to Come as described by the sages.[111] But, once the person has died, the knowledge of the immortal agent intellect cannot be increased, since one no longer has the faculties or organs—the senses, the imagination, and memory—for the attainment of additional knowledge.[112] Thus, the intellectual enjoyment a person experiences after death is but a reflection of that which he or she has accrued during his or her lifetime.

Here we see how the medieval philosophers transformed the nature of rabbinic afterlife theology. For the Rabbis, the doctrine of immortality was unequivocally associated with the notion of reward and punishment, and one's experience in *Olam Ha-Ba* would be a reflection of one's ethical action in the world. However, for Gersonides, like Maimonides, the postmortem existence was understood as a product of the pursuit of intellectual knowledge. One is immortal to the extent that one attains intellectual perfection while alive. This, above all, is Gersonides' main teaching on the afterlife.

THE AFTERLIFE PHILOSOPHY OF NAHMANIDES

Introduction—The Life and Work of Nahmanides

Moses ben Nahman (1194–1270), known as Nahmanides or the Ramban (acronym for Rabbi Moses ben Nahman), was another medieval philosopher who made an important contribution to Judaism's conception of the afterlife.[113] Born in Gerona, Spain, Nahmanides, like his older contemporary, Maimonides, was one of the great creative minds of his generation. A man of many talents, he was renowned as a rabbi, philosopher, artist, talmudist, biblical commentator, and physician. Although he earned his livelihood as a physician, he was active throughout his lifetime as a spiritual leader of the Spanish-Jewish community. During the height of the anti-Maimonidean controversy, the Ramban successfully mediated between the opposing factions. And in the Jewish-Christian public theological debates of the mid-thirteenth century, Nahmanides was called upon to represent his community.

Toward the end of his days, in the wake of increasing anti-Jewish persecutions, Nahmanides was forced into exile by the Catholic Church. The final three years of his life were spent in Palestine, where he had emigrated in 1267. There, the aging Nahmanides was involved in building new Jewish communities and in the founding of a number of synagogues. He also found the time to write his famous *Commentary on the Torah*, an exegetical-homiletic text that is respected and studied to this day.

Nahmanides was educated in Kabbalah, and his writings reflect a philosophical mysticism that contrasts with the scholastic philosophy of Saadia, Maimonides, and Gersonides. Although not an Aristotelian scholastic philosopher, Nahmanides was certainly well versed in medieval Jewish philosophy and in many of his writings responded directly to Maimonides' views. It might be said that while Maimonides represents the voice of logic and reason in Jewish tradition, Nahmanides represents the side of feeling and emotion.[114]

The influence of kabbalistic mysticism on Nahmanides is apparent in his major work, *Torat Ha-Adam* ("The Law of Man"). This lengthy text combines both legalistic and philosophical styles of writing. The bulk of the book deals with laws and customs pertaining to illness, visiting the sick, deathbed confessions, burial, and mourning.[115] The final chapter of the text, entitled *Shaar Ha-Gemul* ("The Gate of Reward"), is the best portrayal of Nahmanides' teachings on the afterlife. There, he diverges from Maimonides on a number of topics as he discusses traditional eschatological themes such as divine judgment, Gan Eden, the World to Come, and the afterlife fate of the soul.

Nahmanides on Divine Judgment

Nahmanides begins *Shaar Ha-Gemul* addressing the topic of divine retribution and the issue of God's judgment for the righteous and the wicked. Offering his own explication of traditional rabbinic notions, he enters into a discussion of the three different judgments that individuals must undergo: on the New Year, at the time of death, and in the World to Come.

According to Nahmanides, at the time of the New Year each individual is judged by a Divine Tribunal, and his or her fate for the coming twelve months is determined. The purpose of this judgment, however, is not to appropriate the individual's destiny in the hereafter; it is a worldly judgment. According to Nahmanides: "Man is judged on the New Year [regarding] matters pertaining only to this world; [the judgment] determines whether he is worthy of life and peace or death and pains."[116]

A second judgment takes place when the individual dies. At this time, the individual's deeds are fully evaluated and due recompense is allocated. There is yet a third judgment that will take place at an unspecified future time when, after reunion of body and soul through physical resurrection, the World to Come will be inaugurated.[117]

Interestingly enough, unlike many other rabbinic and medieval writers, Nahmanides is not only concerned with the notion of a final, collective judgment at the end-of-days. What is refreshingly unique about the Ramban is that he is specifically concerned with the postmortem divine judgment of the individual and develops his philosophy along these lines.

According to Nahmanides, the deceased individual will not have to wait for judgment until the time of collective redemption. Immediately after death, an individual is judged and assigned a portion in the hereafter, according to merit:

Each and every person . . . is subject to judgment at the time of his death, and his fate is decided in accordance with one of . . . three essential groups: the thoroughly righteous are immediately inscribed and sealed and enter into Gan Eden . . . ; the thoroughly wicked are immediately sealed and enter Gehenna and are punished there; the intermediates cry out [in prayer] to be removed therefrom to a place of tranquillity. . . .[118]

For those sentenced to Gehenna, punishment is allocated only in proportion to one's transgression. Hence, the thoroughly wicked must remain "for all generations."[119] But the intermediates are sentenced for only twelve months; then they are released into the hands of Dumah, the guardian angel of the dead.[120] However, since God's judgment is just and equitable, why should all sinners be punished for twelve months? Are there not "among the sinners themselves . . . those whose punishment should be greater than that of their fellows?"[121] According to Nahmanides' explanation,

in Gehenna, there can be more pain and suffering for one sinner than there is for another. Thus, as far as punishment and reward are concerned, there is a distinction between the Gehenna [for one individual] and the Gehenna [for another].[122]

Here, God's judgment of the wicked in Gehenna is not seen as a uniform condemnation for all. Instead, Nahmanides postulates that the suffering of Gehenna varies from person to person, based on one's deeds. This point of view is parallel to the notion that first emerged in apocryphal literature of different realms of Gehenna specifically for various categories of sinners. In Nahmanides this idea is developed even more explicitly, and we see here the formulation of what be regarded as a psychological understanding of the afterlife. The afflictive character of Gehenna is a direct result of the individual's psychological state, at the time of death.

The Fate of the Soul in Gehenna

Nahmanides continues to articulate his understanding of Gehenna, reiterating various talmudic and midrashic descriptions of Gehenna—its characteristics, dimensions, and population of mythological beings.

In fact, as he discusses Gehenna, Nahmanides cites many of the exact same *midrashim* presented in the portrayal of rabbinic views of the afterlife (see Chapter 5). But, as we have begun to see, he brings to traditional Jewish eschatology a somewhat changed perspective. Reading the historical layers of Jewish afterlife philosophy, it so apparent that at every juncture, the themes and motifs of the afterlife build on each other, and what has come before stands as building blocks for the new and the innovative.

For Nahmanides, like the Rabbis, Gehenna "is a place of execution of judgment."[123] One enters that realm immediately after death,[124] and there, it is the soul and not the body that is subjected to punitive afflictions. Consonant with rabbinic tradition, Nahmanides maintains that in Gehenna "the souls of the sinners are punished with suffering and pain which have no parallel in this world."[125] While this is not in itself anything new in Jewish postmortem thought, the way in which he explains the differences between the suffering of soul and the body suggests, once again, how a psychological understanding of the afterlife is superseding a moralistic, ethical one:

> [S]uffering in this world affects the lowly body, which is bulky in [its state of] creation and slow in sensitivity, while the grave punishment and the pain [of Gehenna] affect the soul, which is pure and refined in [its state of] creation. . . . The feeling of the soul in its suffering is . . . very much greater than the suffering of the body because of the soul's greater sensitivity and clearness of its creation. There is no comparison or likeness whatsoever between the extremely great suffering of the soul and the bodily pain of the living creatures.[126]

Once in Gehenna, the judgment of the soul is carried by fire—"the River of Fire which comes forth from beneath the Throne of Glory."[127] And this "refined intangible fire,"[128] unlike the fire of this world, actually has the ability to consume the soul. In fact, this River of Fire was created by God specifically for this purpose:

> He Who placed the soul in this matter [i.e., the body] and joined it to the body can confine it to that place [the Gehenna] and can attach it to the ethereal fire, which is there from a higher source and which was created for the purpose of consuming the soul and changing it in that crucible or completely destroying it.[129]

Continuing his discussion of Gehenna, Nahmanides attempts to clarify the meaning of the term *karet*, excision or "destruction of the soul." "Destruction," he explains, "is only a form of afflictive punishment; it is not that the wicked man dies and his soul is destroyed and becomes like the eradicable soul of an animal."[130] An animal soul can be decomposed into its constituent natural elements. But the human soul originates from a source beyond physical matter. Therefore, it can neither be destroyed nor reverted to an animal soul. According to Nahmanides, "such [destruction of the human soul] is untrue by tradition and is also very remote from [the truth of] this subject."[131]

Yet rabbinic tradition does speak about how after twelve months the souls of the wicked in Gehenna are burned and their ashes are spread "under the soles of the feet of the righteous" (*Rosh Ha-Shanah* 17a).[132] What does this mean, asks Nahmanides, demonstrating his medieval philosophical mind-set. If souls are of an essential, nonphysical nature, how can they be destroyed? Nahmanides attempts to explain this idea of ashes spread "under the soles of the feet of the righteous" in a metaphoric sense. For him, there is a clear postmortem hierarchy. Those subjected to Gehenna for twelve months do afterward ascend, but their subsequent afterlife experience is not in any way as supernal and blissful as that of the righteous. Such sinners, even after they exit from Gehenna, are granted a postmortem repose or a lesser grade—that is, below that of the righteous—hence the phrase "at the feet of the righteous."

Thus, we see within Nahmanides an emerging psychological vantage point in his conceptions of the afterlife. For him, the rabbinic view that "the souls of the wicked are punished in Gehenna immediately after their death according to what they deserve"[133] is understood to mean that each soul experiences the state of consciousness it has evolved during the physical plane life.

Distinction between Gan Eden and the World to Come

Nahmanides continues his philosophical exposition on the afterlife with a discussion of "the concept of reward which the Master of recompense will bestow on us."[134] For the Rabbis, he notes, this reward is designated as either Gan Eden or the World to Come; as well, the talmudic sages speak of the messianic era and the resurrection of the dead. Acclaiming his loyalty to rabbinic doctrine, he asserts:

At the outset, we declare that the reward for [the observance of] all
the commandments and their good recompense are a clear matter
based on the words of our Rabbis that the great principle [of reward]
is life in the World to Come.[135]

However, he then adds a point of clarification. The reward for the
righteous that precedes the future World to Come is a life in Gan Eden;
it is the reward the individual experiences immediately after death.[136]
Now this is important. Here, for Nahmanides, a definite distinction is
made between *Olam Ha-Ba* and Gan Eden. The former is the divine recompense at the end-of-days; the latter, the postmortem reward. With this
clarification a very explicit notion of reward immediately after death of
the body is affirmed, and this is a pivotal point in the development of
Jewish notions of the afterlife.

Elaborating on his understanding of the nature of Gan Eden,
Nahmanides cites numerous talmudic and midrashic references. Like the
Rabbis, he maintains that "Gan Eden is the opposite of Gehenna"[137] and
that it has a physical existence, "an actual garden on the earth."[138] As
for the quality of life in Gan Eden, Nahmanides describes it as follows:

Thus in Gan Eden, which is the chosen place for understanding all
the higher secrets through the imagery of things, the souls of the
dwellers [therein] become elevated by . . . study and they perceive
visions of God in the company of the higher beings of that place. They
attain whatever [degree of] knowledge and understanding created
being can achieve.[139]

Then, in a passage that is somewhat obscure, he suggests that there
are actually two Gan Edens, a lower and a higher one. This is an idea
that is developed further in kabbalistic writings, which we will investigate more fully in the next chapter. In the words of Nahmanides:

You may ask: "Since the subject is mentioned and Gan Eden is on
this lower world, what kind of reward could the souls have there when
they derive no advantage from anything material or from any place
on earth and the world of the lower creatures?" [In reply] we have
. . . explained that the subject is twofold in meaning. This Gan and
Eden of the lower world are [metaphorically speaking] illustrations
of higher secrets, and these higher matters to which they [the lower

Gan and Eden] allude are also termed Gan and Eden, from which
the lower ones derive their names. How is this so? In the higher
[spheres], there is a concept allusively designated Gan in the words
of our Rabbis, and [there is] an even higher concept than that which
is designated Eden. This is termed the bundle of life [*tzror ha-
hayyim*].[140]

In this quote by Nahmanides we see remnants of the ancient rabbinic idea of multiple layers of heaven, or Gan Eden. At the same time,
in speaking of *tzror ha-hayyim*—"the bundle of life"—as a higher supernal realm than even Gan or Eden, Nahmanides is bringing in the Greek-
influenced idea of a storehouse of preexistent souls and the correlate notion of a realm unto which all souls eventually return. Later kabbalists
build on this idea of *tzror ha-hayyim* even further. But with Nahmanides,
once again, we see how various ideas about the afterlife frequently merge
and commingle.

The World to Come and the World of Souls

Recognizing some of the nebulous aspects of traditional rabbinic
eschatology, Nahmanides—probably more than anyone else in the medieval period—does his part to eliminate long-standing conceptual con-
fusions. In the final chapters of *Shaar Ha-Gemul* he takes up the topic of
the World to Come and right at the outset acknowledges the ambiguity
in such rabbinic statements as: "The thoroughly righteous are inscribed
and immediately sealed for life in the World to Come" (*Rosh Ha-Shanah*
16b).[141] But exactly when the World to Come will begin is not specified,
notes Nahmanides, discovering exactly what we did in our earlier journey though rabbinic texts on *Olam Ha-Ba*:

> It is not clearly explained if it means . . . the reward which reaches
> each soul immediately after the [individual's] death . . . or if it is
> another world which will be created and the reward will be experi-
> enced in that newly created era.[142]

So, what does Nahmanides do? To clarify this issue, once and for
all, he introduces a totally new eschatological term—*olam ha-neshamot*,
or "the World of Souls"—in contradistinction to the World to Come,
Olam Ha-Ba. The World of Souls is the realm one enters immediately

on death (what Nahmanides had previously spoken of as Gan Eden). Whereas *Olam Ha-Ba*, the World to Come, will manifest following the resurrection, *olam ha-neshamot*, the World of Souls, exists concurrently with the present one. Further, according to Nahmanides all the statements of the Rabbis

> clearly indicate that the World to Come . . . is not [synonymous with] the World of Souls and the reward which reaches the deceased immediately after death. Rather, it is the world which the Holy One, blessed be He, will create after the era of the Messiah and the resurrection of the dead.[143]

This is very clear. It is a point that Nahmanides enunciates repeatedly:

> In any case, concerning the meaning of the World to Come, we have learned that is a world in which the body, the Sanctuary, and its vessels will be present; it is not the World of Souls in which every man receives his due immediately after death.[144]

With Nahmanides, there is an unequivocal differentiation between the individual's afterlife existence and the time of collective redemption which will inaugurate the World to Come. In a historical perspective, Nahmanides' term *olam ha-neshamot*, the World of Souls, is an important breakthrough in the evolution of Jewish notions of the afterlife.

Having defined the World of Souls as an afterlife realm of disembodied spirits, Nahmanides goes on to discuss the World to Come. As he understands it, it is "an enduring world created for people [to be] resurrected in body and soul."[145] For Nahmanides, the physical body will exist in the World to Come, but in a totally transformed, spiritualized state—"the existence of the body will [then] be like that of the soul."[146] Referring to biblical tradition, he explains: Moses atop Mount Sinai was sustained for forty days because of the "ascendancy of the soul over the body."[147] And both Elijah (2 Kings 2:11) and Enoch (Genesis 5:24) ascended to heaven with body and soul intact. Similarly, in the World to Come the body will exist along with the soul, which "will be cleaving to 'the knowledge of the Most High'" (Numbers 24:6).[148] And at this time, the soul "will be elevated to an even greater [degree of] perception than heretofore, and the existence of all will be forever and ever."[149]

On this point Nahmanides diverges decisively with the Maimonidean view of *Olam Ha-Ba* as an immortal, incorporeal spiritual realm. It is one of the more important and obvious differences between these two medieval philosophers.

Nahmanides' Role in the Evolution of Jewish Afterlife Teachings

Nahmanides' *Torat Ha-Adam* stands out as an important text in the historical development of Jewish teachings on life after death. Prior to Nahmanides, there had always existed within Judaism a tendency to confuse and transpose conceptions of the end-of-days with those pertaining to the postmortem fate of the individual. But in *Torat Ha-Adam* Nahmanides makes a very clear distinction between these two facets of Jewish afterlife eschatology. More than any of his predecessors, Nahmanides differentiates between divine judgment prior to the resurrection and the judgment of the soul immediately after death. Upon death each individual is subjected to reward or punishment; the purgative punishment of Gehenna is meted out in direct proportion to the quality of the life lived. It is not, however, a uniform punishment for all sinners. Rather, it is determined, so to speak, by one's postmortem psychological state.

Torat Ha-Adam serves as an important bridge point in the historical evolution of Jewish afterlife teachings. Certainly among the philosophy of the medieval era it is the clearest Jewish eschatological statement on the fate of the soul immediately following death. In terms of the evolution of Jewish thought, Nahmanides' afterlife philosophy, which has undertones of a psychological orientation, serves as a transitional bridge between the postmortem thinking of the Rabbis and Maimonides and the subsequent generations of kabbalists and *hasidim*.

SUMMARY

In this chapter we have explored the afterlife teachings found within the writings of the medieval philosophers. From the foregoing, we can make the following observations about Jewish afterlife teachings in medieval philosophy:

1. In the writings of the medieval philosophers, an attempt is made to integrate rabbinic teachings on *Olam Ha-Ba* with philosophi-

cal ideas about the essence and substantiality of the soul. That being the case, we find in this body of literature a rationalistic concern with the metaphysics of the immortal soul and little interest in mythic depictions of the postmortem realm.

2. In the substantive philosophical thinking of Saadia Gaon, ethical, moral actions polish the soul, leaving it luminescent and bright; immoral, wicked actions tarnish the soul, leaving it dull. Building on this, for Saadia, Gan Eden is the accumulated luminescence of a righteous soul and Gehenna is the accumulated, purging fire of a wicked, tarnished soul.

3. Saadia reaffirms traditional rabbinic ideas of resurrection but rejects mystical notions about reincarnation and transmigration of souls.

4. For Maimonides, *Olam Ha-Ba* is an immortal spiritual world, a disembodied state of existence bestowed on those souls who have acquired knowledge of the divine.

5. Maimonides replicates the traditional rabbinic confusion of collective and individual eschatology. A close reading of Maimonides suggests that, for him, the immortal, disembodied world of *Olam Ha-Ba* comes into manifestation subsequent to the time of collective redemption. There are contradictions in various Maimonidean writings, and it is not clear that he adds much to the general knowledge of the state of the individual soul immediately after death.

6. For Gersonides, immortality is the result of one's intellectual attainment while alive; once dead, the soul, or rather, in Gersonides' terms, the immortal Agent Intellect, does not continue to grow and evolve, but rather enjoys what was accrued in the way of knowledge during life.

7. Nahmanides, more than the other medieval philosophers, focuses specifically on the fate of the soul after death and introduces an entirely new eschatological term—*olam ha-neshamot*, or the World of Souls. This is a postmortem realm completely different from the *Olam Ha-Ba* at the end-of-days.

8. Influenced by kabbalistic philosophy, Nahmanides' writings reflect an emerging psychological orientation with regard to the afterlife. Increasingly, the experience of life after death comes to be seen as a state of consciousness reflecting the quality of consciousness one has developed during life.

Chapter 8

The Afterlife Journey of the Soul in Kabbalah

THE HISTORICAL CONTEXT

Our historical voyage now takes us into the academies of Jewish mysticism of thirteenth- to fifteenth-century Spain and sixteenth-century Palestine. In this chapter we will explore the texts of kabbalistic Judaism, in particular, the *Zohar*, a mystical commentary on the Torah. Our intention is to investigate some of Judaism's most sophisticated teachings on the afterlife, and in so doing, map out a variegated collection of wisdom on the nature of the soul, its judgment at the time of death, and its postmortem destiny. Even though we now encounter another completely distinct genre of Jewish religious writings, historically, we remain in the medieval period, predominantly in the late Middle Ages.

Something quite curious occurred in the twelfth and thirteenth centuries of Jewish history. At about the same time that the great Jewish rationalist Moses Maimonides was authoring his now-famous *Guide to the Perplexed*, Jewish mystical scholars were composing esoteric treatises with mythological, symbolic depictions of the nature of Godhead quite unlike anything found in medieval philosophy. In similar historical and cultural circumstances, two contrasting religious phenomena—Jewish rationalist philosophy and kabbalistic Jewish mysticism—emerged on the scene, so to speak, in approximately the same era.

While today the word *mysticism* itself holds an aura of both fascina-
tion and revulsion for many, this was not always so. During the Middle
Ages there were times when mystical teachings were normative among
Jews, and on the surface, anyway, there was not much difference between
Jewish "mysticism" and rabbinic tradition. Many of the most famous
Rabbis of the medieval times were both rationalists and mystical kabbalists,
and many ideas and practices of the mystics of Spain and Palestine were
infused into the routines of Jewish life. For example, in his time Rabbi
Joseph Caro, author of the *Shulhan Arukh*, was both a halakhic legalist
and leader of the mystical schools of Judaism. And the now-famous Friday-
night hymn welcoming the Sabbath Bride, *Lekhah Dodi*, was composed
in the kabbalistic community of sixteenth-century Safed but is now a standard part of the Friday-evening Kabbalat Shabbat service.

However, with the ascendance of a rationalistic materialism in the
nineteenth century, religion, in general, but mysticism, in particular, fell
into ill repute—so much so that the nineteenth-century Jewish historian Heinrich Graetz regarded kabbalistic mysticism as an inherently un-
Jewish and polytheistic reaction to rationalistic medieval philosophy. For
Graetz, Maimonides, the rationalistic philosopher, represented the
epitome of Judaism, the highest development of the spirit of Jewish monotheism; but mysticism, as he saw it, was an irrational retrogression and
an aberration.[1] For example, describing the impact of Lurianic Kabbalah
with disdain, Graetz writes: "The harm that the kabbalistic doctrines of
Luria caused is inexpressible. Judaism became surrounded with so thick
a husk of mysticism that it has not yet succeeded in entirely freeing itself, showing its true kernel."[2]

In part, because of Graetz's response to Kabbalah, Jewish mystical
teachings were not taken seriously by most Jewish scholars of the nineteenth and early twentieth centuries. Consequently, the profuse collection of afterlife teachings in Jewish mysticism became increasingly irrel-
evant to modern Jewish sensibilities.

However, in the second half of the twentieth century, Gershom
Scholem's prolific and voluminous scholarship prompted a modern rediscovery of the legacy of Jewish mysticism. In his writings, Scholem
documented the ways in which Jewish mysticism, especially after the sixteenth century, left its impact on the development of modern Jewish
history.[3] Over the course of almost sixty years of scholarly work, Scholem
demonstrated how a mystical strand had been indigenous to Judaism,
taking various unique forms over a period of two millennia.

Contemporaneous with the creation of the Talmud, there were ancient Jewish forms of cosmogonic speculation—what Scholem called Jewish Gnosticism[4]—rooted in the forms of theosophical and esoteric traditions prevalent in the Greco-Roman world.[5] Subsequently, during the Geonic period, there were major schools of Jewish mysticism that based their philosophies on mystical interpretations of the creation story (*Maaseh Bereshit*, or "The Works of Creation") and on Ezekiel's vision of the Chariot (*Maaseh Merkabah*, or "The Works of the Chariot").[6] These forms of Jewish mysticism found expression in the *hekhalot* literature, wherein are to be found detailed descriptions of divine journeys through heavenly regions.

Sometime between 1150 and 1220, the term "Kabbalah" came into use among mystically oriented Jews of Provence.[7] Broadly speaking, the term refers to a large corpus of esoteric and theosophical teachings on the nature of God, humanity, and the universe derived from all esoteric movements in Judaism beginning in the early rabbinic period. However, specifically, Kabbalah describes the form medieval Jewish mysticism assumed from the twelfth century onward.[8]

Kabbalah literally means "to receive," and it is an esoteric tradition passed on from teacher to disciple. Originally, the kabbalists were reluctant to commit to writing many of their esoteric doctrines on the soul and its fate after death. In its earliest phases, prior to the appearance of the first written texts and manuscripts, Kabbalah was essentially an oral tradition.[9] As Moshe Idel has noted:

> When we attempt to reconstruct the various concepts of the different kabbalistic schools, we must remind ourselves that these ideas were meant, from the beginning, to be limited to a small intellectual elite. The main medium of transmission of these traditions was, as the kabbalists themselves indicate time and again, oral teaching.[10]

Eventually, however, kabbalistic teachings were encoded in written form. While innumerable writings of the kabbalists were "lost in the storms of Jewish history," what has survived to this day has been a diverse assortment of texts and manuscripts, often in partial, fragmentary condition, containing ambiguous, arcane, and cryptic symbolism.[11]

Although Gershom Scholem completed a great deal of bibliographic and historical analysis of kabbalistic texts, nonetheless, a relatively small proportion of kabbalistic material has been translated into English. Undoubtedly, with the growing interest in Jewish mysticism and spirituality, important strides are being made to produce a corpus of Jewish mystical texts for an English-speaking audience. While this chapter will analyze ideas on the afterlife in Kabbalah and demonstrate the relationship of these teachings to earlier Jewish postmortem conceptions, above all, the intention here is to provide a resource compilation of kabbalistic teachings on life after death.

THE SOURCES

The central text of medieval Kabbalah is *Sefer Ha-Zohar*, or the "Book of Splendor," a mystical commentary on the Five Books of Moses. Appearing in the Jewish world in the late thirteenth century, the *Zohar* is undoubtedly the most important kabbalistic text for understanding the evolution of afterlife teachings in Judaism.

There is one tradition that claims the author of the *Zohar* was Shimon bar Yochai, a second-century Palestinian Rabbi. According to legend, during the thirteen years he spent in a cave hiding from the Romans, bar Yochai composed the homiletic verses and mystical speculations of the *Zohar*, as revealed to him by the prophet Elijah and accompanying angels. However, historical scholarship has shown that the *Zohar* is filled with concepts, language, and liturgical references that reflect the influence of the medieval Jewish world.[12] As a result, it is now generally assumed by all but the pious fundamentalists that the *Zohar* was written by a kabbalist named Moshe ben Shem Tov de Leon, sometime between 1280 and 1286 in Guadalajara, Spain, a town northeast of Madrid. Essentially, the *Zohar* is regarded as a pseudigraph penned by de Leon, and perhaps some of his kabbalistic colleagues,[13] in the name of bar Yochai, utilizing ancient forms of midrashic interpretation of Torah to communicate emerging kabbalistic doctrines.[14]

Linguistic analysis has revealed that the *Zohar* is not simply one book, but more accurately, should be regarded as a complete genre of literature in and of itself. Written in both Hebrew and Aramaic, the *Zohar* appears in printed editions in five volumes: the first three volumes are a commentary on the Torah (*Sefer ha-Zohar al Ha-Torah*); the other two are *Tikkunei Ha-Zohar* ("Emendations of the *Zohar*") and *Zohar Hadash* ("New *Zohar*"). There is also a later work, dependent upon yet separate from the *Zohar* itself, entitled *Raaya Meheimna*, or "The Faithful Shepherd," composed by an anonymous author.[15]

One of the pivotal topics addressed throughout the *Zohar* is the doctrine of the soul. Repeatedly, we find Rabbis having impassioned discussions about the origins of the soul; the process of its creation and its coming into manifestation from the supernal to the earthly realm; the garments of the soul and its relationship to the body; and the soul's capacity for transcendent awareness of the divine. This intense concern with the soul gave rise to extensive teachings on the soul's reward and punishment after death. Hardly a section of the text passes without some reference to the soul's experience of the dying process; divine judgment; the postmortem worlds of Gehenna and Gan Eden; resurrection; and the unique kabbalistic concept of reincarnation and the transmigration of souls, *gilgul*.

Along with medieval Midrash, the *Zohar* is the richest resource for understanding the Jewish philosophy of the afterlife. However, similar to rabbinic literature, the *Zohar* never systematically outlines teachings on life after death in any one place. Rather, they appear randomly throughout the text, found in the midst of homiletical interpretations of Torah, and often disguised in cryptic kabbalistic symbols. For example, in discussing the death of the patriarch Jacob, the *Zohar* lapses into an elaborate meandering on what occurs to the soul at the time of death. While very little is actually said regarding Jacob's demise, the *Zohar* presents over three pages of varied notions about the afterlife (I, 217b–222a), then moves on to address another seemingly unrelated esoteric topic. This type of patchwork literary style is characteristic of the *Zohar*, and although rich in philosophical content, makes for difficult reading and analysis.

Given that kabbalistic afterlife philosophy was never formally encoded into a credo, nor given definitive form, there was always room for a great deal of improvisation and imagination. Building on the afterlife teachings evidenced in rabbinic literature and in medieval Midrash, the *Zohar* embellishes and elucidates these teachings utilizing the framework of kabbalistic symbolism. As a result, the *Zohar* is replete with a curious synthesis of folkloristic and mystical elements.[16] For this reason, a random perusal of individual chapters or pages of the *Zohar* often reveals conflicting and contradictory ideas on the journey of the soul in the hereafter.

In what follows, our intention is to make some sense of the diverse collection of kabbalistic afterlife teachings, utilizing both primary and secondary source studies.[17]

KABBALISTIC PHILOSOPHY OF THE SOUL

A Tripartite Model of the Soul

Within the *Zohar* there is an underlying assumption that the human soul has a threefold nature; this assumption forms the framework for almost all speculation on what occurs to the individual after death. One cannot understand conceptions of immortality and life after death in the *Zohar* without an awareness of this kabbalistic doctrine of the soul.

In biblical texts we find the terms *nefesh*, *ruah*, and *neshamah* used to imply some form of "spirit" but having no standardized distinction between the varied nomenclature. In medieval philosophy, Saadia Gaon, Abraham ibn Ezra, Maimonides, and Abraham bar Hiyya, among others, envisioned the soul as being composed of three dimensions, or functions, which they labeled *nefesh*, the vegetative soul; *ruah*, the animal soul; and *neshamah*, the intellectual soul.[18] It is this model of the soul that eventually became paramount to the kabbalists.

From the mid-thirteenth century, the acronym *naran*—נר״ן—meaning *nefesh*, *ruah*, and *neshamah*, emerged as the operating term when kabbalists discussed the soul. Even prior to the *Zohar*, in the thirteenth-century kabbalistic text *Sefer Shaarei Orah*, by Rabbi Joseph Gikatilla, we find these terms and the accompanying three-tiered view of the soul.[19]

Progressively, the kabbalists transformed the medieval notion of the soul, and over the course of time it became increasing mystical in nature. What was a rational or intellectual dimension of the soul for the philosophers, became intuitive and mystical for the kabbalists, more closely aligned with the transcendent Godhead.[20] As Isaiah Tishby and Fischel Lachower note:

> we must assume that the transition from the philosophical to the mystical tripartite division of the soul took place at the end of the thirteenth century in the circle of the author of the *Zohar*, who was influenced also by the writings of the Gnostic kabbalists. What happened was that the terminology and the mystical significance of *neshamah*, *ruah*, and *nefesh*, which these kabbalists attributed to dif-

ferent grades of the soul, were combined with the philosophical view that three divisions formed one single human soul.[21]

Nefesh, which translates as "breath," is the lowest level of the soul. It is an individual vital energy that attaches itself to the physical body and serves to animate and preserve it. *Nefesh* is the first element found in an individual; it comes into being at the moment of birth, and vitalizes all psychophysical activities.

Ruah is the second level of the soul. It is awakened when an individual rises above the vitalistic nature. In the *Zohar ruah* is depicted as an intermediary power, which animates and illumines the *nefesh* utilizing the light that emanates from the *neshamah*.

Neshamah is a supernal level of the soul, awakened by attention to study of the Torah and the fulfillment of the commandments. *Neshamah* seems to be a bridge between human and divine realms, between a person and God; its development brings about a higher consciousness, and the ability to perceive the divine mysteries, the nature of the Godhead, and the unfolding of the cosmos.[22]

Thus, in the *Zohar* we find the following statement:

> There are three levels that comprise the soul, and therefore the soul has three names: *nefesh*, *ruah*, and *neshamah*. *Nefesh* . . . is the lowest of all. *Ruah* is the [power of] sustenance, which rules over the *nefesh* and is a higher level than [the *nefesh*], sustaining it throughout as is fitting. *Neshamah* is the highest [power of] sustenance, and rules over all, a holy level, exalted above all. (I, 205b)

And further:

> Rabbi Yehudah asked how many garments there are. Rabbi Eleazar said: "The authorities differ on this point, but in truth there are three. One is for clothing the spirit [*ruah*] in the terrestrial Gan Eden. A second, the most precious of all, is for investing the inner soul [*neshamah*] when among the bundle of the living in the circle of the king. The third is an outer garment which appears and disappears, and with which the vital soul [*nefesh*] is clothed." (I, 224b)

Unity of *Nefesh*, *Ruah*, and *Neshamah*

While elucidating a wide variety of teachings regarding the threefold nature of the soul, the kabbalists continually affirmed the essential unity of this soul.[23] Thus, the *Zohar* affirms without doubt that "all three [aspects of the soul] are one, forming one whole, united in a mystical bond, in which *nefesh*, *ruah*, and *neshamah* constitute together one totality" (I, 142a).

In a similar vein, in other writings of Moshe de Leon, we find the following point of view expressed:

> The mystery of the soul is that it is divided into three parts, but joined together in a single unity. Even though they appear to be separated from one another because of their separate names, they really form one mystery: *nefesh*, *ruah*, *neshamah*. . . . They are indeed a single mystery, without any division.[24]

Elsewhere in the *Zohar*, this stance is articulated as follows:

> The *nefesh* rules by night and [seeks] to gain its level; the *ruah* [rules] by days, as it is written "With my soul [*nefesh*] I desired You in the night"—this is the *nefesh* that rules by night: "and with my spirit [*ruah*] within me have I sought You early" (Isaiah 26:9)—this is the *ruah* that rules by day. Now you might say that there two levels are separated, but it is not so, for they are one level—two in a single unity. There is also a higher one, which rules over them, and it cleaves to them and they to it, and it is called *neshamah*. And all the levels [together] constitute the mystery of wisdom. (I, 83a)[25]

A Fivefold Model of the Soul

In addition to these three parts of the soul, the author of *Raaya Meheimna* speaks of two additional, transcendent dimensions of the soul: *hayyah* and *yehidah*.[26] These other aspects of the soul "were considered to represent the sublimest levels of intuitive cognition and to be within the grasp of only a few chosen individuals."[27] All five component aspects of the soul are closely intertwined and operate in relationship to one another.

Gershon Winkler, in his discussion of the anatomy of the soul, explicates this fivefold kabbalistic notion of the soul as follows: *nefesh*—appetitive awareness; *ruah*—emotional awareness; *neshamah*—intellect; *hayyah*—divine life force; *yehidah*—uniqueness.[28] Explaining the function and interaction of these five levels, he writes:

At the optimum level of *neshamah*, or pure intellect, the individual transcends emotions [*ruah*] and imagination [*nefesh*], and thereby commences the realization of the fourth level, *hayyah*, the ability to experience pleasure without the otherwise necessary faculty of the physical, for at this level his life-experience is consciously or unconsciously connected to the source of Eternal Life, God. The next plane is the optimum, *yehidah*, wherein all the soul's faculties are unified with God. Spontaneously, therefore, the five soul-levels represent successive planes of connection to, and awareness of, the ultimate force which emanates from God.[29]

While this fivefold model is not developed in classical *Zohar*, it does become increasingly important in later Kabbalah[30] and will be used as a basis for developing a contemporary model of the afterlife in Chapter 10.

The Postmortem Fate of the Soul

It is of utmost importance for our purposes to understand the ways in which the kabbalists describe the postmortem fate of these various levels of the soul.

According to teachings found throughout the *Zohar*, after death the *nefesh* remains with the body in the grave. There it undergoes judgment and suffers the punishment of *Hibbut Ha-Kever*, the pangs of the grave:

> *Nefesh* remains in the grave until the body is decomposed and turned into dust, during which time it flits about in this world, seeking to mingle with the living and to learn of their troubles; and in the hour of need it intercedes for them. . . . it wanders about the world and beholds the body which was once its home devoured by worms and suffering the judgment of the grave [*Hibbut Ha-Kever*]. (II, 141b–142a)

Subsequently, the *ruah* goes through its own phase of postmortem judgment in Gehenna, where it is punished for its sins for a period of twelve months. In the words of the *Zohar*,

> the *ruah* is purified in Gehenna, whence it goes forth roaming about the world and visiting its grave. . . . After twelve months the whole is at rest; the body reposes in the dust and the soul is clad in its luminous vestment. (I, 226a–226b)

In the next phases of the postmortem journey, the *ruah* enters a realm called the terrestrial or Lower Gan Eden, known in Hebrew as *Gan Eden Takhton*, or *Gan Eden shel Matah*:

> *Ruah* enters the earthly Garden [i.e., Lower Gan Eden] and there dons a likeness which is in the semblance of the body it tenanted in this world: that likeness being, as it were, a garment with which the spirit robes itself, so that there it may enjoy the delights of the radiant Garden. (II, 141b)

Neshamah, which by all reckoning is not liable to sin, returns to its source, in the Upper Gan Eden, referred to as *Gan Eden Elyon*, or *Gan Eden shel Malah*, where it experiences various forms of divine bliss. As the *Zohar* teaches,

> after death of the body, the *neshamah* . . . ascends at once to her place, the region from whence she emanated [Upper Gan Eden], and for her sake the light is kindled to shine above. She never again descends to earth. . . . (II, 141b)

Thus, we see that the three parts of the soul, *nefesh*, *ruah*, and *neshamah*, enter very distinct abodes or realms of experience at the time of death. This is the essential view of life after death at the core of the *Zohar*, and is summarized in Table 8-1.

The higher faculties of the soul, *hayyah* and *yehidah*, referred to earlier, remain in contact with the infinite Godhead after death. Those who have awakened these dimensions of their being are able to perceive the infinite grandeur of the divine realms, to enter the everflowing celestial stream—described by the *Zohar* as the "bundle of life," *tzror hahayyim*, where all souls are housed (II, 209a).

DIVINE JUDGMENT

Ethical Basis of Afterlife Views in the *Zohar*

The motif of divine judgment permeates all kabbalistic teachings on the afterlife. On numerous occasions before and after death, the human being is subjected to a thorough divine scrutiny. Giving consideration to both body and soul, supernal envoys such as angelic beings or

TABLE 8-1 LEVELS OF SOUL IN KABBALAH

Level of Soul	Soul Function	Postmortem Fate
Neshamah	Higher mind	Enters Upper Gan Eden
Ruah	Emotional awareness	12 months of purgation in Gehenna; enters Lower Gan Eden
Nefesh	Vital awareness	Punishment of the Grave

members of a heavenly tribunal evaluate the merits of the individual's life. Recompense or retribution is apportioned, based on how ethically, honestly, and devotionally the individual has lived his or her life.

While there is no monolithic point of view regarding the type of reward or punishment, the unchanging criterion for judgment itself is the extent to which the individual has abided by the ways of Torah and performed good deeds.

Repeatedly, the *Zohar* teaches that when faced with life's finality, "the only protection . . . a man has is the virtuous deeds that he performs in the world" (I, 202a). At all times, the consequences of a person's actions impacts directly on his or her fate at the time of death, and after. If an individual has lived a life of wrongdoing and wickedness, at the time of postmortem judgment his deeds appear before him ready to testify against him. But for the individual who has been committed "to the study of Torah for its own sake, when he departs this world, the Torah goes before him and proclaims his merit, and shields him from the emissaries of punishment" (I, 175b).

Thus, we see that at the root of the *Zohar*'s pronouncements regarding the afterlife is a simple formula for ethical living, identical to the one inherent in rabbinic writings: Torah and good deeds in life yield divine benevolence in death; wickedness and neglect of Torah result in postmortem chastisement. This basic premise is stipulated quite clearly in the following passages:

> [T]he soul of one who has labored in the study of the Torah, when it leaves this world, ascends by ways of the paths of the Torah—ways and paths familiar to them. They who know the ways and the paths of the Torah in this world follow them in the other world when they leave this world. But those who do not study the Torah in this world and know not its ways and paths, when they leave this world know

not how to follow those ways and paths, and hence stumble therein.
They thus follow other ways which are not the ways of the Torah,
and are visited with many chastisements. (I, 175b)

[I]f a man follows a certain direction in this world, he will be led
further in the same direction when he departs this world; as that to
which he attaches himself in this world, so is that to which he will
find himself attached in the other world: if holy, holy, and if defiled,
defiled. If he cleaves to holiness he will on high be drawn to that
side and be made a servant to minister before the Holy One among
the angels, and will stand among those holy beings. . . . Similarly,
if he clings here to uncleanness, he will be drawn there toward that
side and be made one of the unclean company and be attached to
them. (I, 100a)

Seven Occasions for Divine Judgment

Throughout our survey we have seen that Jewish afterlife conceptions become increasingly complex in successive eras of Jewish history.
This is certainly the case in the kabbalistic period, and in more than one
instance the *Zohar* speaks of a total of seven times for divine judgment
and punishment of the soul. This is evidenced in *Zohar* II, 199b, as well
as in the following passage:

Indeed, what a number of ordeals man has to undergo in passing out
of this world! First comes the judgment from on high . . . when the
spirit leaves the body. Then comes his judgment when his actions
and utterances precede him and make proclamation concerning him.
Another is the judgment when he enters the grave. One more is in
the grave itself. He afterward goes through an ordeal at the hands
of the worms. There is then the judgment of Gehinnom. And finally
there is the ordeal undergone by the spirit when it roams to and from
through the world and finds no place until its deeds have been re-
quited. In truth, "seven times pass over him" (Daniel 4:13). (III,
127a)

Judgment Prior to Death

According to the *Zohar*, divine judgment is an ongoing process.
Annually, at the time of the New Year, Rosh Ha-Shanah, a person's fate
for the coming year is determined in the heavenly spheres. If death is

impending, then at the end of Sukkot, on the night of Hoshana Rabba, angels remove from the human realm the image [Hebrew: *tzelem*, "shadow"] of the person whose death has been decreed (II, 142b). This image is then transported to the netherworlds and placed in the care of Metatron, the chief angelic being who is charged with the sustenance of humanity.[31]

If one of the wandering dead recognizes that this image belongs to a person from his home town, the soul immediately "returns to its place in the grave and announces to the remaining dead: 'So-and-so is coming to join us.' If he is a righteous and good man they all rejoice, but if not they bemoan his fate" (II, 142b). Even prior to death, space is reserved in the lofty spheres for the soul of this soon-to-be-deceased individual, and specific places are allocated for the *nefesh*, *ruah*, and *neshamah* so that they may have appropriate repose after death (II, 142b).[32]

Elsewhere, the *Zohar* suggests that only thirty days prior to death is the individual's image removed from the human to the heavenly realms. This seems to be a time of preparation of the soul for its eventual entry into the postmortem regions. Thus, we find this teaching in the name of Rabbi Jose:

> When a man's appointed time draws near, proclamation is made concerning him for thirty days, and even the birds of the heaven announce his doom; and if he is virtuous, his coming is announced for thirty days among the righteous in Gan Eden. We have learned that during those thirty days his soul departs from him every night and ascends to the other world and sees its place there, and during those thirty days the man has not the same consciousness or control of his soul as previously. (I, 217b)

Judgment on the Sickbed

Another occasion when judgment occurs is on the sickbed. In times of illness, when an individual's fate hangs in the balance, the divine forces evaluate one's actions and determine whether the person shall live or die.[33]

According to the *Zohar*:

> When they judge a man in the world above they bring the soul up before the court and judge according to its evidence, and it testifies

about everything. It testifies about all the man's thoughts, but it does not testify about his deeds, because these are all written in a book. And man is judged on the basis of them all. When they judge a man in the world above he has far more physical suffering than at other times. If they judge him favorably, then he recovers and sweat breaks out over his body, and the soul returns to its place and illumines everything. A man never rises from his sickbed until they have judged him in the world above. (I, 227a–227b)

Judgment on the Day of Death

With regard to judgment on the exact day of one's death, the *Zohar* says the following:

> Rabbi Jose said: Alas for the people who do not know, and who refuse to contemplate the ways of the Torah. Alas for them when the Holy Blessed One, comes to pass judgment on their deeds, and body and soul stand together to give an account of their deeds, before the soul is separated from the body. That day is the Day of Judgment, the day when the books are opened and the accusers appear. At that time the snake is prepared, ready to bite [the body], and all the limbs are afraid of it. And the soul becomes separated from the body and goes on its way, not knowing which path it has to take or the place to which it will be brought. (I, 201b)

DYING AND THE VISIONS OF THE DEATHBED

Attitudes toward Dying

For the mystically oriented kabbalists, the thought of death did not evoke distress, or anxiety. Dying was not the final curtain on human life, but rather a continuation of the process of drawing closer to God, another phase in the journey of the evolution of the soul.

The ideal way to encounter death, according to kabbalistic philosophy, was with an attitude of lucid equanimity. One was not to fear, deny, or be confused by death. In talmudic literature, the process of the soul leaving the body had been described as a gentle, painless experience; the metaphor most often used was "like taking a hair out of milk" (*Berakhot* 8a). The kabbalists reaffirmed this view and developed a variety of spiritual practices that made it possible to identify with spirit over matter, soul over the attachments of the body. Thus, for the righteous who lived a life of spiritual development, death itself could be a peaceful and painless process that served to transport the individual through a portal to other realms of consciousness.[34]

Supernal Visions of the Deathbed

After Nahmanides introduced the term *olam ha-neshamot*, or "World of Souls," to the lexicon of Jewish afterlife teachings, we observe an increasing concern with specific visions and events experienced by the soul on the deathbed itself and in the very process of dying.

According to the *Zohar*, with the approach of death an individual is granted a sense of transcendental vision and the ability to perceive elements in the unseen worlds that ordinary human beings do not see (III, 88a). This is indicated by the *Zohar* in the following way:

> When a man lies [on his deathbed] and judgment rests upon him decreeing that he should leave this world, he is granted an additional supernal spirit that he never had before. And when this dwells with him and cleaves to him, he sees what he has never been worthy enough to see throughout his life, because the additional spirit has now been given to him. And once this has been granted him, and he sees, he departs from this world. (I, 218b)

What are some of these elements the dying person can see? As in rabbinic literature, but with even greater acuity, the *Zohar* repeatedly speaks of angelic beings, visionary guides, deceased relatives, and even some rather unfriendly demonic-looking characters. There is quite a wide assortment of imagistic depictions of deathbed visions and phenomena of the dying process evidenced in the *Zohar*. Whereas we might describe medieval midrashic literature as a videotape of what happens to the soul after death, the *Zohar* sometimes seems more like a slide show of images, vignettes of text in which there are very brief depictions of distinctive phenomena of the dying process. It is not by any means clear that the text suggests that all these varied phenomena are encountered by every dying or deceased individual. Instead, it seems more likely that the various texts, when collated together, present a catalog of potential visionary experiences one might conceivably encounter in the experience of dying.[35]

Visions of Adam

At the time of death, Adam appears to the dying individual and welcomes him to the world of the deceased (I, 65a). Adam and the deceased individual engage in a dialogue, delineated in the *Zohar* as follows:

No man leaves the world without first seeing Adam. He asks the man the reason for his departure from the world, and he replies, "Alas, it is your fault that I have to leave the world!" And [Adam] says, "My son, I transgressed just one commandment and was punished because of it. Consider how many sins you have committed, and how many of your Master's commandments you have transgressed." (I, 57b)

Visions of the *Shekhinah*

Elsewhere, the *Zohar* describes how the dying man is blessed with a vision of the *Shekhinah*, the divine presence of God that appears as a formless, radiant image: "No man dies before he sees the *Shekhinah*, and because of its deep yearning for the *Shekhinah* the soul departs in order to see her" (III, 88a).

The text suggests that at the time of death each individual is given at least a brief glimpse of the *Shekhinah*. However, the ability to abide in continued relationship with this divine presence is not guaranteed, but is, in fact, contingent on the level of one's spiritual attainment:

When a man is on the point of leaving this world, his soul suffers many chastisements along with his body before they separate. Nor does the soul actually leave him until the *Shekhinah* shows herself to him, and then the soul goes out in joy and love to meet the *Shekhinah*. If he is righteous, he cleaves and attaches himself to her. But if not, then the *Shekhinah* departs, and the soul is left behind, mourning for its separation from the body, like a cat which is driven away from the fire. (III, 53a)

In some cases, the envisioned *Shekhinah* is accompanied by three ministering angels:

[I]t has been taught: The time of man's departure is the great day of judgment, for the soul is separated from the body, and no man leaves the world before he sees the *Shekhinah*. This is the meaning of "No man can see Me and live" [Exodus 33:20]. And with the *Shekhinah* there come three ministering angels to receive the soul of the righteous. (I, 98a *Midrash Ha-Ne'elam*)

As to the function of the three accompanying angels, it is maintained that

one of them makes record of all the good deeds and the misdeeds that he has performed in this world; one casts up the reckoning of his days; and the third is the one who has accompanied the man from the time when he was in his mother's womb. (II, 199a)

Visions of the Angel of Death

Along with the visitation of the *Shekhinah*, as might be expected, the Angel of Death makes an appearance. Linking philosophy and practice, the *Zohar* teaches that it is important to quickly close the eyes of the deceased, so that one who looked upon a holy vision of the *Shekhinah* need not be defiled by something as unholy and debased as the Angel of Death[36] (I, 226a; III, 88a). However, if the unsuspecting dying person looks upward—lo and behold, there might appear a rather sinister-looking character, brandishing an unsheathed sword, fully prepared to torture and execute (III, 88a).

The frightening and ghastly Angel of Death is described quite imagistically:

The king's guard descends and stands before him at his feet with a sharpened sword in his hand. The man raises his eyes and see the walls of the room burning with the fire that emanates from him. And then he sees him himself in front of him, covered with eyes, clothed in fire, burning in the man's presence. . . . When he sees him he trembles, in body and spirit, and his heart can find no tranquillity because it is the sovereign of the whole body. His spirit moves through every part of the body and asks leave, like someone asking his friend for permission to go to another place. . . . The man is afraid and tries to hide, but he cannot. When he sees it is impossible, he opens his eyes, and he has to look on him. He looks upon him with open eyes, and then he surrenders his body and his soul. (III, 126a–127a)

The best-known immunization against the ruthlessness of the Angel of Death is a life of Torah and good deeds. When a virtuous person departs this world, there is no way in which his soul can be harmed. Instead, four protective angels appear, and the soul of the righteous person is gracefully escorted out of this world, "with a kiss," completely avoiding the vengeful actions of the Angel of Death (II, 256a).

Furthermore, it is said that the Angel of Death is powerless over the *neshamah*. The *nefesh*, which is closer in its essential nature to the evil inclination, is susceptible to the Angel of Death. However, at the time of death, the angel Gabriel intervenes on behalf of the holy *neshamah*, preventing it from harm and mistreatment (I, 99a, *Sitrei Torah*).

Visions of Deceased Relatives and Friends

Another phenomenon encountered by the disembodied consciousness is the experience of being welcomed into the postmortem realms by previously deceased relatives and friends. It is said that newly deceased souls are oriented into the invisible realms by the likes of those who have gone before. Thus, the *Zohar* teaches that "at the time of a man's death he is allowed to see his relatives and companions from the other world" (I, 219a). Similarly, "we have learned that when a man's soul departs from him, all his relatives and companions in the other world join it and show it the place of delight and the place of torture" (I, 219a).

Elsewhere, the deathbed vision of a deceased ancestor is described in this way:

> R. Simeon then said to R. Isaac: "Have you seen today the image of your father? For so we have learned, that at the hour of a man's departure from the world, his father and relatives gather round him, and he sees them and recognizes them, and likewise all with whom he associated in this world, and they accompany his soul to the place where it is to abide." (I, 217b)

Life Review

The *Zohar* also indicates that on the deathbed the dying person is given the opportunity to see all the deeds of his or her life, a complete review of all life activity: "When God desires to take back a man's spirit, all the days that he lived in this world pass before him in review" (I, 221b). Or, "when a man departs from this world, [he] goes to give an account to his Master of all his actions in this world while the body and soul were still joined together" (I, 65b).

In a different passage, the postmortem life review is described as follows:

> R. Eleazar said: "On the day when man's time arrives to depart from the world . . . three messengers stand over him and take an account of his life and of all that he has done in this world, and he admits all with his mouth and signs the account with his hand . . . the whole account is signed with his hand so that he should be judged in the next world for all his actions, former and later, old and new, not one of them is forgotten." (I, 79a)

Contained in this passage is an unequivocal reiteration of the rabbinic doctrine of individual retribution. Each person, after seeing the life review, is held fully responsible for all his or her actions; subsequently, punishment or reward is meted out accordingly. The three messengers mentioned above are the Angel of Love, whose task it is to record the person's merits; the Angel of Judgment, who keeps account of sins; and the Angel of Mercy, who notes of the length of the persons days.[37]

In a similar vein, the *Zohar* speaks of how a newly deceased individual is approached by two beings—angels acting as scribes on behalf of the court—who "write down all that he did in this world and every word that ever went from his mouth" (III, 126b). Once again, a vivid judgment scene is described in which the person must confess to all his deeds, which are literally called upon to testify against him. After finally signing a written confession, body and soul separate and an even more elaborate process of postmortem torment begins.

Just as we discovered in rabbinic literature, what is described in all the above passages is a process whereby, at the time of death or soon after, an individual experiences an instantaneous recall of all life events. This phenomenon seems to be a spontaneous replay of a person's life experience in its entirety and is documented extensively, both in other religious traditions around the world[38] and in contemporary research on near-death experiences.[39]

DEPARTURE OF THE SOUL FROM THE PHYSICAL BODY

Hibbut Ha-Kever

Although the ideal model for the kabbalists was to experience a painless transition of the soul from the body, traditional teachings indicate that this did not always take place. In fact, it was expected that an individual who had lived a life identified with sensual delights of the body would experience a painfully difficult time as the soul departed. The texts frequently describe how such an individual, lacking an abundance of good deeds to testify on his or her behalf, was almost guaranteed to experience painful torment seeing the body dead and decomposing.

Like the Rabbis and the medieval midrashists, the kabbalists were familiar with the notion of *Hibbut Ha-Kever*, the pain and anguish of the grave. However, the kabbalists further developed and emphasized this postmortem concept, seeing it as a three- to seven-day process that took place as the *nefesh* aspect of the soul was extricated from the body. During this time, any soul with physical plane attachments would remain earthbound, traveling back and forth between the cemetery, where the body lay, and the home of the deceased, where beloved family and possessions were found. Describing this process, the *Zohar* states: "For seven days the soul [*nefesh*] goes to and fro from his house to his grave from his grave to his house, mourning for the body . . . and it grieves to behold the sadness in the house" (I, 218b–219a).

At the same time, due to its unwillingness to surrender attachment to the physical world, the *nefesh* experiences excruciating physical torment. It is said that the *nefesh* "wanders about the world and beholds the body which was once its home devoured by worms and suffering the judgment of the grave" (II, 142a). As we have seen, the medieval *Masekhet Hibbut Ha-Kever* texts elucidate this wandering and torment with elaborate detail. Although not as extensively described, the *Zohar* says the following about the process of separation of soul from body, and the experience of *Hibbut Ha-Kever*:

> All the deeds that man performs in this world are preserved and are ready to offer testimony about him, and they do not leave him. When they take him out for burial they are all there, going before him. And there are three heralds making a proclamation, one in front of him, one on his right, and one on his left, and they say: "This is so-and-so. He has rebelled against his Master . . . rebelled against the Torah, rebelled against His commandments. Look at his deeds! Look at his words! It were better for him if he has not been born!" When he reaches his grave the dead all rise up against him saying: "Alas! Alas! That this man should be buried among us!" His deeds and his words precede him and enter the grave and stand by the body [ready to give evidence] while his spirit wanders abroad, in mourning over the body. Once a man is buried in the cemetery Dumah comes with his three courts that are appointed for judgment at the grave. They have three fiery scepters in their hands, and they judge spirit and body together. (III, 126b–127a)

Separation of Body and Soul

This phenomenon of the soul withdrawing from the body is depicted as being a painful, emotional upheaval:

> "For love is strong as death" (Song of Songs 8:6)—it is as strong as the separation of the spirit from the body. For we have learned: When the time comes for a man to depart from the world, and he sees what he sees, the spirit moves through every part of the body, following all its convolutions, like someone who sets out to sea without oars, going up and down without any peace. And it goes and asks leave of every part of the body, and [no time] is more violent than the day when the spirit separates from the body. (I, 245a)

Elsewhere in the *Zohar*, this process is portrayed with even more acute detail, as follows:

> This moment is the time of great judgment, when man is judged in this world. And then the spirit moves through all the parts of the body and asks leave of them. It traverses all the bodily organs and trembles on all sides, and all the different parts of the body tremble. And when the spirit comes to each part of the body to ask leave of it, sweat breaks out on that particular part, and that part dies right away, and so with them all. (III, 126b)

Remembering One's Name

To facilitate the process of separation from the body, it is said that Dumah, the guardian of the dead, appears and asks the soul its Hebrew names. Since the shock of death allegedly causes a kind of amnesia, the soul needs to be reminded of its true spiritual identity. Thus, in asking the soul its name, the intention is to assist the deceased to recollect their essential identity. And recollecting one's identity—as a spiritual being—facilitates disidentification from the physical world, thereby minimizing the soul's struggle to leave behind the body.

An interesting series of spiritual practices were developed to prepare the individual for this postmortem encounter with Dumah. Specific liturgies were utilized and taught even to young children to help indelibly imprint memory of one's Hebrew name. Rabbi Zalman Schachter-Shalomi describes these liturgical techniques, which demonstrate how a belief in the afterlife permeated Jewish religious practice:

In order to dispel this amnesia, the learning of a mnemonic device while one is alive is recommended: At the conclusion of every *Amidah* [the central prayer of the service], the worshiper is instructed to "sign off" by reciting a biblical verse that begins with the first initial of his name and ends with the last letter of his name. Among Sephardic Jews, the child is initiated into his/her own sentence at the *bar* or *bat mitzvah*. In this way, the worshiper reinforces the memory of his Jewish name at the end of every prayer service. Thus, in death, even if he is unable to remember his name, he will be able to remember the Torah verse, because Torah is eternal and cannot decay. The soul will therefore be able to follow the angels who summon it before the heavenly court.[40]

The Catapult—*Kaf Ha-Kela*

According to kabbalistic tradition, another phenomenon encountered as body and soul separate is the experience of *kaf ha-kela*, best defined as "the catapult." In a number of places the *Zohar* speaks of how, after death, certain unprepared or tainted souls roll about "like a stone inside [the hollow of a] sling" (I, 77b, 217b; II 59a, 99b). *Kaf ha-kela* is a term based on the biblical verse in 1 Samuel 25:29 that speaks of how "the lives of your enemies he will hurl away as from the hollow of a sling." As the biblical image suggests, the concept here is of a soul being thrown about, catapulted through the ethereal postmortem realms.

In explicating the idea of *kaf ha-kela*, the kabbalists drew from ancient rabbinic teaching about two angels that appear after death and catapult the soul back and forth from one end of the universe to the other.[41] According to the kabbalistic view, this act on the part of the angels serves to purify the soul. The experience of *kaf ha-kela* is a "cosmic centrifuge" designed to help eliminate accumulated psychic impurities and prepare the soul for its continued sojourn in the postmortem worlds.[42]

Decomposition of the Body

Another postmortem phenomenon, according to the *Zohar*, is a process of dissolution of bodily elements. In a rather cryptic passage, we find this teaching:

> We have learned that on the dread day when a man's time comes to depart from the world, four quarters of the world indict him, pun-

ishments rise up from all four quarters, and four elements fall quarreling and seek to depart each to its own side. (I, 218a)

In and of itself, this *Zohar* passage remains rather obscure. What are the "four quarters of the world" that indict the deceased? What is meant by the phrase "four elements fall quarreling and seek to depart each to its own side"? Is there a metaphor encoded here intended to describe, symbolically, an actual experience of consciousness? If so, what is it?

Interestingly, material found in the afterlife traditions of Tibetan Buddhism sheds light on this teaching from the *Zohar*. Classical Tibetan postmortem philosophy speaks of an "intermediate state" termed a *bardo*,[43] a transitional state of awareness immediately after death, in which the bodily elements of earth, water, fire, and air begin to dissolve. According to Lama Lodru, author of the *Bardo Teachings: The Tibetan Way of Death and Rebirth*:

> Life depends on the interaction of four basic elements: The essence of earth is flesh, the essence of water is bodily fluid, the essence of fire is bodily heat and the essence of air is breath. The dying process begins with the dissolution of these elements.[44]

Demonstrating a profound understanding of human consciousness, the Tibetan text goes on to describe what occurs during the dying process. As each of these fundamental elements separate, there are both internal, subjective visions and accompanying outward phenomena:

> [First] the element earth dissolves and is absorbed by the element water. This is accompanied by the inner experience that . . . everything is falling apart from great floods and earthquakes. You will not be able to stand because your strength is fast disappearing. . . .
>
> In the second phase, the element water dissolves and is absorbed by the element fire . . . you will experience the sensation that the entire universe has been flooded with water. During this time, those around you perceive that your face and lips are rapidly drying up. You will also feel extremely thirsty.
>
> When the third element, fire, dissolves into the element air you . . . will experience the sensation that everything around you is burning. During this time the heat from your body will go away.
>
> [Finally] the element air will begin to dissolve into consciousness itself. When this happens, you will have the . . . experience that all phenomena in the universe are being blown away by the .

winds of a great storm. You will hear a grinding roar like that of a thousand thunders [and] . . . the external air or breath will be extinguished.[45]

Does this text chronicle internal visions in which "four elements fall quarreling and seek to depart each to its own side"? Perhaps we see in the Tibetan Buddhist text the same process described in the *Zohar*, except with more extensive detail.

With regard to the external phenomena outlined in the *bardo* teachings, consider how when in the presence of a person a terminally ill person, very close to death, one notices that the body becomes very heavy, the limbs difficult to move. The dying individual often becomes dehydrated, needing small chips of ice to keep from becoming totally parched. As death approaches, the body loses heat, the limbs becoming very cold. Finally, the breath ceases. Is this the outer correlate to the dissolution of the earth, water, fire, and air elements?

It may well be that in describing how "the four elements fall quarreling and seek to depart each to its own side," the *Zohar* presents a map of the internal journey and subjective experiences of the dying process, far more sophisticated than that of contemporary medical science.

Guf Ha-Dak

Once the process of separation of body and soul is complete, the individual consciousness continues to exist enveloped in a separate field of light, or a "transparent body"—what is called in some kabbalistic sources *guf ha-dak*. This *guf ha-dak* is regarded as a spiritual postmortem body.[46] Rabbi Eliezer Ha-Rofei Ashkenazi (1513–1586), author of *Maaseh Ha-Shem*, refers to a spiritualized form around the body that continues to exist after death. Similarly, Menasseh ben Israel (1604–1658), author of *Nishmat Hayyim*, writes of a translucent, spiritual body in which all souls are garbed; even after death, this "body" remains attached to the soul.[47]

This view is inherent to kabbalistic tradition, which asserts that "the spiritual body and the physical body are actually one and the same before, during and after life, although manifested on two different planes."[48] After death, the former separates from the latter; while the body begins its process of physical decomposition, the spiritual body, *guf ha-dak*, survives and goes through the stages of the postmortem journey.

After successfully separating from the physical realm, it is through this translucent, postmortem body that the discarnate being experiences the torments of Gehenna and the transcendental bliss of Gan Eden.[49]

In the *Zohar*, the *guf ha-dak*, is spoken of as a "celestial garment," a vehicle of awareness qualitatively different from the garment of the physical body. Just as Prophet Elijah had two bodies, "one in which one in which he appear[ed] below to human kind, another in which he appear[ed] above among the celestial and holy angels" (III, 88b), so human beings are given an earthly body while alive and a celestial vesture after death. According to the *Zohar*,

in the same way as the soul has to be clothed in a bodily garment in order to exist in this world, so is she given an ethereal supernal garment wherewith to exist in the other world. . . . (I, 66a)

Elsewhere, the *Zohar* states that

when the time comes for the spirit to leave this world . . . it cannot do so until the Angel of Death has taken off the garment of this body. When that has been done he again puts on that other [celestial] garment in Gan Eden of which he had to divest himself when he entered this world. And the whole joy of the spirit is in that celestial body. (II, 150a)

In keeping with the ethical basis of all rabbinic and kabbalistic teachings, the receipt of these celestial garments is contingent on one's spiritual attainment and is provided for the righteous, but not the wicked:

God shows kindness to His creatures in not divesting them of their earthly garment until other garments, more precious and finer than these, are prepared for them. But the wicked, they who have never turned to their Lord with a perfect repentance—naked they came into this world, and naked they must return from it, and their souls go in shame to join other souls in like plight, and they are judged in the earthly Gehenna from the fire above. (II, 150a)

The donning of the spiritual garment is seen to be necessary for entry into Gan Eden. Without it, one is condemned to the torments of Gehenna:

If, then, the soul is worthy and wears the precious protecting garment, multitudes of holy hosts stand ready to join her and accompany her to Gan Eden. But if she has not that garment, the "strange"
hosts compel her to take the path which leads to Gehenna. Angels
of destruction and confusion are they, who will gladly take their revenge on her. (II, 97a)

In another place, the Zohar suggests that the receipt of the celestial
garments does not take place immediately after death, but thirty days
later, after the soul first undergoes a process of purification, and "after
purification it receives its garment, in virtue of which it is then assigned
to its appropriate place" (II, 210a).

Thus far, our survey of teachings on the postmortem fate of the
individual reveals a great variability and variety of views regarding that
which occurs at the time of death and as body and soul separate. However, despite the creative improvisation, without variation, underlying
all teachings is rabbinic Judaism's well-established ethical stance—a life
of pursuit of Torah and good deeds makes it easier for the soul to leave
the body and minimizes postmortem punishment.

GEHENNA

Seven Stories of Gehenna

In the next phase of the postmortem journey, the soul enters into
Gehenna. Again we encounter a potpourri of fanciful images, replete with
the same kind of contradictions and inconsistencies evidenced in earlier
strands of Jewish literature. Building on the past, kabbalistic writings
usually replicate the landscape of Gehenna found in rabbinic and medieval Midrash. However, in the Zohar conceptions of Gehenna often assume somewhat of a different character, recast within the philosophical
world of kabbalistic Judaism.[50]

With regard to the time of creation of Gehenna, one passage in
the Zohar maintains that Gehenna is "a blazing fire" (I, 33a) fashioned
on the second day of creation. But, in a compensatory action, on the third
day the quality of mercy was extended to sinners in order to cool the
flames of Gehenna (I, 46a).[51] Elsewhere, it is taught that the light
of Gehenna was fashioned even before the world came into being (III,

34b). Similarly, *Zohar Hadash* teaches that Gehenna came into existence a thousand years before the creation of the world (*Zohar Hadash* 125a).

The *Zohar* maintains the traditional seven-tiered schema for Gehenna. In one place, it is taught that the seven realms of Gehenna correspond directly with the seven names for the *yetzer hara*, "the evil inclination," which causes a person to sin, and to be brought to Gehenna (II, 263a; *Zohar Hadasah* 79a). Elsewhere, Zoharic tradition asserts that the seven regions of Gehenna are designated for particular categories of sinners, who receive specific types of punishment:

> Gehenna has seven doors which open into seven habitations; and there are also seven types of sinners: evildoers, worthless ones, sinners, the wicked, corrupters, mockers, and arrogant ones; and corresponding with them are the habitations in Gehenna, for each kind a particular place, all according to grade. (II, 150b)

There is no consistent tradition on the names of the seven realms of Gehenna. In certain textual passages only some of these netherworld regions are named:

> We have learned that the sinners of Gehinnom are in different stories, and that Gehinnom has a number of gates corresponding to those of Gan Eden, each with its own name. There is one story lower than all the rest which consists of a story on a story, and that is called nether Sheol, "Sheol" being one story and "nether" another below it. (III, 285b)

Other names of Gehenna mentioned in the *Zohar* are Abbadon and "boiling filth" (II, 150b). It is claimed that a person who has never repented descends to Abbadon (III, 286b). In one place, the *Zohar* states that it is possible to ascend upward from Sheol, but not from Abbadon (III, 178b). Typical of the inconsistencies evidenced in kabbalistic eschatology, elsewhere it is taught that "of all the grades of Gehinnom there is none so hard as Sheol" (III, 54b).

Dumah and the Attendants of Gehenna

In this realm of the journey, the disembodied soul encounters various mythical beings who are either patrolling the entry into Gehenna or carrying out specific punishments. Most notable is Dumah, the guardian of Gehenna:

> [A]dventures await the souls when they altogether leave the body to depart from this world. In their attempt to soar upwards they have to pass through many gates at which bands of demons are stationed. These seize the souls that are of their side and deliver them into the hands of Dumah in order that he may take them into Gehinnom. (II,130b)

Dumah does not work alone, but rather, in conjunction with an extensive cadre of helpers. In one place, the *Zohar* speaks of Dumah's 12,000 myriads of "attendants [who are] all charged to punish the souls of sinners" (I, 237b). Elsewhere, it is taught that within Gehenna there are a number of "executioners of judgment" charged with the castiga-tion and punishment of the souls of the wicked:

> [W]hen the souls of the wicked leave this world many executioners of judgment await them and take them to Gehinnom, and subject them there to three tortures every day. Afterwards they go about the world in company with them and mislead the wicked from whom repentance is withheld, and then return to Gehinnom and punish them there. (III, 70a)

In addition, there are special angels appointed for each of the seven habitations of Gehenna, all of whom are "under the direction of Dumah, who has thousands and myriads of angels under him, to punish sinners according to their deserts . . ." (II, 150b).

A parallel passage teaches that Dumah's task is to deliver newly arrived sinners into the hands of the various gatekeepers of the seven regions of Gehenna:

> There are in Gehinnom seven circuits and seven gates, each with several gatekeepers under their own chief. The souls of sinners are delivered by Dumah to those gatekeepers who then close the gates of flaming fire. There are gates behind gates, the outer ones remain-ing open while the inner ones are closed. (I, 237b)

Also included in the underworld entourage of the *Zohar* are three specific chiefs of Gehenna named Destruction, Anger, and Wrath (III, 237a). Although subordinate to Dumah (*Zohar Hadash* 79a), these beings are responsible for regulating the punishment of those sinners who committed murder, incest and idolatry (I, 27b).[52]

We see here a parallel to the medieval midrashic texts discussed in Chapter 6. In *Gedulat Moshe*, "The Revelation of Moses," there are two angels, one named Wrath, the other, Anger. Moses encounters these beings in his travels through the seventh heaven. Although there are comparable images from one set of literature to the next, the use of names of angels and of demons continually changes in Jewish afterlife literature, highlighting the complete lack of any standardized or canonized tradition.

Gehenna as Purgation and Purification

According to kabbalistic philosophy, Gehenna was a purgatorial realm in which the impurities of the soul were cleansed. The defilements that had accumulated from the life lived on earth had to be extricated during the time in Gehenna.[53] While in medieval Midrash we find fanciful mythic depictions of the geography of Gehenna, the attention of the *Zohar* centers on the nature of the soul's purification during this phase of the postmortem journey. For example, in one passage the teaches that

> whoever pollutes himself in the world draws to himself the spirit of uncleanness, and when his soul leaves him the unclean spirits pollute it, and its habitation is among them. For according to man's strivings in this world is his habitation in the next world; hence such a man is polluted by the spirits of uncleanness and cast into Gehinnom. (II, 129b)

Elsewhere, the *Zohar* describes a process of purification that takes place deep within the interior of Gehenna, in a realm referred to as *Ben-Hinnom*, where souls are purified and prepared for entry to Lower Gan Eden:

> At first the soul is taken to a spot called *Ben-Hinnom*, so called because it is the interior of Gehinnom, where souls are cleansed and purified before they enter the Lower Gan Eden. Two angel messengers stand at the gate of Gan Eden and called aloud to the chieftains who have charge of that spot in Gehinnom, summoning them to receive that soul, and during the whole process of purification they continue to utter aloud repeatedly the word *Hinnom* (literally: "here

they are"). When the process is completed, the chieftains take the soul out of Gehinnom and lead it to the gate of Gan Eden, and say to the angel messengers standing there: *Hinnom*, behold, here is the soul that has come out pure and white. (II, 211b)

The cleansing system of Gehenna is described as a process of purification by fire: "In Gehenna there are certain places [where] souls that have been polluted by the filth of this world . . . are purified by fire and made white, and then they ascend toward the heavenly regions" (II, 150b). Similarly, the *Zohar* teaches that every evening the Holy Blessed One judges the wicked in Gehenna, and at that time "seven rivers of fire issue forth and descend on the heads of the wicked, along with burning coals of fire . . ." (III, 64b).

Why is fire utilized to punish souls? According to the *Zohar*, fire represents the quality of human passion: "Says R. Yehudah . . . the fire of Gehenna, which burns day and night, corresponds to the hot passion of sinfulness in man" (II, 150b). The idea here is that the more one has experienced unbridled passion (usually implying sexuality), the more intensely the fire burns. In fact, the *Zohar* overtly states that the character of one's experience in Gehenna is a direct reflection of the kind of life one has lived, and the types of impurities accumulated. The more defiled, the stronger the need for the fires of purification:

When a man's sins are so numerous that he has to pass through the nethermost compartments of Gehinnom in order to receive heavier punishment corresponding to the contamination of his soul, a more intense fire is kindled in order to consume that contamination. (II, 212a)

In some places, the *Zohar* suggests that the punishment of Gehenna consists of both fire and water (I, 68b);[54] in other places, as in the passage below, this punishment is described as a combination of fire and snow:

R. Hizkiah said that sinners are punished in Gehinnom twelve months, half with fire, half with snow. When they go into the fire they say: "This is really Gehinnom!" When they go into the snow they say: "This is the real winter of the Holy Blessed One." They begin by exclaiming "Alas!" and then exclaim "Woe." The supreme punishment is with snow. (I, 238b)

In discussing this motif of the fires of Gehenna, Gershon Winkler emphasizes the importance of recognizing the metaphor encoded in the text. Thus, he writes:

> There is only chemical fire and burning in the world of the physical, but not in the realm of the spiritual. The concept of "hell" [Gehenna] is translated the way it is because, as physical beings, we can only relate to concepts after they have been clothed in physical analogies.[55]

Winkler goes on to describe Gehenna as "a profound spiritual experience which cannot be comprehended by the limited human mind as long as one is restricted within the material world."[56] He offers the following astute contemporary perspective on the purification process of Gehenna:

> How much a person invests in the cultivation of his soul while yet alive, will determine the reaction of the soul when it confronts the ultimate of purity and perfection (G-d) after "death." The less one permits himself to draw from the absolute focal point of reality, G-d, the less prepared he will be, and the more intense will be the contrast when he is faced with that reality after death. For having been preoccupied with the excessive material indulgence while alive, the soul, after death, maintains these same spiritual yearnings but now without the benefit of the physical outlets and faculties to facilitate their satisfaction. The "purification" is then the painful process of "cold turkey" withdrawal of the disembodied consciousness from its heretofore exclusive relationship with the material, enabling it subsequently to bask in the eternal bliss of the purely spiritual [Gan Eden].[57]

Punishment in Gehenna—Finite or Eternal?

The process of purification of the psychic remnants of earthly life is not an indefinite one. The *Zohar*, like the Talmud, maintains that this process lasts only twelve months:

> The punishment of sinners in Gehinnom lasts twelve months, after which the Holy One raises them out of Gehinnom, where they have undergone purification. They remain then sitting at the gate of

Gehinnom, and when they see sinners enter there to be punished, they beseech mercy for them. In time the Holy One takes pity on them and causes them to be brought to a certain place reserved for them. From that day onward the body rests in the dust and the soul is accorded her proper place. (I, 107b–108a)

As noted above, the *ruah* aspect of the soul is subjected to the trials and tribulations of Gehenna. This ordeal of twelve months—which, according to one kabbalist, is the length of time needed for extraction of the soul's impurity[58]—serves to prepare the disembodied soul to continue the postmortem journey. This essential view occurs repeatedly within the *Zohar*:

[T]he *ruah* is purified in Gehinnom, whence it goes forth roaming about the world and visiting its grave until it acquires a vestment. After twelve months the whole is at rest; the body reposes in the dust and the soul is clad in its luminous vestment. (I, 226a; see also I, 225a, I, 130b; III, 53a, 205a)

In spite of a prevalent belief that Gehenna lasted only twelve months, in a number of places the *Zohar* refers to the possibility of an unending purgation in Gehenna.[59] Certain classes of contaminated sinners who never repent are dispatched to a realm of Gehenna named "boiling filth"; once there, they never depart (II, 150b). Similarly, the *Zohar* maintains that even though everyone may be required to pass through Gehenna, they all exit except for "those sinners who never harbored thoughts of repentance . . . who go down and do not come up (III, 220b).

Those individuals who did not respond "Amen" when they heard a prayer or blessing are judged with extreme severity in Gehenna, and sentenced to an abode of perpetual torment:

We have learned that he who ascends to Abbadon, which is called "nether," never ascends again, and he is called "a man who has been wiped out from all worlds." To this place they take down those who scorn to answer to Amen, and for all the amens which they have neglected they are judged in Gehinnom and taken down to the lowest story which has no outlet, and from which they never ascend. (III, 285b–286a)

In addition to this crime of neglecting to answer "Amen," eternal damnation is the due punishment for those who do not believe in the resurrection of the dead:

> Woe to those that sleep with eyes fast closed and do not know or consider how they will arise in the Day of Judgment; for reckoning is exacted when the body is defiled, and the soul flits over the face of the transparent ether, now up and now down. . . . Woe to them! Who shall plead for them? For they shall not be admitted to this joyance, among the delightful habitations of the righteous their places shall be missing, they shall be delivered into the hand of Dumah, they shall descend and not ascend. (I, 77a–77b)

It is clear that these teachings on eternal damnation served an ethical-pedagogical purpose. The idea behind them was to motivate people to a life of good deeds, or at least to repentance. In fact, the *Zohar* teaches that repentance is always an effective antidote to eternal punishment:

> R. Jose said: 'Woe to the wicked who will not repent of their sins before the Holy Blessed One while they are still in this world. For when a man repents of his sins and feels remorse for them, the Holy Blessed One forgives them. But those who cling to their sins and refuse to repent of them will in the end descend to Gehinnom and never come up again."(I, 66a)

Even though there are random teachings on eternal punishment in both kabbalistic and talmudic tradition, this was always a minority view. On the whole, the Jewish masses were taught that the soul's purgation in Gehenna lasted twelve months.

There is an interesting parallel between this teaching and the Jewish practice of saying *Kaddish*. *Kaddish* is a memorial prayer recited by a bereaved individual on behalf of the deceased.[60] In the sixteenth century, Rabbi Moses ben Israel Isserles of Cracow (1525–1572) limited the recital of the *Kaddish* for one's parent to only eleven months. His rationale was that since twelve months was the maximum punishment for sinners in Gehenna, one would not want to assume that one's dead father or mother had been allocated the full punishment time in that postmortem realm.[61] Thus, this little vignette of religious history indicates, first of all, that twelve months in Gehenna was the assumed belief. Second, it demonstrates the extent to which beliefs about the state of the soul in the afterlife influenced Jewish community death practices. To this day, *Kaddish* for a parent is recited for only eleven months.

Further Antidotes to Postmortem Punishment

The *Zohar* maintains that it is possible to bypass the painful fate of Gehenna, primarily by shunning the temptations of "the spirit of uncleanness" during earthly life:

> [W]hoever sanctifies himself and is on guard against defilement in this world finds his habitation in the next world among the supernal holy angels, where they carry out God's messages. (II, 129b–130a)

As we have seen, the essential guideline for avoiding the torments Gehenna is to live a life dedicated to the ways of Torah:

> Why was the Torah given in fire and darkness? In order to show that he who is constantly and diligently occupied with the study of it will be saved from the fire of Gehenna and from the darkness of exile and heathen lands. (II, 86b)

Those who invest time and energy learning Torah are rewarded accordingly; those who do not are undeniably destined for postmortem punishment, as the passages below indicate:

> [T]he Holy One said to Abraham: "As long as your children shall be absorbed in the ways of the Torah they will be saved from punishment, but should they turn from her and forget her paths the fire of Gehenna will have dominion over them. . . ." (II, 86b)
>
> [W]hoever devotes himself to the study of the Torah in this world, will be privileged to study in the world to come. . . . On the other hand, the man who fails to study the Torah in this world, and so walks in darkness, when he leaves this world is taken and cast into Gehinnom, a nethermost place where there will be none to pity him, a place called "tumultuous pit, miry clay" (Psalm 40:3). Hence, of him who has not devoted himself to the study of the Torah in this world, but has besmirched himself with the offscourings of this world, it is written: "And they took him and cast him into that pit," that is,

into Gehinnom, a place where those who have not labored in the Torah are brought to judgment.

According to the *Zohar*, one other antidote, or prophylactic, against the torments of Gehenna is a circumcised penis. It is taught that

> when a man leaves this world, numbers of angels swoop down to seize him, but when they behold this sign of the holy covenant [circumcision] they leave him and he is not delivered into the hands of Dumah, so as to be sent down to Gehinnom. (I, 94a)

In addition, the practice of responding "Amen" to prayers and blessings helps one avoid Gehenna's punishments:

> [W]hen a man who was careful to answer Amen departs from this world, his soul ascends and they proclaim before him: Open the gates before him[62] as he opened every day by being careful to answer Amen. But if one hears a blessing from the reader and is not careful to answer Amen, what is his punishment? As he did not open blessings below, so they do not open for him above, and when he leaves this world and they proclaim before him: Close the gates in the face of So-and-so that he enter not, and do not receive him—woe to him and to his soul! (III, 285b–286a)

Clearly the above teachings are all designed to reaffirm specific beliefs of Jewish law. Circumcision for males is unequivocally important; hence, ignoring this Jewish practice destines one to postmortem retribution. Similarly, prayer is an essential element of Jewish religious life, and attentiveness to prayer mandates one to answer with "Amen" when hearing specific blessings recited by a reader in the synagogue. The ethical message inferred in these afterlife teachings is a simple one: practice the divine commandments of Jewish law, as prescribed by Torah. By doing so, you will be rewarded appropriately in the world of souls after death.

Sabbath: A Day of Rest in Gehenna

One additional pronouncement about Gehenna also serves an ethical-pedagogical purpose. It is taught that with the start of the Sabbath, the gates of Gehenna are opened and all sinners are released from the grips of Dumah's punishments (I, 237b). And further, it is stated that "the moment the Sabbath begins the blaze of fire is imprisoned, all fires of the harmful kind are similarly hidden away and suppressed, including even the fire of Gehenna, so that the sinners obtain a respite" (II, 203b).

In a similar vein, elsewhere the *Zohar* teaches:

> Every Sabbath Eve, at the time of the sanctification of the day, heralds are sent to proclaim throughout the length of Gehenna: "Cease from punishing the wicked! The Holy King is come; the Sabbath is about to be sanctified. He takes them all under His protection," and all chastisements cease and the wicked find rest for a space. But the fire of Gehenna never ceases to burn those souls who have never kept the Sabbath. (II, 150b–151a)

Again the point made by this teaching applies to the realm of Jewish spiritual practice—observe the Sabbath as decreed in the Torah and avoid the punishments of Gehenna. Desecrate the Sabbath and suffer for your sins.

From Gehenna to Lower Gan Eden

As the period of time in Gehenna ends, a new phase of the journey begins. After completing the allocated time for punishment, the soul enters, first Lower, then Upper Gan Eden, to enjoy the delights of the higher worlds:

> The body is punished in the grave and the soul in the fire of Gehinnom for the appointed period. When this is completed she rises from Gehinnom purified of her guilt like iron purified in the fire, and she is carried up to the Lower Gan Eden. . . . (III, 53a)

In Lower Gan Eden the postmortem journey continues. We will now explore further the motif of Gan Eden in kabbalistic Judaism.

GAN EDEN

Entering Gan Eden

Leaving behind the purgatorial realm of Gehenna, the soul begins to sojourn through the interior regions of Gan Eden. According to the *Zohar*, entry into Gan Eden requires passing through a guarded gate. At once, the soul is greeted by Adam, who sits accompanied by the righteous dead:

> For when a man departs from this world . . . [he] meets Adam, the first man, sitting at the gate of Gan Eden, ready to welcome with joy all those who have observed the commands of their Master. Round him are many righteous men, those who in this life have kept clear of the path to Gehinnom and followed the path to Gan Eden. (I, 65b)

Once in Gan Eden, the soul encounters the light of Gan Eden. Using rabbinic Midrash as a basis, the *Zohar* teaches that the light of Gan Eden was formed even prior to creation:

> R. Hizkiah asked R. Eleazar: "How many lights were created before the world was created?" He answered: "Seven: namely the light of Gan Eden, the light of Gehenna, the light of the Temple, the light of the Throne of Glory, the light of repentance, the light of the Messiah." (III, 34b)

The disembodied soul encounters the light of Gan Eden by dipping in what is called the River of Light, or *nehar dinur* (II, 210a; III, 182b). According to kabbalistic tradition, the River of Light is "created from the perspiration that flows from the heavenly hosts as they fervently sing glory to the Highest."[63] Immersion in this divine source of light serves to further purify the soul of any lingering psychic impressions from mundane, earthly existence, so that it may fully perceive the majestic glory of the realm of paradise. After being cleansed in the River of Light, the soul "emerges completely purified and . . . come[s] before the presence of the Master of the Universe purified in every aspect" (II, 121b).

Souls of the Righteous Are in Gan Eden

Gan Eden is the abode of those who lived virtuous lives, and it is said that "every day the spirits of the righteous sit in rows in Gan Eden arrayed in their robes and praise God gloriously . . ." (I, 226b). These robes worn by the righteous are celestial garments that reflect the quality of an individual's spiritual attainment. As the *Zohar* teaches,

> a man's good deeds done in this world draw from the celestial resplendency of light a garment with which he may be invested when he comes to appear before the Holy Blessed One. Appareled in that

raiment, he is in a state of bliss and feasts his eyes on the radiant effulgence. (II, 229b)

After completing the purgations of Gehenna, the *ruah* aspect of the soul then enters Gan Eden. First:

Ruah enters the earthly Garden [Lower Gan Eden] and there dons a likeness which is in the semblance of the body it tenanted in this world: that likeness being, as it were, a garment with which the spirit robes itself, so that there it may enjoy the delights of the radiant Garden. On Sabbath, New Moons and festivals it ascends unto higher regions imbibes the joys thereof, and then returns to its place. . . . (II, 141b)

Subsequently:

Neshamah ascends at once to her place [in Upper Gan Eden], the region from whence she emanated, and for her sake the light is kindled to shine above. She never again descends to earth. . . . (II, 141b)

Lower Gan Eden

As evidenced in the above passages, there is a distinction made between Lower and Upper Gan Eden. This is similar to the distinction between earthly Gan Eden [*Gan Eden shel Ha-Aretz*] and heavenly Gan Eden [*Gan Eden shel Malah*], as described in the medieval midrashic text *Seder Gan Eden*. Inherent to kabbalistic tradition, this twofold distinction is described in the *Zohar* as "a difference between darkness and light" (III, 182b).

Within this kabbalistic schema, Lower Gan Eden serves as a transit point, a staging area found between Gehenna and the more supernal Upper Gan Eden. Those souls who do not immediately merit the supernal delights of Upper Gan Eden "are assigned a lower place according to their deserts" (III, 182b). In Lower Gan Eden the soul continues the process of purification and preparation for entry into the heavenly Gan Eden. During its transitional sojourn in Lower Gan Eden the soul "is cleansed in the waters of Gan Eden and perfumed with its spices, and there she remains till the time comes for her to depart from the abode of the righteous" (III, 53a).

In addition, there are qualitatively different garments that envelop the soul in these separate regions of Gan Eden. In Upper Gan Eden, souls are attired in celestial garments. In Lower Gan Eden, however, disembodied beings find themselves in a more terrestrial type of garment—souls are "clad in a resplendent vesture resembling their corporeal figure in the world" (I, 7a; see also III, 159b). The deeds an individual performed while alive form the constituent elements of the soul's garments in Lower Gan Eden. Thus, according to the *Zohar*, "in Lower Gan Eden a person's soul is thus sustained by these deeds and is clad in garments of glory made out of them" (II, 210b).

By contrast, the soul's garments in Upper Gan Eden are described in this way:

> But when the soul mounts on high through that portal of the firmament [i.e., to Upper Gan Eden], other precious garments are provided for it of a more exalted order, made out of the zeal and devotion which characterized his study of the Torah and his prayer. (II, 210b)

Just as every Sabbath souls in Gehenna are given permission to temporarily enter Gan Eden, so come the Sabbath the soul populace of Lower Gan Eden are permitted to venture into the heavenly Gan Eden. As the *Zohar* teaches:

> On Sabbath, at midnight, when the wise consummate their on Sabbath eve, all those hosts of holy angels who are appointed over Lower Gan Eden bring up from that region the souls which dwell there into . . . Gan Eden above, and bring them before the Throne of Glory. (II, 136a)

Since Lower Gan Eden is directly linked with the upper worlds (III, 159b), eventually the disembodied soul permanently leaves this realm and finally gets to experience the celestial delights of Upper Gan Eden.

Upper Gan Eden

As the soul travels on its postmortem journey, it ascends into the realms of Upper Gan Eden. As the *Zohar* states: "Still further within [Gan Eden] is a compartment reserved for the pious of a higher grade" (II, 130a).

Upon entering Upper Gan Eden, the soul is once again be immersed in the celestial River of Light, or *nehar dinur*. This second immersion heals the soul and purges it of any remaining defilements:

> A second ordeal has to be undergone by the soul on its passage from Lower Gan Eden to Upper Gan Eden; for while in Lower Gan Eden it is not yet entirely purged of the materialities of this world, so as to be fit to ascend on high. They thus pass it through the "river of light" from which it emerges completely purified and so come before the presence of the Master of the universe purified in every aspect. Also the rays of the celestial light afford it healing. This is its final stage. At that stage the souls stand garbed in their raiment and adorned in their crowns before their Master. (II, 211b)

In a number of places, we find mythic depictions of the nature and activities of Upper Gan Eden. It is said that a celestial music can be heard in that realm:

> As soon as the souls arrive at the gate of the firmament . . . [an Eagle with four faces] revolves three times round [Upper] Gan Eden, producing thereby such sweet music that all the souls come forth and listen and behold the rising of the pillar of fire and cloud and smoke and shining brightness, before which they all prostrate themselves. (III, 211a)

In addition, in Upper Gan Eden, it is said that life is organized into schools, or *yeshivot*, for the learning of Torah. One image used repeatedly to describe this region of Gan Eden is the "Celestial Academy," *yeshivah shel maalah* (I, 7a). Within this Celestial Academy, the divine mind of the immortal soul can attain a blissful understanding of God. Each midnight, God Himself appears within the Celestial Academy to visit and take delight in sharing His wisdom with the numerous souls of the righteous congregated there.[64]

Furthermore, within the supernal realms of Gan Eden there are continual gradations, increasingly elevated abodes where the finely purified and righteous dwell, each soul in accordance with the accumulated merit of their life. In the words of the *Zohar*, "there is in the next world a gradation of glorious abodes and resplendent lights, each outshining the other" (II, 130a). The more spiritually developed a soul, the higher the realm in which it abides:

> For there are many abodes prepared by the Holy One, blessed be each
> one according to his grade. . . . As the works of the righteous dif-
> fer in this world, so do their place and lights differ in the next world.
> (I, 129b)

Tzror Ha-Hayyim—Return to the Source

According to kabbalistic tradition, the soul does not repose in Gan
Eden is forever. In fact, there is still one additional, final stopping point
on the afterlife journey. Once souls complete their stay in the realms of
Gan Eden, they enter another region known as tzror ha-hayyim, usually
translated as "the bundle of the living." It is described in the texts as
follows:

> that holy celestial abode which is called "the bundle of the living,"
> where that holy superior grade called the super-soul [neshamah] re-
> gales itself with the supernal delights. (III, 70a)
>   . . . the virtuous who are thought to be worthy to be "bound
> up in the bundle of the living" are privileged to see the glory of the
> supernal Holy King, and their abode is higher than that of all the
> holy angels. (III, 182b)
>   . . . in the same way as the soul has to be clothed in a bodily
> garment in order to exist in this world, so is she given an ethereal
> supernal garment wherewith to exist in the other world, and to be
> enabled to gaze at the effulgence of life radiating from that "land of
> the living." (I, 66a)

This realm of the hereafter called tzror ha-hayyim is a "storehouse
of souls." Upon exiting the celestial Gan Eden, worthy souls enter tzror
ha-hayyim, which seems to be a realm designed specifically for souls returning from a completed postmortem sojourn.

To make a leap in our understanding of the afterlife journey: tzror
ha-hayyim is a region of the celestial realms where a disembodied soul
returns, in order to prepare for eventual rebirth. In contemporary language we might say that tzror ha-hayyim is a center of "Mission Control"
for souls, wherein they are given their assignment for their subsequent
incarnation. After passing through the various phases of the postmortem journey, the individual soul returns to the divine source of all life, in
order to prepare to reenter physical plane life in a newly fashioned body.

This understanding of *tzror ha-hayyim* is implicitly based on the kabbalistic doctrine of *gilgul*, or reincarnation of souls. Presently, we will explore the historical background of *gilgul* and its basis in the *Zohar*.

GILGUL—THE KABBALISTIC DOCTRINE OF REINCARNATION

Reincarnation—A Jewish Belief

Inherent to the kabbalistic view of life after death is the doctrine of reincarnation of souls, an ancient teaching found among religious traditions throughout the world.[65] This philosophical belief asserts that after death a soul eventually returns to earth and assumes a new physical body, appropriate to the evolutionary lessons required for a subsequent lifetime.

Over the course of centuries, the kabbalists repeatedly spoke about how souls, once they have assimilated the spiritual learning of the highest heavenly realm, are subject to reincarnation. Through the process of physical reimbodiment, the soul can bring about a restitution for the wrongdoings of a previous life and attain further perfection.[66]

However, the rationalistic biases that impelled twentieth-century Jews to disregard ancient traditions on the afterlife likewise concealed from awareness the legacy of teachings on reincarnation.[67] As a result, many contemporary Jews, as well as non-Jews, are often astonished to discover that this concept is given expression in Judaism. Yes, kabbalists do believe in reincarnation! And after the twelfth century, reincarnation is as kosher to Judaism as is Mogen David wine.

In fact, this doctrine of reincarnation—termed by the kabbalists as *gilgul*, or "wheel," or "revolution"—had an important and expansive effect on Judaism's teachings on the postmortem fate of the individual. In addition to descriptions of death and the process of separation from the physical plane, Gehenna and its purgations, and the bliss of Gan Eden, we find in kabbalistic writings, including the *Zohar*, a considerable body of teachings on the why and wherefore of the soul's reincarnation.

Historical Background

The notion of transmigration of souls has no basis in Jewish writings of the biblical period. Likewise, there is no reference to this doctrine in either talmudic or midrashic literature.[68] However, by use of allegorical interpretation, the kabbalists did find allusions to *gilgul* in biblical texts. For example, the verse from Ecclesiastes 1:4: "One generation passes away, another generation comes" is interpreted to mean that a generation dies and subsequently returns via the process of reincarnation.[69] However, this is a much later interpretative hermeneutic used to "prove" the biblical roots of reincarnation. But in classical Judaism of biblical and rabbinic times, there is absolutely no evidence of a belief in transmigration of souls.

So, how did the doctrine of reincarnation, with ancient roots in Hinduism and Platonic philosophy, enter into Judaism? From the second century on, these philosophical teachings were part of the worldview of many Gnostic, Orphic, and Manichean sects. As Gershom Scholem suggests, they may have found their way into Judaism via an ancient Jewish Gnostic tradition. In addition, there are parallels between kabbalistic views of reincarnation and those of the twelfth-century Christian Cathars, who lived in close geographical proximity to the kabbalistic communities of southern France. However, ultimately there has been no final determination with regard to the source of Judaism's teachings on reincarnation, and even Scholem himself asserts that many questions about the historical origins of the doctrine of *gilgul* remain unanswered.[70]

Nevertheless, it is clear that during the Middle Ages, the doctrine of reincarnation began to seep into Judaism. In the eighth century, Anan ben David, founder of Karaism, a Jewish sectarian movement, espoused a belief in transmigration and this doctrine is reflected in his writings. In the tenth century, the medieval philosopher Saadia Gaon rejected the notion of transmigration of souls, speaking about the "nonsense and stupidities" of such beliefs.[71] Yet his disapproval suggests that even at that point Jews were embracing some form of teachings on reincarnation.

Despite any philosophical opposition, teachings on the reincarnation of souls became increasingly popular in kabbalistic circles. The first literary expression of this doctrine is found in the *Sefer Bahir*, which dates from c. 1150 to 1200. In the *Sefer Bahir* transmigration is cast as an esoteric doctrine, explicated through metaphor and parable but never directly.[72] By the end of the twelfth century reincarnation had become important to the community of Provençal kabbalists that had produced the *Sefer Bahir*. It was said that one of their spiritual leaders, Isaac the Blind (c. 1200), could observe a person's face and determine whether one was a new soul or an old soul who had reincarnated.[73]

By the fourteenth century, writings on transmigration became even more widespread, particularly among the kabbalists of Gerona. However, this kabbalistic community also viewed reincarnation as a profound mystery and an esoteric doctrine, and still used allegory, hints, and allusions to speak about the subject.[74]

The kabbalists of Gerona had a strong impact on the Spanish kabbalists who produced the *Zohar*. One generation later this esoteric doctrine became much more widespread. From the time of the *Zohar* onward, belief in reincarnation becomes prevalent in kabbalistic circles. Within the *Zohar* there are explicit and eloquent discourses on reincarnation and the transmigration of souls, such as the following:[75]

> Truly, all souls, must undergo transmigration; but men do not perceive the ways of the Holy One, how the revolving scale is set up and men are judged every day at all time, and how they are brought up before the Tribunal, both before they enter into this world and after they leave it. They perceive not the many transmigrations and the many mysterious works which the Holy One accomplishes with many naked souls, and how many naked spirits roam about, in the other world without being able to enter within the veil of the King's Palace. (III, 99b)

Some of the terms used in kabbalistic literature when speaking about the notion of reincarnating souls include *ha-atakah*—"transference"; a translation of the Arabic term *tanasukh*; *hithallefut*—"exchange"; *ibbur*—"impregnation"; and finally, the word that became most popular in mystical and philosophical writings, *gilgul*.[76]

Another term, used by Rabbi Menasseh ben Israel, is *din gilgul neshamot*, literally, "the law of the revolution of souls." Ben Israel, author of *Nishmat Hayyim* ("The Soul of Life"), addresses the topic of transmigration quite extensively. The view he expresses in the following passage demonstrates how deeply reincarnation doctrine penetrated into the Jewish world:

> The belief or the doctrine of transmigration of souls is a firm and infallible dogma accepted by the whole assemblage of our [community] with one accord, so that there is none to be found who would dare to deny it. . . . Indeed, there is a great number of sages in Israel who hold firm to this doctrine so that they made it a dogma, a fundamental point of our religion. We are therefore in duty bound

to obey and to accept this dogma with acclamation . . . as the truth
of it has been incontestably demonstrated by the Zohar, and all books
of the kabbalists.[77]

Purpose of Gilgul

Kabbalistic conceptions of gilgul evolved in stages, and as to be expected, there are a wide variety of often-conflicting views on reincarnation.

Initially, there was an inherent tension between this new notion of
gilgul and the classical doctrine of postmortem purgation in Gehenna. Not
everyone reincarnated. In fact, there was a tendency to limit reincarnation to only particular categories of sinners, and most people were believed to be punished with the torments of Gehenna. However, over time,
there was a philosophical shift, and the doctrine of reincarnation was
applied more widely.[78]

For the early kabbalists, transmigration of souls was not a universal
law. Only those guilty of sexual transgressions and offenses against procreation were to reincarnate. In such cases, gilgul functioned as a way of
administering God's punitive justice.[79] For example, in the main part
of Zohar and in a section entitled Midrash Ha-Ne'elam, it was taught that
a man and woman who did not conceive a child were subjected to reincarnation. Since the commandment to "be fruitful and multiply"
was so highly valued in Judaism, and since the mystical kabbalistic
worldview was replete with teachings about divine union of masculine
and feminine principles, the inability to conceive new life was regarded
as a sin against the cosmic order. Thus, the man who did not propagate
the species would be required by God to return to embodied human existence in order fulfill that duty which he had neglected (II, 186b; III, 25a).[80]

Other kabbalists spoke about how all evildoers [rasha] were subjected to reincarnation. Biblical and rabbinic law taught that those who
had transgressed the Torah's sexual codes were evildoers, to be punished
with karet, meaning "extinction of the soul." However, through the doctrine of gilgul an element of divine mercy was introduced. Transmigration of the soul enabled those who had committed sexual offenses to
experience some form of restitution, and thus avoid being wiped out totally by the punishment of karet. Through reembodiment one could be
given the gift of another lifetime in order to make amends for sins committed.[81]

Thus, for example, Scholem writes about a kabbalist named Rabbi Sheshet des Mercadell, a disciple of Nahmanides, who believed that all evildoers were subjected to reincarnation. According to these teachings,

> only evildoers [rasha] are subject to transmigration. Divine love and severity thus balance out one another; by saving their souls from obliteration in the fires of [Gehenna], God performs an act of mercy, giving them a chance to cleanse themselves by a new, though agonizing transmigration. . . .[82]

With the passing of time, other kabbalistic authors taught that not just evildoers [rasha] but also middling folk [beinonim] and righteous ones [tzaddikim] were subject to transmigration. Why righteous? Because through reincarnation, the perfected righteous person [tzaddik], in a manner similar to the enlightened Buddhist bodhisattva, can assist other aspiring beings to attain greater and greater spiritual perfection.

Regardless of how reincarnation was understood and whether justice or mercy was emphasized, gilgul had as "its singular purpose . . . the purification of the soul and the opportunity, in a new trial, to improve its deeds."[83]

Transmigration into Animal Bodies

One controversial issue among the kabbalists was whether or not souls could transmigrate into the bodies of animals. This idea was originally put forth in Sefer Ha-Temunah (written before 1250) and Taamei Ha-Mitzvot (c. 1290–1300). This was a punishment allocated for sexual acts prohibited by the Torah. Although this belief grew in popularity, both Sefer Ha-Bahir and the Zohar itself are silent on issue of rebirth in the body of an animal and teach only of reembodiment into human form. Nonetheless, there were kabbalists who taught this view of reincarnation.[84]

For example, there was a spiritual leader of Modena, Italy, named Rabbi Barukh Abraham da Spoleto. In 1585 he caused quite an uproar in his community after delivering a Sabbath sermon on the subject gilgul, in which he maintained that the souls of those who sinned against God were condemned to transmigrate into the bodies of animals. When word of his teachings got out into the community, he was directly challenged by other authorities, in particular Abraham ben Hananiah Yagel, who found such a view to be heretical to the kabbalistic philosophy of the *Zohar*.[85]

The reason reincarnation into animal bodies was a problematic issue for the kabbalists was that it contradicted a basic understanding of *gilgul* as a process of purification designed to improve the evolutionary fate of the soul.[86] Rebirth into animal form was seen as a downward movement along the evolutionary ladder. Recognizing this dilemma, certain kabbalists offered a metaphoric interpretation of reincarnation into animal bodies, suggesting that this was equivalent to the sufferings of Gehenna. However, this kind of understanding was not widespread among kabbalists,[87] and this controversy continued unabated throughout the fourteenth, fifteenth, and sixteenth centuries. Over time, however, the philosophical teaching limiting reincarnation to human bodies emerged as the dominant view. Nonetheless, the idea that one could be reborn as an animal was never completely eliminated from Jewish thought and appears centuries later in the Eastern European folk tradition.[88]

Gilgul for the Purpose of Fulfilling the Mitzvot

Kabbalistic teachings on *gilgul* were harmonized with the spirit of rabbinic theology. According to the *Zohar*, the extent of one's obedience to the precepts of Jewish law during life incarnate directly determined whether or not one had to undergo *gilgul*.

In *Tikkunei Zohar*, we find an important new idea that shaped kabbalistic views of *gilgul*. According to Scholem,

> the author of *Tikkunei Zohar* developed another new theory, which acquired major importance in the history of these ideas. The primal shape of man corresponds to the mystical shape of the Godhead. . . . Everything in man, each of his 248 limbs and 365 sinews, corresponds to one of the supernal lights, as these are arranged in the structure of the *Shi'ur Komah*, the primal shape of the highest manifestation of God. Man's task is to bring his own true shape to its spiritual perfection, to develop the divine image within himself. This is done by observing the 248 positive and 365 negative commandments of the Torah, each one of which is linked to one of the organs of the human body, and hence of one of those supernal lights. Whoever fulfills the Torah properly makes his body into a dwelling place for the

Shekhinah. But a person must undergo *gilgul* for every limb that does not become a "Throne for the *Shekhinah*"—that is, for every commandment that a man fails to observe or prohibition that he transgresses—until he has carried out his original task.[89]

This idea is evidenced in the following passage from *Tikkunei Zohar*:

> [I]f there is even one organ in which the Holy Blessed One does not dwell, then he will be brought back into the world in reincarnation because of this organ, until he becomes perfected in his parts, that all of them may be perfect in the image of the Holy Blessed One. (*Tikkunei Zohar*, 70, 132a)

Since there were 613 commandments, each one sacred and requiring specific holy actions, it was necessary to reincarnate to assure that the religious obligation of each would be completed. Thus, at the level of religious practice, *gilgul* would allow for a deeper involvement in the path of fulfillment of *mitzvot*. However, at a spiritual level, the successive reincarnations of *gilgul* enable a soul to evolve and to open to deeper dimensions of divine perception. According to this doctrine, if one has fulfilled all the commandments, or *mitzvot*, it is possible to fully awaken each of the 248 spiritual limbs and 365 spiritual veins of the human form, that is, to develop the spiritual body. If not, *gilgul* was mandated over and over, and the individual would evolve in order to fully awaken the undeveloped spiritual body.

Gilgul and the Soul

According to Chaim Vital, author of *Shaar Ha-Gilgulim*,[90] each of the five levels of the soul must be perfected. If there is a level of the soul not fully actualized during one's lifetime, there must be a *gilgul* to continue the process of the soul's evolution.[91] If during one incarnation an individual perfects the *nefesh*, or vital, level of the soul, in a subsequent life the individual must perfect the *ruah*. Similarly, once the *ruah* is perfected, the task is then to refine *neshamah*. Ultimately, the process of *gilgul* continues indefinitely, so that the *nefesh*, *ruah*, and *neshamah* are able to develop to perfection.[92] Thus, the individual continually reincarnates and ultimately guarantees the complete purification and evolution of the soul.[93]

IBBUR AND *DYBBUK*

Gilgul on the Folk Level

As Lurianic Kabbalah grew as a socioreligious force, *gilgul*—the belief in transmigration of souls—was infused with the superstitious spirit characteristic of Eastern European Jewry. For centuries, the Jewish masses had believed in spirits that wandered among the living. Both biblical and rabbinic texts contained stories describing various forms of spirit possession.[94] It was believed that these wandering spirits, on a moment's notice, could possess the body of one still alive.[95]

It was not a far step from this belief to the notion of possession by one who had died and was preparing for or desiring reincarnation. Two words used in this context are *ibbur*, literally "impregnation"—benign possession; an *dybbuk*, from the Hebrew word meaning "cleaving" or "clinging"—malevolent possession.

Ibbur: Benign Possession

The term *ibbur* evolved in kabbalistic circles in the second half of the thirteenth century. It refers to benign possession, when a soul enters a body and soul of one incarnate on earth. It was believed that such a supplementary soul might occupy the body of a living being for a limited period of time, specifically with the intention of performing a specific task, or fulfilling incomplete *mitzvot*.[96]

Explaining the notion of *ibbur* found in the *Zohar*, Scholem writes:

Not all migrating souls enter the new body at the moment of conception or of birth; sometimes, at special moments during the course of his life, a person receives a second soul that is, so to speak, impregnated within his own soul. This additional soul is not linked to his psychophysical organism from birth and nor does it partake in its development, but it can accompany him until his death or may leave him earlier. According to the *Zohar*, the souls of certain pious figures in the Bible were impregnated with the deceased souls of other righteous men from the past at decisive moments in their lives. Hence the soul of Judah entered that of Boaz, while those of Aaron's two sons, Nadab and Abiihu, entered that of Phineas.[97]

In the kabbalistic communities of Safed, the doctrine of *ibbur* held a place of importance. It fit in well and was a natural extension of the philosophy of reincarnating souls. A righteous, spiritualized soul can come into *ibbur*—impregnated within the soul of another being. Often, through an encounter with an *ibbur*, a living person can be raised to exalted heights of consciousness.[98] The *ibbur* can offer benevolent assistance to the living by providing information on future life events, guidance, and blessing.

In turn, the living person can help the discarnate soul. A righteous soul can avoid a complete additional incarnation by temporary reincarnation as an *ibbur*. Entering the body of a living person, at a fortuitous moment, a disembodied soul can perform an unfulfilled *mitzvah*, and in this way, through contact with the living, receive the merit needed for a minor atonement.[99]

The practice of naming children after deceased relatives may have evolved in connection with the doctrine of *ibbur*. This custom, widespread among Ashkenazic Jews, can be seen as "a means of affording the departed another return to life or of creating affinities so that it, as an *ibbur*, may help their offspring and receive their help in return."[100]

Dybbuk: Malevolent Possession

While the *ibbur* is a benign possession, seventeenth- to nineteenth-century textual traditions record numerous instances of evil possession. The *ibbur* of a wicked person into the soul of another is referred to as a *dybbuk*.

Dybbukim (Hebrew, plural), according to Gershom Scholem,

> were generally considered to be souls, which, on account of the enormity of their sins, were not even allowed to transmigrate and as "denuded spirits" they sought refuge in the bodies of living persons. The entry of a *dybbuk* into a person was a sign of his having committed a secret sin which opened a door for the *dybbuk*.[101]

Gershon Winkler points out the difference between *dybbuk* and *gilgul*:

> A *dybbuk* is a departed soul which cleaves spontaneously to another person prior to its ascent for divine judgment. A *gilgul*, on the other hand, involves a soul which has returned to wander the earth after

having faced the heavenly tribunal. A *gilgul* possession is a complete manifestation of the invading soul in the person of the victim; the victim's own consciousness becomes, in a way, suspended. A *dybbuk* possession, however, is not a total "takeover" of the victim's consciousness; both the *dybbuk* and the victim remain conscious and co-exist in the victim's body.[102]

Historical Background

The word *dybbuk*—from the Hebrew root *davok*, meaning "cleaving" or "clinging"—does not appear in the *Zohar*, but became a common term among German and Eastern European Jews in the seventeenth century.[103] However, "in Jewish folklore and popular belief [there had always been descriptions of] an evil spirit or a doomed soul which enters into a living person, cleaves to his soul, causes mental illness, talks through his mouth, and represents a separate and alien personality."[104]

Talmudic literature refers to this evil spirit as *ruah tezazit*, similar to the New Testament appellation "unclean spirit." *Dybbuk* is an abbreviation of *dibbuk me-ruah raah*, "a cleavage of an evil spirit," or *dibbuk min ha-hizonim*, "a *dybbuk* from the demonic side."[105] Thus, "the attachment of the spirit to the body became the name of the spirit itself."[106]

Originally, *dybbukim* were considered demons possessing the fragile body of a sick person. But later, the explanation was added "that some of the *dybbukim* were the spirits of dead persons who were not laid to rest and thus became demons."[107] With the spread of the doctrine of *gilgul*, *dybbukim* were seen as wicked souls, unable to transmigrate, who would possess selected, weakened, and receptive individuals, often for vengeance.

The earliest literary use of the term *dybbuk* dates from 1602, with the publication of the *Maaseh Book* ("The Book of Stories") in Germany.[108] In this story

> the spirit which took possession of a young man was the spirit of one who in this life had sinned egregiously, and which could therefore find no peace. It had entered the youth's body after having been forced to flee its previous abode, the body of a cow which was about to be slaughtered.[109]

Stories of this nature were widespread in subsequent centuries, demonstrating the influence of kabbalistic teachings on *gilgul*, *ibbur*, and *dybbuk*. Throughout Eastern Europe and Germany there was a fusing of philosophical teachings on *gilgul* with superstitious fears of spirit possession, producing what sometimes amounted to a cultural preoccupation with *dybukkim*.

Exorcism of a *Dybbuk* in Lurianic Kabbalah

The kabbalistic writings of Luria's disciples, as well as hasidic literature, contain innumerable stories on the exorcism of *dybbukim*. Texts by Chaim Vital, Eliezer ben Eliyahua ha-Rofeh, and Menasseh ben Israel provide very specific details for the exorcism ritual.[110] Many hasidic Rebbes were known for their successful exorcisms of *dybbukim*.[111]

In one instance, described by Schachter-Shalomi, the Rebbe convenes a court, a *Bet Din*. Together with two additional judges and the presence of a *minyan*, the court is called to order with the permission of the Heavenly Court.[112] The *dybbuk* is questioned and eventually condemned to return to its realm of discarnate wandering.

Dybbuk stories held the fascination of European Jews for centuries, and became even more popular in the seventeenth to nineteenth centuries. As we shall see in subsequent chapters, this idea of the *dybbuk* emerges as a significant motif in hasidic tales and in Eastern European folk literature. Out of the new kabbalistic doctrine of *gilgul* was born the notion of *dybbuk*. Once again, what is a seminal idea in one era of Jewish history becomes central to, and characteristic of, Jewish afterlife teachings in a subsequent epoch.

RESURRECTION

Resurrection and *Gilgul*

To complete this survey of kabbalistic afterlife teachings, we need to mention, at least briefly, kabbalistic views of resurrection. As Jews committed to rabbinic tradition, the kabbalists embraced the doctrine of the resurrection of the dead. It was an inherent part of their mystical, metaphysical worldview, an underlying perennial truth of Jewish tradition.

The early Kabbalah does not cast any doubt on the notion of a physical resurrection of the dead at the end-of-days, the time of collective redemption. Following "the great day of judgment," the radiant, perfected soul will reenter a fully resurrected body. For the kabbalists, this resurrected body will be totally spiritualized and transformed.

The kabbalists linked resurrection and *gilgul* by asking an important question in Jewish eschatology: If human beings have lived numerous *gilgulim*, incarnations, in different physical bodies, into which body will the resurrected soul enter? This question is discussed in the *Zohar*: "What will happen to a number of bodies which shared in succession the same soul? [it asks]. Only the last that had been firmly planted and took root will come to life."[113]

Resurrection of a Spiritualized Body

In the kabbalistic scheme, the resurrected body, subsequent to the time of messianic redemption, is regarded as a physical body totally infused with the radiant luster of the awakened soul. According to Kabbalah, in this life it is the soul that invigorates the body. But in the future life of resurrection the body will then be invigorated by the soul. This is so, according to the kabbalists, because the physical body—capable of procreating, of creating new things, of doing *mitzvot*—is therefore closer to the absolute of God than is the soul.[114]

Explaining this further, Schachter-Shalomi writes:

> The soul without the body is only able to enjoy the actualization of the potential, but it cannot actualize new potential. The soul living in the resurrected body, and the resurrected soul harboring the reincarnated soul, live in an unobstructed universe infused with the light-radiant infinitude of God, a universe in which creativity is not only possible, but inevitable.[115]

Spiritual Resurrection

In the kabbalistic communities of Safed, from whence evolved clear guidelines to the individual's postmortem soul journey, the notion of a resurrection was downplayed. The belief in a physical resurrection could not be fully harmonized with the spiritual, metaphysical cosmology of Lurianic Kabbalah. Similarly, the early *hasidim* deemphasized the doctrine of bodily resurrection.[116]

The doctrine of resurrection was interpreted by later Jewish mystics in a spiritual sense—"a materialization of the level of the spiritual body that the soul has built for many incarnations." Furthermore, "those souls that have not completed their spiritual body will, at the resurrection, materialize here on earth to perform the remaining *mitzvot* required of them in an environment free of death and evil."[117]

But for the kabbalists, even the resurrection itself is not the ultimate state of being. The fully awakened soul within a spiritualized, resurrected body is actually divinity itself fully realized. This soul merges with the source of the Divine Being, or in the words of the *Zohar*, it becomes "absorbed in the very body of the King."[118] This is the ultimate attainment.[119]

SUMMARY

This chapter has delineated the diverse depictions of the afterlife in the teachings of kabbalistic Judaism, in particular, the *Zohar*. From the material presented, the following observations can be made about the postmortem conceptions of Kabbalah:

1. According to kabbalistic teachings, each dimension of the multileveled soul—*nefesh, ruah, neshamah, hayyah, yehidah*—goes through different experiences on the afterlife journey. The lower levels of the soul are purified and purged of physical and emotional attachments, while the higher levels experience transcendental bliss.

2. Kabbalistic teachings demonstrate an acute understanding of the dying process itself. The *Zohar* and other mystical texts describe deathbed visions, the postmortem life review and judgment, and the painful separation of body from soul/spirit.

3. Within the kabbalistic tradition Gehenna is conceived of as a purification process in which psychic remnants from the previous life are purged and transformed. This purgation process lasts only twelve months and is tormentingly painful in direct proportion to each individual's lived life experience.

4. For the kabbalists, Gan Eden is conceived of in a dual sense. Lower Gan Eden is the realm in which one experiences the bliss of the higher emotions; Upper Gan Eden is yet a more transcendental realm in which one realizes the results of one's lofty, spiritual thoughts of the previous life and communes directly with God.

5. *Gilgul*, the doctrine of reincarnation, became increasingly important in kabbalistic Judaism from the twelfth century onward. For the kabbalists, the process of physical reembodiment made it possible for one to fulfill all the *mitzvot*, or commandments.

6. At the folk level, *gilgul* led to the development of an extensive literary tradition on possession by reincarnating spirits. The terms used in this context were *dybbukkim*, spirits of malevolent possession, and *ibburrim*, souls of benevolent possession.

7. The kabbalists reaffirmed the rabbinic belief in resurrection of the dead. However, they added a spiritual context to this doctrine, understanding the resurrection as being a materialization of the fully awakened spiritual body.

8. In kabbalistic writings, a psychological orientation to the postmortem journey is evident. Although the rabbinic doctrine of divine retribution underlies kabbalistic eschatology, the kabbalists made a significant contribution to Jewish afterlife tradition by developing a more psychologically oriented description of the after-death experiences. The afterlife teachings of the kabbalists are couched more in a psychological tone than uniquely in an ethical one. Gan Eden and Gehenna are not simply regions of reward or punishment; they are postmortem spiritual states of awareness that mirror the quality of one's emotional and mental consciousness while alive in the physical body.

Chapter 9

Death and the Afterlife
in Hasidic Tales

THE HISTORICAL CONTEXT

Continuing our historical journey, we now enter into the world of Hasidism, a mystical movement that burst upon the stage of Jewish history in the mid-eighteenth century. In this chapter we will explore beliefs about life after death afterlife in hasidic folktales.

Hasidism was founded in the Podolia and Volhynia regions of the Ukraine by the charismatic preacher and miracle worker Rabbi Israel Baal Shem Tov. By emphasizing devotional ecstasy and religious fervor over and above scholarship and legalism, the hasidic movement became a force for revolutionary change challenging the overintellectualized severity of talmudic Judaism. During his lifetime the Baal Shem Tov aroused unabated opposition from the rabbinic leaders of his era. Repeatedly, he was accused of downplaying the importance of talmudic learning, undermining religious practice, sabotaging traditional worship, and disrespecting conventional norms of behavior and social relationship.[1]

All the criticism not withstanding, the Baal Shem Tov's teachings appealed to a deep yearning among the uneducated classes of Jews. In less than a generation, Hasidism captivated the Jewish masses, spreading like a raging fire, to become a widespread folk movement. By the early nineteenth century, hasidic enclaves were found throughout Eastern

Europe—in the Ukraine, Eastern Galicia, Poland, Lithuania, White Russia, Rumania, and Hungary.[2]

Philosophically, Hasidism shared a common worldview with kabbalistic Judaism. Whereas Kabbalah was an elitist school of sixteenth-century mysticism, Hasidism was a populist movement that brought the esotericism of Moses de Leon and Isaac Luria to the masses, evolving entirely new forms of divine communion that centered on prayer and devotion, rather than on cosmology and metaphysical speculation.

Unique to Hasidism was the notion of the *tzaddik*, literally the "righteous one," the evolved spiritual leader who was seen as a divine manifestation on earth. According to the Baal Shem Tov, the ideal goal of the spiritual life was to become godlike, embodying God's attributes in human form. Given the Baal Shem Tov's profound spiritual prowess, as long as he was alive, he was regarded as the living symbol and the penultimate embodiment of this ideal.[3] However, knowing that "at least in its material form, this symbol would soon be broken . . . [he] created what is perhaps the most daring innovation of the sect he had founded, the *tzaddik*."[4] The Baal Shem Tov emphasized the importance of loving the *tzaddik* and cleaving to him as a way of drawing closer to God and bringing on oneself God's blessing.

Two disciples of the Baal Shem Tov, Yakov Yosef of Polnoi, author of *Toldot Yakov Yosef*, and Elimelekh of Lyzhansk, author of *Noam Elimelekh* (1787), further expounded upon the doctrine of the *tzaddik*. Yakov Yosef encouraged the aspiring *hasid* to surrender in complete faith to the *tzaddik*, whose actions, he maintained, were carried out exclusively for sake of heaven. As the intermediary between man and God, the *tzaddik* was the vehicle through which divine blessing, *shefa*, was transmitted to humanity, and thus the source of divine grace for the *hasid*. In addition, Yakov Yosef taught that the *tzaddik* was also a spiritual redeemer of souls.

Going even further, Elimelekh of Lyzhansk depicted the *tzaddik* as a superhuman being, one who is endowed with power over the universe, over life and death itself. According to Elimelekh, the *tzaddik*, by the inherent power of his prayers

> provided his followers with health, children, and livelihood: he healed the sick, made barren women fertile, guaranteed success in business, provided protection from persecution, freed captives, and could even nullify a decree by God that a person should die.[5]

The *tzaddik* came to be seen as an individual charged with personal charisma and magical powers who, for the *hasid*, or disciple, played the role of "cosmic redeemer, redeemer of the individual soul, and protector . . . from evil spirits."[6] With God-given powers to influence the heavenly spheres, the *tzaddik* had the ability to affect the destiny of human beings, not only in this world, but ultimately, in the world beyond death.[7]

Integrating the doctrine of the *tzaddik* with kabbalistic notions of the journeying postmortem soul, Hasidism ultimately evolved a model of a holy man who had the ability to control life and death and to sojourn into the worlds beyond death, in ways similar to the shamans of many primordial cultures.[8]

THE HASIDIC TALE

As the hasidic movement spread, there were at first dozens, then literally hundreds of individual hasidic Rebbes who were revered by their disciples as wonder-working *tzaddikim*. Traditions evolved in which the wondrous deeds of the charismatic hasidic masters were told in story form. Since the Baal Shem Tov himself did not do any writing, the earliest hasidic stories were originally preserved through oral transmission. However, Dov Baer, the Maggid of Mezhirich, foremost disciple and successor of the Baal Shem Tov, compiled and authored the first collection of hasidic tales. Known as *Shivhei Ha-Besht*, "In Praise of the Baal Shem Tov,"[9] this collection of legends emphasized the importance of the founder of the hasidic movement and served to exalt his wondrous deeds.

As a folkloristic genre of communication, the art of storytelling was easily adapted and rapidly institutionalized in the grassroots, populist hasidic movement. During the sacred meals of the Sabbath and holy days, it was common to transmit hasidic wisdom via tales and parables highlighting the spiritual achievements of the Baal Shem Tov and his disciples.[10] In subsequent generations, as famous Rebbes died, their legacies were preserved and transmitted through stories and legends. It became a common practice in hasidic circles to hold a sacred feast on a Rebbe's *Yahrzeit*, the anniversary of a death. On such occasions, the *hasidim* would celebrate the elevation of the soul by singing, dancing, teaching Torah, and telling tales in commemoration of the life and deeds of a beloved, deceased Rebbe.[11] In very little time, the hasidic story, or

meiseh, became the characteristic literary genre of Hasidism, and continues as such to this day.[12]

The popularity of hasidic legends can be explained in terms of the
doctrine of the *tzaddik*. Given Hasidism's unique reverence for the *tzaddik*,
it was necessary to communicate the promethean spiritual accomplishments of the Rebbes. Emphasizing the miraculous and heroic over and
above historical biography, the hasidic *meiseh* became the vehicle for such
communication. Hasidic tales served to glorify the Rebbes, validate their
supramundane spiritual abilities, and, in turn, reaffirm the doctrine of
the *tzaddik* as miracle worker. As Ben-Zion Dinur notes:

> Most of the hasidic stories represent a type of propaganda in a liter-
> ary-didactic form, directed in general at "reaffirming belief in
> *tzaddikim*," reinforcing faith in the ability of man to reach a higher
> spiritual plane through his belief in the *tzaddikim*; and sometimes they
> are intended to enhance the influence of other *tzaddikim* in particu-
> lar and to heighten devotion of their followers. Moreover, the reli-
> gious value of a story about a *tzaddik* and his saintly deeds lies in the
> telling itself, regardless of any connection to historical reality or ac-
> tual events.[13]

HASIDIC TALES AS SOURCES
FOR STUDYING THE AFTERLIFE

Hasidic tales focus on all aspects of life experience, but they are especially concerned with transformative events such as birth, marriage, illness, personal calamity, and death.[14] In particular, we find innumerable
stories on the mysteries of death and dying and on encounters with the
spirits of the dead. The sacred moments of the deathbed; ways of dying
peacefully and in communion with the higher spiritual realms; visionary
states of consciousness associated with death; visitations from the spirits
of Rebbes and other departed ones; the nature of life in Gehenna and
Gan Eden; the enigma of reincarnation—all these are the topics of consideration in hasidic tales. Regardless of their historical authenticity, these
types of legends provide a rich repository of afterlife teachings, and demonstrate the inherent beliefs that the *hasidim* held about death, immortality, and postmortem survival. As we will discover, underlying these
kinds of stories is a spiritual worldview that understands death as a tran-

sition to another realm of consciousness, to a state of disembodied awareness in which there is a continued relationship with the realm of the living.

This chapter presents a compilation of hasidic legends highlighting the themes of death, dying, and the postmortem wanderings of the soul. The main sources used here are Martin Buber's two-volume anthology *Tales of the Hasidim*,[15] supplemented by other sources such as *Shivhei Ha-Besht*[16] and *The Hasidic Anthology*, translated and edited by Louis Newman.[17] *Tales of the Hasidim* does contain stories that were edited or reconstructed by Buber himself, in his attempt to "supply the missing links in the narrative."[18] Nonetheless, the various legends collated by Buber certainly depict with acuity ways in which the *hasidim* perceived a life after death. Wherever possible, references to the original Hebrew and Yiddish sources for the various hasidic stories are included in the notes of this chapter.[19]

By way of structure, the hasidic tales presented here are arranged according to a schema moving from the predeath experience to the higher Edenic experiences. Even if not always apparent, this schema is designed to resemble the outline of kabbalistic teachings in Chapter 8.

ATTITUDES TOWARD DEATH

Dying and Living

Rabbi Simhah Bunem lay dying. In her grief, his wife burst into tears. He said to her: "Why are you crying? My whole life was only that I might learn how to die." And with this attitude, he died, peacefully.[20]

This acceptance of death was common among the Rebbes. Dying is part of living; and both life and death are a fulfillment of God's destiny. The *hasid* who devoutly embraced God would accept equally, and with conviction, both life and death.

In commenting on the words from the Book of Psalms, "I shall not die but live" (Psalm 118:17), Rabbi Yitzhak of Vorki said: "In order to really live, a man must give himself to death. But when he has done so, he discovers that he is not to die—but to live."[21]

To accept death, for the *hasid*, is to affirm life; and to affirm the goodness of life is to guarantee oneself a place in *Olam Ha-Ba*, the World to Come. As Rabbi Simhah Bunem taught: "Life is good, for it may bring to a man the joys of the World to Come. Hence if one shows contempt for life by self-destruction, he is deprived of his share in the World to Come."[22]

Death without Fear

For the Rebbe who accepted God's grace into his life, there was absolutely no reason to fear death. Reb Elimelekh of Lyzhansk was extraordinarily cheerful as his death was approaching. When asked by a disciple for an explanation of his behavior, he replied: "Why should I not rejoice, seeing that I am about to leave this world below, and enter into the higher worlds of eternity? Do you not recall the words of the Psalmist: 'Yea, though I walk the valley of the shadow of death, I will fear no evil, for You are with me' (Psalm 23:4). Thus does the grace of God display itself."[23]

For some Rebbes, the fear of death and the acceptance of its inevitability could inspire a person to godliness. Once the Gerer Rebbe was traveling a steep and difficult road with his nephew. The horses found themselves on a dangerously steep incline and became terror-struck. The Rebbe's nephew cried out in fright, but his uncle remained calm and undisturbed. "Why cry out?" he asked. "A man ought to feel terror and premonition of mortal danger always, for he may die at any moment. King David was conscious of the imminence of death all the days of his life, and while under this emotion he composed his greatest psalms."[24]

Death in the Holocaust

Even amidst the terror, dehumanization, and desecration of the Holocaust, many hasidic Rebbes could accept their death, all the while affirming their faith in God through joy and song.

"With a Torah scroll in his hands, Meir Ofen, a kabbalist and *hasid* of the Dzikover Rebbe, led hundreds of Jews during their march to the mass grave, reciting from Psalm 33:1, 'Rejoice in God, righteous ones!'"[25]

"The Dombrover Rebbe, Rabbi Hayyim Yehiel Rubin, prayed the Sabbath meal service, his last, with great fervor, sang the Sabbath meal songs, and led twenty Jews in a hasidic dance prior to death in graves dug by themselves."[26]

"The Grodzisker Rebbe, Rabbi Yisrael Shapira, in an inspiring message before entering the gas chambers of Treblinka, urged Jews to accept

Kiddush Ha-Shem ["sanctification of God's Name in death"] with joy. He led in the singing of *Ani Maamin*."[27]

It was because the Hasidism upheld a belief in the afterlife that they could accept their death in a spirit of joyous devotion. As the Piazesner Rebbe had taught in the Warsaw ghetto: "Those who fail to praise God in death, will neither be aware of Him in the world to come."[28]

PREPARING FOR DEATH

Learning How to Die

There were hasidic Rebbes who invested time learning specifically how to die. The following stories indicate how the *hasidim* believed one could develop the ability to be consciously aware during the process of dying:

> A *hasid* of Rabbi Pinhas of Kinsk, a grandson of Rabbi Yerahmiel, once came into the master's room and found him lying down and playing with his watch. He was surprised because it was almost noon and the rabbi had not yet prayed. Just then Rabbi Yerahmiel said to the *hasid*: "You are surprised at what I am doing? But do you really know what I am doing? I am learning how to leave the world."[29]

> On Hanukkah, when Rabbi Abraham Moshe was in the city of Biala with his mother, he said to her: "Mother, I have a craving to die." She answered: "I heard from your father that one has to learn to die." He answered: "I have learned it." Again she said: "I heard from your father that one has to learn for a very long time, to learn it properly." He answered: "I have learned long enough," and lay down. He died on the seventh day of the feast. Later his mother found out that before going on his journey he had visited his favorite disciples and taken leave of them.[30]

Conscious Preparation for the Final Moment

By accepting the inevitability of death, the hasidic Rebbe could be totally prepared for the final moment of life, the moment of the transition to the other side. There is a story of one Rebbe who called together his disciples toward the end of the Sabbath. He taught them a new *niggun* (wordless melody) and requested they sing it for him. As they did, he leaned back, offering his soul to God, and died leaving this plane of existence consciously and prepared.[31]

Ensuring a Peaceful Death

The hasidic masters knew that the less attached one was to physical plane life and to the drama of one's personal life story, the easier it was to die peacefully. Certain attitudes and actions were considered ideal. Like their rabbinic and kabbalistic predecessors, the *hasidim* believed that an ethical, God-fearing life was always an effective way of preparing for a painless, peaceful death. As the Slonimer Rebbe taught: "Happy is who who end his days in repentance and holy service, and dies with a clear conscience."[32]

The story is told of the Maggid of Koznitz who, prior to his death, prayed ardently to God on the eve of Yom Kippur, asking for forgiveness. Not only did he request to be forgiven by God, but he demanded a definitive reply, exclaiming: "Therefore I beseech Thee: if it has been easy for me to take upon myself the yoke of Thy people, and to perform this service with my suffering body, how can it be burdensome for Thee to speak two words?" Instantly his being was filled with joy as he heard the words descend from on high: "I forgive." Soon after he died.[33]

In leaving behind the material world, everything had to be surrendered, even the fulfillment of the *mitzvot*, or divine commandments. On the day of his death, Rabbi Eisik of Zhydatchov awoke and put on his *tallis* and *tefillin* (prayer shawl and phylacteries) as always. Soon after he began the morning prayers he stopped, rapidly removed the prayer shawl and phylacteries, and said: "Today I am free of *tallis* and *tefillin* and *mitzvot*, and I shall soon be free of the world." He died that evening.[34]

PRECOGNITION OF DEATH

Precognition of One's Own Death

Many of the hasidic masters knew in advance when the end of life would arrive and often predicted their own death, or that of a disciple. Sometimes it was possible to sense the immediate imminence of death, but, on other occasions, there were Rebbes who knew weeks and months in advance that their death was drawing near.

"Today you must know, is the day of my death," said Rabbi Shmelke of Nikolsburg. As his disciples began to weep, he bade them to stop, spoke his last words, and after asking all present to leave him, leaned back and died.[35]

The Rabbi of Morchov, in the Ukraine, was a close friend of Rabbi Levi Yitzhak of Berditchev. When the *tzaddik* died, the Rabbi of Morchov came to the funeral and walked behind his bier. When they had transported the body out of the house, he approached it, leaned down, and whispered in the ear of the dead Rebbe. Only the last words were audible: "As it is written: 'Seven weeks you shall count.'" When seven weeks had passed, he himself died.[36]

Precognition of Another's Death

In a story from *Shivhei Ha-Besht*, the Baal Shem perceives the Angel of Death drawing near to a person, but to no avail for the unsuspecting and unrepentant individual:

A tenant farmer who had bad luck came to the Besht as well. The Besht saw the Angel of Death dancing behind him. He strongly warned him to repent of his sins: "Why do you pursue the affairs of this world? It would be better for you to repent and correct your ways."

The man suspected that the Besht wanted some money. He offered him some coins, but the Besht refused to take them. When the tenant farmer left, the Besht said: "The fool. He will die today or tomorrow, and he worries about his luck." His brother-in-law, the rabbi, our teacher, Rabbi Gershon, scolded him and said: "Why do you speak evil against a Jew?" He answered him: "What can I do about it if you are blind and did not see the Angel of Death following behind him." And the Besht went home.

At that time, the brother-in-law of the Besht, our rabbi and teacher, Jacob, was a widower, and he went on a journey to be remarried. He was accompanied by this same tenant farmer, since both of them had to go the same way.

They slept overnight at an inn neighboring the village of the tenant farmer. The tenant farmer ordered a fine dinner. Rabbi Jacob did not want to eat meat, and they gave him dairy food at the end of the table. The tenant farmer mocked him. Afterward they went to sleep. During the night the tenant farmer awoke with a severe headache and he cried out. He asked that someone say the right of confession with him. Since there was no one else to say the confession with him, Rabbi Jacob said the prayer and the tenant farmer recited the confession after him. Rabbi Jacob wondered about it. Then the tenant farmer's wife left him alone saying, "Perhaps he'll sleep for a while, and then he will feel better." But in a little while she looked at him and saw that he was dead.

Then Rabbi Jacob returned home to tell that indeed we are blind.[37]

Precognition of the Death of Another Rebbe

Many of the *tzaddikim* were deeply connected with each other. Their bond of spiritual kinship transcended physical limitations. There are thus many stories describing how, at the moment of another's death, the *tzaddik*, although in a different geographical location, is aware of the passing of a beloved friend:

> They tell that the hour Rabbi Levi Yitzhak died, a *tzaddik* teaching in a distant city suddenly interrupted his discourse in which he was trying to fuse the power of the doctrine with that of worship, and said to his disciples: "I cannot go on. Everything went dark before my eyes. The gates of prayer are closing. Something must have happened to the great worshiper, to Rabbi Levi Yitzhak."[38]
>
> On the Festival of Simchat Torah, the Ropshitzer stood at the window and saw how the *hasidim* celebrated and danced in the courtyard. He was in an exalted mood and his entire being was illumined with great joy. Suddenly he raised his hand, and everyone stopped, gazing up at him with faltering breath. For a while he stood in silence, his changed facial expressions revealing his frightened dismay. Gradually he recovered himself and turning to his disciples he cried out with great enthusiasm: "When one of the generals falls in battle, do the companies scatter and take flight? The fight goes on! Rejoice and dance!" Later it became known that at the very moment his friend, Rabbi Abraham of Ulanov, had breathed forth his soul, departing the earthly sphere.[39]

In another story, Rabbi Jacob Samson of Spitkova, who resided in the Holy Land, had a very powerful dream vision. He saw the *Shekhinah*, God's Divine Feminine Presence, in the form of a woman in lamentation; he sensed that her lamentation was for a friend of her youth who had died. He immediately awoke, and cried out with grief: "Reb Pinhas of Koretz has died." And so it was at the moment, on the continent of Europe, Reb Pinhas of Koretz had breathed his last.[40]

There is even a story in which the death of a Rebbe is known of in advance in the heavenly spheres:

> An old woman who sold vegetables in the marketplace said to her neighbor: "This morning at dawn—I don't know whether I was awake or dreaming—I saw my husband, may he rest in peace, who has been dead all these years. I saw him rush past without looking at me. Then I burst into tears and cried to him: 'First you go and leave me to a miserable life with my orphaned children and now you don't even look at me!' But he kept on running and didn't turn to give me a glance. As I sat there crying, I saw him come back. He stopped and said: 'I couldn't take any time off before. We had to fumigate the road and cleanse the air because the *tzaddikim* from the land of Israel cannot stand the air here, and they will soon be coming to receive the Rabbi of Apt and escort him to the other side.'"[41]

THE REBBE'S DEATHBED EXPERIENCES

Deathbed Visions

Hasidic literature abounds with stories describing the deathbed experiences of many hasidic Rebbes. These stories are often very detailed and show how many Rebbes made the transition from physical plane life with a sense of equanimity and calm.

There were some Rebbes able to describe the visions they witnessed as death approached. In the hour before he died, Rabbi Shmelke of Sasov saw standing beside him his deceased father, Rabbi Moshe Leib, and his great teacher, Rabbi Mikhal of Zlotchov.[42]

Rabbi Shneur Zalman of Liadi, shortly before his death, turned to his grandson and asked, "Do you see anything?" The boy looked at him in astonishment. Then the Rebbe said: "All I can see is the divine nothingness which gives life to the world."[43]

Transmission to Disciples

Upon his deathbed, Reb Elimelekh of Lyzhansk passed on to his disciples specific spiritual powers or talents he himself had possessed. To the Seer of Lublin he gave his eyes power to see; to Abraham Yeshua, his lips power to pronounce judgment; to Israel of Koznitz, his heart power to pray; and finally to Mendel, he gave his spirit power to guide.[44]

The Baal Shem Tov's Death

When the Baal Shem Tov fell ill shortly before his death, he would not take to his bed. His body grew weak, his voice faint, and he would sit alone in his room meditating. On the eve of Shavuot, the last evening of his life, his disciples gathered around him and he spoke to them about the giving of the Torah at Mount Sinai. In the morning he requested that all of them gather together in his room and he gave his final instructions for burial to members of the *Hevrah Kaddisha*. Afterward he asked for a *siddur* [prayer book] and said: "I wish to spend some time communing with *Ha-Shem Yitbarakh* [the Name, may He be blessed].

Then after his time spent in prayer and preparation for greeting the Angel of Death, he told his disciples that as a sign, at the moment of his death the two clocks in the house would stop.

The Baal Shem Tov then asked his disciples to sing Reb Zlotcher's melody and they did so. . . . After a while the Baal Shem Tov began to describe how the soul was leaving his body, first through the extremities, slowly, slowly . . . slowly. . . . Then in a quiet voice he said: "Now I can no longer speak with you." His disciples looked and noticed that at the moment, one clock in the house had stopped.

The Baal Shem Tov then motioned for his disciples to cover him with blankets and he began to shake and tremble as he did when praying the silent prayer. Finally he grew quiet, inhaled his last breath of air, and there was no exhalation, only stillness, peace. At that moment, the disciples noticed that the second clock in the house had stopped too.

And those who buried the Baal Shem Tov said they had seen his soul ascend toward the heavens as a blue flame.[45]

The Death of Reb Shlomo of Karlin

When Reb Shlomo of Karlin was living in Ludmir, the Russians put down a revolt of the Poles in that region. The Russian commander, who had entered the town, gave his men permission to loot at will for two hours. It was a Sabbath day and the Jews were gathered in the House of Prayer. Rabbi Shlomo was praying in such ecstasy that he heard nothing and saw nothing that went on around him. Just then a tall cossack came limping along, went up to the window, looked in, and pointed his gun. In a ringing voice, the rabbi was saying the words, "For thine, O Lord, is the kingdom," when his little grandson, who was standing beside him, timidly tugged at his coat, and he awoke from ecstasy. But the bullet had already struck him in the side. "Why did you fetch me down?" he asked. When they brought him to his house, he had them open the *Zohar* [the Book of Splendor] at a certain passage and prop it up in front of him while they bound his wound. It stayed there, open before his eyes until the following Wednesday, when he died.[46]

The Death of Reb Mikhal of Zlotchov

In the last two years before his death, Rabbi Mikhal fell into a trance of ecstasy time after time. On these occasions his face would glow and one could see that he clung to the higher life, rather than earthly existence. His children were always careful to rouse him from his ecstasy at the right moment, as they feared his soul only had one small step to pass over from this world. Once, after the third Sabbath meal, he went to the House of Study as usual, and sang songs of praise. He returned home, entered his room unaccompanied, and began to pace the floor. His daughter, who was passing his door, heard him repeat over and over: "Willingly did Moses die! Willingly did Moses die!" She was greatly troubled and called one of her brothers. When he entered he found his father lying on the floor on his back, and heard him whisper the last word of the confession, "One," with his last breath.[47]

The Dying Rebbe: A Model for Conscious Transition

These tales portray a religious environment in which humanity and divinity constantly interact. Through prayer, devotion, meditation, study, and deeds of loving-kindness, the Rebbe and, in turn, the *hasid* grow closer to God. In drawing closer to the moment of death, there is no reason to fear, for even in that experience God is to be found.

For the Rebbe, death is a time of transition from one state of consciousness to another. "This world is like a vestibule before the World to Come" (M. *Avot* 4:21), and death is the gateway between the two worlds, the door into the heavenly spheres.

In the above stories, each Rebbe went through the death experience fully conscious and in tune with God. For the *tzaddik*, in death the body is left behind while the soul continues to commune with its creator.

The description of the Baal Shem Tov's deathbed experience may be seen as an ideal model for dying. His equanimity, control, connectedness with others, self, and God; love; devotion; and consciousness on the deathbed are all exemplary in a society where many die alone and afraid.

The *hasidim* have something to teach our contemporary society about life, the afterlife, and how to die. These stories demonstrate that it is possible for individuals to die, as did Reb Nahman, "bright and clear . . . without any confusion whatsoever, without a single untoward gesture, in a state of awesome calmness."[48]

ENTERING THE POSTMORTEM REALMS

Life Review

The *hasidim* were aware of the experiences that the individual encountered subsequent to physical death. The Gerer Rebbe spoke of the life review that would occur after death. "Why is a man afraid of dying?" he asked, "for does he not then go to his Father! What man fears is the moment he will survey from the other world everything he has experienced on this earth. In the World to Come a man obtains a clear retrospect of all his deeds on the earth."[49]

Judgment

The *hasidim* envisioned that they would have to undergo a judgment before the Heavenly Tribunal in the postmortem world. This Heavenly Tribunal would question them on the activities of their life and determine their merit in the World to Come. Many of the Rebbes advocated an attitude of honesty and self-acceptance in the face of this judgment process.

For example, before his death Reb Zusya said: "In the coming world, they will not ask me: 'Why were you not Moses?' They will ask me: 'Why were you not Zusya?'"[50]

And in another story:

Reb Elimelekh once said: "I am certain to have a share in the coming world. When I stand in the court of justice above, and they ask me: 'Have you studied all you should?' I shall answer 'No.' Then they will ask: 'Have you prayed all you should?' And again I shall answer: 'No.' And they will put a third question to me: 'Have you done all the good you should?' And this time too, I shall have to give the same answer. Then they will pronounce the verdict: 'You told the truth. For the sake of truth, you deserve a share in the coming world.'"[51]

Judgment and Near-Death Experiences

In *Shivhei Ha-Besht* we find a long story that highlights the theme of divine judgment. This story also depicts a near-death experience. In the tale, a sick child is brought before a celestial tribunal for judgment. For the successful intercession of the Baal Shem Tov, the child is released from the grips of death and returned to the world of the living:

Once, the son of the holy rabbi, our teacher and rabbi Mikhel of Zolochev, was very sick. At that moment news reached the rabbi that in a certain country they wanted to burn the holy books of the rabbi, our teacher, Jacob Joseph of Polonnoye. The rabbi left his home, and he told the members of his household that if, God forbid, his son should die, they should wait with the burial until he returns home. After his departure, the boy fell into a lethargy . . . and they thought the boy was dead. After three days he began to perspire, and his soul returned to his body. When he recovered he told them all that had happened.

As soon as his soul left his body an angel took him and brought him to a palace. The angel did not have permission to enter into the palace, and he entered the palace alone. He stood at the door and saw that the great court was in session. He saw two messengers carrying a book containing his good deeds, but the scale was unbalanced until they brought in a third book, which was the book of the sufferings he had endured. . . . Then, many of the sins were eliminated. Nevertheless, they wanted to sentence him to death because of what remained. They were about to pronounce the sentence. At that moment his father, our rabbi and teacher, Mikhel, made a noisy entrance and cried out that they wanted to burn the books of Jacob Joseph. . . . When he saw his son standing at the door, he said to him, "My son, what are you doing here?"

He answered him: "I have been standing here for a long time, and I do not know why. Please say something in my favor."

He said: "If I do not forget, I will speak well of you." And again he shouted about the books as he had done the first time.

The court answered: "This matter does not belong to our court but to the one who is *higher than the high watcheth* (Ecclesiastes 5:7), and so on."

The rabbi departed and he did not remember to mention his son. In the meantime the holy rabbi, our teacher, the author, Jacob Joseph, ascended to this palace, and he also cried out, weeping and complaining greatly because they wanted to burn his holy books. Jacob Joseph saw him standing at the door, and he asked him, "Joseph, what are you doing here?" He answered him as he had before, and he asked him to speak in his favor. Jacob Joseph answered him as his father had: "If I do not forget, I will speak well of you." Afterward he went away as well, and the boy stood in despair because he had no one to support him. Immediately a great sound was heard and all the worlds resounded, and they announced: "Clear the way. The Besht himself is coming into the palace." The Besht saw him standing at the door and asked him: "Joseph, what business do you have here?"

He answered him as he had before: "I asked my master, my father, and the rabbi of the holy community of Polonnoye to speak in my favor, but they forgot. Therefore, I ask you, your holy honor, to speak."

The rabbi asked the court to let the boy go in peace. He told him to return home. He wanted to stay there a little longer to see what the Besht was going to do there. At once two men came and took him with them. They found a putrid corpse lying on the floor and they told him, "Enter into that corpse," but he absolutely refused. He cried and appealed to them but they hit him and made him enter in spite of himself. When he entered the corpse he began to perspire.[52]

The World of Confusion

According to the teachings of kabbalistic tradition, after physical death the soul remains close to the body for some time. Reb Simhah Bunem explained this teaching by use of a metaphor.

Once one of his favorite disciples lost his scarf and searched everywhere for it with ardent zeal. His companions, seeing his plight, laughed at him. "Do not laugh," said Reb Bunem. "He is right to treasure a thing which has served him. Just so after death the soul visits the body that has sunk and leans above it."[53]

Those souls who remain attached to the physical body and the material world would find themselves in "the world of confusion," *olam ha-tohu*.[54] By recognizing that one was in such a state, attached to the illusion of a physical world, it was possible to leave this *olam ha-tohu* and enter other postmortem regions:

> To Rabbi Yisakhar of Wolborz there came a dead man whom he had once known when he was alive and prominent in his community, and begged the rabbi's help, saying that his wife had died some time ago and now he needed money to arrange for his marriage to another.
>
> "Don't you know," the *tzaddik* asked him, "that you are no longer among the living, that you are in the world of confusion?" When the man refused to believe him, he lifted the tails of the dead man's coat and showed him that he was dressed in his shroud.
>
> Later Rabbi Yisakhar's son asked: "Well, if that is so—perhaps I too am in the world of confusion?" "Once you know there is such a thing as that world," answered his father, "you are not in it."[55]

In a similar story, Reb Simhah Bunem sends such a lost, wandering soul to the place of eternal rest:

> One day Reb Bunem said to the Kotzker: "Let's go out into the fields." When the horses were hitched to the cart, they left town and arrived in the open. "Well, what do you see?" asked Reb Bunem. "I see peasants mowing wheat." "Call one of them over," suggested Reb Bunem.
>
> When he stood before them, Reb Bunem continued, "You think he is wearing clothes, don't you? Well, he's not. He is enveloped in a shroud. He belongs to the world of phantoms. Let him go to his eternal rest."[56]

THE REBBE REDEEMS SOULS FROM GEHENNA

Bargaining with God

The *hasidim*, like the kabbalists and talmudic Rabbis, saw Gehenna as a realm of purification for one's earthly sins. In order to avoid the purgations of Gehenna, the *hasidim* practiced God's commandments, the *mitzvot,* and regularly evaluated their lives (*heshbon ha-nefesh,* literally, an "accounting of the soul") in order to correct their unrighteous ways.

As spiritual leaders, the Rebbes worked to save their disciples from sin and negativity, and when possible from God's wrathful punishment. Many imagined that they would continue this work even after death. The Apter Rebbe, for example, anticipated that he would enter Gehenna and, once there, bargain with God to redeem the souls residing in that tormented abode:

> "Master of the Universe," he said, "I know that I have no virtue and no merit for which, after my death, you could set me in Gan Eden among the righteous. But if you are thinking of putting me in Gehenna among the evil-doers, please remember that I cannot get along with them. So I beg of you to take all of the wicked out of Gehenna, so you can put me in."[57]

Similarly, the Ropshitzer Rebbe taught:

> We are told by our sages that the wicked rest on Sabbath in Gehenna. It stands to reason that if a man was accustomed during his lifetime to spend his Sabbath at a Rebbe's, and that the Rebbe is now in Gan Eden, he should be granted permission to visit his Rebbe there. And what a foolish person the Rebbe would be if he allowed his adherent to be returned to Gehenna.[58]

Standing before Gehenna Unafraid

The Rizhyner Rebbe, confident of his relationship with God, declared: "They can't punish me with anything. Because if God says to me go to hell, I will do it. So they can't punish me with anything."[59]

Another Rebbe was able to successfully negotiate with the "prince of Gehenna" in order to rescue souls from Gehenna:

> Upon his death, Reb Moshe Leib of Sasov said to himself: "Now I am free from fulfilling the commandments. What can do now that will be in obedience to the will of God?" He thought for a while. "It must surely be God's will that I be punished for my countless sins!" And immediately he began to run with all his might and jumped straight into Gehenna. Gan Eden was very much perturbed at this,

and soon the prince of Gehenna was told not to stoke his fires while the Rabbi of Sasov was down there. Thereupon the prince begged the *tzaddik* to take himself off to Gan Eden, for this was clearly not the place for him. It just would not do to call a holiday in Gehenna for his sake.

"If that is the case," said Moshe Leib, "I won't stir from here until all the souls are allowed to go with me. On earth I made it my business to ransom prisoners, and so I will certainly not let this big crowd suffer in this prison." And they say that he had his way.[60]

Gehenna Preferred to *Gilgul*

Another hasidic tale suggests how, in some cases, the *hasidim* preferred a brief period of punishment in Gehenna, as a way of atoning to past sins, rather than a mandated rebirth in another lifetime.

This story is about Reb Noah [the father of the Tsemakh Tzedek]. He was a student of Lubavitch. He died and came to the Court of Heaven. They looked into his case and they found out that all his life he had observed everything that he should in the highest way. Angels came who were born from his good deeds and they were witnesses for him: "I was born from this good deed." Thousands of angels came who had been born from the good deeds of this *tzaddik*. And the Court was going to decide that he should go immediately to [Gan Eden].

All of a sudden an angel appeared and he said, "Wait a second! I have to tell something about him." And he said, "I was created from one bad deed that this *tzaddik* did in his lifetime." And he brought out what he did.

The Court of Heaven deliberated and they said he should have either one half hour in Gehenna or he should be reborn on earth to fix what he had failed to do the first time. Reb Noah answered the court that all his life everything that he had to decide he asked his Rebbe. He never did anything without asking the Rebbe; therefore, he wanted to ask the Rebbe to tell now what he should decide. They looked over his records in the Court of Heaven and they found out that he was right. Everything he did he asked the Rebbe's permission.

The Rebbe, Rabbi Shneur Zalman, was sitting with his *hasidim* and he said to them, "Reb Noah is asking now what he should select: either Gehenna, a half hour of hell, or be reborn in the world a second time." They had nothing to say. They were waiting. And the Rebbe put his holy hand on his forehead and he rested his head on the table a short time. Then he said: "Gehenna . . . Gehenna." In the second when the Rebbe said the word Gehenna, they heard a voice, "Oy, Rebbe!" And they saw on the wall by the door, the mark of a burned hand—the fingers of a hand burned into the wall.[61]

From Gehenna to Gan Eden

There is yet another story from the collection of hasidic tales on Gehenna, where a Rebbe prepares for and expects to enter Gehenna, only to discover that he is destined for a blissful life in Gan Eden:

> Reb Shlomo of Karlin used to say: "I have to prepare for what I shall have to do in Gehenna," for he was certain that no better end was in store for him. Now when his soul ascended after death, and the serving angels received him joyfully, to guide him to the highest paradise, he refused to go with them. "They are making fun of me," he said. "This cannot be the world of truth." At last the *Shekhinah* herself said to him: "Come my son! Out of mercy I shall give you my treasure." Then he gave in and was content.[62]

GAN EDEN—A REFLECTION
OF ONE'S OWN CONSCIOUSNESS

Each Person Creates Their Own Gan Eden

All the hasidic tales on Gan Eden point out one essential teaching: what will be experienced in the postmortem realms of paradise is a direct reflection of one's life experience and spiritual awareness. As the Maggid of Mezhirich said: "A man's kind deeds are utilized by the Lord as seed for the planting of trees in Gan Eden; thus each man creates his own Paradise. The reverse is true when he commits transgressions."[63]

In another instance, the Maggid taught: "After my death I anticipate being in Gan Eden. For even if admittance should be denied me, I shall loudly begin to recite and discuss new Torah, and all the *tzaddikim* in Gan Eden will assemble to hear me. The place where I will stand will become Gan Eden."[64]

The Blaze and Ecstasy of Gan Eden

Rabbi Shlomo of Karlin said: "When he, who has done all the commandments of the Torah, but has not felt the blaze of holy ecstasy in so doing, comes to that other world, they open the gates of Gan Eden for him. But because he has not felt the blaze of ecstasy in this world, he does not feel the ecstasy of Gan Eden. Now if he is a fool, and complains and grumbles: "And they make so much to-do about Gan Eden!" he is instantly thrown out. But if he is wise, he leaves of his own accord, and goes to the *tzaddik*, and he teaches the poor soul how to feel ecstasy.[65]

Gan Eden Is in the Tannaim

For the *hasidim*, Gan Eden was not a physical locale as much as a state of consciousness. This idea is expressed in a story about Reb Moshe Teitelbaum. Once Reb Moshe dreamed that he was in Gan Eden and was conducted to the room of the *Tannaim*, the early rabbinic Sages. He beheld a *Tanna* studying the Talmud. Somewhat disappointed with what he was seeing, he exclaimed: "Is this all there is to Gan Eden?" Suddenly, he heard a voice answer him: 'Moshe, you believe the *Tannaim* are in Gan Eden. You are wrong. Gan Eden is in the *Tannaim*.'"[66]

Gan Eden for the Wicked

According to the *hasidim*, the wicked person who entered Gan Eden would be unable to enjoy its spiritual delights. Said Reb Yakov Yosef of Polnoi:

No Gehenna can be worse for the wicked than permission to enter Gan Eden. They find there no pleasure to which they were addicted in life; no eating or drinking or any other pleasures of the body. They see merely *tzaddikim*, deriving great joy from the nearness of the Lord. And who are these *tzaddikim* who occupy places of prominence in Gan Eden? They are the very persons upon whom the wicked poured out their scorn in life, and whose learning they thoroughly despised. What, then, can these persons feel in Gan Eden but bitterness? Can they know the joy of the *Shekhinah*'s nearness, inasmuch as they never trained themselves in their lifetime for the enjoyments of the spirit?[67]

Gan Eden for the Unlearned

In another tale, the Gan Eden experience for the righteous but unlearned person is described. This tale, quite popular in hasidic circles, reflects the folk and populist dimension of the hasidic movement. Attributed to Baal Shem Tov, this story originally appears in a text entitled *Meir Einei Ha-Golah*:

> A *tzaddik* was traveling in the early spring in a wagon. The roads were in terrible condition; the axles of the wheels broke several times, and the horses ploughed with difficulty through the slush and mire. Friday morning came and a great distance was yet to be covered before the *tzaddik* could reach his destination. He turned to the *baalegoleh* [literally, "master of the wagon"; teamster or truck driver] and said: "It is important I arrive at my goal before the advent of the Sabbath." The *baalegoleh* promised to do his best. A horse fell dead from exhaustion, but the *baalegoleh* continued with the second horse, and succeeded in reaching the *tzaddik*'s destination before the Sabbath.
>
> On Sunday the *tzaddik* heard that the second horse had also died from exhaustion, and that the *baalegoleh*'s grief was so great that he was stricken with illness. The *tzaddik* ordered the best medical attention for him, but in vain; the man died. When his soul came before the Heavenly Tribunal, the counsel for the defense won the case, and Gan Eden was ordered for the poor *baalegoleh*. His soul arrived there, but it found no pleasure whatsoever in the spiritual and cultural atmosphere of even the lowest region.
>
> He was then sent into an imaginary world where he was presented a beautiful carriage to four magnificent horses, and where the roads stretched before him, always dry and level. The *baalegoleh* was able to enjoy only an imaginary Gan Eden, not the true one.[68]

In another version of the story, it is the Baal Shem Tov who intervened with the Heavenly Tribunal to ensure this humble man was given a Gan Eden experience in which he could enjoy existence itself, albeit in an imaginary physical universe.

Gan Eden: An Evolutionary Journey

For the kabbalists, and hence the *hasidim*, Gan Eden itself is not a static experience nor an ultimate resting place. Within Gan Eden there are regions within regions within regions, the seven heavens or levels of Gan Eden depicted in midrashic literature. The soul on its postmortem journey progresses through these heavenly domains advancing toward evermore lofty, transcendent, spiritual heights. In other words, in the postmortem realm of Gan Eden, the soul continues its evolutionary journey of light and consciousness.

This teaching was brought forth in Hasidism by Reb Zvi Hirsh of Zhydatchov. The young rabbi had been a disciple of Yehiel Mikhal of Zlotchov. Many years after dying, his Rebbe appeared to him in a dream saying: "Know, that from the moment I died, I have been wandering from world to world. And the world which yesterday was spread over my head as Gan Eden, is today the earth under my feet, and the Gan Eden of today is the earth of tomorrow."[69]

For the *hasidim*, Gan Eden is a state of consciousness reflecting one's own acquired psychic reality; at the same time, it is a series of transcendent realms in which the soul continues to learn and grow.

SPIRITS AND SOULS ON THE OTHER SIDE

Encounters with the Spirit World

For the *hasidim*, the soul survived bodily death. This soul, understood as *naran* (the acronym for the three levels of soul: *nefesh*, *ruah*, *neshamah*), often would remain in contact with the living. There are numerous stories documenting encounters with those who have died either through dreams or spirit visitations.

One story, for example, is told of the Maggid of Koznitz,

[who] had a sister who had died at a young age. The Heavenly Tribunal has allocated to her permission to live her brother's home. The Maggid, who saw to it that clothing was made for poor orphans, was often advised by his sister on how to buy good, durable material at the best price. She also kept a close watch on the activities of the servants. Once when one of them stole a loaf of bread, she instantly reported the theft to her brother. He detested this tale-bearing, but he could not break her of it. Once his temper grew short and he said to her: "Wouldn't you like to take a rest?" From that time on, she was gone.[70]

Visitation by the Soul of a Dead Grandfather

One night, the wife of Rabbi Mendel of Lubavitch, the rav's grandson, was awakened by a loud noise coming from her husband's room which was next to hers. She ran to him and saw Rabbi Mendel lying on the floor by his bed. In reply to her questions, he told her that his grandfather had been to see him. She tried to calm him, but he said: "When a soul from the world above and a soul from this world want to be together, the one must put on a garment, the other must take one off."[71]

The Rebbe Descends from Gan Eden

Some guests had attended the wedding of the daughter of Reb Schmelke of Sasov, who was Reb Moishe Leib's son, paid a visit to Reb Meir of Primishlan on their way home. He questioned them eagerly as to what special thing they had seen at the celebration, refused to be satisfied with what they had told him, and kept on asking: "And what else happened?" Finally they said: "While the traditional dances with the bride and groom were going on, an enormous man completely disguised as a bear leaped into the circle and did a most magnificent bear's dance. Everybody marveled at his really wonderful bounds, and there was a clapping of hands. And then just as suddenly as he had come, he was gone. No one knew him."

"I'll tell you," said Reb Meir. "That was none other than our holy teacher Reb Moishe Leib of Sasov—may his memory help us—who came down from the uppermost Gan Eden to rejoice with his family."[72]

Connection with the Rebbe Transcends Death

Hasidism was a pietistic devotional movement in which the relationship between Rebbe and disciple was of paramount importance. This was so in life; and for many *hasidim*, likewise in death.

After the death of Reb Simhah Bunam, his disciple, Yitzhak of Vorki, went to visit his Rebbe's son, Abraham Moshe, to speak words of comfort to him. The son, in his grief, lamented, "And who will teach me now?"

"Take courage," said the disciple. "Up to now your father has taught you in his coat; from now on he will teach you without his coat on."[73]

Another story is told of a disciple, Reb Menahem Mendel of Kotzk, who was greatly troubled after the death of his Rebbe, the Yehudi. He was uncertain as to who would now be his teacher. The Yehudi appeared to him in a dream and tried to comfort him, saying that he was willing to continue to teach him. For Reb Mendel, however, this was not a suitable solution. "I do not want a teacher from the other world," he retorted.[74]

Personal Relationships Continue after Death

There are stories that indicate that the relationship between the living and the dead continues after the physical body has been buried. These relationships can often have an intense, emotional quality to them, both for the living and for the disembodied deceased.

For example, the following story is told about Reb Abraham (the Angel):

> In the night after the seven days of mourning for Reb Abraham the Angel, his wife had a dream. She saw a vast hall, and in it thrones, set in a semicircle. On each throne sat one of the great. A door opened, and one who looked like those others, entered. It was Abraham, her husband. He said: "Friends, my wife bears me a grudge because in my earthly life I lived apart from her. She is right, and therefore I must obtain her forgiveness." His wife cried out: "With all my heart I forgive you," and awoke comforted.[75]

For the living, there is one very simple message to this story. Consciousness does survive bodily death, and whatever relationships are incomplete and charged with negative emotions and resentments prior to one's death require resolution for both the discarnate soul and the surviving bereaved.

According to other tales, Reb Abraham (the Angel) had somewhat of a stormy relationship with his father, the Maggid of Mezhirich, after the latter's death:

> After his death, the Maggid appeared to his son and—invoking the commandment to honor one's parents—ordered him to give up his life of perfect seclusion, for whoever walks a way such as this, is in danger. Abraham (the Angel) replied: "I do not recognize a father in the flesh. I recognize only one merciful Father of all that lives."
>
> "You accepted your inheritance," said the Maggid. "With that you recognized me as your father even after my death."

"I renounce my father's inheritance," cried Reb Abraham. At that moment a fire broke out in the house and consumed the few small things the Maggid had left his son—but nothing besides.[76]

A short time after the fire in which the clothing and utensils the Maggid had left his son were burned, Reb Abraham's brother-in-law made him a present of a robe of white silk the Maggid had worn on High Holy Days, the famous white "pekeshe." On the eve of the Day of Atonement, Abraham put it on to honor his father. The lights in the House of Prayer had already been lit. With a fervent gesture the *tzaddik* leaned over to one of them. The robe caught on fire. They snatched it from his body. With a long understanding, he watched it crumble to ash.[77]

These stories have somewhat of an enigmatic quality to them. However, once again the essential message here is that human relationships do continue after the time of physical death; there is a communion between the disembodied soul and the surviving beloved ones.

Reincarnating Souls

Finally, within the hasidic tradition there are tales of souls who are aware of their own process of reincarnation. The Baal Shem Tov himself claimed to be a reincarnation of Rabbi Saadia Gaon;[78] Dov Baer of Mezhirich was said to be the reincarnation of Rabbi Akiba; and Reb Israel Stolin had the soul of the famous tenth-century scholar Rashi.[79]

Reb Moshe Teitelbaum, the Satmarer Rebbe, was aware of numerous previous lives. He spoke of having been alive in ancient times—as one of the sheep of Jacob when he worked for his father-in-law Laban, as one of the many Jews who left Egypt with Moses, and as a witness to the destruction of the Temple. In this latter incarnation he claimed to be the prophet Jeremiah.[80]

There is also a legend told of Reb Abraham Joshua Heschel of Apt who was said to have been able to remember all his previous incarnations. Thus, during the *Avodah* service on Yom Kippur, when reading the liturgy about the High Priest of the Jerusalem Temple, the Apter Rebbe would say: "Thus did I say" and not "Thus did he say."[81]

In another story, an individual is reborn to atone for misdeeds of a previous lifetime:

On a certain New Year's night, the Maggid of Zlotchov saw a man who had been a reader in his city and who had died a short time ago. "What are you doing here?" he asked. "The rabbi knows," said the dead man, "that in this night, souls are incarnated anew. I am such a soul." "And why were you sent out again?" asked the Maggid. "I led an impeccable life here on earth," the dead man told him. "And yet you are forced to live once more?" the Maggid went on to ask. "Before my death," said the man, "I thought over everything I had done and found that I had always acted in just the right way. Because of this my heart swelled with satisfaction and in the midst of this feeling I died. So now they have sent me back into the world to atone for my pride."

At that time a son was born to the Maggid. His name was Reb Wolf of Zbarazh. He was very humble.[82]

Finally, in one other reincarnation story, quite characteristic of hasidic literature, at the exact time when one individual dies, a new life is born, obviously a reincarnation of the person who has died:

A rich and powerful man by the name of Shalom, who was generally called Count Shalom, fell dangerously ill. His son at once set out for the Rabbi of Lublin, to ask him to pray for mercy. But when, after his long journey, he stood before the *tzaddik* and gave him a slip of paper with his request, Rabbi Yakov Yitzhak said: "Help is no longer possible. He has already passed from the sphere of ruling into that of learning." When the man reached home, he discovered that his father had died that very same hour, but that, in the same hour, his wife had borne him a son. He was named Shalom after his grandfather, and grew up to be a master of the teachings.[83]

Thus, in this story we see how the hasidic movement took complex philosophical concepts of Kabbalah—in this case, the doctrine of *gilgul*—and through the art of storytelling transformed these teachings into popular folk beliefs, which became the material of hasidic legends.

SUMMARY

The compilation of hasidic tales presented in this chapter conveys the understanding the *hasidim* had toward dying and a life after death. From the material presented, the following observations can be made about hasidic stories on dying and the postmortem experience:

1. Hasidic stories indicate how deeply the notion of immortality and life after death was integrated into the life experience and teachings of Hasidism. For *hasidim*, there was never any sense of doubt or question about the continuation of some form of existence after bodily death.
2. Hasidic stories provide a folk-level understanding of the afterlife. These stories include and reflect the central elements of the postmortem experience evidenced in kabbalistic afterlife teachings.
3. Hasidic tales provide an ideal model for approaching the deathbed experience today. Hasidic deathbed stories indicate how, with a spiritual attitude, one may die peacefully and accepting of death as a spiritual transition to another realm of existence.

Chapter 10

A Contemporary
Psychological Model
of the Afterlife

AFTERLIFE TEACHINGS AS A REFLECTION OF CULTURE

On our voyage to explore the afterlife in Judaism we have traversed over three thousand years of Jewish history, traveling from ancient Canaan to premodern Poland, stopping along the way in places such as Alexandria, Egypt; Babylonia; Italy; Provence; Spain; and Safed. Our investigation of the vast treasure house of Jewish sacred texts reveals how Judaism's varied and diverse conceptions of an individual afterlife experience developed progressively, from the sixth century B.C.E. onward. At each stage, a more fully evolved and complex notion of an individual postmortem immortality emerged, culminating in the mythic visionary writings of the medieval midrashists and the mystical afterlife philosophy of the kabbalists.

As we have seen with each unique genre of literature, views of life after death in each historical period directly reflect the worldview and cultural experience of that age. Thus, the tribal society of the early biblical period envisioned the postmortem world as an ancestral family clan of the dead. In the later biblical period, the emerging Israelite nation, loyal to an authoritative monotheistic deity, conceived of the afterlife as a realm over which the all-powerful God YHVH had complete control. Subsequently, the talmudic Rabbis, who were deeply concerned with ethical living and correct religious practice in a world without the Holy Temple, evolved a philosophy of the hereafter based on a belief in divine retribution and reward and punishment. In the superstitious Middle Ages, when the world was populated with demons and spirits, the mythic midrashists authored visionary portraits of an extraordinary and dynamic multileveled heaven and hell. And as scholastic thought came into vogue, Jewish philosophers begat radically new ideas of the hereafter focusing on a rationalistic preoccupation with the essential substance of the soul and its essential nature during life and after death. Around the same time, in the medieval era, the kabbalists came onto the scene of Jewish history. Concerned with the mysterious ways in which macrocosm and microcosm, universe and soul, came into existence, in their understanding of the afterlife they focused on the psychological and spiritual experiences of the soul, and mapped out the postmortem journey from the moment of death onward. And then, as we observed at the beginning of this study, as materialistic science and logical positivism came to predominate in the modern mind, in the nineteenth and twentieth centuries, the very idea of life after death simply disappeared from the scene, or in some cases, came to be reinterpreted in nonspiritual, metaphoric terms. We have passed from "tribal netherworld" to "dead is dead" in less than four millennia. What now?

Since Jewish notions of the afterlife evolve in consonance with the changing consciousness of each age, the questions to be addressed now are these: Given the vast ancient legacy of Judaism's teachings on the afterlife, how can we best understand life after death in this era? In this ever-changing contemporary age, which is itself a time of transformation and paradigm shift, not only in the sciences, but in the very way we think about religion and spirituality, how do we make sense of the whole notion of postmortem survival? Given the reality of human mortality—all human beings die, plain and simple—what meaning do teachings about survival in the hereafter have for us today? Perhaps we have come full circle and must ask what contemporary, postmodern Jews are to believe about life after death. It is the intention of this final chapter to address these questions, by presenting a contemporary psychological explication of the postmortem journey of the soul, synthesizing Judaism's traditional afterlife teachings with contemporary thought.

THE CULTURAL CONTEXT

As we navigated through each age of Jewish civilization, we endeavored to note historical developments and cultural influences. What are the cultural parameters operating in this age? What are the cultural influences and the intellectual building blocks that will assist us in constructing a contemporary Jewish model of life after death, personally meaningful and spiritually relevant for men and women today?

At the very beginning of this book, in Chapter 2, two major trends of cultural influence were noted: (1) the Jewish renewal movement—the grassroots renaissance of Jewish spirituality, and (2) thanatology—the study of death and dying, also known as the death awareness movement. The Jewish renewal movement is very much of a neokabbalistic, neo-hasidic mystical revival, and much of what follows in this chapter is based on the sources of kabbalistic Judaism but presented in contemporary metaphor. At the same time, the practical concern with the teachings on the afterlife as it affects the dying and bereaved grows out of the innovative pathways carved by Elisabeth Kübler-Ross and her colleagues and students, who have pioneered new approaches in thanatology. This chapter is a by-product of these two cultural trends.

Besides the Jewish renewal movement and thanatology, other important influences come into play in the creation of a contemporary Jewish model of the afterlife: research on near-death experiences; Eastern philosophy, in particular, Buddhist and Hindu teachings on life after death; and contemporary transpersonal psychology.

Near-Death Experiences

In 1976 Raymond Moody, Jr., a philosopher and medical doctor, published his observations on "near-death experiences," or NDEs, in a now-famous book, entitled *Life after Life*.[1] In this study, Moody interviewed men and women who had been on the verge of death, or even pronounced clinically dead, and later returned to life to report vivid descriptions of an interim world between life and death. Moody chronicled the various inner phenomena these people claimed to expe-

rience. Repeatedly, individuals perceived that they were actually dying
and that their consciousness was no longer contained within the physical body. They reported encountering a luminosity of great intensity and
loving angelic beings, and claimed to have experienced a transcendent
sense of peace and well-being. Subsequent to these NDEs, individuals
felt little fear about dying and developed a strong belief that some form
of consciousness would continue to survive after biological death.

From the beginning, Moody's work attracted a great deal of attention and spawned a widespread professional and popular fascination with
NDEs. As a result of NDE research, since the mid-1970s new ways of thinking about death and the life beyond have emerged. First of all, the nature
of the NDE indicates that there is an awareness that transcends the limitations of the physical body and continues to exist even after the biological functions have ceased. In addition, NDE research sheds light on the
nature of the experiences one might encounter after death. Various phenomena of the NDE parallel motifs of afterlife experience in religious texts,
and certainly NDE literature presents an invaluable perspective in an attempt to understand traditional teachings about life after death.

In earlier chapters we did note some correlations between afterlife
themes in Judaism and the NDE. In this chapter we will use some of the
findings from NDE research literature to elucidate our contemporary Jewish model of the afterlife.

Tibetan Buddhist *Bardo* Teachings

Another influence in creating a contemporary Jewish model of the
afterlife is, oddly enough, Tibetan Buddhism. Throughout history, Jews
have always been influenced by the surrounding religious cultures, and
this generation is no exception. Even more so, in this age of interconti-
nental travel, it is now possible to leave behind the familiar Western world
and within twenty-four hours land in New Delhi or Katmandu. And with
Eastern swamis, lamas, and gurus having established centers throughout
North America and Europe, more Jews have access to the study and practice of Eastern religions than at any other point in history. For reasons
that are beyond the scope of this study, there is an exceptionally high
percentage of Jews participating in Hindu, Buddhist, Taoist, and Sufi
spiritual communities. In various ways, there continues to be an infu-
sion of Eastern religious thought and practice into Judaism, at least within
Jewish renewal circles.

Within Tibetan Buddhism, the afterlife, or *bardo*, teachings, first encoded in the *Tibetan Book of the Dead*, present an exceptionally clear and evolved understanding of the postmortem experience.[2] There are numerous parallels between Tibetan Buddhist and Jewish views of the afterlife, and the Buddhist philosophy of life after death does provide a valuable framework for understanding many of the elements of Jewish afterlife beliefs. By way of background, in articulating the afterlife model presented in this chapter, we will draw on certain elements of Tibetan Buddhist philosophy of postmortem survival.

Transpersonal Psychology and the Afterlife

Transpersonal psychology is a spiritually based approach to psychology that focuses on that which is "trans" or beyond the individual ego, that is, the spiritual dimension of the human person. The term "transpersonal" was originally coined by Abraham Maslow.[3] Given the tenor of the first half of the twentieth century, the early psychologists were predominantly secularists. However, in the late 1960s, as people increasingly reported mystical or peak experiences and wrestled with the impact of those experiences on their lives,[4] Maslow and his colleagues developed a psychological framework giving due consideration to the spiritual potentialities of each individual being and to the various states of consciousness beyond normal, ordinary waking consciousness. Through the work of such individuals as Robert Assagioli,[5] Stanislav Grof,[6] Jean Houston,[7] and especially Ken Wilber,[8] there has been a rapidly growing body of knowledge describing the interior regions of the human psyche and the enormous potentialities of expanded levels of consciousness.

One of the most important theoreticians of transpersonal psychology, Stanislav Grof, has authored two important books—*The Human Encounter with Death*[9] and *Beyond Death—The Gates of Consciousness*[10]—which bring a transpersonal psychological perspective to the study of the afterlife. In these books Grof summarizes his years of experimental psychedelic psychotherapy research with cancer patients.[11] In supervised psychedelic sessions and follow-up interviews, terminally ill individuals were given an opportunity to focus on unresolved life issues and on the problems in accepting the inevitability of death. During the research, Grof noted that the themes of death and rebirth repeatedly recurred in people's inner, subjective visions. Time and time again subjects encountered a profound symbolic experience of their own death, literally witnessing themselves die and be reborn. These types of visions, such as the one described below, frequently helped patients feel more prepared to accept cancer, illness, and death without fear:

> There was a long episode during which Jesse saw numerous scenes of junkyards strewn with corpses, carcasses, skeletons, rotting offal, and trash cans spreading foul odors. His own body lay there, wrapped in stinking bandages, eaten by cancer, its skin cracking, leaking, covered with cancerous ulcerations. Then a gigantic ball of fire appeared suddenly out of nowhere and all this mess and garbage was dumped into its purifying flames and consumed. Jesse's flesh and bones were destroyed in this fire, yet his soul survived the procedure. He found himself in a Last Judgment scene where God ("Jehovah") was weighing his good and evil deeds. Numerous memories from his life were passing through his mind in what felt like a final reckoning. The positive aspects of his life were found stronger than his sins and transgressions. It felt as if he heard sounds of celestial music and angelic singing, and started to understand the meaning of his experience. The following message was coming to him through some supernatural, nonverbal channels and was permeating his whole being: "When you die, your body will be destroyed, but you will be saved; your soul will be with you all the time. You will come back to earth, you will be living again, but you do not know what you will be on the next earth."[12]

Grof went further in his research, investigating the meaning of these death–rebirth experiences. He noticed that there were striking resemblances between the subjective visions of death and dying in psychedelic psychotherapy, and depictions of the afterlife journey of the soul in religious texts and traditions throughout the world.[13] In contradistinction to secularist, psychological thinking, Grof does not reject religious afterlife teachings as being a product of primitive, magical thinking. He suggests that depictions of life after death in religious literature may represent, symbolically, an experiential reality of human consciousness. Writes Grof:

> Psychedelic research conducted in the last two decades has resulted in important phenomenological and neurophysiological data indicating that experiences involving complex mythological, religious and mystical sequences before, during, and after death might well represent clinical reality. Reports describing subjective experiences

of clinical death, if studied carefully and with an open mind, contain ample evidence that various eschatological mythologies represent actual maps of unusual states of consciousness experienced by dying individuals.[14]

As Grof understands it—and this is of central importance for this study—postmortem teachings in the sacred texts of world religions depict, in symbolic form, those realms of the psyche encountered during and following the process of dying. Each mythological or philosophical image represents a particular quality or state of consciousness; and the complete myth or the total compilation of teachings on all facets of the afterlife experience provides a map, or psychological cartography, which reveals the specific changes in consciousness that take place during the death moment and afterward.[15] In other words, as Rabbi Zalman Schachter-Shalomi often explains, "eschatology equals psychology"[16]— eschatological and philosophical teachings on life after death are, in reality, *metaphoric depictions of the various psychological states of experienced by the disembodied consciousness after death.*

Following Grof's thinking, in this chapter we will approach Jewish afterlife teachings from a psychological vantage point. We will synthesize material from Jewish sources and compile a phenomenological cartography of Jewish after-death imagery. We will then work to translate the images and motifs of Jewish afterlife teachings into a psychological framework that explicates the states of consciousness one encounters after death.

A Kabbalistic-Psychological Cartography of the Afterlife

By way of method, this chapter proceeds by first summarizing background material on the model of the soul in kabbalistic Judaism and explicating that model in terms of contemporary transpersonal psychology. Then, using the kabbalistic understanding of the soul as a framework, we delineate a composite model of the specific stages of the afterlife journey, describing in psychological terms the experiential realities of the dying process and the states of consciousness encounter after death. Employing the teaching methods of the hasidic masters—storytelling— we draw on an elaborate hasidic story on life after death as a way of reiterating and synthesizing the various elements of the multileveled model developed herein. Integrating classical Jewish sources and contemporary psychological thought, the overall goal of this chapter is to create a kabbalistic-psychological cartography of the postmortem journey of the soul.

One caveat: The kabbalistic-psychological model to be delineated here should be regarded as a working hypothesis for understanding Judaism's traditions of the afterlife. Any attempt to describe the nature of life after death—especially by a living, embodied human being, sitting in front of a computer—will invariably be partial, incomplete guesswork, or simply incorrect. Even more, someone might come along and say, "Life after death! Who are you kidding? When you're alive, you're alive! Dead is dead! Never mind the afterlife!" There is no room for further exploration and discussion because an adversarial situation is created. However, the intention here is to not to market any particular belief, but rather to catalyze people to think more about life after death and its meaning in the face of grief and loss. Therefore, the best way to look at this chapter is as a speculative model, a working hypothesis that may help one comprehend what is encoded in Judaism's traditions of the afterlife. What is presented is offered as one way—not the only way—of understanding the mysteries of the world beyond. By using not only the rational but also the intuitive mind, each individual can determine for himself or herself the personal applicability of this kabbalistic-psychological view of the afterlife.

BACKGROUND—THE KABBALISTIC FRAMEWORK

Before we can understand life after death, we need to be clear about how we conceive of life. Before we can articulate a philosophy or a psychology of what transpires after the body dies, we need to examine our assumptions about the human being and about the nature of reality itself.

In Judaism, the central operating principle of the religion, the baseline faith statement that conditions the entire Jewish worldview is the prayer declaring the oneness of God: *Shema Yisrael, Adonai Eloheinu, Adonai Ehad*—"Hear, O Israel, the Lord Our God, the Lord is One." This is Judaism's central doxology, recited day and night, from practically womb to tomb. God is oneness, indivisible; this is the central idea communicated here.

The Jewish mystical view of *Shema Yisrael*, and the theology that comes out of it, adds a whole other dimension of understanding to

Judaism's view of reality. God's name, *Adonai,* is spelled in Hebrew with the letters YHVH (pronounced by the names of the original Hebrew letters *yod, hey, vav, hey*).[17] This is the tetragrammaton, the ineffable Divine Name of God. According to Jewish mysticism, the Divine Name YHVH represents the totality of all reality, the oneness of the entire created order. "Hear, O Israel . . . YHVH is One" means that God, YHVH, is the totality of Being, manifest and unmanifest, transcendent and immanent.

From this starting point, the kabbalists go further and proclaim that God's Oneness manifests on four different levels of reality, from the highest to the lowest realm of the created order. In other words, within the universe there are four different worlds or realms of discourse through which God's unity is expressed; each letter of the fourfold Divine Name YHVH is symbolic of one of those four worlds. Symbolically, the *yod* (ʾ) of the Divine Name is the World of *Atzilut,* or Emanation; the first *hey* (ה) is the World of *Beriyah,* or Creation; the *vav* (ו) is the World of *Yetzirah,* or Formation; and the second *hey* (ה) is the World of *Assiyah,* or Function.

Interpreting traditional kabbalistic terms in a contemporary way, Schachter-Shalomi explains that the *yod* (ʾ) of the Divine Name is the world of spirit, the realm of being, or essence; the first *hey* (ה) is the world of mind, the realm of thought; the *vav* (ו) is the world of emotion, the realm of feeling; and the second *hey* (ה) is the physical world, the realm of the body, and of action, or doing.[18] Thus, on a microcosmic level, the individual, who is made in the image of God, is an aggregate of four interrelated worlds of being, or states of consciousness: physical, emotional, mental, and spiritual. Table 10-1 delineates the relationship of each of these worlds to the Divine Name YHVH (*yod hey-vav hey*).

This kabbalistic model of the four worlds is directly related to the model of the soul developed in *Zoharic* literature and in Lurianic Kabbalah. Reiterating what was presented in Chapter 8, later Kabbalah (in the *Raaya Meheimna* additions to the *Zohar*) speaks of five levels of the soul; from the lowest to the highest aspect they are *nefesh, ruah, neshamah, hayyah, yehidah,* translated by Gershon Winkler as appetitive awareness, emotional awareness, intellect, divine life force, and uniqueness.[20] Each of the lower three aspects of the soul—*nefesh, ruah, neshamah*—are related to a specific world of Kabbalah[21] and to one of the letters of the Divine Name. *Hayyah* and *yehidah* are related to the fourth world, the spiritual world of *Atzilut,* and correlate with the *yod* of

TABLE 10-1   THE FOUR WORLDS OF KABBALAH[19]

Letter of Divine Name— Hebrew	World of Kabbalah	English Translation	Realm of Consciousness
ʼ *yod*	*Atzilut*	Emanation	Spiritual; being; essence
ה *hey*	*Beriyah*	Creation	Mental; mind; thought
ו *vav*	*Yetzirah*	Formation	Emotional; feeling
ה *hey*	*Assiyah*	Function	Physical; action; body

the Divine Name. Table 10-2 outlines the kabbalistic model of the soul, using both traditional and psychological terminology.

To elaborate on Table 10-2, the kabbalistic model of the soul postulates that the individual is an organism comprised of interconnected, interpenetrating fields of awareness, or qualities of soul-nature. These are fields of conscious energy that surround the physical body and connect the individual to the infinite.

The *nefesh* aspect of the soul is a field of vital energy or bioenergy, which surrounds and animates the physical body. The *ruah* aspect of the soul is a field of emotional energy; it may also be considered the center of the personality, or personal self. The *neshamah* aspect of the soul is a field of mental energy, the higher mind; it is also the receptor of the energy of the transpersonal self that connects the individual to the spiritual dimensions of existence. The *hayyah* and *yehidah* are the transcendental aspects of the soul. The *hayyah* may be seen as the universal self, or "soul-body,"[22] and the *yehidah* is a transcendental field of light, the source of pure spirit where the individual soul and Godhead actually merge.

While the person is alive, these different aspects of the soul are vitally interconnected: bioenergy, emotions, mind, soul, and spirit interact and are expressed through the vehicle of the body. After the death of the body, however, the different energy fields that comprise the totality of the soul begin to separate. Death, and what follows, is regarded as

TABLE 10-2 FOUR WORLDS OF KABBALAH AND LEVELS OF THE SOUL

Letter of Divine Name	World of Kabbalah	Level of Soul	Level of Soul (Winkler)	Level of Soul (Transpersonal Psychology)
ʾ yod	Atzilut	Yehidah	Uniqueness	Transcendental Field of light; Oneness; Spirit
	Spiritual	Hayyah	Divine life force; soul	Universal Self
ה hey	Beriyah	Neshamah	Intellect	Transpersonal Self; Higher Mind
	Mental			Mental Energy Field
ו vav	Yetzirah Emotional	Ruah	Emotion	Emotional Energy Field
ה hey	Assiyah Physical	Nefesh	Vitality	Bioenergetic Field

an unraveling of the various interconnected dimensions of the human person.

Kabbalistic tradition describes how each aspect of the soul has a different experience in the postmortem realms. To build on what was presented in our exploration of Kabbalah in Chapter 8, the *nefesh*, or bioenergetic aspect of the soul, remains closely attached to the physical body and experiences "the pangs of the grave," *hibbut ha-kever*. The *ruah*, or emotional energy field, experiences the twelve-month purgations of Gehenna and then, according to the doctrine of the *Zohar*, passes into Lower Gan Eden. The *neshamah* aspect of the soul enters the sublime regions of Upper Gan Eden. *Hayyah* and *yehidah*, which are usually linked in kabbalistic sources, eventually enter into what is called *tzror ha-hayyim*, "the bundle of life," the divine region where souls are stored.

These kabbalistic teachings on the postmortem destiny of the soul can be correlated with the four-lettered Divine Name. Each aspect of the soul corresponds with a specific phase of the postmortem journey and, symbolically, with another letter of the name of God. Thus, in a symbolic sense, according to these kabbalistic teachings, life after death is a process whereby the disembodied soul progressively extricates itself from the physical realm, moving in stages from the lowest to the highest cosmic worlds: from the first *hey* of the Divine Name to the *yod*, the highest realm of transcendental consciousness. Table 10-3 summarizes these kabbalistic postmortem teachings.

A STRUCTURAL FRAMEWORK FOR UNDERSTANDING THE AFTERLIFE

The next step in evolving a contemporary Jewish model of the afterlife is to create an overarching framework that helps to define even more specifically the stages of the soul's postmortem wanderings. Understanding

TABLE 10-3   KABBALISTIC MODEL OF THE SOUL AND THE POSTMORTEM WORLDS

Letter of Divine Name	Level of Soul	Level of Soul (Transpersonal Psychology)	Postmortem Experience
׳ *yod*	*Yehidah* *Hayyah*	Transcendental Field of light; Oneness; Spirit Universal self	*Tzror ha-hayyim* Source of life; Storehouse of Souls
ה *hey*	*Neshamah*	Transpersonal Self; Higher Mind; Mental Energy Field	Gan Eden Realm of Heavenly Delights
ו *vav*	*Ruah*	Personal Self Emotional Energy Field	Gehenna Realm of Purgation and Purification
ה *hey*	*Nefesh*	Bioenergetic Field	*Hibbut ha-kever* Pangs of the Grave

the structure of the afterlife journey is important because it allows us to highlight those postmortem adventures of the soul that seem to be archetypal, in other words, common to human spiritual experience. Certainly, research on life after death in religions around the world indicates there is commonality to the structure of the postmortem journey. What changes from culture to culture, from tradition to tradition, is the content and symbolism used to describe the nature of the hereafter; but time and time again the overriding structure of the afterlife experience remains similar. Almost all myths of the postmortem voyage demonstrate a discernible and replicable pattern of experience consisting of an encounter with celestial light, meeting of divine beings who show the way through the landscapes of the beyond, a review of life experience, a process of judgment, and individual realms of torment and of bliss.[23]

Undeniably, our exploration of Jewish sacred writings throughout the ages also reveals a progressive structural order evident in descriptions of the afterlife. From the rabbinic era on, there are commonly occurring imagistic depictions of the soul's experiences at the moment of death; there is almost always some notion of an early postmortem cleansing, *hibbut ha-kever*, or "the pangs of the grave"; this is followed by purgatorial torments of Gehenna and then by the resplendent delights encountered as the soul enters Gan Eden. Following Gan Eden there is, at least in some sources, an experience of *tzror ha-hayyim*, seemingly a return to "the storehouse of souls." In order to elaborate more fully on the various elements of the afterlife encounter, we can take this structural framework even further and divide the postmortem journey into a series of progressive phases, which we are calling here "transit stages."[24]

A note on terminology: The term "transit stage" is an interpretative translation of the Tibetan Buddhist concept of *bardo*. *Bardo*, frequently rendered as "intermediate state," is a condition of awareness, or transition between two other kinds of existences.[25] Consciousness is constantly in flux: one state of awareness leads to another, leads to another. So it is with the various *bardos*. There are differing stages of consciousness, each having its own quality and characteristics. When alive, one can experience a continuum of consciousness of waking states, dream states, sleep states, or meditation states.[26] Similarly, in death there are varied states of consciousness—*bardos* or transit stages. The *Tibetan Book of the Dead* speaks of three postmortem *bardos*: (1) the *bardo* of the process of death (*Chikai Bardo*)—this includes the dying of the physical body and the cessation of the vital functions, and the final departure of the awareness principle from the body; (2) the *bardo* of the state after death (*Chonyi Bardo*)—this is a state in which the deceased experiences both beneficent and malevolent postmortem visions, referred to as the peaceful and wrathful deities, and somewhat similar to Gan Eden and Gehenna; and (3) the *bardo* of seeking rebirth (*Sipai Bardo*)—this is the process of preparation for physical reimbodiment.[27] Though an in-depth analysis of the relationship between the *Tibetan Book of the Dead* and Jewish afterlife teachings is beyond the scope of this study,[28] the postmortem pattern of Tibetan Buddhism provides a useful backdrop in developing a Jewish structural model of the afterlife.

Based on a synthesis of various sources, Judaism's afterlife journey of the soul can be divided into the following Transit Stages:

1. The Dying Process
2. *Hibbut ha-kever*—Separation from the Physical Body
3. Gehenna—Emotional Purification
4. Lower Gan Eden—Final Completion of the Personality
5. Upper Gan Eden—Heavenly Repose for the Soul
6. *Tzror ha-hayyim*—Return to the Source
7. Preparation for Rebirth

These stages can be interrelated with the kabbalistic map of reality and the Divine Name of God outlined earlier. Transit Stages 1 and 2, the dying process and *hibbut ha-kever*—Separation from the Physical Body—affect the *nefesh*, or bioenergy level of the soul, and occur in the realm associated with the first *hey* (ה) of the Divine Name. Transit stages 3 and 4, Gehenna—Emotional Purification, and Lower Gan Eden, Final Completion of the Personality—affect the *ruah*, or emotional level of the soul, and occur in the realm associated with the letter *vav* (ו) of the Divine Name. Transit Stage 5, Upper Gan Eden—Heavenly Repose for the Soul—affects the *neshamah*, or mental level of the soul, and occurs in the realm associated with the second *hey* (ה) of the Divine Name. Transit Stages 6 and 7, *tzror ha-hayyim*—Return to the Source and Preparation for Rebirth—affect the *hayyah* and *yehidah*, the universal and transcendental levels of the soul, and occur in the realm associated with the letter *yod* (י) of the Divine Name. These correlations are summarized in Table 10-4. In essence, what we have here is a systematized way of describing the ongoing transformation of the soul after death.

TABLE 10-4   YHVH MODEL OF THE AFTERLIFE JOURNEY OF THE SOUL

Letter of Divine Name	World of Kabbalah	Level of Soul	Transit Stage	State of Consciousness
׳ yod	Atzilut	Yehidah	7. Preparation for Rebirth	Prewomb/ In-womb
	Spiritual	Hayyah	6. Tzror ha-hayyim	Return to the Source
ה hey	Beriyah	Neshamah	5. Upper Gan Eden	Heavenly Repose for the Soul
	Mental			
ו vav	Yetzirah	Ruah	4. Lower Gan Eden	Final Completion of the Personality
	Emotional		3. Gehenna	Emotional Purification
ה hey	Assiyah		2. Hibbut ha-kever	Separation from Physical Body
	Physical	Nefesh	1. Dying Process	Dying Process

TRANSIT STAGE 1: THE DYING PROCESS

Each person ultimately must die. We are all given a certain life span, and a certain destiny as to how death takes us from this life. According to ancient Jewish wisdom, the moment of physical death itself is absolutely painless. The Talmud (*Berakhot* 8a) describes how death, for the righteous, is effortless, like taking a hair out of milk. Have you ever taken a hair out of milk? No resistance, no obstruction, only a graceful yielding.

Eyewitness reports from the deathbed bear out the accuracy of the talmudic claim. Numerous people have described the death experiences of terminal cancer patients, individuals painfully tormented by a ravaging cancer. In spite of all the suffering, at the exact moment of death it is not uncommon to see a peaceful smile of radiance overtake a person. Death ends the suffering of physical life; as the life force departs from the physical body, there is no longer pain, only peace. With that peace comes a recognition of death as being "another transformation through which we move, an adventure to surpass all adventures, an opening, an incredible moment of growth, a graduation."[29]

The notion of death as a peaceful and painless transition is confirmed by studies of NDEs. People have described experiencing a blissful peace at the exact moment they were pronounced clinically dead by attending doctors and nurses. According to NDE experiencers, at the time of death they "couldn't feel a thing in the world except peace, comfort, ease— just quietness."[30] All have affirmed that there is nothing to fear and no pain in the experience of dying.

During the dying process—Transit Stage 1—there are a number of accompanying visions. The exact order of these visions cannot be determined with precise accuracy and surely vary from person to person, depending on the spiritual development of the person and the circumstances of the death. There is obviously a difference in the death experience of one who dies suddenly or violently and another who dies of a long-lingering disease. However, the following may be considered as the subjective visions associated with Transit Stage 1: (1) the experience of the clear light; the River of Light; (2) the encounter with angelic spirits and deceased relatives; (3) the life review; and (4) the dissolution of the elements.

The Experience of the Clear Light—The River of Light

During the dying process one can often (although not always) glimpse the radiance of the higher aspects of the soul as it separates from its connection to the physical body. While it may be difficult to determine exactly when this vision occurs, evidence from both religious texts and descriptions of NDEs indicate that this phenomenon of an encounter with intense luminosity occurs soon after the death of the body.

Kabbalistic sources describe how the soul, at this time, takes a dip in the River of Light, *nehar dinur*. Similarly, in the *Zohar*, we encounter the statement "No man dies before he sees the *Shekhinah*" (III, 88a); perhaps what is implied is that the deceased person beholds a radiant image of divine luminescence. Cross-culturally, in the sources of Tibetan Buddhism we find evidence of a similar encounter with radiant light at the time of death. The traditions of the *Tibetan Book of the Dead* frequently speaks of the Ground Luminosity, or Clear Light, "where consciousness itself dissolves into the all-encompassing space of truth."[31]

Whether or not one will actually be able to notice this inner light and not be frightened by its intensity depends on the level of consciousness attained during life. The *Zohar* makes this point in the following way:

> When a man is on the point of leaving this world . . . the *Shekhinah* shows herself to him, and then the soul goes out in joy and love to meet the *Shekhinah*. If he is righteous, he cleaves and attaches himself to her. But if not, then the *Shekhinah* departs, and the soul is left behind, mourning for its separation from the body. . . . (III, 53a)

Individuals who have practiced a meditative discipline and become familiar with altered states of consciousness may recognize the vision of the *Shekhinah*, or the River of Light, as the inner luminosity of the soul and receptively bask in its radiance. Those who have not acquired a familiarity with the higher experiential realities of consciousness may actually be completely unaware and unconscious during this early phase of the postmortem journey. Or perhaps, the intensity of the River of Light may evoke fear and fright. However, the sacred religious texts frequently encourage the deceased being to welcome the light and embrace it. Kabbalistic teachings suggest that by dipping in the River of Light, one may be purified from the defilements of earthly life. In other words, this encounter with the light of the radiant soul assists the dying person in leaving behind the physical world and in becoming identified with the spiritual world.

The Encounter with Angelic Spirits and Deceased Relatives

Another phenomenon characteristic of the dying process is an encounter with divine beings or with deceased relatives and beloved ones. Phenomenologically, religious texts and NDE studies indicate that there are two qualitatively different types of visionary encounters: a meeting with an angelic or divine being—some type of archetypal entity with very concrete mythic features; and a rendezvous with familial beings—most often beloved friends or family members. Jewish tradition speaks of both types of experience.

Rabbinic literature (*Pesikta Rabbati* 2:3), medieval Midrash (*Masekhet Hibbut Ha-Kever* I, 3), and Kabbalah (*Zohar* I, 79a) all have references to three angels (or three groups of angels) who appear after death and greet the departed being. Elsewhere, in the *Zohar*, it is claimed that Adam himself is present when one dies (I, 65b). Sephardic burial liturgy speaks of how, after death, the archangel Michael, the Cherubim, the *kohanim* (priests) and Levites, and seven orders of the *tzaddikim* and *hasidim* greet the soul of the deceased person.[32]

This phenomenon is also documented in NDE studies where people claim to be greeted by a being of light:

> I heard the doctors say I was dead. . . . Everything was very black, except that, way off from me, I could see this light. . . . I was trying to get to that light at the end, because I felt it was Christ.[33]

Evidence suggests that the kind of archetypal vision a person experiences frequently reflects their own cultural framework, or religious belief system. Thus, the Buddha may appear to a dying Buddhist, Christ to a dying Christian; but a Protestant is less likely to have a vision of Mary; a Jew, unlikely to see a vision of Jesus. One man, who had been a nonpracticing Jew, had a vision of an angel—nonspecific and culturally generic—that appeared to him as his death approached.[34] Anecdotally, there is another story of an elderly Jewish man who, although he had lived a secular lifestyle all his adult life, in his youth in Europe had been educated in a traditional hasidic *yeshivah*. At one point, in his late eighties he had an illness that brought him close to death, and on recovery reported that Rabban Gamliel had appeared and told him it was not yet time for him to leave the world.[35] Who was this Rabban Gamliel? One of the famous talmudic Rabbis familiar to him from his long-forgotten education almost seventy-five years earlier. This was the archetypal image evoked in his consciousness.

A second type of apparition is reported in the early phase of the dying process. It is very common for a person in the throes of death to be visited by the spirit of a deceased relative or friend, who is ready to welcome them into the postmortem worlds. There are certainly countless reports of people who, just prior to death, have a dream in which a deceased spouse, parent, or sibling informs them they will soon be reunited. It is also common at the moment of death for a person to see before their eyes the spirit of a deceased loved one.[36] In like fashion, NDE experiencers report seeing a loving family member who, at the right time, is prepared to assist the person to make the transition from the physical plane. (In the case of NDEs, the beloved one often tells the person their time to die has not yet come.)

Further along these lines, Elisabeth Kübler-Ross tells a fascinating story about a man who had witnessed a hit-and-run accident in which a woman was seriously injured. He stopped his car and offered help, but the woman told him there was nothing he could do except convey a message to her mother that she was okay and happy now because she was with her father. The woman then died in his arms. The man was so profoundly moved by the experience that he drove seven hundred miles to the Native American reservation where this woman's mother lived. He delivered the daughter's message, only to discover that the young woman's father had died from a coronary approximately an hour before the fatal accident, and she had absolutely no way of knowing this news.[37] An anecdote like this suggests that there is a mysterious connection between the world of the living and the world of the dead, a connection that we often cannot fully comprehend.

However, thousands of years before Raymond Moody and Elisabeth Kübler-Ross, Jewish tradition seemed to know something about this link between the dying and the dead. For example, the Talmud recounts how, at the time of his death, Rabbi Yohanan ben Zakkai proclaimed that King Hezekiah, of Judah, was coming to meet him (*Berakhot* 22b). In like manner, the *Zohar* indicates quite explicitly that "at the hour of a man's departure from the world, his father and his relatives gather round him . . . and they accompany his soul to the place where it is to abide" (II, 218a). And perhaps when biblical tradition uses the phrases "gathered unto one's fathers" or "sleeping with one's ancestors" to speak of death, conceivably these terms are not metaphoric, but allude to the experiential reality of encountering one's deceased relatives and friends at the time of death.

The convergence of evidence from NDE studies, deathbed observations, and religious literature suggests that at the time of death one is not alone. A disembodied being, or guide—either an archetypal, angelic wise being or a beloved parent, grandparent, or special friend—makes its presence known to the dying individual and actively assists in the transition from the world of the living to the world beyond. These guides have a very specific function: to initiate the neophyte into the realm of post-mortem consciousness.

The Life Review

Another frequently documented vision associated with the dying process is the postmortem review of life experience. This phenomenon is noted in the rather explicit talmudic teaching: "When a man departs to his eternal home all his deeds are enumerated before him and he is told: Such and such a thing have you done, in such and such a place on that day" (*Taanit* 11a). Likewise, the *Zohar* proclaims: "When God desires to take back a man's spirit, all the days that he has lived pass in review before Him" (II, 222a). Elsewhere in the *Zohar* it is taught that three angelic messengers help a person complete the process of life review—they "count up the days that a man has lived, the sins that he has committed, and all the works which he has accomplished" (I, 79a).

The life review is also attested in descriptions of NDEs, as in the following example:

> When the light appeared, the first thing he said to me was "What do you have to show me that you've done with your life?" or something to that effect. And that's when these flashbacks started . . . all of a sudden I was back early in my childhood. And from then on, it was like I was walking from the time of my very early life, on through each year of my life, right up to the present.[38]

Describing the subjective phenomenology of the life review experience Moody writes:

> This review can only be described in terms of memory, since that is the closest familiar phenomenon to it, but it has characteristics which set it off from any normal type of remembering. First of all, it is extraordinarily rapid. The memories, when they are described in temporal terms, are said to follow one another swiftly in chronological order. Others recall no awareness of temporal order at all. The remembrance was instantaneous; everything appeared at once, and they could take it all in with one mental glance. However, it is expressed all seem in agreement that the experience is over in an instant of earthly time.[39]

An experiential review of life history is also mentioned in various religious depictions of the afterlife, such as in ancient Egyptian tradition, the *Tibetan Book of the Dead*, and St. Augustine's *City of God*.[40] It appears to be a facet of the dying process that all individuals undergo on death. Some NDE researchers have suggested that this life review is a kind of holographic experience in which everything occurs at once, synchronously.[41] Others have suggested that at the time of death, the consciousness is released from the limitations of time and space and is thus "able to embrace all of the forgotten experiences of the past and link them together with the conscious mind, creating an expanded or superconscious state of awareness."[42] Regardless of how we understand the life review, this phenomenon seems to be a naturally occurring by-product of death. Even in our patterns of speech we find the idea of a life review: "I saw my life pass before my eyes," people often exclaim. The likelihood is that this phrase emerged out of a genuine perceived threat of death that, in fact, evoked a life review experience.

What all this suggests is that perhaps the human bioorganism possesses a "black box" recorder and along with it, the ability to chronicle and record all life events. Then, with the encroachment of death a spontaneous reactivation of all recorded memories is triggered—the "black box" goes into rapid review mode.

Although both NDE studies and religious literature suggest that the life review usually transpires in an instantaneous flash, it is conceivable that in cases of a slow and lingering approach of death, the "black box" begins its process of replay even earlier, and as a consequence, the life review takes places more slowly, over hours, or even days. Certainly there are countless deathbed stories about dying people, in a fitful coma, who seem to be in a confused state of consciousness, between dream and sleep state, calling out names of deceased family members. It often appears that these people are reliving earlier life experiences in a dream state. Perhaps these are also life review experiences; conceivably the storehouse of memory within the recesses of consciousness is actively replaying all the events of the life lived, preparing the soul for its departure from the body.

Whether it occurs slowly or rapidly, whether we explain it in mythical terms as an angel who records human deeds or in psychological terms as disembodied consciousness beyond time-space in which past, present, and future knowledge coalesce in one holographic whole, it appears this phenomenon of a life review is characteristic of the early stages of the dying process. We do not fully understand just how it happens, but that this life review takes place, somehow, is increasingly obvious as we continue to study the mysteries of life after death.

The Dissolution of Elements

Another experience associated with the process of dying is the dissolution and separation of the constituent elements of the physical body. Although NDE studies have nothing to say about this aspect of the postmortem journey, our Jewish sources are illuminated by the afterlife lore of Tibetan Buddhism.

As noted in Chapter 8, according to Tibetan *bardo* teachings, during the dying process the four essential components of biological existence—earth, water, fire, and air—begin to dissolve and disconnect from each other. (There are actually five elements, ether or space being the fifth.) Accompanying this experience are very specific inner visions and corresponding outer physical manifestations, all part of the dissolution process and chronicled with extensive detail in numerous Tibetan writings.[43] According to Ken Wilber, what transpires at this point is that the more subtle dimensions of consciousness—bodily awareness, sensation, perception, impulse, and eventually, the capacity for gross conceptualization—each dissolve.[44] The elemental foundations of the human psyche unravel.

Within Jewish tradition, there is one unique text that alludes to this aspect of the dying process, a cryptic *Zohar* passage that states: "[W]hen a man's time comes to depart from the world, four quarters of the world indict him . . . and four elements fall to quarreling and seek to depart each from its own side" (I, 218b). The author of the *Zohar*, like the ancient Tibetan sages, may well have been aware of the subtle, subjective intricacies of dying. Nonetheless, for contemporary people trying to understand what goes on when a human being dies, the *Zohar* does not provide any elaboration that enables us to fully comprehend the experiential reality of dying alluded to in this passage.

However, Tibetan *bardo* tradition suggests that the "four elements" the *Zohar* speaks of are the elements of earth, water, fire, and air as they dissipate and leave the body; the "quarreling" is the potentially tumultuous process that takes place in the inner dimensions of consciousness.

It is apparent that the inner experience of dying is far more complex, than evident to objective observation. As we study ancient esoteric models of the afterlife, it becomes increasingly clear that dying is not simply a momentary event that takes place only on a physical level, but rather a complex process of consciousness transformation. Although scientific instrumentation cannot record physiological activity after the advent of biological death, it seems that, nonetheless, the more subtle and gradual internal aspects of dying continue for some time after pulse, heartbeat, and brain wave measurements go flat. In fact, some traditions teach that it takes anywhere from twenty minutes to several hours for consciousness to leave the body.[45]

Obviously, our current state of knowledge about dying is still incomplete; and at times all we can do is speculate. However, a synthesis of Tibetan Buddhist and Jewish afterlife sources can help us to comprehend more fully the inner dimensions of the dying process. It is evident that some kind of process of dissolution of the elements is particular to the earliest phases of the postmortem journey. We need to learn more about the naturally occurring visionary phenomena associated dying and continue to develop more elaborate cartographies of inner experience for this phase of the postmortem journey. Ultimately, through thorough knowledge and a deeper understanding of these inner experiences, we can help alleviate the fear individuals often experience on the deathbed.

Passing through the Tunnel—Rending the "Silver Cord"

Our description of Transit Stage 1, the Dying Process, is not yet complete. There is one subsequent transition that occurs during the dying process. Traversing an impermeable boundary line between life and death, the soul takes leave of its connection to the physical body and passes through a celestial corridor into the world beyond. This is an important transformative occurrence in the postmortem journey, but most of the available evidence we have for this stage of the journey comes from non-Jewish sources. To explain this stage more fully, we need to draw once again from NDE research and also from Theosophy, a body of metaphysical writings about the spiritual life.

Many of Moody's subjects reported entering a tunnel or some kind of passageway between this world and the world beyond. Although coming very close to the edge of the tunnel, they never finally crossed over to the other side. In all cases, the individual reached a limit beyond which he or she could not pass, and had to turn back.[46]

In Jewish sources, we find the tunnel phenomenon hinted at in the teaching of the *Zohar*, that as the soul leaves the world, it enters the Cave of Makhpelah, which functions as a passageway to Gan Eden (I, 81b).[47] Perhaps the Cave of Makhpelah, metaphorically speaking, is the psychic bridge between life and death.

With the NDE experience, all the people who entered the tunnel returned; they never died. These were "near-death" encounters. But what happens when people die? Is there, in fact, a boundary line the dying person traverses, making death totally irreversible?

Theosophy, from *theo*, meaning "divine," and *sophia*, meaning "wisdom"—the divine wisdom, which claims to be a synthesis of ancient mystical teachings from the various world religions—offers an interesting perspective on this transitional passage between life and death.[48] Theosophy speaks of a "silver cord," a connective link between the body and the soul. When a person is alive, there is an etheric thread of connection between the physical body and the more subtle energy fields that surround and interpenetrate the physical form. Upon death, this silver cord is irreparably snapped. There is no longer any possibility of a return from a "near death"—body and soul are permanently separated.

The Theosophists claim the following passage from the Book of Ecclesiastes refers to this silver cord:

> For the almond tree may blossom,
> The grasshopper be burdened,
> And the caper bush may bud again;
> But man sets out for his eternal abode,
> With mourners all around in the street.
> Before the silver cord snaps
> And the golden bowl crashes. . . .
> And the dust returns to the ground
> As it was
> And the lifebreath returns to God. . . .
> (Ecclesiastes 12:5–7)

Bringing the wisdom of Theosophy to NDE research, we might conjecture that the experience of crossing the tunnel corresponds with the final rending of the silver cord. Once the tunnel is crossed, death is irreversible, the silver cord linking body and soul is severed. Physical resuscitation is out of the question; there is no longer a possibility of reentering and reanimating the body. Now, in the inner planes of awareness, a whole other stage of the postmortem journey begins to unfold.

TRANSIT STAGE 2: *HIBBUT HA-KEVER*— SEPARATION FROM THE PHYSICAL BODY

Strictly speaking, Transit Stage 1, the Dying Process, is not separate and distinct from Transit Stage 2, Separation from the Physical Body. The two are actually part of the same process that has to do with the completion of all experiences related to the physical realm, symbolized by the first *hey* (ה) of the Divine Name. Together, these two transit stages are a continuum of experience transpiring just prior to and immediately following the death moment. One transit stage merges with the other, and both are of variable lengths of time, depending on the individual and the circumstances of the death itself.

Here, however, for the purposes of clarification, a distinction is being made between the earlier visions of the dying process (most of which are evidenced in NDE studies) and what may be a longer process, lasting days or weeks, in which consciousness is completely extricated from the physical body.

Transit Stage 2 is usually described as a process of surrendering one's attachments to the physical body and progressively accepting the reality of one's own death. This Transit Stage corresponds with the phenomenon described in Jewish sources as *hibbut ha-kever*, the "pangs of the grave." It is a three- to seven-day period in which the deceased individual goes through a very painful and anguishing ordeal, releasing attachments to the body and the material world. Often unaware and confused during this time, the deceased may try to communicate with loved ones, or even attempt to reenter the physical body.

In a psychological context, this process of Transit Stage 2 can be elucidated by referring to the kabbalistic model of the soul. During this stage of the postmortem journey, the *nefesh*, or bioenergy aspect of the soul, dissipates and eventually severs its identification with the body. Symbolically represented by the first *hey* (ה) of the Divine Name, the *nefesh* is the energy that animates the physical body; it is a gross form of energy that, according to the kabbalists, is the source of vital energy in the human being.

For those closely identified with the physical body and its passions, extricating oneself from the attachment to the material world after death can be painfully severe. It is an arduous task to relinquish something one clutches with an unyielding grasp: one whose soul has been strongly tainted by sensual indulgences will find it exceptionally difficult to think of oneself separate from the body. Hence, for such an individual, the *nefesh*, or vital energy, remains very closely identified with the body and with all aspects of the material world. As a result of this kind of tenacious clinging, the deceased individual is forced to go through the painful anguish of *hibbut ha-kever*. "Like a needle in living flesh, so does the corpse feel the worms," declares the Talmud (*Berakhot* 12b); *hasidim* understood this to mean that a person was eaten alive by the "worms of his wants."[49] The pain of *hibbut ha-kever* is like an incessant gnawing craving; it is a craving of the desire nature that, like an addiction, can never be fulfilled with any inherent satisfaction.

The length of time and the quality of experience in Transit Stage 2 depends directly on how an individual lived his or her life. If a person cultivated only the physical body, the senses and the desire nature, and if he or she developed addictions to nicotine, alcohol, drugs, sex, and so on, then the bonds of attachment to the body are much stronger. This being the case, the process of separation from the physical body and dissipation of the *nefesh* energy creates much pain for the deceased and likely requires a greater length of time.

However, if an individual has lived more of a pure life, treating the physical body as a temple of the soul, avoiding toxic substances and impurities, cultivating an appreciation of the nonmaterial dimensions of life, and not identifying uniquely with the physical body and the lower vital or *nefesh* energy, then this period of separation from the physical body is a much easier and rapid one. Essentially, if one can discern that there is a sense of self that transcends body and senses, then it is feasible to avoid the pain and anguish of the grave. In such cases, the Transit Stage of *hibbut ha-kever* may not be a lengthy or painful ordeal at all.

It is interesting to note the relationship of Jewish mourning customs to this particular transit stage of the postmortem journey. Interestingly, this phase of *hibbut ha-kever* corresponds with the Jewish tradition of *shivah* (literally, "seven"), a seven-day mourning ritual during which time memorial prayers are recited for the deceased, within the context of community. Throughout the week of *shivah*, mourners are given the opportunity to grieve the loss of the departed one and to receive support from family and friends. For the bereaved, *shivah* serves as a communal vessel for healing and helps to prepare for the eventual reintegration into community life.[50]

On an entirely different level, however, this seven-day process of mourning serves another function: to assist the deceased in the process of disengaging the *nefesh* energy from attachment to the material world. The *Zohar* teaches that during the time of *shivah*, the soul lingers close to the physical plane: "For seven days the soul [*nefesh*] goes to and fro from the house to the grave and from the grave to the house, mourning for the body" (II, 26a). But this is a transitional stage; to continue along the journey, the soul must relinquish physical attachments. This is what the process of sitting *shivah* does for the soul of the deceased.

From a perspective that recognizes that consciousness survives bodily death, *shivah*, in essence, is a spiritual send-off party for the soul of the deceased. At a spiritual level, *shivah* assists the soul to give up its longing for the physical world. During the week of *shivah*, the act of gathering together in prayer to remember and mourn the deceased enables the *nefesh* aspect of the soul to progressively yield material plane entrapments. If the being who has died perceives that beloved ones are mourning his or her passing from the world, the reality of the body's death becomes obvious. *Shivah* brings the soul of a deceased person to the awareness that he or she is no longer among the living and can now leave behind old attachments to life in a physical body.

At the conclusion of *shivah*, there is an interesting custom that relates directly to the psychological function of Transit Stage 2. After being in the house for a week, as the *shivah* ends, family members arise and go outside for a walk around the block. (This practice has local variations and is not practiced universally in all Jewish communities.) For the mourners, this ritual act is a way of saying: "This time of intense mourning has ended; we are now preparing to return to the world of the living to continue life." For the deceased whose consciousness is completing Transit Stage 2, Separation from the Physical Body, this act seems to be a statement from the bereaved to the soul of the deceased: "We have just spent seven days mourning your death and giving up our attachments to you as a physical being. We will walk you out of the house where you have always lived and around the block. But now you must go on your way. Now you must leave the world of the living forever and begin your journey of the afterlife worlds."

Jewish tradition points out that not all souls instantly pass through this transit stage and overcome the process of *hibbut ha-kever* in three, four, or even seven days. There are some deceased individuals who refuse to give up their attachments to the physical body and the material world; there are also those who may have died suddenly or violently, unaware that their death has taken place. These beings, according to Jewish sources, may remain in *olam ha-tohu*, "the world of confusion."[51] Here they remain, as ghoulish spirits who have not accepted their death and attempt to stay in close contact with the living.

However, this experience of souls in *olam ha-tohu* is likely more the exception than the rule; certainly, the sources we examined earlier in no way suggest this happens to everyone. Eventually, the *nefesh* energy completely dissipates and the individual surrenders to the reality of death. The energy of attraction to the physical world is completed symbolically, it is the end of the energy associated with the letter *hey* (ה) of the Divine Name. Then, there begins yet another stage of the postmortem journey.

TRANSIT STAGE 3: GEHENNA—
EMOTIONAL PURIFICATION

Transit Stage 3 corresponds with Gehenna, the postmortem realm of purgation described in Jewish sources. After finally surrendering attachments to the physical body, at this point in the postmortem journey the individual soul next has to deal with unresolved emotional dimensions of one's being. According to the kabbalistic model, Transit Stage 3 is concerned with the energies of the *ruah* aspect of the soul—the emotional energy field. This is the world of emotions, symbolized by the *vav* (ו) of the Divine Name.

During life, an individual experiences a wide variety of ever-changing emotional states. Love, hate, joy, anger, sadness, ecstasy, passion, and aggression are among the many multifaceted emotions of human existence. Also in the course of life itself the individual experiences emotional and psychological wounds, disappointments, rejections, missed opportunities in relationship, deaths of loved ones, and so on; all these have the potential to leave deep level emotional scars. But day-to-day existence, with its pressures of time and social conditioning, often inhibits the full expression of painful emotion. Who can be angry and fully experience one's rage when there are children to send off to school or an employer to satisfy? Who can deal with sadness or grief when daily life demands full concentration on the prosaic and mundane? So often societal norms and physical plane demands necessitate the suppression of emotions that may be "inappropriate" to a particular time or place, emotions that are negative, hostile, or aggressive.

In addition, as human beings, even with the best intentions, it is quite common to live life not fully in tune with the highest ethical, moral values we hold. In relationships, we may hurt others by our actions and words. Whether consciously or unconsciously, intentionally or unintentionally, we may transgress personal or culturally determined boundaries of acceptable behavior. In theological terms, we can talk about sins—recall the traditional Jewish perspective that says Gehenna is a process of purgation for one's sins. In this age of relativity of values, it is probably more appropriate to speak of a failure to live up to one's highest and holiest potential. In either case, in the course of life human beings experience all kinds of raw, negative emotions that are forgotten and repressed, forced into the recesses of the unconscious. There, such festering emotions become psychological complexes—what Stan Grof calls COEX systems (systems of condensed experience)[52]—and at an energy level abide within the emotional energy field, or *ruah* aspect of the soul.

Gehenna, or Transit Stage 3, provides a concentrated opportunity to encounter the dark and dishonorable, unresolved negative emotions. It is easier to deal with intense and conflicting emotion when you no longer have to attend to such irritations of embodied life as flossing teeth, answering the telephone, taking a car in for repairs, or paying Visa bills. Even though it may feel like hell, the experience of consciousness without a body allows for a much more intense connection with one's previously hidden inner reality. As someone once said, "There is no rug in the universe to sweep the shit under."[53] Death of the body serves to lift up the rug and allows a being to have full contact with everything hidden under the rug.

Like it or not, after death and separation from the physical body, the deceased being can no longer hide from years of accumulated and unexpressed anger, rage, fear, sadness, pain, desire, grief, guilt, and shame. Perhaps during this period of time the disembodied being gets to feel the consequences all destructive, negative actions committed and experience with full intensity the pain, shame, and guilt that may have been repressed during life.

Psychologically, we might speak of the purging function of Gehenna as being one of abreaction, discharge, and catharsis. But along with purgation, it is said that Gehenna is also a time of purification for the *ruah* (*Zohar* I, 226a), and as such, may also allow for a progressive resolution of painful, incomplete emotions. In some sense, the Transit Stage of Gehenna might be envisioned as a prolonged psychotherapy intensive, a period of time in which one gets to deal with the consequences of one's unresolved and unconscious emotional issues. Like psychotherapy, Gehenna moves the soul toward healing, transformation, and completion with the past. Although characterized by a fierce emotional agony that may seem interminable, eventually this transit stage reaches its conclusion. As Jewish sources have reiterated throughout the ages, after a maximum of twelve months, the soul of the deceased completes its stint in Gehenna.

It is important to remember that, according to the mystical view of the kabbalists and hasidim, Gehenna is not a locale, so much as a state of consciousness, an experiential realm reflecting one's own emotional state. As Grof's work suggests, descriptions of the torments of Gehenna, which abound in rabbinic and medieval Midrash and Kabbalah, are to be seen as symbolic and not literal. Like the bardo visions of the Tibetan Book of the Dead and Christian images of hell, they describe in allegory and metaphoric language different aspects of the process of purgation and emotional purification.

One midrashic text, for example, speaks of the five different kinds of fire of Gehenna;[54] in another place, the text describes both the ice and the fire of Gehenna.[55] Metaphorically, we might say that these passages refer to specific kinds of emotional and psychological experiences. When the emotions are aroused, one may speak of the burning fires of passion; and emotional states of varying intensity may be described as different kinds of fire. Think of what happens when you get angry. Are you a hothead? What is your type of fire—do you smolder, or burn up full force? Similarly, when the emotional nature is blocked or repressed, one may speak of being a cold person. Is your style to give someone an icy, cold shoulder? From a symbolic standpoint, the textual references to the ice and freezing of Gehenna relate to specific states of consciousness in which the emotional nature is frozen and repressed.

In addition, midrashic tradition over the course of at least a thousand years continually speaks of the seven realms of Gehenna, each one being of a progressively tormenting nature. If, as we are hypothesizing, Gehenna is a direct reflection of one's emotional state, then each person will experience a Gehenna reflecting the depth and quality of his or her unresolved emotions. Obviously, for some, Gehenna will be a more difficult experience; for others, less so.

Above all, Gehenna is a process of purgation and purification, and ultimately during the course of this transit stage the soul of the deceased is again tempered and transformed.

Like Transit Stage 2, Transit Stage 3 bears a particular relationship to Jewish mourning customs. After the death of a beloved family member, the traditional period of mourning lasts twelve months, during which time the *Kaddish* memorial prayer is recited for eleven months, less one day.[56] Interestingly, and not coincidentally, this period of mourning corresponds with the length of time the soul spends in Gehenna.

For the living, reciting the *Kaddish* prayer daily helps the individual adjust to the loss of a beloved one. The mourner is able to grieve more fully, and in so doing experience—in Kübler-Ross's terms[57]—the denial, anger, bargaining, depression, and acceptance that are the inherent stages of the bereavement process. Eventually, the mourner is moved toward an acceptance of death in the face of personal pain and suffering.

On another level, the ritual act of saying *Kaddish* may also have a direct effect on the soul of the deceased. Our secular-influenced society emphasizes how *Kaddish* is for the bereaved; but traditionally Judaism has recognized that by saying the Mourner's *Kaddish*, in the year after a death, the living have the capacity to influence the postmortem fate of the dead. For example, the Talmud tells the following story:

> Rabbi Akiva once saw in a vision the shadowy figure of a man carrying a load of wood on his shoulders. "What ails you?" asked the Rabbi. "I am one of those forlorn souls condemned for his sins to the agony of hell-fire," replied the shadow. "And there is no hope for you?" inquired the Rabbi further in great compassion. "If my little son, who was a mere infant when I died, could be taught to recite the *Kaddish*, then and only then would I be absolved." The Rabbi took the boy under his care and taught him to lisp the *Kaddish*. He was then assured that the father had been released from Gehenna.[58]

What we see in the story is the Jewish belief that saying *Kaddish* functions as a way of assisting the disembodied soul through its purgations in Gehenna. Judaism teaches quite overtly that after death there is a continued emotional connection between the living family member and the soul of the person who is being mourned. And that connection is mediated through the ritual act of saying *Kaddish*.

Conceivably, what this means is that the bereavement process of the mourner has the capacity to either free or hinder the soul of the deceased in Gehenna. In the course of the first year after a death, grief for the living is most intense; for the soul of the deceased, it is a time of emotional purification. If the mourner can reach a feeling of peace, forgiveness, and resolution about the death of a beloved one, does this not directly affect the soul of the deceased in its process of emotional cleansing? If a child can forgive a parent for any hurt or injustice, does this not enable the soul of the dead parent to resolve incomplete and unresolved feelings of guilt? On the other hand, if the mourner cannot get beyond resentment, anger, and hostility toward the person who has died, perhaps such feelings will maintain the intensity of purgation for the deceased soul in Gehenna.

On the other hand, perhaps the converse is true: if through the process of purgations in Gehenna a soul can be purged of anger or guilt toward a child, sibling, or spouse and discover a deeper sense of love, peace, and forgiveness, would this not assist the mourner in reaching similar feelings of resolution? While all this is speculative, it makes the point that if we understand that consciousness survives bodily death with awareness intact, then at a deeper spiritual level the bereaved and the deceased do continue to work on transforming and resolving their relationship. We know that, psychologically, a person in grief goes through a profound and often gut-wrenching process of resolving a relationship with the person who has died, and the more problematic the relationship was, the more difficult the work of resolution. What this Jewish afterlife model adds to our understanding of bereavement is the awareness that the relationship between the bereaved and the deceased is an interactive one that endures even after the body is interred in the earth. The year of saying *Kaddish* is, at a spiritual level, a process of guiding the soul through the journey of emotional purification in the Transit Stage of Gehenna. It is a time for both the living and the dead to "finish old business,"[59] to make peace with the past and to awaken to the possibilities of new dimensions of existence.

As Jewish tradition teaches, Transit Stage 3 is finite in time and eventually ends. The emotional work of Gehenna is eventually completed; the consequences of the emotional experience and learning of the past life are integrated and assimilated. The postmortem soul is ready to continue its journey, prepared to enter yet another Transit Stage.

TRANSIT STAGE 4: LOWER GAN EDEN— FINAL COMPLETION OF THE PERSONALITY

At this point in the postmortem journey, another important transition takes place. According to the *Zohar*, after the *ruah*, or emotional energy field, goes through the purgations of Gehenna, it then enters Lower Gan Eden.

Lower Gan Eden is a transitional state between Gehenna and Upper Gan Eden. Here, the consciousness of the departed one experiences a world of emotional bliss. All the highest emotions of ecstasy, joy, fervor, and so on, can be experienced freely, without limitation or inhibition.

Psychologically, Lower Gan Eden appears to be a time for the final completion of the last vestiges of desire in the finite personality. Hence, whatever inspired emotions are left over from the physical plane life, they must be experienced before the departed one can move into the transcendent realms of Upper Gan Eden. Similarly, if there are any other incomplete desires, they must be given expression. Only when the last vestiges of one's personal life are played out can the soul finally bask in Gan Eden *Ha-Elyon*—the eternal or Upper Gan Eden.

In another sense, perhaps Lower Gan Eden represents a process in which all the acquired learning and experience of the *ruah*, or personal self, are passed on to the *neshamah*, or transpersonal self. Thus, in this Transit Stage, the integrated merit and experience of the personal life are transferred to the immortal dimensions of the soul, in preparation for the transcendent Upper Gan Eden part of the postmortem journey.

To explain the Lower Gan Eden transit stage as a state of consciousness, or a specific psychological function, according to the four-fold kabbalistic model: At this point in the journey of postmortem existence, that which is personal and impermanent—symbolized by the *vav* and *hey* (ו and ה) of the Divine Name, the two lower worlds—comes to an end. Up until this point the postmortem journey has dealt primarily with the vestiges of the physical and bioenergetic worlds, and the personal and emotional energy field. With the passage through the state of Lower Gan Eden, the postmortem being enters into the world of the infinite, the divine.

Thus, the importance of Lower Gan Eden is that it connotes the time of completion of the postmortem experiences having to do with the individual personality. From this point onward in the postmortem journey, the experiences of consciousness relate to the transcendent levels of the soul, the worlds symbolized by *yod* and *hey* (י and ה), of the Divine Name.

The latter stages of the postmortem journey are transcendent states of consciousness experienced through the higher dimensions of the soul.

TRANSIT STAGE 5: UPPER GAN EDEN—
HEAVENLY REPOSE FOR THE SOUL

Prior to entry into Upper Gan Eden, the disembodied being again takes a dip in the River of Light, and also experiences a second review of life experience. This time, all the events of the life just lived, their meaning and consequences, are seen from the perspective of many lifetimes. The meaning of all that has been experienced in the most recent life becomes instantly apparent from the vantage point of the eternal, transpersonal self.[60]

Upper Gan Eden is described in kabbalistic sources as a world of transcendental bliss. This is a world that correlates with the *neshamah* level of the soul, symbolized by the second *hey* (ה) of the Divine Name. Here, the soul experiences the "greater delights of knowing God through understanding."[61] This is an archetypal realm in which familiar souls of like mind and consciousness congregate together in what is referred to as the "Celestial Academy."[62] In his book *Afterlife: The Other Side of Dying*, Morton Kelsey offers a description of heaven that accurately augments the Jewish understanding of Upper Gan Eden:

> It is that state of being in which we will be comforted, made heirs of all of the earth's richest treasure, filled to the brim so that our deep-est longest are satisfied. . . . Then we will behold God and work and play with him among those who love him. . . . Heaven [i.e., Upper Gan Eden] is the place where we will find those kindly, fine, noble, courageous, self-effacing humble, understanding, forgiving, striving spirits whom we have loved on earth. It is the place and state of being where they are happy and at home.[63]

During the Transit Stage of Upper Gan Eden, the soul experiences the spiritual rewards it has merited. This is the vision of paradise described in religious traditions throughout the world—Christianity speaks of heaven, the *Tibetan Book of the Dead* describes the *bardo* visions of the peaceful deities. In the language of the psychology of consciousness, Upper Gan Eden is a state of transpersonal awareness in which one is able to perceive the universe as an integrated unified whole, a state in which the world is seen as inherently beautiful, good, desirable, bounti-ful with perceptions of the wonder, awe, and reverence in the face of a grand, magnificent order; in this state of consciousness the distinctions between the individual soul and the infinite divine are blurred.[64] Thus,

Upper Gan Eden may be such a state of consciousness, experienced some time after death, in which this transcendent, transpersonal awareness is present at all times.

Jewish tradition, however, points out that the quality of one's experience in Upper Gan Eden is reflective of the consciousness the individual has developed during life; this is similar to the declaration of the *Bardo Thodol* that all the visions of the peaceful deities are emanations of mind.[65] Thus, if a person has concentrated solely on the accumulation of material possessions, paying little attention to the spiritual dimensions of life, then the transcendent realms of Upper Gan Eden will be barely perceptible to such a being. On the other hand, if a person lived a life of spiritual questing and has experienced transpersonal states of consciousness during embodied life, then that soul will be able to reap the rewards of such spiritual pursuits and enjoy the transcendent bliss of Upper Gan Eden.

It would appear that even in Upper Gan Eden, the soul continues the evolutionary journey—Gan Eden is not a static experience, but one of ongoing spiritual transformation. Thus, when the Midrash speaks of the seven heavens of Gan Eden (*Sifre Deuteronomy* 10:67a; *Maaseh de R. Joshua ben Levi*) it may be that one moves through these seven heavens, experiencing the increasingly transcendental states of consciousness of the *neshamah* level of the soul.

Again, there is a Jewish mourning practice that correlates with this phase of the postmortem journey. At the time of an anniversary of a death, what is known as a *Yahrzeit*, one recites the *Kaddish* prayer in memory of the deceased. Doing so, according to Jewish tradition, provides spiritual benefit to the soul of the deceased. Even more, according to the kabbalists, the act of reciting a *Kaddish* at the time of a *Yahrzeit* "elevates the soul every year to a higher sphere in Gan Eden."[66]

It is a common custom, at least in some communities, to remember the dead by toasting *Le-Hayyim* ("To life!") and saying *de neshomah zol hobben an aliyah*—"may the soul further ascend." In other words, by remembering the person who has made the transition into the postmortem realms, the living have the ability to assist the disembodied soul in its spiritual journey through the realms of Gan Eden.

Eventually, the time spent in Upper Gan Eden is complete. At this point, the energy of the *neshamah* aspect of the soul, symbolized by the second *hey* (ה) of the Divine Name, completes its heavenly repose. Then, it begins yet another Transit Stage of the postmortem journey.

TRANSIT STAGE 6: TZROR HA-HAYYIM— RETURN TO THE SOURCE

This Transit Stage appears to involve the highest aspects of the soul, the *hayyah* and *yehidah*, corresponding with the *yod* (ʼ) of the Divine Name. At this stage of the afterlife journey, there are far less sources to draw from, and our psychological vantage point is replaced by more of a metaphysical one. If the Transit Stage of Upper Gan Eden may be described as "seeing God," this Transit Stage is the one of "being with God." Jewish sources speak of how the soul returns to *tzror ha-hayyim*, the "storehouse of souls," often translated as "the bundle of life" (*Zohar* II, 209a). It is the place of the origin and terminating point for all souls in the universe. Speculatively, we might suggest that here, in *tzror ha-hayyim*, the soul returns to receive its message for the next incarnation.

We might also correlate this Transit Stage, together with the next one, with another Jewish mourning ritual—the *Yizkor*, or memorial service for the dead, which takes place four times a year, on selected Jewish holy days.[67] Jews have always held the belief that it is possible for the deceased to intervene favorably on behalf of the living. People go to synagogue at the time of *Yizkor* and offer petitionary prayers for health, financial security, family stability, and fertility. In fact, there is a whole premodern liturgical tradition of such prayers.[68] In Jewish folklore and hasidic legend there are stories of barren women who, at the time of *Yizkor*, petition a mother or father in the world beyond, requesting spiritual assistance to be able to conceive and bear a child. We might even imagine that the next year, at *Yizkor*, the woman appears in synagogue pregnant and offers prayers of thanks to the soul of the deceased parent as it continues its postmortem sojourn.

At every stage of the afterlife journey there appears to be some correlation between the experiences of the transiting soul and the ritual practices of the bereaved. Table 10-5 summarizes the correspondence between transit stages of the afterlife journey and Jewish mourning rituals.

TRANSIT STAGE 7: PREPARATION FOR REBIRTH

One final transit stage brings this model to completion. The kabbalists speak about *gilgul*, or reincarnation. Whereas Tibetan Buddhist *bardo* teachings provide a description of the rebirth process,[69] Jewish afterlife

TABLE 10-5   TRANSIT STAGES OF THE AFTERLIFE AND JEWISH MOURNING RITUALS

Letter of Divine Name	Transit Stage	State of Consciousness	Jewish Mourning Ritual
׳ yod	7. Preparation for Rebirth	Prewomb/In-womb	Yizkor
	6. Tzror ha-hayyim	Return to the Source	
ה hey	5. Upper Gan Eden	Heavenly Repose for the Soul	Yahrzeit
ו vav	4. Lower Gan Eden	Final Completion of the Personality	Kaddish
	3. Gehenna	Emotional Purification	
ה hey	2. Hibbut ha-kever	Separation from Physical Body	Shivah
	1. Dying Process	Dying Process	

sources really do not. However, there are certain midrashic teachings that do describe the nature of life in the womb, and we want to include these sources in this model.

A medieval text entitled *Seder Yetzirat Ha-Vlad*, "The Creation of the Embryo,"[70] written in a style similar to the visionary Midrash of Chapter 6, describes how the soul prepares for birth into the world. There in the womb, claims the Midrash, the soul is accompanied by two angels. A light is set above the soul, making it possible to see from one end of the world to the other.

First, the soul is accompanied by the angels to Gan Eden and shown the fate of the righteous. The angels tell the soul that she, too, can experience such a blissful reward by following the ways of God's Torah and commandments. Next, the soul is shown the fate of the sinners in Gehenna. The soul is warned to avoid such a fate when the time comes to depart from the world. Subsequently, the soul is shown a vision of the life that it will live. It is, in a sense, a prelife review.

The text describes the soul in-womb experiences as follows:

> Between morning and evening the angel carries the soul around and shows her where she will live and where she will die, and the place

where she will be buried, and he takes her through the whole world, and points out the just and the sinners and all things. In the evening, he replaces her in the womb of the mother, and there she remains for nine months. . . .

Finally, the time comes for the soul to enter the world. It is reluctant to leave; but the angel touches the baby on the nose, extinguishes the light above the head and sends it forth into the world. Instantly, the soul forgets all that it has seen and learned and enters the world, crying have just lost a place of shelter, rest and security.[71]

With the birth of a new being into the world, the postmortem journey is complete. A soul has finished its transition through the afterlife; another life of physical incarnation begins.

A HASIDIC TALE ON THE AFTERLIFE JOURNEY OF THE SOUL

Our contemporary model of the afterlife has many facets to it and needs to be reiterated once more to enhance clarification. To do so, the following story will demonstrate at least the first five Transit Stages of the afterlife model outlined above. The emphasized passages document specific phenomena and elements of the postmortem journey. The story and the brief discussion that follows are another way of communicating the essential teachings of Judaism on the afterlife experience.

A story is told concerning Reb Elimelech of Lizhensk who, in his youth, had a close friend who was great in Torah and an exalted *tzaddik*. Between Reb Elimelech and this young man there was a great love and friendship.

Suddenly the young man took sick and was very close to death. Reb Elimelech went to visit him and his friend wept before him, begging him to raise his small son, whom he would leave behind at his death. Reb Elimelech promised to do this on the condition of a handshake promise that after his death his friend would come to him and tell him how he fared in judgment. This handshake and promise he gave to him. Reb Elimelech then promised to raise the child and his friend, leaving life to the living, passed on.

When the lad's time of courting came, the Rebbe bound him with the bond of matrimony to a rich man's daughter. On the day of the nuptial canopy all the citizens of the city gathered and the holy master Reb Elimelech entered his room, where he sat in seclusion. The people who had come to the ceremony waited unto despair, and yet the Rebbe did not come. They came close to the door and, spying through the keyhole, they saw him sitting on his chair completely lost in his thoughts and they were very much afraid to disturb him from his meditation. After several hours had passed, the Holy Master came to the canopy and performed the ceremony according to the Law.

At the time of the meal he turned to those who sat near him and said, "Do you know why I tarried so long to come to the canopy? I will tell you why. Behold this young man. The father of the groom was as close a friend as a brother to me from the day of my youth and he promised me before his death that he would come to tell me how he fared in judgment, as long as I would raise his child, and to this he gave me his handshake. I kept my promise, but he did not stand up to his word. Therefore, I would not go to the canopy before he came to see me. Several moments before the ceremony he came to see me. I was in full possession of my consciousness and he seemed to me like a fully living person. I asked him, what happened in your judgment? He answered me in the following words:

"'At the *moment of death I did not feel any pain. It was like taking a hair from milk. But it seemed to me as if I were asleep. After those who had washed and cleaned my body had done their duty, I wished to rise up and send them away. I could not do so and all seemed to me like a dream.* After they had put me into the grave and covered it with the ground, and the people who had accompanied my body to the grave had gone home, *I rose from my grave.* It seemed to me that I was very *amazed that I had come to the cemetery and I wanted to go from there to my home.* I did not know where the gate was. So I climbed up on the surrounding wall and climbed down the other side and started off for home. The day was almost gone and the sun had set in the west. The road led across a small brook. As I wanted to pass through the brook I saw the waters rose and I feared to pass through them. I found a piece of wood and wanted to make a bridge. But the water became suddenly very deep and I was unable to build this bridge. To my dismay the rain began to pour and all my clothes became wet from the rain. I did not know where to turn, for on one side there was the cemetery and on the other side the river. The sun had set and *my soul so desired to return to its former home. Such a fierce desire I never had experienced before.* From my great despair I began to cry His blessed name. Suddenly *a man as tall as from the earth to the sky appeared to me.* He asked me why I wept. I told him that I wished to return to my home, but that I was unable to do so. Whereupon the man said to me, "You fool: Do you think that you are still in that world? You are already in *the Universe of Truth!*"

"'And he took me and raised me up from the earth and put me *before the Heavenly Court. There they began to weight and measure my record. They did not find any stain on me which would obligate me to go to Gehinnom, but because of a small damage they were unable to assign me to Gan Eden.* For this reason it was decreed that I was to sit in a mansion whose one door would open to Gehinnom and the second door to Gan Eden. And *because of the fact that I would be able to see the path of the wicked in Gehinnom and feel with them, my sin too would be removed and my transgression forgiven.* And thus they placed me in the hands of an overseer to seat me in that mansion that they had prepared for me. As I looked into Gehinnom I saw many people of my acquaintance and *heard their outcries and painful sobs.* I was unable to look there and closed my eyes so I would not see.

"'*I was also able to see the great bliss of the righteous in Gan Eden on the other side* and this too I was unable to bear, for it was apparent that I had not yet merited this. But when the Sabbath came, all the souls of Gehinnom were freed, and so I spoke to my overseer and said that I too wanted to be freed from my mansion. My overseer replied that he had no permission to free me. So I said to him, "Would you please go and ask the Heavenly Court." This he did and returned to me with the reply that permission was granted. I then went out of the mansion and raised my eyes and saw thousands of souls soaring and rising up in a to and fro motion to welcome the countenance of the Sabbath Queen. Suddenly a very exalted angel was seen and all approached him and embraced him. I asked who he was and they told me that he was the angel that was created out of the holy teachings that Reb Elimelech had just uttered. When I heard this I remembered that I was to him a friend as close as a brother and it seemed to me in my heart that since Reb Elimelech is so well reckoned with in heaven and since I was his close friend and served, some sort of reward was coming to me on account of this. So when on the Sabbath end, the overseer again came and wanted to return me to my previous mansion, I told him that I had no desire to go back there. So he said to me: "So what else will you do? I can't help it, I am merely an emissary of the Heavenly Court and thus I must fulfill my obligation." So I said to him, "Listen, please, to my word. Speak to the Heavenly Court and say to them that I was a good friend of Reb Elimelech's and therefore I have no desire to return to my mansion." So the overseer went to the Heavenly Court and there they agreed that this was true and that the right was with me. But *since I had given a promise on a handshake to Reb Elimelech that I would come to tell him what had happened, unless I kept the word, I could not be admitted to Gan Eden.* Therefore, I stood in need of return to my own place. So I began to go to Reb Elimelech, and now that I've come to tell you, to keep my promise (between then and now many a year has passed, because I erred on the way until my son became fourteen or fifteen years old).'"

And so Reb Elimelech finished his tale and said, "Thus the man spoke to me and begged for a note saying that he had fulfilled his promise. I replied, 'With honor I will do as you ask, but do stay for the wedding of your son, since you have already come to sojourn under the rafters of my roof.' But he said to me, 'Do not hold me back, for *it is impossible to describe the great bliss that is in Gan Eden* and all things of this world not important to me at all.' So I gave him his note and he left and I went to the canopy."[72]

Reb Elimelech's friend died peacefully. Once again, the death moment is described as being "like taking a hair out of milk"—an easy, painless, and effortless experience. The passage from life to death is likened to a time of sleep, unconsciousness. At this point, Reb Elimelech's friend enters the first stages of the postmortem journey—the two interrelated stages we have termed Transit Stages 1 and 2, the period when the *nefesh* or bioenergy is beginning to separate itself from the physical body.

As the story indicates, this process of separation does not occur immediately. First, Reb Elimelech's friend is able to witness his body being prepared for burial. He is in a dreamlike state, and though he attempts to communicate with the people attending to his corpse, he is unable to do so. In the cemetery, he is still unaware and unaccepting of his own death. He struggles to leave his grave, to return to his former home. But he finds himself in a growing state of anguish—"such a fierce desire I had never experienced before." This is the process described in Jewish sources as *hibbut ha-kever*, the pangs of the grave. The story documents quite explicitly the psychological experience of this early stage of the postmortem journey where the attachment to the physical body and the material world persists. The greater the attachment, the greater the pain and anguish.

After calling out in despair, Reb Elimelech's friend was greeted by a being of light—"a man as tall as from the earth to the sky." This is the image of a guide or wise being who assists the deceased one to enter the afterlife realm. Reb Elimelech's friend is then transported by this being to a scene of judgment before the Heavenly Court, "where they began to weigh and measure my record." This is the image of the life review that recurs in religious literature and in NDE descriptions.

The other visions of the dying process mentioned above—the River of Light, the dissolution of the elements, and the appearance of beloved ones—are not replicated in this story. However, these are phenomena of the early stage of the postmortem journey and would likely occur at the time of or soon after death.

In this story, the man is assigned an interesting role in the afterlife: he is to remain seated between Gehenna and Gan Eden. Metaphorically speaking, this refers to the Lower Gan Eden, Transit Stage 4, which occurs between Gehenna, Transit Stage 3, and Upper Gan Eden, Transit Stage 5. This image conveys the nonlinear nature of the postmortem experience: the postmortem experiences of Gehenna, Lower Gan Eden, and Upper Gan Eden all operating simultaneously here. The man is able to witness the purgations of Gehenna—"I looked into Gehinnom [and] I saw many people of my acquaintance and heard their outcries and painful sobs." His Gehenna experience is a short and vicarious one: by seeing the path of the wicked in Gehinnom and feeling their pain, he is cleansed of his own sin and transgression. Perhaps he is able to avoid a prolonged and painful Gehenna experience because, as a man of God who fulfilled spiritual practices, he died relatively unburdened with unresolved emotional complexes.

His assignment to the world between Gan Eden and Gehenna indicates that he is at first not prepared to fully leave behind his own personal life. Besides the necessary emotional purgation, there remains something from his life on earth that is not yet fulfilled: his vow to Reb Elimelech. Before he can fully enter the transcendent realm of Upper Gan Eden, he is required to return to Reb Elimelech himself, thereby completing the last vestiges of his personal life on earth. Only after doing so can he fully experience the "great bliss" reserved for the righteous in Upper Gan Eden.

This story does not go on to describe the final stages of the postmortem journey—Transit Stage 6, *tzror ha-hayyim*—Return to the Source —and Transit Stage 7, Preparation for Rebirth. However, were there to be an imagined postscript to this story, eventually Reb Elimelech's friend would conclude his time in Upper Gan Eden. He might first return to that transcendent realm where all souls are created, and from there receive an impulse toward his next reincarnation on earth. He might even choose to be reborn as a child of the marriage of his son and daughter-in-law.

SUMMARY

The above hasidic story and the model of the afterlife presented earlier are designed to bring together into a systematic statement the essential Jewish teachings on the afterlife journey of the soul. Although the model consists of seven different Transit Stages, it would appear that the psychological reality of the postmortem experience is a fourfold process corresponding with the Four Worlds of Kabbalah, and symbolically with the four letters of the Divine Name.

In the first stage, the physical body dies, and accompanying this death of the body are very specific visions such as the life review, the appearance of guides or beings of light, the encounter with the River of Light, and the dissolution of the elements of the physical body. The essential psychological process of this first stage of the postmortem experience has to do with consciousness separating from the physical body, from the kabbalistic World of Body/Action. This process of the afterlife journey is identical to the experience of *hibbut ha-kever* and deals with the part of the soul known as *nefesh*, bioenergy, and corresponds symbolically with the first *hey* (ה) of the Divine Name.

The second process of the postmortem journey is one of emotional purification. This is identical to the experience of Gehenna and Lower Gan Eden and involves the level of the soul known as *ruah*, the emotional energy field, and relates to the kabbalistic World of Emotion, corresponding symbolically with the *vav* (ו) of the Divine Name.

The third process of the postmortem journey is one of spiritual repose for the soul. This is a transpersonal process involving the level of the soul known as *neshamah*. This process is identical to the experience of Upper Gan Eden and relates to the kabbalistic World of Mind, corresponding symbolically with the second *hey* (ה) of the Divine Name.

The final process of the postmortem journey is one in which the soul returns to its source, the storehouse of souls known as *tzror ha-hayyim*. This stage involves the levels of the soul known as *hayyah* and *yekhidah*. This process relates to the kabbalistic World of Essence and corresponds symbolically with the *yod* (י) of the Divine Name. Ultimately, taking this process to its final culmination, through the experience of *gilgul*, or rein-carnation, the soul is reborn into the world in another physical body. Death, afterlife, rebirth: human existence is a continuous cycle.

CONCLUSIONS

We come to the end of our journey exploring Jewish views of the after-life. The terrain we have covered brings to light an extensive accumula-tion of images and themes on the fate of the disembodied soul and makes it overwhelmingly clear that, historically, Judaism has always affirmed a belief in life after death.

The kabbalistic-psychological model developed in this chapter pro-vides a way to bring into a coherent whole the variegated assortment of afterlife teachings throughout the ages. Even more, there are a number of contemporary implications of this model that affect our understand-ing of the experience of death, dying, and mourning. First of all, this model suggests to us that beyond the limitations of the physical form, there exists a timeless, immortal dimension of the individual personality, a soul, a consciousness, that survives bodily death. Although signifying the ter-mination of physical life, death is not the endpoint of conscious exis-tence. Individual awareness transcends physical death, and death itself is simply a transition to another state of consciousness. This being the case, death is not to be feared. With the death of the body, one enters a nonmaterial, spiritual world wherein a whole series of transformational experiences occur. The experience of the soul after death is best described as a journey of consciousness in which the disembodied being encoun-ters a sequence of visionary experiences and tribulations, designed to resolve various incomplete aspects of the life just completed.

Further, our model suggests that with spiritual preparation, one can die consciously and remain aware of the subjective, moment-to-moment changes that occur prior to, during, and subsequent to the death mo-ment. This being the case, we need to develop an expanded spiritual approach to the care of the dying. If we see death as a profound experi-ence of inner transformation, what role can people present at the time of death—medical and mental health professionals, clergy, or friends and family—play in assisting dying individuals to leave behind the physical world and enter the postmortem realms? Perhaps we need to train people to serve as "deathing guides" in the same way that midwives assist in the birthing process; such individuals can play a "soul guiding" role at the time of death, supporting the dying individual to remain conscious and without fear during the trials and tribulations of the death moment, and beyond. This might be done in a number of different ways: within the context of Jewish hospice work; by reinstituting community Jewish burial societies, *Hevrei Kaddisha*, where, along with preparation for burial, people are trained to do spiritual work with the dying; and by creating "caring community" models within synagogues.[73] A training program for such "soul-guiding" practitioners could be created based on the understanding of the afterlife developed in this study.

Additionally, our kabbalistic-psychological model suggests that the period immediately after death and throughout the first year is a profoundly important time for the postmortem soul. During this time, the Jewish rituals associated with death and mourning, besides the ways in which they catalyze psychological healing for the bereaved, also function to mediate the relationship between the living and the deceased. Jewish tradition suggests that the living can functionally influence the fate of the soul in the realms of the afterlife. Perhaps through the processes of burial, *shivah*, *Kaddish*, *Yahrzeit*, and *Yizkor* bereaved friends and family, and appropriate "soul guiding" professionals can consciously attune to the inner worlds and help the disembodied soul to progress through the various phases of the postmortem journey. But what would it take to bring this "soul guiding" perspective into the contemporary Jewish world, both liturgically and ritually? No doubt, we need to develop functional soul guiding liturgical resources on dying, death, and bereavement, as well as personal and community healing processes that take into consideration the ongoing spiritual relationship between the bereaved and the deceased.

In the realm of professional training, we need to teach rabbis, educators, helping professionals, and Jewish funeral directors about Judaism's afterlife teachings—many still do not know that Judaism has an extensive view of postmortem survival. It is also vital to train such professionals to incorporate an experiential "soul guiding" dimension into the Jewish rituals associated with burial and bereavement.

In the sphere of public education, it is important to develop specific modules for Jewish death awareness education that incorporate teachings on the afterlife with information on the traditional rituals of death and bereavement. Different kinds of programs may be developed for Hebrew day schools and work with younger children and teens; university Jewish Studies programs; synagogues and Jewish community centers; and work with Jewish elders.

Above all, we need to create a contemporary Jewish death manual that integrates recent psychological perspectives on dying and bereavement with the vast legacy of Jewish tradition on death and the afterlife. Designed for healing the bereaved and Jewish death-awareness education, such a manual, "A Jewish Book of Life," can be used in hospice and hospitals, at funerals, in *shivah* houses, for memorial services, and in other ritual moments that deal with dying and death.

In the final analysis, our kabbalistic-psychological model teaches us that between the world of the living and the world of the dead there is a window and not a wall. From earliest times, Jewish tradition has recognized that the living and the dead continue to interact in important and intimate ways. Jewish tradition teaches us to remember the dead: doing so will, in the long run, help us enhance the quality of life. Long after people die, their legacy lives on inside us. Within the wellsprings of our infinite souls we find the window of connection between the living and the dead.

Notes

CHAPTER 1

1. See Moses Mendelssohn, *Phaedon; or the Death of Socrates*, trans. from the German (New York: Arno Press, 1973; originally published in 1789).

CHAPTER 2

1. An earlier version of this chapter was published as "Is There Afterlife after Auschwitz? Reflections on Jewish Views of Life after Death in the Twentieth Century" in *Judaism—A Quarterly Journal of Jewish Life and Thought and Response* 41:4 (Fall 1992): 346–360.

2. This story is found in Stephen Levine, *Who Dies? An Investigation of Conscious Living and Conscious Dying* (Garden City, NY: Anchor Books, 1982), p. 272.

3. Quoted in Jean Herschaft, "Patient Should Not Be Told of Terminal Illness: Rabbi," *The Jewish Post and Opinion*, 13 March 1981, p. 12.

4. There is a rabbinic teaching that proclaims: "Better is one hour of bliss in the World to Come than the whole of life in this world." However, this statement is immediately followed by the claim, "Better is one hour of repentance and good works in this world than the whole life of the World to Come (M. *Avot* 4:17). The juxtaposition of these two ideas in the same place serves to

emphasize that embodied, physical plane life does have a primary value in the Jewish schema of things.

5. Abraham Joshua Heschel, "Death as Homecoming," in *Jewish Reflections on Death*, ed. Jack Riemer (New York: Schocken Books, 1974), p. 73.

6. Aaron Berechia ben Moshe Mi'Modina, *Maavor Yabok* (B'nai Brak: Yishpah, 1967).

7. Jacob R. Marcus, *Communal Sick-Care in the German Ghetto* (Cincinnati: Hebrew Union College Press, 1947), pp. 229–230.

8. Menasseh ben Israel, *Nishmat Hayyim* (New York: Sinai Offset, n.d.; originally published in 1651).

9. For biographical information, see Cecil Roth, *A Life of Menasseh ben Israel* (Philadelphia: Jewish Publication Society, 1934).

10. Dante Alighieri, *The Inferno*, trans. John Ciardi (New York: New American Library, 1954); *The Paradiso*, trans. John Ciardi (New York: New American Library, 1961); *The Purgatario*, trans. John Ciardi (New York: New American Library, 1961).

11. Dov Yardin, ed., *Mahbarot Immanuel HaRomi*, vol. 2 (Jerusalem: Mosad Bialik, 1954), pp. 511–554.

12. This is not only a problem of language; it is more complex, as we will see. Even in modern-day Israel, where Hebrew is the predominant language, it is often difficult to find in bookstores copies of medieval texts on life after death. And topics such as the soul's postmortem destiny, Gehenna, Gan Eden, and reincarnation are not high on the agenda in the Orthodox, *yeshivah* world.

13. See Theodore J. Lewis, *Cults of the Dead in Ancient Israel and Ugarit* (Atlanta: Scholars Press, 1989), pp. 99–181.

14. R. H. Charles, *Eschatology: The Doctrine of a Future Life in Israel, Judaism and Christianity* (New York: Schocken Books, 1963), pp. 19–20. Originally published in 1899, Charles's book is one of the classic studies of afterlife teachings in biblical times.

15. Herschel J. Matt, "An Outline of Jewish Eschatology," *Judaism* 17:2 (Spring 1968): 186–196.

16. Moses Maimonides, *Mishneh Torah*, vol. 1: *The Book of Knowledge*, trans. and ed. Moses Hyamson (Jerusalem: Boys Town Publishers, 1965), p. 91a.

17. Maurice Lamm, *The Jewish Way in Death and Mourning* (New York: Jonathan David, 1969), p. 225.

18. Leo Baeck, *The Essence of Judaism*, trans. Victor Grubenwieser and Leonard Pearl (New York: Schocken Books, 1948, 1976), p. 185.

19. Sir George James Frazer, *The Belief in Immortality and the Worship of the Dead*, 3 vols. (London: Dawsons, 1968).

20. A. Rust, "Der primitive Mensch," quoted in Hans Kung, *Eternal Life?* trans. Edward Quinn (Garden City, NY: Doubleday, 1974), p. 51.

21. Ian Wilson, *The After Death Experience* (New York: William Morrow, 1987), pp. 7–26.

22. See Mircea Eliade, *Death, Afterlife and Eschatology* (New York: Harper & Row, 1967, 1974), and Stanislav and Christina Grof, *Beyond Death—The Gates of Consciousness* (New York: Thames and Hudson, 1980).

23. Bertrand Russell, *Why I Am Not a Christian* (London: Unwin Paperbacks, 1957), p. 45.

24. Quoted in John Bowker, *The Meanings of Death* (New York: Cambridge University Press, 1991), p. 6.

25. Max Schur, *Freud: Living and Dying* (New York: International Universities Press, 1972), p. 136.

26. Sigmund Freud, *The Future of an Illusion* (Garden City, NY: Anchor Books, 1961; originally published 1927).

27. Sigmund Freud, "Totem and Taboo," in *Standard Edition of the Complete Psychological Works of Sigmund Freud*, trans. and ed. James Strachey (London: Hogarth Press, 1953–1974), 13:1–161; quoted in Schur, *Freud: Living and Dying*, 298.

28. Sigmund Freud, "Thoughts for the Times on War and Death," *Standard Edition* 14:273–302.

29. Allan Arkush, "Immortality," in *Contemporary Jewish Religious Thought*, ed. Arthur A. Cohen and Paul Mender-Flohr (New York: Scribner's, 1987), pp. 479–482.

30. Hermann Cohen, *Religion of Reason out of the Sources of Judaism*, (1971), p. 308; quoted in Arkush, "Immortality," p. 481.

31. Quoted in Arkush, "Immortality," p. 481.

32. Kenneth L. Woodward, "Heaven," *Newsweek*, 27 March 1989, pp. 52ff.

33. See Arthur Waskow, *These Holy Sparks—The Rebirth of the Jewish People* (New York: Harper & Row, 1983). See also David Teutsch, ed., *Imagining the Jewish Future: Essays and Reponses* (New York: State University of New York Press, 1992).

34. See Colleen McDannell and Bernhard Lang, *Heaven: A History* (New Haven, CT: Yale University Press, 1988), pp. 47–68. See also Jacques Le Goff, *The Birth of Purgatory*, trans. Arthur Goldhammer (Chicago: University of Chicago Press, 1984).

35. See, for example, Richard Cavendish, *Visions of Heaven and Hell* (London: Orbis, 1977), and Robert Hughes, *Heaven and Hell in Western Art* (New York: Stein and Day, 1968).

36. Quoted in Kung, *Eternal Life?*, p. 130.

37. George Gallup, *Adventures in Immortality* (New York: McGraw-Hill, 1982), p. 212. Another survey of American beliefs about life after death was done in 1980–1981. However, unlike the earlier polls, this one was not broken down according to religion. In this study, Gallup indicates that nationwide, 67 percent of Americans believe in life after death, 27 percent do not, and 6 percent have no opinion.

38. Richard Siegel, Michael Strassfeld, and Sharon Strassfeld, eds., *The First Jewish Catalog* (Philadelphia: Jewish Publication Society of America, 1973).

39. In 1981, the figure of 125,000 was presented by Elisabeth Kübler-Ross. The figure of 200,000 is a projected estimate, based on this earlier figure. See "Playboy Interview: Elisabeth Kübler-Ross," *Playboy* 28 (November 1981): 96ff.

40. According to *Psychological Abstracts*, there are between 100 and 150 articles a year on the topic "Death and Dying." Two bibliographies on thanatological literature, one by Kutsher et al., the other by Miller and Acri, list 4,844 and 3,848 entries, respectively.

See Martin L. Kutsher et al., *A Comprehensive Bibliography of Thanatology Literature* (New York: MSS Information Corporation, 1975), and Albert J. Miller and Michael James Acri, *Death: A Bibliographical Guide* (Metuchen, NJ: Scarecrow Press, 1977).

41. Geoffrey Gorer, *Death, Grief and Mourning* (Garden City, NY: Anchor Books, 1967).

42. See Elisabeth Kübler-Ross, *On Death and Dying* (New York: Macmillan, 1970).

43. American Psychiatric Association, *DSM-III-R* (Washington, DC: APA, 1987).

44. This story is related in Riemer, *Jewish Reflections on Death*, p. 1, and Derek Gill, *Quest—The Life of Elisabeth Kübler-Ross* (New York: Ballantine, 1980), p. 131.

45. Two notable exceptions to the prevalent dearth of Jewish writings on the spirituality of death and afterlife are Rifat Sonsino and Daniel B. Syme, *What Happens after I Die?* (New York: UAHC Press, 1990), and Anne Brener, *Mourning and Mitzvah* (Woodstock, VT: Jewish Lights Publishing, 1993). The latter is one of the most exciting new contributions to Jewish perspectives on death.

46. Quoted in Riemer, *Jewish Reflections on Death*, p. 2.

CHAPTER 3

1. For an overview of biblical chronology, see Manahem Mansoor, *Jewish History and Jewish Thought—An Introduction* (Hoboken, NJ: Ktav, 1991). See also Max I. Margolis and Alexander Marx, *A History of the Jewish People* (Philadelphia: Jewish Publication Society, 1927).

2. For a discussion on the dating of biblical texts see Norman K. Gottwald, *A Light to the Nations* (New York: Harper & Row, 1959), pp. 103–109. The classic study on dating of biblical sources is Julius Wellhausen, *Prolegomena to the History of Ancient Israel*, trans. J. Sutherland Black (New York: Meridian Books, 1957; originally published in 1878), pp. 6ff. Changing contemporary perspectives on the dating of biblical texts are brilliantly elucidated by

Richard Elliott Friedman, *Who Wrote the Bible?* (New York: Harper & Row, 1987).

3. Throughout this book we will use the notation YHVH to refer to the Divine Name. This appellation comprises the four Hebrew letters *yod, hey, vav,* and *hey,* which is likely the most accurate English language representation of the name of the biblical God. See Arthur Waskow, "The Rainbow Seder," in *The Shalom Seders,* ed. New Jewish Agenda (New York: Adama Books, 1984), p. 35.

4. For a discussion of the understanding of human consciousness in this historical era, see Ken Wilber, *Back to Eden—A Transpersonal View of Human Evolution* (Garden City, NY: Doubleday, 1981).

5. R. H. Charles, *Eschatology: The Doctrine of a Future Life in Israel, Judaism and Christianity* (New York: Schocken Books, 1963), pp. 19–20. Originally published in 1899, Charles's book is one of the classical studies of afterlife teachings in Biblical times. In some places, however, his historical dating has been proven incorrect by later scholarship.

6. Albrecht Alt, *Essays on Old Testament History and Religion,* trans. R. A. Wilson (Garden City, NY: Doubleday, 1967), p. 61. Alt notes how such biblical references as "the God of Abraham, the God of Isaac, the God of Jacob" (Exodus 3:6), "the Fear of Isaac" (Genesis 31:53), and "the Mighty One of Jacob" (Genesis 49:24) are indicative of cults of worship centered on a particular tribal leader.

7. It is likely that phrases such as these were understood quite literally. Archaeological evidence indicates that the dead were laid to rest on rock shelves within family burial caves, and later the bones may have been gathered and placed in a collective depository. See Walter Eichrodt, *Theology of the Old Testament,* vol. 2, trans. J. A. Baker (London: SCM Press, 1967), pp. 213ff.; Eric Meyers, *Jewish Ossuaries: Reburial and Rebirth* (Rome: Biblical Institute Press, 1971).

8. Herbert Chanan Brichto, "Kin, Cult, Land and Afterlife—A Biblical Complex," *Hebrew Union College Annual* 44 (1973): 8.

9. Ibid., 1–54; Eichrodt, *Theology of the Old Testament,* pp. 213ff.; Charles, *Eschatology,* p. 32. Raphael Patai, *Sex and Family in Bible and the Middle East* (Garden City, NY: Doubleday, 1959), pp. 233ff.

10. Colleen McDannell and Bernhard Lang, *Heaven: A History* (New Haven, CT: Yale University Press, 1988), pp. 3–6.

11. Cited by W. O. E. Oesterly and Theodore H. Robinson, *The Hebrew Religion—Its Origin and Development* (London: Society for Promotion of Christian Knowledge, 1930), p. 322.

12. William Foxwell Albright, *The Archaeology of Palestine* (New York: Pelican Books, 1961), p. 93; S. G. F. Brandon, *Man and His Destiny in the Great Religions* (Manchester: Manchester University Press, 1962), pp. 110–112;

Rolland de Vaux, *Ancient Israel*, vol. I: *Social Institutions* (New York: McGraw-Hill, 1965), p. 60.

For historical background on early biblical burial practice see Emanuel Feldman, *Biblical and Post-Biblical Defilement and Mourning: Law as Theology* (New York: Yeshiva University Press, 1977), and Audrey Gordon, "Death and Dying—Past, Present and Future," in *Ancient Roots and Modern Meanings*, ed. Jerry Diller (New York: Bloch, 1978), pp. 201–215.

13. Called a *vidui maaser*, "A Confession of the Priestly Tithe." See Maimonides, *Mishneh Torah*, "*Hilkhot Bikkurim*," 4:1. See also *Bikkurim* 2:2, *Sotah* 7:1, and Saul Lieberman, *Hellenism in Jewish Palestine* (New York: Jewish Theological Seminary of America, 1962), p. 140, n. 11.

14. Charles, *Eschatology*, p. 24.

15. See, for example, 1 Kings 11:8; 14:22–24; 16:31–33, 22:53–54; 2 Kings 3:2, 13:6, 16:3.

16. Rolland de Vaux, *Ancient Israel*, vol. 2: *Religious Institutions*, (New York: McGraw-Hill, 1965), pp. 284–285.

17. Ibid., p. 286. For a further description, see Raphael Patai, *The Hebrew Goddess* (New York: Avon Books, 1967), pp. 16–41. See also 2 Kings 18:4, 23:13–14; 2 Chronicles 14:2.

18. William Foxwell Albright, *Yahweh and the Gods of Canaan* (London: Athlone Press, 1968), pp. 177ff., 205; de Vaux, vol. 1, p. 58; vol. 2, p. 287. See also "Cult Places, Israelite," *Encyclopaedia Judaica*, vol. 5, 1167. Not all scholars have agreed on the association between *bamot* and the dead. See, for example, W. Boyd Barrick, "The Funerary Character of 'High-Places' in Ancient Palestine: A Reassessment," *Vetus Testamentum* 25 (1975): 565–595.

19. de Vaux vol. 2, p. 287.

20. Ernest Klein, *A Comprehensive Etymological Dictionary of the Hebrew Language for Readers of English* (Jersualem: Carta, 1987).

21. Charles, *Eschatology*, pp. 21ff.

22. Ramban, *Commentary on the Torah*, Gen. 31:19, trans. Charles B. Chavel (New York: Shilo, 1973).

23. For a discussion of *teraphim* and divination, see W. O. E. Oesterley, *Immortality and the Unseen World—A Study in Old Testament Religion* (London: SPCK, 1921), pp. 135–136.

24. Brichto, "Kin, Cult, Land and Afterlife," p. 46.

25. Oesterley, *Immortality and the Unseen World*, p. 134.

26. See Harry A. Hoffner, "Second Millennium Antecedents to the Hebrew *Ob*," *Journal of Biblical Literature* 86 (1967): 385–401.

27. Charles, *Eschatology*, pp. 33ff.; Johs. Pederson, *Israel—Its Life and Culture* (London: Oxford University Press, 1926, 1959), pp. 461–462.

28. This particular passage from Genesis is dated from the tenth century B.C.E. by Francis Brown, S. R. Driver, and C. A. Briggs, *Hebrew and English*

Lexicon of the Old Testament (Oxford: Clarendon Press, 1907, 1968), pp. 982–983.

29. Eichrodt, *Theology of the Old Testament*, p. 210 n. 1. See also M. Jastrow, "The Babylonian Term *su'alu*," *American Journal of Semitic Languages and Literature* 14 (1897–1898): 165–170, who argues that Sheol is etmologically related to *su'alu*, a Babylonian term for the netherworld, cited by Nicholas J. Tromp, *Primitive Conceptions of Death and the Nether World in the Old Testament* (Rome: Pontifical Biblical Institute, 1969), p. 21, n. 3.

30. Charles, *Eschatology*, p. 34.

31. S. G. F. Brandon, *The Judgement of the Dead—The Idea of Life after Death in the Major Religions* (New York: Scribner's, 1967), p. 57.

32. John Hick, *Death and Eternal Life* (San Francisco: Harper & Row, 1976), p. 57.

33. McDannell and Lang, *Heaven*, p. 4.

34. Charles, *Eschatology*, pp. 35–36; Brandon, *Judgement of the Dead*, p. 58.

35. Charles, *Eschatology*, p. 33.

36. For a further discussion on Sheol, see George Foote Moore, *Judaism*, vol. 2 (Cambridge: Harvard University Press, 1927, 1962), pp. 290ff. For an elaborate investigation of the motifs associated with the underworld in the early biblical period, see Tromp, *Primitive Conceptions*.

37. See Oesterley, *Immortality and the Unseen World*, p. 73.

38. *Genesis Rabbah* 26:7 makes a clear association between these different names stating: "They were called by seven names: Nephilim, Emim, Rephaim, Gibborim, Zamzumim, Anakin, and Awim."

39. See 1 Enoch 7–16; Jubilees 5:6; Wisdom 14:6; *Pirkei de Rabbi Eliezer*, chapter 22.

40. Oesterley, *Immortality and the Unseen World*, pp. 73–74

41. Pederson, *Israel—Its Life and Culture*, p. 153.

42. Hans Walter Wolff, *Anthropology of the Old Testament*, trans. Margaret Kohl (Philadelphia: Fortress Press, 1974), p. 10. For further illumination of the biblical concept of *nefesh*, see Alan Cooper, *Body, Soul and Life Everlasting* (Grand Rapids, MI: Eerdmans, 1989).

43. D. S. Russell, *The Method and Message of Jewish Apocalyptic* (London: SCM Press, 1964), p. 353.

44. Charles, *Eschatology*, p. 41.

45. For a clear analysis of the evolution of a retributive postmortem eschatology in the postexilic biblical period, see Brandon, *Judgement of the Dead*, pp. 59–60.

46. Jewish tradition (*Baba Batra* 15a) teaches that Jeremiah authored Lamentations, the biblical text describing the Babylonian pillage and destruction of Jerusalem.

47. Hick, p. 70.

48. Wilber, *Back to Eden*, pp. 179ff.

49. Russell, *Method and Message*, p. 356.

50. Another English translation of Job 19:25–26, from the Jewish Publication Society edition, reads:

But I know that my Vindicator lives,
In the end He will testify on earth—
This, after my skin will have been peeled off.
I would behold God while still in the flesh.

This translation suggests another possible interpretation: that Job's suffering and vision of God occurs in this life and not in a postmortem afterlife. See *Tanakh—The Holy Scriptures* (Philadelphia: Jewish Publication Society, 1988).

51. Charles, *Eschatology*, pp. 71ff.

52. On messianism in the biblical era, see Joseph Klausner, *The Messianic Idea in Israel*, trans. W. F. Stinespring (New York: Macmillan, 1955), pp. 49–55.

53. See Charles, *Eschatology*, pp. 86–104, who presents an elaborate analysis of biblical collective eschatology.

54. Ibid., p. xi. On Persian dualistic eschatology, see Brandon, *Judgement of the Dead*, pp. 149–164.

55. See John F. Sawyer, "Hebrew Words for the Resurrection of the Dead," *Vetus Testamentum*, 23, (1973): 218–234.

56. Reform Judaism never accepted Jewish philosophical conceptions of physical resurrection. With the creation of Reform prayer books, liturgical references to resurrection were substituted with the notion of immortality. See Jakob J. Petuchowski, *Prayerbook Reform in Europe* (New York: World Union for Progressive Judaism, 1968), pp. 215ff.

With the development of Mordecai Kaplan's Reconstructionism, there was a rejection of all supernaturalistic conceptions of Judaism, and the doctrine of resurrection was likewise reinterpreted. Reconstuctionist liturgy speaks of the God who "gives and renews life." See *Kol Haneshama—Shabbat Eve*, ed. David Teutsch et. al. (Wyncote, PA: The Reconstuctionist Press, 1989).

57. Charles, *Eschatology*, p. 130. See also Harris Birkeland, "The Belief in the Resurrection of the Dead in the Old Testament," *Studia Theologica* 3 (1950): 60–78.

58. Charles, *Eschatology*, p. 131.

59. Other references to a national resurrection include Hosea 6:1–3 and Isaiah 53:10.

60. McDannell and Lang, *Heaven*, p. 12

61. Bernhard Lang, "Street Theater, Raising the Dead, and the Zoroas-

trian Connection in Ezekiel's Prophecy," in *Ezekiel and His Book*, ed. John Lust (Leuven: Leuven University Press, 1986), pp. 297–316.

62. Helmer Ringgren, "Resurrection," *Encyclopedia of Religion*, vol. 12 (New York: Macmillan, 1987).

63. The doctrine of the resurrection of the physical body is consistent with biblical notions of the nonduality of the body and soul. If there was to be a re-newed life after death—the coming kingdom—according to Hebrew concep-tions of the human being, it could not be without a physical body. Ibid., p. 64.

64. While this is the earliest direct reference to the resurrection of the dead, according to Leonard Greenspoon, centuries earlier there were biblical teachings indicating a long, slow evolutionary process in the development of a doctrine of resurrection. See Leonard J. Greenspoon, "The Origin of the Idea of Resurrection," in *Traditions in Transformation: Turning Points in Biblical Faith*, ed. Baruch Halpern and Jon D. Levenson (Winona Lake, IN: Eisenbrauns, 1981), pp. 247–321.

65. Ibid. Even as late as the first century C.E., the two dominant schools of Jewish life, the Pharisees and the Sadducees, were still in disagreement with regard to acceptance of the doctrine of resurrection. See Louis Finkelstein, *The Pharisees*, 2 vols. (Philadelphia: Jewish Publication Society, 1938, 1962), vol. 1, pp. 145–159; vol. 2, pp. 742–747.

66. Charles, *Eschatology*, p. 131.

67. Greenspoon, "Origin," p. 259. Helmer Ringgren, *Israelite Religion*, trans. David E. Green (Philadelphia: Fortress Press, 1966), p. 247.

68. Charles, *Eschatology*, p. 132 n. 3.

69. Apocalyptic is a designation applied to "a whole body of literature whose existence . . . stretches over the period of the fifth century B.C.E. through to the first century C.E. These works generally consist of a compendium of visions which an angel interprets for the visionary, who is often a hero from antediluvian times, or from the beginnings of history." See Andre Lacoque, *The Book of Daniel*, trans. David Pellauer (Atlanta: John Knox Press, 1979), pp. 4–5.

CHAPTER 4

1. For a scholarly history of this period, see Victor Tcherikover, *Helle-nistic Civilization and the Jews*, trans. S. Applebaum (Philadelphia: Jewish Pub-lication Society of America, 1966), and Elias J. Bickerman, "The Historical Foundations of Post-biblical Judaism," in *The Jews: Their History*, ed. Louis Finkelstein (New York: Schocken Books, 1970), pp. 72–118.

2. For a portrayal of the diversity of Jewish views within this period, see Lawrence H. Schiffman, *From Text to Tradition: A History of Second Temple and Rabbinic Judaism* (Hoboken, NJ: Ktav, 1991), and Michael E. Stone, *Scriptures*,

Sects and Visions (Philadelphia: Fortress Press, 1980). On the wide-ranging literary activity of this period, see Michael E. Stone, ed., *Jewish Writings of the Second Temple Period* (Philadelphia: Fortress Press, 1984).

3. Jewish settlement in Alexandria began in the third century B.C.E. See Bickerman, "Historical Foundations," p. 284.

4. Raphael Patai, *Gates to the Old City: A Book of Jewish Legend* (New York: Avon Books, 1980), pp. 122–123.

5. With the exception of 2 Esdras and the Prayer of Manasseh. On the history and canonization of the Apocrypha, see James H. Charlesworth, ed., *The Old Testament Pseudepigrapha*, vol. I: *Apocalyptic Literature and Testaments* (Garden City: Doubleday, 1983) pp. xxiiiff.; Donald E. Gowan, *Bridge between the Testaments* (Pittsburgh: Pickwick Press, 1976), p. 337; and George W. E. Nickelsburg, *Jewish Literature between the Bible and the Mishnah* (Philadelphia: Fortress Press, 1981), pp. 5–6.

6. See, for example, *The Holy Bible*, New American Catholic Edition, 1961; for a non-Catholic Bible that includes apocryphal texts, see *The New English Bible* (New York: Oxford University Press, 1971).

7. Charlesworth, *Old Testament Pseudepigrapha*, vol. 1, p. xxv.

8. This number is comprised of five books of Torah—Genesis, Exodus, Leviticus, Numbers, and Deuteronomy; eight books of the prophets—Joshua, Judges, 1 and 2 Samuel (together forming one book), 1 and 2 Kings (together forming one book), Isaiah, Jeremiah, Ezekiel, and the twelve minor prophets (one book); and eleven books of the Writings: Psalms, Proverbs, Job, Song of Songs, Ruth, Lamentations, Eccelsiastes, Esther, Daniel, Ezra-Nehemiah (as one book), and 1 and 2 Chronicles (as one book). Ibid., p. 555.

9. M. *Yadayim*, 3:5.

10. Charlesworth, *Old Testament Pseudepigrapha*, vol. 1, p. xxii.

11. Rashi's commentary on Mishnah *Megillah* 4:8.

12. Erwin R. Goodenough, *Jewish Symbols in the Greco-Roman Period* (New York: Pantheon Books, 1958), especially vols. 9–11.

13. On the relationship between the apocryphal and pseudepigraphic traditions and normative Judaism, see D. S. Russell, *The Method and Message of Jewish Apocalyptic* (London: SCM Press, 1964), pp. 20ff.

14. Exceptions to this are the Book of Maccabees and the Book of Judith, which provide source documentation on the postbiblical holiday of Hanukkah.

15. R. H. Charles, ed., *The Apocrypha and Pseudepigrapha of the Old Testament in English*, vol. 2: *Pseudepigrapha* (Oxford: Oxford University Press, 1919, 1963).

16. Abraham Kahana, ed., *Ha-Sefarim Ha-Hitzonim*, 2 vols. (Tel Aviv: Hozaath M'qoroth Publishers, 1936).

17. James H. Charlesworth, *The Old Testament Pseudepigrapha*, 2 vols. (Garden City, NY: Doubleday, 1985).

18. Russell, *Method and Message*, pp. 357ff.

19. Ibid., p. 357.

20. Patrick W. Skehan, ed., *The Wisdom of Ben Sira* (New York: Doubleday, 1987), pp. 8ff.

21. *Sanhedrin* 100b; *Hagigah* 13a; *Niddah* 16b; *Berakhat* 11b.

22. J. T. Milik attributes this text to a Qumran scribe and studies have documented a clear relationship between this text and the Zadokite Fragments found at Qumran. Russell, *Method and Message*, p. 42.

23. Ibid., 358.

24. This text is also known as *The Life of Adam and Eve*. See Charlesworth, *Old Testament Pseudepigrapha*, vol. 1, pp. 249ff.

25. For historical background, see R. H. Charles, "The Book of the Secrets of Enoch," in *The Apocrypha and Pseudepigrapha of the Old Testament in English*, vol. 2 (Oxford: Oxford University Press, 1913, 1963), p. 425. See also R. H. Charles, *The Book of Enoch (1 Enoch)* (London: SPCK, 1917) and Charlesworth, *Old Testament Pseudepigrapha*, vol. 1, pp. 5–12, 91–100, 223–254.

26. J. T. Milik and M. Black, *The Book of Enoch: Aramaic Fragments of Qumran Cave* (Oxford: Oxford University Press, 1976).

27. Stone, *Scriptures, Sects and Visions*, p. 31.

28. See Gershom Scholem, *Major Trends in Jewish Mysticism* (New York: Schocken Books, 1954), pp. 43–44, and *Jewish Gnosticism, Merkabah Mysticism and Talmudic Tradition* (New York: Jewish Theological Seminary, 1965).

29. This passage relies on the translation of George W. E. Nickelsburg, *Resurrection, Immortality and Eternal Life in Intertestamental Judaism* (Cambridge: Harvard University Press, 1972), pp. 134–136.

30. According to T. F. Glasson's interpretation, there are four: the righteous who have been martyred, and those who have died a natural death; and the wicked who have been judged in this life, and those who have not. R. H. Charles maintains that there are only three categories of the dead: one for the righteous, two for the wicked. See T. Francis Glasson, *Greek Influence in Jewish Eschatology* (London: SPCK, 1961), p. 16, and Charles, *Eschatology*, p. 217.

31. Charles, *Eschatology*, pp. 161–162.

32. Martha Himmelfarb, *Tours of Hell—An Apocalyptic Form in Jewish and Christian Literature* (Philadelphia: Fortress Press, 1985), pp. 51ff. See also Richard Bauckham, "Early Jewish Visions of Hell," *Journal of Theological Studies* 41:2 (October 1990): 355–385.

33. On the dating of the different sections of 1 Enoch, see Charles, *Eschatology*, pp. 213, 220, 250.

34. F. I. Anderson, "2 (Slavonic Apocalypse of) Enoch," in Charlesworth, *Old Testament Pseudepigrapha*, vol. 1, pp. 91ff.

35. Nickelsburg, *Jewish Literature*, p. 185.

36. Charles, "Introduction," p. 425ff.; Anderson, pp. 91ff.

37. German-Jewish scholars of the nineteenth century, among them Heinrich Graetz, believed that 3 Enoch was part of a literary genre dating from the seventh to eleventh centuries. J. T. Milik also affirms the text is quite late, from the twelfth to fifteenth centuries C.E. On the other hand, Hugh Odeberg, who translated 3 Enoch in the early twentieth century, maintained that this text was a product of the second century C.E. However, Gershom Scholem has demonstrated the origin of this texts is in the fifth or sixth century C.E., although he acknowledges that much of the material within stems from an earlier period.

On dating of 3 Enoch, see P. Alexander, "3 (Hebrew Apocalypse of) Enoch," in Charlesworth, *Old Testament Pseudepigrapha*, vol. 1, pp. 225–229; Hugh Odeberg, ed. and trans., *3 Enoch or the Hebrew Book of Enoch* (New York: Ktav, 1973); Scholem, *Jewish Gnosticism*, p. 7 n. 19.

38. See Louis Jacobs, *Jewish Mystical Testimonies* (New York: Schocken Books, 1978), pp. 26ff.

39. Adolph Jellinek, ed., "Sefer Hekhalot," in *Beit Ha-Midrash*, vol. 5 (Jerusalem: Wahrmann Books, 1967), pp. 170–176.

40. *Yebamot* 62a, 63b.; *Avodah Zarah* 5a; *Niddah* 13b.

41. Odeberg, *3 Enoch*, p. 176.

42. Nickelsburg, *Resurrection*, p. 138. See also Jacob M. Meyers, trans., *The Anchor Bible—I and II Esdras* (Garden City, NY: Doubleday, 1974), pp. 107–134.

43. B. Metzger, "Fourth Book of Ezra," in Charlesworth, *Old Testament Pseudepigrapha*, vol. 1, p. 520.

44. Russell, *Method and Message*, p. 361.

45. Charles, *Eschatology*, pp. 299ff.

46. Russell, *Method and Message*, pp. 372ff.

47. Ibid., p. 380.

48. Ibid., p. 381.

49. This is a term developed by Raymond Moody, *Life after Life* (New York: Bantam, 1976).

50. Alexander, "3 Enoch," p. 245.

51. Russell, *Method and Message*, p. 384.

52. Nickelsburg, *Jewish Literature*, pp. 252–253, and "Eschatology in the Testament of Abraham," in George W. E. Nickelsburg, ed., *Studies on the Testament of Abraham* (Missoula, MO: Scholars Press, 1976), pp. 23–64.

53. Brandon, *Judgement of the Dead*, pp. 64–65.

CHAPTER 5

1. On the history and theology of the rabbinic period, see Max Kaddushin, *The Rabbinic Mind* (New York: Bloch, 1972); George Foote Moore,

Judaism in the First Centuries of the Christian Era, 2 vols. (Cambridge: Harvard University Press, 1927, 1962); and Ephraim E. Urbach, *The Sages: Their Concepts and Beliefs*, trans. Israel Abrahams (Cambridge: Harvard University Press, 1979).

2. See Jacob Neusner, *From Politics to Piety: The Emergence of Pharasaic Judaism* (Englewood Cliffs, NJ: Prentice-Hall, 1973), especially chap. 6.

3. For a comprehensive overview of talmudic thought, see Adin Steinsaltz, *The Essential Talmud* (New York: Bantam, 1976). On the literature of the rabbinic period, see R. C. Musaph-Andriesse, *From Torah to Kabbalah: A Basic Introduction to the Writings of Judaism* (New York: Oxford University Press, 1982), pp. 20ff.

4. For a discussion of the categories of midrashic literature, see Hermann L. Strack, *Introduction to the Talmud and Midrash* (New York: Harper & Row, 1965). See also "Midrash," *Encyclopaedia Judaica*, vol. 11, 1507–1514.

5. W. Hirsch, *Rabbinic Psychology—Beliefs about the Soul in Rabbinic Literature of the Talmudic Period* (London: Edward Goldston, 1947), p. 12.

6. Ibid.

7. For a portrayal of the character of rabbinic postmortem conceptions, see the following anthologies: A. Cohen, *Everyman's Talmud* (New York: Schocken Books, 1975), and C. G. Montefiore and H. Loewe, eds., *A Rabbinic Anthology* (New York: Schocken Books, 1974).

8. Urbach, *The Sages*, p. 4.

9. For a discussion of Christian views of the world beyond, see Colleen McDannell and Bernhard Lang, *Heaven: A History* (New Haven, CT: Yale University Press, 1988).

10. Levi A. Olan, *Judaism and Immortality* (New York: UAHC, n.d.), p. 39.

11. Urbach, *The Sages*, p. 4.

12. From the Sabbath morning liturgy. See *The Authorized Daily Prayer Book*, rev. ed., trans. with commentary by Joseph I. Hertz (New York: Bloch Publishing Co., 1948), pp. 426ff.

13. This passage by an unknown author is from a liturgical poem, or *piyyut*, composed in Palestine as early as the fifth century C.E. However, it was not included in regular Sabbath liturgy until as late as the eleventh or twelfth century. See Abraham E. Millgram, *Jewish Worship* (Philadelphia: Jewish Publication Society, 1971), 175–176; Kaddushin, *Rabbinic Mind*, p. 363.

14. See also *Sanhedrin* 108a–110b.

15. Cohen, *Everyman's Talmud*, p. 364.

16. The complete textual passage from *Leviticus Rabbah* is: "As the vine is the lowliest of trees and yet rules over all the trees, so Israel is made to appear lowly in this world but will in *Olam Ha-Ba* inherit the world from end to end. As the vine is at first trodden under the foot but is afterward brought upon the

table of kings, so Israel is made to appear contemptible in this world . . . and in the *Olam Ha-Ba* the Lord will set him on high" (*Leviticus Rabbah* 36:2).

17. Strack, *Introduction*, p. 226.

18. Julius Guttmann, *Philosophies of Judaism* (Philadelphia: Jewish Publication Society, 1964), p. 33.

19. See Hirsch, *Rabbinic Psychology*, pp. 238ff.

20. The Rabbis come to this figure based on a homelitical interpretation of Psalm 68:21: "He that is our God is the God of salvation; and to God, the Lord belongs the issues of death." The significant phrase here—"issues of death"—is, in Hebrew, *toza'ot mavet*. According to the system of *gematria*, the numerical value of the word *toza'ot* is 903. Hence, 903 different kinds of death.

21. Stanislav Grof and Christina Grof, *Beyond Death—The Gates of Consciousness* (New York: Thames and Hudson, 1980), pp. 79ff.

22. Material in this section is adapted from A. P. Bender, "Beliefs, Rites, and Customs of the Jews, Connected with Death, Burial and Mourning," *Jewish Quarterly Review* 6 (1894): 317ff., and Hirsch, *Rabbinic Psychology*, pp. 239–244.

23. See "Angel of Death," *Encyclopaedia Judaica*, vol 2, 952.

24. Bender, "Beliefs," p. 323.

25. Ibid., p. 325.

26. Ibid., p. 328.

27. See Saul Lieberman, "Some Aspects of After Life in Early Rabbinic Literature," in *Harry Austryn Wolfson, Jubilee Volume*, vol. 2 (Jerusalem: American Academy for Jewish Research, 1965), pp. 495–532, especially pp. 506ff.

28. Ibid., p. 507.

29. Hirsch, *Rabbinic Psychology*, pp. 256ff.

30. See Rashi's commentary on *Nazir* 54a.

31. Hirsch, *Rabbinic Psychology*, p. 261. Much later, within the early medieval rabbinic world, necromancy is given somewhat of a Jewish flavor by rabbinic leaders, as they attempt to keep out pagan elements in a folk practice that was likely widespread in Central European Jewish communities. See Joshua Trachtenberg, *Jewish Magic and Superstition—A Study in Folk Religion* (New York: Athenum, 1974), pp. 62ff.

32. Lieberman, "Aspects of After Life," p. 506.

33. The two terms are used interchangeably in rabbinic literature.

34. That is, it is not based on the texts of the Hebrew Bible but is ascribed to the original revelation Moses received at Sinai. See Cohen, *Everyman's Talmud*, p. 379 n. 2.

35. See also *Sotah* 10b and Louis Ginzberg, ed., *Legends of the Jews*, vol. 5, trans. Henrietta Szold (Philadelphia: Jewish Publication Society, 1967–1969), p. 20 n. 57. For an elaborate discussion of the various names of Gehenna, see Samuel J. Fox, *Hell in Jewish Literature* (Northbrook, IL: Whitehall, 1972), pp. 11–14.

36. According to the midrashic text *Pirke de Rabbi Eliezer*, while Gehenna came into existence prior to creation, on the second day the fire of Gehenna was created (*Pirkei de Rabbi Eliezer*, chap. 4).

37. See Dan Cohn-Sherbok, "The Jewish Doctrine of Hell" *Religion* 8 (1978): 196–209.

38. See also *Gittin* 7a; *Baba Batra* 10a; *Midrash on Proverbs* 11:4.

39. It was taught that "every man is under the obligation to teach his son Torah that he may rescue him from Gehenna" (*Song of Songs Rabbah* 4:1). Hence, if one fulfilled that task for an ignorant man unable to do so, the teacher of Torah and the son of the ignoramus were duly rewarded.

40. Montefiore and Loewe, *Rabbinic Anthology*, p. 582. See also Gerald Walsh et al., trans., *St. Augustine—The City of God* (Garden City, NY: Image Books, 1958).

41. See Cohen, *Everyman's Talmud*, pp. 380–381. See also Fox, *Hell in Jewish Literature*.

42. Fox, *Hell in Jewish Literature*, pp. 23–24.

43. Genesis 2:8, 3:23–24; Ezekiel 36:35; Joel 2:3.

44. "Garden of Eden," *Encyclopaedia Judaica*, vol. 7, 326–327.

45. Hirsch, *Rabbinic Psychology*, pp. 268–269.

46. Ibid., p. 18.

47. Ibid.

48. The term used in this text is *Olam Ha-Ba*, but it is clearly a parallel tradition to the one appearing in *Sifre Deuteronomy* 10, 67a.

49. On the dating of this passage from *Yalkut Shimeoni*, see Cohen, *Everyman's Talmud*, p. 387.

50. Ibid., pp. 387–389.

51. Hirsch, *Rabbinic Psychology*, p. 177.

52. In this text the saying is attributed to R. Assi.

53. Hirsch, *Rabbinic Psychology*, p. 176.

54. Moore, *Judaism*, vol. 2, p. 323

55. William Whiston, trans., *The Works of Flavius Josephus* (London: Simms and McIntyre, 1843), *Wars*, II, viii, 14; see also *Antiquities*, XVIII, i, 4.

56. Ibid., *Antiquities*, XVIII, i, 4.

57. Matthew 22:23–34; Mark 12:23–26; Luke 20:27–45.

58. Salo Wittmayer Baron, *A Social and Religious History of the Jews*, vol. 2: *Ancient Times* (Philadelphia: Jewish Publication Society, 1951), p. 311.

59. Term generally used as a designation for Judeo-Christian. See Soncino English translation of the Babylonian Talmud, *Sanhedrin*, 90b n. 12.

60. Lester T. Whitelock, *The Development of Jewish Religious Thought in the Intertestamental Period* (New York: Vantage Press, 1976), p. 91. On the place of the doctrine of resurrection in rabbinic theology, see A. Marmorstein, *Studies in Jewish Theology* (New York: Oxford University Press, 1950), pp. 145–161.

61. *Siddur Tehillat Hashem*, trans. Nissan Mangel (Brooklyn, NY: Merkos L'Inyonei Chinuch, 1978), pp. 51–52.

62. Millgram, *Jewish Worship*, p. 102.

63. This was based on the rabbinic principle of reward and punishment, referred to as *Middah ke'neged middah*—"a measure for a measure" (*Sanhedrin* 90a). The Rabbis believed that every human action would be either rewarded or punished in accordance with the merit of the particular action. Thus, if an individual denied the resurrection, he or she would therefore be punished by being denied resurrection at the end-of-days.

64. Meyers, *Jewish Ossuaries*, pp. 72–96. See also *Pesikta Rabbati* 1:6.

65. Cohen, *Everyman's Talmud*, p. 362.

66. On the folk-level customs associated with Jewish burial, see Theodor Gaster, *The Holy and the Profane—Evolution of Jewish Folkways* (New York: William Morrow, 1980).

CHAPTER 6

1. For a concise history of the development of rabbinic Midrash, see "Midrash," *Encyclopaedia Judaica*, vol. 11, 1511–1512.

2. Meyer Waxman, *A History of Jewish Literature*, vol. 1 (New York: Thomas Yoseloff, 1933, 1960), p. 147. For a sampling of the kinds of midrashic texts authored in this era, see David Stern and Mark Jay Mirsky, eds., *Rabbinic Fantasies—Imaginative Narratives from Classical Hebrew Literature* (Philadelphia: Jewish Publication Society, 1990).

3. Stern and Mirsky, *Rabbinic Fantasies*, p. 5.

4. See "Cairo Geniza," *Encyclopaedia Judaica*, vol. 16, 1333–1342.

5. Moses Gaster, ed. and trans., *The Chronicles of Jerahmeel* (New York: Ktav, 1971; originally published in 1899), pp. 1–3.

6. Elijah de Vidas, *Reishit Hokhma* (Brooklyn, NY: Josef Sacks, 1984; originally published in 1579).

7. Moses Gaster, ed., *Studies and Texts in Folklore, Magic, Medieval Romance, Hebrew Apocrypha and Samaritan Archaeology*, vol. 1 (New York: Ktav, 1971). See also Gaster, *Jerahmeel*. See also Moses Gaster, "Hebrew Visions of Hell and Paradise," *Journal of the Royal Asiatic Society* (July 1893): 571–612.

8. Ginzberg, *Legends*.

9. Saul Lieberman, "On Sins and Their Punishments," in *Texts and Studies* (New York: Ktav, 1974), pp. 29–57.

10. Martha Himmelfarb, *Tours of Hell* (Philadelphia: Fortress Press, 1986).

11. Stern and Mirsky, *Rabbinic Fantasies*, pp. 239–252.

12. Adolph Jellinek, *Beit Ha-Midrash*, 6 vols. (Jerusalem: Wahrman Books, 1967).

13. J. D. Eisenstein, ed., *Otzar Midrashim*, 2 vols. (New York: Grossman's, 1915).

14. Abraham Wertheimer, *Batei Midrashot*, 2 vols. (Jerusalem: Ktav Yad V'Sefer, 1989).

15. Elijah de Vidas, *Reishit Hokhmah* (Brooklyn, NY: Josef Sacks, 1984).

16. Dov Yardin, ed., *Mahbarot Immanuel HaRomi*, vol. 2 (Jerusalem: Mosad Bialik, 1954), pp. 511–554.

17. Gaster, *Jerahmeel*, p. 2.

18. For background on Eleazar ben Asher Ha-Levi, see Haim Schwartzbaum "Prolegomenon" in Gaster, *Jerahmeel*, pp. 1–7. Waxman, *Jewish Literature*, vol. 1, pp. 527–530.

19. Gaster, *Jerahmeel*, ix–xxi.

20. Gaster, *Studies and Texts*, vol. 1, pp. 125–141. See also "Visions," 572–588.

21. Hermann Gollancz, trans., *Tophet and Eden* (London: University of London Press, 1921).

22. English: *Jerahmeel*, XI. Schwartzbaum, in Gaster, *Chronicles of Jerahmeel*, p. 29, notes a relationship between R. Abahu's parable described in this text and a similar parable of three different men narrated in *Pirkei de Rabbi Eliezer*, chap. 34. Hebrew: Jellinek, *Beit Ha-Midrash*, vol. 1, pp. 151ff. Gaster relates this text to *The Pearl of Rab*, found in Jellinek, *BHM*, vol. 2, 120–122.

23. English: *Jerahmeel*, XII. Hebrew: Jellinek, *BHM*, vol. 5, pp. 48–49. Eisenstein, *Otzar*, vol. 1, pp. 92–93.

24. This is the main text on *Hibbut Ha-Kever*; the two previous texts are included in various other recensions. English: *Jerahmeel*, XIII. Hebrew: Jellinek, *BHM*, vol. 1, pp. 150–151, from the second paragraph on (additional material found in Jellinek). Eisenstein, *Otzar*, vol. 1, pp. 93–94. Elijah de Vidas, *Reishit Hokhmah* (*Shaar Yirah*, chapter 12). Avraham Azulai, *Hesed L'Avraham* (B'nai Brak: Agudat Yad Avraham, 1986; orginally published in 1685); also includes kabbalistic commentary on this text.

25. This sentence contains an important concept: three days of judgment at the time of *Hibbut Ha-Kever*, three days of judgment in Gehenna, and three days in heaven. However, while this sentence is in Gaster's English edition, it does not appear in the four Hebrew versions consulted: *Beit Ha-Midrash*, *Hesed L'Avraham*, *Otzar Midrashim*, and *Reishit Hokhmah*. I also have not found this notion expressed in any other Jewish writings. Consequently, it is hard to say whether this is an indigenous Jewish concept (which seems unlikely), a Christian amendation that entered the text used by Gaster, or even the unique creation of the author of the *Chronicles of Jerahmeel*.

26. See Himmelfarb, *Tours of Hell*, especially chapter 1, where she delineates the wide range of texts.

27. Ibid., p. 45.

28. This is based on rabbinic traditions found in *Ketubbot* 77b and *Berakhot* 51a. For legendary material on Rabbi Joshua ben Levi, see Gershom Bader, *The Encyclopedia of Talmudic Sages* (Northvale, NJ: Jason Aronson, 1988), pp. 535ff.

29. Himmelfarb, *Tours of Hell*, p. 75.

30. Lieberman, "On Sins and Their Punishment," p. 48.

31. Ginzberg, *Legends*, vol. 5, p. 20 n. 56.

32. English: *Jerahmeel*, XIV. Hebrew: Jellinek, *BHM*, vol. 1, pp. 147–148. Eisenstein, *Otzar*, vol. 1, pp. 91–92. Elijah de Vidas, *Reishit Hokhmah* (*Shaar Yirah*, chap. 13).

33. Translation of text from Bible, "The leech has two daughters, [crying], 'Give! Give!'"

34. English: *Jerahmeel*, XV. Hebrew: Jellinek, *BHM*, vol. 1, pp. 148–149. Eisenstein, *Otzar*, vol. 1, p. 92. Elijah de Vidas, *Reishit Hokhmah* (*Shaar Yirah*, chap. 13).

35. English: *Jerahmeel*, XVI. Hebrew: selections found in Jellinek, *BHM*, vol. 5, pp. 49–51, Eisenstein, *Otzar*, vol. 1, pp. 94–95, under title of *Keitzad Din Ha-Kever*.

36. English: *Jerahemeel*, XVII; Hebrew: selections found in *Seder Rabba de Breishit*, in Wertheimer, *Batei Midrashot*, vol. 1, pp. 36ff.; and in *Midrash Konen*, Jellinek, *BHM*, vol. 2, pp. 35–36.

37. English: *Jerahmeel* XXI. Hebrew: similar to Jellinek, *BHM*, vol. 2, pp. 48–51. Also in *Midrash Konen*, Jellinek, *BHM*, vol. 2, pp. 30–31. Paragraphs 4 through 11 are found in Jellinek, *BHM*, vol. 5, pp. 43–44, an Aramaic text entitled *Agudat Rabbi Yehoshua ben Levi*. Eisenstein, *Otzar*, vol. 1, p. 213.

38. There are discrepant versions with regard to the names of the angels. The angels' names used here appear in the Aramaic version of the text. Jellinek, *BHM*, vol. 5, 43–44.

39. Ginzberg, *Legends*, vol. 5, p. 31 n. 90.

40. See Israel Abrahams, ed., *Hebrew Ethical Wills*, vol. 1 (Philadelphia: Jewish Publication Society, 1923), pp. 31–50.

41. "Orchot Hayyim," *Encyclopaedia Judaica*, vol. 12, 1457–1458.

42. Gershom Scholem, *Major Trends* (New York: Schocken Books, 1954), p. 183.

43. Alternate version: *Tehmimim*.

44. See Stern and Mirsky, *Rabbinic Fantasies*, pp. 246–248. Also *Zohar* II, 167b.

45. Chava Weissler, "Women in Paradise," *Tikkun* 2:2 (1987): 43–46, 117–120.

46. See *Berakhot* 5:3.

47. English: *Jerahmeel* XVIII; A. Cohen, *Everyman's Talmud* (New York: Schocken Books, 1975), pp. 387–389; Ginzberg, *Legends* vol. 1, pp. 19–20. Hebrew: Jellinek, *BHM*, vol. 2, pp. 52–53. Eisenstein, *Otzar*, vol. 1, pp. 83–84. This is a more elaborate version of the text quoted from *Yalkut Shimoni* in the previous chapter.

48. According to a discrepant text, 800 tastes.

49. English: Gaster, "Visions," 591–596. A text that consists of paragraphs 10 through 17 of this text appears in *Jerahmeel*, XX. See Gaster, "Introduction," in *Jerahmeel*, p. lxix. See also Ginzberg, *Legends*, vol. 5, pp. 32–34 n. 97. Hebrew: Jellinek, *BHM*, vol. 2, 48–51, *Maaseh de Rabbi Joshua ben Levi*; Eisenstein, *Otzar*, vol. 1, pp. 212–213, where it appears under the title *Iggeret Rabbi Joshua ben Levi*.

50. Based on a talmudic legend, told about Rabbi Hanina ben Papa, found in *Ketubbot* 77b.

51. What follows here is Rabbi Joshua ben Levi's tour of Gehenna, which is in *Rabbi Joshua ben Levi and the Seven Compartments of Gehinnom*.

52. English: *Jerahmeel*, XIX. Hebrew: Jellinek, *BHM*, vol. 5, p. 43. Eisenstein, *Otzar*, vol. 1, p. 89.

53. English: George Wesley Buchanan, ed. and trans., *Revelation and Redemption: Jewish Documents of Deliverance from the Fall of Jerusalem to the Death of Nahmanides* (Dillsboro, NC: Western North Carolina Press, 1978), pp. 556–568. Hebrew: Jellinek, *BHM*, vol. 3, pp. 131–140; Eisenstein, *Otzar*, vol. 1, pp. 85–89. On the origin of the women in Gan Eden, see Ginzberg, *Legends*.

54. Throughout this section, Buchanan uses the word *degree*, which I have translated as "realm."

55. Buchanan translates this phrase: "without erring for the age."

56. English in this previous section is an abridged version of Jellinek, *BHM*, vol. 3, pp. 135–136.

57. See M. *Berakhot* 5:3.

58. There are two different terms in the text, *Gan Eden Ha-Elyon*, which is translated here as Upper Gan Eden, and *Gan Eden shel Malah*, translated as Heavenly Gan Eden. The two terms are used synonymously.

59. Term here is used synonymously with *Gan Eden shel Ha-Aretz*.

60. Lieberman, "On Sins and Their Punishments," p. 29.

61. Ginzberg, *Legends*, vol. 5, p. 416 n. 117.

62. Wertheimer, *Batei Midrashot*, vol. 1, pp. 273–275.

63. Ibid.

64. The rabbinic midrashic text, *Pesikta Rabbati*, which dates from the sixth or seventh century C.E., contains a lengthy decription of Moses' encounter with angelic beings and ministering angels who show him the supernal worlds, q.v. *Pesikta Rabbati* 20:4.

65. English: Gaster, "Visions," 572–588. Ginzberg, *Legends*, vol. 2, pp. 304–316. Hebrew: Wertheimer, *Batei Midrashot*, vol. 1, pp. 273–286, where it is titled *Ke-Tapuakh Be-Atzei Ha-Yaar*. Also, cited by Jellinek, *BHM*, vol. 2. pp. x., xiv. ff., and xix–xx. For background souces on the text, see Ginzberg, *Legends*, vol. 5, pp. 416–419 n. 117–118.

66. The Hebrew word here is *shamayim*.

67. According to talmudic tradition, Gabriel is the strongest of all the angels (*Berakhot* 4a).

68. In the version of the text translated by Gaster, the names of the angels do not appear. However, in the Hebrew the names of the angels are included. Wertheimer, *Batei Midrashot*, vol. 1, pp. 273–286.

69. In the text used by Wertheimer, the angel named here is Nuriel. However, Ginzberg notes that the angel Moses encountered in the third heaven is Sandalphon, and Nuriel, who appears in the second heaven is, according to Ginzberg, a scribal error in Wertheimer's text. q.v. Ginzberg, *Legends*, vol. 5, p. 416 n. 117.

70. This phrase, "the one who said and the world was created," is found in a prayer called *Barukh She-Amar*.

71. This paragraph contains materials from two discrepant texts used by Gaster and Wertheimer. The occurrence of the phrase "teaching souls which were created by God at the time of the Creation" suggests an editiorial amendment representing the stream of Jewish thought emphasizing the notion of preexistence of souls.

72. This is based on a passage in Proverbs 28:9: "He who turns his ear away from hearing Torah, even his prayer is abomination."

73. This paragraph and the one above have briefer versions translated in Gaster, "Visions," 581. See Hebrew edition, Wertheimer, *Batei Midrashot*, vol. 1, pp. 281–282.

74. This paragraph is translated from Wertheimer, *Batei Midrashot*.

75. See *Berakhot* 54b.

76. This paragraph combines material from Wertheimer, Gaster, and Ginzberg. In Wertheimer, the angel tells Moses the name of this locale is *Tit Ha-Yaven*, a duplication of the name given earlier. What is clear from these variant textual readings is that there was never a monolithic tradition with regard to the seven names of the underworld of Gehinnom.

77. Here there is a play on words using gematria: the word *she-kakhah*, שככה (as in *Ashrei ha-am she-kakhah lo*) is numerically equivalent to the word Moshe, משה.

78. The Hebrew word here is *Baalei Teshuvah*.

79. This is from the twenty-eighth composition of the *Mahbarot Immanuel*. Hebrew: Yardin, *Mahbarot Immanuel HaRomi*, vol. 2, pp. 511–554. English: Gollancz, *Tophet and Eden*. For a varied form of English translation, see B. Halper, ed., *Postbiblical Hebrew Literature—An Anthology* (Philadelphia: Jewish Publication Society, 1921), pp. 188–193.

80. According to Cecil Roth, his date of birth was 1261. Cecil Roth, *The Jews in the Renaissance* (New York: Harper & Row, 1965), p. 89.

81. For background on Immanuel Ha-Romi, see ibid., pp. 86–103; Waxman, *Jewish Literature*, vol. 2, pp. 65ff. Israel Zinberg, *A History of Jewish*

Literature, trans. Bernard Martin (Cleveland: Press of Case Western Reserve University, 1973), vol. 2, pp. 205–217.

82. Roth, *Jews in the Renaissance*, p. 90.

83. Ibid., p. 91.

84. *Shulhan Arukh, Orah Hayyim, Hilkhot Shabbat*, chap. 307, sec. 16.

85. Zinberg, *History*, vol. 2, p. 216.

86. Waxman, *Jewish Literature*, vol. 2, p. 72.

87. Gollancz has demonstrated numerous parallels between Dante and Immanuel Ha-Romi. Gollancz, *Tophet and Eden*, pp. 11–13.

88. Yardin, *Mahbarot Immanuel HaRomi*, vol. 2, pp. 511–554.

89. Psalm 39:4.

90. Gollancz, *Tophet and Eden*, p. 14

91. Daniel 9:23.

92. Psalm 39:5.

93. Gollancz, *Tophet and Eden*, pp. 14–15.

94. This is the same name for one of the realms of Gehenna found in *Masekhet Gehinnom* texts.

95. Genesis 3:24. This is the flaming sword outside Gan Eden.

96. 1 Chronicles 26:16.

97. Gollancz, *Tophet and Eden*, pp. 16–17.

98. Ibid., pp. 17–18.

99. Ibid., p. 35.

100. Ibid., pp. 37–38.

101. Ibid., p. 44.

102. Genesis 31:19; Judges 7:5; 1 Samuel 19:13.

103. Gollancz, *Tophet and Eden*, p. 46.

104. Ibid., pp. 51–52.

105. Ibid., p. 55.

106. Ibid., p. 56.

107. Genesis 28:12.

108. *Hagigah* 12b; Isaiah 30:26.

109. 1 Samuel 25:29. The Hebrew phrase here, *be-tzror ha-hayyim tz'rurot*, is derived from *el maleh rahamim*, a memorial prayer for the dead. See Yardin, *Mahbarot Immanuel HaRomi*, p. 539 n. 665.

110. Gollancz, *Tophet and Eden*, pp. 60–61.

111. *Berakhot* 17a.

112. Gollancz, *Tophet and Eden*, p. 64.

113. Based on the traditional rabbinic teaching "The righteous of the nations of the world have a share in the World to Come."

114. Gollancz, *Tophet and Eden*, pp. 64–65.

115. Exodus 24:10.

116. Genesis 49:9.

117. Genesis 49:10.

118. Golllancz, *Tophet and Eden*, pp. 65–66.

119. "Our Holy Teacher," name given to Rabbi Judah the Prince, encoder of the Mishnah.

120. Gollancz, *Tophet and Eden*, p. 78.

121. Ibid., pp. 80–82.

122. Ibid., p. 85.

123. Daniel 12:3; Gollancz, *Tophet and Eden*, pp. 85–86.

CHAPTER 7

1. See Julius Guttmann, *Philosophies of Judaism* trans. David W. Silverman (New York: Schocken Books, 1973), and Isaac Husik, *A History of Mediaeval Jewish Philosophy* (Philadelphia: Jewish Publication Society, 1940).

2. "Philosophy, Jewish," *Encyclopaedia Judaica*, vol. 13, 427–428.

3. For background on this period, see Seymour Feldman, ed. and trans., "Introduction" to Levi Ben Gershom (Gersonides) *The Wars of the Lord*—Book 1: *Immortality of the Soul* (Philadelphia: Jewish Publication Society, 1984), and Meyer Waxman, *A History of Jewish Literature*. vol. 1 (New York: Thomas Yoseloff, 1933, 1960), pp. 318ff.

4. Husik, *Mediaeval Jewish Philosophy*, pp. xvi–xvii.

5. Norbert Samuelson, "Medieval Jewish Philosophy," in *Back to the Sources*, ed. Barry Holtz (New York: Summit Books, 1984), pp. 262ff.

6. Harry Blumberg, "The Problem of Immortality in Avicenna, Maimonides and St. Thomas Aquinas," in *Studies in Maimonides and St. Thomas Aquinas*, ed. Jacob I. Dienstag (New York: Ktav, 1975), p. 29. Also published in the *Harry Austryn Wolfson Jubilee Volume* (Jerusalem: American Academy for Jewish Research, 1965), pp. 165–185.

7. Guttmann, *Philosophies*, p. 61.

8. Saadia Gaon, *The Book of Beliefs and Opinions*, ed. and trans. Samuel Rosenblatt (New Haven, CT: Yale University Press, 1948, 1976), p. xxiii.

9. Ibid., p. xxiv.

10. Husik, *Medieval Jewish Philosophy*, p. 26.

11. A. J. Wensinck, *The Muslim Creed*, pp. 23, 35, cited by Israel Efros, *Studies in Medieval Jewish Philosophy* (New York: Columbia University Press, 1974), p. 91.

12. Efros, *Studies*, p. 94.

13. Guttmann, *Philosophies*, p. 73.

14. For additional background, see Henry Malter, *Saadia Gaon, His Life and Works* (Philadelphia, 1921).

15. The original Arabic title was *Kitab al-Amanat wa'l-I'tikadat*. The Hebrew translation was done by Yehuda ibn Tibbon.

16. Joseph L. Blau, *The Story of Jewish Philosophy* (New York: Random House, 1962), p. 141.

17. The English edition of *Emunot Ve-Daot* used throughout this chapter is Samuel Rosenblatt's Yale University series translation, *Saadia Gaon—The Book of Beliefs and Opinions* (referred to below as *Beliefs*).

18. *Beliefs*, VI, chapter 1, p. 236. See also Phillip David Bookstaber, *The Idea of the Development of the Soul in Medievel Jewish Philosophy* (Philadelphia: Morris Jacobs, 1950), p. 26.

19. *Beliefs*, VI, chapter 1, p. 235.

20. Bookstaber, *Development of the Soul*, p. 28

21. *Beliefs*, VI, chapter 3, p. 242.

22. Ibid., chapter 7, p. 255.

23. Ibid., chapter 3, p. 243. This threefold distinction used by Saadia is based on Aristotle. See Efros, *Studies*, p. 108 n. 35.

24. Ibid., chapter 5, p. 250.

25. Efros, *Studies*, pp. 107–108.

26. Ibid., p. 87; *Beliefs*, VI, chapter 4, p. 247.

27. *Beliefs*, I, chapter 1, p. 207.

28. Ibid., VI, chapter 4, p. 247.

29. Ibid., V, chapter 1, p. 207.

30. Ibid., IX, chapter 3, p. 331.

31. Guttmann, *Philosophies*, p. 71.

32. *Beliefs*, IX, chapter V, p. 337.

33. Ibid., p. 338

34. Efros, *Studies*, p. 120

35. *Beliefs*, IX, chapter V, p. 340.

36. Efros, *Studies*, p. 114.

37. Ibid.

38. Ibid., p. 116.

39. Guttmann, *Philosophies*, p. 73.

40. For biographical information on Maimonides, see Abraham Joshua Heschel, *Maimonides—A Biography*, trans. Joachim Neugroschel (New York: Farrar, Straus, Giroux, 1982).

41. Salo W. Baron, "Moses Maimonides," in *Great Jewish Personalities in Ancient and Medieval Times*, ed. Simon Noveck (Washington, DC: B'nai Brith Adult Jewish Education, 1969), pp. 204ff.

42. See "Maimonidean Controversy," *Encyclopaedia Judaica*, vol. 11, 745ff.

43. Baron, "Moses Maimonides," pp. 204ff. See also R. C. Musaph-Andriesse, *From Torah to Kabbalah* (New York: Oxford University Press, 1982), pp. 73ff.

44. "Eschatology," *Encyclopaedia Judaica*, vol. 6, 338.

45. Among the translations of this text are Moses Maimonides, *Commentary on the Mishnah—Tractate Sanhedrin*, trans. and ed. Fred Rosner (New York: Sepher-Hermon Press, 1981), and Zalman Schachter-Shalomi, trans., "Moses Maimonides' Commentary on the Mishnah Sanhedrin, Chapter 10," photocopied ed. (Philadelphia: B'nai Or Religious Fellowship, n.d.).

46. *Commentary on the Mishnah*, p. 135. Unless otherwise indicated, all translations of this text are from the Rosner translation.

47. Ibid.

48. Ibid.

49. Ibid.

50. Ibid., pp. 135–136.

51. Ibid., p. 136.

52. Ibid., 136. Translation here is from Schachter-Shalomi, "Moses Maimonides Commentary on the Mishnah Sanhedrin, Chapter 10," 3.

53. *Commentary on the Mishnah*, p. 143.

54. Ibid., p. 143.

55. "Eschatology," *Encyclopaedia Judaica*, vol. 6, p. 338; and Guttmann, *Philosophies*, pp. 199–200.

56. Guttmann, *Philosophies*, pp. 199–200.

57. *Commentary on the Mishnah*, p. 144.

58. Ibid., pp. 144–145.

59. Moses Maimonides, *The Guide of the Perplexed*, trans. and ed. M. Friedlander (New York: Hebrew Publishing, 1881), pt. 1, chap. XLI.

60. Blumberg, "Problem of Immortality," pp. 174–175. See also *Commentary on the Mishnah*, pp. 172–173 n. 189.

61. *Mishneh Torah*, "Hilkhot Yesodei Ha-Torah" IV, 9.

62. Blumberg, "Problem of Immortality," p. 175

63. A. Cohen, *The Teachings of Maimonides* (New York: Ktav, 1968), pp. 230ff.

64. *Commentary on the Mishnah*, p. 145.

65. Schacher-Shalomi, "Mishnah Sanhedrin," p. 15.

66. Ibid., p. 15.

67. Ibid., p. 16. *Commentary on the Mishnah*, p. 146.

68. Hebrew term used here is *le-atid-la-vo*. *Commentary on the Mishnah*, p. 146.

69. Ibid.

70. Ibid., p. 147.

71. Schacher-Shalomi, "Mishnah Sanhedrin," p. 17.

72. Ibid. p. 20.

73. Rosner, "Introduction," *Commentary on the Mishnah*, p. 17.

74. *Mishneh Torah*, vol. 1: *The Book of Knowledge*, p. 92a.

75. Ibid., p. 90a.

76. Ibid.

77. Ibid.

78. Ibid., p. 91a.

79. Ibid., p. 91b.

80. Ibid., pp. 91b–92a.

81. Ibid., p. 91a.

82. Joshua Finkel, "Maimonides Treatise on Resurrection: A Comparative Study," in *Essays on Maimonides*, ed. Salo Wittmayer Baron (New York: Columbia University Press, 1941), pp. 94ff.

83. For more information on the resurrection controversy, see Daniel Jeremy Siller, "The Resurrection Debate," in *Moses Maimonides' Treatise on Resurrection*, trans. and ed. Fred Rosner (New York: Ktav, 1982), pp. 71–102.

84. Rosner, *Treatise on Resurrection*, p. 21.

85. Ibid., p. 25.

86. Ibid., p. 32.

87. Ibid., p. 40.

88. Ibid., pp. 40–41.

89. Ibid., p. 35.

90. Ibid., p. 15.

91. Ibid., p. 33.

92. Ibid.

93. Blumberg, "Problem of Immortality," p. 42.

94. Joseph Sarachek, *The Doctrine of the Messiah in Medieval Jewish Literature* (New York: Hermon Press, 1968), p. 158.

95. A complete listing of Gersonides' writings can be found in Feldman, pp. 8–30.

96. Ibid., p. 45.

97. Ibid., p. 21. This instrument, known as "Jacob's Staff" (Hebrew: *maqel*), is described and pictured in B. Barry Levy, *Planets, Potions and Parchments: Scientific Hebraica from the Dead Sea Scrolls to the Eighteenth Century* (Montreal: McGill Queen's University Press, 1990), pp. 28–29; 120.

98. Feldman, *Wars of the Lord*, p. 21.

99. Ibid., pp. 3–7.

100. Ibid., pp. 31–32. "Provence," *Encyclopaedia Judaica*, vol. 13, 1259–1264. See also I. Twersky, "Aspects of the Social and Cultural History of Proveçal Jewry," in *Jewish Society Through the Ages*, ed. H. H. Ben Sasson and S. Ettinger (New York: Schocken Books, 1971), pp. 185–207.

101. Feldman, *Wars of the Lord*, Book 1, "Introductory Remarks," p. 98.

102. Husik, *Mediaeval Jewish Philosophy*, p. 331.

103. Feldman, *Wars of the Lord*, Book 1, p. 98.

104. Discussion of *Milhamot HaShem* is found in Husik, *Mediaeval Jewish Philosophy*, pp. 331–361. Guttmann, *Philosophies*, pp. 237–254.

105. Samuelson, "Medieval Jewish Philosophy," p. 279.

106. An "Analytical Table of Contents" of all six books of *The Wars of the Lord* is found in Feldman, pp. 243–256.

107. Feldman, *Wars of the Lord*, Book 1, p. 109.

108. Ibid., p. 244.

109. Ibid., p. 79.

110. Ibid., p. 81.

111. *Wars*, Book I, XIII, p. 225.

112. Ibid.

113. For biographical information on Nahmanides, see Solomon Schechter, *Studies in Judaism: Essays on Persons, Concepts, and Movements of Thought in the Jewish Tradition* (Philadelphia: Jewish Publications Society, 1958), specifically chapter 7.

114. Ibid.

115. Ramban, *The Gate of Reward*, trans. and ed. Charles B. Chavel (New York: Shilo Publishing House, 1983), pp. v–vi.

116. Ibid., p. 4.

117. Ibid., pp. 4–5.

118. Ibid., pp. 7–8.

119. Ibid., p. 8.

120. Based on *Berakhot* 18b.

121. *Gate of Reward*, p. 8.

122. Ibid.

123. Ibid., p. 81.

124. Ibid., p. 69.

125. Ibid., p. 81.

126. Ibid.

127. Ibid., p. 60.

128. Ibid., p. 61.

129. Ibid., p. 62.

130. Ibid., p. 64.

131. Ibid., p. 65.

132. Ibid.

133. Ibid., p. 69.

134. Ibid., p. 82.

135. Ibid.

136. Ibid.

137. Ibid.

138. Ibid., p. 88.

139. Ibid., pp. 87–88.

140. Ibid., p. 90.

141. Ibid., p. 97.

142. Ibid.

143. Ibid., p. 105.

144. Ibid., p. 107.

145. Ibid., p. 109.

146. Ibid., p. 114.

147. Ibid., p. 110.

148. Ibid., p. 116.

149. Ibid.

CHAPTER 8

1. Joseph Dan, *Gershom Scholem and the Mystical Dimension of Jewish History* (New York: New York University Press, 1987), pp. 147–148. Gershom Scholem, *Origins of the Kabbalah*, trans. Allan Arkush (Philadelphia: Jewish Publication Society, 1987), pp. 1–12.

2. H. Graetz, *History of the Jews*, 6 vols. (Philadelphia: Jewish Publicaton Society, 1894), vol. 4, p. 625.

3. Dan, *Gershom Scholem*, p. 31.

4. Gershom Scholem, *Jewish Mysticism, Merkabah Mysticism and Talmudic Tradition*, 2nd ed. (New York: Jewish Theological Seminary, 1965).

5. Scholem, *Origins of the Kabbalah*, p. 8.

6. On the historical development of Jewish mysticism, see Dan, *Gershom Scholem*; Ernest Muller, *History of Jewish Mysticism*, trans. M. Simon (Brooklyn, NY: Yesod Publishers, n.d.); Gershom Scholem, *Kabbalah* (New York: New American Library, 1978); Gershom Scholem, *Major Trends in Jewish Mysticism*, 3rd ed. (New York: Schocken Books, 1961); and Scholem, *Origins of the Kabbalah*.

7. Scholem, *Kabbalah*, pp. 6–7.

8. Ibid., p. 3.

9. Moshe Idel, *Kabbalah—New Perspectives* (New Haven, CT: Yale University Press, 1988), p. 20.

10. Ibid.

11. Scholem, *Origins of the Kabbalah*, p. 4.

12. See Scholem, *Major Trends in Jewish Mysticism*, pp. 156–243.

13. More recent *Zohar* scholarship suggests that de Leon did not author the *Zohar* single-handedly but had literary assistance from a number of other kabbalists. See Yehuda Leibes, *Studies in the Zohar*, trans. Arnold Schwartz et al. (Albany, NY: SUNY Press, 1993), especially chapter 2.

14. On the history of the *Zohar*, see Daniel Channan Matt, ed., *Zohar: The Book of Enlightenment* (New York: Paulist Press Classics of Western Spirituality, 1983), pp. 3–39. See also Scholem, *Kabbalah*, pp. 57–61, 213–243.

15. Scholem, *Kabbalah*, pp. 213–220.

16. Ibid., p. 160.

17. The standard English translation of the *Zohar* is taken from Harry Sperling and Maurice Simon, trans., *The Zohar*, 2nd ed., 5 vols. (London: Soncino Press, 1984). Although numerous sections are missing from this translation, it is the most complete English translation of *Zohar* available.

Partial translations of the *Zohar* are Gershom Scholem, trans., *The Zohar* (New York: Schocken Books, 1963), and Matt, trans. *Zohar: The Book of Enlightenment*.

Another important source for the study of *Zohar* is Isaiah Tishby and Fischel Lachower, eds., *The Wisdom of the Zohar*, 3 vols., trans. David Goldstein (London: Oxford University Press, 1989). This monumental study includes both primary source translation and secondary source analysis by topic. Unfortunately, although the authors had intended to finish an additional volume with a complete analysis of postmortem eschatology of the *Zohar*, this was never done.

A complete Aramaic edition of the *Zohar*, with Hebrew commentary (*Perush Ha-Sulam*), is Yehuda Ashlag, *Sefer Ha-Zohar*, 14 vols. (Jerusalem: Press of Yeshivat Kol Yehuda, 1991).

An excellent *Zohar* concordance, *Otzar Ha-Zohar*, provides topical listings of afterlife terms used in the *Zohar*: *Otzar Ha-Zohar*, ed. Daniel Frish, 5 vols. (Jerusalem: Aleph-Beit Press, 1976).

18. Scholem, *Kabbalah*, p. 155.

19. Tishby and Lachower, *Wisdom of the Zohar*, vol. 2, p. 692.

20. For more background information, see the discussion of the stages of the emergence of the kabbalistic notion of the soul, Ibid., vol. 2, pp. 677–722.

21. Ibid., vol. 2, p. 692.

22. Scholem, *Kabbalah*, p. 155. Tishby and Lachower, vol. 2, pp. 684–685.

23. On the relationship between the three aspects of the soul, Gershom Scholem writes:

> Only a soul in its perfect state—that is, one that had realized the Torah and its mysteries—could possess three parts [*nefesh, ruah,* and *neshamah*]. The normal psychophysical constitution of the human being is already included in full on the lowest level—*nefesh*. In other words, the *nefesh* itself already encompassed the three "preparations," "potentialities," or "parts" (the terminology depended on the various philosophical schools that inspired the kabbalists). The two higher levels of the soul, *ruah* and *neshamah*, are intuitive degrees or levels of the soul, achieved by the mystics only after much practice and contemplation of the secrets of the Torah. Everyone is born with a *nefesh*, but whether or not he will succeed in bringing down his own

ruah and *neshamah* from the treasure-house of souls, or some other heavenly source where these higher forms of his own soul abide, depends on his own choice and spiritual development.

Gershom Scholem, *On the Mystical Shape of the Godhead*, trans. Joachim Neugrosschel (New York: Schocken Books, 1976), p. 218.

24. Moshe de Leon, *Sefer Ha-Nefesh Ha-Hakhmah*, pt. 1, sig. 2, fol. 4b. Cited by Tishby and Lachower, *Wisdom of the Zohar*, vol. 2, p. 711.

25. According to Tishby's comment on this passage: "The different levels of the soul indicate the kabbalistic mysteries in their apprehension of the divine, because they parallel and reflect the different *sefirot* [emanations of the Tree of Life inherent to kabbalistic cosmology]. Ibid., vol. 2, p. 731 n. 66.

26. *Zohar* II, 158b (*Raya Meheimna*).

27. Scholem, *Kabbalah*, p. 157.

28. Gershon Winkler, *The Soul of the Matter* (New York: Judaica Press, 1982), p. 7.

29. Ibid., pp. 7–8.

30. This model is used extensively by the contemporary exponent of Kabbalah Rabbi Zalman Schachter-Shalomi. Schachter-Shalomi, "Exploring the Worlds of Jewish Mysticism," audiocassette of class series, no. 5 (Philadelphia: P'nai Or Religious Fellowship, 1981).

31. Tishby and Lachower, *Wisdom of the Zohar*, vol. 2, pp. 771, 831.

32. Ibid., vol. 2, p. 831.

33. Ibid., vol. 2, p. 832.

34. Edward Hoffman, *The Way of Splendor—Jewish Mysticism and Modern Psychology* (Boulder, CO: Shambhala Publications, 1981), p. 190.

35. Tishby and Lachower, *Wisdom of the Zohar*, vol. 2, pp. 832ff., delineates much of the material included here outlining the various phenomena of dying.

36. Ibid., p. 834. On the origins of this custom, see also *Maavor Yabok*, 128a.

37. Tishby and Lachower, *Wisdom of the Zohar*, vol. 2, p. 844 n. 63.

38. Stanislav Grof and Christina Grof, *Beyond Death—The Gates of Consciousness* (New York: Thames and Hudson, 1980).

39. Raymond Moody, *Life after Life* (New York: Bantam, 1976); Raymond Moody, *Reflections on Life after Life* (New York: Bantam, 1977); Michael Sabom, *Recollections of Death—A Medical Investigation* (New York: Simon & Schuster, 1982).

40. Zalman Schachter-Shalomi, "Life in the Hereafter: A Tour of What's to Come," in *The Jewish Almanac*, ed. Richard Siegel and Carl Rheins (New York: Bantam, 1980), p. 594.

41. Ibid., p. 595. See also *Shabbat* 152b.

42. Ibid.

43. See Detlef Ingo Lauf, *Secret Doctrines of the Tibetan Books of the Dead* (Berkeley, CA: Shambhala Publishers, 1977), pp. 33ff.

44. Lama Lodru, *Bardo Teachings: The Tibetan Way of Death and Rebirth* (Boulder, CO: Karma Dawa Tashi, 1979), p. 3.

45. Ibid., pp. 3–5.

46. Winkler, *Soul of the Matter*, p. 64.

47. Ibid., pp. 64–65. See also Menasseh ben Israel, *Nishmat Hayyim* (New York: Sinai Offset Co., n.d.; originally published in Amsterdam, 1651).

48. Ibid.

49. Ibid. p. 65.

50. See Raoul B. Nass, *The Road to Eternal Life and to Resurrection from Death, after Death* (Montpelier, VT: Capital City Press, 1976), pp. 246ff.

51. The discussion that follows this passage in the *Zohar* indicates that this teaching is bound up with kabbalistic doctrine of the *sefirot*, the emanations of the Tree of Life. A more complete investigation of the philosophical background of the Tree of Life would take us far beyond the scope of our present inquiry.

52. Nass, *Road*, p. 248; Samuel J. Fox, *Hell in Jewish Literature* (Northbrook, IL: Whitehall, 1972), p. 64.

53. Schachter-Shalomi, "Life in the Hereafter," p. 595.

54. See also Nass, *Road*, p. 248.

55. Winkler, *Soul of the Matter*, p. 19.

56. Ibid.

57. Ibid., p. 20.

58. Meir ben Ezekiel ibn Gabbai, *Avodat HaKodesh* (Warsaw, 1883), 31, 48b, cited by Fox, *Hell in Jewish Literature*, p. 113.

59. Nass, *Road*, pp. 246–248.

60. On the *Kaddish*, see Tzvi Rabinowicz, *A Guide to Life—Jewish Laws and Customs of Mourning* (Northvale, NJ: Jason Aronson, 1989), pp. 69–79.

61. Ibid., p. 75.

62. *Shabbat* 119b.

63. Schachter-Shalomi, "Life in the Hereafter," p. 595. See also *Zohar* II, 211b.

64. Ibid.

65. See, for example, Joseph Head and S. L. Cranston, eds., *Reincarnation: The Phoenix Fire Mystery* (New York: Juliam Press, 1977).

66. Schachter-Shalomi, "Life in the Hereafter," p. 596.

67. According to one modern Jewish thinker: "Very few modern Jews believe in reincarnation and the doctrine is certainly not very prominent even among those who do." From Louis Jacobs, *What Does Judaism Say About?* (New York: New York Times Book Co., 1973), p. 268.

68. Scholem, *Kabbalah*, p. 344.

69. Scholem, *Godhead*, p. 203. *Zohar Hadash*, 33a.

70. Scholem, *Godhead*, pp. 198ff; *Kabbalah*, p. 344. See also R. Tzvi Werblowsky, "Transmigration," in *Death, Afterlife and the Soul*, ed. Lawrence E. Sullivan (New York: Macmillan, 1989), p. 134.

71. Scholem, *Godhead*, p. 198. See also Saadia, *Beliefs*, VI, chapter 8.

72. Scholem, *Kabbalah*, pp. 344–345; *Godhead*, p. 207.

73. Recanti, *Perush Ha-Torah* (Venice, 1545, f. 79a, 209a), cited by Scholem, *Godhead*, p. 207 n. 17.

74. Scholem, *Godhead*, p. 207.

75. Ibid., p. 209.

76. Scholem, *Kabbalah*, pp. 344–345.

77. Quoted by William Judge, "Reincarnation in Judaism and the Bible," in *Reincarnation*, W. Q. Judge Series, no. 1 (Los Angeles: Theosophy Co., n.d.), p. 8.

78. Scholem, *Godhead*, p. 211.

79. Ibid.

80. Scholem, *Godhead*, p. 209; Nass, *Road*, p. 164.

81. Ibid., pp. 209–210.

82. Ibid., p. 210.

83. Scholem, *Kabbalah*, p. 346

84. Ibid., p. 347.

85. On this controversy, and on the life of Abraham ben Hananiah Yagel, see David B. Ruderman, *Kabbalah, Magic and Science—The Cultural Universe of a Sixteenth-Century Jewish Physician* (Cambridge: Harvard University Press, 1988), pp. 121ff.

86. Scholem, *Godhead*, p. 225.

87. Ibid., p. 226.

88. Scholem, *Kabbalah*, p. 347. See also A. B. Gotlober, "The Gilgul or the Transmigration," in *Yenne Velt—The Great Works of Jewish Fantasy and Occult*, trans. and ed. Joachim Neugroschel (New York: Pocket Books, 1976), pp. 386–434. This story demonstrates that teachings on reincarnation into animal bodies remained within folk-level Judaism for centuries.

89. Scholem, *Godhead*, p. 219.

90. Chaim Vital, *Shaar Ha-Gilgulim* (Jerusalem: 1981). Originally published in 1666.

91. Winkler, *Soul of the Matter*, pp. 17–18.

92. Ibid., p. 18.

93. Schachter-Shalomi, "Some Thoughts on the Hereafter," unpublished paper, n.d., p. 6.

94. Gershon Winkler, *Dybbuk* (New York: Judaica Press, 1981), pp. 1–5.

95. Joshua Trachtenberg, *Jewish Magic and Superstition* (New York: Atheneum, 1974), pp. 153–180.

96. Scholem, *Kabbalah*, p. 348.

97. Scholem, *Godhead*, pp. 221–222.

98. Schachter-Shalomi, "Life in the Hereafter," p. 596.

99. Ibid. Scholem, *Godhead*, pp. 222–223.

100. Schachter-Shalomi, "Life in the Hereafter," p. 596.

101. Scholem, *Kabbalah*, p. 349.

102. Winkler, *Dybbuk* , p. 9.

103. Scholem, *Godhead*, p. 222.

104. Scholem, *Kabbalah*, p. 349.

105. Ibid.

106. Ibid.

107. Ibid.

108. Trachtenberg, *Jewish Magic and Superstition*, p. 50. See also Moses Gaster, trans. and ed., *Maaseh Book* (Philadelphia: Jewish Publicaton Society, 1934, 1981).

109. Trachtenberg, ibid.

110. Daniel R. Shevitz, "Rituals for Jewish Exorcism," in *The Jewish Almanac*, ed. Richard Siegel and Carl Rheins (New York: Bantam, 1980), pp. 568–570.

111. Zalman Schachter-Shalomi, "Dybbuk and Exorcism," cassette tape (Philadelphia: P'nai Or Religious Fellowship, 1982).

112. Ibid.

113. Hoffman, *Way of Splendor*, p. 202.

114. Schachter-Shalomi, "Some Thoughts on the Hereafter," p. 7.

115. Ibid.

116. Hoffman, *Way of Splendor*, p. 202.

117. Schachter-Shalomi, "Some Thoughts on the Hereafter," p. 7.

118. Ibid.

119. Ibid.

CHAPTER 9

1. Jacob S. Minkin, *The Romance of Hasidism* (North Hollywood, CA: Wilshire Book Co., 1971), p. 99.

2. Benzion Dinur, "The Origins of Hasidism and Its Social and Messianic Foundations," in *Essential Papers of Hasidism: Origins to Present*, ed. Gershon David Hundert (New York: New York University Press, 1991), pp. 86–208.

3. Minkin, *Romance*, p. 97.

4. Ibid., p. 98.

5. Stephen Sharot, *Messianism, Mysticism, and Magic: A Sociological Analysis of Jewish Religious Movements* (Chapel Hill: University of North Carolina Press, 1982), p. 161.

6. Ibid., 158.

7. On the *tzaddik*, see Aryeh Rubinstein, *Hasidism* (New York: Leon Amiel Publisher, 1975), pp. 44ff.; Samuel H. Dresner, *The Zaddik* (New York: Abelard Schuman, 1960); Arthur Green, "Typologies of Leadership and the Hasidic Zaddiq," in *Jewish Spirituality*, vol. 2: *From the Sixteenth Century Revival to the Present*, ed. Arthur Green (New York: Crossroad Publishing, 1987), pp. 127–156; and Sharot, *Messianism, Mysticism, and Magic*, pp. 155ff.

8. Mircea Eliade, *Shamanism—Archaic Techniques of Ecstacy*, trans. William R. Trask (Princeton, NJ: Princeton University Press, 1972).

9. Dan Ben-Amos and Jerome P. Mintz, trans. and eds., *Shivhei Ha-Besht—In Praise of the Baal Shem Tov* (Bloomington, IN: Indiana University Press, 1970).

10. Jerome Mintz, *Legends of the Hasidim: An Introduction to Hasidic Tradition and Oral Culture in the New World* (Chicago: University of Chicago Press, 1968), pp. 3ff.

11. Sharot, *Messianism, Mysticism, and Magic*, p. 161.

12. See, for example, Howard Schwartz, *The Dream Assembly: Tales of Rabbi Zalman Schachter-Shalomi* (Amity, NY: Amity House, 1988). This is a contemporary collection of hasidic tales about Rabbi Zalman Schachter-Shalomi.

13. Dinur, "Origins of Hasidism," pp. 93–94.

14. Sharot, *Messianism, Mysticism, and Magic*, p. 161.

15. Martin Buber, *Tales of the Hasidim*, 2 vols. (New York: Schocken Books, 1975 and 1977).

16. Ben-Amos and Mintz, *Shivhei Ha-Besht*.

17. Louis Newman, ed. and trans., *The Hasidic Anthology—Tales and Teachings of the Hasidim* (New York: Schocken Books, 1975).

18. Describing his editing work with the original legends, Buber writes:

One like myself, whose purpose it is to picture the *tzaddikim* and their lives from extant written (and some oral) material, must above all, to do justice simultaneously to legend and to truth, supply the missing links in the narrative. In the course of this long piece of work I found it most expedient to begin by giving up the available form (or rather formlessness) of the notes with their meagerness of excessive detail, their obscurities or digressions, to reconstruct the events in question with the most accuracy (wherever possible with the aid of variants and other relevant material), and to relate them as coherently as I could in a form suited to the subject matter. Then, however, I went back to the notes and incorporated in my final version whatever felicitous turn or phrase they contained. On the other hand, I considered it neither permissible nor desirable to expand the tales or to render them more colorful and diverse. Only in a few cases where the notes at hand were quite fragmentary did I compose a connected whole by fusing what I had with other fragments, and filling the gap with relate material. (Buber, *Tales*, vol. 1, p. viii)

19. In *The Hasidic Anthology*, Newman provides the original sources for the stories cited and includes in his bibliography publication information on the various texts cited. In the English version of Buber's *Tales of the Hasidim*, references to the original Hebrew and Yiddish sources are not given. However, they are to be found in the Hebrew edition of Buber's *Tales*, entitled *Or Ha-Ganuz* ("The Hidden Light"). Martin Buber, *Or Ha-Ganuz* (Tel Aviv: Schocken Publishing House, 1946).

20. Ibid., vol. 2, p. 268. M. Lipson, *Midor Dor* (Tel Aviv, 1929), p. 244.

21. Ibid., vol. 2, p. 291; M. Walden, *Ohel Yitzhak* (Piotrkov, 1914).

22. Newman, *Hasidic Anthology*, pp. 4–5; S. Shinaver, *Ramathaim Tzofim* (Warsaw, 1881), p. 164.

23. Ibid., p. 70; Chaim Bloch, *Gemeinde des Chassidim* (Vienna, 1920), p. 145.

24. Ibid., p. 73; Abram Alter, *Meir Einei Ha-Golah*, vol. 1 (Piotrkov, 1928), p. 110.

25. Story cited by Pesach Schindler, "The Holocaust and the Kiddush Hashem in Hasidic Thought," in *Religious Encounters with Death*, ed. Frank Reynolds and Earle W. Waugh (University Park: Pennsylvania State University, 1977), p. 172.

26. Ibid.

27. Ibid.

28. Ibid., p. 171.

29. Buber, *Tales*, vol. 2, p. 234; J. K. K. Rokotz, *Tiferet Ha-Yehudi* (Warsaw, 1911).

30. Ibid., vol. 2, p. 269. *Marom Ha-Rayam*.

31. Zalman Schachter-Shalomi, "Some Thoughts on the Hereafter" (Unpublished paper, n.d.), p. 4.

32. Newman, *Hasidic Anthology*, p. 67; *Or Yesharim* (Piotrkov, 1924), p. 202.

33. Ibid., p. 69; M. Buber, *Die Chassidischen Buecher* (Hellerau, 1928), pp. 490–491.

34. Buber, *Tales*, vol. 2, p. 223; I. Berger, *Esser Kedushoth* (Warsaw, 1925).

35. Ibid., vol. 1, p. 194. *Rahmei H'av*.

36. Ibid., vol. 1, p. 234; I. Berger, *Esser Orot* (Warsaw, 1913).

37. Ben-Amos and Mintz, *Shivhei Ha-Besht*, pp. 37–38.

38. Buber, *Tales*, vol. 2, pp. 233–234; *Shelosha Adirei Tzon* (Piotrkov, 1930).

39. Ibid., vol. 1, p. 197: Newman, *Hasidic Anthology*, p. 70; I. Berger, *Esser Tzachtzochoth* (Piotrkov, 1910), p. 89.

40. Newman, *Hasidic Anthology*, p. 71; Chaim Bloch, *Priester des Liebe* (Vienna, 1930), p. 86.

41. Buber, *Tales*, vol. 2, p. 121; *Ha'shva Toldot Yosef* (Berdichev, 1908).

42. Ibid., vol. 2, p. 95; *Beit Shlomo* (Warsaw, 1929).

43. Ibid., vol. 1, p. 271; *Shivhei HaRav*.

44. Ibid., vol. 2, p. 126; A. S. B. Michaelson, *Ohel Elimelekh* (Prezemysl, 1910).

45. Ibid., vol. 1, pp. 83–84; see also Ben-Amos and Mintz, *Shivhei Ha-Besht*, pp. 255–257; Jack Riemer, ed., *Jewish Reflections on Death* (New York: Schocken Books, 1974), pp. 26–27.

46. Ibid., vol. 1, p. 284; E. I. Stand, *Seder Ha-Dorot Ha-Hadash* (Lemberg, 1865).

47. Ibid., vol. 1, p. 156; *Nativ Mitzvotekha*.

48. Edward Hoffman, *The Way of Splendor* (Boulder, CO: Shambhala, 1981), quoting *Rabbi Nahman's Wisdom*, p. 445. For a detailed depiction of the death of Reb Nahman of Bratslav, see Arthur Green, *Tormented Master—A Life of Rabbi Nahman of Bratslav* (New York: Schocken Books, 1981), pp. 275–282.

49. Buber, *Tales*, vol. 2, p. 311; Abram Alter, *Meir Einei ha-Golah*, ii (Warsaw, 1931), p. 78.

50. Buber, *Tales*, vol. 1, p. 251.

51. Ibid., vol. 1, p. 253; Elimelekh of Lyzhansk, *Noam Elimelekh* (Warsaw, 1881), p. 40.

52. Ben-Amos and Mintz, *Shivhei Ha-Besht*, pp. 260–261.

53. Buber, *Tales*, vol. 2, p. 250; I. Berger, *Simchat Yisrael* (Piotrkov, 1910).

54. Zalman Schachter-Shalomi, "Life in the Hereafter: A Tour of What's to Come," in *The Jewish Almanac*, ed. Richard Siegel and Carl Rheins (New York: Bantam, 1980), pp. 594–596.

55. Ibid., vol. 2, p. 182; *Ohel Yissachar* (Lublin, 1933).

56. Story told by Abraham Joshua Heschel, *A Passion for Truth* (New York: Farrar, Strauss, Giroux, 1973), pp. 20ff.

57. Buber, *Tales*, vol. 2, p. 111. *Mekor Hayyim* (Bilguray, 1912).

58. Newman, *Hasidic Anthology*, p. 2; I. Berger, *Esser Tzachtzochoth* (Piotrkov, 1910), p. 92.

59. Mintz, *Legends of the Hasidim*, p. 193.

60. Buber, *Tales*, vol. 2, p. 94; *Beit Yisrael*.

61. Mintz, *Legends of the Hasidim*, pp. 251–252.

62. Buber, *Tales*, vol. 1, p. 285; *Beit Aharon*.

63. Newman, *Hasidic Anthology*, p. 1; I. Berger, *Esser Orot* (Warsaw, 1913), p. 32.

64. Ibid., pp. 5–6; Alter, *Meir Einei ha-Golah*, i (Piotrkov, 1928), p. 85.

65. Buber, *Tales*, vol. 1, pp. 276–277; *Beit Aharon*.

66. Newman, *Hasidic Anthology*, p. 1; B. Ehrman, *Peer Ve-Kavod* (Muncats, 1912), p. 12a.

67. Newman, *Hasidic Anthology*, p. 3. Abraham Kahana, ed., *Ha-Sefarim Ha-Hitzonim* (Tel Aviv: Hozoath M'goroth Publishers, 1936), p. 134.

68. Newman, *Hasidic Anthology*, p. 5; Alter, *Meir Einei ha-Golah*, i (Piotrkov, 1928), pp. 81–82.

69. Buber, *Tales*, vol. 1, p. 157; *Tefillah Le-Moshe* (Lvov, 1856).

70. Ibid., vol. 1, pp. 295–296; *Sefaran shel Tzaddikim*.

71. Ibid., vol. 1, pp. 271–272; *Shivhei Ha-Rav*.

72. Ibid., vol. 2, pp. 94–95; *Beit Shlomo* (Warsaw, 1929).

73. Ibid., vol. 2, p. 269; *Simhat Yisrael*.

74. Ibid., vol. 2, p. 271; J. K. K. Rokotz, *Siach Sarfei Kodesh*, vol. 4 (Lodz, 1929).

75. Ibid., vol. 1, p. 117; *Kahal Hasidim*.

76. Ibid., vol. 1, p. 115; *Tiferet Yisrael*.

77. Ibid., vol. 1, p. 116; *Devarim Eruvim*.

78. Ben-Amos and Mintz, *Shivhei Ha-Besht*, p. 106.

79. Mintz, *Legends of the Hasidim*, p. 93.

80. Ibid.; see also Ben-Amos and Mintz, *Shivhei Ha-Besht*, pp. 190–191.

81. Louis Jacobs, *Jewish Mysticial Testimonies* (New York: Schocken Books, 1978), p. 267.

82. Buber, *Tales*, vol. 1, p. 158; Rokotz, *Shiftei Kodesh*, vol. 4 (Lodz, 1929).

83. Buber, *Tales*, vol. 1, p. 310; *Niflaot Ha-Rabi Bunam* (Warsaw, 1926).

CHAPTER 10

1. Raymond Moody, *Life after Life* (New York: Bantam, 1976).

2. Actually, the term "Tibetan Book of the Dead" is a Western misnomer. What W. Y. Evans-Wentz first called the Tibetan Book of the Dead was actually a translation of seven of seventeen chapters of the text *Bar-do thos-grol chen-mo*—"Great Liberation through Hearing in the Bardo." This particular text, also called the *Bardo Thodol*, is only one of innumerable Tibetan texts on death and the postmortem experience. The Tibetan scholar Detlef Ingo Lauf has listed over thirty-nine different versions of various death texts from Tibet. See Detlef Ingo Lauf, *Secret Doctrines of the Tibetan Books of the Dead* (Berkeley, CA: Shambhala, 1977), p. x, and W. Y. Evans-Wentz, ed., *The Tibetan Book of the Dead* (New York: Oxford University Press, 1960).

3. Anthony Sutich, "The Emergence of the Transpersonal Orientation," *Journal of Transpersonal Psychology* 8:1 (1976): 5–19.

4. This term was also coined by Maslow. See Abraham Maslow, *Religions, Values and Peak-Experiences* (New York: Viking, 1970).

5. Roberto Assagioli, *Psychosynthesis* (New York: Viking, 1974).

6. Stanislav Grof, *Beyond the Brain—Birth, Death and Transcendence in Psychotherapy* (Albany, NY: SUNY Press, 1985), *Realms of the Human Unconscious* (New York: Dutton, 1976), and *The Holotropic Mind* (San Francisco: Harper, 1993).

7. Jean Houston, *Life Force—The Psycho-Historical Recovery of Self* (New York: Delacorte, 1980).

8. Ken Wilber, *The Atman Project* (Wheaton, IL: Quest Books, 1980), and *The Spectrum of Consciousness* (Wheaton, IL: Quest Books, 1977).

9. Stanislav Grof and Joan Halifax, *The Human Encounter with Death* (New York: Dutton, 1978).

10. Stanislav Grof and Christina Grof, *Beyond Death—The Gates of Consciousness* (New York: Thames and Hudson, 1980).

11. See Grof and Halifax, *Human Encounter*, pp. 26ff.

12. Ibid., pp. 82–83.

13. Ibid., pp. 158 ff. In both *The Human Encounter with Death* and *Beyond Death* Grof examines such texts as the *Egyptian Book of the Dead*, *Tibetan Book of the Dead*, *Ars Moriendi*, and *Garuda Purana*, as well as Indian and Greek mythology.

14. Ibid., p. 159.

15. Ibid.

16. Zalman Schachter-Shalomi, *Spiritual Intimacy—A Study of Counseling in Hasidism* (Northvale, NJ: Jason Aronson, 1991), pp. 38ff.

17. See Chapter 3 n. 3.

18. D. M. Dooling, "Worlds of Discourse: A Conversation with Zalman Schachter," *Parabola* 2:2 (Summer 1977): 84–95.

19. Adapted from Zalman Schachter-Shalomi, *Fragments of a Future Scroll* (Philadelphia: Leaves of Grass Press, 1975), pp. 24–25.

20. Gershom Winkler, *The Soul of the Matter* (New York: Judaica Press, 1982), p. 7.

21. Moses de Leon, *Sefer Ha-Nesfesh Ha-Hakhamah*, vol. 1, sig. 2, fol. 4b; sig. 3, fol. 1a, quoted by Isaiah Tishby and Fischel Lachower, eds., *The Wisdom of the Zohar*, vol. 2, trans. David Goldstein (London: Oxford University Press, 1989), p, 688.

22. Also referred to as the "auric-egg" in theosophical philosophy. See Geoffrey A. Barborka, *The Divine Plan* (Wheaton, IL: Theosophical Publishing House, 1972).

23. Grof and Grof, *Beyond Death*, pp. 60–95.

24. E. J. Gold, *American Book of the Dead* (Nevada City, CA: I.D.H.H.B., 1978).

25. Chogyam Trungpa and Francesca Fremantle, trans., *The Tibetan Book of the Dead* (Berkeley, CA: Shambhala, 1981), pp. 10–11.

26. According to traditional Tibetan doctrine, these three *bardos* are *Kye*

Nes Bardo—the *bardo* of having taken birth; *Milam Bardo*—the *bardo* of the dream state; and *Samten Bardo*—the meditation *bardo*. Lama Lodru, *Bardo Teachings—The Tibetan Way of Death and Rebirth* (Boulder, CO: Karma Dawa Tashi, 1979), pp. 1–2.

27. Ibid.

28. For a fuller treatment of this subject, see my doctoral dissertation: Simcha Steven Paull [Simcha Raphael], "Judaism's Contribution to the Psychology of Death and Dying" (Ph.D. dissertation, California Institute of Integral Studies, 1986; University Microfilms Publication Number 86–25,140), especially chapter 5.

29. Stephen Levine, *Who Dies?* (Garden City, NY: Anchor Books, 1982), p. ix.

30. Moody, *Life after Life*, p. 29.

31. Sogyal Rinpoche, *The Tibetan Book of Living and Dying* (San Francisco: Harper, 1992), p. 259.

32. A. ben Baruch Crehange, trans., *L'Arbre de la Vie: Prieres pour les malades, les mourants et les morts* (Tel Aviv: Sinai Publishers, 1972), pp. 64–67.

33. Moody, *Life after Life*, p. 62.

34. Karlis Osis and Erlendur Haraldsson, *At the Hour of Death* (New York: Avon, 1977), p. 85.

35. Personal conversation with my late great-uncle, John Cornfield.

36. The work of Osis and Haraldsson is based on deathbed observations, with information gathered from thousands of attending physicans and nurses. See Osis and Haraldsson, *At the Hour of Death*, pp. 26ff.

37. Elisabeth Kübler-Ross, *On Life after Death* (Berkeley, CA: Celestial Arts, 1991), p. 60.

38. Moody, *Life after Life*, pp. 65–66.

39. Ibid., pp. 64–65.

40. F. Gordon Greene and Stanley Krippner, "Panoramic Vision: Hallucination or Bridge into the Beyond?" in *What Survives: Contemporary Explorations of Life after Death*, ed. Gary Doore (Los Angeles: Tarcher, 1990), pp. 61–75.

41. Kenneth Ring, *Life at Death* (New York: Coward, McCann and Geoghegan, 1980), cited by Greene and Krippner, "Panoramic Vision," p. 71.

42. Greene and Krippner, "Panoramic Vision," p. 70.

43. Lati Rinpochay and Jeffrey Hopkins, *Death, Intermediate State and Rebirth in Tibetan Buddhism* (Valois, NY: Snow Lion Publications, 1981), pp. 16–18.

44. Wilber, "Death, Rebirth and Meditation," in Doore, *What Survives*, pp. 179–184.

45. Levine, *Who Dies?* pp. 268–271.

46. Moody, *Life after Life*, pp. 30–34, 73–84.

47. Jonathan Neumann, "Near-Death Experiences in Judaic Literature," *Journal of Psychology and Judaism* 14:4 (Winter 1990): 225–251.

48. Theosophy has been described as the perennial ancient wisdom/religion that has always existed on earth. In its modern context, Theosophy emerged in the Western world and in India via the teaching inspiration of Helena P. Blavatsky, a Russian woman who lived in the late 1800s. Blavatsky brought the esoterica of Eastern philosophy to the Western world through the founding of the Theosophical Society in the late 1800s. Within Theosophy can be found a significant core of teachings on the postmortem journey of the soul and the doctrine of reincarnation. See H. P. Blavatsky, *The Key to Theosophy* (Pasadena, CA: Theosophical University Press, 1972), and Laurence J. Bendit, *The Mirror of Life and Death* (Wheaton, IL: Quest Books, 1968).

49. Schachter-Shalomi, *Spiritual Intimacy*, p. 42.

50. Tzvi Rabinowicz, *A Guide to Life—Jewish Laws and Customs of Mourning* (Northvale, NJ: Jason Aronson, 1989), pp. 45–54.

51. Zalman Schachter-Shalomi, "Life in the Hereafter: A Tour of What's to Come," in *The Jewish Almanac*, ed. Richard Siegel and Carl Rheins (New York: Bantam, 1980), pp. 594–596.

52. Grof, *Realms of the Human Unconscious*.

53. Werner Erhard, founder of Erhard Seminars Training (est), frequently used this phrase.

54. *Massekhet Gehinnom* I:4.

55. 2 Enoch 10:1–6.

56. One recites *Kaddish* for a mother or father for eleven months; for a sister, brother, spouse, or child for thirty days. See Rabinowicz, *Guide to Life*, pp. 69–79.

57. Elisabeth Kübler-Ross, *On Death and Dying* (New York: Macmillan, 1970).

58. Cited in Rabinowicz, *Guide to Life*, p. 73. In *Seder Eliyahu Rabbah* the story is told in the name of Rabban Yohanan ben Zakkai.

59. Elisabeth Kübler-Ross, *To Live Until We Say Goodbye* (Englewood Cliffs, NJ: Prentice-Hall, 1978), p. 55.

60. This idea of a second life review is clearly from Theosophical sources than from Jewish ones. See Geoffrey Farthing, *Exploring the Great Beyond* (Wheaton, IL: Quest Books, 1978), p. 78.

61. Schachter-Shalomi, "Life in the Hereafter," p. 595.

62. Ibid.

63. Morton Kelsey, *Afterlife: The Other Side of Dying* (New York: Crossroad Publishing, 1979), p. 185.

64. This descriptive language is adapted from: Maslow, *Religions, Values, and Peak-Experiences*, pp. 59–68.

65. Sogyal Rinpoche, *Tibetan Book of Living and Dying*, pp. 274ff.

66. From a ritual code entitled *Or Zarua* by Rabbi Isaac ben Moses of Vienna, and attributed to Isaac Luria; quoted in Rabinowicz, *Guide to Life*, pp. 91–92.

67. Ibid., pp. 95–97.

68. A text entitled *Maaneh Lashon*, containing all kinds of memorial prayers, was extremely popular for centuries in Eastern Europe. Within this text are prayers spoken directly to the soul of the deceased. It is based on and reflects an extensive tradition of making supplications at the grave of a dead relative or teacher. Developed originally in the 1600s, by 1800 it had been printed in over forty editions in both Hebrew and Judeo-German. An English translation of this text, from the early twentieth century is G. Selkovitsch, trans., *Memorial Prayers and Meditations* (New York: Hebrew Publishing, 1910). On the history of the *Maaneh Lashon* liturgical traditions, see Jacob R. Marcus, *Communal Sick-Care in the German Ghetto* (Cincinnati: Hebrew Union College Press, 1947), pp. 222ff.

69. Sogyal Rinpoche, *Tibetan Book of Living and Dying*, pp. 295–298.

70. This selection is from Louis Ginzberg, ed., *Legends of the Jews*, vol. 1, trans. Henrietta Szold (Philadelphia: Jewish Publication Society, 1967–1969), pp. 57–58. The complete English text is found in Moses Gaster, ed. and trans., *The Chronicles of Jerahmeel*, IX (New York: Ktav, 1971; originally published in 1899); the complete Hebrew text is in Adolph Jellinek, ed., *Beit Ha-Midrash*, vol. 1 (Jerusalem: Wahrmann, 1967), pp. 153–158, and J. D. Eisenstein, ed., *Otzar Midrashim*, vol. 1 (New York: Grossman's, 1915), pp. 243–244.

71. Ginzberg, ibid.

72. Zalman Schachter-Shalomi, "Some Thoughts on the Hereafter" (unpublished paper, n.d.), p. 2.

73. Richard Address, ed., *The Synagogue as a Caring Community—A Resource Book for Congregational Leaders*, 3 vols. (Philadelphia: UAHC, 1982–1989).

Bibliography

Abrahams, Israel, ed. *Hebrew Ethical Wills*, 2 vols. Philadelphia: Jewish Publication Society, 1923.

Albright, William Foxwell. *The Archaeology of Palestine*. New York: Pelican, 1961.

———. *Yahweh and the Gods of Canaan*. London: Athlone Press, 1968.

Alighieri, Dante. *The Inferno*. Trans. John Ciardi. New York: New American Library, 1954.

———. *The Paradiso*. Trans. John Ciardi. New York: New American Library, 1961.

———. *The Purgatario*. Trans. John Ciardi. New York: New American Library, 1961.

Alt, Albrecht. *Essays on Old Testament History and Religion*. Trans. R. A. Wilson. Garden City, NY: Doubleday, 1967.

American Psychiatric Association. *Diagnostic and Statistical Manual-III-R*, 3rd ed., rev. Washington, DC: American Psychiatric Association, 1987.

Arkush, Allan. "Immortality." In *Contemporary Jewish Religious Thought*, ed. Arthur A. Cohen and Paul Mender-Flohr, pp. 479–482. New York: Scribner's, 1987.

Assagioli, Roberto. *Psychosynthesis*. New York: Viking, 1974.

Azulai, Avraham. *Hesed L'Avraham*. B'nai Brak: Agudat Yad Avraham, 1986; originally published in 1685.

The Babylonian Talmud. Ed. and trans. I. Epstein. London: Soncino Press, 1935–1965.

Bader, Gershom. *The Encyclopedia of Talmudic Sages*. Northvale, NJ: Jason Aronson, 1988 pp. 535ff.

Baeck, Leo. *The Essence of Judaism*. Trans. Victor Grubenwieser and Leonard Pearl. New York: Schocken Books, 1948, 1976.

Barborka, Geoffrey A. *The Divine Plan*. Wheaton, IL: Theosophical Publishing House, 1972.

Baron, Salo Wittmayer. *A Social and Religious History of the Jews*. Vol. 2: *Ancient Times*. Philadelphia: Jewish Publication Society, 1951.

Barrick, W. Boyd. "The Funerary Character of 'High-Places' in Ancient Palestine: A Reassessment." *Vetus Testamentum* 25 (1975): 565–595.

Bauckham, Richard. "Early Jewish Visions of Hell." *Journal of Theological Studies* 41:2 (October 1990): 355–385.

Ben Gershom, Levi [Gersonides]. *The Wars of the Lord*. Book 1: *Immortality of the Soul*. Ed. and trans. Seymour Feldman. Philadelphia: Jewish Publication Society, 1984.

ben Israel, Menasseh. *Nishmat Hayyim*. New York: Sinai Offset Co., n.d.; originally published in Amsterdam, 1651.

ben Moshe Mi'Modina, Aaron Berechia. *Maavor Yabok*. B'nai Brak: Yishpah, 1967.

Ben-Amos, Dan, and Mintz, Jerome P., trans. and eds. *Shivhei Ha-Besht—In Praise of the Baal Shem Tov*. Bloomington, IN: Indiana University Press, 1970; Northvale, NJ: Jason Aronson, 1993.

Bender, A. P. "Beliefs, Rites, and Customs of the Jews, Connected with Death, Burial and Mourning." *Jewish Quarterly Review* 6 (1894): 317–347, 664–671.

———. "Beliefs, Rites, and Customs of the Jews, Connected with Death, Burial and Mourning." *Jewish Quarterly Review* 7 (1895): 101–118, 259–269.

Bendit, Laurence J. *The Mirror of Life and Death*. Wheaton, IL: Quest Books, 1968.

Birkeland, Harris. "The Belief in the Resurrection of the Dead in the Old Testament." *Studia Theologica* 3 (1950): 60–78.

Blau, Joseph L. *The Story of Jewish Philosophy*. New York: Random House, 1962.

Blavatsky, H. P. *The Key to Theosophy*. Pasadena, CA: Theosophical University Press, 1972.

Blumberg, Harry. "The Problem of Immortality in Avicenna, Maimonides and St. Thomas Aquinas." In *Studies in Maimonides and St. Thomas Aquinas*, ed. Jacob I. Diesenstag, pp. 174–180. New York: Ktav, 1975.

Bookstaber, Phillip David. *The Idea of the Development of the Soul in Medievel Jewish Philosophy*. Philadelphia: Morris Jacobs, 1950.

Bowker, John. *The Meanings of Death*. New York: Cambridge University Press, 1991.

Brandon, S. G. F. *Man and His Destiny in the Great Religions*. Manchester, England: Manchester University Press, 1962.

————. *The Judgement of the Dead—The Idea of Life After Death in the Major Religions*. New York: Scribner's, 1967.

Brener, Anne. *Mourning and Mitzvah*. Woodstock, VT: Jewish Lights Publishing, 1993.

Brichto, Herbert Chanan. "Kin, Cult, Land and Afterlife—A Biblical Complex." *Hebrew Union College Annual* 44 (1973): 1–54.

Brown, Francis, et al. *Hebrew and English Lexicon of the Old Testament*. Oxford: Clarendon Press, 1907, 1968.

Buber, Martin. *Or Ha-Ganuz*. Tel Aviv: Schocken Publishing House, 1946.

————. *Tales of the Hasidim*. Vol 1: *The Early Masters*. New York: Schocken Books, 1975.

————. *Tales of the Hasidim*. Vol. 2: *The Later Masters*. New York: Schocken Books, 1977.

Buchanan, George Wesley, ed. and trans. *Revelation and Redemption: Jewish Documents of Deliverance from the Fall of Jerusalem to the Death of Nahmanides*. Dillsboro, NC: Western North Carolina Press, 1978.

Cavendish, Richard. *Visions of Heaven and Hell*. London: Orbis, 1977.

Charles, R. H. *The Book of Enoch (1 Enoch)* London: SPCK, 1917.

————. *Eschatology: The Doctrine of a Future Life in Israel, Judaism and Christianity*. New York: Schocken Books, 1963.

————, ed. *The Apocrypha and Pseudepigrapha of the Old Testament in English*, 2 vols. Oxford: Oxford University Press, 1919, 1963.

Charlesworth, James H., ed. *The Old Testament Pseudepigrapha*, 2 vols. Garden City, NY: Doubleday, 1983.

Cohen, A. *The Teachings of Maimonides*. New York: Ktav, 1968.

————, ed. *Everyman's Talmud*. New York: Schocken Books, 1975.

Cohn-Sherbok, Dan. "The Jewish Doctrine of Hell." *Religion* 8 (1978): 196–209.

Cooper, Alan. *Body, Soul and Life Everlasting*. Grand Rapids, MI: Eerdmans, 1989.

Crehange, A. ben Baruch, trans. *L'Arbre de la Vie: Prieres pour les malades, les mourants et les morts*. Tel Aviv: Sinai Publishers, 1972.

Dan, Joseph. *Gershom Scholem and the Mystical Dimension of Jewish History*. New York: New York University Press, 1987.

de Vaux, Rolland. *Ancient Israel*, 2 vols. New York: McGraw-Hill, 1965.

de Vidas, Elijah. *Reishit Hokhmah*. Brooklyn, NY: Josef Sacks, 1984; originally published in Venice, 1579.

Dinur, Benzion. "The Origins of Hasidism and Its Social and Messianic Foundations." In *Essential Papers of Hasidism: Origins to Present*, ed. Gershon David Hundert, pp. 86–208. New York: New York University Press, 1991.

Dooling, D. M. "Worlds of Discourse: A Conversation with Zalman Schachter." *Parabola*, 2:2 (Summer 1977): 84–95.

Doore, Gary, ed. *What Survives: Contemporary Explorations of Life after Death.* Los Angeles: Tarcher, 1990.

Dresner, Samuel H. *The Zaddik.* New York: Abelard Schuman, 1960.

Efros, Israel. *Studies in Medieval Jewish Philosophy.* New York: Columbia University Press, 1974.

Eichrodt, Walter. *Theology of the Old Testament.* Trans. J. A. Baker London: SCM Press, 1967.

Eisenstein, J. D., ed. *Otzar Midrashim,* 2 vols. New York: Grossman's, 1915.

Eliade, Mircea. *Death, Afterlife and Eschatology.* New York: Harper & Row, 1974.

———. *Shamanism—Archaic Techniques of Ecstacy.* Trans. William R. Trask. Princeton, NJ: Princeton University Press, 1972.

Encyclopaedia Judaica. Jerusalem: Macmillan, 1971.

Farthing, Geoffrey. *Exploring the Great Beyond.* Wheaton, IL: Quest Books, 1978.

Fathers According to Rabbi Nathan. Trans. Judah Goldin. New Haven, CT: Yale University Press, 1955.

Feldman, Emanuel. *Biblical and Post-Biblical Defilement and Mourning: Law as Theology.* New York: Yeshiva University Press, 1977.

Finkel, Joshua. "Maimonides Treatise on Resurrection: A Comparative Study." In *Essays on Maimonides,* ed. Salo Wittmayer Baron, pp. 93–121. New York: Columbia University Press, 1941.

Finkelstein, Louis. "The Jewish Doctrine of Immortality." *Harvard Divinity School Bulletin* 30 March 1945, pp. 5–34.

———. *The Pharisees,* 2 vols. Philadelphia: Jewish Publication Society, 1938, 1962.

———, ed. *The Jews: Their History.* New York: Schocken Books, 1970.

Fox, Samuel J. *Hell in Jewish Literature.* Northbrook, IL: Whitehall, 1972.

Foxman, Jean H., et al. *Index to Jewish Periodicals.* Cleveland Heights, OH, 1978–1984.

Frazer, Sir George James. *The Belief in Immortality and the Worship of the Dead,* 2 vols. London: Dawsons, 1968.

Freud, Sigmund. *Standard Edition of the Complete Psychological Works of Sigmund Freud.* Ed. and trans. James Strachey. London: Hogarth Press, 1953–1974.

———. *The Future of an Illusion.* Garden City, NY: Anchor Books, 1961.

Friedman, Richard Elliott. *Who Wrote the Bible?* New York: Harper & Row, 1987.

Frish, Daniel, ed. *Otzar Ha-Zohar,* 5 vols. Jerusalem: Aleph-Beit Press, 1976.

Gallup, George. *Adventures in Immortality.* New York: McGraw-Hill, 1982.

Gaon, Saadia. *The Book of Beliefs and Opinions.* Ed. and trans. Samuel Rosenblatt. New Haven, CT: Yale University Press, 1948, 1976.

Gaster, Moses. "Hebrew Visions of Hell and Paradise." *Journal of the Asiatic Society* (July 1883): 571–612.

———, ed. and trans. *The Chronicles of Jerahmeel.* New York: Ktav, 1971; originally published in 1899.

————, ed. *Studies and Texts in Folklore, Magic, Medieval Romance, Hebrew Apocrypha and Samaritan Archaeology*, 3 vols. New York: Ktav, 1971.

————, trans. and ed. *Maaseh Book*. Philadelphia: Jewish Publication Society, 1934, 1981.

Gaster, Theodor. *The Holy and the Profane—Evolution of Jewish Folkways*. New York: William Morrow, 1980.

Gill, Derek. *Quest—The Life of Elisabeth Kübler-Ross*. New York: Ballantine, 1980.

Ginzberg, Louis, ed. *Legends of the Jews*, 7 vols. Trans. Henrietta Szold. Philadelphia: Jewish Publication Society, 1967–1969.

Glasson, T. Francis. *Greek Influence in Jewish Eschatology*. London: SPCK, 1961.

Gold, E. J. *American Book of the Dead*. Nevada City, CA: I.D.H.H.B., 1978.

Gollancz, Hermann, trans. *Tophet and Eden*. London: University of London Press, 1921.

Goodenough, Erwin R. *Jewish Symbols in the Greco-Roman Period*. New York: Pantheon, 1958.

Gordon, Audrey. "Death and Dying—Past, Present and Future." In *Ancient Roots and Modern Meanings*, ed. Jerry Diller, pp. 201–222. New York: Bloch Publishing, 1978.

Gorer, Geoffrey. *Death, Grief and Mourning*. Garden City, NY: Anchor Books, 1967.

Gotlober, A. B. "The Gilgul or the Transmigration." In *Yenne Velt—The Great Works of Jewish Fantasy and Occult*, trans. and ed. Joachim Neugroschel, pp. 386–434. New York: Pocket Books, 1976.

Gottwald, Norman K. *A Light to the Nations*. New York: Harper & Row, 1959.

Gowan, Donald E. *Bridge Between the Testaments*. Pittsburgh: Pickwick Press, 1976.

Graetz, H. *History of the Jews*, 6 vols. Philadelphia: Jewish Publicaton Society, 1894.

Green, Arthur. *Tormented Master—A Life of Rabbi Nahman of Bratslav*. New York: Schocken Books, 1981.

————, ed. *Jewish Spirituality*. 2 vols. New York: Crossroad Publishing, 1987.

Greenspoon, Leonard J. "The Origin of the Idea of Resurrection." In *Traditions in Transformation: Turning Points in Biblical Faith*, ed. Baruch Halpern and Jon D. Levenson, pp. 247–321. Winona Lake, IN: Eisenbrauns, 1981.

Grof, Stanislav. *Beyond the Brain—Birth, Death and Transcendence in Psychotherapy*. Albany, NY: SUNY Press, 1985.

————. *The Holotropic Mind*. San Francisco: Harper, 1993.

————. *Realms of the Human Unconscious*. New York: Dutton, 1976.

Grof, Stanislav, and Grof, Christina. *Beyond Death—The Gates of Consciousness*. New York: Thames and Hudson, 1980.

Grof, Stanislav, and Halifax, Joan. *The Human Encounter with Death*. New York: Dutton, 1978.

Guttmann, Julius. *Philosophies of Judaism*. Trans. David W. Silverman. New York: Schocken Books, 1973. Published as *The Philosophy of Judaism*. Northvale, NJ: Jason Aronson, 1988.

Halper, B., ed. *Post-Biblical Hebrew Literature—An Anthology*. Philadelphia: Jewish Publication Society, 1921.

Head, Joseph, and Cranston, S. L., eds. *Reincarnation: The Phoenix Fire Mystery*. New York: Juliam Press, 1977.

Herschaft, Jean. "Patient Should Not Be Told of Terminal Illness: Rabbi." *The Jewish Post and Opinion*, 13 March 1981, p. 12.

Hertz, Joseph I., ed. and trans. *The Authorized Daily Prayer Book*, rev. ed. New York: Bloch, 1948.

Heschel, Abraham Joshua. *A Passion for Truth*. New York: Farrar, Straus, Giroux, 1973.

———. *Maimonides—A Biography*. Trans. Joachim Neugroschel. New York: Farrar, Straus, Giroux, 1982.

Hick, John. *Death and Eternal Life*. San Francisco: Harper & Row, 1976.

Himmelfarb, Martha. *Ascent to Heaven in Jewish and Christian Apocalypses*. New York: Oxford University Press, 1993.

———. *Tours of Hell—An Apocalyptic Form in Jewish and Christian Literature*. Philadelphia: Fortress Press, 1985.

Hirsch, W. *Rabbinic Psychology—Beliefs about the Soul in Rabbinic Literature of the Talmudic Period*. London: Edward Goldston, 1947.

Hoffman, Edward. *The Way of Splendor—Jewish Mysticism and Modern Psychology*. Boulder, CO: Shambhala, 1981; Northvale, NJ: Jason Aronson, 1989.

Hoffner, Harry A. "Second Millennium Antecedents to the Hebrew *Ob*." *Journal of Biblical Literature* 86 (1967):385–401.

Holtz, Barry, ed. *Back to the Sources*. New York: Summit, 1984.

The Holy Bible. New American Catholic ed., 1961.

Houston, Jean. *Life Force—The Psycho-Historical Recovery of Self*. New York: Delacorte, 1980.

Hughes, Robert. *Heaven and Hell in Western Art*. New York: Stein and Day, 1968.

Husik, Isaac. *A History of Mediaeval Jewish Philosophy*. Philadelphia: Jewish Publication Society, 1940.

Idel, Moshe. *Kabbalah—New Perspectives*. New Haven, CT: Yale University Press, 1988.

Jacobs, Louis. *Jewish Mystical Testimonies*. New York: Schocken Books, 1978.

———. *What Does Judaism Say About?* New York: New York Times, 1973.

Jellinek, Adolph, ed. *Beit Ha-Midrash*, 6 vols. Jerusalem: Wahrmann, 1967.

Judge, William. "Reincarnation in Judaism and the Bible." In *Reincarnation*. W. Q. Judge Series, no. 1. Los Angeles: Theosophy Co., n.d.

Kaddushin, Max. *The Rabbinic Mind*. New York: Bloch, 1972.

Kahana, Abraham, ed. *Ha-Sefarim Ha-Hitzonim*, 2 vols. Tel Aviv: Hozaath M'qoroth Publishers, 1936.

Kelsey, Morton. *Afterlife: The Other Side of Dying*. New York: Crossroad Publishing, 1979.

Klausner, Joseph. *The Messianic Idea in Israel*. Trans. W. F. Stinespring. New York: Macmillan, 1955.

Klein, Ernest. *A Comprehensive Etymological Dictionary of the Hebrew Language for Readers of English*. Jersualem: Carta, 1987.

Kol Haneshama—Shabbat Eve. Ed. David Teutsch et al. Wyncote, PA: The Reconstructionist Press, 1989.

Kübler-Ross, Elisabeth. *On Death and Dying*. New York: Macmillan, 1970.

———. *On Life after Death*. Berkeley, CA: Celestial Arts, 1991.

———. *To Live Until We Say Goodbye*. Englewood Cliffs, NJ: Prentice-Hall, 1978.

Kung, Hans. *Eternal Life?* Trans. Edward Quinn. Garden City, NY: Doubleday, 1974.

Kutsher, Martin L., et al. *A Comprehensive Bibliography of Thanatology Literature*. New York: MSS Information Corporation, 1975.

Lacoque, Andre. *The Book of Daniel*. Trans. David Pellauer. Atlanta: John Knox Press, 1979.

Lamm, Maurice. *The Jewish Way in Death and Mourning*. New York: Jonathan David, 1969.

Lang, Bernhard. "Street Theater, Raising the Dead, and the Zoroastrian Connection in Ezekiel's Prophecy." In *Ezekiel and His Book*, ed. John Lust, pp. 297–316. Leuven, Belgium: Leuven University Press, 1986.

Lauf, Detlef Ingo. *Secret Doctrines of the Tibetan Books of the Dead*. Berkeley, CA: Shambhala, 1977.

Lauf, Detlef Ingo, and Evans-Wentz, W. Y., eds. *The Tibetan Book of the Dead*. New York: Oxford University Press, 1960.

Le Goff, Jacques. *The Birth of Purgatory*. Trans. Arthur Goldhammer. Chicago: University of Chicago Press, 1984.

Leibes, Yehuda. *Studies in the Zohar*. Trans. Arnold Schwartz et al. Albany, NY: SUNY Press, 1993.

Levine, Stephen. *Who Dies? An Investigation of Conscious Living and Conscious Dying*. Garden City, NY: Anchor Books, 1982.

Levy, B. Barry. *Planets, Potions and Parchments: Scientific Hebraica from the Dead Sea Scrolls to the Eighteenth Century*. Montreal: McGill Queen's University Press, 1990.

Lewis, Theodore J. *Cults of the Dead in Ancient Israel and Ugarit*. Atlanta: Scholars Press, 1989.

Lieberman, Saul. *Hellenism in Jewish Palestine*. New York: Jewish Theological Seminary of America, 1962.

————. "On Sins and Their Punishments." In *Texts and Studies*, pp. 29–57. New York: Ktav, 1974.

————. "Some Aspects of After Life in Early Rabbinic Literature." In *Harry Austryn Wolfson, Jubilee Volume*, vol. 2. Jerusalem: American Academy for Jewish Research, 1965.

Lightstone Jack. "The Dead in Late Antique Judaism." *Cahiers de researches en sciences de la Religion* 6 (1986): 51–79.

Lodru, Lama. *Bardo Teachings—The Tibetan Way of Death and Rebirth*. Boulder, CO: Karma Dawa Tashi, 1979.

Maimonides, Moses. *Commentary on the Mishnah—Tractate Sanhedrin*. Trans. and ed. Fred Rosner. New York: Sepher-Hermon Press, Inc., 1981.

————. *The Guide of the Perplexed*. Trans. and ed. M. Friedlander. New York: Hebrew Publishing, 1881.

————. *Mishneh Torah*. Trans. and ed. Moses Hyamson. Jerusalem: Boys Town Publishers, 1965.

Malter, Henry. *Saadia Gaon, His Life and Works*. New York: G. Olms, 1921.

Mansoor, Manahem. *Jewish History and Jewish Thought—An Introduction*. Hoboken, NJ: Ktav, 1991.

Marcus, Jacob R. *Communal Sick-Care in the German Ghetto*. Cincinnati: Hebrew Union College Press, 1947.

Margolis, Max I., and Marx, Alexander. *A History of the Jewish People*. Philadelphia: Jewish Publication Society, 192.

Marmorstein, A. *Studies in Jewish Theology*. New York: Oxford University Press, 1950.

Maslow, Abraham. *Religions, Values and Peak-Experiences*. New York: Viking, 1970.

Matt, Daniel Channan, ed. *Zohar: The Book of Enlightenment*. New York: Paulist Press Classics of Western Spirituality, 1983.

Matt, Herschel J. "An Outline of Jewish Eschatology." *Judaism* 17:2 (Spring 1968): 186–196.

McDannell, Colleen, and Lang, Bernhard. *Heaven: A History*. New Haven, CT: Yale University Press, 1988.

Mendelssohn, Moses. *Phaedon; or, the Death of Socrates*. Trans. from the German. New York: Arno Press, 1973; originally published in 1789.

Meyers, Eric. *Jewish Ossuaries: Reburial and Rebirth*. Rome: Biblical Institute Press, 1971.

Meyers, Jacob M., trans. *The Anchor Bible—I and II Esdras*. Garden City, NY: Doubleday, 1974.

Midrash on Proverbs. Trans. Burton L. Visotzky. New Haven, CT: Yale University Press, 1992.

Midrash on Psalms. 2 vols. Trans. William G. Braude. New Haven, CT: Yale University Press, 1959.

Midrash Rabbah. 10 vols. Trans. H. Freedman. New York: Soncino Press, 1983.

Midrash Tanhuma. Trans. John T. Townsend. Ed. Martin Buber. Hoboken, NJ: Ktav, 1989.

Milik, J. T., and Black, M. *The Book of Enoch: Aramaic Fragments of Qumran Cave 4.* Oxford: Oxford University Press, 1976.

Miller, Albert J., and Acri, Michael James. *Death: A Bibliographical Guide.* Metuchen, NJ: Scarecrow Press, 1977.

Millgram, Abraham E. *Jewish Worship.* Philadelphia: Jewish Publication Society, 1971.

Minkin, Jacob S. *The Romance of Hasidism.* North Hollywood: Wilshire Book, 1971.

Mintz, Jerome. *Legends of the Hasidim: An Introduction to Hasidic Tradition and Oral Culture in the New World.* Chicago: University of Chicago Press, 1968.

The Mishnah. Trans. Herbert Danby. London: Oxford University Press, 1933.

The Mishnah—A New Translation. Trans. Jacob Neusner. New Haven, CT: Yale University Press, 1988.

Mishnayot, 12 vols. Ed. Pinchas Kahati. Jerusalem: Keter, 1977.

Montefiore, C. G., and Loewe, H., eds. *A Rabbinic Anthology.* New York: Schocken Books, 1974.

Moody, Raymond. *Life After Life.* New York: Bantam, 1976.

———. *Reflections on Life After Life.* New York: Bantam, 1977.

Moore, George Foote. *Judaism.* 2 vols. Cambridge: Harvard University Press, 1927, 1962.

Moss, Steven A. "The Attitudes toward Sickness, Dying, and Death as Expressed in the Liturgical Works *Maavor Yabok* and *Sefer Hahayyim.*" Rabbinic thesis, Hebrew Union College—Jewish Institute of Religion, 1974.

Muller, Ernest. *History of Jewish Mysticism.* Trans. M. Simon. Brooklyn, NY: Yesod Publishers, n.d.

Musaph-Andriesse, R. C. *From Torah to Kabbalah: A Basic Introduction to the Writings of Judaism.* New York: Oxford University Press, 1982.

Nass, Raoul B. *The Road to Eternal Life and to Resurrection from Death, after Death.* Montpelier, VT: Capital City Press, 1976.

Neumann, Jonathan. "Near-Death Experiences in Judaic Literature." *Journal of Psychology and Judaism* 14:4 (Winter 1990): 225–251.

Neusner, Jacob. *From Politics to Piety: The Emergence of Pharasaic Judaism.* Englewood Cliffs, NJ: Prentice-Hall, 1973.

New English Bible. New York: Oxford University Press, 1971.

Newman, Louis, ed. and trans. *The Hasidic Anthology—Tales and Teachings of the Hasidim.* New York: Schocken Books, 1975; Northvale, NJ: Jason Aronson, 1987.

Nickelsburg, George W. E. *Jewish Literature Between the Bible and the Mishnah.* Philadelphia: Fortress Press, 1981.

————. *Resurrection, Immortality and Eternal Life in Intertestamental Judaism.* Cambridge: Harvard University Press, 1972.

————, ed. *Studies on the Testament of Abraham.* Missoula, MO: Scholars Press, 1976.

Noveck, Simon, ed. *Great Jewish Personalities in Ancient and Medieval Times.* Washington, DC: B'nai Brith Adult Jewish Education, 1969.

Odeberg, Hugh, ed. and trans. *3 Enoch or the Hebrew Book of Enoch.* New York: Ktav, 1973.

Oesterley, W. O. E. *Immortality and the Unseen World—A Study in Old Testament Religion.* London: Society for Promotion of Christian Knowledge, 1921.

Oesterley, W. O. E., and Robinson, Theodore H. *The Hebrew Religion—Its Origin and Development.* London: Society for Promotion of Christian Knowledge, 1930.

Olan, Levi A. *Judaism and Immortality.* New York: UAHC Press, n.d.

Osis, Karlis, and Haraldsson, Erlendur. *At the Hour of Death.* New York: Avon, 1977.

Otzar Ha-Aggadah, 3 vols. Ed. Moshe David Gross. Jerusalem: Mossad Harav Kook, 1986.

Otzar Ha-Zohar, 3 vols. Ed. Daniel Frish. Jerusalem: Aleph Beit, 1976.

Patai, Raphael. *Gates to the Old City: A Book of Jewish Legends.* New York: Avon, 1980.

————. *The Hebrew Goddess.* New York: Avon, 1967.

————. *Sex and Family in Bible and the Middle East.* Garden City, NY: Doubleday, 1959.

Paull, Simcha Steven [Simcha Raphael]. "Judaism's Contribution to the Psychology of Death and Dying." Ph.D. dissertation, California Institute of Integral Studies, 1986.

Pederson Johs. *Israel—Its Life and Culture.* London: Oxford University Press, 1926, 1959.

Pesikta Rabbati, 2 vols. Trans. William G. Braude. New Haven, CT: Yale University Press, 1968.

Petuchowski, Jakob J. *Prayerbook Reform in Europe.* New York: World Union for Progressive Judaism, 1968.

Pirke de Rabbi Eliezer, 4th ed. Trans. Gerald Friedlander. New York: Sefer-Hermon Press, 1981.

"Playboy Interview: Elisabeth Kübler-Ross." *Playboy* 28 (November 1981): 96ff.

Rabinowicz, Tzvi. *A Guide to Life—Jewish Laws and Customs of Mourning.* Northvale, NJ: Jason Aronson, 1989.

Ramban. *Commentary on the Torah.* Trans. Charles B. Chavel. New York: Shilo Publishing, 1973.

————. *The Gate of Reward.* Ed. and trans. Charles B. Chavel. New York: Shilo Publishing, 1983.

Raphael, Simcha Paull. "Is There Afterlife After Auschwitz? Reflections on Jewish Views of Life After Death in the Twentieth Century." *Judaism* 41:4 (Fall 1992): 346–360.

Richard Address, ed. *The Synagogue as a Caring Community—A Resource Book for Congregational Leaders*, 3 vols. Philadelphia: UAHC, 1982–1989.

Riemer, Jack, ed. *Jewish Reflections on Death*. New York: Schocken Books, 1974.

Ringgren, Helmer. *Israelite Religion*. Trans. David E. Green. Philadelphia: Fortress Press, 1966.

———. "Resurrection." *Encyclopedia of Religion*, vol. 12. New York: Macmillan, 1987.

Rinpochay, Lati, and Jeffrey Hopkins. *Death, Intermediate State and Rebirth in Tibetan Buddhism*. Valois, NY: Snow Lion Publications, 1981.

Rinpoche, Sogyal. *The Tibetan Book of Living and Dying*. San Francisco: Harper, 1992.

Roth, Cecil. *The Jews in the Renaissance*. New York: Harper & Row, 1965.

———. *A Life of Mensaaeh Ben Israel*. Philadelphia: Jewish Publication Society, 1934.

Rubinstein, Aryeh. *Hasidism*. New York: Leon Amiel Publisher, 1975.

Ruderman, David B. *Kabbalah, Magic and Science—The Cultural Universe of a Sixteenth-Century Jewish Physician*. Cambridge: Harvard University Press, 1988.

Russell, Bertrand. *Why I Am Not a Christian*. London: Unwin, 1957.

Russell, D. S. *The Method and Message of Jewish Apocalyptic*. London: SCM Press, 1964.

Sabom, Michael. *Recollections of Death—A Medical Investigation*. New York: Simon and Schuster, 1982.

Sarachek, Joseph. *The Doctrine of the Messiah in Medieval Jewish Literature*. New York: Hermon Press, 1968.

Sawyer, John F. "Hebrew Words for the Resurrection of the Dead." *Vetus Testamentum*, 23, (1973): 218–234.

Schachter-Shalomi, Zalman. "Dybbuk and Exorcism." Audiocassette tape. Philadelphia: P'nai Or Religious Fellowship, 1982.

———. "Exploring the Worlds of Jewish Mysticism." Audiocassette of class series, no. 5. Philadelphia: P'nai Or Religious Fellowship, 1981.

———. *Fragments of a Future Scroll*. Philadelphia: Leaves of Grass Press, 1975.

———. "Life in the Hereafter: A Tour of What's to Come." In *The Jewish Almanac*, ed. Richard Siegel and Carl Rheins, pp. 594–596. New York: Bantam, 1980.

———. "Some Thoughts on the Hereafter." Unpublished paper, n.d.

———. *Spiritual Intimacy—A Study of Counseling in Hassidism*. Northvale, N.J: Jason Aronson, 1991.

————, trans. "Moses Maimonides' Commentary on the Mishnah Sanhedrin, Chapter 10." Photocopied ed. Philadelphia: P'nai Or Religious Fellowship, n.d.

Schechter, Solomon. *Studies in Judaism: Essays on Persons, Concepts, and Movements of Thought in the Jewish Tradition*. Philadelphia: Jewish Publication Society, 1958.

Schiffman, Lawrence H. *From Text to Tradition: A History of Second Temple and Rabbinic Judaism*. Hoboken, NJ: Ktav, 1991.

Schindler, Pesach. "The Holocaust and the Kiddush Hashem in Hasidic Thought." In *Religious Encounters with Death*, ed. Frank Reynolds and Earle W. Waugh, pp. 170–180. University Park: Pennsylvania State University, 1977.

Scholem, Gershom. *Jewish Gnosticism, Merkabah Mysticism and Talmudic Tradition*, 2nd ed. New York: Jewish Theological Seminary, 1965.

————. *Kabbalah*. New York: New American Library, 1978.

————. *Major Trends in Jewish Mysticism*. New York: Schocken Books, 1954.

————. *On the Mystical Shape of the Godhead*. Trans. Joachim Neugrosschel. New York: Schocken Books, 1976.

————. *Origins of the Kabbalah*. Trans. Allan Arkush. Philadelphia: Jewish Publication Society, 1987.

————, trans. *The Zohar*. New York: Schocken Books, 1963.

Schur, Max. *Freud: Living and Dying*. New York: International Universities Press, 1972.

Schwartz, Howard. *The Dream Assembly: Tales of Rabbi Zalman Schachter-Shalomi*. Amity, NY: Amity House, 1988.

Selkovitsch, G., trans. *Memorial Prayers and Meditations*. New York: Hebrew Publishing, 1910.

Sharot, Stephen. *Messianism, Mysticism, and Magic: A Sociological Analysis of Jewish Religious Movements*. Chapel Hill: University of North Carolina Press, 1982.

Shapiro, David S. "Death Experiences in Rabbinic Literature." *Judaism* 28:1 (Winter 1979): 90–94.

Shevitz, Daniel R. "Rituals for Jewish Exorcism." In *The Jewish Almanac*, ed. Richard Siegel and Carl Rheins, pp. 568–572. New York: Bantam, 1980.

Shneidman, Edwin S., ed. *Death: Current Perspectives*. Palo Alto, CA: Mayfield Publishing, 1976.

Siddur Tehillat Ha-Shem. Trans. Nissan Mangel. Brooklyn, NY: Merkos L'Inyonei Chinuch, 1978.

Siegel, Richard, et al. *The First Jewish Catalog*. Philadelphia: Jewish Publication Society, 1973.

Sifre: A Tannaitic Commentary on the Book of Deuteronomy. Trans. Reuven Hammer. New Haven, CT: Yale University Press, 1986.

Silver, Daniel Jeremy. "The Resurrection Debate." In *Moses Maimonides' Treatise on Resurrection*, ed. and trans. Fred Rosner, pp. 71–102. New York: Ktav, 1982.

Skehan, Patrick W., ed. *The Wisdom of Ben Sira*. New York: Doubleday, 1987.

Sonsino, Rifat, and Syme, Daniel B. *What Happens after I Die?* New York: UAHC Press, 1990.

Steinsaltz, Adin. *The Essential Talmud*. New York: Bantam, 1976; Northvale, NJ: Jason Aronson, 1992.

Stern, David, and Mirsky, Mark Jay, eds. *Rabbinic Fantasies—Imaginative Narratives from Classical Hebrew Literature*. Philadelphia: Jewish Publication Society, 1990.

Stone, Michael Edward. *Scriptures, Sects and Visions*. Philadelphia: Fortress Press, 1980.

——, ed. *Jewish Writings of the Second Temple Period*. Philadelphia: Fortress Press, 1984.

Strack, Hermann L. *Introduction to the Talmud and Midrash*. New York: Harper & Row, 1965.

Sutich, Anthony. "The Emergence of the Transpersonal Orientation." *Journal of Transpersonal Psychology* 8:1 (1976): 5–19.

Tanakh—The Holy Scriptures. Philadelphia: Jewish Publication Society, 1988.

Tcherikover, Victor. *Hellenistic Civilization and the Jews*. Trans. S. Applebaum. Philadelphia: Jewish Publication Society, 1966.

Teutsch, David, ed. *Imagining the Jewish Future: Essays and Reponses*. Albany, NY: SUNY Press, 1992.

Tishby, Isaiah, and Lachower, Fischel, eds. *The Wisdom of the Zohar*, 3 vols. Trans. David Goldstein. London: Oxford University Press, 1989.

Torah Ha-Ketubah Ve-Ha-Messurah, 3 vols., 2nd ed. Ed. Aaron Hyman and Arthur Hyman. Tel Aviv: Hotza'at Dvir Publishing, 1979.

Trachtenberg, Joshua. *Jewish Magic and Superstition—A Study in Folk Religion*. New York: Atheneum, 1974.

Tromp, Nicholas J. *Primitive Conceptions of Death and the Nether World in the Old Testament*. Rome: Pontifical Biblical Institute, 1969.

Trungpa, Chogyam, and Fremantle, Francesca, trans. *The Tibetan Book of the Dead*. Berkeley, CA: Shambhala, 1981.

Twersky, I. "Aspects of the Social and Cultural History of Provencal Jewry." In *Jewish Society through the Ages*, ed. H. H. Ben Sasson and S. Ettinger, pp. 185–207. New York: Schocken Books, 1971.

Urbach, Ephraim E. *The Sages: Their Concepts and Beliefs*. Trans. Israel Abrahams. Cambridge: Harvard University Press, 1979.

Vital, Chaim. *Shaar Ha-Gilgulim*. Jerusalem: 1981; originally published in 1666.

Walsh, Gerald, et al., trans. *St. Augustine—The City of God*. Garden City, NY: Image Books, 1958.

Waskow, Arthur. "The Rainbow Seder." In *The Shalom Seders*, ed. New Jewish Agenda, pp. 13–37. New York: Adama Books, 1984.

———. *These Holy Sparks—The Rebirth of the Jewish People*. New York: Harper & Row, 1983.

Waxman, Meyer. *A History of Jewish Literature*, 6 vols. New York: Thomas Yoseloff, 1960.

Weissler, Chava. "Women in Paradise." *Tikkun* 2:2 (1987): 43–46; 117–120.

Wellhausen, Julius. *Prolegomena to the History of Ancient Israel*. Trans. J. Sutherland Black. New York: Meridian Books, 1957; originally published in 1878.

Werblowsky, R. Tzvi. "Transmigration." In *Death, Afterlife and the Soul*, ed. Lawrence E. Sullivan, pp. 130–137. New York: Macmillan, 1989.

Wertheimer, Abraham. *Batei Midrashot*, 2 vols. Jerusalem: Ktav Yad V'Sefer, 1989.

Whiston, William, trans. *The Works of Flavius Josephus*. London: Simms and McIntyre, 1843.

Whitelock, Lester T. *The Development of Jewish Religious Thought in the Inter-Testamental Period*. New York: Vantage Press, 1976.

Wilber, Ken. *The Atman Project*. Wheaton, IL: Quest Books, 1980.

———. *Back to Eden—A Transpersonal View of Human Evolution*. Garden City, NY: Doubleday, 1981.

———. *The Spectrum of Consciousness*. Wheaton, IL: Quest Books, 1977.

Wilson, Ian. *The After-Death Experience*. New York: William Morrow, 1987.

Winkler, Gershon. *Dybbuk*. New York: Judaica Press, 1981.

———. *The Soul of the Matter*. New York: Judaica Press, 1982.

Wolff, Hans Walter. *Anthropology of the Old Testament*. Trans. Margaret Kohl. Philadelphia: Fortress Press, 1974

Woodward, Kenneth L. "Heaven." *Newsweek*, 27 March 1989, pp. 52ff.

Yardin, Dov, ed. *Mahbarot Immanuel Ha-Romi*, 2 vols. Jerusalem: Mosad Bialik, 1954.

Zinberg, Israel. *A History of Jewish Literature*, 12 vols. Trans. Bernard Martin. Cleveland: Press of Case Western Reserve University, 1973.

The Zohar. 5 vols. Trans. Harry Sperling and Maurice Simon. London: Soncino Press, 1933, 1956.

Acknowledgments

The author gratefully acknowledges permission to quote from the following sources:

From "Is There Afterlife After Auschwitz? Reflections on Jewish Views of Life After Death in the Twentieth Century" by Simcha Paull Raphael. *Judaism* 41:4 (Fall 1992): 346–360. Copyright © 1992 by the American Jewish Congress. Used by permission.

From *Revelation and Redemption: Jewish Documents of Deliverance from the Fall of Jerusalem to the Death of Nahmanides* by George Wesley Buchanan, ed. and trans. Copyright © 1978 by Western North Carolina Press. Published by Western North Carolina Press. Used by permission.

From *Legends of the Hasidim: An Introduction to Hasidic Tradition and Oral Culture in the New World* by Jerome Mintz. Copyright © 1968 by Jerome Mintz. Published by University of Chicago Press. Used by permission of the author.

From "Some Thoughts on the Hereafter," unpublished manuscript by Rabbi Zalman Schachter-Shalomi. Copyright © 1994 by Zalman Schachter-Shalomi. Used by permission.

Index

ABOUT THE AUTHOR

Simcha Paull Raphael received a doctorate in psychology from the California Institute of Integral Studies in San Francisco and ordination as a rabbinic pastor from Rabbi Zalman Schachter-Shalomi. He is currently an assistant professor in the Department of Religion and Jewish chaplain at LaSalle University. Dr. Raphael is also in private practice as a psychotherapist specializing in bereavement. Originally from Montreal, he and his wife, Geela Rayzel, now reside in Philadelphia with their son, Yigdal.